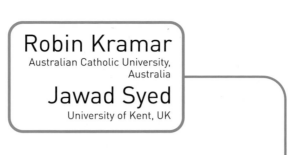

Robin Kramar
Australian Catholic University,
Australia

Jawad Syed
University of Kent, UK

HUMAN RESOURCE MANAGEMENT IN A GLOBAL CONTEXT

A CRITICAL APPROACH

palgrave
macmillan

First published 2012 by
PALGRAVE MACMILLAN

Palgrave Macmillan in the UK is an imprint of Macmillan Publishers Limited,
registered in England, company number 785998, of Houndmills, Basingstoke,
Hampshire RG21 6XS.

Palgrave Macmillan in the US is a division of St Martin's Press LLC,
175 Fifth Avenue, New York, NY 10010.

Palgrave Macmillan is the global academic imprint of the above companies
and has companies and representatives throughout the world.

Palgrave® and Macmillan® are registered trademarks in the United States,
the United Kingdom, Europe and other countries.

ISBN: 978–0–230–25153–3

This book is printed on paper suitable for recycling and made from fully
managed and sustained forest sources. Logging, pulping and manufacturing
processes are expected to conform to the environmental regulations of the
country of origin.

A catalogue record for this book is available from the British Library.

A catalog record for this book is available from the Library of Congress.

10 9 8 7 6 5 4 3 2 1
21 20 19 18 17 16 15 14 13 12

Printed in China

Brief contents

Contents

Case study matrix

Chapter 1	**HRM in Brunei's public sector** Country focus: Brunei	27
Chapter 2	**Strategic human resource management: insights from Deloitte ME's experience** Region focus: Middle East	51
Chapter 3	**View Corporation** Country focus: Belgium, United Kingdom	71
Chapter 4	**Samina's experiences in Retail Co.** Country focus: United Kingdom	93
Chapter 5	**Global working hours at HDS** Country focus: United States, Germany, Australia, Dubai	122
Chapter 6	**The Australian Cladding Company** Country focus: Australia	145
Chapter 7	**Job design at TechCo** Country focus: Australia	172
Chapter 8	**The design of a new multinational personnel selection system at MobilCom** Country focus: Malaysia, China, Australia, Germany	204
Chapter 9	**Performance appraisals in the not-for-profit sector** Country focus: United States	239
Chapter 10	**The strategy and practice of rewards in Chinese MNCs** Country focus: China	280
Chapter 11	**Sanyo** Country focus: Japan	310
Chapter 12	**Change management in TV Middle East** Region focus: Middle East	341
Chapter 13	**Employee involvement at Paper Co** Country focus: Sweden, United Kingdom, United States	368
Chapter 14	**Balancing work and life in a non-Western economy** Country focus: Nigeria	391
Chapter 15	**ABC** Country focus: South Korea	419
Chapter 16	**HPWSs in a European context** Country focus: United Kingdom, France	442

About the authors

The editors

ROBIN KRAMAR is Professor of Human Resource Management at the Faculty of Business, Australian Catholic University, Australia. Professor Kramar is the co-author of *Human Resource Management in Australia* (McGraw-Hill), now in its 4th edition, and she has also authored or edited five other books on aspects of human resource management.

JAWAD SYED is Senior Lecturer in Human Resource Management and Industrial Relations at Kent Business School, University of Kent, UK, and co-founder of the South Asian Academy of Management (SAAM). Dr Syed is also the co-author of *Managing Cultural Diversity in Asia: a research companion* and *Managing Gender Diversity in Asia: a research companion* (Edward Elgar).

The contributors

FIDA AFIOUNI Assistant Professor, Suliman S. Olayan School of Business, American University of Beirut, Lebanon

TINEKE CAPPELLEN Researcher, Faculty of Business and Economics, Katholieke Universiteit Leuven, Belgium

JULIA CONNELL Professor, Curtin Business School, Curtin University, Australia

MARK W. GILMAN Senior Lecturer in Industrial Relations and Human Resource Management, Kent Business School, University of Kent, UK

PETER HOLLAND Senior Lecturer in HRM and Employee Relations, Faculty of Business and Economics, Monash University, Australia

DIMA JAMALI Associate Professor, Suliman S. Olayan School of Business, American University of Beirut, Lebanon

MADDY JANSSENS Professor, Research Centre for Organization Studies, Katholieke Universiteit Leuven, Belgium

NICOLINA KAMENOU Senior Lecturer, School of Business and Management, Heriot-Watt University, UK

CHRISTINA KIRSCH Senior Researcher and Consultant, Change Track Research, Australia

OLIVIA KYRIAKIDOU Assistant Professor, Athens University of Economics and Business, Greece

DIANNAH LOWRY Principal Lecturer in HRM, Bristol Business School, University of the West of England, UK

JANE MALEY Lecturer, Macquarie Graduate School of Management, Australia

PETER A. MURRAY Associate Professor of Business, University of Southern Queensland, Australia

DK NUR'IZZATI PG OMAR Research student, Kent Business School, University of Kent, UK

AMANDA PYMAN Senior Lecturer in Human Resource Management and Employment Relations, Monash University, Australia

SIMON O. RABY Research Associate, Kent Business School, University of Kent, UK

CATHY SHEEHAN Senior Lecturer, Faculty of Business and Economics, Monash University, Australia

JOHN SHIELDS Professor and Associate Dean, University of Sydney Business School, University of Sydney, Australia

EBRAHIM SOLTANI Reader in Operations Management, Kent Business School, University of Kent, UK

TRACY WILCOX Lecturer, Australian School of Business, University of New South Wales, Australia

PATRIZIA ZANONI Associate Professor, Faculty of Business and Economics, Katholieke Universiteit Leuven, Belgium

Acknowledgements

I would like to acknowledge all the contributors to the book for their engagement with the spirit of the book, my colleagues at ACU for their dedication and support of excellent education and research, and my very special daughters, Claire and Ingrid, who inspire and enthuse me.

Robin Kramar

First and foremost, I would like to thank all the expert contributors, without whom this book would not exist. Their commitment to the quality of content, consistency of structure and blending of theory and practice and their patience in responding to editors' and reviewers' comments are highly appreciated. I also take this opportunity to thank Joanna McGarry, our Development Editor at Palgrave Macmillan, for unwearyingly and persistently coordinating the editing and publishing of this book. Ursula Gavin, publisher at Palgrave Macmillan, liked the original idea and encouraged me to translate that idea into the tangible product that is this book. Thanks to all at Aardvark Editorial, especially to Carrie Walker for copyediting, Jo Booley for page layout and Linda Norris for project management. Last but not least, I want to thank my mother Khalida, wife Faiza and two little angels Haider and Pernian, who tolerated my ever-increasing hours on the computer and generously accepted a few days' vacation in compensation.

Jawad Syed

Publisher's acknowledgements

The Publishers are grateful to the organisations listed below for permission to reproduce material from their publications:

John Wiley for Figure 7.2. Original source is Oldham, G. (1996) Job design. In Cooper, C. L. and Robertson, I. T. (eds), *International Review of Industrial and Organisational Psychology*. New York: John Wiley, 11: 33–60.

Emerald Group Publishing for Table 15.1. Original source is Wilkinson, A., Marchington, M. and Dale, B. G. (1993) Human resource's function. *TQM Magazine*, 5(3): 31–5.

The Academy of Management for Table 15.3. Original source is Blackburn, R. and Rosen, B. (1993) Total quality and human resource management: lessons learned from Baldrige Award-winning companies. *Academy of Management Executive*, 7(3): 49–66.

Taylor and Francis Group for Figure 16.1. Original source is Goss, D. (1991a) *Small Business and Society*. London: Routledge

Tour of book

Key objectives

At the start of every chapter, key objectives guide your reading and provide a useful reference for revision

After reading this chapter, you should
☐ Develop a vocabulary for discuss resources practices from an eth
☐ Identify how and why human activities have an ethical d
☐ Recognize the connecti human resources

Critical Thinking boxes

Look for the lightbulb to develop your critical thinking skills, by exploring contemporary debates in HRM and some of the issues facing human resources managers in the global workplace

went fur
Thus, Ford
and job design
dominance as th
(Lipietz, 1987).

Critical thinking 7.1
The case of Schmidt
In Taylor's most famous experiment, he studied m
shovelling pig iron. He noted that one particular r
Schimdt – finished the day's work and jogged h
finish building his own house. Taylor therefore p
Schimdt for his experiment. After restructuring
shovel and how the work was to be undertak
(eliminating all superfluous activity), Tayl
en to shovel and when to rest. Fro
as able to demonstrate

Exercises

Exercises in many chapters give you the chance to test your understanding and apply your reading to your own experiences

reward
more endu
245–51) asserts
non-cash award th
m
The
non-
'win
edly
(whe
ma
re

Exercise
• When it comes to recognizing and rewarding individual performance, what are the three main advantages and three chief disadvantages of using non-cash recognition plans?

Collective pe

In certain
in th

For discussion and review

Assignments, revision questions and topics for discussion at the end of each chapter help guide your class discussion and revision

surrounding in

For discussion and re

Questions
1 How has globalization cha
2 How does performance ap
3 What are the challenges i different culture?
4 How can leaders influen MNC?

Exercise
1 Go to the

Case studies

At the end of each chapter, extended case studies give insight into HRM in practice in companies and countries around the world

Case Study The design of a

On Monday morning at 7.30 am,
leaving his apartment, one specific
expatriates, and was heading towards
Kuala Lumpur's central business distr
way, he listened to the voice messages on
phone, one of which was from the assis
firm's owner, Frank. The message stated
was expected to call back before his m
the human resources (HR) team th
leading. The team meeting was sched
to bring together Hans and Chinese
form a crossfunctional project tea
the development and impleme
personnel process within th
structuring, in order

Mini case studies

There are also mini case studies throughout the book, providing a glimpse into real-world HRM in a global context.

of st
high ethica
be successful.

Mini Case Study 9.1
Ethics: performance appraisal at Travelscenc
In 2004, Keith Gavin became financial controller a
member of the executive committee of Travelscen
medium-sized, family-owned travel agency in the
Hunter valley, 2 hours' drive north of Sydney, Aus
Keith sold his home in Sydney and relocated to
Hunter valley with his wife and two young chil
8 and 10 to take up the position. He was th
from outside the family running the comp
ior position in it or to be included
ee, and he took the job

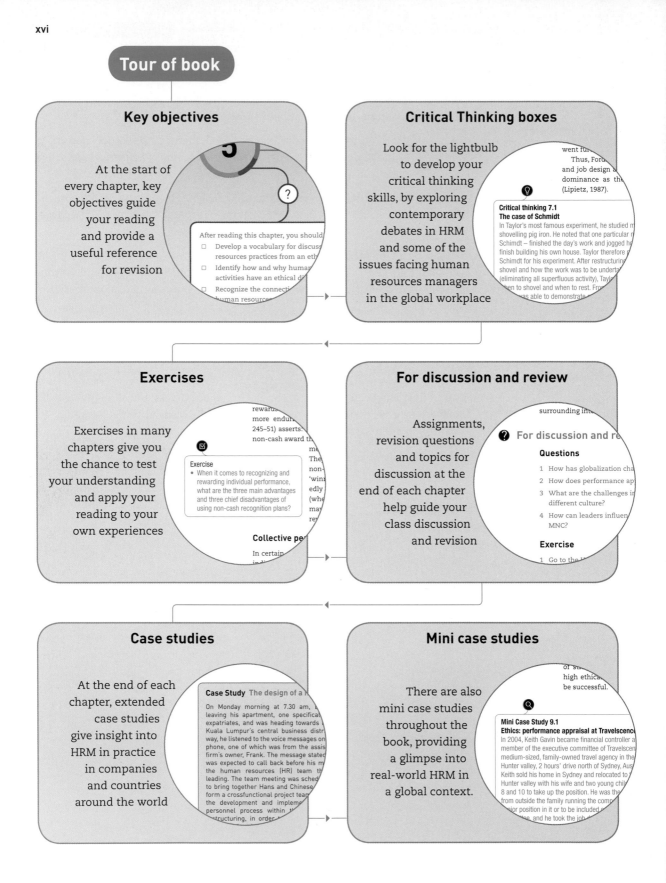

Making critical sense of human resource management in a globalized world

Jawad Syed and Robin Kramar

Welcome to the first edition of *Human Resource Management in a Global Context: A Critical Approach*. The book has been written with the aim of developing our understanding and practice of human resource management (HRM) in an increasingly globalized world of work. The book uses a critical lens to develop an approach to HRM that is not only business-focused but also context-sensitive and socially responsible – we will explain our rationale for this below.

The emergence of HRM in the 1980s was accompanied by a sustained theoretical assault on its pretensions, highlighting the gap between the rhetoric of HRM and the reality, which was focused on impersonal economic rationalism. The reconstruction of the employment relationship as a singularly individual market exchange did not go uncontested in management education. However, whereas the proponents of HRM once felt the need to engage and respond to critique, the field now seems to have narrowed as the major concerns relate merely to strategic 'fit' and identifying mechanisms to facilitate 'high-commitment' and 'high-performance' organizations.

We consider the overemphasis of HRM on strategic performance to be problematic in view of the considerable gap between the policy and practice of strategic HRM. Vaughan (1994) argues that although organizational mission statements usually hold that employees are their most important asset, organizational reality is characterized by impersonal economic rationalism. Wilmott (1993) asserts that the rhetoric of HRM tends to turn employees into 'willing slaves' who negate their own interests, assuming the organization will take care of them. Seen from this angle, HRM's unitary rhetoric may compromise the individual and collective needs of employees and may instill an HRM culture that advantages organizations at the expense of employees. This is particularly true in periods of economic recession and instability. Although the economic gains for the organization are always a priority, issues related to individuals and societies remain subject to various concerns and tensions. Furthermore, a number of changes have occurred in factors influencing the way people are used in organizations, for example globalization, migration, environmental sustainability, governance, ethics, work–life balance and workforce diversity.

Bringing together eminent international scholars, this book places a premium on the critical thinking and analytical abilities that can be successfully applied to HRM. We take a different view of HRM theory and practice from that of often mechanically prescriptive orthodox texts. Our take on the theory and practice of HRM is far from US- or UK-centric: our choice of the topics as well as geographies covered in the text (that is, continental Europe and Asia-Pacific) is an attempt to situate the critical issues facing HRM in a global context.

Each chapter in this volume addresses a core topic and reflects the current state of critical scholarly activity in the field, highlighting some enduring theories and approaches, and then pushing the boundaries of HRM beyond those ideas. Our approach differs most widely when we consider that the practice and theory of HRM involves a number of key issues, including but not limited to managing diversity, ethics, corporate social responsibility, national context, knowledge management, relationship between work and non-work, implementing HRM (which often requires managing change), understanding the expectations and motivations of individuals and groups, and the role of external factors, for example legal and regulatory requirements, in influencing HRM. We consider these topics to lie at the heart of real-life HRM situations, and we believe that a critical approach offers a more effective outcome. We identify and challenge assumptions, develop an awareness of the context, seek alternative ways of seeing a situation and relate these to real-world examples in contexts as diverse as Europe and the Asia–Pacific region.

Each chapter follows a common structure by first identifying learning outcomes, and then moving on to a discussion of fundamental theories and key concepts related to the chapter, an integration of contextual and critical insights with the HRM literature, and one or more case studies exemplifying the application of theory to the world of HRM practice.

Each case study is designed for students who are taking a course in HRM with a significant international component. The aim is to provide a dynamic example and critical illustration of the HRM theory that readers are studying. As a learning tool, Clegg et al. (1984) and Hoffman and Ruemper (1991) identify several advantages of the case study approach:

☐ For students, case studies provide an opportunity to think logically and imaginatively, to experiment and to debate ideas free of risk.
☐ Cases provide an opportunity for experiential learning with particular reference to interpersonal skills and group work.
☐ Cases provide an opportunity to evaluate critically some of the theories covered in the textbook and on the course.

☐ A series of set case tasks typically provides an opportunity to improve a student's ability to write business communications.

The case studies we present in this book are expected to encourage students to integrate knowledge and skills relating to HRM and to avoid 'compartmentalizing' or 'silo' thinking and action. They also encourage students to look for multicausality when examining workplace problems and solutions, to think across disciplines and subdisciplines, and to think logically. We hope that students and practitioners alike will find these cases useful for testing and developing human resources theories, stimulating a critical insight into and a contextual understanding of this subject.

Structure of the book

There are 16 chapters in this book, and these are divided into three parts: The Human Resource Management Arena (five chapters), Human Resource Management in Practice (six chapters) and Human Resource Management and Contemporary Issues (five chapters).

Part 1: The Human Resource Management Arena

Syed and Pg Omar's chapter on 'Contextualizing Human Resource Management' (Chapter 1) begins with a literature review of the contextual forces that influence the design and practice of HRM. The authors also consider certain latent tensions between globalization and HRM. The case study presents an empirical study of HRM practices in Brunei Darussalam. It describes the influence of the macroenvironmental context on the design and implementation of HRM strategies, policies and practices in government sector organizations. The study reveals that culture, especially the Malay Islamic Monarchy ideology, plays a significant role in shaping HRM in Brunei.

In their chapter on 'A Critical Perspective on Strategic Human Resource Management' (Chapter 2), Jamali and Afiouni provide a critical assessment of strategic HRM (SHRM), shedding light on its differentiating attributes and theoretical foundations, as well as on the lingering gaps and challenges in this rapidly growing field. This chapter shows that SHRM undoubtedly presents significant advances and new insights in relation to people management, but it is not a panacea and is still plagued by both conceptual ambiguity and a dearth of empirical support. These challenges, coupled with the difficulty of translating theory into practice, are possibly stumbling blocks in the way of a fully fledged maturation of SHRM and are fleshed out and discussed in detail in Chapter 2.

In their chapter on 'Human Resource Management in Contemporary Transnational Companies' (Chapter 3), Cappellen, Zanoni and Janssens discuss the latest evolution in HRM in transnational organizations and the emergence of the global professional as a new profile within these organizations. For each topic presented in the chapter, the authors first discuss the 'mainstream' approaches and then reflect on them by drawing on more critical literature.

Kamenou and Syed's chapter on 'Diversity Management' (Chapter 4) explains the concepts of managing diversity and equal opportunities in employment. Given the demographic transformation of the population and the labour force in many countries, workforce diversity is a major issue facing managers and organizations. There is, however, evidence of an application of unrelenting stereotypes and discriminatory attitudes and behaviours that not only permeate the workplace, but are also found in abundance on a societal and institutional level. The authors introduce students to various forms of employment discrimination, as well as legislation in various countries to tackle discrimination. With respect to theorizing diversity management, two key approaches are discussed: the business case approach and the social equity approach. The authors also discuss some methodological issues in conducting research on diversity and equal opportunity, and present a case study on ethnic minority women in the UK.

In their chapter on 'Human Resource Management and Ethics' (Chapter 5), Wilcox and Lowry discuss human resources practices from an ethical perspective. The authors identify how and why human resources activities have an ethical dimension and also highlight the connections between ethical human resources practices and ethical global business operations. In addition, the chapter identifies some key distinctions between ethical relativism (the view that the definition of right or wrong depends on culture, history and the individual) and ethical pluralism (the view that there are multiple, possibly incompatible definitions of right or wrong that may be equally correct and fundamental; see also Chapter 5), and describes some of the features of critical business ethics.

Part 2: Human Resource Management in Practice

In her chapter on 'Human Resource Planning' (Chapter 6), Sheehan explains how current changes in socioeconomic circumstances require innovative responses and careful HRM planning. The author explains that, as a custodian of the people resource in organizations, it is the function of the HRM role to assist in the development of human resource planning initiatives that match changes in the supply and demand for labour, and also manage initiatives for attracting and retaining talent strategically rather than reactively. Sheehan's chapter broadly reviews approaches to human resource planning and also critically analyses some of the strategic responses to issues associated with the supply and demand of labour that impact on talent management.

Holland, in his chapter on 'Job and Work Design' (Chapter 7), examines the development of modern job and work design to better understand the contemporary nature of work organization. The chapter reviews the literature on work organization and provides a contextual analysis for the development of 'modern' job and work design, explaining how it has already evolved and continues to evolve.

In her chapter on 'Recruitment and Selection' (Chapter 8), Kyriakidou explores the classical theories and current research that underpin the three basic elements of a personnel selection system: (1) studying the job to be performed, (2) recruiting a pool of applicants for the job, and (3) selecting the 'best' people from the applicant pool. Such an exploration is enriched by international considerations and implications for recruitment and selection, with a special focus on expatriate managers. Finally, the author adopts a critical perspective that tries to reveal the ethical issues underpinning personnel staffing and questions the current emphasis on connecting selection practices with performance.

Maley's chapter on 'Performance Management' (Chapter 9) discusses an organization's most critical procedures, that is, the performance management system. These systems are now widely and routinely used for many employees. Their use increased through the 1990s as a result of the pressures of globalization, increased competition and a greater analysis of all the characteristics of employee performance. Performance management systems were originally used for managers, professionals and technical employees, but today they are frequently used to appraise staff at all levels in many parts of the world. The author explains the purpose, criteria and ethics of performance management, and also considers approaches to and effective methods of conducting appraisals, the limitations of the process and the value of multiple sources. The chapter includes various suggestions to help improve the performance management process and evaluates performance management in an international context. Finally, the chapter discusses the need for a critical evaluation of and future direction for performance appraisal.

In his chapter on 'Reward Management' (Chapter 10), Shields explains how reward strategies, programmes and policies are structured in both domestic and international contexts. The chapter discusses the variety of reward possibilities and practices covered by the notion of 'total reward' and the different motivational and behavioural assumptions associated with particular types of reward. It also explains how social and cultural factors affect employees' perceptions of pay fairness and how these perceptions affect the design and effectiveness of pay programmes. Finally, the chapter explains the worth of a constructively critical (pluralist) approach to understanding reward management theory and practice.

Murray's chapter on 'Training, Development and Learning' (Chapter 11) discusses and explores a number of critical issues related to training, development and learning in organizations. It does so by highlighting the differences between the terms, reflecting on older, more classical approaches to training compared with more contemporary and recent trends that are more situation- or context-specific. The latter mean that the older approaches to training, albeit useful, have to be rethought. More recent trends in global organizations, such as technological advances, human expectations of what constitutes a valuable job, the organization's expectations related to capabilities that match strategic business needs, and increased social interaction, have meant that the older approaches are less valuable. The chapter explores the nuances and differences between individual and organizational learning, including, but not limited to, developing versus recruiting workers, needs assessments linked to training design and performance issues, various training and learning methods, the link between learning and knowledge, and critical issues within an international context. The chapter is designed to take the reader from existing normative and traditional views of training, development and learning to a more critical creative view that is context-specific.

Part 3: Human Resource Management and Contemporary Issues

In their chapter on 'Change Management and Human Resource Management' (Chapter 12), Kirsch and Connell discuss several eras in the literature on the management of organizational change. The authors explain the various approaches, drivers and change measurements utilized in the last few decades. They also explain some of the key roles associated with change agents and human resource managers concerned with implementing organizational change. The chapter offers two case studies depicting different change management approaches and identify the key issues associated with each case.

Pyman's chapter on 'Human Resource Management, Productivity and Employee Involvement' (Chapter 13) deals with a critical evaluation of the relationship between employee involvement (EI) and productivity. The chapter focuses on direct and indirect means of EI, which can take a wide variety of forms. EI is management-initiated and management-led, and has a number of objectives. Some examples of the objectives of EI are summarised for the reader. The chapter demonstrates that management introduce EI for a variety of reasons, with the overarching objective of improving productivity and competitiveness.

In her chapter on 'Work–Life Balance in the 21st Century' (Chapter 14), Kamenou engages in key debates on work–life balance through a global context perspective, acknowledging national and cultural differences in how work–life balance is perceived and how flexible working arrangements are negotiated. She also notes the diverse legal frameworks and workplace practices involved in dealing with work and employment, as well with rights for parents, carers, and so on. The experiences of social groups, including among others women, older workers and ethnic minority groups, in relation to work–life balance issues are also explored. A range of work–life balance organizational initiatives and flexible working types are presented, together with the legal protection associated with these practices. A discussion on the social and economic benefits of a healthy, fulfilled workforce is presented, as is an evaluation of the costs of inaction by organizations and the government, such as the costs of high absenteeism and work-related stress.

Soltani's chapter on 'Managing Human Resources and Quality' (Chapter 15) explores and analyses the link between total quality management and HRM. By reviewing the relevant literature, the author presents a case for compatibility between the two concepts. In doing so, he makes use of the frequently cited elements of the 'HRM cycle' to discuss the vital role of human resources in enhancing quality and organizational productivity. The author also provides empirical verification for the link in order to base his arguments on inferences made from a range of theoretical and previously published research in the domains of both quality and HRM.

Finally, in their chapter on 'Human Resource Management in Small to Medium-sized Enterprises' (Chapter 16), Raby and Gilman address the role of HRM in small to medium-sized enterprises (SMEs), and in doing so will explore the following: how SMEs are defined; the importance and contribution of SMEs to national economies; the employment relations environment within SMEs; and the role of HRM and its influence on performance within SMEs. The chapter also offers an extensive case study of HRM in SMEs by drawing upon detailed action research conducted during a 2-year Knowledge Transfer Partnership programme, a UK government scheme that creates a strategic partnership between a company and a knowledge base (for example, universities) to transfer and develop the latest in management thinking.

Finally, we summarise the book in the Conclusion, providing a critical synthesis of the various topics and themes covered in the book and highlighting a number of challenges and opportunities for HRM scholars and practitioners.

Features of the book

By virtue of the range of topics as well as the geographical regions covered in the theoretical discussions and practical examples offered in the various chapters, we believe that this volume will be equally beneficial for undergraduate and postgraduate students in business and management studies, particularly those pursuing a major in HRM. Courses on HRM or/and industrial relations or/and international HRM are generally compulsory in undergraduate and postgraduate management programmes across a number of universities in the UK, Australia and other countries. This book will be useful for students enrolled on such programmes.

Although the book is primarily designed for students, it will be of equal interest to research scholars as well as practitioners of HRM. Academic as well as governmental libraries and academic associations, such as the Chartered Institute of Personnel and Development and the Society for Human Resource Management, may be interested in procuring copies of this book.

The book has several important features:

☐ It has been specially designed to relate to HRM in the UK, Australia, continental Europe and Asia, but it is, however, accessible to a wider international audience.
☐ It is suitable for undergraduate and graduate teaching programmes on general HRM, as well as for specialist modules on critical HRM and international HRM.
☐ It is an international text, written for an international audience, with the ability to be adapted for various countries and continents.
☐ It offers a critical perspective on HRM, integrating fundamental theories and practices of HRM with critical insights.
☐ Original case studies provide critical and contextual insights into HRM practice.
☐ The text is jargon-free but deals with cutting edge research, and it is easily accessible to scholars from non-English speaking backgrounds.

☐ The book has a logical structure and pedagogy that is useful for teachers, students and practitioners alike.

☐ Contributions have been made by eminent scholars in the field.

☐ There is a common structure for all the chapters.

With a view to reconnecting a critical HRM perspective to the mainstream, we feel that the time is right for an in-depth evaluation of the phenomena of HRM. Although old debates cannot be ignored, our concern is to provide a critical text integrating the fundamental theories and practices of HRM with critical insights and relevant practical examples from a variety of international contexts. This book is expected to stimulate a discussion of how to destabilize the prevailing orthodoxy in the field of HRM and deconstruct some aspects of the HRM paradigm. While the book has been designed and written primarily for students, we believe that it will be equally useful for academics and practitioners who want to understand and meet the increased challenges facing HRM in the current global crisis and beyond.

References

Clegg, C., Kemp, N. and Legge, K. (1984) *Case Studies in Organizational Behaviour*. London: Paul Chapman Publishers.

Hoffman, R. and Ruemper, F. (1991) *Organizational Behavior: Canadian Cases and Exercises*. Whitby, ON: Captus Press.

Vaughan, E. (1994) The trial between sense and sentiment: a reflection on the language of HRM. *Journal of General Management*, 19(3): 20–32.

Wilmott, H. (1993) Strength is ignorance; slavery is freedom: managing culture in modern organizations. *Journal of Management Studies*, 30(4): 515–53.

Part 1
The human resource management arena

Contextualizing human resource management

Jawad Syed and Dk Nur'Izzati Pg Omar

1

?

After reading this chapter, you should be able to:

- ☐ Understand the importance of local context and its implications for HRM
- ☐ Identify the external contexts that affect the policies and actions involved in HRM
- ☐ Learn how to design context-appropriate HRM
- ☐ Understand the pros and cons of a crosscultural transfer of HRM practices
- ☐ Identify future directions for contextualizing HRM

Introduction

Human resource management (HRM) as a management concept originated in the 1950s in North America with the seminal works of Drucker (1954) and McGregor (1957), and has subsequently been adopted and widely used across the world. HRM is defined as the managing of people within employer–employee relationships. This usually involves maximizing employees' performance (Harris, 2002), and human resources need to be effectively utilized in order to obtain maximum productivity and performance. By the 1980s, the concept of HRM had gained wider international recognition, particularly in English-speaking countries (Sparrow and Hiltrop, 1994).

The theories and practices of HRM have since made inroads into continents other than North America and Europe, such as their adoption and integration into Asia and Africa (see, for example, Bennington and Habir, 2003; McCourt and Foon, 2007). However, despite more than two decades of academic research and practice, the HRM literature has been only partly successful in offering a universal solution for the complexities of managing people that can transcend national, institutional, cultural and economic divides. Özbilgin's (2004) survey of academic scholarship and journals in the field of international HRM points towards a limited geographical coverage by the 'mainstream' scholarship in HRM, which remains dominated by North American and Western European theorization and empirical studies. In other words, HRM is not culturally neutral. The limited geographical reach of HRM is also highlighted by other authors, such as Baruch (2001) and Clark et al. (2000), who have argued for an ethical duty on the part of HRM scholars and journals to widen their geographical spread. Critical Thinking 1.1 highlights the parochial nature of HRM resulting from its geographical and theoretical limitations.

Although HRM is today an international phenomenon, the nature and scope of its links with local institutions, labour laws, corporate strategies and industrial relations vary greatly across national borders (Özbilgin, 2004). Despite the fact that the mainstream HRM theories, which were overwhelmingly formulated in management schools in North America (see, for example, Beer et al., 1985; Schuler and Jackson, 1987) and the UK (Storey, 1992) in the 1980s, quickly found their way to other developed countries (Maurice et al., 1986; Tung, 1993) and later to developing countries (Budhwar and Debrah, 2001), few models of HRM found in the mainstream literature derive from outside the English-speaking world. This is despite an increasing consensus that mainstream human resources theories and practices are inadequate in addressing the human resource issues facing international and multinational companies (Clark et al., 2000). As a result, and also because of a growing pursuit of effective ways of managing human resources in crosscultural contexts (Taylor et al., 1996), it is important to develop a contextualized understanding and operationalization of HRM. The interest of scholars and practitioners in this topic is expected to grow further due to the relevance of issues such as crossnational and comparative HRM, expatriate management and diversity management (Caligiuri, 1999).

This chapter begins with a literature review on the adoption and implementation of HRM and the contextual forces that influence it. We also consider certain latent tensions between globalization and HRM. The case study at the end of the chapter presents an empirical study of HRM practices in Brunei Darussalam, describing the influence of the macroenvironmental context on the design and implementation of HRM strategies, policies and practices in government sector organizations in Brunei.

Critical Thinking 1.1
Parochialism in the HRM literature

In the 'mainstream' English-language texts on HRM, there are hardly any references to resources in other languages (Özbilgin, 2004). Exceptions to this rule are some European languages, for example French-, German- and Spanish-language publications, which are also only very occasionally cited in English-language texts. The inclusion of materials not written in English is hardly encouraged and is often left to the linguistic competence of individual authors. As a consequence, the mainstream writing in the field of HRM remains influenced and dominated by the English-speaking world.

Adler (1991) refutes any claims of universal reach and offers the notion of 'parochialism' in management writing. Clark et al. (1999) identify two forms of parochialism in the international HRM texts: (1) that a sole reliance on English-language sources poses a major challenge; and (2) that the texts often fail to acknowledge the methodological complexities of studying crossnational and international management issues. The limiting impact of the English language appears to be the most insidious as it simply demarcates our knowledge of and imagination related to HRM practice to those geographies where the English language is spoken.

Similarly, the difficulty of formulating overarching conceptual frameworks, theoretical models and critical approaches is a recurring theme in the international HRM literature. Large-scale empirical studies in this field are rare, and such studies come with long descriptions of the limitations of their method and analysis. However, due to their rarity, great significance is attributed to the studies that are available, and their findings are often overstated, misinterpreted or used out of context. For example, although Hofstede's work in the 1960s and 70s challenged the assumption that the theoretical frameworks developed in the USA would be universally applicable (Schneider, 2001), Hofstede's IBM studies were later quoted as a clear indicator of the convergence and divergence of management practices, without much questioning of the nature of his study.

Questions

1 What are the implications of the dominance of English-language literature for theories and practices in HRM?
2 How can scholars and practitioners of HRM benefit from the literature on HRM that has been published in languages other than English?

Source: Adapted from Özbilgin (2004)

Contextualizing HRM in a global village

Global integration has driven dramatic changes in the economic and institutional contexts of HRM. Globalization refers to the shift to a more integrated and interdependent world economy (Hill, 2009). It focuses on the maximization of profits and, as an economic driver, has had a significant effect on the way in which human resources are managed. Globalization has also changed the image of a company. Companies have become multinational, each one seeking to attain the competitive advantage, and the human resources of a company may just be the key to that. For this reason, HRM policies are changing in order to better respond to different cultural and institutional contexts.

Context is multilayered, multidimensional and interwoven (Collin, 2007), and different contexts may have dynamic and divergent influences on the organization of work within their sphere of influence. Globalization has steadily and gradually created a world in which:

> barriers to cross-border trade and investment are declining; material culture is starting to look similar the world over; and national economies are merging into an interdependent, integrated global economic system. (Hill, 2009: 4)

During current times, when the world economy and businesses are shaped and structured by the process of globalization, it is imperative to understand and contextualize the policies and practices of HRM.

Although it is no longer possible to divide the world economy into separate, distinct national economies isolated from foreign markets and influences, it would be wrong to ignore the fact that employment relationships in almost all countries remain largely shaped by national systems of employment legislation and the cultural contexts in which they are operationalized. Critical Thinking 1.2 highlights the case of varying perspectives on working hours in the European Union (EU).

Although factors such as culture, history and language underlie much of the variation in management practices, the practice of HRM is, more than that of any other business function, closely linked to national culture (Gaugler, 1988). Culture can mean many different things for people with different backgrounds. Culture, according to Tylor (1924: 1), is 'that complex whole which includes knowledge, belief, art, morals, law, custom, and any other capabilities and habits acquired by man as a member of society'. Within employment contexts, there is ample evidence that people's behaviours are affected by specific national cultures. Hofstede (1991) suggests that the significance of national culture is that most inhabitants of a country share the same mental program. Based on that, other researchers have sought to discover to what extent individuals' national culture influences their way of working and thinking, and to identify how people in different countries may have a collective programming, that is, a predisposition to behave in a certain way (Stredwick, 2005).

Although globalization is pervasive, it is not without serious criticism. Critics argue that globalization has demoted national governments as regulators of the free market system (Chomsky, 1999). Among other things, globalization may at times create inequality and environmental challenges. In 1996, the United Nations reported that the assets of the world's 368 billionaires exceeded the combined incomes of 45 per cent of the planet's population (Faux and Mishel, 2001). The Kyoto Protocol in 1997 and subsequent agreements at the Copenhagen climate summit in 2009 have highlighted issues (the need to reduce emissions of carbon dioxide and greenhouse gases) that directly affect the behaviour of organizations and countries. Organizations will lobby their governments to prevent the ratification of such treaties and lessen other external pressures that may affect their economic interests. For example, in 2002, Canada potentially faced unemployment losses through plant closures and costs in the manufacturing sector relating to curbing their emissions (Chase, 2002). When firms seek foreign investment or outsourcing to take advantage of economies of scale, lay-offs of workers in the home country may drain the economy through welfare benefits, and the demand for cheaper services in the host country of globalizing firms may entail making adjustments in the local labour markets.

Globalization has created dynamic alternatives for multinational firms. Corporations can outsource production and services to more economically viable locations, allowing multinational enterprises to drive down costs and increase their efficiency. For example, several clothing giants in the UK and the USA now outsource much of their manufacturing to South Asia, where production costs are much lower. And the displacement of workers caused by transferring resources away from Europe to Asia is not occurring just in the clothing industry. Many telecommunication firms too are transferring their back-office operations to India and other countries where costs are cheaper. This adversely affects the labour market in home countries that may face unemployment of the manual working classes.

In recent years, it has become increasingly evident that the global economic crisis that began in 2008 may leave many nations in recession. Many firms have reacted to this by making thousands of workers redundant, especially in sectors where the recession has hit hardest, for example financial services and the construction industry in 2009. This approach places pressure on organizations in terms of issues outside of their control, at times forcing them to relocate or restructure their operations. In these circumstances, it is essential to consider how HRM can be contextualized in its design and implementation.

Critical Thinking 1.2
Geographical variation in philosophy

Scholars and scientists list a large number of variations between countries and point towards a 'wide diversity in philosophies of people management' (Price, 1997: 122). When comparing one country with another, certain tasks that need to be completed within a line of work are given different priorities and are completed in a different way (Price, 1997). An example of this is the EU voting for a decree stating that its Member States should introduce legislation to decrease the number of working hours for employees. Every country then had to set a chosen number of hours, and it was apparent that the number of working hours thought suitable was different between different countries: the UK believed that 48 hours was reasonable, whereas France decided 35 hours was enough (Stredwick, 2005).

Questions
1 Why is it important to consider a country's sociocultural context when designing HRM?
2 What factors affect the number of working hours per week in a country?

Contextual influences on HRM

This section highlights different contextual forces that may influence HRM – we will start with a discussion of sociocultural context. Hofstede (1980) identified five dimensions of culture, and culture serves as an umbrella for all other contexts: legal, political, economic and technological contexts are all influenced by the role culture plays in a society. Noe et al. (2008) state that culture shapes people's respect and obedience for laws and regulations, hence affecting a country's legal and political system. And the way in which human capital and technology are valued by a particular society influences the economy of that country. Various HRM practices, such as recruitment and selection, training and development, compensation systems, performance appraisal and the employment relationship, are affected by the macrocontextual factors that this section will cover (Table 1.1).

Table 1.1 An organization's macroenvironment

Legal and political factors	Economic factors
National legislation (current and future)	Home economy
International legislation	Trends in the economy
Regulatory bodies and processes	Overseas economies
Government policies	General taxation
Government term and change	Taxation specific to the product/service
Trading policies	Seasonality issues
Funding, grants and initiatives	Market/trade cycles
Home market pressure groups	Specific industry factors
International pressure groups	Distribution trends
Ecological/environmental issues	Customer/end-user drivers
Wars and conflicts	Interest/exchange rates
	International trade and monetary issues
Sociocultural factors	**Technological factors**
Lifestyle trends	Information and communications
Demographics (age, gender, literacy)	Development of competing technology
Language	Associated/dependent technologies
Ethnicity/race	Replacement technology/solutions
Religion/sect	Maturity of technology
Ethical issues	Manufacturing maturity and capacity
Social policy	Research funding
Technology	Technology legislation
Media views	Innovation potential
Consumer attitudes and opinions	Intellectual property issues
Company image	Global communications
Fashion, brand, role models	
Major events and influences	

Table 1.1 suggests that the strategies and practices of human resources ought to be examined in a broader context, and that social, legal, economic, political and technological influences all have a different impact when putting HRM into a context. For example, the global economic crisis and the near collapse of the banking system in 2008 are powerful contextual events that affect both national economies and organizations. Macrocontextual analysis will lay the groundwork for an investigation of the extent to which and how local cultural and institutional contexts affect HRM (Figure 1.1).

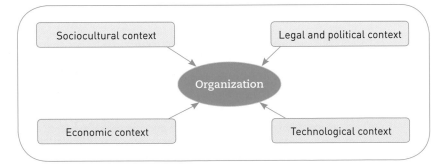

Figure 1.1 Key factors of the macroenvironment.

Sociocultural context

Several elements in the sociocultural context have consequences for the design and efficacy of HRM. Culture dynamics and population demographics affect many aspects of the business environment. Rousseau (1990) argues that culture is a set of common values, beliefs, expectations and understandings that are obtained through socialization; it is learnt and shared by the members of the community (Noe et al., 2008). Culture can be defined as a system of values and norms that are shared among a group of people (Hill, 2009). It is dynamic and changes over time, for example when a nation becomes more affluent.

According to Tayeb (2005), HRM is a 'soft' aspect of an organization. Hence it is more influenced by culture than are financial and technical matters, which are considered to be the 'hard' aspects of an organization. Culture has a significant role in attracting, motivating and retaining individuals in organizations. Other key areas that are usually influenced by culture are training, performance management and compensation.

Table 1.2 Hofstede's cultural dimensions

Individualism	The degree to which individuals are integrated into groups
Power distance	The extent to which the less powerful members of organizations and institutions accept and expect that power is distributed unequally
Uncertainty avoidance	A society's tolerance for uncertainty and ambiguity
Masculinity	The distribution of emotional roles between the genders
Long-term orientation	Long-term-oriented societies foster pragmatic virtues oriented towards future rewards, in particular saving, persistence and adapting to changing circumstances. Short-term-oriented societies foster virtues related to the past and present, such as national pride, respect for tradition, preservation of 'face' and fulfilment of social obligations

Source: Adapted from http://www.geerthofstede.nl/culture/dimensions-of-national-cultures.aspx (accessed July 2011)

Hofstede's (1984) five dimensions of culture can influence management practices and the culture of organizations. The five categories are outlined in Table 1.2 and are also discussed below.

Individualism versus collectivism

This dimension describes the strength of the relationship between individuals in a society, that is, the degree to which people act as individuals rather than as members of a group, or the extent to which the individuals are integrated into groups. In individualist cultures such as the USA, the UK and The Netherlands, people are expected to look after their own interests and the interests of their immediate families. South-East Asian countries are more collectivist – they look after the interests of the larger community. Collectivist cultures tend to owe total loyalty to their group.

Low versus high power distance

This cultural dimension concerns hierarchical power relationships and refers to the unequal distribution of power. It describes the degree of inequality among people that is considered to be normal in different countries. For example, Denmark and Israel have a small power distance, whereas India and the Philippines have a larger one. Another obvious example is the way people are addressed. In a business context, Mexican and Japanese people always address each other using titles, for example Señor Smith or Smith-San, but in the USA, first names are preferred. The reason for this is to minimize power distance.

Low versus high uncertainty avoidance

This dimension deals with the fact that the future is not perfectly predictable. For example, in Singapore and Jamaica, cultures of weak uncertainty avoidance, individuals are socialized to accept uncertainty and take each day as it comes. However, Greek and Portuguese culture socializes people to seek security through technology, law and religion.

Masculinity versus femininity

This dimension indicates the extent to which the dominant values in a society tend to relate to assertiveness and a greater interest in things than in people and quality of life. A 'masculine' culture is one in which dominance and assertiveness are valued, as is evident in the USA, Japan and Venezuela, for example. A 'feminine' culture, as can be found in The Netherlands and Sweden, promotes values that have been traditionally regarded as feminine, leaning more towards quality of life and relationships in society. Hofstede (1984) notes that most South-East Asian countries fall the between the masculine and feminine poles.

Long-term versus short-term orientation

Long-term orientation focuses on the future and holds values in the present that will not necessarily provide an immediate benefit; examples of countries adopting this approach are Japan and China. The USA, Russia and West Africa have a short-term orientation, being oriented towards the past and present, and promoting respect for tradition and the fulfilment of social obligations.

It is, however, important to acknowledge the criticism raised by some authors who view Hofstede's conceptualization of culture as static and essential. For example, Ailon (2008) and McSweeney (2002) caution against an uncritical reading of Hofstede's cultural dimensions, particularly because of their allegedly ethnocentric interpretations, which may lead to stereotyping.

Other scholars have identified additional dimensions of culture, including its informal, material or dynamic orientation (Adler, 1991; Ronen, 1994). They have compared HRM across countries and observed that cultural values and orientations are determinants of the differences found between them (see, for example, Arvey et al., 1991; Brewster and Tyson, 1991; Triandis et al., 1994; Brewster, 2007). However, culture may not explain all the differences in HRM found across countries (Lincoln, 1993; Jackson and Schuler, 1995) – such differences may also be an outcome of variations in economic and political conditions (see, for example, Carroll et al., 1988), laws and social policies (see, for example, Florkowski and Nath, 1993), industrial relations systems (Strauss, 1982) and labour market conditions (see, for example, Levy-Leboyer, 1994).

Legal and political context

The legal and political context is represented by national laws and sociopolitical policies and norms. Given that culture is a codification of right and wrong that exists in a country's laws, political systems and laws often reflect what constitute the legitimate behaviour and norm of a particular country (Tayeb, 2005; Noe et al., 2008). These contexts have the power to shape the nature of the employment relationship and the way in which HRM practices and policies are enacted (Bratton and Gold, 2007). Jackson and Schuler (1995) claim that almost all aspects of HRM are influenced by political and legal regulations, and Noe et al. (2008) have identified training, compensation, hiring and lay-offs as some of the HRM practices most commonly affected by this context.

The UK, the USA and most European countries, for example, place a strong emphasis on eliminating discrimination in the workplace; hence, equal employment regulations are put into effect. To focus on one example, in the UK the Sex Discrimination Act 1975, the Disability Discrimination Act 1995, the Race Relations Act 1976, the Employment Equality (Age) Regulations 2006, the Employment Equality (Religion or Beliefs) Regulations 2003 and the Equality Act (Sexual Orientation) Regulations 2007 are the laws that are included under the heading of Equality Employment Regulations. These regulations play a major role in developing HRM policies in relation to recruitment and dismissal procedures (Noe et al., 2008). Not only that, but pay and compensation can also be affected, with the setting of minimum wages for employees and a determination of the extent to which unions have the legal right to negotiate with the management.

The role of the state and its political system is crucial in determining the nature of employment relations in a country. Tayeb (2005) points out that workers in Germany have a legal right to 'co-determination', in which their participation in management is ensured; therefore, any HRM matter must abide by such laws (Noe et al., 2008). The Brunei case study at the end of this chapter provides another example of how the state impacts on employment relations. Furthermore, the European Economic Community can also affect the political-legal system relating to HRM because it provides workers' fundamental social rights. These rights include freedom to be fairly compensated, freedom of association and collective bargaining, and equal treatment for men and women.

Legal influences affecting HRM practices can take the form of how local regulations affect the labour market (see Critical Thinking 1.3). Different countries will impose regulations on minimum wages and working hours as well as the involvement of trade unions, as has been seen in most Western developed economies. In the UK, government legislation has gradually worn down the power of trade unions and given rise to managerial flexibility and decentralized employment regulation. Although it is employers who control the design of HRM practice at an organizational level, managers need to be aware or informed of external developments in the legal context.

Politically related external conflicts may have acute implications for firms operating in a particular country, and managers need to be aware of political manoeuvrings relevant to their interests. The state does not, however, have a monopoly of control over the conduct of business – firms too can lobby and influence state policies to meet their needs (Needle, 2004). This was the case with the USA's mohair farmers, who were paid numerous cash payments from the Federal budget (Wheelan, 2003). The mohair agricultural subsidy has now disappeared, but it highlights the importance and power of organized institutions.

External pressures in the global political environment may directly affect how business and employee relationship are conducted. The collapse of the Communist system in 1989 in East Europe and Central Asia paved the way for new market economies based on the Western capitalist market system. Employment regulation and managerial responsibility were taken away from government and replaced by the power of institutions and organizations.

Critical Thinking 1.3
Employment relations in India

Labour unrest haunts auto sector in Tamil Nadu
Madhu Bharati, May 4, 2010 (Chennai)

In recent decades, the Indian State of Tamil Nadu has been attracting enormous investment into automobile and accessories manufacturing. However, investors and manufacturers have of late become quite worried about repeated labour unrest, which is also impeding future investment in the state.

Hyundai, the second largest car maker in the country, is facing a similar situation. In May 2010, Hyundai employees threatened a sit-in strike after the company refused to reinstate 35 employees who had been dismissed for alleged misconduct. According to a news report, the company was not able to meet the agreed deadline to reinstate the dismissed workers. The company has been making frantic efforts for a possible settlement with the dismissed employees, offering them certain financial compensation as a part of the settlement.

If the strike announced in May 2010 does go ahead, it will be the third strike at Hyundai over the past year. Previously, in April 2009, employees went on strike for 18 days after the company laid off 65 workers. Then again, in July 2009, employees went on strike protesting at a wage agreement that had allegedly been signed by a minority union (or pocket union).

However, Hyundai is not the only company suffering as a result of labour unrest. In May 2009, workers at MRF struck work for several months, demanding recognition of their union. In September 2009, a senior official at Pricol was killed in workers' unrest in the auto-ancillary hub of Coimbatore, which resulted in a work closure lasting more than a month.

According to Abdul Majeed, an auto sector leader at PWC, labour laws are to be blamed: 'Our labour laws need an amendment. No one wins when it comes to dealing with labour. There has to be a give and take to some level amongst everyone. But our labour laws are the biggest of problems.'

The existing labour laws in India require large companies to seek prior permission from state governments before laying off workers or hiring workers on contract. These laws have been blamed by managers for encouraging workers to go on frequent strikes. With India positioning itself as the hub of small car production, such labour unrest may not send the right message to international investors.

Questions
1 In the light of this example, is it correct to blame laws for encouraging workers to strike?
2 Is it always possible to reconcile the ethical and business implications of labour laws?

Source: Adapted from NDTV Profit, May 4 2010

Economic context

Although the economic context of a country is hardly predictable and stable, it is most likely to have long-term consequences for HRM (Tayeb, 2005). The attitudes and values that are embedded in every individual are formed by culture (Noe et al., 2008), hence the claim of human capital theory that a culture that encourages continuous learning is most likely to contribute to the success of the economy. Jackson and Schuler (1995) argue that skills, experience and knowledge are of significant value for the economy, and enhancing them can make individuals more productive and more adaptable to changing economic conditions.

The need to improve human capabilities relates back to whether the economic system supplies sufficient incentives for developing human capital. For example, Tayeb (2005) found that socialist economies offer a free education system, which provides an opportunity for human capital to be developed, thus enabling employees to obtain greater monetary rewards based on their competencies. This is evident in the USA, where levels of human capital are reflected in the differences in individuals' salaries, higher skilled employees, for example, earning better compensation than lower skill ones (Noe et al., 2008). In fact, it has been discovered that for each additional year of schooling, individuals' wages increase by about 10–16 per cent (Noe et al., 2008). Conversely, the opportunity to enhance human capital is smaller in capitalist systems due to the high costs of training employees; hence, human resource development is lower in capitalist countries (Tayeb, 2005).

Tayeb (2005) highlights the role of market conditions in determining employees' rights in capitalist countries that have 'centre right' policies. According to Flamholtz and Lacey (1981), investments in human capital are usually made in anticipation of future returns; besides improving employees' competencies, the costs also include factors such as motivating, monitoring and retaining these employees in order to benefit from their gains in productivity (Jackson and Schuler, 1995). Chapter 3 in this book offers a detailed discussion of HRM in contemporary transnational businesses.

Of course, different forms of political capitalism, for example in terms of their socialist or free-market orientation, will have different effects on the way in which HRM is practised domestically as well as internationally. Even the most global of companies may be deeply rooted in the national business systems of their country of origin. For example, Edwards (2004), Hu (1992) and Ruigrok and van Tulder (1995) have argued that, on several dimensions, multinational corporations exhibit national characteristics.

There are various ways in which HRM can increase organizations' human capital, for instance offering attractive compensation and benefits packages to individuals, what Jackson and Schuler (1995) claim is 'buying' human capital, which is apparent in recruitment and selection processes. Creating equal opportunities in training and development can also help to 'make' human capital in an organization; at times of tight labour supply, this method is usually adopted. Training and developing existing employees' capabilities, as well as enhancing their wages, benefits and working conditions, can help in retaining them, especially when there is a scarce supply of human capital in the economy.

At times of economic boom and similarly in times of recession, the supply and demand of labour forces may vary in relation to a country's unemployment level. When the economy is booming and the level of unemployment is low, employees have much greater power and influence over their working conditions, pay and other employment rights (Tayeb, 2005). Having said that, managers in return gain more prerogatives during recessions and periods of high unemployment by controlling employees' working conditions and compensation, thus weakening the power and influence of both workers and trade unions. Jackson and Schuler (1995) note that it is common in such periods for absenteeism and turnover rates to fall because competition for jobs is more intense and employees' poor performance may result in retrenchment. It has been identified that, in the USA, excess demand typically relates to low unemployment, whereas high unemployment is reported to be associated with excess supply (Jackson and Schuler, 1995).

Technological context

Technology has evolved along with globalization, which is often associated with advances in communication and information technology. The way people throughout the world communicate, exchange information and learn about their world has changed as computer usage has become more prevalent in almost every part of the globe, further enhanced by the increase in the number of information technology-literate individuals (Burton et al., 2003). The influence of technology is also apparent in HRM (Critical Thinking 1.4), especially with the transformation of traditional HRM to IT-based HRM, or what is known as e-HRM (Bondarouk and Ruel, 2009), as a result of the growing sophistication of IT.

e-HRM, for example, deals with the implementation of HRM strategies, policies and practices through the full use of web-based technologies. Bondarouk et al. (2009) believe that e-HRM can reduce the cost of traditional methods of processing and administration of paperwork, as well as speeding up transaction processing, reducing information errors and improving the tracking and control of human resources actions. However, the effectiveness of e-HRM may depend upon the types and levels of knowledge that are required by the system and the extent to which tasks and people are interdependent (Jackson and Schuler, 1995).

When face-to-face HRM services become obsolete, higher levels of motivation and commitment are required (Othman and Teh, 2003). This is because employees are expected to work independently with little supervision, so the supervisor's role is greatly reduced as control over employees' work behaviour can no longer be exerted through direct observation. According to Bondarouk and Ruel (2009), e-HRM eliminates the 'human resources middleman' who is initially responsible for dealing with human resources matters.

Besides ensuring independent work through the introduction of e-HRM, IT also enables organizational learning to help employees improve their capability, adaptation, knowledge and understanding (Othman and Teh, 2003) because the use of teams is practised, which helps the transfer of learning from the individual to the organization. Othman and Teh claim that, with the growing usage of IT, people are expected to think critically, be able to solve problems, communicate and work in teams, creatively and proactively, as well as bring diverse and newer perspectives to their work. This requires a change in organizational structures and processes, for example selection processes, training, performance appraisals and rewards. Put simply, this means that the way employee performance is monitored has to rely on data interpretation and on assessing outputs.

There are, however, some critiques of the usage of IT in organizations. Based on findings from Othman and Teh (2003), the workforce is deskilled and controlled by managers through the use of IT. There is less chance for employees to develop their intellectual skills when their role has already been weakened by IT. Additionally, while most management invests heavily in acquiring technology, insufficient resources tend to be allocated to managing the organizational change process; thus HRM issues are neglected, and technology usage fails to meet expectations.

Critical Thinking 1.4
Technological context and HRM

The correlation between new technology and work can be identified in many different forms. Academics have, however, pinpointed three specific areas in which HRM practices are directly affected (Millward and Stevens, 1986):

- *Advanced technology change:* new plant machinery and equipment that has incorporated microprocessor technology.
- *Conventional technological change:* machinery and equipment not aided by microprocessor technology.
- *Organizational change:* substantial changes in work organizations not involving new plant, machinery or equipment (Bratton and Gold, 2007).

Across many workplaces, microprocessor technology plays an active role: in 1998, 87 per cent of manufacturing workplaces in the UK used microprocessor-based technology, a large jump from 44 per cent in 1984 (Bratton and Gold, 2007). This reflects how great an influence the technological context may have on designing HRM. Entire organizations are administered based on their information system. In addition, manufacturing process concepts are part of the technological context that are able to directly impact upon organizations. Similarly, performance enhancement and organizational restructuring have vigorously shaped business processes in order to gain a competitive advantage.

Total quality management (TQM) focuses on maximizing profits by increasing service and product quality and decreasing costs (Hill, 2005). TQM and other quality management innovations such as Six Sigma are ground-breaking institutional approaches to improving organizations and are an example of how the technological context has influenced the design of HRM. However, quality management may also pose a problem for managers and organizations: although the system welcomes key aspects of quality – between suppliers and customers – it demands mutual commitment from every party involved in the organization and requires rigorous implementation and corporate governance, which may cause a hegemonic conflict between top and mid-level management and the workforce whom they direct.

Questions
1 Do technological advances always have positive implications for employees in organizations?
2 What role can HRM play in coping with changes in the technological context of an organization?

Critical discussion and analysis

HRM is constantly being reshaped by new economic, sociocultural and political realities. Changes in the levels of unemployment, structural transformation (for example, privatization and deindustrialization) and social trends (an ageing population) will all shift the balance of power in individual and collective contract negotiations.

Furthermore, increasing globalization and advances in information and communication technologies are fast transforming the world into a global village in which management practices cannot remain isolated from external influences. As demonstrated in this chapter, we will be ill-advised to believe that globalization will cause organizations to become isolated or aloof from the society in which they operate. Conversely, local contexts will remain a key influence on the way in which human resources are treated and managed.

It is, however, a fact that some types of HRM system may be used effectively across countries that are culturally quite dissimilar (Wickens, 1987; MacDuffie and Krafcik, 1992), and that organizational and industry characteristics remain key determinants of managerial practices and employee behaviours (Hofstede, 1991). Our understanding of the role of national culture in HRM could also benefit from investigations examining how multinational corporations develop HRM systems that are simultaneously consistent with multiple and distinct local cultures and yet internally consistent in the context of a single organization (cf. Heenan and Perlmutter, 1979; Tung, 1993; Jackson and Schuler, 1995).

From an academic perspective, certain specialized fields, for example industrial-organizational psychology and social work psychology, may be very useful in advancing our understanding of HRM in context. In this age of unprecedented internationalization as well as sociocultural specificity, the dearth of comparative publications in HRM is both surprising and alarming (Özbilgin, 2004). Several shifts in approach may be required: from treating organizational settings as sources of error variance to attending as closely as possible to individual characteristics; from focusing on individuals to treating social systems as the target for study; from focusing on single practices or policies to adopting a holistic approach to conceptualizing HRM systems; from research conducted in single organizations at one point in time to research comparing multiple organizations across time, space and culture; and from a search for the 'one best way' to a search for the many possible ways to design and maintain effective HRM systems (Jackson and Schuler, 1995) .

Conclusion

In conclusion, it is imperative that local contextual factors are considered when designing and operationalizing HRM policies. Although HRM and organizations are currently evolving due to the evolving nature of globalization, culture continues to have a vital effect on people and organizations. As Stredwick notes 'indeed to the observer in one country, the workplace practices in another might seem downright absurd … any attempt to impose the ways and methods that he or she knows best in that other national context might be doomed to failure' (2005: 442).

The chapter has demonstrated that the field of HRM will have limited value if it does not adequately take into account cultural and institutional contexts. Global policies may seem an easy solution, but the issue of the expatriate workers, diversity and institutional and cultural variances must not be neglected. As Sparrow and Hiltrop (1994) suggest, care must be taken to escape the trap of ignoring significant differences between national cultures.

In this chapter, we have identified a number of elements in the macrolevel environment, that is, the sociocultural, legal, political, economic and technological contexts, that affect HRM in different ways. Economy is an important context that influences the design and outcomes of HRM; the financial crisis occurring at the time of writing this book has affected employment environment across many nations, and this is in turn affecting the behaviour of local labour markets. Similarly, cultural values, such as age and gender traditions and stereotypes, are significant social contexts relevant to HRM.

Managers also need to be aware of legal contexts that have the potential to affect employment relations. Local culture and other external pressures will influence the design of HRM, but institutions can, in their turn, influence the contexts affecting them – political leveraging and lobbying has, for example, been conducted by corporations against agreements that have had the potential to affect employment behaviour, such as the Kyoto agreement.

External contexts can also be linked to the pursuit for competitive advantage, as is usually emphasized in organizations in industrialized Western economies linking HRM strategy to competitive advantage. Towards that end, HRM practitioners will need to analyse and respond to external contextual issues and deal with them in a coherent and strategic manner.

❓ For discussion and revision

1 How do macrocontextual factors affect the design and operationalization of the following HRM functions:
  - Recruitment and selection
  - Training
  - Performance management
  - Reward management
  - Career management.

2 Make a study of HRM policies and practices in a specific company. Identify the various ways in which the HRM policies and practices in that company are affected by its sociocultural, political, legal and economic contexts.

3 What are various tensions between the globalization and contextualization of HRM? What are implications of such tensions for the future of HRM?

4 Identify at least one resource in a language other than English which deals with issues related to HRM. Feel free to seek help from a friend who speaks a language other than English. What can you learn from this resource?

5 How does the dominance of US and UK literature in the field of HRM affect the contextualization of HRM?

6 According to Hofstede (1991), organizational and industry characteristics may be more important than national cultures as determinants of managerial practices and employee behaviours. Discuss.

Further reading

Books

Dowling, P. J., Festing, M. and Engle, A. D. (2008) *International Human Resource Management. Managing People in a Multinational Context* (5th edn). London: Thomson Publishing.

Price, A. (2007) *Human Resource Management in a Business Context* (3rd edn). London: Thomson Learning.

Quinn, J. B., Mintzberg, H. and James, R. M. (eds) (1988) *The Strategy Process: Concepts, Context, and Cases*. Englewood Cliffs, NJ: Prentice Hall International.

Journals

Budhwar, P. and Khatri, P. (2001) HRM in context: the applicability of HRM models in India. *International Journal of Cross Cultural Management*, 1(3): 333–56.

Jackson, S. E. and Schuler, R. S. (1995) Understanding human resource management in the context of organizations and their environment. *Annual Review of Psychology*, 46: 237–64.

Kamoche, K. (2002) Introduction: human resource management in Africa. *International Journal of Human Resource Management*, 13(7): 993–7.

Khatri, N. (1999) Emerging issues in strategic HRM in Singapore. *International Journal of Manpower*, 20(8): 516–29.

Schmidt, V. (1993) An end to French economic exceptionalism? The transformation of business under Mitterand. *California Management Review*, (Fall), 75–98.

Selmer, J. and Leon C. D. (2001) Pinoy-style HRM: human resource management in Philippines. *Asia Pacific Business Review*, 8(1): 127–44.

Wan, D. (2003) Human resource management in Singapore: changes and continuities. *Asia Pacific Business Review*, 9(4): 129–46.

Other resources

Institut Perkhidmatan Awam (2008) About IPA. Available from: http://ipa.gov.bn/ipaonline/ipa_information/ipa_history.aspx [accessed 31 December 2009].

Laman Rasmi Jabatan Pekhidmatan Awam (n.d.) Hal Ehwal JPA. Available from: http://jpa.gov.bn/hal_ehwal/index.htm [accessed 31 December 2009].

Case Study   HRM in Brunei's public sector

Brunei is a monarchical government that is governed by Sultan Haji Hassanal Bolkiah Mu'izzaddin Waddaulah, who has executive authority and is assisted and advised by five constitutional bodies. The concept of 'Malay Islamic Monarchy' (MIB) is often thought of as a 'national philosophy', incorporating both the official Malay language, culture and customs and the importance of Islam as a religion and a set of guiding values.

Brunei, situated in South-East Asia, has an estimated population of 390,000, of whom 67 per cent are Malay and 15 per cent are Chinese, the remaining 18 per cent comprising indigenous groups, expatriates and immigrants. About 54 per cent of the overall population is made up of the 20–54-year age group, which is the economically productive group. The main source of income for Brunei is the oil and gas industry, followed by the private and government sectors. The public sector is the main employer for the majority of citizens and residents of Brunei (Brunei Economic Development Board, n.d.).

Owing to Brunei's distinct political system, it has different employment structures from those of other South-East Asian countries. Brunei is ruled by a strict essence of conformity and consensus that does not allow organization or individuals to challenge the government and its policies. Brunei's public sector may be seen as a 'model employer' (Beattie and Osborne, 2008), in the sense that the public sector sets an example to the private sector in terms of the fair treatment of employees and providing good conditions of service – this includes high levels of job security, better leave entitlement and generous pensions (Black and Upchurch, 1999). In this case study, we seek to explore how HRM policies and practices in the public sector are shaped by contextual influences in Brunei.

In the public sector, the *General Order and State Circulars* shape HRM practices. The General Order dates back to 1962; its content covers many key elements of HRM, for example appointments, promotions, benefit entitlement, work etiquette and discipline, although certain current issues related to HRM may not be present in the booklet. State Circulars cover more current HRM issues not addressed in the General Order, including those which have just arisen. All government bodies are sent Circulars whenever any new issues arise. Circulars often call upon the command of the Sultan of Brunei, who holds the absolute power in the way Brunei should be managed.

All civil servants are required to have a detailed knowledge of – and abide by – both the General Order and State Circulars in order to carry out their jobs and to progress in their careers. Every officer, supervisor or clerk who is aspiring towards promotion or a rise in salary will have to sit a written examination based on the content of both these sets of government policies.

A recent innovation within HRM in the Brunei public sector is the *Government Employee Management System* (GEMS), which is currently being trialled. This is a web-based system that enables efficient data input and greater transparency, which allows a better management of HRM practices such as recruitment and selection, compensation and benefits, as well as human resources administration. In addition, this will reduce paper usage and help Brunei to become more 'green'. Human resources administrators, government employees and the public are the three main stakeholders that GEMS is focusing on.

GEMS allows human resources administrators to manage job advertisements, and update and approve allowance and benefit applications. Government employees can apply for allowances and benefits online, retrieve useful information such as the latest policies that have been introduced, check their balance of leave entitlement and participate in surveys and forums where they can express their suggestions for how to improve the civil service. The public, on the other hand, can check job vacancies online, submit job applications and track their progress (Government Employee Management System, 2010).

Interviews conducted with a number of mangers and non-managerial staff in three departments within the Brunei public sector have provided an insight into how the local context has an impact on the design and implementation of HRM practices.

Socioculture

Many interviewees felt that Brunei's close-knit socioculture was an important factor in HRM practices. In particular, family relationships have a significant impact on workplace relations with supervisors and colleagues alike. As one interviewee stated:

> Working in the public sector, we are expected to respect our supervisors and officers. Supervisors and officers, regardless of their age, are like a father or leader to us; we share an informal relationship and talk to them in person if we have any issues or problems. A very family-like relationship is what motivates me, in particular, because it gives me a feeling of belonging and

security. Although we have an informal relation-ship, it does not mean that we respect our supe-riors any less.

Previous research in other countries has high-lighted that close-knit relationships often result in subjective and informal recruitment and selection processes (see, for example, Myloni et al.'s [2004] research in Greece). The majority of the employees interviewed for this case study claimed that family connections do not influence the way people are employed. This is evident in the following except:

Yes we have a very close relationship in our culture, but I must say that it has no direct influ-ence on the way we recruit and select appli-cants. Because everyone goes through the same procedure, that is, a written exam and then interviews for short-listed applicants. Further-more, there are guidelines and procedures that need to be followed when recruiting people. Also, there is a group of committee members who decides on the final result'; this is based on consensus agreement. There is no room for favouritism. ... Personally, when the one who is newly recruited happens to be the son/daughter of an authority figure in the public sector, it is because he/she is qualified for the position, he/she might have already been trained with the kind of traits and skills that we are looking for. That is not nepotism.

However, the above account contradicts statements made by at least three other participants, who felt that 'nepotism' is still the essence of recruitment and selection, particularly in the government sector. Overall, the interviews suggest that close-knit social relationships in Brunei society have an impact on employment relationship in the work-place. However, the impact is moderated in HRM practices, particularly in recruitment and selec-tion, because governmental regulations still affect HRM policies.

Law and politics

The national philosophy of MIB has an important influence on the way HRM works in the public sector. One interviewee noted that:

Malay culture teaches us to be respectful and courteous to others. Islam instils honesty, trust, loyalty and good faith in oneself. Monarchic government means that His Majesty the Sultan holds the ultimate power in decision-making; no one is allowed to go against His Majesty's command. So, basically MIB influences us, in terms of the way we bring ourselves, the way we

perform our work as a loyal subject of His Majesty. Every aspect of government affairs revolves around the concept of MIB.

The political influence of the state has in other studies been shown to either strengthen or under-mine the role of HRM (Tayeb, 2005): a more cooper-ative government will have a better chance of adopting HRM efficiently, and vice versa. When asked whether monarchical government hinders employee participation in decision-making, one interviewee stated that:

Any grievances, complaints or suggestions that are made by employees are attended to by respective supervisors or officers. Obviously in a monarchical government like Brunei, His Majesty holds the absolute powers in major decisions. But other than that, we do value employees' suggestions and points of view. We always take their opinions into consideration. In my position as an officer, I make sure that my door is always open for them to come in and express any problem or suggestion that they may have. We ensure that we include them into any problem-solving and decision-making, because it is important that they feel included.

When asked about how the General Order and State Circulars are dealt with by public sector workers, managers underlined the critical impor-tance of these, not only for their own careers, but also to provide a basis for all government servants for what should and should not be done while working in the public sector. As one interviewee noted:

Every circular is by command of His Majesty The Sultan; we are obliged to obey them. Officers are directed to encourage and make employees aware of existing circulars.

Non-managerial staff, however, tended to take a less rigorous approach and were sometimes unfa-miliar with the content of these documents. Regula-tions were still poorly enforced regardless of the availability of the General Order and State Circulars.

With regards to the content of the General Order, benefits entitlements and working hours are usually included and practised in workplace policies. Partici-pants generally felt that the policies adopted by the government are flexible and family-friendly. For example, one married female participant stated that:

Yes it is very family-friendly. One of the most obvious aspect is the working hours in the government sector. In the regulation book, General Order, it states that one should work maximum 8 hours from 7.45 am to 4.30 pm, but there is some flexibility when it comes to family responsibility, such as sending or picking up children to/from school. Also, in terms of leave entitlement, a married woman can take unpaid leave to follow her husband who was sent to work abroad and her job is still available when she comes back.

Economics

Research suggests that, for individuals to be more productive and adaptable to changing economic conditions, experience and knowledge have to be significantly valued (Jackson and Schuler, 1995). In the Brunei public sector, this valuation of education and human capital seems to have been achieved. When asked whether different economic situations influenced the need for educated or experienced workforce, one manager noted that:

> In the government sector education plays a very important role because we believe fresh graduates have new ideas, which would ultimately benefit the organization over a person with experience who might not have anything new to bring to the organization.

From an economic perspective, Brunei is currently facing an excess supply of labour in the job market. An officer thus explained this:

> This is a very challenging issue Brunei is facing. The demand for jobs is overwhelmingly high but the supply of jobs to accommodate the demand is rather low. This is because a new post will only be available when someone retires, resigns, there is end of contract of an employee or a budget is allocated to create new posts.

This is consistent with Jackson and Schuler's observation that a country is likely to experience high unemployment in times of oversupply of its labour force. Brunei is currently experiencing this problem, and thus many students are sponsored to study abroad to temporarily alleviate the number of workers currently seeking jobs. The problem with an oversupply of labour is that very few vacant positions are usually available in the government sector. For example, in response to a recent advertisement (at the time of this research) for a clerical position, 1,000 applications were received for only four vacancies.

Technology

Technology is a new element in the government sector in Brunei. The Sultan has allocated billions of dollars for IT to be used effectively. In particular, the introduction of GEMS, described above, is indic-

ative of a new approach to technology in HRM practice. Public sector workers have mixed reactions to this new system. One manager noted that:

> It's very convenient because there's less paperwork and sharing of documents will be easier as it is computerised. Leave applications, benefits entitlement, car and house loans, all are accessible any time and anywhere.

Another, less positively, argued that:

> We currently have an online method of inputting data called SIMPA; it is in Malay and it is very straightforward. But it is only for data entry and nothing else. Well, GEMS from what I have tried is a bit too complex for me because there are so may folders to click on and most importantly, it is in English. To be honest, I am not good in English language, so I don't know how I will be able to get used to the changes.

Officers in general tend to agree with the technological changes that the government intends to implement, whereas the staff are slightly hesitant about the changes. For example, a training officer stated that:

> Every human resources development representative of each government department is given courses to train their respective employees on the usage of this new system. Emphasis is given to clerical positions as they are the ones who handle most paperwork.

From the interview data, one obvious challenge facing HRM in Brunei relates to how well individuals can adjust themselves to technological changes. Moving away from the traditional face-to-face HRM services may cause some difficulty and stress for some employees. Training, on the other hand, may assist staff and officers to adapt effectively to such changes.

Conclusion

This study of HRM in Brunei makes clear that the macroenvironmental context has a huge impact on the way HRM polices are designed and implemented. Culture serves as the overarching umbrella for all the other contexts, such as the legal and political system, the economy and adaptation to technology. In the main, HRM in Brunei revolves around the MIB ideology, which signifies the extent to which Western-originated HRM practices are customized and applied in the country. Human capital is given great importance and has high value in the job market; incentives are, therefore, given to improve human capital. However, the monarchical government of Brunei limits the ability for freedom of speech, freedom of associations and collective bargaining.

A hierarchical relationship is present in the government sector, but power distance is not a key concern, as is evident from the interview data. These show that Brunei does have a hierarchical relationship as claimed by Hofstede (1984) but that the power distance is not very great and is often a sign of respect for authority and for one's superiors. The relationship shared between officers and subordinates positively affects employees' participation rates in problem-solving and decision-making. However, close-knit relationships seem not to excessively influence the recruitment and selection process, which is regulated by state laws and procedures.

From a legal and political context perspective, the MIB ideology seems to have a visible impact on HRM. It enhances the initiatives of various departments in ensuring that everyone gets 100 hours of training and development. It also prohibits employees from setting up or joining trade unions, instead encouraging a more peaceful and harmonious negotiation with officers and supervisors. The General Order and State Circulars are still weakly enforced, although superiors tried to stress their importance. In addition, MIB and state laws help to create a family-friendly policy that is flexible for working parents and employees with dependants.

From an economic context perspective, human capital, education, knowledge and skills are encouraged through continuous learning for all employees and officers. The benefits offered by the public sector create the perception of its being the most stable and secure workplace, and hence provide an advantage when recruiting and retaining human capital. Oversupply of the workforce is a prominent issue in Brunei. This affects HRM processes in making sure that the public sector recruits the right people for the right jobs.

Technology seems to be an upcoming aspect in the government sector. Not much information could be gleaned, except for the perceptions of older workers that there is a shift towards an online-based system of HRM. Some older workers find it difficult to adjust to this, but they are still able to do so slowly. Also, when officers and staff were asked whether this would increase convenience, most participants answered positively, saying that IT is helping to speed up their work and lessen their workload.

It can be concluded that local culture and politics (MIB) have a much greater impact on the implementation of HRM in Brunei. We recommend that further research be conducted on a larger scale to explore the contextualization of HRM in Brunei and other national contexts. Preferably, academia–industry partnership-based research in these government departments might allow for a deeper understanding of the topic.

Questions

1 How do culture and politics affect the design and implementation of HRM in Brunei?
2 Culture serves as the overarching umbrella for all the other contexts, such as the legal and political system, the economy and adaptation to technology. Critically discuss this.
3 How can HRM enable individual employees to adjust themselves to technological changes in their organizations?
4 How does HRM in Brunei different from HRM in a Western country?

References

Adler, N. J. (1991) *International Dimensions of Organizational Behavior*. Boston, MA: PWS-KENT Publishing.

Ailon, G. (2008) Mirror, mirror on the wall: culture's consequences in a value test of its own design. *Academy of Management Review*, 33(4): 885–904.

Arvey, R. D., Bhagat, R. S. and Salas, E. (1991) Cross-cultural and cross-national issues in personnel and human resources management: where do we go from here? *Personnel and Human Resource Management*, 9: 367–407.

Baruch, Y. (2001) Global or North American top management journals? *Journal of Cross-cultural Management*, 1(1): 131–47.

Beattie, R. S. and Osborne, S. P. (2008) *Human Resource Management in the Public Sector*. London: Routledge.

Beer, M., Lawrance, P. R., Mills, D. Q. and Walton, R. E. (1985) *Human Resource Management*. New York: Free Press.

Bennington, L. and Habir, A. D. (2003) Human resource management in Indonesia. *Human Resource Management Review*, 13(3): 373–92.

Black, J. and Upchurch, M. (1999) Public sector employment. In Hollinshead, G., Nicholls, P. and Tailby, S. (eds) *Employee Relations*. London: Financial Times Management.

Bondarouk, T. V. and Ruel, H. J. M. (2009) Electronic human resource management: challenges in the digital era. *International Journal of Human Resource Management*, 20(3): 505–14.

Bondarouk, T., Ruel, H. and Heijden B. V. D. (2009) e-HRM effectiveness in a public sector organization: a multi-stakeholder perspective. *International Journal of Human Resource Management*, 20(3): 578–90.

Bratton, J. and Gold, J. (2007) *Human Resource Management: Theory and Practice* (4th edn). New York: Palgrave Macmillan.

Brewster, C. (2007) Comparative HRM: European views and perspectives. *International Journal of Human Resource Management*, 18(5): 769–87.

Brewster, C. and Tyson, S. (eds) (1991) *International Comparisons in Human Resource Management*. London: Pitman.

Brunei Economic Development Board (n.d.) Introducing Brunei. [Online]. Available from: http://www.bedb.com.bn/ [Accessed 9 November 2009].

Budhwar, P. S. and Debrah, Y. A. (2001) *Human Resource Management in Developing Countries*. London: Routledge.

Burton, J. P., Butler, J. E. and Mowday, R. T. (2003) Lions, tigers and alley cats: HRM's role in Asian business development. *Human Resource Management Review*, 13(3): 487–98.

Caligiuri, P. M. (1999) The ranking of scholarly journals in international human resource management. *International Journal of Human Resource Management*, 10(3): 515–19.

Carroll, G. R., Delacroix, J. and Goodstein, J. (1988) The political environments of organizations: an ecological view. *Research in Organizational Behavior*, 10: 359–92.

Chase, S., 2002. Ratifying Kyoto. *Globe and Mail*, 27 February, p. B6.

Chomsky, N. (1999). *Profit over People: Neoliberalism and the Global Order*. New York: Seven Stories Press.

Clark, T., Gospel, H. and Montgomery, J. (1999) Running on the spot? A review of twenty years of research on the management of human resources in comparative and international perspective. *International Journal of Human Resource Management*, 10(3): 520–44.

Clark, T., Grant, D. and Heijltjes, M. (2000) Researching comparative and international human resource management. *International Studies of Management and Organization*, 29(4): 6–17.

Collin, A. (2007) Contextualising HRM: developing critical thinking. In Beardwell, J. and Claydon, T. (eds) *Human Resource Management: A Contemporary Approach*. Harlow: FT Prentice Hall, pp. 83–116.

Drucker, P. (1954) *The Practice of Management*. New York: Harper & Row.

Edwards, T. (2004) The transfer of employment practices across borders in multinational companies. In Harzing, A.-W. and Ruysseveldt, J. V. (eds) *International Human Resource Management*. London: Sage, pp. 389–410.

Faux, J. & Mishel, L. (2001) Inequality and the global economy. In Hutton, W. and Giddens, A. (eds.) *On the Edge: Living with Capitalism*. London: Vintage Books.

Flamholtz, E. G. and Lacey, J. M. (1981) Personnel management, human capital theory, and human resource accounting. Cited in Jackson, S. E. and Schuler, R. S. (1995) Understanding human resource management in the context of organizations and their environments. *Annual Review of Psychology*, 46: 237–64.

Florkowski, G. W. and Nath, R. (1993) MNC responses to the legal environment of international human resource management. *International Journal of Human Resource Management*, 4: 305–24.

Gaugler, E. (1988) HR management: an international comparison. *Personnel*, (August): 24–30.

Government Employee Management System (2010) About GEMS: GEMS Background. [Online]. Available from: http://www.jpa.gov.bn/gems/EN/About_GEMS/background.htm [Accessed 10 January 2010].

Harris, L. (2002) The future for the HRM function in local government: everything has changed – but has anything changed? *Strategic Change*, 11(7): 369–78.

Heenan, D. A. and Perlmutter, H. V. (1979) *Multinational Organization Development*. Reading, MA: Pearson Addison Wesley.

Hill, T. (2005) *Operations Management*. Basingstoke: Palgrave Macmillan.

Hill, C. (2009) *International Business: Competing in the Global Marketplace* (7th edn). New York: McGraw-Hill.

Hofstede, G. (1980) *Culture's Consequences: International Differences in Work Related Values*. Beverly Hills: Sage.

Hofstede, G. (1984) Cultural dimension in management and planning. *Asia Pacific Journal of Management*, 1(2): 81–99.

Hofstede, G. (1991) *Cultures and Organizations*. London: McGraw-Hill.

Hu, Y.-S. (1992) Global or stateless corporations are national firms with international operations. *California Management Review*, (Winter): 107–26.

Jackson, S. E. and Schuler, R. S. (1995) Understanding human resource management in the context of organizations and their environments. *Annual Review of Psychology*, 46: 237–64.

Levy-Leboyer, C. (1994) Selection and assessment in Europe. In Triandis, H. C., Dunnette, M. D. and Hough, L. M. (eds) *Handbook of Industrial and Organizational Psychology* (2nd edn, Vol. 4). Palo Alto, CA: Consulting Psychology Press, pp. 173–90.

Lincoln, J. R. (1993) Work organization in Japan and the United States. In Kogut, B. (ed.) *Country Competitiveness: Technology and the Organizing of Work*. Oxford: Oxford University Press, pp. 93–124.

McCourt, W. and Foon L. M. (2007) Malaysia as model: policy transferability in an Asian country. *Public Management Review*, 9(2): 211–29.

MacDuffie, J. P. and Krafcik, J. (1992) Integrating technology and human resources for high performance manufacturing. In Kochan, T. and Useem, M. (eds) *Transforming Organizations*. New York: Oxford University Press, pp. 210–26.

McGregor, D. (1957) *The Human Side of Enterprise. Fifth Anniversary Convocation of the MIT School of Industrial Management*. Cambridge, MA: MIT Press.

McSweeney, B. (2002) Hofstede's model of national cultural differences and their consequences: a triumph of faith – a failure of analysis. *Human Relations*, 55(1): 89–118.

Maurice, M., Sellier, F. and Silvestre, J.-J. (1986) *Bases of Industrial Power*. Cambridge, MA: MIT Press.

Millward, N. and Stevens, M. (1986) *British Workplace Industrial Relations 1980–1984*. Aldershot: Gower.

Myloni, B., Harzing, A. K. and Mirza, H. (2004) Host country specific factors and the transfer of human resource management practices in multinational companies. *International Journal of Manpower*, 25(6): 518–34.

Needle, D. (2004) *Business in Context* (4th edn). London: Thomson.

Noe, R. A., Hollenbeck, J. R., Gerhart, B. and Wright, P. M. (2008) *Human Resource Management: Gaining a Competitive Advantage* (6th edn). New York: McGraw Hill.

Othman, R. and The, C. (2003) On developing the informated work place: HRM issues in Malaysia. *Human Resource Management Review*, 13: 393–406.

Özbilgin, M. (2004) Inertia of the international human resource management text in a changing world: an examination of the editorial board membership of the top 21 IHRM journals. *Personnel Review*, 33(2): 205–21.

Price, A. (1997) *Human Resource Management in a Business Context*. London: International Thomson Business Press.

Ronen, S. (1994) An underlying structure of motivational need taxonomies: a cross-cultural confirmation. In Triandis, H. C., Dunnette, M. D. and Hough, L. M. (eds) *Handbook of Industrial and Organizational Psychology* (2nd edn, Vol. 4). Palo Alto, CA: Consulting Psychology Press, pp. 241–70.

Rousseau, D. M. (1990). Assessing organizational culture: the case for multiple methods. In Schneider, B. (ed.), *Organizational Climate and Culture*. San Francisco: Jossey-Bass, pp. 153–92.

Ruigrok, W. and van Tulder, R. (1995) *The Logic of International Restructuring*. London: Routledge.

Schneider, S. (2001) Introduction to the international human resource management special issue. *Journal of World Business*, 36(4): 341.

Schuler, R. S. and Jackson, S. E. (1987) Linking competitive strategies with human resource management practices. *Academy of Management Review*, 1(3): 207–19.

Sparrow, P. R. and Hiltrop, J.-M. (1994) *European Human Resource Management in Transition*. London: Prentice Hall.

Storey, J. (1992) *Developments in the Management of Human Resources: An Analytical Review*. Oxford: Blackwell.

Strauss, G. (1982) Workers participation in management: an international perspective. *Research in Organizational Behavior*, 4: 173–265.

Stredwick, J. (2005) *An Introduction to Human Resource Management* (2nd edn). London: Elsevier.

Tayeb, M. H. (2005) *International Human Resource Management: A Multinational Company Perspective*. New York: Oxford University Press.

Taylor, S., Beechler, S. and Napier, N. (1996) Toward an integrated model for strategic international human resource management. *Academy of Management Review*, 21(4): 959–71.

Triandis, H. C., Dunnette, M. D. and Hough, L. M. (eds) (1994) *Handbook of Industrial and Organizational Psychology* (2nd edn, Vol. 4). Palo Alto, CA: Consulting Psychology Press.

Tung, R. L. (1993) Managing cross-national and intra-national diversity. *Human Resource Management Journal*, 23(4): 461–77.

Tylor, E. B. (1924). *Primitive Culture* (7th edn, Vols 1 and 2). New York: Brentano's.

Wheelan, C. (2003) *Naked Economics: Undressing the Dismal Science*. New York: W. W. Norton.

Wickens, P. (1987) *The Road to Nissan*. London: Macmillan.

A critical perspective on strategic human resource management

Dima Jamali and Fida Afiouni

2

?

After reading this chapter, you should be able to:

☐ Recognize recent transformations and dynamic change in the human resources management (HRM) field

☐ Demonstrate good knowledge of the various theoretical approaches to strategic HRM

☐ Discuss how human resources can be a source of sustainable competitive advantage

☐ Critically examine choices and contingencies in the HRM field

☐ Recognize the significant advances brought about by the strategic HRM paradigm, as well as lingering challenges, particularly the gap that remains between human resources policies and practices

Introduction

From personnel management to SHRM: an evolutionary road map

Differentiating attributes, key contributions and underlying theories

Critical analysis and discussion

Conclusion

For discussion and revision

Further reading

Case study: Strategic human resource management: insights from Deloitte ME's experience

References

Introduction

Over the past two decades, there has been a vibrant change and evolution in the field of human resource management (HRM). Schuler and Jackson (2007) categorize changes in the field into two major transformations. The first has entailed a transformation from personnel management to HRM, and the second constituted a leap forward into what is commonly referred to today as strategic HRM (SHRM). According to its proponents, SHRM constitutes a new orthodoxy and is mainly differentiated by its macro or strategic orientation, as well as its focus on outcomes and performance (Delery and Doty, 1996). Although it is certainly a discipline that is still taking shape and form, SHRM has enjoyed an astounding ascendancy in recent years, and has attracted significant interest from the academic and practitioner community (Becker and Huselid, 2006).

The aim of this chapter is to provide a critical assessment of SHRM, shedding light on its differentiating attributes and theoretical foundations, as well as the persistent gaps and challenges in this rapidly growing field. SHRM undoubtedly presents significant advances and new insights in relation to people management, but it is not a panacea and there is still no consensus on an exact definition of SHRM among scholars. These challenges, coupled with the difficulty of translating theory into practice, are possible stumbling blocks in the way of the fully fledged maturation of SHRM and will be fleshed out and discussed further in the sections below.

The structure of this chapter is as follows. First, we will explore the evolutionary road map from personnel management to SHRM and examine the various theoretical approaches to SHRM, namely the universalist, contingency and resource-based views (RBVs). This exploration will be enriched by practical exercises and critical questions that allow for a better understanding of the strategic role of HRM. Finally, we will adopt a critical perspective that aims to reveal the global and ethical issues that underpin SHRM and sensitize the reader to the potential gaps that remain between the policy and practice of SHRM.

From personnel management to SHRM: an evolutionary road map

The traditional personnel management approach was prevalent in the first part of the 20th century and reflected management currents revolving around Weberism, Taylorism and scientific management. The focus was on maximizing labour productivity and efficiency, and in response to this, the personnel management function adopted a uniquely inward and operational focus, with an obsessive concern with legal compliance and streamlining basic administrative and personnel processes. Personnel management was therefore commonly characterized as a transactional, low-level, record-keeping and maintenance function with a short-term micro-orientation and a preoccupation with operational issues, practices and policies, to the neglect of broader business issues and the overall direction of the organization (Guest, 1987; Redman and Wilkinson, 2009).

This approach to the management of people was essentially anchored in a view of labour as a commodity to be used efficiently and discarded as appropriate.

The first major transformation or turning point came about in the 1970s and reflected the ascendancy of the human relations and organizational behaviour paradigms (Mahoney and Deckop, 1986; Anthony et al., 2002). These new theoretical traditions highlighted the complexity of human behaviour and the importance of soft aspects of management, including leadership and motivation, in impacting work outcomes in a positive way. The challenge for HRM was therefore to reposition 'employees as valued organizational resources' (Dunn, 2006: 71) and to better orchestrate policies and practices that affected their behaviour and productivity at work (Schuler and Jackson, 2007).

Although HRM retained essentially its tactical short-term orientation, it was heralded as 'a new era of humane people oriented employment management' (Keenoy, 1990: 375) capitalizing on systematic and professional management practices, and the improved coordination and integration of human resources practices. Valuing employees as an important human capital – an investment rather than a cost (Wright et al., 2001) – was the prevailing assumption permeating this first transformation of the function. This transformation of the HRM function was in turn accompanied by the emergence of the total quality management (TQM) paradigm, as highlighted by Soltani in Chapter 15 of this book. Despite differences in the nature of and approaches to TQM and HRM, both concepts share the paramount importance of people-focused organizational efforts. These shared characteristics of the two concepts suggest a resurgence of the value attached to managing human resources, as both focus on a systematic and careful approach to the recruitment of employees, the use of teamwork and group problem-solving, egalitarian work structures, a commitment to training, and performance and reward systems.

The second major transformation in the field occurred more recently, starting in the 1990s in response to large-scale organizational change and an intensely competitive global economic environment (Calakoglu et al., 2006). In the context of new trends including organizational transience, corporate restructuring (for example, mergers and acquisitions, and downsizing), a renewed focus on quality and customers, and the war for talent among others (Conner and Ulrich, 1996; Amit and Belcourt, 1999; Pilbeam and Corbridge, 2006), the need for agility and efficiency has been accentuated. In addition, the role of human resources has been brought to the fore as it has been realized that employees can have a significant impact on the overall success of the organization. SHRM is therefore anchored in a recent appreciation that human resources and the effective management of people are critical to profitability (Boxall and Purcell, 2011) and the overall ability of a firm to thrive and compete (Meilich, 2005). As suggested by Boxall and Purcell (2011), the adjective 'strategic' implies a concern with the ways in which HRM is critical to the firm's survival and relative success', and SHRM has come to denote 'a strategic and coherent approach to the management of an organization's most valued assets – the people working there, who individually and collectively contribute to the achievement of its objectives' (Armstrong, 2006: 3).

Figure 2.1, adapted from Pilbeam and Corbridge (2006) and Brockbank (1999), outlines this ongoing process of transformation or evolution from traditional personnel management to SHRM. Figure 2.1 also highlights interesting nuances at both sides of the continuum. On the left-hand side, we can note nuances between reactive and proactive operational orientations with an operationally reactive human resources function focused on day-to-day demands and implementation of the regular and mundane; this contrasts with a more proactive orientation concerned with improving the basics, as suggested by Brockbank (1999). We can also highlight interesting nuances between strategically reactive and strategically proactive human resources orientations on the right-hand side of the continuum, with the strategically reactive human resources generally concerned with implementing and realizing strategy, and more strategically proactive human resources concerned with creating and forging strategic alternatives (Brockbank, 1999).

Figure 2.1 From traditional personnel management (TPM) to strategic human resource management (SRHM).

Source: Adapted from Pilbeam and Corbridge (2006), Bockbank (1999)

Mini Case Study 2.1

HRM at Algorithm: good strategic alignment

Algorithm is a pharmaceutical plant operating in the Middle East, having existed under this name since 1989. The firm's business line is manufacturing pharmaceutical products and sending them to its distributors and exporters (it does not handle any distribution activities itself). Algorithm belongs to a group of three sister companies employing a total of 320 employees, 170 of whom are employed by Algorithm. It manufactures products under license, as well as its own generic products. It has a development laboratory – the Product Development Lab – but this mainly copies generic products and designs new products without creating molecules. The organization does not outsource any technical or production activities as it has all the necessary departments and assets. This means that it manufactures, analyses and registers all its products. The plant's production includes over-the-counter (OTC) and prescription drugs, but no cosmetic products.

An interview was conducted with Mrs Nicole Bakhache, the HR and administration manager at Algorithm Lebanon and a member of Algorithm's strategy-setting team. The human resources function at Algorithm has been given much greater importance over the past 5 years, and no major decision related to people or structure is taken without human resources input. Mrs Bakhache explained that some personnel activities involve a more reactive role (for example, benefits and payroll), whereas other human resources activities, such as recruitment, training and career planning, involve a more proactive and strategic role.

At Algorithm, the human resources department also

▷ plays a substantial role in ensuring the success of general business strategies, and helping to accomplish business goals. It is expected to translate business strategy into action, and to focus on aligning human resources strategies and practices with business strategies. The department has forged a partnership with line managers, and together they formulate and manage processes to help meet business objectives. Furthermore, line managers now view human resources as a partner and are themselves involved in the management of human resources – working along with the human resources function on activities such as recruitment, people development and personnel-related issues.

The human resources manager explained that the strategies of the human resources function are aligned with the general business strategies, and that line management involves human resources in meetings where future strategies are being formulated. They are, for example, involved in strategic meetings discussing company expansion (since they will have to recruit the qualified staff needed for this), budgeting and planning. Mrs Bakhache explained that the technical departments do not have regular meetings with human resources, but hold periodic meetings to discuss budgets, management reviews, expansion plans, recruitment and a review of training needs. The input of human resources is required when discussing issues related to staff, such as filling internal vacancies and retaining key staff if ever they should consider leaving the company.

Questions

1 How does the human resources department at Algorithm help to accomplish its business goals?
2 Use Figure 2.1 to evaluate the role of the human resources department in terms of its strategic/operational orientation as well as proactive/reactive orientation.

Differentiating attributes, key contributions and underlying theories

At the heart of SHRM lies the idea that the way in which people are managed is one of the most crucial factors in the array of competitiveness-inducing variables, with a view that labour is an asset that should be leveraged in the pursuit of competitive advantage (Boxall and Purcell, 2011). Strategic choices associated with labour processes in turn reflect on the firm's performance. Hence, human resource policies need to be integrated with each other, as well as linked to the strategies and overall direction of the organization (Schuler and Jackson, 2007). In this context, the core differentiating attributes of SHRM have come to be theorized as revolving around commitment, flexibility, quality and integration (Guest, 1987), a strategic thrust informing decisions about people management and a new set of levers to shape the employment relationship (Storey, 2001). Armstrong (2006) identifies core differentiating features of SHRM revolving around strategic orientation, commitment, people as a core asset and business values/results. Some of these core themes are reflected in Table 2.1.

In essence, SHRM is more fluid, organic and strategy-driven practice and is associated with *commitment*-based systems of control (Guest, 1990: 152). SHRM is therefore based on the assumption that people are not only assets, but also have value-creating properties. This insight derives essentially from the RBV of the firm, a concept that emerged in 1984 and has enjoyed increasing popularity within the strategic management and HRM literatures. According to Wright et al. (2001), the RBV has been clearly instrumental to the development of the SHRM field of study, primarily because it has promoted a rebalancing of the strategy literature away from external factors (such as industry position) towards the firm's internal resources as sources of competitive advantage.

Table 2.1 Definitions and differentiating attributes of strategic human resource management (SHRM)

Author(s)	Definition of SHRM
Boxall and Purcell (2000)	A concern with the ways in which HRM is critical to organizational effectiveness
Buyens and De Vos (2001)	The linking of the human resources function with the strategic goals and objectives of the organization in order to improve business performance and develop organizational cultures that foster innovation and flexibility
Redman and Wilkinson (2009)	A concept entailing strategic integration and a positive approach to the management of employees, with an emphasis on staff as a resource rather than a cost
Guest (1987)	SRHM has four key dimensions: commitment, flexibility, quality and integration
Armstrong (2006)	SHRM is differentiated by its strategic thrust, emphasis on integration, commitment orientation, belief that people are core assets and focus on business values and results
Storey (2001)	Four key aspects of SHRM entailing a particular constellation of beliefs and assumptions, a strategic thrust informing decisions about people management, the central involvement of line managers, and a reliance upon a new set of levers to shape the employment relationship

Indeed, one of the key contributions of the RBV to date has been a theory of competitive advantage and how firms can achieve and sustain their competitive advantage (Fahy, 2000). The RBV contends that the answer to this question lies in the nurturing and deployment of certain key resources. From an RBV perspective, not all resources are of equal importance – certain resources have an edge in terms of creating competitive advantage (Fahy, 2000). Barney (1991) posits that desirable resources must meet four conditions, namely value, rareness, inimitability and non-substitutability. Collis and Montgomery (1995) suggest along the same lines that value-creating resources are characterized by inimitability, durability, appropriability, non-substitutability and competitive superiority. The RBV has therefore contributed significantly in terms of putting people on the strategy radar screen and highlighting the importance of people to competitive advantage.

Following the logic of the RBV, human capital constitutes a very important intangible asset or resource that is resistant to duplication by competitors. However, what is equally important from this perspective is the way in which this asset is deployed and managed, which has been captured through the notion of 'capabilities' that was introduced by Leonard-Barton as early as 1992. Capabilities are the tangible and intangible assets that firms use to develop and implement their strategies (Wernerfelt, 1995). Essentially, capabilities encompass the skills of individuals

Exercise

Barney (1991) posits that desirable resources must meet four conditions – value, rareness, inimitability and non-substitutability – in order to be a source of sustainable competitive advantage. Based on these characteristics, critically examine how human resources are a possible source of competitive advantage.
- Where does the advantage come from?
- Is it a human capital advantage deriving from the quality of the employees, or is it a human process advantage deriving from the set of human resources policies and practices that has been applied?

and groups, as well as the organizational routines and interactions through which all the firm's resources are coordinated (Grant, 1991). Typical of the latter are, among others, teamwork, communication, collaboration, learning, knowledge management, work design, organizational culture, trust between management and workers, and leadership. In this respect, human resources is not limited to its effects on employee skills and behaviour. Instead, its effects are more encompassing in that they help weave those skills and behaviours within the broader fabric of organizational systems, processes and ultimately competencies (Wright et al., 2001).

Capabilities that give an organization a strategic advantage over its competitors have been called core capabilities (Leonard-Barton, 1992), although a number of alternative terms have been used to refer to the same or similar concepts. An important article by Prahalad and Hamel (1990) that helped to disseminate the RBV refers to developing core competence within an organization. Core competence develops from collective learning in an organization, especially from being able to coordinate diverse sets of skills and integrate different technologies. Teece et al. (1997) define dynamic capabilities as the ability to integrate, build and reconfigure internal and external competencies to address rapidly changing environments. Similarly, Leonard-Barton (1992) posits that dynamic capabilities reflect an organization's ability to achieve new and innovative forms of competitive advantage given path dependencies and market positions.

In other words, human resources do not automatically confer a sustainable competitive advantage, and the managerial role is critical in nurturing, deploying and protecting key firm resources over time (Williams, 1992). Whereas exceptional human talent confers human capital advantage (HCA), firms need to supplement or pair the latter with what has been referred to as human process advantage (HPA), through the nurturing of specific processes, routines and practices, and their constellation, operation and application over time (Boxall, 1996). Therefore, organizations face a dual challenge – or the management of mutuality (Wright et al., 2001) – that entails the creation of a committed and talented workforce, as well as nurturing the right processes that support this talent and shape its competencies, cognitions and attitudes (Boxall, 1996). The contemporary theories of job design, as outlined by Holland in Chapter 7 in this book, are important in conferring such a HPA in the sense that they focus on human needs and psychological aspects of job content. In other words, SHRM needs to take into account job design aspects relating to variety and challenge, continuous learning, decision-making autonomy and social relationships, particularly in creating HPA.

These two sources of competitive advantage, when effectively combined, reinforce the systemic quality of highly effective human resources architectures and confer human resource advantage, as illustrated in Figure 2.2. SHRM posits in turn a relationship between a firm's human resources architecture and that firm's performance (Becker and Huselid, 2006).

The link between the human resources architecture and the firm's performance is not direct but is usually mediated by an appropriate match between the

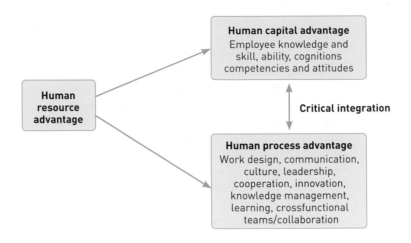

Figure 2.2 The resource-based view and human resource advantage.
Source: Adapted from Boxall (1996)

human resources architecture and strategic choice – what is commonly referred to as the human resources–strategy fit (Schuler and Jackson, 1987). In other words, the human resources architecture needs to be aligned with the larger competitive strategy of the firm. As Mohrman and Lawler (1997: 160) write, 'in order for the human resources function to contribute to its organization's performance, it must ensure that all of its human resources practices "fit with each other and with the strategy and design of the organization".' Although the latter has tended to be a salient underlying premise of SHRM – that firms adopting a particular strategy require human resources practices that are different from those required by organizations adopting alternative strategies (Delery and Doty, 1996) – there is no consensus on this point. This is reflected in the emergence of three different modes of theorizing in the field of SHRM:

☐ the universalistic perspective;
☐ the contingency perspective;
☐ the configurational approach.

These are described briefly below.

The universal approach, also commonly referred to as the best practice approach, to SHRM posits that some human resources practices are always better than others, and that all organizations should adopt these best practices (Delery and Doty, 1996). The logic is that all firms are likely to see improvements in their performance if they identify and implement best practice, and that the link between human resources and the firm's performance is universal across the population of organizations. The most renowned model in the best practice approach is that of Pfeffer (1994), who argued that the greater adoption and use of 16 management practices, such as employment security, selectivity in hiring, incentive pay, high wages, empowerment, participation, training and skill development and promotion from within, would result in higher productivity and profit across firms. Osterman (1994) similarly suggested that innovative work practices, such as teams, quality circles, job rotation and TQM, stimulate productivity gains across companies. These practices identified by Pfeffer (1994) and others have been labelled as high-performance work practices as they induce higher performance (Delery and Doty, 1996).

Contingency theorizing, or what is commonly referred to as the best fit approach, argues that the human resources strategy will be more effective when it is appropriately integrated with its specific organizational and broader environmental context (Boxall and Purcell, 2011). For example, the rate of product, service or market innovation has frequently been treated as a critical contingency, with firms that are highly innovative considered as prospectors, firms that are moderately innovative considered as analysers, and firms that rarely innovate considered as defenders (Miles and Snow, 1984). Basically, the successful implementation of any of those business strategies relies heavily on human resources and its moulding of appropriate employee behaviour (Delery and Doty, 1996). Schuler and Jackson (1987), for example, argue that human resources practices should be designed to reinforce the behavioural implications of the various generic strategies defined by Porter (1985), as illustrated briefly in Figure 2.3 and Table 2.2. Therefore, to the extent that an organization's strategy demands behavioural requirements for its success, the use of human resources practices can reward and control employee behaviour (Delery and Doty, 1996).

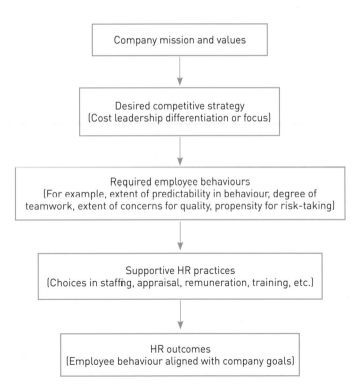

Figure 2.3 Linking human resources (HR) practices to competitive strategy.
Source: Adapted from Schuler and Jackson (1987: 208)

Table 2.2 Different competitive strategies and different employee competitive role behaviours

Strategy	Employee role behaviours needed
Innovation	• Highly innovative behaviour • Very long-term behaviour • Highly cooperative behaviour • Moderate concern for quality • Moderate concern for quantity • Equal concern for process and results • Flexibility for change and risk-taking • High tolerance for ambiguity and unpredictability
Cost leadership	• Repetitive and predictable behaviour • Short-term behaviour or focus • Autonomous or individual activity • Modest concern for quality • High concern for quantity of outputs • Primary concern for results • Low risk-taking activity • High degree of comfort with stability

Source: Adapted from Schuler and Jackson (1987: 209)

A third approach, the configurational approach to HRM, bridges the gap between the universal and the contingency approaches and suggests that a firm will perform better through an appropriate internal fit between its HRM practices (the configuration fit) and an appropriate external fit between the firm's business strategy and its HRM practices. MacDuffie (1995) argues that the appropriate unit of analysis for studying the strategic link between different HRM practices and performance does not involve individual practices as much as interrelated and internally consistent practices, called 'bundles'. He explains that a bundle creates the multiple, reinforcing conditions that support employee motivation, given that employees have the necessary knowledge and skills to perform their jobs effectively.

Mini Case Study 2.2
HRM at Fattal: a continuous improvement journey

Fattal Holding is a regional organization operating in the Middle East and North Africa region, with a total of 932 employees in Fattal Lebanon, 220 in Syria, 140 in Jordan, 110 in Iraq, 50 in the UAE and 50 in Sudan. It specializes in distribution, sales and marketing. The human resources director at Fattal, Mr Samir Messara, has worked there for 24 years, for the last 6 years as human resources director, reporting to the chief operating officer, and previous to that as a line manager.

The human resources department at Fattal has existed since 1982, and has developed from a personnel department in charge of administrative activities to a strategic human resources department that started off in 1996–1997. There are currently seven employees in the human resources department working in the following divisions: personnel administration, training, compensation and benefits, recruitment, and communication and bonding – better known in Fattal as 'the five pillars of human resources', as Mr Messara describes them.

In the past 3 years, the human resources function has shifted its techniques and adopted a competency-based approach in which all functions (for example, recruitment, selection and performance appraisal) are linked back to core skills and competencies. Mr Messara explained that Fattal's CEO has announced to all the directors that the human resources department is the most strategic asset in the company because it deals with people. Mr. Messara asserted that senior management, as well as line management, at Fattal recognize the significance of the human resources function and appreciate its added value, considering it to

▷

▷ be as important as the other functions in contributing to the organization's performance. He also stressed that the operational and strategic pillars are equally important parts of the human resources department: 'operational does not mean that it is not important, and strategic does not mean that it is theoretical'. Subdividing functions into operational and strategic is thus a secondary issue as one without the other does not work or succeed – in other words, there is a 'duality'.

The human resources function therefore plays both a reactive and a proactive role. A reactive role is adopted when a decision is taken and the human resources department 'cascades it' through its systems and procedures; human resources monitors its execution and follows it to completion or finalization. Human resources operations are now expanding in terms of new people – new assignments and recruitment for human resources in Syria and Iraq – a reactive role in which human resources has been deeply involved.

The proactive role comes from the strategic part of human resources. Human resources is always invited to be part of the 'think-tank' of the company and is invited by the CEO and Director to join in the decision-making about the next steps to be taken. Human resources is involved in the organization's major business decisions and takes part in strategy-setting meetings wherein they offer their own input. Their input is considered in the final outcome, and the department also maintains open lines of communication with the Chairman, CEO, and all the general managers and country managers.

The proactive role of human resources can therefore be seen to be quite important in Fattal. For example, the firm had an issue regarding whether or not to open a subsidiary in Libya – this would need investment, the country was new to the firm's operations, and it would need new suppliers. Mr Messara explained that the human resources department was involved from day one in discussing the viability, feasibility and implications of opening up in Libya, as well as in how to go about it.

Questions

1 How has the human resources department evolved at Fattal during the last 28 years?
2 Mr Messara stressed that the operational and strategic pillars are equally important parts of the human resources department: 'operational does not mean that it is not important, and strategic does not mean that it is theoretical.' Critically examine this statement and elaborate more on the 'duality' of HRM's role, as well as on factors critical to success.

Critical analysis and discussion

The succinct review presented above clearly highlights new directions and a significant advance in the scholarship of SHRM. SHRM has partly evolved in response to a dramatically more competitive economic environment. But there are those who argue that the ascendancy of SHRM should be viewed in the context of the long-standing battle that the human resources function has faced in justifying its position and demonstrating its value to business firms (Wright et al., 2001). At the heart of SHRM is the question of how much of a difference HRM can make in terms of organizational performance, and more specifically how the management of human capital can make this difference (Colakoglu et al., 2006). SHRM has certainly matured over the past few years, and has benefited from some empirical support and from the reinforcement provided by the RBV; however, there are lingering issues that are worth accounting for when discussing SHRM, most notably the frequently raised criticism that the field still lacks a solid theoretical foundation, as highlighted below (Dyer, 1984; Delery and Doty, 1996). According to Wright and McMahan (1992: 297):

> Without good theory, the field of SHRM could be characterized as a plethora of statements, regarding empirical relationships and prescriptions for practice that fail to explain why these relationships exist or should exist.

The RBV of the firm has provided a core theoretical rationale for the potential role of human resources as a strategic asset in the firm, and has broadened the foundation for exploring the impact of human resources on strategic resources. Several authors have, however, expressed concern about the level of abstraction in RBV theory and in SHRM theory in general (Priem and Butler, 2001; Becker and Huselid, 2006). According to Becker and Huselid (2006), the link between the human resources architecture and most RBV concepts remains too abstract and too indirect to explain the link between that architecture and a firm's subsequent performance, or how human resources contributes to a firm's sustained competitive advantage. Implementation from this perspective should be given more attention in SHRM theory because the link between the human resources system and the firm's performance is not as direct as suggested by previous SHRM literature (Wright and Sherman, 1999). There are also intermediate outcomes that are central and crucial to a more complete understanding of how the human resources architecture drives a firm's performance, and very few attempts have been made to demonstrate that the human resources practices actually impact the skills or behaviours of the workforce, and that these skills or behaviours are related to concrete performance measures (Wright et al., 2001; Becker and Huselid, 2006).

Another common criticism is the reliance in the RBV on constructs that are difficult to operationalize in practice, which limits the prescriptive value of the theory for managers (Priem and Butler, 2001). What we need, according to Priem and Butler (2001), is a more careful delineation of the specific mechanisms purported to generate competitive advantage and more actionable prescriptions. According to Wright et al. (2001), a major step forward in the SHRM literature will be simply to move beyond the application of RBV logic to human resource issues, and towards research that directly tests the core concepts of the RBV. According to Fahy (2000), the vast majority of contributions within the RBV have been of a conceptual rather than an empirical nature, with the result that many of its fundamental tenets remain to be validated. Colbert (2007) posits that although the RBV has been helpful and relevant to the field of SHRM, there are aspects of the view that scholars have deemed critical but that are difficult to deal with in research and practice. Another important and salient criticism relates to the preoccupation of the RBV with internal resources, undermining the fact that countries provide variable contextual inputs and resources in terms of physical infrastructure, sociopolitical systems, and educational and technical infrastructure. Hence, there is a danger of becoming too absorbed with the firm as the unit of analysis (Boxall and Purcell, 2011).

There is also a continuing debate and various expressed concerns about best practice (universal) versus best fit (contingency) streams of theorizing in SHRM. A common concern with the best practice approach is whether there is indeed a best human resources architecture that creates value for all firms. Despite the appeal of the notion of universally applicable HRM practices, some problems persist including the following:

☐ subjectivity and a lack of agreement on a definitive prescription of the best bundle;

□ the implicit assumption that a particular bundle of practices is feasible for all organizations;

□ the way in which best practices sometimes become ends in themselves dissociated from company goals (Boxall and Purcell, 2011).

Moreover, research suggests that national contexts matter, and the wide variations in labour laws and unionism across nations undermine support for best practice models. There are also salient differences across sectoral and organizational contexts (for example, sectors exposed to international competition). Generally, the evidence points to the adoption of innovative human resources bundles or high-performance work systems in sectors where quality is a major competitive factor and where firms need to exploit advanced technology. Cost-effectiveness is also certainly an important consideration in the limited diffusion of best practice models (Boxall and Purcell, 2011).

There is also a parallel set of concerns with best fit or contingency models. The most important concern relates to the purported simplicity of arranging a firm's assets and resources given a specific choice of strategy (Wright et al., 2001). Specifically, according to Cappelli and Singh (1992), most SHRM models based on fit assume: (1) that a certain business strategy demands a unique set of behaviours and attitudes on the part of employees; and (2) that certain human resources policies produce a unique set of responses from employees. But both assumptions are simplistic. There is also a lack of sophistication in existing descriptions of competitive strategy in the sense of concrete evidence that resilient firms in some sectors tend to successfully and simultaneously pursue different kinds of strategy (for example, cost leadership and differentiation). In addition, there are concerns that best fit models emphasizing the alignment of HRM and competitive strategy tend to overlook employee interests (Boxall and Purcell, 2011). In other words, the strategic goals of HRM are plural. Although they do involve supporting the firm's competitive objectives, they also involve meeting employee needs and complying with social requirements for labour management (Boxall and Purcell, 2011). Multiple fits are required, and there is always a strategic tension inherent in a changing environment between performing optimally in the present context and building the capacity of the organization and preparing for the future.

One of the main reasons for lingering ambiguity and complexity in this area is that the choice of performance measures used in SHRM research studies varies widely. SHRM tries to link and synthesize multiple metrics, but this has been neither simple nor straightforward. Whereas traditional HRM research has tended to focus on individual-level outcomes such as job performance, job satisfaction and motivation, SHRM has focused on firm-level outcomes related to labour productivity, sales growth, return on assets and return on investment. This latter category of financial and accounting outcomes is more distal to human resources practices than individual-level employee outcomes (Colakoglu et al., 2006). Although corporate- or firm-level performance metrics are important to

Exercise

Many qualified human resources managers often fail to manage the function strategically. Who is to blame? The human resources manager? Organizational factors? Environmental factors? List and discuss all possible factors that might impede proper SHRM initiatives.

examine, they are, according to some authors, not definitely and necessarily more important than others. The focus on organizational performance is illuminating and convincing for managers looking for concrete evidence of a significant impact of human resources on distal outcomes such as market or financial performance (Colakoglu et al., 2006). But these organizational performance outcomes are inevitably rooted in lower level outcomes to which SHRM does not seem to accord enough attention.

These complexities become even more accentuated in the context of international SHRM research, which considers the growing importance of multinational corporations (MNCs) and the influence of complex global strategic business decisions on the human resource activities of these MNCs (Sparrow and Braun, 2007). Complexity arises from the multiplicity of independent variables as influencing factors, and from the importance of linking HRM policies and practices with the organizational strategies of the MNC. This is rooted in the realization that MNCs are geographically dispersed and vary in their goals, and that different levels of integration and responsiveness are also invariably affected by whether or not the parent company actually has a global strategy, or more specifically 'a strategic international HRM system orientation'. In addition, it comes from the degree of similarity of affiliates' human resources systems to those of the parent company, and the extent to which top management believes that HRM capability is indeed a source of strategic advantage (Sparrow and Braun, 2007).

On a final note, there is also enduring concern about whether human resources strategy theories developed in Western countries do actually apply to other cultures, and how human resources strategies may be made to apply better in other cultures, which has been the domain of comparative HRM research. The answer to the first part of the question is clearly no, in the sense that human resources theories developed in Western countries do not necessarily apply universally, and there are important contingency variables and institutional realities and multilevel factors that affect the practice of SHRM. Generally, the conclusion reached is that companies are not as global or international as is often assumed, and that a clear country of origin effect is still evident (Sparrow and Braun, 2007). US MNCs, for example, tend to be more formalized and centralized than others in the management of HRM issues ranging from pay systems to collective bargaining and employee recognition. There is also a stream of literature that considers how the transfer of human resources practices can happen successfully, with convergence of practice depending, according to Kostova (1999), on internationalization and the implementation of human resources rules by subsidiaries.

Looking back on the last two decades, Paauwe and Boselie (2005) point to major similarities between the development of HRM and the developments in strategic management theorizing. In the 1980s, HRM was influenced by Porter-like outside–in approaches, for example reflected in the work of Schuler and Jackson (1987), emphasizing the necessity of strategic fit – the fit between the overall strategy (based on the external environment) and the human resources strategy. The introduction of the RBV in the 1990s also led to a transition from the former outside–in approaches (based on contingency assumptions) to an inside–out approach, in which human resources play a key role in the search for the sustained competitive advantage of an organization (Paauwe and Boselie, 2005).

Recently, institutional theory has been increasingly used as a framework to analyse human resource practices. It looks at the influence that environmental factors and institutions such as social and political systems, legislation and the power of labour unions and trade associations have on the adoption of human resources practices (Chow, 2004). The rationale of institutional theory is, according to Paauwe and Boselie (2003), that organizations are embedded in a wider institutional context that plays a role in shaping HRM practices and policies. Institutional mechanisms (for example, legislation with respect to conditions of employment, collective bargaining agreements, employment security, trade union influence and employee representation) shape employment relationships and human resources decision-making in organizations. Paauwe (2004) acknowledges institutional differences at both a country level and an industry level. Institutional mechanisms (mimetic, normative and/or coercive) affect the relationship between HRM and performance and should therefore be taken into account in future research (Paauwe and Boselie, 2003).

Conclusion

The aim of this chapter was to provide a critical assessment of SHRM, shedding light on its differentiating attributes and theoretical foundations, as well as on the lingering gaps and challenges in this field. The opening sections highlighted the evolution in the field from personnel management to HRM and, most recently, SHRM. Although some suggest that the changes in the field are revolutionary (Storey, 1993; Hope-Hailey et al., 1997; Hoque and Noon, 2001), it is more accurate to characterize the change process as one of metamorphosis, evolution or adaptation rather than of completely new creation (Torrington et al., 2002; Redman and Wilkinson, 2009). Each phase basically constitutes an improvement that has effectively leveraged or built on, rather than replaced, the preceding knowledge base of the discipline (Schuler and Jackson, 2007).

SHRM is essentially posited as constituting the highest level of sophistication or maturation in the field, and as an apt response to existing business trends and challenges. It has brought to the fore a set of new assumptions relating to strategic thrust, an emphasis on integration, an orientation towards commitment, a belief that people are the core assets, and a focus on business values and results. In the process, SHRM has raised and addressed an array of important questions, probing the link between HRM and organizational effectiveness. For example, which human resources practices lead to greater organizational performance? How does a firm ensure that its human resources practices fit with its strategy? How does it ensure that its individual human resources practices fit with each other? The key constructs and central debates in SHRM have grown out of the above questions: best practice versus best fit, horizontal and vertical fit, fit versus flexibility, univariate and multivariate effects, and appropriate theoretical frames (Colbert, 2007). What is common to all this work though is a focus on the links between human resources practices, the human resource pool and organizational outcomes (Colbert, 2007).

The applications and implications of the RBV within the SHRM literature have clearly led to an increasing convergence between the fields of strategic management and SHRM (Snell et al., 2001). In relation to both areas of the literature, the RBV has helped to put people on the radar screen and to highlight the importance of human knowledge and a firm's processes and capabilities in general as sources of competitive advantage. With its emphasis on the firm's internal resources as sources of competitive advantage, the RBV has gained increasing popularity within SRHM and has become by far the most often used theory within SHRM, both for the development of theory and for the rationale underlying empirical research. The RBV has triggered at the very least a deeper understanding of the interplay between HRM and competitive advantage, as well as a substantial advance in the SHRM literature.

But although the RBV has formed an integrating ground or backdrop for most of the work in SHRM over the past decade, it offers little in an explicit sense in the way of prescriptions for managers, thus not answering the 'how' questions central to SHRM. Delery (1998) notes that while the RBV provides a nice backdrop explaining the importance of human resources to a firm's competitiveness, it does not specifically deal with how an organization can develop and support the human resources it needs for competitive advantage.

Although many continue to refer to best practice versus best fit, perhaps a broader conceptualization, as suggested by Wright et al. (2001) and also nicely captured in Figure 2.2 above, is to focus on the people management system within an organization. The word 'system' denotes attention to the importance of understanding the multiple practices that impact employees, rather than focusing on a single practice. The term 'people', rather than 'human resources', expands the relevant practices to those beyond the direct control of the human resources function, such as to communication, work design, culture, leadership and a host of others that affect employees and shape their competencies, cognitions and attitudes. In other words, sustained competitive advantage is not just a function of single or isolated components, but rather a combination of human capital elements such as the development of stocks of skills, strategically relevant behaviours and supporting people management systems. The recognition of the systemic quality of highly effective human resources and people management systems has been a key insight brought to the fore through the RBV and SHRM paradigm.

❓ For discussion and revision

1 Explain the evolutionary road map from personnel management to SHRM. What are the factors that triggered this evolution?

2 Why is the application of 'best practice' models of SHRM in organizations problematic?

3 In what way have the contingency and the configurational approaches to HRM contributed to your understanding of SHRM?

4 How does the RBV contribute to your understanding of SHRM?

5 The link between HRM practices and organizational performance is not direct, and HRM scholars often refer to the existence of a 'black box' between the two concepts. Divide the class into groups of three. Each group should discuss what this black box entails. Then share your findings with other groups and discuss them.

6 Defining the effective human resource manager:

- What does an effective human resources manager look like? What skills, competencies and knowledge do they require to become a business partner? Try to collect information from a range of sources, for example corporate websites, human resources practitioner journals (*HR magazine, Personnel Today, People Management*), other journals (*Human Resource Management Journal, International Journal of Human Resource Management, Personnel Review*), the Chartered Institute of Personnel Development and The Society for Human Resource Management websites and HRM textbooks to develop a profile of an effective human resources manager in the 21st century.

- Discuss your findings with other students in your class. What conclusions can you draw?

Further reading

Books

Boxall, P. and Purcell, J. (2011) *Strategy and Human Resource Management* (3rd edn). New York: Palgrave Macmillan.

This book is a classic work integrating HRM and strategic management, explaining the latest theoretical and practical developments in this fascinating area and bridging the gap between theory and practice. It also integrates both HRM and employment relations in a critical and constructive way.

Schuler, R. and Jackson, S. (2007) *Strategic Human Resource Management* (2nd edn). Malden, MA: Blackwell Publishing.

This book provides students with a complete and updated guide to the latest work in the field. This selection of important and highly readable articles from authors around the world charts key developments that have changed the theory and practice of SHRM over the last decade.

Journals

Legnick-Hall, M. L., Legnick-Hall, C. A., Andrade, L. S. and Drake B. (2009) Strategic human resource management: the evolution of the field. *Human Resource Management Review*, 19: 64–85.

This article takes an evolutionary and chronological perspective on the development of the SHRM literature. The authors trace how the field has evolved to its current state, articulate many of the major findings and contributions, and discuss how they believe it will evolve in the future. This approach contributes to the field of SHRM by synthesizing work in this domain and by highlighting areas of research focus that, while promising, have remained largely unexamined.

Paauwe, J. and Boselie, P. (2003) Challenging 'strategic HRM' and the relevance of the institutional setting. *Human Resource Management Journal*, 13(3): 56–70.

In this article, the authors use the theory of new institutionalism as a better way to understand the shaping of human resources policies and practices in different settings. After a concise review of the latest debates in the area of SHRM, in which the RBV is the dominant perspective, they turn to an analysis of HRM in different institutional settings, which suggests the need for additional theory – that is, new institutionalism.

Wright, P. M., McMahan, G. C. and McWilliams, A. (1994) Human resources and sustained competitive advantage: a resource-based perspective. *International Journal of Human Resource Management*, 5(2): 301–26.

The RBV of the firm has influenced the field of SHRM in a number of ways. This paper explores the impact of the RBV on the theoretical and empirical development of SHRM. It explores how the fields of strategy and SHRM are beginning to converge around a number of issues, and proposes a number of implications of this convergence.

Case Study Strategic human resource management: insights from Deloitte ME's experience

The Deloitte Middle East Firm (Deloitte ME) is a member of the global professional services firm Deloitte Touche Tohmatsu, which employs 169,000 people in 140 countries and had revenues of US$27 billion in the 2009 fiscal year. Deloitte ME is one of the longest established professional services firms in the region and has been operating since 1926 in 15 countries with 26 offices and a team of over 2,300 professionals. It has enjoyed a compounded revenue growth rate of 31 per cent in the region over the 3 years to 2010.

This case study is based on several rounds of interviews with Mrs Rana Ghandour Salhab, the first woman admitted as partner in the Middle East in the 80-year history of the firm in the region. She is currently the partner in charge of human resources and communications in the Middle East and a member of the Deloitte ME Board Advisory Council and the Deloitte ME Partner Screening Committee. It is worth noting that, in April 2009, Deloitte ME was recognized as one of the best 10 employers in the Middle East by Hewitt Associates, the global human resources consulting firm that runs best employer surveys across the world.

Based on a recent survey asking Deloitte employees what they expect from their employer, Deloitte ME adopted a 'develop, deploy and connect' model as a talent strategy and a Career Value Map tool to reinforce the steps that individuals can take to own their careers and leverage Deloitte's resources and tools within each of the model areas. According to Mrs Salhab, organizations can, by focusing on these three elements, generate capability, commitment and alignment in key workforce segments (Figure 2.4), which in turn improves business performance: 'When this happens, the attraction and retention of skilled talent largely take care of themselves'.

Deloitte has an interesting regional Talent Attraction Program and e-recruitment, revolving around a Middle East referral scheme, university relationships, an alumni and experienced hire programme, supplier relations, web and social networks sourcing, and Google ad words. The Deloitte Invites Top Talent programme also aims to attract top students from leading universities around the region to source offices with nationals of the Gulf Cooperation Council and Arabic-speaking professionals. Their screening techniques focus on assessment centres, competency-based behavioural interviewing, psychometric testing and a global development programme for their workforce. The Deloitte

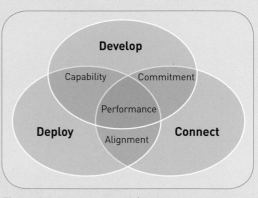

Figure 2.4 The Deloitte ME 'develop, deploy and connect' model.

performance management system is the key development employee tool, with a technical and shared skills competency model that facilitates year round career conversations and a coaching culture. Through the ME Deloitte Retention and Advancement for Women Program, the firm is committed to creating an environment where high achieving women and men both reach leadership roles.

Deloitte ME has been striving for a balance between a strategic human resources agenda with a long-term impact and operational day-to-day human resources activities. The company realizes that the drivers and challenges for the business are transitioning the core efforts of human resources towards providing the business with a competitive advantage. This will happen by moving away from a focus on administration (for example, payroll, benefits, compliance and record-keeping), or what they refer to as value maintenance, to a focus on value creation through the selection and design of human resources practices that support the firm's strategy (Figure 2.5). Mrs Salhab recognizes that assuming the human resources partner role depends on the level of maturity of the organization; it also illustrates nicely how the Deloitte ME function has made a successful transition from roles revolving around analyst and advisor to human resources roles entailing effective advocacy and partnering. This transformation has, according to Mrs Salhab, required a proactive approach combining flexible and specialist human resources orientations, combined with the redirecting of administration queries and a more active involvement of line managers in different sorts of people management activities.

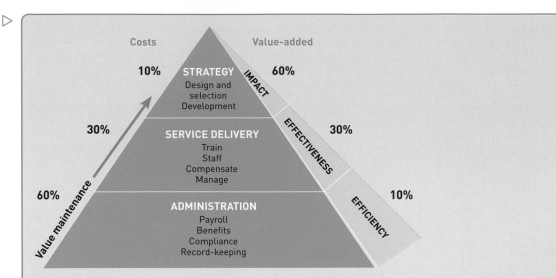

Figure 2.5 Deloitte ME value creation through strategic human resources.

Mrs Salhab admits that the transformation of human resources into strategic roles is not always easy and may in some companies be typically undermined by a number of risks and pitfalls that have to be avoided. These may be, for example:

☐ reduced client satisfaction (in the sense that a one-size-fits-all approach to service delivery may not recognize the diversity of employees);
☐ insufficient market insight into and innovation in human resources policies;
☐ low morale in human resources, with no clear career path or longer term development programme for some human resources professionals;
☐ overly expensive running costs and poor-quality outsourcing contracts;
☐ ineffective human resources business partners who are unable and ill-equipped to deliver the level of business advice expected;
☐ a continued erosion of data quality, and therefore human resources credibility, as a result of poorly constructed processes;
☐ dissatisfaction with self-service technologies due to their low-quality implementation and the poor education of line managers.

These failings have led the business to question whether human resources is best placed to fix the issues or whether the business itself should take control and address them. Mrs Salhab also admits that, despite the global change in paradigms of SHRM, human resources professionals are still spending too much time on low-impact activities (for example, responding to queries, responding to complaints, enforcing policies, managing conflicts and basic administrative transactions) as opposed to forging strategy, developing metrics and nurturing talent and leaders.

According to Mrs Salhab, human resources cannot just become strategic overnight. They have to drive a strategic agenda around things that matter, strengthen leadership capability, create an adaptable workforce and advise on strategies that can maintain and enhance performance. This requires a number of key organizational and cultural changes that need to be crafted together, revolving around establishing the role of the chief human resources officer, optimizing shared service centres, measuring success through value operation centres, and freeing business partners and the chief human resources officer to reflect the strategic focus. Other important changes revolve around adjusting human resources strategies to respond to changing needs, identifying critical human resources metrics and business strategies, identifying talent issues and prioritizing human resources needs, redesigning structures around strategic objectives and, importantly, understanding the talent needs of the business. In this context, the onus also falls on human resources to nurture the right skills and competencies, including, among others, the following:

☐ behavioural competencies as in leadership skills, negotiation and conflict resolution, change leadership and communication skills;
☐ technical competencies, as in functional human resources knowledge, project management and the management of strategic resources;

◻ business competencies, as in business acumen, industry and organizational awareness, strategy and business planning, and consulting skills.

In conclusion, for Mrs Salhab, human resources is clearly at a turning point. For a decade now, it has been undergoing a process of transformation. But for many, this has been a process that has increasingly failed to produce the results expected of it: 'During these times of rapidly changing economics, we believe human resources is faced with a stark choice. It can either evolve and make a significant contribution, or be diminished and dispersed in the business.'

Questions

1 Mrs Salhab stated that 'During these times of rapidly changing economics, we believe human resources is faced with a stark choice. It can either evolve and make a significant contribution, or be diminished and dispersed in the business.' Use Figures 2.4 and 2.5 to explain how the human resources department at Deloitte adds value to the business.

2 Mrs Salhab is the first woman admitted as a partner in the Middle East in the 80-year history of the firm in the region. What additional challenges and opportunities can this provide for the successful development of the human resources department?

3 Do some further research and investigate whether the same human resources practices and policies are applied at Deloitte in various regions of the world. What lessons can you draw?

References

Amit, R. and Belcourt, M. (1999) Human resources management processes: a value-creating source of competitive advantage. *European Management Journal*, 17(2): 174–81.

Anthony, W., Kacmar, M. and Perrewe, P. (2002) *Human Resource Management: A Strategic Approach* (4th edn). Cincinnati, OH: South-Western.

Armstrong, M. (2006) *Strategic Human Resource Management. A Guide to Action* (3rd edn). London: Kogan Page.

Barney, J. (1991) Firm resources and sustained competitive advantage. *Journal of Management*, 17(1): 99–120.

Becker, B. and Huselid, M. (2006) Strategic human resources management: where do we go from here?' *Journal of Management*, 32(6): 898–925.

Boxall, P. (1996) The strategic HRM debate and the resource based view of the firm. *Human Resource Management Journal*, 56(3): 59–75.

Boxall, P. and Purcell, J. (2000) Strategic human resource management: where have we come from and where should we be going? *International Journal of Management Reviews*, 2(2): 183–203.

Boxall, P. and Purcell, J. (2011) *Strategy and Human Resource Management* (3rd edn). New York: Palgrave Macmillan.

Brockbank, W. (1999) If HR were really strategically proactive: present and future directions in HR's contribution to competitive advantage. *Human Resource Management*, 38(4): 337–52.

Buyens, D. and De Vos, A. (2001) Perceptions of the value of the HR function. *Human Resource Management Journal*, 11(3): 70–89.

Cappelli, P. and Singh, H. (1992) Integrating strategic human resources and strategic management. In Lewin, D., Mitchell, P. and Sherer, P. (eds) *Research Frontiers in Industrial Relations and Human Resources*. Madison, WI: IRRA, pp. 165–92.

Chow, I. (2004) The impact of institutional context on human resource management in three Chinese societies. *Employee Relations*, 26(6): 626–42.

Colakoglu, S., Lepak, D. and Hong, Y. (2006) Measuring HRM effectiveness: considering multiple stakeholders in a global context. *Human Resource Management Review*, 16: 209–18.

Colbert, B. (2007) The complex resource based view: implications for theory and practice in strategic human resource management. In Schuler, R. and Jackson, S. (eds) *Strategic Human Resource Management* (2nd edn). Malden, MA: Blackwell Publishing, pp. 98–123.

Collis, D. and Montgomery, C. (1995) Competing on resources: strategy in the 1990s. *Harvard Business Review*, 73: 118–28.

Conner, J. and Ulrich, D. (1996) Human resource roles: creating value, not rhetoric. *Human Resource Planning*, 19(3): 38–49.

Delery, J. (1998) Issues of fit in strategic human resource management: implications for research. *Human Resource Management Review*, 8: 289–309.

Delery, J. and Doty, D. (1996) Modes of theorizing in strategic human resource management: tests of universalistic, contingency, and configurational performance predictions. *Academy of Management Journal*, 39(4): 802–35.

Dunn, J. (2006) Strategic human resources and strategic organization development: an alliance for the future? *Organizational Development Journal*, 24(4): 69–76.

Dyer, L. (1984) Linking human resource and business strategies. *Human Resource Planning*, 7(2): 79–84.

Fahy, J. (2000) The resource based view of the firm: some stumbling blocks on the road to understanding sustainable competitive advantage. *Journal of European Industrial Training*, 24: 94–104.

Grant, R. (1991) The resource based theory of competitive advantage: implications for strategy formulation. *California Management Review*, 33: 114–35.

Guest, D. (1987) Human resource management and industrial relations. *Journal of Management Studies*, 24(5): 503–21.

Guest, D. (1990) Personnel management: the end of orthodoxy? *British Journal of Industrial Relations*, 29(2): 149–75.

Hope-Hailey, V., Gratton, L., McGovern, P., Stiles, P. and Truss, C. (1997) A chameleon function: HRM in the '90s. *Human Resource Management Journal*, 3(3): 5–18.

Hoque, K. and Noon, M. (2001) Counting angels: a comparison of personnel and HR specialists. *Human Resource Management Journal*, 11(3): 5–22.

Keenoy, T. (1990) HRM: rhetoric, reality, and contradiction. *International Journal of Human Resource Management*, 23(1): 363–84.

Kostova, T. (1999) Transnational transfer of strategic organizational practice: a contextual perspective. *Academy of Management Review*, 24(2): 308–24.

Leonard-Barton, D. (1992) Core capabilities and core rigidities: a paradox in managing new product development. *Strategic Management Journal*, 13: 111–25.

MacDuffie, P. (1995) Human resource bundles and manufacturing performance: organizational logic and flexible production systems in the world auto industry. *Industrial and Labor Relations Review*, 48(2): 197–221.

Mahoney, T. and Deckop, J. (1986) Evolution of concept and practice in personnel administration/human resource management. *Journal of Management*, 12(2): 223–41.

Meilich, O. (2005) Are formalization and human asset specificity mutually exclusive: a learning bureaucracy perspective. *Journal of American Academy of Business*, 6: 161–9.

Miles, R. and Snow, C. (1984) Designing strategic human resource systems. *Organizational Dynamics*, 13(1): 36–52.

Mohrman, S. and Lawler, E. III (1997) Transforming the human resource function. *Human Resource Management*, 36(1): 157–62.

Osterman, P. (1994) How common is workplace transformation and who adopts it? *Industrial and Labor Relations Review*, 47: 173–88.

Paauwe, J. (2004) *HRM and Performance: Unique Approaches for Achieving Long-term Viability*. Oxford: Oxford University Press.

Paauwe, J. and Boselie, P. (2003) Challenging 'strategic HRM' and the relevance of the institutional setting. *Human Resource Management Journal*, 13(3): 56–70.

Paauwe, J. and Boselie, P. (2005) HRM and performance: what's next? *Human Resource Management Journal*, 15(4): 68–83.

Pfeffer, J. (1994) *Competitive Advantage Through People: Unleashing the Power of the Workforce*. Boston, MA: Harvard Business School Press.

Pilbeam, S. and Corbridge, M. (2006) *People Resourcing: Contemporary HRM in Practice* (3rd edn). London: Prentice Hall.

Porter, M. (1985) *Competitive Advantage*. New York: Free Press.

Prahalad, C. K. and Hamel, G. (1990) The core competence of the corporation. *Harvard Business Review*, (May–June): 79–91.

Priem, R. and Butler, J. (2001) Is the resource based view a useful perspective for strategic management research? *Academy of Management Review*, 26(1): 22–40.

Redman, T. and Wilkinson, A. (2009) *Contemporary Human Resource Management: Text and Cases* (3rd edn). Harlow: Prentice Hall.

Schuler, R. and Jackson, S. (1987) Linking competitive strategies with human resource management practices. *Academy of Management Executive*, 1(3): 207–19.

Schuler, R. and Jackson, S. (2007) Preface. In *Strategic Human Resource Management* (2nd edn). Malden, MA: Blackwell Publishing.

Snell, S., Shadur, M. and Wright, P. (2001) The era of our ways. In Hitt, R., Freeman, R. and Harrison, J. (eds) *Handbook of Strategic Management*. Oxford: Blackwell Publishing, pp. 627–9.

Sparrow, P. and Braun, W. (2007) Human resource strategy in international context. In Schuler, R. and Jackson, S. (eds) *Strategic Human Resource Management* (2nd edn). Malden, MA: Blackwell Publishing, pp. 162–99.

Storey, J. (1993) The take-up of human resource management by mainstream companies: key lessons from research. *International Journal of Human Resource Management*, 4(3): 529–33.

Storey, J. (2001) *Human Resource Management: A Critical Text* (2nd edn). London: Routledge.

Teece, D. J., Pisano, G., and Shuen, A. (1997) Dynamic capabilities and strategic management. *Strategic Management Journal*, 18(7): 509–33.

Torrington, D., Hall, L. and Taylor, S. (2002) *Human Resource Management*. London: FT/Prentice Hall.

Wernerfelt, B. (1995) The resource based view of the firm: ten years after. *Strategic Management Journal*, 16: 171–4.

Williams, J. (1992) How sustainable is your competitive advantage? *California Management Review*, 34: 29–51.

Wright, P. and McMahan, G. (1992) Theoretical perspectives for strategic human resource management. *Journal of Management*, 18: 295–320.

Wright, P. and Sherman, W. (1999) Failing to find fit in strategic human resource management: theoretical and empirical problems. *Research in Personnel and Human Resources Management*, Supplement 4: 53–74.

Wright, P., McMahan, G., Snell, S. and Gerhart, B. (2001) Comparing line and HR executives' perceptions of HR effectiveness: services, roles, and contributions. *Human Resource Management*, 40(2): 111–23.

Human resource management in contemporary transnational companies

Tineke Cappellen, Patrizia Zanoni and Maddy Janssens

3

After reading this chapter, you should be able to:

- ☐ Understand the implications of globalization for today's workers
- ☐ Explain how human resource management can facilitate integration and differentiation within transnational organizations
- ☐ Discuss the role of global professionals within organizations
- ☐ Critically reflect on the new forms that power relations take in contemporary transnational organizations

Introduction

In today's economy, the majority of national companies are converting into international companies, entering new markets and creating value-adding activities in geographies outside their home country (Galbraith, 2000). They have grown from an international towards a multinational, then a global and finally a transnational mentality (see, for example, Ghoshal and Nohria, 1993; Bartlett et al., 2004). In the transnational form, which is the highest level of international development (Galbraith, 2000), subsidiaries are no longer independent national subunits (a multinational form), and global authority is no longer centralized in the company's native headquarters (a global form). Rather, the transnational scope moves beyond the global one, aiming for a combination of homogenized global products characterized by high quality and low cost along with local responsiveness that reasserts national preferences (Bartlett et al., 2004). Subsidiaries take leading and contributory roles to generate value-adding advantages, creating a power structure that is distributed throughout the firm.

Due to this increasing transnational character of their activities within a global economy (Bartlett et al., 2004), companies are today changing their approach to employees' mobility and cross-border transfers. Traditionally, they relied mainly on expatriate assignments, whereby employees were sent from headquarters to foreign branches for a period spanning 2 years or more. Today, companies instead make use of a range of alternative forms of international work, such as short-term assignments, commuter assignments, international business travel and virtual assignments (Collings et al., 2007). Alongside these assignments, which are short term and directed towards specific purposes, globalization has given rise to 'global professionals' who coordinate functional domains on a global scale (Bartlett and Ghoshal, 1992).

In this chapter, we will discuss the latest evolution in human resource management (HRM) in transnational organizations and the emergence of the global professional as a new profile within these organizations. The structure of the chapter is as follows. In the first section, we will discuss the global context within which transnational companies and global professionals need to work. Afterwards, we present an overview of classical theories and key concepts relevant to transnational companies and their employees. In the third section, we will discuss the implications of the transnational form of international development for several HRM issues within contemporary companies. For each section presented in this chapter, we will first discuss the 'mainstream' approaches and then reflect on them by drawing on more critical literature. Finally, the chapter ends by discussing the benefits of studying HRM from a critical perspective and making recommendations in terms of organizations, managers and employees.

The global context

According to Govindarajan and Gupta (2001), the global context refers to the interdependence of countries, industries and companies as reflected in an increasing cross-border flow of three things: goods and services, capital, and know-how. As such, it reflects a dynamic complexity in which the dimensions of multiplicity, interdependence and ambiguity interact to multiply each other's effects (Lane et al., 2006):

- First, *multiplicity* reflects the different models for organizing and conducting business that should enable organizations to function in an environment characterized by more (number) and different (nature) players.
- Second, *interdependence* points to the cross-border flows and exchanges that remove the isolated status of organizations through interdependent arrangements such as outsourcing, alliances and network arrangements.
- Finally, *ambiguity* refers to the vast amount of information available, which is unclear because of the multiple meanings, incorrect attributions, erroneous interpretations and conflicting interests that hinder effective guidance of the organization's actions.

Overview of classical theories and key concepts

Transnational organizations in a global economy

The activities of multinational corporations (MNCs) have been increasingly global in scope, reflecting the growing interdependence of countries, industries and companies (Box 3.1) (Govindarajan and Gupta, 2001). In the earliest stages of internationalization, foreign operations used to be distant outposts of the parent company fully controlled by headquarters, whose main task was to sell the company's products in foreign markets. Nowadays, organizations are increasingly organized along a transnational structure that enables them to deal with simultaneous demands for global efficiency and worldwide innovation on the one hand, and national responsiveness on the other (Bartlett and Ghoshal, 1989; Galbraith, 2000).

Organizations rely on a strong global management to ensure communication and coordination between the units across geographical, cultural and functional boundaries (Galbraith, 2000). In this way, they can identify customers across the world, realize cost-minimizing economies of scale and scope, and exchange information, products and people (Bartlett and Ghoshal, 1989, 2000; Ghoshal and Nohria, 1993). However, they also need a strong national subsidiary management that understands and can meet the changing needs of local customers, as well as dealing with the pressures (that is, employment and tax legislation, health standards, and so on) that host governments and regulatory agencies put upon them (Rosenzweig and Singh, 1991). As a result of this evolution, key activities and resources are today disseminated across different locations, turning subsidiaries into sources of a given product or expertise that can enhance value globally (Bartlett and Ghoshal, 2000). Accordingly, transnational organizations are structured as integrated networks of distributed and interdependent resources and capabilities.

> **Box 3.1 Characteristics of a transnational firm**
>
> **Organization structure**
>
> ☐ Subsidiaries take leading and contributing roles in generating advantages
> ☐ There is a distributed power structure
> ☐ An integrated and interdependent network is present
>
> **Management process**
>
> ☐ Headquarters does not evidently play a dominant role
> ☐ There is an awareness of location-specific advantages and lead markets outside the home country
> ☐ The firm seeks to achieve both global efficiency and local responsiveness
> ☐ There is a large flow of products, people and information between the subsidiaries

This transnational, networked structure of the organization has generally been interpreted as an evolution towards less hierarchical relations between headquarters and subsidiaries, with power being less centralized and more evenly distributed (Galbraith, 2000). More critically oriented scholars have, however, challenged this view. Some have argued that subsidiaries in 'developing countries' continue to be cheap production centres owing to their lower labour costs, reproducing a classical international division of labour to the advantage of the West (Banerjee and Linstead, 2001; Mir et al., 2006).

Others, drawing on post-colonial theory, have rather argued that, under globalization, inequality is reproduced in a more subtle way through new types of control (Westwood, 2004). Whereas power was previously directed towards changing the behaviour of the colonized peoples, to serve the colonizer's interests, more subtle types of control today aim to change identity and the very sense of self (Prasad, 1997). It is a subjugation process that passes primarily through the symbolic and the cultural dimensions of relationships, rather than being solely one of military, political and economic domination. Drawing on Bhabha's notion of 'mimicry' (1994), Frenkel has recently argued that those who are colonized are expected and encouraged to imitate the colonizer, yet such imitation can never be perfect, excluding colonized individuals from becoming 'an essential and legitimate part of the colonizing society' (2008: 927).

Owing to unequal relations at the macro level, the subsidiaries and the company's headquarters can never be equivalent parties within transnational organizations. Yet others have shown how knowledge originating in non-Western countries continues to lack legitimacy in the eyes of the West (Wong-MingJi and Mir, 1997; Özbilgin, 2004; Frenkel, 2008), affecting the unequal exchange of practices and technologies throughout organizations (Frenkel, 2008; Leonardi, 2008; Mir et al., 2008).

Mini Case Study 3.1
The changing management process at Farmers' Future

Farmers' Future is a non-governmental organization (NGO) with roots in the Christian civil society movement of a Western European country. Their mission is to promote sustainable agriculture and a better future for farmers all over the world. Farmers' Future carries out two main types of activity: awareness-raising and education in the home country, and rural development programmes abroad. To achieve its goals, the organization raises funds from private and public donors and collaborates with rural organizations in developing countries. Seven regional offices led by expatriates support development programmes in Africa, Asia and Latin America that involve 152 local rural partners, one third of which are farmers' organizations.

Farmers' Future emerged over a decade ago from the merger between four NGOs operating in agriculture. At that time, public donors were asking for more professional management of NGOs and cooperation with local parties that focused on capacity-building to enhance market functioning while the grassroots transnational movement for sustainable agriculture was emerging. Facing the distinct approaches and expertise of the merging organizations, the rising institutional pressures and their increasingly important transnational advocacy role, the staff at Farmers' Future needed to build a new shared understanding of the organization's activities, structure and working practices.

Attempting to address donors' new demands, the headquarters identified a new strategic approach for the activities of Farmers' Future abroad. The focus shifted from agricultural production to capacity-building aimed at overcoming structural problems in all phases of the product chain, including enhancing farmers' access to markets. The organization also reorganized into two units covering local education and advocacy, and programmes abroad, respectively. Finally, a new, more professional financial reporting system was created and implemented in the organization.

Although the headquarters frequently discussed the changes with the regional officers, the new strategy, structure and practices clearly reflected external pressures on the headquarters. These external pressures were, however, felt much less in the overseas offices. As a result, new systems and procedures were increasingly perceived as being an imposition from headquarters. Pressures on regional representatives to reformulate their programmes to meet the new strategy met with much resistance as they were used to managing their programmes autonomously. The regional representatives were increasingly becoming executors of headquarters' global programme, but they were receiving little extra support to do this and remained fully accountable for the success or failure of their programme.

Questions
1 How does a transnational company differ from companies that operate under a more ethnocentric orientation?
2 What types of management structures and processes are essential for becoming a transnational firm?

Global professionals as key actors

Transnational organizations rely for their functioning on global professionals (Peiperl and Jonsen, 2007), managers who ensure that people and activities are coordinated and integrated into a worldwide value-added network contributing to the success of the organization as a whole (Martinez and Jarillo, 1989; Bartlett and Ghoshal, 1992; Galbraith, 2000). Unlike expatriate managers, who transferred knowledge and values from the headquarters to subsidiaries (Edström and Galbraith, 1977; Adler and Bartholomew, 1992), global professionals need to understand the complexities of working in an interdependent and complex global network (Box 3.2) (Adler and Bartholomew, 1992; Kedia and Mukherji, 1999). Their task is to recognize opportunities and risks across national and functional boundaries (Pucik and Saba, 1998) and to decide when it is opportune to be locally responsive and when to emphasize global integration (Adler and Bartholomew, 1992).

Box 3.2 Characteristics of a global professional (Adler and Bartholomew, 1992)

A global professional needs to:

☐ Understand the worldwide business environment from a global perspective
☐ Learn about the perspectives, tastes, trends, technologies and approaches involved in conducting business in many foreign cultures
☐ Work with people from many cultures simultaneously
☐ Use crosscultural skills on a daily basis
☐ Interact with foreign colleagues as equals

Because of working with multicultural teams, workforce diversity is a major challenge facing global professionals (see Chapter 4 on 'Diversity Management'). Conceptual literature indicates that they are expected to learn about the perspectives and approaches to conducting business that many foreign cultures use, be flexible and open-minded towards a multitude of cultures, and have a broad cultural perspective and appreciation for cultural diversity (Adler and Bartholomew, 1992; Pucik and Saba, 1998). However, recent empirical research questions this ability to gain an in-depth knowledge on a multitude of cultural contexts (Janssens and Cappellen, 2008).

More important than their cognitive ability, authors agree, is that global professionals are expected to overcome an ethnocentric mindset and develop an openness to other perspectives, selectively incorporating foreign values and practices into the global operations (Box 3.3) (Adler and Bartholomew, 1992; Janssens and Cappellen, 2008). These types of competency differ significantly from the ones of expatriate managers who, working within a particular foreign culture for a predetermined period of time, need to become knowledgeable in that specific culture (Adler and Bartholomew, 1992; Pucik and Saba, 1998). The working style of global professionals is also necessarily more collaborative. This is due, first, to the interdependence between team members, and second, to the lack of clearly defined hierarchies of structural and/or cultural dominance and subordination that once defined interactions between expatriates and their foreign colleagues (Adler and Bartholomew, 1992; Pucik and Saba, 1998).

Box 3.3 The global mindset

Global professionals need a global perspective that consists of a global mindset supported by appropriate skills and knowledge (Kedia and Mukherji, 1999). Not only do they need to be competent to operate across borders, but competent global professionals are also forced to adapt to the demands of significantly greater

▷

3

▷

> complexity. These may include a heightened need for cultural understanding, a greater need for a broad knowledge that spans functions and nations, wider and more frequent boundary-spanning, more stakeholders, a more challenging and expanded list of competing tensions, heightened ambiguity and more challenging ethical dilemmas (Bird and Osland, 2006).
>
> A global mindset is the ability to develop and interpret criteria for personal and business performance that are independent of the assumptions of a single country, culture or context, and to implement those criteria appropriately in different countries, cultures and contexts (Kedia and Mukherji, 1999). It reflects an openness to and an awareness of diversity across cultures and markets, with a propensity and ability to integrate this diversity.

Expatriates based in the host country could exert control over subsidiaries through a mixture of direct and indirect mechanisms (Edström and Galbraith, 1977; Jaeger, 1983; Shenkar et al., 2008). The direct mechanisms stand for formalized norms imposing a certain type of behaviour on individuals fulfilling established criteria (that is, position in the hierarchy). The indirect mechanisms represent the ideological control that shapes employees' sense of the self in a way that fits with and is productive in terms of managerially defined objectives (Alvesson and Willmott, 2002). Global professionals, who are not steadily present in the host country and coordinate teams dislocated across the world, necessarily rely more on ideological forms of control. Locally embedded managers have a greater degree of discretion over how to implement ideas, yet the two work together to construct professional identities that achieve commitment and compliance. This shift reflects a more general trend within organizations from direct to indirect modes of control, yet in culturally diverse organizations the intercultural dimension is key to this process (Peltonen, 2006; Zanoni and Janssens, 2007).

Mini Case Study 3.2
The quest for a global mindset

One of the main challenges for people working in a transnational organization is to have a global mindset. Alice, a worldwide sales and marketing manager of a utility company, explains this challenge as follows:

> The most difficult thing is to create a worldwide team, you know. And making people understand that by doing something local, they help the world. That's the first point. Second point, by doing something local, they may have an impact in another part of the world, because our customers are global as well. Because, for example, I know Kakogawa in Japan; he is investing in Dubai for a big project, and the decision-maker will be in Japan. And if the sales guy doesn't meet the decision-maker in Japan, we will never get the order in Dubai. But how do you convince the sales guy in Japan that he has to spend time on a project in which he will never see an order, because the order will come in Dubai?

So Alice wants to convince her local sales manager in Japan to talk to a Japanese company in order to generate an order in Dubai.

Questions

1 What is the main problem that Alice is encountering?
2 What are some solutions for this problem? How would you go about convincing the local sales manager?

The contentious nature of HRM in transnational companies

The transnational nature of organizations brings with it a shift in the goals and approach of HRM. In order to contribute to the success of the company, HRM is expected to attract, develop and deploy talented employees who can work together effectively despite differences in their culture, language and location. Organizations today are still discovering the complexities of managing and organizing work in this new context (Lane et al., 2006; Boussebaa, 2009).

On the one hand, as transnational organizations are characterized by a range of employees with heterogeneous cultural, cognitive and emotional orientations, they need to have a set of explicit or implicit corporate values and shared beliefs that facilitate interpersonal collaboration and integration across the different parts of the organization (Bartlett et al., 2004). Yet, at the same time, management practices arising from the corporate level must be adopted to fit local cultural and legally mandated expectations (Paik and Sohn, 2004). Studies show that HRM is the function within organizations with the strongest tendency to diversify its practices to fit the local environment (Rosenzweig, 1994), as these are often mandated by local regulation or shaped by strong local conventions. It is therefore important for the central human resources department to adopt an appropriate 'parenting style' towards the diverse local human resources units. Techniques that are more formalized and centralized are used to provide consistent practice, to reduce uncertainty and to underpin the legitimacy of the corporate decision-making process (Ghoshal and Bartlett, 1990).

Critical perspectives view corporate values and global practices not just as facilitators of collaboration and integration, but rather as powerful culture-specific tools that emanate largely from the mother company to exert control over employees across the organization (Peltonen, 2006). At the same time, some authors have observed that culture is strategically used to justify not applying headquarters' employment conditions throughout MNCs but to allow less favourable conditions in the subsidiaries (Adler, 2002; Shimoni and Bergmann, 2006; Frenkel, 2008).

International employee resourcing

Today, organizations compete on the effectiveness and competence of their human talent pool around the world (Caligiuri and Tarique, 2006). As a result, one of the main challenges is to identify and develop talent to function effectively within a transnational organization. Careful selection practices are essential for global leaders (Osland et al., 2006). In contrast to expatriates, who are home-country nationals, transnational organizations no longer select talent exclusively from within their home country. Operating as a network across the globe, transnational organizations make use of their worldwide presence to select employees from a worldwide pool of human resources.

Given the fact that specific values and motivations are necessary to develop global leadership skills (Cappellen and Janssens, 2008), Caligiuri (2006) suggests selecting individuals on that basis. According to Spencer and Spencer (1993), this is the most cost-effective approach because motive and trait competencies cannot be taught. They also argue that people's values and motivations distinguish superior performers from good performers and are therefore a suitable way of selecting employees.

In a similar vein, a cultural intelligence (CQ) approach could be used to select superior performers for positions as global professionals (Janssens and Cappellen, 2008). Following Spencer and Spencer's reasoning (1993), this is especially true as CQ goes beyond other forms of intelligence, including not only cognitive, but also behavioural and motivational abilities, to deal with cultural contexts (Ang et al., 2007). As such, CQ may serve as a selection instrument, specifically selecting candidates based on their skills and values/motivations to work effectively in culturally diverse settings. In a similar vein, Kyriakidou (see Chapter 8 on 'Recruitment and Selection') refers to a renewed interest in personality testing as part of effective personnel selection. Technical knowledge and skills, which are complementary to motive and trait competencies, can be acquired in organizational training sessions. Therefore, they do not necessarily need to be part of the process to resource international staff.

International management development

Whereas the management development literature on expatriation focused on individuals' adjustment, performance and repatriation (Mendenhall et al., 1987; Thomas, 1998; Lazarova and Caligiuri, 2001), the more recent literature increasingly focuses on globally mobile professionals viewed as strategic human resources (Peltonen, 2006) with competencies considered to be crucial to the success of these organizations (Makela and Suutari, 2009). But unlike the situation for expatriates, recent research has indicated a lack of human resources support for alternative types of international work, because these individuals do not need to be relocated with their families (Mayerhofer et al., 2004; Collings et al., 2007). With the burden then placed on employees themselves, global professionals increasingly rely on self-management, building their career competency profile by focusing on their personal identification with work (Cappellen and Janssens, 2008). Instead of referencing their careers to the organization, these competencies enable them to reference their career to the global economy and thereby fulfil their career aspirations to work across borders and cross borders to work (Cappellen and Janssens, 2010a). This does not, however, imply that global professionals are job-hoppers; rather, they take agency over their own career even within the context of a single employer (Cappellen and Janssens, 2010b).

So far, the careers of global professionals have not been studied from critical perspectives. Peltonen (2006: 531) argues that a strategic human resources approach:

> makes it more difficult to think about and theorize expatriates as individuals-in-context, especially to understand how internationally mobile employees' work and career processes are affected and affect the wider circuits of power and control in international businesses.

However, running the organizational and individual perspectives of global professionals in counterpoint might offer a fruitful path that would better reflect the complexity of power dynamics in international management, abandoning the assumption that the interests of organizations and their global professionals are in agreement.

Developing crosscultural understanding

In an increasingly global business environment, employees must interact effectively with colleagues and customers from different cultural backgrounds. For expatriate managers, organizations have developed specific language and culture training programmes directed at working in one specific culture (Forster, 2000). Empirical research on global professionals indicates that they themselves question their ability to acquire in-depth cultural knowledge because of the multitude of cultural contexts they have to deal with and the cursory nature of their contact with them (Janssens and Cappellen, 2008). Rather than focusing on knowledge, they stress the importance of cultural awareness in intercultural communication, acknowledging the participants' differing perspectives and searching for compromises that will integrate these differences.

According to Friedman and Berthoin Antal (2005), the ability to recognize and use cultural differences as a resource for learning and to design action in specific contexts is the core intercultural competence today. Instead of learning the specific cultural values and norms of a single culture, as expatriates do, global professionals may benefit from approaching every intercultural situation as a unique and distinct one. This requires an awareness of their own cultural frame of reference, and an understanding of how this affects their thinking and behaviour. If the professional can then apply this to their counterpart in intercultural communications, reality can be negotiated, leading towards a jointly designed best way of generating ideas, decisions and actions (Friedman and Berthoin Antal, 2005).

Mini Case Study 3.3
Worldwide coordination and its mechanisms of control

Inherent in global professionals' core task of worldwide coordination is the need to be responsible for work that is remotely implemented. Steve, a worldwide quality manager at a water company, recounts how he experiences this challenge:

> You are obliged to work in a very different way. If you need to get something done across borders, you need to send an e-mail, but in case he doesn't answer this e-mail, you can guess. Or he didn't bother, or he is overloaded, doesn't understand it, something which happens quite often, or he feels there is no need to answer, so you need to do it quite differently. You need to start calling him, and then he can still say yes, but in the end, you have to guess whether or not he has done it. So you need to check, whereas when it is in your own surroundings, you can see it.
>
> So actually, you need to learn how to let them feel your presence, with all those people, from top to

bottom, and in the end to occupy yourself with the right issues in quite a different way. Each time you do something, you need to get these people to go along, buy in, saying explicitly where it is you want to go, checking whether they have understood. It sounds very simple and sometimes quite stupid, but … And then in the end, you need to check whether they have implemented it in the right way.

Questions
1 Can you help Steve to facilitate his work with people who are dislocated across the world?
2 How would you resolve Steve's problems to check whether your own team members have implemented the work in a correct way? Can you think of two additional strategies?
3 Reflect on the nature of your control strategies. Do you use direct or indirect mechanisms of control? Do you rely on more ideological forms of control?

Critical scholars of international management are unanimously supportive of conceptualizations of culture as being continuously constructed and reconstructed through interactions between individuals in specific contexts (Frenkel, 2008). In this sense, their perspectives are closer to those of the global professional, whose competencies are based on recognizing culture as a dynamic and relational process, than to the traditional expatriate, who was trained to acquire a specific culture, understood as a fixed set of values and rules, in order to be able to enact 'culturally appropriate' behaviour in the host country (Forster, 2000). Yet, differently from the mainstream literature on global professionals, critical scholars examine the power dynamics underlying such interactions, highlighting the participants' diverging interests (Ybema and Byun, 2009). Along these lines, Shenkar and colleagues (2008) have recently proposed replacing the metaphor of 'cultural distance', largely dominant in the international management literature, with the one of 'cultural friction', to better reflect the power dimension of intercultural relations.

Also focusing on power dynamics in intercultural interactions, Janssens et al. (2006) have examined how female managers can actively shape relations in a way that is more favourable to them. Here, culture is seen as one of the power-laden identity discourses affecting intercultural interactions, rather than as something monolithic and 'given'. Individuals, as agents, do not necessarily need to conform to culture but can rather draw from the alternative discourses available to them – in this case gender and hierarchy – to actively shape intercultural interactions, thus enhancing their professional success.

Mini Case Study 3.4
The search for effective crosscultural training
CULTRAINING is an organization in Belgium that has created a new training concept for those who want to interact more consciously and effectively with other cultures. In order to acquire knowledge, insight and inspiration for a specific cultural context, the organization organizes trips to new economies such as China, India, Indonesia, Turkey and the United Arab Emirates that are currently being explored by Belgian MNCs as business locations. Participating in these training exercises, people should become acquainted

▷ with the culture in terms of living and working in each of these contexts. For foreigners working in Belgium, CULTRAINING organizes exploration sessions that introduce them to the Belgian cultural context.

The organization offers a multifaceted training programme, including formal and informal encounters, introductions to the history of the country and its business context, visits to tourist highlights and remarkable projects, gastronomic experiences and entertainment. Because of its local embeddedness, the organization promises to guide participants outside the beaten paths.

Besides a cultural training programme, participation in these training episodes also provides access to valuable local contacts and networks. Through intense exchange, a theoretical framework and debriefing, individuals should be enabled to develop a strong connection with the country or region they have visited. People who have participated in such training have indicated that they not only learnt how others lived and worked, but were also enabled to reflect on their own cultural framework and learn to value other alternatives. In sum, the organization aims to create and/or heighten cultural sensitivity, which in turn teaches people to communicate and conduct business more effectively in a context of cultural diversity.

Questions
1 What challenges do companies face in managing the complexities of working with global professionals?
2 How can human resources activities support the creation of a global mindset?

Ethical considerations in transnational organizations

Traditionally, the focus of corporate governance has been on financial performance, reporting to and protecting shareholders (De Cieri and Dowling, 2006). Organizations are, however, increasingly expected to behave ethically, be transparent and be responsive to the needs of society in general and employees and customers in particular. They need to find ways of including environmental, social and governance considerations in their management systems (DeCieri and Dowling, 2006) and human practices (see Chapter 5 on 'Human Resource Management and Ethics'). As a result of large-scale business failure to meet societal expectations – as, for example, with energy company Enron's financial dealings, or the case of chemical company Union Carbide in Bhopal – ethics has in recent years become the object of much debate among business scholars and practitioners (Carroll and Buchholtz, 2009).

Transnational organizations face a particularly large challenge in terms of identifying and enforcing ethical standards in multiple contexts. Although some basic values – such as honesty, integrity and the protection of society – are found in all cultures, appropriate behaviour to conform with those values differs strongly in different societal contexts characterized by different cultures, styles and institutions (Schneider and Barsoux, 2003). International business therefore has to deal with global ethical pluralism (DeGeorge, 1993): it needs to consider not only a variety of ethical norms and standards (ethical pluralism), but also cultural ones (globalization), making it a difficult exercise to find out what is shared and what is culture-specific. International business scholars have argued that only in this way can a level playing field be created where the rules of the game can be negotiated and clearly spelled out (Schneider and Barsoux, 2003). As global citizens, global professionals need to be aware of the heterogeneity of ethical norms in the multiple cultural contexts they encounter; in this way, they will be able to build a shared consensus on what is expected and acceptable behaviour across them. As a result, the organization will be able to deal with ethical dilemmas and operate in an ethically responsible way when conducting its international business.

Overall, critical scholars are much more sceptical about the possibility that businesses can genuinely embrace social and environmental concerns. In radical critical thought, the very reason for the existence of companies, which is the maximization of profit, is in itself unethical because it derives from the exploitation of human and environmental resources (Marx, 1976; Adler, 2009). Accordingly, a focus on ethical norms and behaviour is, from a critical perspective, misplaced as it shifts attention away from the structural problem of capitalism as an economic system to the moral dimension of the organization's and the individual's behaviour (Jones et al., 2005; Banerjee, 2008).

The contradictions inherent in business ethics are particularly visible in transnational organizations as the power inequalities between these companies and the locally embedded actors with which they deal, such as employees and states, are particularly large. These local entities are generally in a relatively weak position to enforce what is best for local employees or the country as a whole. In a recent book on business ethics, Jones and colleagues (2005) straightforwardly identified 'global capital' as the denial of ethics. Arguably, the transnational structure of contemporary organizations is in itself a strategy to find contexts with more advantageous institutional conditions for the company, such as a cheaper labour force, as well as weaker trade unions and lower levels of legislative protection for consumers and the environment.

Although the increasingly global circulation of information has facilitated international campaigns publicly condemning the most extreme forms of exploitation of labour and natural resources – such as Nike's employment standards in Asia and Nestlé's unethical marketing practices for baby formula food in Africa – critics argue that these few cases are only the tip of the iceberg of a widespread 'dark' business reality on which the wealth of Western corporations and consumers is based. Although such campaigns can raise awareness in (Western) consumers, they might also have unintended negative effects as they do not address the structural problems in developing countries. For instance, Khan and colleagues (1997) have shown how a well-meant international campaign to ban child labour in the production of soccer balls in Pakistan in fact negatively affected the living conditions of women and children. This case suggests that ethical issues might be so inherently complex that it is hard to envisage what the 'ethical' behaviour of individuals and organizations might be.

Critical analysis and discussion

Studying HRM in transnational organizations from a critical perspective allows future managers to gain a better understanding of the multiple perspectives of the different actors involved. This should be one taking into consideration not only their 'cultural difference', but also structural inequalities that exist at the multiple levels of interpersonal relations, teams, the organization and different countries. Interpreting transnational phenomena by taking into account differences in both culture and power (and the relationship between the two) will in turn enable future managers to better assess situations, diagnose problems and find appropriate solutions.

Conclusion

This chapter has discussed the contentious nature of globalization and its implications for the organization and its employees. It has shown how contradicting forces of global integration and local responsiveness need to be balanced in transnational organizations, and how global professionals are deployed in order to coordinate functional domains on a worldwide basis. Taking a critical perspective, this chapter has also questioned the proclaimed power relations in these transnational organizations, discussing how new and more subtle types of control are being executed. The critical literature, however, does agree with recent research arguing that global professionals should negotiate reality in each crosscultural interaction rather than aiming for in-depth cultural knowledge. Albeit for different reasons, both types of literature in the end conclude that culture is continuously constructed in every interaction between people from different contexts.

For global professionals, the multicultural nature of their work strongly suggests the need for a 'culture-general' knowledge (Hofstede, 2001). This type of knowledge is based on people's awareness of their own mental make-up and the fact that this (may) differ from that of other cultures. Global professionals should start their work with a mindfulness of their own cultural background and how this influences them to approach issues in a certain way.

According to Thomas (2006), mindfulness is a linking process between knowledge and behavioural ability in which people are aware of their own assumptions, ideas and emotions, and their selective perception, attribution and categorization. It implies an enhanced attention to the particular current experience or present reality and its context, while creating new mental maps of other people's personalities and cultural backgrounds as a basis for immediate action (Thomas and Inkson, 2004). Being mindful, global professionals will be able to approach a situation with an open mind, focusing their attention on personal and context-specific details (Thomas, 2006). In this way, they can open themselves up to divergent cultural influences and experiences (Koehn and Rosenau, 2002) and negotiate reality (Friedman and Berthoin Antal, 2005).

Organizations can help global professionals to become mindful by training them to have an active awareness of their own cultural framework and how this may influence their perceptions and behaviours. At a later stage, training interventions may focus on an exploration of underlying assumptions in other cultures and their use as a basis for learning new ways of seeing and doing things in an effective way in a different cultural context.

This chapter has also shown that, up until now, organizations have had no equivalent in terms of repatriation programmes for expatriates. As such, global professionals are left with the burden of being responsible for their own management development. Being aware of this lack of support might challenge organizations to use personal development plans that guide the careers of global professionals throughout the organization. By discussing and revising these plans jointly on a regular basis, organizations can support the further development of global managers by providing them with viable career opportunities for the future.

❓ For discussion and revision

Questions

1 Can you think of three localizing and three globalizing forces in business today?

2 Can you think of other functions within transnational companies besides human resources that might show a strong tendency to diversify in line with local conventions?

3 Would you prefer to work as a global professional or as an expatriate manager? Why?

4 What do you think of the argument that specific culture knowledge (for example, on eating and greeting rituals) promotes stereotypical thinking?

5 How does the notion of the global professional match the nature of the transnational organization?

6 Identify the main challenges for organizations working with global professionals?

7 How has globalization changed the nature of intercultural competencies?

Exercises

1 You are a crosscultural training advisor. Your client is a transnational organization that has employed you to train its employees in crosscultural communication. Divide your class into two groups:

- The first group of training advisors will design a training programme for a home-country employee who will be sent to Japan as an expatriate, managing the corporation's subsidiary in Tokyo.
- The second group of training advisors will design a training programme for a host-country employee (coming from one of the corporation's subsidiary countries) who has been promoted to a position as a global professional within the corporation. Working as a global professional, she will have to deal with the following countries: the USA, Mexico, Brazil, South Africa, Morocco, Egypt, the United Arab Emirates, Italy, Germany, France, China, Russia, Japan, Australia and the Philippines.

Compare the two training programmes in class. What are the main similarities and differences? Why?

2   Discuss ideological, more subtle types of control that can be executed within transnational organizations. Develop a role-play to present in class that illustrates these types of control.

Further reading

Books

De Cieri, H. and Dowling, P. J. (2006) Strategic international human resource management in multinational enterprises: developments and directions. In Stahl, G. K. and Björkman, I. (eds) *Handbook of Research in International Human Resource Management*. Cheltenham: Edward Elgar, pp. 15–35.

Janssens, M. and Cappellen, T. (2008) Contextualizing cultural intelligence: the case of global managers. In Ang, S. and Van Dyne, L. (eds) *Handbook of Cultural Intelligence. Theory, Measurement and Applications*. Armonk, NY: M. E. Sharpe, pp. 356–71.

Journals

Adler, N. J. and Bartholomew, S. (1992) Managing globally competent people. *Academy of Management Executive*, 6: 52–65.

Collings, D. G., Scullion, H. and Morley, M. J. (2007) Changing patterns of global staffing in the multinational enterprise: challenges to the conventional expatriate assignment and emerging alternatives. *Journal of World Business*, 42: 198–213.

Case Study View Corporation

View Corporation started as a Belgian television manufacturer in the mid-1930s. Even back then, the company had international connections, as it imported parts from the USA for its televisions. By the end of the 20th century, it had acquired several other companies and established a number of foreign subsidiaries, becoming a truly global company.

Today, View is a global technology company active in more than 90 countries and employing 3,300 people worldwide. It designs and develops visualization solutions for a variety of selected professional markets such as media and entertainment, security and monitoring, medical imaging, presentation, and simulation and avionics. View's headquarters are located in Brussels, yet the company has branches for sales and marketing, customer support, research and development and manufacturing in Europe, America and the Asia-Pacific region.

View Corporation is structured along its professional markets into five divisions. Each of these divisions has functional units in operations, research and development, marketing and sales, finance, and human resources. At the group level, similar functional units across the divisions collaborate, ensuring an integration of policies and practices and the creation of economies of scale and scope. Being a truly transnational organization, the company has a policy of capitalizing on location-specific advantages. For instance, the medical imaging division recently acquired a company in northern Italy with specific expertise in hospital display technology. View decided to make the unit a centre of excellence within the company rather than transferring the expertise to Belgium.

Although the company traditionally relied on expatriates to manage its foreign subsidiaries, expatriate assignments are now rather rare. They are only used for specific purposes such as carrying out an acquisition or in response to an employee's explicit request to move. The company is exploring new ways of working across borders, such as commuter assignments.

After the acquisition of a company in Edinburgh (UK), the president of the medical imaging division suggested that one of his vice-presidents move there. He told them it was an important acquisition, costing View some €35 million, so it would be important to have someone on site. Based on his loyalty towards View, Pete decided that he would go, given the fact that the other vice-president had small children, whereas his son was already 16 years old. But instead of relocating to Edinburgh, he commuted. The company rented an apartment there, enabling him to leave his wife and son every Sunday evening to go to Edinburgh, and come back home every Friday evening, taking the last flight home.

Although this meant that Pete's family did not have to relocate, he experienced this commuter assignment very negatively:

> My family didn't go along, and that damaged our relationship. And it was very lonely. Why? Because at night, you're sitting there alone. In general, you're working longer hours, often until 9 pm, and then you go to your apartment, but to do what? You're sitting there, on your own, nothing to do. You are also away from your company. I was very surprised about that. Physically, you're not present, you're no longer in the action, and you really have to make an effort to make sure you can stay in the action, because they forget you really fast.

After this negative experience, Pete decided never to commute again. However, he liked working in an international business environment, so he continued his work as a global professional. At View, global professionals make sure that coordination is ensured and knowledge is transferred. This can be done in a number of ways, combining trips with telephone and video-conferencing, and Pete uses this approach: 'I got a phone call today from India, yesterday I had a videoconference with Switzerland, and last week I was in the US, where I had to deal with some Japanese problems.' View uses global management positions to ensure a flexible presence across the globe, without the costs associated with relocating workers and their families. Even in early stages of their career, from their junior or middle management position at headquarters onwards, View's employees are already being given responsibility for worldwide coordination.

Although global professionals in View frequently use the communication facilities described above, travelling remains necessary. Throughout the years, Pete has travelled a lot:

> You cannot believe where I have been. I save all my flight tickets, it's a large pile, I save them in my attic, and when I retire, I'm going to input all that into a spreadsheet, to see how many miles I've travelled. To give you an idea: I have about a million frequent flyer miles with American Airlines, eight hundred thousand with Air France, about one and a half million miles with Sabena and six hundred thousand with Lufthansa. Apart from Africa and South America, I have visited all states of the USA, Australia, China, you name it.

Travelling is important as it remains the only way to establish a sound relationship with colleagues around the world. For Pete, these local visits are the only opportunity to have face-to-face contact, getting to know his local counterparts, 'Because as a foreigner, I cannot understand all of them. They tell me something and they think I understand. It's not about language, it's about the way one looks at life.' According to Pete, getting to know this way of life through face-to-face contact facilitates future telephone and video-conferences because it allows him to better understand others' perspectives.

To support their employees who are working internationally, View organizes cultural training sessions. Recently, a training course on the cultural differences between Belgium and China was delivered by a university professor. As a global professional at View, Pete considers the world his working space, yet he questions a person's need and ability to acquire in-depth knowledge of all the cultural contexts he and his colleagues come across:

> I always had a very strong interest in meeting people and different cultural contexts, because I believe that you need to open yourself to these experiences. So you need to use chopsticks in China to eat, and have burgers with a large dollop of mustard in the States, while drinking large beers. For me, that's getting the feeling of a culture. How should I say? With an American, you have to run along and say yeah, great, wow, and with Germans, you have to yell along, raising your voice in a discussion. In Japan, you have to stroll along, be quiet and at ease, while the Chinese, you have to laugh and play fun with them. And somehow, that's my ... I don't think about that and I try not to figure out these cultures, cause I think that's not useful. For example, in the States, you have to go once to a baseball game; you cannot understand why it's such an event. How these things are ... you can't imagine. But I don't make the effort. There are

colleagues here who try to unravel these cultures ... I don't take the time. Just go with the flow, join them in talking, yelling and so on ... and you'll be accepted as a business partner.

Questions

1 Although Pete likes to work in an international context, he clearly experiences some frustration in the way in which View Corporation manages its international work. What kind of advice would you give the organization to improve this?
2 How do you evaluate View's training policy? Why?
3 What are the specific needs of global professionals in terms of crosscultural interaction?
4 Reflect on Pete's strategy for working effectively with his colleagues across the world.

Critical analysis of the case study

This case study above portrays the perspective of a global professional working at the headquarters of a transnational organization. Such individual experience highlights the difficulties of combining a career as a global professional with the private sphere, the pressure managers feel to take up jobs, and the need to find effective ways of dealing with the heterogeneous cultural contexts they constantly encounter. In other words, it shows the 'human' dimension (including the human cost) of a career as a global professional.

Such an individual perspective from a global professional based in a company's headquarters does not, however, allow us to unveil the structural privilege that this employee actually enjoys within the broader context of the transnational organization. Unequal power relations are much more likely to emerge from voices at the periphery of organizations and in subordinate positions, because those employees are more likely to experience disadvantage and marginalization, reflecting the underlying power relations.

References

Adler, N. (2002) *International Dimensions of Organizational Behavior*. Cincinnati, OH: South-Western.

Adler, N. J. and Bartholomew, S. (1992) Managing globally competent people. *Academy of Management Executive*, 6: 52–65.

Adler, P. S. (2009) Marx and organization studies today. In Adler, P. S. (ed.) *Oxford Handbook of Sociology and Organization Studies: Classical Foundations*. New York: Oxford University Press, pp. 62–91.

Alvesson, M. and Willmott, H. (2002) Identity regulation as organizational control: producing the appropriate individual. *Journal of Management Studies*, 39: 619–44.

Ang, S., Van Dyne, L., Koh, C., Ng, K., Templer, K. J., Tay, C. and Chandrasekar, N. A. (2007) Cultural intelligence: its measurement and effects on cultural judgment and decision making, cultural adaptation, and task performance. *Management and Organization Review*, 3(3): 335–71.

Banerjee, S. B. (2008) Corporate social responsibility: the good, the bad and the ugly. *Critical Sociology*, 34(1): 51–79.

Banerjee, S. B. and Linstead, S. (2001) Globalization, multiculturalism and other fictions: colonialism for the new millennium? *Organization*, 8(4): 683–722.

3

Bartlett, C. A. and Ghoshal, S. (1989) *Managing Across Borders: The Transnational Solution*. Boston: Harvard Business School Press.

Bartlett, C. A. and Ghoshal, S. (1992) What is a global manager? *Harvard Business Review*, 70: 124–32.

Bartlett, C. A. and Ghoshal, S. (2000) *Transnational Management: Text, Cases and Readings* (3rd edn). Irwin: McGraw-Hill.

Bartlett, C. A., Ghoshal, S. and Birkinshaw, J. (2004) *Transnational Management: Text, Cases and Readings* (4th edn). Irwin: McGraw-Hill.

Bhabha, H. K. (1994) Of mimicry and man: the ambivalence of colonial discourse. In Bhabha, H. K. (ed.) *The Location of Culture*. London: Routledge, pp. 85–92.

Bird, A. and Osland, J. (2006) Global competencies: an introduction. In Lane, H. W., Maznevski, M. L., Mendenhall, M. E. and McNett, J. (eds) *Handbook of Global Management. A Guide to Managing Complexity*. Malden, MA: Blackwell Publishing, pp. 57–80.

Boussebaa, M. (2009) Struggling to organize across national borders: the case of global resource management in professional service firms. *Human Relations*, 62: 829–50.

Caligiuri, P. (2006) Developing global leaders. *Human Resource Management Review*, 16(2): 219–28.

Caligiuri, P. and Tarique, I. (2006) International assignee selection and cross-cultural training and development. In Stahl, G. K. and Björkman, I. (eds) *Handbook of Research in International Human Resource Management*. Cheltenham: Edward Elgar, pp. 302–22.

Cappellen, T. and Janssens, M. (2008) Global managers' career competencies. *Career Development International*, 13(6): 514–37.

Cappellen, T. and Janssens, M. (2010a) The career reality of global managers: an examination of career triggers. *International Journal of Human Resource Management*, 21: 1884–919.

Cappellen, T. and Janssens, M. (2010b) Enacting global careers: organizational career scripts and the global economy as co-existing career referents. *Journal of Organizational Behavior*, 31: 687–706.

Carroll, A. B. and Buchholtz, A. K. (2009) *Business and Society: Ethics and Stakeholder Management*. Cincinnati, OH: Cengage Learning.

Collings, D. G., Scullion, H. and Morley, M. J. (2007) Changing patterns of global staffing in the multinational enterprise: challenges to the conventional expatriate assignment and emerging alternatives. *Journal of World Business*, 42: 198–213.

De Cieri, H. and Dowling, P. J. (2006) Strategic international human resource management in multinational enterprises: developments and directions. In Stahl, G. K. and Björkman, I. (eds) *Handbook of Research in International Human Resource Management*. Cheltenham: Edward Elgar, pp. 15–35.

DeGeorge, R. T. (1993) *Competing with Integrity in International Business*. New York: Oxford University Press.

Edström, A. and Galbraith, J. R. (1977) Transfer of managers as a coordination and control strategy in multinational organizations. *Administrative Science Quarterly*, 22: 248–63.

Forster, N. (2000) The myth of the 'international manager'. *International Journal of Human Resource Management*, 11(1): 126–42.

Frenkel, M. (2008) The multicultural corporation as a third space: rethinking international management discourse on knowledge transfer through Homi Bhabha. *Academy of Management Review*, 33(4): 924–42.

Friedman, V. J. and Berthoin Antal, A. (2005) Negotiating reality: a theory of action approach to intercultural competence. *Management Learning*, 36(1): 69–86.

Galbraith, J. R. (2000) *Designing the Global Corporation*. San Francisco: Jossey-Bass.

Ghoshal, S. and Bartlett, C. (1990) The multinational corporation as an interorganizational network. *Academy of Management Review*, 15: 603–25.

Ghoshal, S. and Nohria, N. (1993) Horses for courses: organizational forms for multinational corporations, *Sloan Management Review*, 34(2): 23–35.

Govindarajan, V. and Gupta, A. K. (2001) *The Quest for Global Dominance. Transforming Global Presence into Global Competitive Advantage*. San Francisco: Jossey-Bass.

Hofstede, G. (2001) *Culture's Consequences. Comparing Values, Behaviors, Institutions, and Organizations Across Nations*. Thousand Oaks: Sage Publications.

Jaeger, A. M. (1983) The transfer of organizational culture overseas: an approach to control in the multinational corporation. *Journal of International Business Studies*, 14(2): 91–113.

Janssens, M. and Cappellen, T. (2008) Contextualizing cultural intelligence: the case of global managers. In Ang, S. and Van Dyne, L. (eds) *Handbook of Cultural Intelligence. Theory, Measurement, and Applications*. Armonk, New York: M. E. Sharpe, pp. 356–74.

Janssens, M., Cappellen, T. and Zanoni, P. (2006) Successful female expatriates as agents: positioning oneself through gender, hierarchy and culture. *Journal of World Business*, 41(2): 133–48.

Jones, C., Parker, M. and ten Bos, R. (2005) *For Business Ethics*. Oxon: Routledge.

Kedia, B. L. and Mukherji, A. (1999) Global managers: developing a mindset for global competitiveness. *Journal of World Business*, 34(3): 230–51.

Khan, F. R., Munir, K. A. and Willmott, H. (1997) A dark side of institutional entrepreneurship: soccer balls, child labour and postcolonial impoverishment. *Organization Studies*, 28(7): 1055–77.

Koehn, P. H. and Rosenau, J. N. (2002) Transnational competence in an emergent epoch. *International Studies Perspectives*, 3(2): 105–27.

Lane, H. W., Maznevski, M. L. and Mendenhall, M. E. (2006) Globalization: Hercules meets Buddha. In Lane, H. W., Maznevski, M. L., Mendenhall, M. E. and McNett, J. (eds) *Handbook of Global Management: A Guide to*

Managing Complexity. Malden, MA: Blackwell Publishing, pp. 3–25.

Lazarova, M. and Caligiuri, P. (2001) Retaining repatriates: the role of organizational support practices. *Journal of World Business*, 36(4): 389–401.

Leonardi, P. M. (2008) Indeterminacy and the discourse of inevitability in international technology management. *Academy of Management Review*, 33(4): 975–84.

Makela, K. and Suutari, V. (2009) Global careers: a social capital paradox. *International Journal of Human Resource Management*, 20: 992–1008.

Martinez, J. I. and Jarillo, J. C. (1989) The evolution of research on coordination mechanisms in multinational corporations. *Journal of International Business Studies*, 20: 489–514.

Marx, K. (1976) *Capital*, Vol. I. London: Penguin Classics.

Mayerhofer, H., Hartmann, L. C., Michelitsch-Riedl, G. and Kollinger, I. (2004) Flexpatriate assignments: a neglected issue in global staffing. *International Journal of Human Resource Management*, 15: 1371–89.

Mendenhall, M., Dubar, E. and Oddou, G. (1987) Expatriate selection, training and career-pathing: a review and critique. *Human Resource Management*, 26(3): 331–45.

Mir, R., Mir, A. and Wong, D. J. (2006) Diversity. The cultural logic of global capital? In Konrad, A. M., Prasad, P. and Pringle, J. K. (eds) *Handbook of Workplace Diversity*. Thousands Oaks, CA: Sage, pp. 167–88.

Mir, R., Banerjee, S. B. and Mir, A. (2008) Hegemony and its discontents: a critical analysis of organizational knowledge transfer. *Critical Perspectives on International Business*, 4(2/3): 203–27.

Osland, J. S., Bird, A., Mendenhall, M. and Osland, A. (2006) Developing global leadership capabilities and global mindset: a review. In Stahl, G. K. and Björkman, I. (eds) *Handbook of Research in International Human Resource Management*. Cheltenham: Edward Elgar, pp. 197–222.

Özbilgin, M. (2004) 'International' human resource management: academic parochialism in editorial boards of the 'top' 22 journals on international human resource management. *Personnel Review*, 33(2): 205–21.

Paik, Y. and Sohn, J. D. (2004) Expatriate managers and MNC's ability to control international subsidiaries: the case of Japanese MNC's. *Journal of World Business*, 39(1): 61–72.

Peiperl, M. and Jonsen, K. (2007) Global careers. In Gunz, H. and Peiperl, M. (eds) *Handbook of Career Studies*. Los Angeles: Sage, pp. 350–72.

Peltonen, T. (2006) Critical theoretical perspectives on international human resource management. In Stahl, G. K. and Bjorkman, I. (eds) *Handbook of Research in International Human Resource Management*. Cheltenham: Edward Elgar, pp. 523–35.

Pucik, V. and Saba, T. (1998) Selecting and developing the global versus the expatriate manager: a review of the state-of-the-art. *Human Resource Planning*, 21: 40–53.

Prasad, A. (1997) The colonizing consciousness and representations of the other: a postcolonial critique of the discourse of oil. In Prasad, P., Mills, A. J., Elmes, M. and Prasad, A. (eds) *Managing the Organizational Melting Pot: Dilemmas of Workplace Diversity*. Thousand Oaks, CA: Sage, pp. 285–311.

Rosenzweig, P. M. (1994) Management practices in U.S. affiliates of foreign-owned firms: are 'they' just like 'us'? *Thunderbird International Business Review*, 36(4): 393–410.

Rosenzweig, P. M. and Singh, J. V. (1991) Organizational environments and the multinational enterprise. *Academy of Management Review*, 16(2): 340–61.

Schneider, S. C. and Barsoux, J.-L. (2003) *Managing Across Cultures* (2nd edn). Harlow: Prentice Hall.

Shenkar, O., Luo, Y. and Yeheskel, O. (2008) From 'distance' to 'friction': substituting metaphors and redirecting intercultural research. *Academy of Management Review*, 33(4): 905–23.

Shimoni, B. and Bergmann, H. (2006) Managing in a changing world: from multiculturalism to hybridization – the production of hybrid management cultures in Israel, Thailand, and Mexico. *Academy of Management Perspectives*, 20(3): 76–89.

Spencer, L. M. and Spencer, S. M. (1993) *Competence at Work. Models for Superior Performance*. New York: John Wiley.

Thomas, D. (1998) The expatriate experience: a critical review and synthesis. *Advances in International Comparative Management*, 12: 237–73.

Thomas, D. C. (2006) Domain and development of cultural intelligence. The importance of mindfulness. *Group and Organization Management*, 31(1): 78–99.

Thomas, D. C. and Inkson, K. (2004) *Cultural Intelligence. People Skills for Global Business*. San Francisco: Berrett-Koehler.

Westwood, R. (2004) Towards a postcolonial research paradigm in international business and comparative management. In Welch, C. (ed.) *Handbook of Qualitative Research Methods for International Business*. Cheltenham: Edward Elgar, pp. 56–83.

Wong-MingJi, D. and Mir, A. H. (1997) How international is international management? Provincialism, parochialism and the problematic of global diversity. In Prasad, P., Mills, A., Elmes, M. and Prasad, A. (eds) *Managing the Organizational Melting Pot: Dilemmas of Workplace Diversity*. Thousand Oaks, CA: Sage, pp. 340–66.

Ybema, S. and Byun, H. (2009) Cultivating cultural differences in asymmetric power relations. *International Journal of Cross-Cultural Management*, 9(3): 339–58.

Zanoni, P. and Janssens, M. (2007) Minority employees engaging with (diversity) management: an analysis of control, agency, and micro-emancipation. *Journal of Management Studies*, 44(8): 1371–97.

Diversity management

Nicolina Kamenou and Jawad Syed

4

?

After reading this chapter, you should be able to:

- ☐ Understand and distinguish between diversity management and equal employment opportunity
- ☐ Understand how demographic transformation of the population and the workforce affects the future of diversity management in the workplace
- ☐ Understand various forms of employment stereotypes and discrimination
- ☐ Know about various laws and regulations in place in several countries to tackle workplace discrimination
- ☐ Distinguish between the business case and social equity approaches to diversity management
- ☐ Understand methodological considerations in diversity management research

Introduction

The aim of this chapter is to introduce students to the concepts of managing diversity and equal opportunities in employment. Given the demographic transformations of the general population and the labour force in many countries, workforce diversity is a major issue facing managers and organizations. There is, however, evidence of unrelenting stereotypes and discriminatory attitudes and behaviours that not only permeate the workplace, but are also found in abundance on a societal and an institutional level. Chapter 14 further expands on issues related to diversity and the experiences of social groups in relation to balancing their work and personal life, and interested readers can review this related work in that chapter.

This chapter will introduce students to various forms of employment discrimination, as well as legislation in various countries to tackle discrimination. Chapter 14 also focuses on some equality legislation in relation to the experiences of diverse groups, mainly in relation to work–life balance. With respect to theorizing diversity management, two key approaches will be discussed: the business case approach and the social equity approach. The chapter also discusses some methodological issues related to conducting research on diversity and equal opportunity, and presents a case study on ethnic minority women in the UK.

Key concepts of diversity management

In the last few decades, diversity management has been gaining increasing attention within the field of human resource management (HRM) and international HRM. Cox (1994) noted that diversity management was initially seen to be a 'North American affair', and that the emphasis in other countries (for example, Canada and the UK) was on learning lessons from the US experience. Local context, however, remains a major determinant of the approach to diversity and diversity management in any country. For example, British identity or Britishness is a key factor in diversity management in the UK 'because most of the disadvantaged women and men in our society have ancestral roots in the colonies of Britain's erstwhile empire, and it is they who bear the brunt of racism and discrimination' (Lorbiecki, 2001: 2).

Most definitions of and discussions related to diversity management focus on the organizational benefits it can provide, that is, the business case for diversity. A large number of organizations in the US, UK and elsewhere are now attempting to 'embrace diversity', both as a result of the advocated benefits of having a diverse group of staff, but also because of demographic changes. Legislative pressures are also crucial in organizations' attempts to present themselves as diversity-friendly.

In the UK, there is extensive legislation covering diversity, including the Race Relations Act 1976, the Race Relations Amendment Act 2000 and the Sex Discrimination Act 1975, as well as EU discrimination provisions that cover religion or belief, sexual orientation and age. The new UK single Equality Act, which came into force in October 2010, brings together a number of existing laws and includes age, disability, gender reassignment, marriage and civil partnership, pregnancy and maternity, race, religion and belief, gender and sexual orientation. The general equality duty in the public sector is set out in the Equality Act 2010 (Equality and Human Rights Commission, 2011), which states that those subject to the equality duty must make efforts to:

☐ eliminate unlawful discrimination, harassment and victimization and other conduct prohibited by the Act;
☐ advance equality of opportunity between people who share a protected characteristic and those who do not;
☐ foster good relations between people who share a protected characteristic and those who do not.

In New Zealand, institutions concerned with a single group in society have recently been replaced by an overarching human rights body that is concerned with various equality strands (Parker and Douglas, 2010).

With some notable exceptions, mainly in the US (for example, Thomas, 1992; Nkomo and Cox, 1996; Thomas and Ely, 1996) but also with some UK examples (Dickens, 1994, 1999; Liff, 1997, 1999; Lorbiecki and Jack, 2000, Kamenou, 2000, Kirton and Greene, 2005; Kamenou and Fearfull, 2006), diversity management has received limited attention from academic scholars. There has been more sociological work on the effects of discrimination and prejudice in organizations and society as a whole (see, for example, Anthias, 1992; Afshar and Maynard, 1994; Brah, 1994; Blackstone et al., 1998) than on diversity management research within business or management schools, although this situation has slowly improved over the last few years. There is a dire need for more academic research on diversity and equality within the 'human-focused' management topics, such as HRM, and organizational behaviour, but also within more general management and business areas such as strategic management, economics and critical accounting. Discussions surrounding equality should be mainstream in both management research and teaching, instead of being considered as a 'soft extra' within more sociological aspects of the curriculum and of research.

The diversity management discourse and its limitations

In the literature addressing specific approaches to diversity and their limitations, 'equal employment opportunity' (EEO), 'affirmative action' and 'diversity management' are frequently used terms (see, for example, Deluca and McDowell, 1992; Syed and Kramar, 2009). Demographic changes in both the population in general and the labour market in many countries mean that employers today need to manage a far broader diversity of groups in their current employment practices compared with the numbers managed in the past (Pool and Sceats, 1990). Accordingly, much literature is now available to organizations informing them how best to handle a diverse workforce (see, for example, Ferris et al., 1994; Thomas and Ely, 1996; Härtel and Fujimoto, 2000; Ely and Thomas, 2001; Ashkanasy et al., 2002; Murray and Syed, 2005; Bell, 2007).

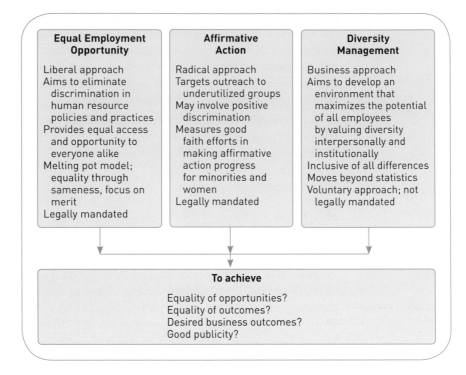

Figure 4.1 Usual approaches to managing diversity.

Source: Based on University of California (1999) and Gagnon and Cornelius (2000)

Figure 4.1 offers three popular approaches to workforce diversity in various international contexts. It highlights the key features of each approach, for example:

- ☐ the emphasis of EEO on eliminating discrimination in human resources policies and practices;
- ☐ the emphasis of affirmative action on equality of outcomes;
- ☐ the emphasis of diversity management on the inclusion of all forms of diversity and business outcomes.

All of these approaches have their origins in the US labour market. Whereas the first two approaches are generally legally mandated, the diversity management approach is based on voluntary corporate measures. Diversity management was adopted as an alternate approach to affirmative action because the realities facing organizations were 'no longer the realities affirmative action was designed to fix' (Thomas, 1990: 107). Affirmative action failed to 'deal with the root causes of prejudice and inequality and did little to develop the full potential of every man and woman in the company' (1990: 117).

Within the Australian context, diversity management has been described as 'second-generation' EEO opportunity that followed a wave of antidiscrimination legislation (Teicher and Spearitt, 1996). The diversity agenda has been described as one that 'has come to Australia from the USA as an HRM workplace strategy' (Strachan et al., 2004: 199), an agenda that has traditionally focused on gender (De Cieri and Kramar, 2005). However, certain other groups of people, such as indigenous Australians and persons from non-English speaking backgrounds, continue to be disadvantaged in employment (Syed and Ali, 2005).

Traditionally, diversity policies have been externally driven, influenced by social responsibility doctrines. However, since the mid-1990s, there has been a shift in public policy towards the business case of diversity. Managing a diverse workforce is now closely linked to business performance (that is, it is internally driven) and is generally considered to be a part of corporate strategy (Bertone and Leahy, 2003). Accordingly, diversity management is described as a programme that was 'needed, not only to meet employee needs, but to reduce turnover costs and ensure that customers receive the best service possible' (De Cieri and Kramar, 2005: 28–9). In Chapter 14 of this book, Kamenou argues that government and organizational initiatives relating to work–life balance are also often based on business case arguments, that is, how different social groups can be 'utilized' in a manner that is good for business and profitability.

Critical Thinking 4.1
The discourse of diversity management
Some scholars suggest that managers now talk about diversity both to keep on the right side of the law, and to ensure the commitment of diverse employees to the organization and its objectives (Antonios, 1997). Employers' approaches generally range from a straight lack of interest to a more inclusive approach and positive potential for a long-term business strategy. Some organizations devote little attention to the area, whereas others devote much. There is also some evidence of a negative reaction against EEO endeavours. In particular, the emphasis on affirmative action has sparked most resistance (D'Netto et al., 2000). Previous research suggests that, in most organizations, diversity policies appear to represent a renaming of EEO rather than being an integrated management approach in their own right (Kramar, 2004). An integrated approach is, however, hard to achieve through single-level conceptualizations of diversity management (Syed and Kramar, 2009; Syed and Özbilgin, 2009).

Scholars have expressed some concern that a shift from social-equity driven EEO to business-benefits driven diversity management may exacerbate the debatable employment conditions of women, ethnic minorities and other disadvantaged groups. For example, Humphries and Grice (1995) argue that while diversity management may be seen as a new social division between the core, the periphery and the unemployed, it ignores the categories that 'illustrate women and other people as not having achieved proportionate representation in the statistics of privilege' (1995: 30–1). The replacement of the discourse of equity with the discourse of diversity may relegate many people from diverse backgrounds to the 'insecure periphery' (1995: 31). In other words, there are serious concerns about the direction and scope of diversity management in improving the conditions of disadvantaged people in the workplace.

There are also some concerns about a predominant emphasis on individuality within the discourse of diversity management. Social identity theory proposes that individuals identify with groups that positively affect their self-esteem, and evaluate their own groups by social comparisons to other groups (Tajfel and Turner, 1986). Previous research also suggests that organizational interventions that fail to address the underlying problem of cultural disintegration will not be able to alleviate social disadvantage within and outside organizations (Appo and Härtel, 2003).

Although collective identity is generally ignored in employment contexts, employers are reportedly more concerned about legal regulations. Managers generally seem to be driven by a legal compliance approach (Antonios, 1997), but legislation is generally limited in its ability to bring about cultural and attitudinal change in organizations (Pyke, 2005). Most probably, this is because of the narrow, single-level conceptualizations of diversity management, so that issues related to national culture, structural conditions, and multiple and intersectionality (overlapping) of various forms of identity remain generally neglected.

A relational framework for diversity management

In order to enable organizations to pursue an integrated approach, Syed and Özbilgin (2009) propose a relational framework that treats diversity management from a layered and intersectional perspective. The framework is informed by Bourdieu's relational sociology, which treats social reality as being layered across agency and structure (see, for example, Bourdieu, 1998). Syed and Özbilgin discuss the need for a relational framework with which equality of opportunities could be studied in dynamic (that is, always evolving), overlapping (in terms of structure and agency and of various forms of identity) and context-specific (instead of universalistic) terms. They argue that single-level conceptualizations of equal opportunities fail to capture the interplay between agentic and structural concerns of equality. Therefore, they propose a relational framework that bridges the divide between large-scale macro-national, medium-sized meso-organizational and small-scale micro-individual insights to arrive at a realistic conceptualization of diversity management.

At the *macro-national* level, the relational framework of diversity management discusses the impact of national structures and arrangements, such as laws, social organization, national culture, and gender and race relations. At the *meso-organizational* level, the framework takes into account the organizational processes, rituals and routinized behaviours at work that establish the rules of middle-level gender and race relations. An absence of debate on equality of rights at work and a lack of recognition of multicultural traditions mean that meso-level relationships may reflect a hierarchical organization of discriminatory practices, embedded within broad social relations. At the *micro-individual* level, the relational framework deals with issues related to individual identity, aspirations and agency that affect change, these phenomena also being viewed in terms of gender and race.

Advantages of diversity

Cox and Blake (1991) identify six dimensions that can help organizations to create a competitive advantage from effectively managing the diversity of their workforce, namely cost, human resource acquisition, marketing, creativity, problem-solving and organizational flexibility.

Cost

Issues such as high employee turnover rates and absence from work cost businesses significant amounts of money. A recent survey by Kronos and Mercer

(2008) showed that unplanned and extended absences cost companies 9.2 per cent of their payroll. According to Cox and Blake (1991), women and racial minority groups had high turnover rates and absenteeism in the workplace due to issues such as pregnancy and fixed work schedules. However, studies prove that organizations have reduced women's turnover rates by 63 per cent as a result of providing in-house childcare facilities (Youngblood and Cook, 1984), and that introducing flexible working times has significantly reduced absenteeism (Kim and Campagna, 1981).

Resource acquisition

Organizations today are involved in a persistent struggle to attract and retain top-quality employees. Cox and Blake (1991) suggest that by using positive publicity to recruit women and individuals from racial minorities, companies can indirectly boost their recruiting efforts.

Marketing and creativity

Markets are becoming more diverse (Cox and Blake, 1991), and each market has its own cultural preferences and sensitivities (Hill, 2008). From a team perspective, a diverse mix of team members is likely to be more creative than a group of identical individuals. A diverse team holds different attitudes and perspectives that are not possessed by an identical team. Therefore, discussions within a diverse group are likely to result in a higher level of analysis and lower conformity in thought, whereas the members of a group who are identical may have little to talk about or may commit identical mistakes (Cox and Blake, 1991). Diversity encourages more creativity and innovation, which can in turn lead to more effective decision-making (Gibson and Gibbs, 2006).

Problem-solving and system flexibility

Companies such as HSBC Bank and Proctor and Gamble (P&G) have achieved global success by hiring talented employees and making sure they gain international experience by relocating them to countries with cultural identities completely different from their own (Ready and Conger, 2007). In this way, employees exchange information about each other's cultures. The knowledge gained in this way can help employees to understand subtle details such as valuable cultural dimensions and how business deals are negotiated (Hofstede, 1984). This can in turn lead to greater flexibility in the system and better problem-solving in organizations (Ready and Conger, 2007).

Critical thinking 4.2
The challenges of managing diversity
Managing diversity is not an easy task. Several issues, such as conflict, isolation and discrimination, may exist within diverse work groups.

In certain situations, diversity may trigger social isolation, which is probably caused by not only social stereotypes, but also unique individual dispositions (Putnam, 2007). Kreitz (2008) suggests that managers in organizations should be able to identify whether people are keeping to themselves and rectify this by promoting an organizational culture in which each group is enabled to embrace each other's identities rather than trying to 'make everyone the same' (Putnam, 2007).

In addition, conflict may arise in diverse groups. In-groups and out-groups can be created as a result of racial and gender differences (Richard et al, 2004). Richard et al. explain that strong identification between people of the same race and gender results in 'poor intergroup communication' and increased conflict during group work.

Research has also suggested that the majority group may feel resentful towards diversity initiatives, especially if these initiatives are not communicated sensitively and constructively by organizations. This often leads to resistance and tensions among different groups, and also to a reluctance on the part of minority groups to engage with diversity initiatives, such as positive action, in case they are seen as 'tokens' (Kamenou, 2003).

Questions
1　If the majority group remains resentful towards disadvantaged employees, is it at all useful to implement diversity management in the workplace?
2　What can organizations do to alleviate any apprehensions in the majority group?

Discrimination is a major issue in organizations with a diverse workforce. International Labour Organization (2004) studies show that qualified migrants in Western industrialized countries face a discrimination rate of 35 per cent (that is, one in three are unfairly excluded in employment procedures). The social identity of employees is reported to be responsible for differing career path trajectories and significant income differences, for instance, for migrant workers who face both 'glass door' and 'glass ceiling' discrimination based on their race and gender (Syed, 2008).

From positive discrimination to positive action

Although positive discrimination (or affirmative action) is now disallowed in many countries (for example, Australia, the UK and the USA) because it allegedly violates the principle of merit and equality, there is evidence of governmental initiatives in order to encourage employment of the previously disadvantaged groups. Positive action may take many forms, as seen, for example, in targeted advertising campaigns encouraging ethnic minority candidates to join the police force.

From a legal perspective, section 47 of the Sex Discrimination Act 1975 in the UK allowed for the use of 'positive action' in a number of specific circumstances. Similarly, sections 37 and 38 of the Race Relations Act 1976 allowed an employer to give special encouragement and provide specific training for a particular racial group. These two Acts have now been replaced by the Equality Act 2010, which also provides for positive action in recruitment and promotion. From an organizational perspective, positive action may include initiatives such as the introduction of non-discriminatory selection procedures and training programmes, or policies aimed at preventing sexual harassment.

Box 4.1 provides some examples of positive action in organizations and also a guide to assess the need for positive action.

Box 4.1 Does your company need positive action?

Before deciding to introduce positive action to encourage underrepresented groups to apply for jobs, employers must look at their own employees to establish how many underrepresented groups have been doing the kind of work in question during the previous 12 months. If the number of underrepresented groups is comparatively small, consideration can be given to encouraging them to apply for the relevant vacancies. For example:

☐ A local government authority in the UK used 'statements of encouragement' in adverts to women to encourage applications in areas where women had traditionally been underrepresented.
☐ London's Metropolitan Police has a positive action team who are undertaking a series of job fairs to encourage ethnic minority and female candidates to join their service.

Useful contacts
☐ See http://www.equalityhumanrights.com/ for further information on gender-positive action and other equality related policies and actions
☐ For resources on Age Positive, a diversity-related initiative from the UK government see http://www.dwp.gov.uk/age-positive/

Source: Equality Advice Centre; http://www.equality-online.org.uk/equality_advice/index.html

Strategies to manage diversity

Managing diversity is not a 'one-off problem'. Hence, organizations need a coherent strategy to understand and manage it, for example in the shape of top management commitment, training and extensive organizational knowledge (Kreitz, 2008). To be more specific, organizations need to create respect for all identity groups by valuing and respecting diversity (Cox and Blake, 1991). Moreover, diversity should be represented in all levels and networks across the organization (Ely and Thomas, 2001). Box 4.2 provides some examples of best practices in diversity management.

Box 4.2 Successful business stories of diversity management

It's not that difficult to find examples of good diversity practice. Here are a few.

☐ UK supermarket giant Tesco does not impose an age limit on its employees. They say that 'It's attitude not age that creates customer satisfaction'. Tesco recruits people from all ages since they believe that customers love people from different age groups dealing with them. Tesco's employees also report that they prefer working in an age-diverse team (Chartered Institute of Personnel and Development, 2005).
☐ BC Tel, a telephone company in Canada, set up an Indo-Canadian phone line. This helped the company to provide Indian- and Chinese-language services and fostered their relationship with diverse customers (Affiliation of Multicultural Societies and Service Agencies of BC, 2000).

▷

□ Ebco Industries, Ltd., a Canadian manufacturing company, has received several prestigious awards, for example the federal government's Excellence in Race Relations Award and the Boeing Company's Eagle Award for Outstanding Cost Reduction and Quality Performance. The company has 900 employees from 48 nationalities. Hugo Eppich, the founder of the company, says that their philosophy is to respect individuals and their uniqueness; he also says that they focus more on strengths rather than differences. Among the diversity practices of this company are multicultural food festivals for all employees and displaying flags of all nationalities in the reception area (Affiliation of Multicultural Societies and Service Agencies of BC, 2000).

□ Corporate Rabobank (based in The Netherlands) has an intranet site that is dedicated to diversity management. This site gives information about the bank's policies, improvements and planned activities. The most interesting thing about this site that it has a page called 'intercultural management', which talks about the reasons behind Rabobank choosing to adopt a multicultural environment (Subeliani and Tsogas, 2005).

□ The military of a country usually reflects its society. The social composition of the US Air Force has altered in recent years as a result of increasing diversity of the USA's population. The military leadership is devoted to education and training on equal opportunities and non-discrimination. Several short courses are offered on sexual harassment, equal opportunities and cultural diversity. Moreover, 2-day courses are offered to senior management on areas such as racism, crosscultural socialization and others.

The US Air Force's leadership encourages contributions from all people without any regard to their origins (Moon, 1997).

Questions

Undertake the following as a class exercise. Based on your personal knowledge or research, identify a successful story of diversity management in a local or international organization.

1　What works well in that organization?

2　Where is there room for improvement?

The US Government Accountability Office (2005) has consulted experts on diversity and suggested nine leading practices organizations that should follow, as described below.

1. Leadership commitment

A good leader's commitment to diversity should be visible based on how well he or she communicates the vision of diversity in an organization. The Government Accountability Office (2005) further recommends that an organization's support for diversity should be communicated in the form of policies, procedures, speeches, meetings and newsletters. Moreover, this support should exist throughout the organization all the way from senior management to the lowest level (Kreitz, 2008). Roosevelt (2006) identifies the following three skills a leader should have for managing diversity, namely the ability to:

□ recognize and analyse diversity in a group;

□ determine whether action is required with respect to a particular group;

□ respond appropriately to a problem.

2. Diversity as part of an organization's strategic plan

Managing diversity is not an isolated issue (Kreitz, 2008): it can take 5–7 years for an organization to successfully integrate its related policies into the strategic plan (Government Accountability Office, 2005). The strategic plan to manage diversity should be in line with the organization's goals (Jayne and Dipboye, 2004).

3. Diversity linked to performance

Managing diversity should be effectively focused on increasing productivity and innovation. For example, positive promotion of diversity can boost an organization's overall recruiting effort (Cox and Blake, 1991) and help a company to extend its services to a more diverse customer base (Ely and Thomas, 2001).

4. Measurement

Organizations can measure the impact of diversity on their performance by collecting and analysing empirical data drawn from interviews, focus groups and surveys (Government Accountability Office, 2005). In order to successfully measure the impact (for example, cost and effort) of diversity, managers must set goals at the start of the year and then review them at the end (Roosevelt, 1999).

5. Accountability

In order to promote the achievement of an organization's diversity goals, managers should be rewarded through adequate performance management and reward systems (Government Accountability Office, 2005). According to the Government Accountability Office, this implies that managers at all levels of the organization should be reviewed based on their ability to manage diverse teams and achieve diversity-specific goals.

6. Succession planning

Organizations should actively identify diverse talent pools and develop them into potential future leaders (Government Accountability Office, 2005). For example, Ready and Conger (2007) explain how the banking organization HSBC has a system of talent pools that tracks the careers of employees with good potential within the organization. The selected candidates are first trained by local managers or business heads, after which they are given assignments overseas. Managers then identify the most capable candidates, who are put in a higher level pool of talent. These candidates can become executive managers in 3–5 years and may in the long term reach top management level.

7. Recruitment

In order to keep up with international competition and a growing diverse market place (Kreitz, 2008), firms need to attract a skilful and diverse workforce. This may help organizations to solve problems and achieve their goals using the multicultural exchange of knowledge, innovation and creativity (Cox and Blake, 1991; Richard et al., 2004).

8. Employee involvement

Organizations should involve employees in their diversity management efforts. According to the Government Accountability Office (2005), this will lead employees to form networks, task forces, councils and committees that help an organization to identify issues, raise opinions and so on, which will ultimately lead the organization to recommend actions while keeping its employees' interest first.

9. Diversity training

To reap the benefits of diversity, organizations need to ensure that management and staff understand the advantages and challenges of diversity (Government Accountability Office, 2005). According to Jayne and Dipboye (2004), the training provided needs to emphasize that a diverse group brings with it new skills and perspectives that can be used to improve task performance. Moreover, team-building exercises should be carried out in such a way that members are able to understand each other's cultural background. Training is essential as team members who are unaware of diversity and its complexities may not work together effectively, and may instead contribute to negative stereotypes and discrimination in the workplace (Ely and Thomas, 2001).

So far, this chapter has provided an overview of key areas of diversity and equality, engaging with key concepts, frameworks and the advantages and challenges faced when managing diversity. The next section will focus on methodological issues that researchers should consider when conducting research on diversity management.

Methodological considerations in conducting research on diversity management: the case of ethnic minority women

This section presents some key methodological considerations to be taken into account when conducting research in the diversity management area. The discussion will engage with the career experiences of ethnic minority women as a means of illustrating key issues related to methodology and the position of the researcher and the researched. Reflexivity on the researchers' role and influence must be considered, particularly in situations where one group is historically seen as more dominant than another. Lorbiecki and Jack (2000: S22) have argued that reflexivity:

> encourages social actors, be they academics or practitioners, to look more deeply at what they are doing and to consider the political, cultural and social implications of the knowledge they are constructing.

Ethnic minority women are seen as social actors within organizational and social group structures and cultures, which may affect their strategies and plans; in turn, they may also be affected by these structures and cultures. In the same vein, researchers are also seen as social actors placed within a specific context at a specific point in time, where their experiences may be informed by a number of factors including their ethnicity, gender, class, education and geographical location. An ethnic minority woman may have different realities from those of a white woman, a white man, an ethnic minority man or an ethnic minority woman of a different ethnic group or class. At the same time, one should avoid essentializing (that is, stereotyping) groups as having specific traits – the above argument should be extended to remind researchers that ethnic minority women of the same ethnic group or class can still have different experiences.

If we acknowledge the fact that there is a need for a better understanding of how researchers can conduct work within diversity management, it is important to examine and identify appropriate methodologies that are sensitive to our topic of investigation and overcome biased perspectives that limit the validity and usefulness of the research.

By focusing on the career experiences of ethnic minority women, one should be aware of the dangers of adopting a feminist research methodology, since the second-wave Western feminist literature has been accused of ignoring the experiences of ethnic minority women (hooks, 1981, 1984, 1989, 1991; Collins, 1990; Maynard, 1994). For example, Finch (1984) and Oakley (1981, 1987) have been criticized for assuming unity by gender and ignoring other divisive factors (Lee, 1993). In some respects, however, a feminist methodology may be appropriate as it is open to giving participants voices to express themselves in their own words, and to setting up non-hierarchical relations between the researcher and the participants.

It is important to identify and engage with non-ethnocentric feminist methodologies, which have been sensitive to multicultural studies and have allowed for an interaction of gender with other subidentities such as class, race, culture and religion. The work of Edwards (1990, 1993) is especially useful in this respect as she has provided a detailed discussion of feminist research methodologies that need to be sensitive to racial and class divisions. She has also discussed her own position as a white woman interviewing Caribbean women, and has engaged with debates on how white researchers can conduct sensitive research on minority groups without imposing their own power or privilege.

Most feminist research writers agree that there is no one method that can be deemed 'the feminist methodology' – to use Edwards' (1993: 182) original emphasis. It seems that there is not one specific feminist philosophy or methodology, but rather a number of overlapping feminist methodologies. Thus, there are no feminist 'how-to-recipes' (Duelli Klein, 1983: 90). Nevertheless, Edwards (1990: 479) has argued that even though there is no single feminist methodology, there are certain elements that characterize the overall approach: 'a feminist methodology has as its base a critique of objectivity, of the supposedly rational, detached, value-free research as traditionally espoused'. Edwards goes to present three key principles that guide feminist research:

1   Women's lives need to be addressed in their own terms: 'women's round lives have been pushed into the square holes of male-defined theories, and where their experiences do not fit those experiences have been invalidated, devalued, or presented as deviant' (Edwards, 1990: 479).

2   Feminist research should not just be 'on women' but 'for women' (Edwards' original emphasis). Edwards (1990) argues that the final aim of research should be to improve women's situations, and this raises concerns on the relationship between the researcher and the researched. The researched should not be treated as 'objects' of research, and their voices and concerns should be heard.

3   The researcher should locate herself (Edwards wrote from a perspective that women should interview women and therefore only acknowledges the female in her discussions) in the research and the process of production of results. She should do this by making explicit the reasoning procedures she has used in carrying out the research and, on a reflexive level, by focusing on the 'researcher's effect upon the actual process of the research, her class, race, assumptions, and beliefs', as well as the effect these have upon the research and its analysis (Edwards, 1990: 479).

Carrying out a study across racial and ethnic lines raises certain issues for the researcher, for example practical, strategic, ethical and epistemological concerns (Stanfield and Dennis, 1993, cited in Kamenou, 2007). Andersen (1993) has argued that research focusing on race has often been distorted as it has been centred on the perspectives and experiences of dominant group members. This could have the unwelcome consequence that the production of knowledge has been 'ideologically determined and culturally biased' (Stanfield, 1993: 4).

Alvesson and Willmott (1992) argue that it is important, when conducting research, to allow people to speak for themselves through ethnographic studies. This 'is a vital means of moderating "totalizing" accounts of management and organization' (p. 442) and of allowing a detailed analysis of perceptions of cultural life through the eyes of the participants (Hammersley and Atkinson, 1995). With regard to interviewing women from ethnic minority groups, some feminists have attributed to the open-ended interview 'an ability to help counter any implicit racism on the part of white researchers' (Edwards, 1993: 184). Open-ended interviews allow women to speak for themselves, and this can avoid the production of data that 'pathologize' women (Edwards, 1993, p. 184) and treat them as passive agents.

Edwards (1993: 184), however, goes on to discuss possible dangers if the female researcher and the female participant(s) derive from a different race or class:

> if we accept that there are structurally based divisions between women on the basis of race and/or class that may lead them to have different interests and priorities, then what has been said about woman-to-woman interviewing may not apply in all situations.

In terms of women interviewing women, Minister (1991) argued that women are not comfortable with hierarchical same-sex systems, and that researchers should therefore attempt to minimize the hierarchical relationship. This argument is perhaps simplistic as it falls into the trap of stereotyping all women as behaving in a similar way and having similar preferences and goals. Some women may be comfortable in a given scheme of hierarchies and may even encourage a power relationship with other women, whereas some may not see themselves as having a bond with other women, or as feeling any need to provide them with help or support.

It is important to look at some of the arguments proposed by black feminists who have criticized white feminists for attempting to involve themselves in research into black people's experiences. Black feminists have argued that white researchers are not capable of, and should not be, conducting research involving ethnic minority men and women as they do not have first-hand experience, insight or understanding. Carby (1982) was a main voice in black feminism and argued that studies by white researchers involving black people are operating within white Western supremacist assumptions. A central argument lies in whether white researchers can contribute to the understanding of the experiences of different racial groups, and whether dominant groups can comprehend the experiences of outsiders (Andersen, 1993). Andersen (1993: 41), a white female researcher, suggested that there are certain problems in conducting research involving ethnic minority groups because of the social distance imposed by class and race relations when the interviewers are white and middle-class and those being interviewed are not:

> How can white scholars study those who have been historically subordinated without further producing sociological accounts distorted by the political economy of race, class and gender?

Standpoint feminists (that is, scholars who propose that feminist social science should be practised from the standpoint of women instead of men) have advocated that members of subordinated groups have unique viewpoints on their own experiences and on society as a whole, arguing that one's race, class and gender are both the origin and the object of sociological knowledge (Andersen, 1993). Kamenou (2002, 2007) has contended, however, that people may be able to gain knowledge without having first-hand experience, and be able to produce research and 'represent the other' (Kitzinger et al., 1996), provided they adopt reflexivity, being sensitive to their own position and the ways in which that position can affect their perceptions and attitudes.

When attempting to conduct culturally sensitive research, there are concerns over how researchers' identities and positions might affect their understanding of situations in which they are not involved. Andersen (1993) has contended that white academics conducting research on race and ethnicity need to acknowledge the influence of institutional racism in their research. This is a great challenge for researchers in white-dominated academic institutions. Academic scholars wanting to conduct research within the diversity management area need to understand the sensitivity of the topic if they want to embark on research involving groups that are diverse in terms of ethnicity, gender, culture, religion and so on. In addition, this research needs to be placed within the broader historical and geographical context in which it is taking place.

To conduct research within the diversity management field and examine the work and life experiences of ethnic minority groups, we advocate for a non-hierarchical, empathy-driven approach in which participants are given a voice to express their opinions and discuss their experiences (Kamenou, 2002, 2007; Syed and Pio, 2010). One cannot deny that profit-making organizations will inevitably focus on any benefits they can accrue from diversity, as well as on cost–benefit analysis in relation to legal sanctions if they do not adhere to equality policies and practices. Management academics, however, need to look beyond the narrow spectrum of conducting research on yet another management topic and recognize that this research needs to be placed within its historical context and geographical location (Kamenou, 2007; Syed, 2009).

There is an urgent need for more work exploring *how* research in equality and diversity should be conducted. Again, work has been conducted in this area of studying 'others' (Davis et al., 2000) in anthropological and cultural studies (see, for example, Rosaldo, 1989; Alcoff, 1991/1992), but this has not occurred to any great extent within management studies. It is not suggested that there is one best model to be adopted when conducting research in this area, but it is important to highlight the fact that there are some methodological considerations that scholars ought to be aware of when working in the field of diversity management.

Conclusion

This chapter has demonstrated that the current ongoing demographic transformation of both the workforce and the general population in many countries has immense implications for the future of HRM, including diversity management, in the workplace. The chapter discussed key concepts of diversity management and distinguished between the EEO and diversity management approaches to managing workforce diversity. It also discussed the distinction between affirmative action and positive action, and identified a gradual transition to the latter in many countries.

In our theorization of diversity management, we criticized the usual organization-focused approaches to diversity management and instead argued for a multilevel approach to diversity that takes into account the overlapping (macro-national, meso-organizational and micro-individual) dimensions of diversity. We discussed the issue of the various laws and regulations in place in several countries to tackle workplace discrimination. Finally, we offered a detailed case study of ethnic minority women in the UK in order to highlight important methodological considerations in understanding and researching diversity management.

An understanding of or interest within management research on equality and diversity, although fundamental, needs to be informed by historical, socio-political and economic factors, as well as by an understanding of post-colonialism and institutional racism in organizations. We explored here the methodological considerations of conducting research within the diversity management field, illustrating the key points through a focus on the work and career experiences of ethnic minority women. Certain issues have a universal appeal, for example:

☐ the need for an informed understanding of the context in which research is conducted;

☐ an acknowledgement of how this context affects participants from diverse social groups, in terms of, for example, gender, ethnicity, culture, age and disability;

☐ an understanding of the issues surrounding reflexivity and self-awareness within research.

Conducting sensitive research within diversity management is therefore dependent on context, but the methodological process allows for some elements of convergence across locations and populations. There is a real need for more work in this area that will improve the baseline of diversity and equality-related research within management settings so that such research will adopt a relevant and context-specific methodology and acknowledge the historical, political and geographical context within which it functions.

❓ For discussion and revision

Questions

1 Why is it inappropriate to treat diversity management as an organization-specific issue?

2 Critically review the legislative framework of diversity management in your country. What are its strengths and weaknesses?

3 What key steps can an organization take in order to manage diversity effectively?

4 Why is it important to understand the local context in order to manage or research diversity?

5 What are current best practices in organizations in your country to manage diversity?

Exercises

1 What are the pros and cons of affirmative action? Debate your answers.

2 Study diversity management policies and practices in a specific company. Identify the various ways in which diversity management policies and practices in that company are affected by its sociocultural, political, legal and economic contexts.

3 Through an Internet search, identify and compare the diversity management policies or visions of at least three companies. Which policies or visions do you prefer, and why?

📖 Further reading

Books

Anthias, F. and Yuval-Davis, N. (1992) *Racialized Boundaries: Race, Nation, Gender, Colour and Class and the Anti-racist Struggle*. London: Routledge.

Bell, M. (2007) *Diversity in Organizations*. Mason, OH: Thomson/South-Western.

Bhavnani, R. (1994) *Black Women in the Labour Market: A Research Review*. London: Organization Development Centre, City University.

Blaine, B. E. (2007) *Understanding the Psychology of Diversity*. London: Sage.

Davidson, M. J. (1997) *The Black and Ethnic Minority Woman Manager: Cracking the Concrete Ceiling*. London: Paul Chapman.

Harvey, C. and Allard, M. J. (eds) (2005) *Understanding and Managing Diversity: Readings, Cases, and Exercises* (3rd edn). New York: Prentice Hall.

Konrad, A., Prasad, P. and Pringle, J. (eds) (2006) *Handbook of Workplace Diversity*. London: Sage.

Modood, T., Berthoud, R., Lakey, J., Nazroo, J., Smith, P., Virdee, S. and Beishon, S. (1997) *Ethnic Minorities in Britain: Diversity and Disadvantage. Fourth National Survey on Ethnic Minorities*. London: Policy Studies Institute.

Özbilgin, M. (2009) *Equality, Diversity and Inclusion at Work: A Research Companion*. Cheltenham: Edward Elgar.

Özbilgin, M. and Syed, J. (eds) (2010) *Managing Cultural Diversity in Asia: A Research Companion*. Cheltenham: Edward Elgar.

Özbilgin, M. and Tatli, A. (2008) *Global Diversity Management: An Evidence-based Approach*. New York: Palgrave Macmillan.

Journals

Amos, V. and Parmar, P. (1984) Challenging imperial feminism. *Feminist Review*, 17: 3–20.

Fearfull, A. and Kamenou, N. (2006) How do you account for it?: a critical exploration of career opportunities for and experiences of ethnic minority women. *Critical Perspectives on Accounting*, 17(7): 883–901.

Kamenou, N. (2008) Reconsidering work–life balance debates: challenging limited understandings of the 'life' component in the context of ethnic minority women's experiences. Special Issue on Gender in Management: New Theoretical Perspectives. *British Journal of Management*, 19: S99–S109.

McGuire, G. M. (2000) Gender, race, ethnicity and networks: the factors affecting the status of employees' network members. *Work and Occupations*, 27: 500–23.

McGuire, G. M. (2002) Gender, race and the shadow structure: a study of informal networks and inequality in a work organization. *Gender and Society*, 16(3): 303–22.

Mason, D. (1996) Themes and issues in the teaching of race and ethnicity in sociology. *Ethnic and Racial Studies*, 19(4): 789–806.

White, Y. E. (1990) Understanding the black woman manager's interaction with the corporate culture. *Western Journal of Black Studies*, 14(3): 182–6.

Case Study Samina's Experiences in Retail Co.

Samina has been working in Retail Co. for almost 8 years. She rose through the organizational ranks and has recently been appointed store manager for the company's newest store. Today was a rare occasion on which she actually had some time to take a quick lunch break so was picking at her sandwich and sipping her coffee. She was in a reflective mood.

She remembered arriving on her first day at work as a shopfloor-level assistant aged 24. She had planned to work at Retail Co. over that summer as she had just completed her university degree. She had wanted to apply for a 'proper job' after the summer. But her plans changed when she was selected early on by her line manager, Mark, as 'someone with a lot of potential', as he put it. He had supported her in getting a position on the organization's fast-track management scheme a year after she had been recruited. Samina always fondly remembered Mark, who took her under his wing and showed her the ropes. He had retired 2 years ago, and they had spoken only occasionally since then. She missed their chats and the support that Mark had always provided. He was great for bouncing ideas off, and he 'always had her back', as he used to say.

Samina was proud of her achievements and for succeeding in reaching her own career goals. With the help of Mark and some of the other managers, she had developed a clear career plan, and she had clearly stated her ambition of becoming a store manager before she reached 34. Colleagues often joked that she was a well-oiled machine, always efficient, very organized and very focused. This sometimes created conflict with some of her workmates, who had not adopt the same management style. At times, she found that upsetting, but it had no an effect on her drive to succeed.

Her family, especially her mother, often told her how proud they were of her work achievements. Samina was the daughter of a Pakistani family who had migrated to the north of England in the 1970s. There were always high expectations of Samina and her two brothers to do well professionally. In the last couple of years, however, her parents had started hinting that maybe she had been focusing 'too much' on her career, at the expense of other areas. Samina knew his really meant having a husband and children!

Samina was aware that, at the moment, she was focusing solely on her career, but she felt she did not have a choice. As a new store manager, her days were very demanding and made up of long hours in the store. She felt the pressure to succeed and prove her critics wrong. Although she had a good working relationship with most of the staff and managers, she was very aware of some resentment, especially from some older white managers, who had assumed they would be made this store's manager once it opened.

The focus of Retail Co. on equality and diversity issues over the last few years had been great and, in Samina's opinion, much needed. There were very few ethnic minority staff in any management positions, but they were especially sparse at senior management levels. The Chief Executive had clearly communicated her commitment to equality in all areas such as gender, ethnicity, disability and age. She had focused on the benefits that diversity could bring to the organization and the need for the stores to represent local communities. As part of these diversity initiatives, stores were given 'aspirational targets' to reach within 2 years, including a higher representation of ethnic minority male and female staff at management levels. Samina knew she had all the right credentials for a store manager's post as she had gained the required management experience in her time at Retail Co.

Increasingly, however, she was feeling like an outsider. Discussions would suddenly halt once she entered the staff canteen; staff would be whispering after she had passed them in the corridor. Indeed, some comments were loud enough for her to hear. 'She is so young; what does she know about managing a whole store?' The most recent comment she had heard the day before was from a Bakery manager, Tom, who had worked for Retail Co. for 20 years: 'Everyone knows she was placed in that position to reach ethnic targets. Actually, it's one tick for race and one tick for gender. It's not right. Why can't they just promote people on merit?'

Samina knew that Tom was very resentful of the organization's diversity initiatives as he perceived these as positive discrimination, despite clear communication from senior managers that they could not lawfully positively discriminate in favour of any group. Thankfully, she was aware that not everyone shared his views and that some staff at least were in support of the initiatives and her promotion. But the negative comments still dominated in her mind.

Anna, a shopfloor-level assistant in her 50s, had come to see her the day before and congratulated her on her promotion. Samina felt touched by this as most staff did not openly wish her well, which she saw that as another sign of resentment or assumptions of tokenism. Her good mood quickly vanished though as Anna went on to say: 'I think it's a great achievement Samina, don't get me wrong ... But I think you are now at an age that you should be focusing on marriage and having kids; you're not that young any more!' Samina felt she could never win. She was worn down by people's expectations, especially her family's views of what it meant to be a single woman in her 30s, focusing on her career. Despite all her achievements in the workplace, she was often made to feel less of a woman – that is, when she was not made to feel like a token promoted to make up Retail Co.'s aspirational targets.

Samina's lunch break was now over and she still had a long day ahead of her. She emptied her tray and started walking back to her office, reluctantly passing three of her colleagues chatting in the corridor. The last thing she needed was more 'well-meaning' comments ...

Questions

1 What are some of the issues that Samina seems to be facing in relation to her work and recent promotion?
2 What are your views on the positive action initiatives that Retail Co. has put in place?
3 What challenges is Samina facing in balancing her work and personal life demands?
4 Could these challenges be influenced by different factors (for example, race, religion, gender or age)?
5 Do you think Samina's experiences may be different from those of white women or ethnic minority men in her organization? Why or why not?
6 During her lunch break, Samina was reflecting on her early experiences in Retail Co. and on having a mentor. How important is mentoring in one's career? What issues could people from minority groups face in selecting a mentor?

References

Affiliation of Multicultural Societies and Service Agencies of BC (2000) Cultural Diversity in Organizations and Business: Gaining a Competitive Advantage. Vancouver, Canada. Available from: http://www.amssa.org/pdf/diversity2000.pdf [accessed 10 May 2010].

Afshar, H. and Maynard, M. (1994) (eds) The Dynamics of Race and Gender. London: Taylor & Francis.

Alcoff, L. (1991/1992) The problem of speaking for others. Cultural Critique, 20: 5–32.

Alvesson, M. and Willmott, H. (1992) On the idea of emancipation in management and organization studies. Academy of Management Review, 17(3): 432–64.

Andersen, M. L. (1993) Studying across difference: race, class and gender in qualitative research. In Stanfield, J. H. II and Dennis, R. M. (eds), Race and Ethnicity in Research Methods. California: Sage, pp. 39–52.

Anthias, F. (1992) Connecting race and ethnic phenomena. Sociology, 6(3): 421–38.

Antonios, Z. (1997) Speech delivered by the Race Discrimination Commissioner at the Women, Management and Industrial Relations Conference, 29 July. Available from: http://www.humanrights.gov.au/speeches/race/managing_diversity.html [accessed 10 June 2006].

Appo, D. and Härtel, C. E. J. (2003) Questioning management paradigms that deal with Aboriginal development programs in Australia. Asia Pacific Journal of Human Resources, 41(1): 36–50.

Ashkanasy, N. M., Härtel, C. E. J. and Daus, C. S. (2002) Diversity and emotion: the new frontiers in organizational behavior research. Journal of Management, 28: 307–38.

Bell, M. P. (2007) Diversity in Organizations. Mason, OH: South-Western.

Bertone, S. and Leahy, M. (2003) Multiculturalism as a conservative ideology: impacts on workforce diversity. Asia Pacific Journal of Human Resources, 41(1): 101–15.

Blackstone, T., Parekh, B. and Sanders, P. (eds) (1998) Race Relations in Britain: A Developing Agenda. London: Routledge.

Bourdieu, P. (1998) Practical Reason: On the Theory of Action. Cambridge: Polity Press.

Brah, A. (1994) Race and culture in the gendering of labour markets: South Asian young Muslim women and the labour market. In Afshar, H. and Maynard, M. (eds), The Dynamics of Race and Gender. London: Taylor and Francis, pp. 151–71.

Carby, H. V. (1982) White women listen! Black feminism and the boundaries of sisterhood. In Centre for Contemporary Cultural Studies, The Empire Strikes Back. London: Hutchinson, pp. 45–54.

Chartered Institute of Personnel and Development (2005) Diversity Management: Linking Theory and Practice to Business Performance. London: CIPD.

Collins, P. H. (1990) Black Feminist Thought. London: Unwin Hyman.

Cox, T. (1994) A comment on the language of diversity. Organization, 1(1): 51–7.

Cox, T. H. and Blake, S. (1991) Managing cultural diversity: implications for organizational competitiveness. Academy of Management Executive, 5(3): 45–56.

Davis, O. I., Nakayama, T. K. and Martin, J. N. (2000) Current and future directions in ethnicity and methodology. *International Journal of Intercultural Relations*, 24: 525–39.

De Cieri, H. and Kramar, R. (2005) *Human Resource Management in Australia: Strategy, People, Performance.* Sydney: McGraw-Hill.

Deluca, J. M. and McDowell, R. N. (1992) Managing diversity: a strategic 'grass-roots' approach. In Jackson, S. E. and Associates (eds), *Diversity in the Workplace: Human Resources Initiatives.* New York: Guilford Press, pp. 227–47.

Dickens, L. (1994) The business case for equal opportunities: is the carrot better than the stick? *Employee Relations*, 16(8): 5–18.

Dickens, L. (1999) Beyond the business case: a three-pronged approach to equality action. *Human Resource Management Journal*, 9(1): 9–19.

D'Netto, B., Smith, D. and Pinto, C. (2000) *Diversity Management: Benefits, Challenges and Strategies.* DIMA Project No. 1. Carlton, Victoria: Mt Eliza Business School, Victoria.

Duelli Klein, R. (1983) How to do what we want to do: thoughts about feminist methodology. In Bowles, G. and Duelli Klein, R. (eds), *Theories of Women's Studies.* London: Routledge & Kegan Paul, pp. 88–102.

Edwards, R. (1990) Connecting method and epistemology: a white woman interviewing black women. *Women's Studies International Forum*, 13(5): 477–90.

Edwards, R. (1993) An education in interviewing: placing the researcher and the research. In Renzetti, C. M. and Lee, R. M. (eds), *Researching Sensitive Topics.* California: Sage, pp. 181–96.

Ely, R. J. and Thomas, D. A. (2001) Cultural diversity at work: the effects of diversity perspectives on work group processes and outcomes. *Administrative Science Quarterly*, 46: 229–73.

Equality and Human Rights Commission (2011) Public Sector Duties. Available from: http://www.equalityhumanrights.com/advice-and-guidance/public-sector-duties/ [accessed 31 March 2011].

Ferris, G. R., Frink, D. D. and Galang, M. C. (1994) Diversity in the workplace: the human resources management challenges. *Human Resource Planning*, 16: 41–51.

Finch, J. (1984) 'It's great to have someone to talk to': the ethics and politics of interviewing women. In Bell, C. and Roberts, H. (eds), *Social Researching: Politics, Problems, Practice.* London: Routledge & Kegan Paul, pp. 166–80.

Gagnon, S. and Cornelius, N. (2000) Re-examining workplace inequality: a capabilities approach. *Human Resource Management Journal*, 10(4): 68–87.

Gibson, C. B. and Gibbs, J. L. (2006) Unpacking the concept of virtuality: the effects of geographic dispersion, electronic dependence, dynamic structure, and national diversity on team innovation. *Administrative Science Quarterly*, 51(3): 451–95.

Government Accountability Office (2005) Diversity Management: Expert-identified Leading Practices and Agency Examples. Available from: http://www.gao.gov/new.items/d0590.pdf [accessed 10 June 2010].

Hammersley, M. and Atkinson, P. (1995) *Ethnography: Principles in Practice.* London: Routledge.

Härtel, C. E. J. and Fujimoto, Y. (2000) Diversity is not a problem to be managed by organizations but openness to perceived dissimilarity is. *Journal of Australian and New Zealand Academy of Management*, 6(1): 14–27.

Hill, C. W. L. (2008) *International Business Competing in the Global Market Place* (7th edn). New York: McGraw-Hill.

Hofstede, G. (1984) Cultural dimensions in management and planning. *Asia Pacific Journal of Management*, 1(2): 81–98.

hooks, b. (1981) *Ain't I a Woman?* London: Pluto.

hooks, b. (1984) *Feminist Theory: From Margin to Center.* Boston: South End Press.

hooks, b. (1989) *Talking Back: Thinking Feminist, Thinking Black.* London: Sheba Feminist Publishers.

hooks, b. (1991) *Yearning.* London: Turnaround.

Humphries, M. T. and Grice, S. (1995) Equal employment opportunity and the management of diversity: a global discourse of assimilation? *Journal of Organizational Change Management*, 8(5): 17–32.

International Labour Organization (2004) Facts on Migrant Labour. Available from: http://www.ilo.org/public/english/bureau/inf/download/factsheets/pdf/migrants.pdf [accessed 15 February 2010].

Jayne, M. E. A. and Dipboye, R. L. (2004) Leveraging diversity to improve business performance: research findings and recommendations for organizations. *Human Resource Management*, 43(4): 409.

Kamenou, N. (2002) Ethnic Minority Women in English Organizations: Career experiences and Opportunities. Unpublished PhD thesis, University of Leeds.

Kamenou, N. (2003) Critical issues in the implementation of diversity strategies: a case study of UK organizations. *International Journal of Knowledge, Culture and Change Management*, 3: 507–20.

Kamenou, N. (2007) Methodological considerations in conducting research across gender, 'race', ethnicity and culture: a challenge to context specificity in diversity research methods. *International Journal of Human Resource Management*, 18(11): 1995–2009.

Kamenou, N. and Fearfull, A. (2006) Ethnic minority women: a lost voice in HRM. *Human Resource Management Journal*, 16(2): 154–72.

Kim, J. S. and Campagna, A. F. (1981) Effects of flexitime on employee attendance and performance: a field experiment. *Academy of Management Journal*, (December), 729–41.

Kirton, G. and Greene, A.-M. (2005) *The Dynamics of Managing Diversity: A Critical Approach* (2nd edn). Oxford: Elsevier.

Kitzinger, D. P., Bola, M., Campos, A. B., Carabine, J., Doherty, K., Frith, H., McNulty, A., Reilly, J. and Winn, J.

4

(1996) The spoken work: speaking of representing the other. *Feminism and Psychology*, 6(2): 217–35.

Kramar, R. (2004) Does Australia really have diversity management? In Davis, E. and Pratt, V. (eds), *Making the Link 15: Affirmative Action and Employment Relations*. Sydney: CCH Australia, pp. 19–26.

Kreitz, P. A. (2008) Best practises for managing organizational diversity. *Journal of Academic Librarianship*, 34(2): 101–20.

Kronos and Mercer (2008) The Total Financial Impact of Employee Absences. Available from: http://www.kronos.com/AbsenceAnonymous/media/Mercer-Survey-Highlights.pdf [accessed 1 December 2009].

Lee, R. M. (1993) *Doing Research on Sensitive Topics*. London: Sage Publications.

Liff, S. (1997) Two routes to managing diversity: individual differences or social group characteristics. *Employee Relations*, 19(1): 11–26.

Liff, S. (1999) Diversity and equal opportunities: room for a constructive compromise? *Human Resource Management Journal*, 9(1): 65–75.

Lorbiecki, A. (2001) Openings and Burdens for Women and Minority Ethnics Being Diversity Vanguards in Britain. Gender, Work and Organization Conference, University of Keele, June 2001.

Lorbiecki, A. and Jack, G. (2000) Critical turns in the evolution of diversity management. *British Journal of Management*, 11, Special Issue, S17–S31.

Maynard, M. (1994) 'Race', gender and the concept of 'difference' in feminist thought. In Afshar, H. and Maynard, M. (eds), *The Dynamics of Race and Gender*. London: Taylor & Francis, pp. 9–25.

Minister, K. (1991) A feminist frame for the oral history interview. In Gluck, S. and Patai, D. (eds), *Women's Worlds: The Feminist Practice of Oral History*. New York: Routledge, pp. 27–42.

Moon, M. M. K. (1997) Understanding the impact of cultural diversity on organizations. The Research Department Air Command and Staff College, Research Paper No. AU/ACSC/0607C/97-03. Maxwell, AB: Air University.

Murray, P. and Syed, J. (2005) Critical issues in managing age diversity in Australia. *Asia Pacific Journal of Human Resources*, 43(2): 210–24.

Nkomo, S. and Cox, T. Jr (1996) Diverse identities in organizations. In Clegg, S. R. et al. (eds), *The Handbook of Organization Studies*. London: Sage, pp. 338–56.

Oakley, A. (1981) Interviewing women: a contradiction in terms. In Roberts, H. (ed.) *Doing Feminist Research*. London: Routledge & Kegan Paul, pp. 30–61.

Oakley, A. (1987) Comment on Malsteed. *Sociology*, 21: 63.

Parker, J. and Douglas, J. (2010) The role of women's groups in New Zealand, UK and Canadian trade unions in addressing intersectional interests. *International Journal of Comparative Industrial Relations and Labour Law*, 26(3): 295–319.

Pool, I. and Sceats, J. (1990) Population: human resource and social determinant. In Green, P. F. (ed.) *Studies in New Zealand Social Problems*. Palmerston North: Dunmore Press, pp. 31–53.

Putnam, R. D. (2007) E pluribus unum: diversity and community in the twenty-first century. The 2006 Johan Skytte Prize Lecture. *Scandinavian Political Studies*, 30: 137–74.

Pyke, J. (2005) Productive Diversity: Which Companies are Active and Why? Master's thesis, Victoria University, Melbourne, Australia.

Ready, D. A. and Conger, J. A. (2007) Make your company a talent factory. *Harvard Business Review*, 85(6): 68–77.

Richard, O. C., Barnett, T., Dwyer, S. and Chadwick, K. (2004) Cultural diversity in management, firm performance, and the moderating role of entrepreneurial orientation dimensions. *Academy of Management Journal*, 47(2): 255–66.

Roosevelt, T. R. Jr (1999) Diversity management: some measurement criteria. *Employer Relations Today*, 25: 49–62.

Roosevelt, T. R. Jr (2006) Diversity management: an essential craft for leaders. *Leader to Leader*, 41 (Summer): 45–9.

Rosaldo, R. (1989) *Culture and Truth: The Remaking of Social Analysis*. Boston: Beacon Press.

Stanfield, J. H. (1993) Epistemological considerations. In Stanfield, J. H. II and Dennis, R. M. (1993) (eds), *Race and Ethnicity in Research Methods*. London: Sage, pp. 16–36.

Stanfield, J. H. and Dennis, R. M. (eds) (1993) *Race and Ethnicity in Research Methods*. California: Sage.

Strachan, G., Burgess, J. and Sullivan, A. (2004) Affirmative action or managing diversity: what is the future of equal opportunity policies in Australia? *Women in Management Review*, 19(4): 196–204.

Subeliani, D. and Tsogas, G. (2005) Managing diversity in the Netherlands: a case study of Rabobank. *International Journal of Human Resource Management*, 16(5): 831–51.

Syed, J. (2008) Employment prospects for skilled migrants: a relational perspective. *Human Resource Management Review*, 18, 28–45.

Syed, J. (2009) Contextualising diversity management. In Özbilgin, M. (ed.) *Equality, Diversity and Inclusion at Work: A Research Companion*. Cheltenham: Edward Elgar, pp. 101–11.

Syed, J. and Ali, F. (2005) Minority ethnic women in the Australian labour market. In Davis, E. and Pratt, V. (eds), *Making the Link: Affirmative Action and Employment Relations*. Sydney: CCH Australia, pp. 48–54.

Syed, J. and Kramar, R. (2009) Socially responsible diversity management. *Journal of Management and Organization*, 15(5): 639–51.

Syed, J. and Özbilgin, M. (2009) A relational framework for international transfer of diversity management practices. *International Journal of Human Resource Management*, 20(12): 2435–53.

Syed, J. and Pio, E. (2010) Veiled diversity: workplace experiences of Muslim women in Australia. *Asia Pacific Journal of Management*, 27(1): 115–37.

Tajfel, H. and Turner, J. C. (1986) The social identity theory of intergroup behaviour. In Worchel, S. and Austin, W. G. (eds), *Psychology of Intergroup Relations*. Chicago: Nelson, pp. 7–24.

Teicher, J. and Spearitt, K. (1996) From equal employment opportunity to diversity management: the Australian experience. *International Journal of Manpower*, 17(4/5): 109–33.

Thomas, D. and Ely, R. (1996) Making differences matter: a new paradigm for managing diversity. *Harvard Business Review*, 74(5): 79–90.

Thomas, R. R. (1990) From affirmative action to affirming diversity. *Harvard Business Review*, (March–April), pp. 107–17.

Thomas, R. R. (1992) Managing diversity: a conceptual framework. In Jackson, S. E. (ed.) *Diversity in the Workplace: Human Resource Initiatives*. New York: Guilford.

University of California (1999) *Staff Affirmative Action Office Policy*. Berkeley: University of California.

Youngblood, S. A. and Cook, K. C. (1984) Child care assistance can improve employee attitudes and behaviour. *Personnel Administrator*, (February), 93–5.

4

Human resource management and ethics

Tracy Wilcox and Diannah Lowry

5

?

After reading this chapter, you should be able to:

☐ Develop a vocabulary for discussing human resources practices from an ethical perspective

☐ Identify how and why human resources activities have an ethical dimension

☐ Recognize the connections between ethical human resources practices and ethical global business operations

☐ Describe the key features of ethical thinking in the context of ethics, business and human resources

☐ Recognize some of the various ethical frameworks that can apply to human resources in a global context

☐ Distinguish between ethical relativism and ethical pluralism

☐ Describe some of the features of critical business ethics

Introduction

Ethical considerations emerge in most if not all of areas of human resource management (HRM) practice, including performance management, work organization and workplace relations. Furthermore, human resources practitioners have what Kochan (2004) has called a 'special professional responsibility'. They are expected to act as stewards of the social contract, to uphold accepted social standards in workplaces and to 'balance the needs of the firm with the needs, aspirations, and interests of the workforce and the values and standards society expects to be upheld at work' (Kochan, 2004: 133).

In recent times, there has been much debate about the relationships between business and society, and about the unintended consequences of the functioning of the global economic system. Faced with economic and environmental uncertainty, recession and, in some regions, the near-collapse of national economies, some of the assumptions and practices we have taken for granted are showing their fragility. The predominance of neo-liberal economic logics, with its narrow view of corporate social responsibility (CSR), has been questioned. These questions and debates have provided an additional impetus for a more critical examination of human resources-related issues, such as the remuneration of executives, performance management systems and downsizing practices.

Implicit in contemporary critiques of human resources practice are notions of trust, responsibility, rights, duties and authority – all components of a frame of reference suggested by the study of *ethics*. Ethical inquiry is intrinsically concerned with *human actions and interactions, their effects and motivations*.

Human resources decisions and actions can have far-reaching consequences, and there is potential for the ethical treatment of employees within the discourse and practice of HRM. This is especially the case for human resources activities in the global sphere as global business activities raise important and highly complex ethical issues. Tensions between the diversity of positions in international business considered to be 'ethical' can pose moral dilemmas with few easy solutions. Despite codes of conduct and various sanctions, multinational companies are able to use their economic might to pressure developing countries reliant on foreign investment to accept values that are not their own. Large global firms may, for example, employ local labour with inadequate health and safety provision, providing poor working conditions and low pay rates.

In this chapter, we argue that the use of human resources practices and their ethical implications in the arena of global business demands serious scrutiny where the human and social embeddedness of human resources practice is typically viewed against a background of other market-oriented concerns. We argue that human resources practices are all too often underpinned by assumptions from Western populist psychology that should be acknowledged and problematized. Hence we have 'absentee management' programmes based on assumptions that workers are absent due to lack of motivation or laziness, or recruitment centres perpetuating unjust assessment procedures, or attempts to engender 'organizational citizenship behaviours' such as 'protecting the organization', 'endorsing, supporting and defending organizational objectives', and '[tolerating] the inevitable inconveniences and impositions of work without complaining' (Podsakoff et al., 2000: 517; see also Organ, 1990).

This chapter starts with an examination of what is meant by the term 'ethics' and a discussion of the key elements of ethical thinking and behaviour. We will then review some of the key frameworks for identifying and making sense of ethical issues in business. These frameworks will provide us with a vocabulary for discussing business practices from an ethical perspective. The frameworks are grounded in the field of moral philosophy, much of which can be applied across cultures (Donaldson and Dunfee, 1994). Following this discussion, we will move to a consideration of contemporary critiques of traditional approaches to ethics. Finally, we will consider a case study of an human resources ethical issue within an organization.

Ethics and human resources

The word *ethics* comes from the Greek word *ethos*, meaning 'character' or 'custom'. Ethics can be defined, in action-oriented terms, as 'the principles, norms and standards of conduct governing an individual or group' (Treviño and Nelson, 2007: 13). Ethics places human beings, or humanity, centre stage. This is what makes ethics so important and in some senses countercultural, particularly in light of the changing expectations of human resource managers.

Ethics is underpinned by the discipline of moral philosophy, which provides theoretical tools and frameworks for reasoning and reflecting on whether something is right and good. Ethics differs from other areas of study such as psychology, science, sociology or economics, in that understanding ethics entails adopting a *normative* perspective. The aim of ethical thinking is to discover what *ought to be*, rather than simply describing what is, or predicting what will probably happen (Enderle, 2000). For example, although a great number of people around the globe are not protected from dangerous conditions in their workplace, whether this be exposure to harmful chemicals or unsafe practices on building sites, for example, this fact does not imply that things *ought* to be this way (Boxes 5.1 and 5.2). Thus, ethical reasoning involves an evaluation of a situation and its context, and reaching conclusions about whether a particular action or decision *should* be taken.

Box 5.1 What 'is' ethics?

In understanding what ethics *is*, it is important to recognize what ethics *isn't*.

Ethics is not the same as *values*. While values are important in shaping ethical (and unethical) practice, prevailing social values may not further human 'good', or be 'right'. For example, in Western industrialized countries up until the mid-19th century, it was widely held that the practice of slavery could be justified by solid economic arguments. The idea that the fundamental human rights of those enslaved were being violated gradually became more widely accepted, but it took centuries for the recognition that slavery was *wrong* to become the 'majority view'. So we cannot assume that just because the majority of members of a society consider something to be right, it is ethical. This is particularly the case in the business arena.

▷

▷

Similarly, *ethics* and the *law* are not equivalent. Legislation typically reflects a society's ideals, norms and values at a particular time and place. However, the law can be slow to change and often reflects only the values and norms of those in positions of power. Moreover, in business, legislation is generally *reactive*: laws are often triggered by problems that have already occurred, for better or for worse. Occupational health and safety laws, for example, have typically been developed in response to catastrophic industrial accidents and employee deaths – examples of laws developed *after* something has gone wrong.

Box 5.2 Ethical relativism: when in Rome ...

The phrase 'When in Rome, do as the Romans do' implies that we should follow the customs and behaviours of the cultures we are visiting. For many elements of our life, this does not present problems, but what happens if a behaviour or practice has moral content? Or if someone might be harmed by the practice? This presents us with an ethical dilemma.

Some people may argue that we should adjust our ethical standards in accordance with the culture we are living in (or the culture our organization is operating in). There may be practices that are common, and considered acceptable, in some places but not others (or in some industries but not others). Recognizing and accepting this variation, or pluralism, constitutes what is known as *cultural relativism*.

But what if you were to translate this understanding of cultural differences to a stance that saw *any* action as ethically permissible, as long as it was in keeping with the cultural standards held by the majority of people in a society? This position is known as *ethical relativism*. Just because practices are widespread does not mean that they are right, or ethical. Cultural practices reflect *values* but not necessarily *ethics*. We have already considered the abhorrent practice of slavery, which was not only widespread in the Western business world in the 18th and 19th centuries, but was also considered *right*.

There are a number of possible reasons why responses to ethical issues may differ across cultures, whether these are national cultures, industry cultures or organizational cultures. Practices may differ because their moral content has not been recognized. For example, as recently as 25 years ago, chemical companies in Australia were dumping industrial waste in waterways and soil, with only the economic value of such practices being considered. Many managers simply did not recognize that such a decision had a moral content as people were likely to be harmed. (Others, of course, may have recognized the moral content but ignored the associated ethical dilemma.) Societies (or industries) can sometimes simply be wrong in evaluating whether something is ethical; the acceptance of slavery provides a good example in this case. Practices can also differ across cultures because of different factual understandings. Differing responses to the issue of global warming provide an example of this, with some people believing that there is still insufficient evidence for action.

On the other hand, we need to beware of automatically judging the practices and behaviours of other cultures as wrong just because they are different. The idea that there is only ever *one* acceptable or right moral principle is known as *ethical absolutism*. In the early days of business ethics education, some Western educators were rightly criticized for adopting this perspective. Both ethical relativism and its flip side, ethical absolutism, involve the oversimplification of complex issues.

Ethicists argue that it is important to recognize that ethics should always be seen in the context of a particular situation. Although there is often no 'absolutely right' answer to an ethical question, there is usually a *better* answer, which involves finding the best or most fitting position in the circumstances. Basic principles can

▷

5

▷ be shared across cultures, even though practices may differ. For example, perhaps the basic principle of respect for one another can be manifest in different ways, with, say, the right of individual liberty given more precedence in the USA than in some Pacific Island communities, where community well-being is considered more important when operationalizing 'respect'.

The alternative to ethical relativism or ethical absolutism, one advocated by many business ethicists, is one in which social and cultural diversity is accepted, alongside *ethical pluralism*. Crane and Matten (2007: 84) explain ethical pluralism as a viewpoint that:

> accepts different moral convictions and backgrounds while at the same time suggesting that a consensus on basic principles and rules in a certain social context can, and should, be reached.

Ethical pluralism implies an acknowledgement that ethical decisions in fact involve balancing various demands and perspectives, which are often in tension with each other. An understanding of ethical relativism, ethical absolutism and ethical pluralism is particularly relevant to human resource practitioners in multinational organizations, or organizations where work is outsourced to contractors in other countries. Organizations such as Unilever, Pirelli, MSD and Novartis, for example, have clearly defined guidelines for their global operations that are applied by local counterparts.

Ethical issues may present to the human resource practitioner at an individual, organizational or macro level, as Figure 5.1 shows:

☐ At the *individual* level fall questions about the rightness or wrongness of a person's decisions and actions, such as unfair recruitment or termination decisions.

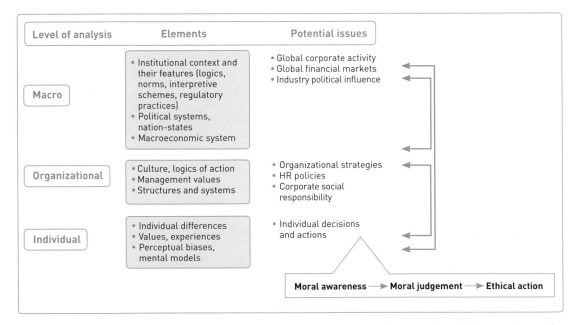

Figure 5.1 The interrelationships between ethical action and contextual issues (adapted from Treviño and Nelson, 2007: 16).

□ Ethical issues can also arise in the *organizational* realm and relate to an organization's policies, practices or culture. In the past, there has been some debate about the moral status (and responsibility) of organizations, but it is now widely held that organizations can make decisions and take action, just as individuals do, and can therefore be evaluated for the rightness or wrongness of those actions and decisions. The notion of CSR reflects this assumption.

□ Finally, *macro* or systemic ethical issues relate to ethical questions concerning the economic, political, legal and social systems in which businesses operate. Systemic ethical issues include the negative consequences of political decisions reflecting the dominant logics of deregulation and market capitalism.

Ethical thinking and behaviour

Ethics provides a means through which business practices can be critiqued and alternatives offered. The practice of ethical reasoning allows those interested in human resources decisions to evaluate a range of possible actions and determine what is 'right' in a particular set of circumstances. The three interrelated elements of ethical practice are thus:

1 *moral awareness* – recognizing the existence of an ethical dilemma;
2 *moral judgement* – deciding what is right;
3 *ethical behaviour* – taking action to do the right thing (Treviño and Nelson, 2007).

As Figure 5.1 illustrates, the ethical (or unethical) behaviour of individuals is best viewed as the outcome of a process involving moral awareness and moral judgement, but shaped by the individual, organizational and broader contextual features pertinent to a particular situation. It is important to situate this process of ethical thinking and action within the individual, organizational and contextual features relevant to a situation. All of these features are interrelated. An individual's own value system and cultural background can influence the nature of the philosophical frameworks he or she chooses to resolve an ethical dilemma, whereas an organization's culture or management systems can influence the type of action (or inaction) taken in response to an ethical dilemma. It is thus important to take into account the social, psychological and political factors that can shape all three elements, or stages of reflective ethical practice. We will now consider each of these stages in turn.

Moral awareness

An important element of ethical practice is the ability to bring ethical issues and dilemmas to the foreground – to make the 'invisible' visible. Doing this entails *moral imagination* or *moral awareness* – a 'recognition that [a] potential decision or action could affect the interests, welfare or expectations' of others in such a way as to harm' (Butterfield et al., 2000: 982). This in turn requires the ability to consider an issue and how others might be affected from various perspectives. Business issues with ethical or moral content can be distinguished from those without by considering the possible unintended consequences of a decision, particularly the question of whether someone might be harmed. In the case of HRM, a potential for affecting the welfare of others is inherent in the human resource manager's role, and many, if not most, HRM decisions have a moral content.

In business, it is not uncommon for managers to fail to 'see' the existence of an ethical issue in the first place. Sense-making practices – in other words, the ways in which people 'see' some elements of their immediate environment and fail to 'see' others, framing their responses according to this filtered perception – can render moral dilemmas 'invisible' to the managers in an organization (Werhane, 2002). This is perhaps not surprising given the nature of the logics and systems of meaning that predominate in a particular business context (Friedland and Alford, 1991). Human resource managers have, within organizations, the logics of capitalist markets, the logics of professional practice (if they consider themselves to be 'human resource professionals') and the logics of state interpretations of the employment relationship as potential influences on their sense-making practices. As Thornton and Ocasio (1999) explain, these logics shape what is considered to be important, the 'rules of the game', and 'what answers and solutions are available and appropriate' to a given social actor, hence influencing processes of moral awareness.

Moral judgement

Even if an ethical issue has been identified, resolving it may not be simple. So moral imagination – the ability to see an ethical dilemma in a particular situation – needs to be augmented by the practice of *ethical reasoning*. Ethical reasoning in turn involves the application of decision tools based on ethical theories, which provide a template or framework against which to evaluate a particular practice or decision. Some of the most well-known ethical frameworks will be considered below.

Ethical behaviour

Choosing to act ethically in a given situation is the third element of reflective ethical practice. Of course, this is not always easy due to the contextual constraints that may be present – including the cultures, norms and values that predominate in an organization. But here we argue that human resource managers do not have to be 'morally mute' (Watson, 2003). An understanding of some of the key elements of ethical thinking, along with an appreciation of the contextual factors discussed here, will go some way towards enabling ethically 'assertive' behaviour on the part of managers (see Lowry, 2006).

> **Exercise**
> Reflect on the activities associated with HRM in your own organization, or in one in which you have worked.
> • Can you identify any ethical issues (issues with moral content) associated with such activities?
> • What are they?

Ethical thinking enables questions about the rightness or wrongness of organizational practice to be considered, in effect placing a critical lens on current business practice (Crane and Matten, 2003: 8) (Box 5.3). Ethics, as Preston (2007: 12) reminds us, can be a 'counter-hegemonic exercise built around a rhythm of action and reflection'. In the next section, we go on to consider some

> **Box 5.3 Ethical thinking and behaviour**
>
> Ethical thinking implies the ability to:
>
> ☐ Think critically
> ☐ Recognize issues or practices that have moral content
> ☐ See beyond one's own personal experience
> ☐ Consider the interconnections between human resources decisions and the contexts within which they are made
> ☐ Address issues from all sides, considering the perspectives of a range of stakeholders
> ☐ Consider the consequences of decisions, whether intended or unintended, on all the stakeholders
> ☐ Evaluate the best arguments from each perspective
> ☐ Arrive at a conclusion based on a systematic analysis of these arguments
> ☐ Defend viewpoints, and analyse new information or perspectives

theoretical ethical frameworks that can be used as thinking tools to enable such reflection. A consideration of human resources practice informed by ethical reasoning enables a nuanced and action-focused critique of unethical human resources practice.

Ethical theories and frameworks

Each of the frameworks discussed in this chapter is grounded in the field of moral philosophy, in the ideal moral perspectives that provide us with ways of thinking about moral issues. A knowledge of normative ethical theories provides a common language with which to debate and evaluate ethical issues and critically reflect on the way in which organizations are managed. There is no one right framework to adopt in all circumstances as each has its usefulness, and each has its limitations. They all contribute normative principles that can underpin moral judgement and moral behaviour (Cohen, 2004). In practice, when faced with ethical issues, more than one framework may be adopted. In the business world, many people do not think about which particular framework they are using when they are faced with an ethical issue. The approach they take will depend in part on their mental models and in part on their cultural and social development.

Consequences of actions (consequentialism)

Consequentialist frameworks enable ethical issues to be examined by *considering the consequences* (both intended and unintended) of decisions, in order to decide the right course of action. This approach is sometimes referred to as 'teleology', from the Greek word *telos*, which means 'end' or purpose. Consequentialism means deciding whether an action is right or wrong based on the possible consequences of that action.

The best-known consequentialist framework is utilitarianism. Adopting this framework, we would say that the best decision is that which maximizes 'utility', or leads to the greatest good for the greatest number of people. The best course of action is, then, one that *brings about the best outcome for most people*, so that overall good (or utility) is maximized. Utilitarianism is based on writings of British Enlightenment philosophers Jeremy Bentham and John Stuart Mill. Both these philosophers thought about how to operationalize the idea of 'the good'. Bentham defined 'good' as pleasure, while Mill developed this further, defining good as the general happiness or well-being of society.

Using this framework, we can argue that certain actions are morally right even if they violate a particular individual's right. For example, a manager may argue that the construction of a new manufacturing plant in a disadvantaged area will provide employment for the local community, even if the buildings may encroach on part of a nature reserve. The manager may argue that the overall benefits of the new facility (the good) outweigh the harm caused (environmental damage) and provide the greater good for the greater number of people. In this example, the employment needs of the local community would be given greater weight by the manager than the ecological needs of future generations (of both humans and animals).

Utilitarian thinking tools are familiar to most managers, and this framework is useful when working through complex issues with multiple stakeholders. Indeed, the idea of conducting a cost–benefit analysis is based on utilitarian thinking. In the business world, however, underlying assumptions about how 'the good' should be defined are not typically subject to critical examination. Cost–benefit analyses are congruent with economics, but 'the good' is traditionally assumed to be economic gain, with profit, return on investment or share price considered acceptable surrogate measures, particularly in Anglo-American cultures. See, for example, the approach of ethical egoism in Box 5.4. But whose good is this? Rarely are the total benefits and harms relating to *all* the stakeholders who are affected by a decision fully considered when cost–benefit analyses are undertaken. Similarly, public goods are not typically taken into account when calculating costs and benefits. This type of narrowly applied and hollow utilitarianism does not consider, at its core, *overall human well-being* as the 'good'.

Box 5.4 Ethical egoism: distorted consequentialism

Another type of consequentialist thinking – one that is in many ways 'anti-'ethical – is known as ethical egoism. This approach to resolving an issue holds that the best action is one that benefits oneself – as either an individual or an organization. At the core of ethical egoism lies a desire to maximize self-interest, however it may be operationalized. Ethical egoism lies behind arguments that individuals should treat others well, not for any intrinsic reason, but because otherwise they may themselves be harmed. Similarly, claims of 'looking out for number one' or 'if we didn't do it, somebody else would' reflect the distorted consequentialism of ethical egoism. The neo-classical economic assumption that people will only act to pursue their own interests, which is particularly prevalent in Anglo-American capitalism, is based on an application of ethical egoism.

Another concern relating to utilitarian thinking is the implication that 'the ends justify the means'. Does this suggest that 'anything goes'? Or are there some things we should *never* do, regardless of the net benefits? These are valid questions. One of the criticisms of consequentialist utilitarian frameworks is that they can be used to rationalize actions that are clearly wrong. This brings us to the next framework.

Deontological principles

The second framework commonly used in ethical reasoning is sometimes known as 'non-consequentialism'. Using this framework, we can judge actions as *right or wrong in themselves*, regardless of the consequences. Ethicists refer to this approach as deontology, which derives from the Greek word *deon*, which means duty. Deontology means deciding whether an action is right or wrong by considering the principles or duties that relate to that action. The essence of this approach to deciding what is right or good is that there are some universal, duty-based principles or rules that apply to everyone and should be used to guide our actions.

Religious ethics are probably the best-known examples of deontological rules. The so-called 'Golden Rule' – treat others as you would like to be treated yourself – or versions of it, can, for instance, be found in religious traditions across the globe (Della Costa, 1998). People who follow religious maxims when faced with ethical issues are drawing on deontological ethical tools to guide their decision-making, even if they are not conscious of so doing.

Another well-known set of deontological principles are those developed by the German philosopher Immanuel Kant. Kant's moral philosophy focuses on humans as moral agents with the ability to make reasoned decisions about what is right or wrong. According to Kant, 'the first proposition of morality is that to have genuine moral worth, an action must be done from duty' (cited in Bowie, 1999: 120). He argued that we are all part of a moral community and hence have duties to one another.

Kant's approach to ethical decision-making revolves around his idea of a 'categorical imperative', which sets in place universal moral principles that should guide human behavior:

☐ His first formulation of the categorical imperative holds that *any principle or maxim should be able to be applied universally*. This forces one to ask the question, 'What if everyone did this?' when considering a moral principle or duty. If, for example, you think it is acceptable to lie to someone, you should also accept their lying to you (Jones et al., 2005).

☐ The second formulation essentially states that *all people have an intrinsic humanity and should never be treated merely as a means to an end*. In other words, we should never 'use' other humans as instruments to achieve our own purposes, as humans possess an innate dignity that should not be violated. As Bowie (1999: 1) acknowledges, this 'respect for persons' principle has fairly radical implications for business and, we might add, human resources, practice because '[at] a minimum, labour cannot be treated as a commodity like land, money, and machines'. Respect for humanity also implies that people should not be coerced or deceived by others in pursuit of their own ends (Bowie, 1999).

☐ Kant's third version of his categorical imperative in essence states that we should act as if *we are all part of a moral community* (what he called an ideal 'kingdom' where one is both 'ruler and ruled at the same time' (Jones et al., 2005: 46).

Kant's framework forms the basis of human rights arguments. It is generally accepted (by reasoning, autonomous people who 'look into their own hearts', as Kant would suggest; Jones et al., 2005) that *all people have rights*, by virtue of their intrinsic humanity – although there may be some debate about precise the nature and scope of those rights. Here we are interested in moral rather than legal rights. Rights can be *negative* – in other words, others are obliged *not* to interfere with a person's right to, for example, privacy or safety. *Positive* rights, on the other hand, relate to the *entitlements* that people have to necessities they may not be able to provide themselves (Velasquez, 2006). In the aftermath of World War II, the United Nations codified a set of universal (positive) human rights. Part of this declaration is reproduced in Box 5.5 below. Although the language is a reflection of the time it was written, the principles remain important.

Box 5.5 **Extract from United Nations Universal Declaration of Human Rights**

Preamble
Whereas recognition of the inherent dignity and of the equal and inalienable rights of all members of the human family is the foundation of freedom, justice and peace in the world,

Whereas disregard and contempt for human rights have resulted in barbarous acts which have outraged the conscience of mankind, and the advent of a world in which human beings shall enjoy freedom of speech and belief and freedom from fear and want has been proclaimed as the highest aspiration of the common people,

Whereas it is essential, if man is not to be compelled to have recourse, as a last resort, to rebellion against tyranny and oppression, that human rights should be protected by the rule of law,

Whereas it is essential to promote the development of friendly relations between nations...

Article	Principle
1	All human beings are born free and equal in dignity and rights. They are endowed with reason and conscience and should act towards one another in a spirit of brotherhood.
2	Everyone is entitled to all the rights and freedoms set forth in this Declaration, without distinction of any kind, such as race, colour, sex, language, religion, political or other opinion, national or social origin, property, birth or other status. Furthermore, no distinction shall be made on the basis of the political, jurisdictional or international status of the country or territory to which a person belongs, whether it be independent, trust, non-self-governing or under any other limitation of sovereignty.

▷

Article	Principle
3	Everyone has the right to life, liberty and security of person.
4	No one shall be held in slavery or servitude; slavery and the slave trade shall be prohibited in all their forms.
5	No one shall be subjected to torture or to cruel, inhuman or degrading treatment or punishment.
6	Everyone has the right to recognition everywhere as a person before the law.
7	All are equal before the law and are entitled without any discrimination to equal protection of the law. All are entitled to equal protection against any discrimination in violation of this Declaration and against any incitement to such discrimination.
8	Everyone has the right to an effective remedy by the competent national tribunals for acts violating the fundamental rights granted him by the constitution or by law.

Source: United Nations; http://www.un.org/en/documents/udhr/

5

Kant's moral philosophy, along with the notion of rights, provides a conceptual foundation for a critique and reformulation of human resources practices. Deontological approaches to ethical dilemmas are not, however, without their problems. There are instances, for example, when principles, rights or duties conflict with each other. For example, one person's right to a healthy workplace may contradict another's right to smoke cigarettes at their desk. Other ethical frameworks, such as utilitarianism, may be needed to resolve these types of conflict.

A consideration of rights leads us to another important derivative of deontological ethics, the idea of *justice* as a universal principle and a fundamental human right. What a person deserves or is entitled to can be evaluated using rules or laws that relate to principles such as equality, non-discrimination, fairness and retribution. Employment laws and practices are heavily reliant on such rules. The word 'justice' is used broadly to cover both the principles and the specific rules derived from these principles (Beauchamp and Bowie, 2004).

Some interesting ideas on justice have been set out by the contemporary philosophers John Rawls and, more recently, Amartya Sen (2009). Rawls' seminal theory of justice holds that people should have the equal access to goods and services regardless of their race, gender, intelligence or family background; Rawls' focus is thus on *social justice* (Boatright, 2003). Rawls uses an interesting thought experiment to convey his argument, challenging us to imagine a society where we are covered by a hypothetical 'veil of ignorance', which means that we would have no idea of our position in that society in terms of race, class, gender, intelligence or physical ability, for example. Rawls called this situation the 'original position'. What kind of arrangements would we agree to if we did not know where in society we would be placed? We would be compelled to be impartial, and to live by principles of fairness that would not favour our own situation. For Rawls (Velasquez, 2006: 96), justice means that:

1 Each person has an equal right to the most extensive basic liberties compatible with similar liberties for all, and
2 Social and economic inequalities are arranged so that they are both:
   □ To the greatest benefit of the least advantaged persons
   □ Attached to offices and positions open to all under conditions of fair equality of opportunity

Nobel Prize recipient Amartya Sen extended Rawls' more theoretical idea of justice to a more practical domain in his 2009 book *The Idea of Justice*. He draws on both Western and Eastern philosophical traditions to support his arguments.

Both of these philosophers are primarily concerned with *distributive* justice, which, as the term suggests, relates to the distribution of resources and opportunities. *Procedural* justice, on the other hand, relates to the processes that are used to come to a decision, and whether these processes themselves are intrinsically fair. The notion of due process is particularly applicable to HRM, as much unethical human resources activity relates to the absence of fair processes of recruitment, performance management and termination. In human resources terms, procedural justice can be operationalized through the provision of employee voice, justifiable explanations of practices and compassionate interpersonal treatment (Margolis et al., 2007). *Interactional* justice implies fairness in interpersonal relations, for example honest, respectful and open communication (Barling and Phillips, 1993). This principle ties directly into Kant's 'respect for persons' dictum and into the need to avoid deception. In the business world, decisions to withhold financial information from employees prior to downsizing would violate interactional justice principles.

Virtues

Another important framework used in resolving ethical dilemmas in the workplace is known as virtue ethics. This framework, which has seen a resurgence in the past two decades, is based on the idea that humans should and do cultivate a set of virtues or qualities in their day-to-day living. Virtue ethics is hence concerned with *the actor rather than the action* (Treviño and Nelson, 2007); virtues are *practised* rather than thought about. Using this framework, we do not ask 'What should we do?' but 'Who ought we become?'(Preston, 2007). Virtues relate to a person's character and are qualities that can be admired in others. They are the character traits that help define what being a 'good person' entails.

This framework is commonly associated with the ideas of the ancient Greek philosopher Aristotle, and religious thinkers such as Confucius or Thomas Aquinas. Aristotle argued that a life well-lived was a virtuous one. Across most cultures, individual role models are often used to educate others in what it means to live a 'good' life, providing a grounding in virtue ethics. Virtues can be taught and are acquired through practice – the more someone practises the virtue of *honesty*, the more *honest* they become. As Velasquez (2006: 112) explains, moral virtues comprise 'those habits that enable a person to *live* a human life well and not merely to do well in social practices'. Every individual has the potential for virtue.

This approach to ethical thinking and, more accurately, *behaving*, overcomes the criticism that sometimes people know what is right but *choose* not to do it (Preston, 2007). It also precludes the more instrumental approach to character traits seen in models such as 'emotional intelligence'. In recent times, there has been a resurgence of interest in virtue ethics among business ethicists, particularly after the corporate scandals of the past 20 years.

Which virtues should be valued? Many philosophers and religious thinkers have tried to develop a list of those virtues necessary for individuals and communities to experience the good life. Such lists tend to include:

- □ honesty
- □ generosity
- □ courage
- □ selflessness
- □ compassion
- □ empathy
- □ self-control
- □ justice
- □ trustworthiness
- □ prudence.

Contemporary philosopher Alasdair MacIntyre (1999) adds two core virtues to this mix: *integrity* in one's character across different social contexts; and *constancy*, or showing the same moral character across time.

Without most of these virtues, it would be difficult for people to live and work together or resolve day-to-day community issues. Virtue ethics tends to emphasis the interrelatedness of people rather than their status as impartial, rational individuals. In recent times, however, it has become clear that some of the role models and heroes of Western business culture have lived anything but 'the good life'. The virtues a society views as worthy (and the vices viewed as repellant) reveal much about the dominant values and mental models within that society.

The main shortcoming of a virtue ethics framework is that, like universal principles, virtues can sometimes contradict each other. Virtue ethics may be insufficient in themselves to resolve a dilemma. For example, human resource managers may be faced with a choice between acting with honesty or with loyalty. Other frameworks, such as justice or utilitarianism, would be needed to examine this dilemma from the perspective of those affected by the human resource manager's choices.

Care ethics

An alternative approach to resolving ethical dilemmas is what has been termed an ethic of care. Within this framework, the main considerations are a *recognition of, and responsiveness to, others' well-being needs*. The care framework is an important recent, and somewhat radical, contribution to moral philosophy which, like virtue ethics, differs from more conventional approaches. Unlike deontological or utilitarian frameworks, this approach does not require impartiality when facing an ethical choice. Instead of considering an abstract or generalized 'other' in approaching an issue (for example, justice), the 'other' is seen as concrete, relational and specific to a particular context.

In care ethics, the *connection* between others is recognized and valued, which also distinguishes this approach from the moral philosophies of Kant and others, with their notions of an autonomous, rational individual (Borgerson, 2007). Finally, care ethics acknowledges the 'different voices' of males and females, an acknowledgement often missing in traditional philosophy (Gilligan, 1995).

Rather than restricting this conceptualization of care to that of a mother–child relationship, as earlier formulations did, contemporary feminist philosophers see care ethics as 'something that develops out of a sense of obligation and the acceptance of responsibility towards the individual cared for' (Machold et al., 2008: 672). Care is seen to have multiple dimensions and is not simply based on familial relationships. Machold et al. (2008) argue that the practice of care specifically involves:

☐ *caring about* – a recognition of another's need, which is a form of *moral awareness*;
☐ *taking care of* – acting when care is needed, entailing a sense of *responsibility*;
☐ *care-giving* – ensuring that care needs are met, entailing both *empathy* and *competence*;
☐ *care-receiving* – the interaction between the carer and the recipient, entailing *responsiveness* and *receptiveness*.

Like virtue ethics and *quanxi* ethics (Box 5.6), care ethics emphasizes practice and social (rather than cognitive) processes, in this case with the aim of empowering and emancipating others (Machold et al., 2008). Both care-givers and care-receivers grow as a result. A consideration of rights is not excluded from this approach, but here rights are seen as *relational* in nature, depending in part on the power relationships between the care-giver and the care-receiver (Baier, 1995). Similarly, justice and care are seen as interconnected, as a just society would acknowledge the fact that all people are dependent (and need care) at some stage in their lives (Kittay, 1998). Care ethics' recognition of relationships, power and needs has also been at the forefront of feminist philosophy, hence the association between the two; feminism, like other critical theories, also rejects the 'liberal individualism' that lies at the heart of conventional economics-informed conceptions of society (Nedelsky, 1998).

An example of care ethics in action can be seen in the actions of the Australian greengrocer chain Harris Farm Markets, who actively employ and train asylum-seekers across their operations, in addition to supporting their employees' religious observance (Doogue, 2003). In choosing to assist the often traumatized refugees by providing them with training and meaningful work, they are exercising a care relationship. This was not an impartial decision for the Harris managers – they actively sought out a group of people whom they knew, and whom they felt they could empower and emancipate through the care they could offer.

The concrete, relationship-specific features of care ethics have meant that this approach has been criticized in the past as relativist. Box 5.6 outlines an example of how the notion of an emphasis on care and relationships can lead to different ethical positions. Care ethicists have, however, argued that, unlike ethical relativism (see Box 5.2), the *idea* of care itself can be universalized, because all humans are entitled to be cared for. Early versions of care ethics – now labelled 'feminine' rather than 'feminist' – have also been criticized for conflating sex and gender, and implying a type of biological determinism and essentialism in their insistence that caring is a uniquely female or 'mothering' quality (Borgerson, 2007).

Box 5.6 *Guanxi* **business practices and ethics**

Like care ethics, *guanxi* ethics places an emphasis on the particulars of relationships and contexts when approaching a moral issue. *Guanxi*, which means 'interpersonal connectedness' or networks, is a central part of business culture in Chinese business (Po, 2009). Its key principles include an acknowledgement of interdependence, reciprocity, traditional social relationships and the sharing of scarce resources (Su et al., 2003). Relationships are viewed in particularistic terms, with norms based on both the relative position and level of intimacy of individuals (Tan and Snell, 2002).

There has been much debate about whether *guanxi* practices encourage unethical behaviour or corruption in business practices. While gift-giving and norms of reciprocity are indeed embodied in a *guanxi* orientation, this does not mean that *guanxi*-focused individuals necessarily make decisions that are less ethical (Su et al., 2003). This Confucian-influenced approach to social practice in fact discourages self-interested practice and recognizes the interconnectedness of people within a differentiated society. Morality is seen as 'both role- and act-dependent', with Confucian virtues such as honesty, sincerity, loyalty and benevolence expected to guide behaviour alongside particular role and relationship features (Po, 2009).

Although a number of frameworks have been presented here, it is important to remember that ethical thinking is not:

> a set of absolute principles, divorced from and imposed on everyday life … It is the awareness that one is an intrinsic part of a social order, in which the interests of others and one's own interests are inevitably intertwined. (Solomon, 1998: 89)

The ethical frameworks provided in this section can all be used as the basis for recognizing and critiquing HRM practice. In the following section, we will explore alternative conceptions of ethics and how they may apply to human resources.

Critical Thinking 5.1
Applying the frameworks

David worked for a brake parts manufacturer while he was studying at university in the mid-1980s. Thirty years later, he was diagnosed with mesothelioma, an incurable lung cancer associated with exposure to blue asbestos fibres. At the time David was working with asbestos, the links between asbestos use and lung diseases such as asbestosis and mesothelioma had been clearly established, and companies using asbestos had sufficient evidence to know of its danger (Haigh, 2006).

Asbestos-related illnesses contribute to the deaths of more than 100,000 people worldwide (International Labour Organization, 2006). Around the world, employees, customers, contractors and their families

▷

are still suffering the consequences of its use. In 2009, the directors of one Australian asbestos products firm, the James Hardie Corporation, faced court charges for their failure to disclose the inadequate resources put aside for an asbestos victims' compensation fund (Moran, 2009).

Question

1 How would each of the four ethical frameworks presented here view this situation:

- A *utilitarian* perspective?
- A *rights* perspective?
- A *virtue* perspective?
- A *care* perspective?

Critical business ethics: the problem of being 'charmed'

So far, we have presented the view that ethics is an essential part of any critical treatment of management practice. We have also argued the case for a potential and legitimate ethics of human resources *in action*. Furthermore, underpinning our discussion is the assumption that ethics has an essence and can be defined, albeit in many ways. But, as students of HRM, you need to explore alternative viewpoints. Consider the following two quotes:

> in its most visible manifestations, business ethics has become an exercise in proclamations: the publishing of admonitions, inducements, seductions. (Roberts, 2003: 250)

> ethical behaviour takes place within a complex interaction of social forces and vested interests ... Ethics as philosophical reflection is never enough but must interact with a realistic and accurate interpretation of social conditions and the prospects from their transformation. (Preston, 2007: 12)

This apparent incongruity between the perspectives of Roberts (2003) and Preston (2007) underscores the tension in any treatment of business ethics. In perhaps one of the most engaging texts on business ethics in recent years, Jones et al. (2005) explore and discuss the 'charm of business ethics'. Drawing creatively on the writings of the French philosopher Bachelard, they argue that a definition of business ethics (and hence human resources ethics) is as elusive yet as charming as the notion of 'fire' despite the discovery of oxygen and the associated identification of heat and fuel:

> In the course of time the chapters on fire in chemistry textbooks have become shorter and shorter. There are, indeed, a good many modern textbooks on chemistry in which it is impossible to find any mention of flame or fire. (Bachelard, 1938: 2, cited in Jones et al., 2005: 69)

Following the reasoning of Bachelard, Jones et al. (2005: 70) argue that fire is difficult to treat objectively due to its seductive, almost hypnotic, charm and warming properties. In the same way, they argue, business ethics has its own particular charm, for after all: 'who could be against business ethics? Business ethics is a charming and attractive idea, seemingly irresistible to many' (Jones et al., 2005: 70).

Charming? Business ethics and human resources ethics may well be charming, but we perhaps need to be aware of the potential pitfalls of charming objects. They may hold us 'spellbound', thus preventing us from reflecting on their meaning and significance and possible dangers. In the case of business ethics and indeed human resources ethics, the critical distance is thwarted by the entrancement and 'warmth' of the phenomenon itself.

We are thus drawn into arguments about the very *meaning* of ethics and associated ethical frameworks. As discussed above, most ethical frameworks tend to assume the meaning of ethics. Yet the meaning of ethics does not lie solely within the object; rather – and here is the contentious proposition – ethics relates to the subject who observes ethics. In short, as Jones et al. (2005: 73) simply state, 'People disagree about ethics'. In other words, the essence of ethics is mutable. This stance implies a non-essentialist approach to ethics (Box 5.7).

Box 5.7 Critical business ethics: an anti-essentialist view

Ethics can be conceived in many different ways. The essence of, say, business ethics is not hiding waiting to be found, nor is it found in a *clear* code of rules prescribing specific forms of ethical behaviour.

The key proponent of a non-essentialist (or even anti-essentialist) ethics is Emmanuel Levinas (1906–1995). His works have had a profound impact on European philosophy that has sought to critically transform and question the meaning of ethics. A comprehensive review of Levinas and his contribution to the notion of a 'critical business ethics' is far beyond the scope of this chapter yet is important enough to warrant discussion. What is presented here is a distillation of his foundational thoughts related to an approach to the study of business ethics and the associated notions of ethics and human resources.

It is worthwhile knowing a little of Levinas' own personal history here. As a Jew in World War II, he was captured by German soldiers, sent to a prison camp and while there befriended a dog. He observed that the dog exhibited an openness to the prisoners that was of a higher ethical order than the German town folk, who treated the Jews as subhuman. The dog recognized him as human, unlike the townspeople whose 'expressions were clear' (Levinas, 2001: 41).

In order to understand where Levinas is 'coming from', it is most useful to consider a story offered by Levinas himself (1999). The story is the children's story of *The Little Prince*, in which the narrator finds himself in the company of a young boy. The narrator had hoped to be an artist, but instead was made to learn other more concrete and diverse disciplines that led him to become a pilot. One day, he crashed his plane in the desert. There he met the special little boy (the prince), who insisted he draw a picture of a sheep. The pilot attempts this, but all of his efforts are disregarded by the little prince. In the end, the pilot draws a small box and explains to the little prince that this box has little holes in it and that in the box is the sheep that he wanted. Happy, the prince does not disturb the sheep since he thinks it is sleeping.

In this story, Levinas attempts to relate his approach to ethics. Rather than drawing (or defining) ethics, an undertaking likely to be rejected by all the little princes and princesses who think they know what ethics 'is', he attempts to draw the box in which ethics may be sleeping. As Jones et al. (2005: 74) observe:

> this suggests that ethics is not something that we can approach directly or something that is easy to represent, but neither should we deny that it is important, or give up because minor royalty are confidently telling us what is in the box.

Where to next?

This chapter has touched on many issues associated with HRM and ethics and the global context of HRM. We have outlined the complexities associated with ethics and human resources, coupled with a critical perspective on human resources and ethics.

Despite the complexities and paradox inherent in any ethics of HRM, we do believe that there is the need, and potential, for ethical human resources practices. These could arguably be achieved through the embedding of ethical considerations into the human resources systems associated with performance management, recruitment and selection, termination, reward, human resources development and the gamut of other such activities. The design and operation of these systems could draw on multiple perspectives and recognize the important role that unions have to play in providing employees with a voice. If human resource managers were to bring a consideration of ethics as part of their role to a strategic level, they would presumably need to be able to challenge and critique strategies as they were formulated, as well as respond to any ethical dilemmas created after the fact by the need to implement predetermined strategies. An overarching aim, then, of *best* human resources practice is to ensure the ethical treatment of employees during the formulation and implementation of organizational strategies.

HRM practices that enable individual, organizational and societal well-being can be framed as an element of socially responsible business practice (Wilcox, 2006) (Box 5.8). The United Nation's Principles for Responsible Investment, for example, provide investors and fund managers with tools for assessing organizations based on their environmental, social and corporate governance, with the signatories to these principles making up around one-fifth of global capital markets (a value of $20 trillion; www.unpri.org). Similarly, the United Nations Global Compact, which has over 5,300 participating business organizations, commits organizations to adhering to the 10 principles shown in Table 5.1, most of which can be linked back to HRM practice (http://www.unglobalcompact.org). There are over 5,300 signatories to the Global Compact from 130 countries including Volvo (Sweden), Carrefour (France), Copel (Brazil), Tata Steel (India), Deloitte (US), PGE (Poland), Westpac Bank (Australia) and SAP (Germany).

Frameworks such as these provide legitimacy for socially responsible human resources practice. But how can these aims be translated into human resources practice, and what might ethically informed HRM entail?

Box 5.8 CSR and HRM

Over the past two decades, we have seen a growing discontent with what appears to be a lack of social and ethical responsibility on the part of some organizations. This discontent has been exacerbated by the failure of some of the key players in the financial crisis of 2008–10 to act responsibly, resulting in widespread harm to stakeholders (Stiglitz, 2009). But what might CSR mean? Is it reasonable to expect that this responsibility encompasses not only an avoidance of harm to society, but also an active consideration of the public good?

Argandoña and Hoivik (2009: 225) have noted difficulties in pinning down a universal, globally relevant notion of CSR given the differing views of the role of business in society. However, they go on to describe CSR in relational terms as:

> the set of moral duties towards other social actors and towards society that the firm assumes ... and ... the set of moral duties that the other agents and society attribute to the firm as a consequence of the role it assumes and its relationships with those actors.

This *relational* conception of CSR is particularly relevant to human resource practitioners, whose daily work has, at its core, relational practices.

For human resource practitioners, the social actors of most relevance are the organization's employees, their families, contractors/outsourcing partners, trade unions or staff associations, and the state institutions concerned with regulation of the employment relationship. Distinct moral duties relate to each of these stakeholders, but for our purposes we are most concerned with those who have limited power.

Building on the work of Margolis and Walsh (2003), Wilcox (2006) discusses three types of duty relevant to human resource practitioners:

- ☐ The first relates to the duty to respond to situations or conditions caused by the organization, for example a duty to prevent harm to employees working with hazardous materials through the provision of safe working environments or common safety training standards across all workplaces.
- ☐ The second type of duty is that owed when organizations benefit from unjust or harmful conditions. Wilcox cites the example of child labour in unregulated economies and the actions of some companies to mitigate the harm through the provision of on-site classrooms.
- ☐ The third form of duty is that of beneficence, the duty to aid others simply because one is in a position to do so. The earlier example of employment of asylum seekers fits into this category.

In the case of human resources development, there are a number of socially responsible policies that human resource practitioners can introduce to enact their moral duties. Some of these can directly address broader social issues (Wilcox, 2006), for example:

- ☐ the redesign of junior jobs to allow exposure to a variety of tasks of differing complexity;
- ☐ equity, access and affirmative action programmes;
- ☐ regular training and life-long learning opportunities for low-skilled employees and junior, older and contingent workers;
- ☐ the regular review of training needs, linked to employee development plans;
- ☐ clear and transparent career progression paths;
- ☐ two-way flexibility of working time, and progression available to part-time employees;
- ☐ family-friendly policies available to *all* grades of employee.

Human resource managers also have a role to play in the promulgation of cultural norms and values that have social responsibility at their heart.

▷

> A number of organizations have responded to calls to move to socially responsible practices. In Europe, for example, the European Commission has instituted the 'European Alliance for CSR', which is composed of three 'peak organizations': CSR Europe, Business Europe and UEAPME (European Association of Craft, Small and Medium-Sized Enterprises). This alliance, which includes CSR Europe members Group Danone, TetraPak, Unilever, Volkswagen, France Telecom Orange and Pirelli, aims to 'further focus [business] efforts to innovate their CSR strategies and initiatives, in cooperation and dialogue with their stakeholders' (http://www.eyv2011.eu/about-the-alliance/84-csr-europe). Each of the member organizations has in turn developed policies and practices that directly relate to their duties towards employees, contractors' employees and local communities.

Table 5.1 United Nations Global Compact Principles for Business Practice

Category	Principle	
Human rights	1	Businesses should support and respect the protection of internationally proclaimed human rights; and
	2	make sure that they are not complicit in human rights abuses
Labour standards	3	Businesses should uphold the freedom of association and the effective recognition of the right to collective bargaining;
	4	the elimination of all forms of forced and compulsory labour;
	5	the effective abolition of child labour; and
	6	the elimination of discrimination in respect of employment and occupation
Environment	7	Businesses should support a precautionary approach to environmental challenges;
	8	undertake initiatives to promote greater environmental responsibility; and
	9	encourage the development and diffusion of environmentally friendly technologies
Anti-corruption	10	Businesses should work against corruption in all its forms, including extortion and bribery

Source: http://www.unglobalcompact.org/AboutTheGC/TheTenPrinciples/index.html

Vuontisjarvi (2006a, 2006b) has provided a detailed overview of practical strategies for socially responsible HRM, which are summarised in Table 5.2. Each of these elements can be translated into principles, process indicators and performance indicators. For example, the principle of 'Long, secure contracts' has associated *process indicators* of 'proactive measures to avoid redundancies and professional support for redundant employees' and *performance indicators* including 'number of redundancies or dismissals, number of internal rotations, breakdown by fixed term or regular, and perception measures'.

Table 5.2 Elements of socially responsible human resources practice

Element	Principle
Training and development	Life-long learning; employability of an employee
Pay and benefits	Just, equal pay
Participation and staff involvement	Open and two-way communication (for example, employee representation, trade unions and teams)
Values and principles	Values, mission, vision statements, and articulated ethical or social responsibility principles
Employee health and well-being	Stress on preventative activities; zero accidents
Measurement of policies	Job satisfaction or other internal surveys
Employment policy	Diversity; access for those who are unemployed or low-skilled (social inclusion)
Security in employment	Long, secure contracts
Equal employment opportunities	Non-discrimination; equal opportunities
Work–life balance	Support for work–life balance

Source: Vuontisjarvi (2006a, 2006b)

Although these principles and their enactment reflect a particular contextual arena, they can be adapted for a broad range of social, political and regional contexts. For example, the Swiss firm Novartis have operationalized their commitment to socially responsible human resources practice in part through their undertaking to implement a 'living wage' globally, drawing on research from Asia and India. Their policy states their commitment to 'fair working conditions', among other things:

> Novartis believes that paying a living wage locally is an important benchmark of its commitment to the UN Global Compact – as well as evidence of the company's determination to be a good corporate neighbor in communities where it operates … Local management bears the ultimate responsibility for acceptance of a living wage as a core principle of a company's operations and culture … For Novartis, the living wage initiative is an essential dimension of the commitment to fair working conditions … We pay competitive and fair wages, which clearly exceed what is needed to cover basic living needs. … [Novartis wants] to be recognized as an innovative, ethical and trustworthy company, fostering a culture where employees are expected to behave ethically, not just lawfully. (http://www.corporatecitizenship.novartis.com/downloads/cc-in-action/Living_Wage.pdf)

Conclusion

The question remains of whether ethical human resources practices and outcomes are possible or simply quixotic musings. Do the harsh realities of global economic systems mean that human resources managers, as Watson (2007: 228) suggests, have little choice but to act as 'agents of industrial capitalist corporations'?

MacIntyre (1999) has argued that the ability of actors to transcend the narrow confines of their organizational roles depends on their habitual questioning of institutionalized social orders. Central to moral agency is a capacity to 'stand back from and consider [one's] engagement with the established role structures' (MacIntyre, 1999: 317) – in other words, the contexts within which individuals find themselves. The importance of such critical and reflective questioning is also acknowledged by McKenna and Tsahuridu (2001: 71), who argue that individuals' ability to act ethically will typically depend on their 'freedom to rationally examine society's values, choose what values to make [their] own and use them in making ethical decisions'.

The sense of who one is as a human being also needs to remain solid in spite of pressures to 'be something else' in accordance with one's social role (in other words, integrity and constancy of character is needed). We would thus caution against overly deterministic conclusions; individuals continue to demonstrate this type of reflective practice, and human resource practitioners can hence find space for ethically informed action. Here we have advocated an ethically pluralistic stand – one in which deontological principles, a sense of virtue and considerations of care also have a place alongside calculations of consequences.

Acting ethically is not easy. As Jones et al. (2005: 51) put it, 'morality in daily life is a struggle'. However, as these authors also later assert, the struggle should not prevent us from trying to 'strive for the good' as we navigate our way through the dilemmas that human resources practice presents to us.

❷ For discussion and revision

Questions

1 How has 'globalization' impacted on ethics and human resources?

2 In what realms may human resources decisions have an ethical impact?

3 How do ethics and 'values' differ?

4 Discuss the relationship between ethical reasoning and moral imagination using two human resources activities to illustrate your answer.

5 In what ways are neo-classical economics and 'ethical egoism' linked?

6 How do consequentialism and deontological principles differ?

7 How do both virtue and care ethics differ from utilitarian frameworks? Illustrate your discussion by reference to two human resources activities.

📖 Further reading

Books

Bolton, S. C. and Houlihan, M. (2007) *Searching for the Human in Human Resource Management: Theory, Practice and Workplace Contexts*. Basingstoke: Palgrave Macmillan.

Explores a variety of issues associated with ethics and HRM.

Crane, A., McWilliams, A., Matten, D., Moon, J. and Siegel, D. (2008) *The Oxford Handbook of Corporate Social Responsibility*. Oxford: Oxford University Press.

An excellent collection of chapters for readers interested in the wider subject of CSR.

Fisher, C. and Lovell, A. (2003) *Business Ethics and Values*. London: Prentice Hall.

An informative book on the general area of business ethics.

Grace, D. and Cohen, S. (2009) *Business Ethics* (4th edn). Oxford: Oxford University Press.

An interesting text on general business ethics.

Hatcher, T. (2002) *Ethics and HRD: A New Approach to Leading Responsible Organizations. New Perspectives on Organizational Learning, Performance and Change*. Cambridge, MA: Perseus.

A good text for readers specifically interested in human resource development issues.

Jones, C., Parker, M. and ten Bos, M. (2005) *For Business Ethics*. London: Routledge.

A very readable text providing a critical approach to business ethics.

Pinnington, A., Macklin, R. and Campbell, T. (2007) *Human Resource Management: Ethics and Employment*. Oxford: Oxford University Press.

Text covering a range of issues associated with ethics and HRM.

Preston, N. (2007) *Understanding Ethics* (3rd edn). Sydney: Federation Press.

Provides an accessible general introduction to ethical thinking and action in a variety of contexts.

Treviño, L. K. and Nelson, K. A. (2007) *Managing Business Ethics: Straight Talk About How to Do It Right* (4th edn). Hoboken, NJ: Wiley.

A text covering general business ethics.

Winstanley, D. and Woodall, J. (2000) *Ethical Issues in Contemporary Human Resource Management*. Basingstoke: Macmillan.

Investigates a variety of issues associated with ethics and HRM.

5

Case Study   Global working hours at HDS

Houston Data Systems (HDS) is a global IT solutions firm based in Houston, Texas. A well-established global player, the company operates in the Middle East (Dubai), Europe (Berlin) and Australia (Sydney). The headquarters in Houston has a strong organizational culture of long working hours and company loyalty, whereby employees are expected to be available for work at any time of day. HQ workers are paid significant annual bonuses, linked to their performance management system.

Human resources operations vary significantly from the Houston base to the host countries. The human resources practices also vary between Berlin, Dubai and Sydney. Berlin and Dubai pay higher salaries than their Australian counterparts and have generous bonus systems in place, whereas Australian HDS employees do not have any bonus system. Australian employees are subject to a 6-monthly performance review that is not linked to training and development plans, while Berlin and Dubai have fully integrated performance management and development systems whereby performance is reviewed annually and associated career development needs are discussed and provided. Berlin and Dubai have established a Career Development Scheme facilitating career opportunities and advancement. Due to the relative isolation of Sydney, however, there is no such scheme available. Promotion in the Sydney office is dependent on vacancies arising, and since the external labour market is tight in Australia, there is little movement internally. On very rare occasions, medium-level host country managers visit the HDS headquarters in Houston, while senior executives are flown around the globe on a regular basis.

Given the time difference between the three cities, a large part of the global operations in HDS is through teleconferencing and web meetings facilitated by the use of mobile technologies. As a rule, three meetings are set every week, each scheduled at between 2 and 3 pm Houston time. Generic training for host country employees is offered by Houston through webcasts, and these occur at the same time as the scheduled meetings. The meetings last approximately 1 hour, depending on the issues arising. Time zone differences (depending on GMT Summer Time) mean that the virtual meetings take place at 9 pm in Germany, 10 pm in Dubai and 5 am in Sydney.

The Senior Programme Manager in Dubai, Vera Schneider (a recipient of the Career Development Scheme), believes that she is unfairly treated since her working day is significantly lengthened by the meetings. She moved to Dubai on the understanding that her employment conditions would be a standard working day. With a small child and an executive husband working long hours (also in Dubai), Vera is becoming increasingly tired and irritated.

This fatigue is shared by the Sydney Project Manager, Josh Baker. Josh is a good employee, ambitious and prepared to work hard, but he struggles to be productive so early, especially since he is awake at 4.30 am preparing comprehensive reports for the 5 am meetings. Additionally, his partner is not impressed with having her sleep disturbed on weekdays. The virtual meetings mean that Josh is out of the house later than he wants and is then stuck in peak hour traffic on a long commute to his workplace in order to 'clock in' by 8.30 am. He too ends up working a very long day. Josh also finds the generic headquarters e-learning sessions – his only means of potential career progression – to be a problem: 'How can I move up the ladder if I don't do the training?', he yawns to his partner on a regular basis.

Meanwhile Gustav Weiss, the Programme Director in Berlin, finds that the virtual meetings interfere with sitting down with his family for their evening meal. Gustav thrives on routine in his life, both at home and at work. He is a hard worker yet is also very much the 'family man'. After a hard day's work, he would like to relax over a hearty meal with his family, a stein of Pils in his hand.

The Houston staff are oblivious to why it is so difficult to get Vera, Josh and Gustav to simply 'attend' each of the meetings every week. After several months of fairly unsuccessful attendance at virtual meetings, they are in the process of having corporate human resources investigate the performance and commitment of all three employees. This is despite the fact that while their attendance may have been sporadic, all the operations and projects in their regions are progressing very smoothly. Randy Sheen, the human resource manager in charge of the investigation, has notified his counterparts in the various host cities that they are to contact and question the employees on their performance and attendance. He notes that the Berlin human resources office is not responding to his requests, and after finding the relevant employee's ID number and e-mail address, he simply sends an e-mail directly to Gustav.

Vera Schneider has just been informed by the Dubai human resources department that questions have been raised over her 'attendance at work' and resulting performance. 'This is really too much', she thinks to herself. 'Working such hours was never discussed when I was selected for the Career Development Scheme. This is just too much too ask.'

Meanwhile Josh Baker has been rung at home at 8.30 pm to be told he has a meeting with Sydney human resources at 9.10 am the following morning that relates to a complaint from HQ, something about difficulties accessing his 'project updates and reports'. Stuck in traffic the next day, his mouth is dry and he feels sick with anxiety. 'I'm as prepared as I can be for those wretched pre-dawn meetings', he says out loud to no-one in the car. 'Plus I need to get the training; it's the only training offered to us', he exclaims, as if to an invisible passenger. 'What if I'm made redundant?', he thinks. 'How will we pay the mortgage?'

Gustav arrives at his desk promptly at 7.45 am to find an e-mail direct from human resources at headquarters. The human resource manager in Berlin has been on a 3-day training course so has been unable to respond to Randy Sheen's original message. Gustav finds the tone of the e-mail to him very disrespectful and accusing. He cannot believe

that he, Gustav Weiss, could be questioned about his performance. 'What's this?' he exclaims out loud. 'Who is this "Randy Sheen"? Why am I being treated like this after all my years here? What's going on?'

Back at the Houston office next day at 2 pm, Randy Sheen taps his pen repeatedly on his desk waiting for a phone call or webcast. 'Why is it taking so long for these people to respond to a simple request?', he comments to the unfamiliar colleague hot-desking next to him.

Question

1   How would each of the four ethical frameworks presented earlier view this situation? (Be sure to comment on ethical relativism, ethical absolutism and ethical pluralism in your responses.)

☐ A *utilitarian* perspective?
☐ A *rights* perspective?
☐ A *virtue* perspective?
☐ A *care* perspective?

References

Argandoña, A. and Hoivik, H. von W. (2009) Corporate social responsibility: one size does not fit all. *Journal of Business Ethics*, 89: 221–34.

Baier, A. C. (1995) The need for more than justice. In Held, V. (ed.) *Justice and Care: Essential Readings in Feminist Ethics*. Boulder, CO: Westview: 47–58.

Barling, J. and Phillips, M. (1993) Interactional, formal, and distributive justice in the workplace: an exploratory study. *Journal of Psychology*, 127(6): 649–56.

Beauchamp, T. and Bowie, N. (2004) *Ethical Theory and Business* (7th edn). Upper Saddle River, NJ: Pearson.

Boatright, J. R. (2003) *Ethics and the Conduct of Business*. Upper Saddle River, NJ: Pearson.

Borgerson, J. (2007) On the harmony of feminist ethics and business ethics. *Business and Society Review*, 112(4): 477–509.

Bowie, N. E. (1999) *Business Ethics: A Kantian Perspective*. Malden: Blackwell.

Butterfield, K. D., Klebe Treviño, L. and Weaver, G. R. (2000) Moral awareness in business organizations: influences of issue-related and social context factors. *Human Relations*, 53(7): 981–1018.

Cohen, S. (2004) *The Nature of Moral Reasoning*. Melbourne: Oxford University Press.

Crane, A. and Matten, D. (2003) *Questioning the Domain of the Business Ethics Curriculum: Where the Law Ends or Where it Starts?* Research Paper No. 21–2004.

Nottingham: International Centre for Corporate Social Responsibility.

Crane, A. and Matten, D. (2007) *Business Ethics: Managing Corporate Citizenship and Sustainability in an Age of Globalization* (2nd edn). Oxford: Oxford University Press.

Della Costa, T. (1998) *The Ethical Imperative: Why Moral Leadership is Good Business*. Reading, MA: Addison-Wesley.

Donaldson, T. and Dunfee, T. (1994) Toward a unified conception of business ethics: integrative social contracts theory. *Academy of Management Review*, 19(2): 252–84.

Doogue, G. (2003) *Compass: Seeking Asylum*, ed. Australian Broadcasting Commission. Australia: ABC Television.

Enderle, G. (2000) Whose ethos for public goods in the global economy? *Business Ethics Quarterly*, 10(1): 131–44.

Friedland, R. and Alford, R. (1991) Bringing society back in: symbols, practices and institutional contradictions. In Powell, W. W. and Di Maggio, P. J. (eds) *The New Institutionalism in Organizational Analysis*. Chicago: University of Chicago Press, pp. 232–66.

Gilligan, C. (1995) Moral orientation and moral development. In Held, V. (ed.) *Justice and Care: Essential Readings in Feminist Ethics*. Boulder, CO: Westview, pp. 31–46.

Haigh, G. (2006) *Asbestos House: The Secret History of James Hardie Industries.* Melbourne: Scribe.

International Labour Organization (2006) Asbestos: The Iron Grip of Latency. Available from: www.ilo.org/global/About_the_ILO/Media_and_public_information/Press_releases/lang--en/WCMS_076282/index.htm [accessed 6 September 2011].

Jones, C., Parker, M. and ten Bos, M. (2005) *For Business Ethics.* London: Routledge.

Kittay, E. F. (1998) Human dependency and Rawlsian equality. In Gatens, M. (ed.) *Feminist Ethics.* Aldershot: Ashgate, pp. 445–92.

Kochan, T. (2004) Restoring trust in the human resource management profession. *Asia Pacific Journal of Human Resources,* 42(2): 132–46.

Levinas, E. (1999) *Alterity and Trancendence,* trans. Michael Smith. New York: Columbia University Press.

Levinas, E. (2001) *Is it Righteous to Be? Interviews with Emmanuel Levinas,* ed. Jill Robbins. Stanford, CA: Stanford University Press.

Lowry, D. (2006) HR managers as ethical decision-makers: mapping the terrain. *Asia Pacific Journal of Human Resources,* 44(2): 171–83.

Machold, S., Ahmed, P. K. and Farquhar, S. S. (2008) Corporate governance and ethics: a feminist perspective. *Journal of Business Ethics,* 81: 665–78.

Macintyre, A. (1999) Social structures and their threats to moral agency. *Philosophy,* 74(289): 311–29.

McKenna, R. and Tsahuridu, E. (2001) Must managers leave ethics at home? Economics and moral anomie in business organizations. *Reason in Practice,* 1(3): 67–75.

Margolis J. and Walsh J. (2003) Misery loves companies: rethinking social initiatives by business. *Administrative Science Quarterly,* 48: 268–305.

Margolis, J. Grant, A., and Molinsky, A. (2007) Expanding ethical standards of HRM: necessary evils and the multiple dimensions of impact. In Pinnington, A., Macklin, R. and Campbell, T. (eds), *Human Resource Management: Ethics and Employment.* Oxford: Oxford University Press, pp. 237–51.

Moran, S. (2009) More Hardie directors join bid to overturn court. *The Australian,* 17 October 2009: 32.

Nedelsky, J. (1998) Reconceiving autonomy: sources, thoughts and possibilities. In Gatens, M. (ed.) *Feminist Ethics.* Aldershot: Ashgate, pp. 391–420.

Organ, D. (1990). The subtle significance of job satisfaction. *Clinical Laboratory Management Review,* 4: 94–8.

Po, K. I. (2009) Is Confucianism good for business ethics in China? *Journal of Business Ethics,* 88: 463–76.

Podsakoff, P. M., MacKenzie, S. B., Paine, J. B. and Bachrach, D. B. (2000) Organizational citizenship behaviors: a critical review of the theoretical and empirical literature and suggestions for future research. *Journal of Management,* 26(3): 513–63.

Preston, N. (2007) *Understanding Ethics* (3rd edn). Sydney: Federation Press.

Roberts, J. (2003) The manufacture of corporate social responsibility: constructing corporate sensibility. *Organization,* 10(2): 249–65.

Sen, A. (2009) *The Idea of Justice.* Harvard: Harvard University Press.

Solomon, R. C. (1998) The one-minute moralist. In Hartman, L. P. (ed.) *Perspectives on Business Ethics.* Chicago: McGraw-Hill, pp. 88–90.

Stiglitz, J. E. (2009) The current economic crisis and lessons for economic theory. *Eastern Economic Journal,* 35: 281–96.

Su, C., Sirgy, M. J., and Littlefield, J. E. (2003) Is Guanxi orientation bad, ethically speaking? A study of Chinese enterprises. *Journal of Business Ethics,* 44(4): 303–12.

Tan, D. and Snell, R. S. (2002) The third eye: exploring Guanxi and relational morality in the workplace. *Journal of Business Ethics,* 41: 361–84.

Thornton, P. H. and Ocasio, W. (1999) Institutional logics and the historical contingency of power in organizations: executive succession in the higher education publishing industry. *American Journal of Sociology,* 105(3): 801–43.

Treviño, L. K. and Nelson, K. A. (2007) *Managing Business Ethics: Straight Talk About How to Do It Right* (4th edn). Hoboken, NJ: Wiley.

Velasquez, M. G. (2006) *Business Ethics: Concepts and Cases* (6th edn). Upper Saddle River, NJ: Pearson Prentice Hall.

Vuontisjarvi, T. (2006a) Corporate social reporting in the European context and human resource disclosures: an analysis of Finnish companies. *Journal of Business Ethics,* 69: 331–54.

Vuontisjarvi, T. (2006b) The European context for corporate social responsibility and human resource management. *Business Ethics: A European Review,* 15(3): 271–91.

Watson, T. (2003) Ethical choice in managerial work: the scope for moral choices in an ethically irrational world. *Human Relations,* 56(2): 167–85.

Watson, T. J. (2007) HRM, ethical irrationality and the limits of ethical action. In Pinnington, A. H., Macklin, R. and Campbell, T. (eds) *Human Resource Management: Ethics and Employment.* Oxford: Oxford University Press: 223–36.

Werhane, P. H. (2002) The very idea of a conceptual scheme. In Donaldson, T. Werhane, P. and Cording, M. (eds) *Ethical Issues in Business.* Upper Saddle River, NJ: Prentice Hall: 83–97.

Wilcox, T. (2006) Human resource development as an element of corporate social responsibility. *Asia Pacific Journal of Human Resources,* 44(2): 184–96.

Part 2
Human resource management in practice

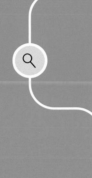

Human resources planning

Cathy Sheehan

6

?

After reading this chapter, you should be able to:

- ☐ Discuss the rise of human resource planning (HRP) as a strategic priority
- ☐ Explain the techniques associated with forecasting the supply and demand of human resources
- ☐ Outline the role of job analysis in the HRP process
- ☐ Describe and analyse the impact of restructuring on HRP responses
- ☐ Explain the role of HRP in talent management
- ☐ Discuss international HRP considerations

Q

Introduction

In the Introduction to this book, Syed and Kramar emphasized the increasing globalization of the world of work and the capacity of events in one country to impact on others. International social and economic change and resultant changes in the international labour market pose particular challenges for the human resource management (HRM) function. The global financial crisis of 2008–09 was a good example of a situation in which the HRM function had to provide leadership in managing potential workforce reductions while still attracting and retaining critical talent in order to maintain businesses' viability.

At a time when many organizations internationally were struggling to manage skill shortages (see Rudd et al., 2007), economic uncertainty created a further level of complexity. The Corporate Leadership Council (2008) advised that those companies which avoided reactionary approaches to HRM and managed to maintain morale and retain skilled employees during the period of downsizing would come through the crisis in a stronger competitive position. These circumstances require innovative responses and careful HRM planning. As custodians of the people resource in organizations, it is the role of the HRM function to assist in the development of human resource planning (HRP) initiatives that match changes in the supply and demand for labour, and also manage initiatives to retain and attract talent strategically rather than reactively.

The purpose of this chapter is, first, to broadly review approaches to HRP, and second, to critically analyse some of the strategic responses to issues associated with the supply and demand of labour. The chapter starts with a discussion of the stages that the HRP activity has moved through and of the emerging recognition of the strategic importance of this area. Techniques for HRP are then explored, including quantitative and qualitative approaches. Following on from this, a discussion of job analysis highlights the connections between the analysis of what a job involves and the HRP requirements for it. Having explained HRP techniques, the discussion will then move on to an examination of the more strategic issues associated with HRP, such as HRP as part of restructuring initiatives and the role of HRP in decisions related to talent management and globalization.

Approaches to HRP

The evolution of HRP

Huselid (1993: 36) has explained that HRP essentially matches 'projected human resource demand with its anticipated supply, with explicit consideration of the skill mix that will be necessary throughout the firm'. HRP is a dynamic process affected by both predictable and unpredictable forces. The economic change experienced during the global financial crisis, for example, in 2008–09 impacted on markets and resulted in swings in consumer demand that affected the level of labour required to meet the product output thus needed. These unplanned changes in the demand for labour occurred at a time when there were ongoing forecasted demographic shifts in the profile of the available workforce (Rudd et al., 2007). These environmental challenges potentially pose major threats to organizational viability, but careful management of the HRP process can make a substantial contribution to the ultimate success or failure of the business.

In Chapter 2, Jamali and Afiouni consider the change and evolution that has occurred in the field of HRM and the increasing awareness of the value of strategic HRM for improving organizational outcomes that has become apparent in the past two decades. HRP activity is a good example of how HRM can provide this strategic value. Industry shifts away from manufacturing to a greater focus on service and knowledge work have led to a recognition of the potential for human capital to make a substantial and lasting impact on sustainable competitive advantage (Wright et al., 1994; Barney and Wright, 1998; Zula and Chermack, 2007).

Historically, the manufacturing industry has provided a large source of work, but its contribution to the number of employed people has been in decline. As a result, the primary focus of employment in many developed countries has increasingly become service-oriented. By the late 1980s, for example, more than 60 per cent of employees in the Organisation for Economic Co-operation and Development as a whole were working in the services sector (Blyton, 1989). In Australia in 1990–91, the manufacturing industry was the main source of employment, but in 2004–05 manufacturing was ranked third after retail trade and the property and business services industries (Australian Bureau of Statistics, 2006).

The impact of this shift towards services has implications for the type of employee who is now in demand:

☐ As most service work requires *face-to-face or voice-to-voice interaction* with customers (Macdonald and Sirianni, 1996), the service interaction may involve high levels of emotional labour or 'the management of feeling to create a publicly observable facial and bodily display' (Hochschild, 1983: 7).

☐ Another feature of employment conditions in the service sector is *flexibility in work arrangements* (Smith, 2005). Australian studies suggest evidence of the common pattern also seen in other industrialized countries: employment is moving from the 'traditional' forms of full-time, permanent work towards a wider variety of working arrangements, including part-time work, temporary employment and contract employment (Van den Heuvel and Wooden, 1997; Kalleberg, 2000).

The growth in the service sector has therefore changed expectations of the type of worker who is now in demand and the structure of working arrangements. Firms that can effectively adjust their human capital base to meet these economic challenges and maintain a workforce mix that supports strategic priorities are well placed to maintain their competitive advantage.

Despite the current priority given to HRP, it has in fact moved through a number of stages to get to this position. Initially, in the '*regulation*' phase, HRP activity ensured that managerial behaviour and organizational systems were compliant with government regulations. The role of HRP was to ensure alignment with laws in areas such as industrial relations, equal employment opportunity, minimum wages and salaries, and employment conditions. The compliance element at this stage actually meant that HRP at times worked against strategic planning rather than with it. In the period spanning the 1960s, 70s and 80s, the compliance activity that dominated HRP meant that activities were confined to operational and reactive activities that did not factor in the need to be strategic (Ulrich, 1987).

As global competition increased, however, proactive strategic initiatives were given greater priority, and HRP entered the second, '*control*' phase. During this period, HRP was used as a control mechanism to align individual behaviour with organizational strategy. Performance management and reward systems, for example, were designed to develop human behaviour in line with strategic priorities. Although HRP was now connected to strategic planning, it was still largely an implementation tool.

It was not until phase three, the '*shape*' phase, that HRP effectively became a potential source of strategic competitive advantage. Ulrich (1987) explains that it was during this stage that key stakeholders such as employees, customers and unions agreed on HRM configurations that would create strategic unity.

Before moving on to a discussion of some of these strategic issues, it is useful to consider how the HRP process actually works. The next section will therefore review how an organization can approach matching human resource demand to supply, before moving into a broader discussion of the strategic impact of HRP activity.

Techniques of HRP

Demand forecasting in HRM determines the quantity and quality of employees required to meet the organization's goals. These forecasts are usually associated with particular job categories and skill areas that support the organization's current and future goals. There are a variety of approaches that provide useful data, differing in their approach and level of sophistication. Demand forecasting may be undertaken either *quantitatively* or *qualitatively*.

Quantitative demand forecasting

Quantitative approaches rely on statistical techniques and mathematical modelling, whereas qualitative approaches gather expert opinions to determine possible changes in demand. Two forms of quantitative analysis include trend projections and multiple regression.

Trend projection is time series analysis that processes past and present information on the number of people hired in various departments, job categories or skills areas and, based on any observed increases or decreases, forms predictions into the future. Although such information is quite easy to understand, the underlying assumption is that previous trends will determine future trends, which does not take into account unexpected environmental developments.

The aim of the *multiple regression* approach is to broaden the determinants of future demand to determine reliable indicators of future demand. Specific independent variables, or predictors, may include variables such as sales in a retail store, student numbers in a school or hospital bed capacity in a hospital. In the situation facing Holden, outlined in Box 6.1, labour demand was affected by adjustments to internal operating decisions as well as changes in consumer taste. The greater the number of independent variables that can be used to predict the labour demand, the more accurate will be the prediction. The restrictions on using multiple regression are, however, the availability of the data and also the size of the sample, with larger datasets providing more accurate information. There is also an expectation that those working in the HRM area are comfortable dealing with both datasets and the computer programs that accompany the technique.

Qualitative demand forecasting

An alternative to the quantitative approach is provided by qualitative techniques that draw in information from key stakeholders. Data collection can be quite informal or can be structured in a formal manner using approaches such as the Delphi technique.

Using a Delphi survey, HRM planners contact a group of expert informants and ask them to respond anonymously to some questions on HRP. Responses are collected and fed back to respondents together with another set of questions. The process continues until a consensus has been obtained (Rothwell, 1995). The benefits of this approach are that expert information is gathered without face-to-face pressure within the group to conform to a particular line of thinking. The approach is also useful when conditions are changing and there are few existing precedents on how to proceed.

Exercise

Under what conditions would a qualitative approach to demand forecasting be more feasible or appropriate than a quantitative approach?

Box 6.1 Factors impacting on labour demand at Holden

During March 2007, car maker Holden made a decision to cut 600 jobs at its assembly operations in Adelaide, Australia. The fall in labour demand was associated with a range of demand determinants including adjustments to internal operating decisions as well as changes in broader consumer demand.

With respect to the internal operating changes, Director of Manufacturing Rod Keane said that the decision to reduce the workforce at the Elizabeth plant followed a major investment at the plant that had increased efficiencies and allowed the car maker to maintain production levels with fewer staff. It also came as the company moved to end the production of its older VZ range of vehicles and concentrate on the new VE models.

Broader reasons for the decline in labour demand were related to a slide in sales of the locally built Commodore range in 2006, with sales down 15.4 per cent. Holden had also cut 1,400 jobs in August 2005, when it axed its third shift at Elizabeth due to a falling local and global demand for large cars.

Ian Jones, federal secretary of the Australian Manufacturing Workers Union vehicle division, commented on environmental pressures that had contributed to this decline in sales. 'Petrol pricing, currency costs, unabated entry of imported products, declining assistance and increased cost of finance are all factors that by themselves would cause major problems for industry,' Mr Jones said.

Federal Industry Minister Ian Macfarlane confirmed that the global automotive industry was going through challenging times and that Australian car producers were not immune from this.

Source: Adapted from http://theage.drive.com.au/motor-news/holden-axes-600-jobs-in-adelaide-20070305-140fo.html [accessed 15 August 2011].

Supply forecasting

Supply forecasting draws from both internal and external sources of HRM information related to supply of employees. Internal labour supply information considers the range of people within the organization who can be promoted, transferred or developed to meet supply needs. When undertaking such a review, a skills inventory – a system for keeping track of employee skill development – is a useful source of information. These data can be kept manually, especially in smaller organizations, but in larger organizations well-developed human resources information systems and detailed performance management information may assist in identifying employees with high potential and the appropriate skills. Along with internal sources of supply, organizations scan labour supply sources external to the organization. This sort of analysis takes into account environmental analysis relating to demographic trends in order to assess the qualitative and quantitative impacts.

In terms of the usefulness of efforts to match the demand and supply of labour, evidence suggests that firms adopting clear HRM planning objectives and a formal planning process obtain useful information for strategic planning (Huselid, 1995; Lam and Schaubroeck, 1998). Despite the logic of external and internal labour scanning, there is evidence that people planning is not always formally developed and implemented. The impact of unplanned environmental events, for example, means that it is frequently difficult to estimate internal labour demand. Indeed, Huselid (1993) established that environmental volatility had an important impact on the adoption of HRP approaches. The most common use of HRP occurred in firms that were experiencing moderate levels of workforce volatility. Firms characterized by high or low levels of workforce volatility, however, tended to have a lower use of HRP. Huselid (1993) observed that higher levels of volatility may render HRP ineffective, whereas low levels of volatility make it unnecessary.

Rothwell (1995) also commented on the lack of HRP within the development of human resource strategy. Consistent with Huselid (1993), the argument is made that the rate of environmental change renders HRP so problematic that it becomes infeasible. Plans are developed but fail to be implemented as further internal or external changes negate the relevance of any proposed initiatives. Policy priorities may also shift as competing interest groups vie for primacy and existing plans are sidelined in the process.

Rothwell (1995) also suggests that the abilities and skills of those who are expected to take on these planning tasks may impact on the quality of HRP. Line managers, for example, who are given the task of making planning projections may not have the background skills or the time to dedicate to developing labour models. Kulik and Bainbridge (2006), in a survey of both HRM professionals and line managers covering a range of HRM responsibilities, established that, with respect to HRP, the collective view confirmed that HRP is best managed centrally by HRM rather than by the line. Although this assigns responsibility to those who may have the skills, line managers often still need to be involved as the decisions ultimately impact on the capacity of line management to complete the organization's output requirements.

Job analysis

Within the HRP process, matching the demand and supply of labour informs decision-makers about potential trends and changes in labour requirements, and also provides information about the best labour mix. Job analysis refines and complements this information to determine exactly what each job involves and who is required before specific staffing decisions can be made (Schneider and Konz, 1989).

Broadly speaking, job analysis refers to the process of getting detailed information about jobs (Brannick et al., 2007). Organizational conditions often change in response to new technology and machinery, as well as legislative and market requirements. Job analysis therefore becomes important in interpreting what the job currently involves. Having identified the objective of the job analysis, the HRM analyst must determine the type of information that needs to be collected, the source of the information, the method of data collection and how the data will be analysed.

The type of information that is collected is usually associated with the development of a job description, or the list of tasks, duties and responsibilities of the job. Additionally, a job specification, or person specification, is derived that lists the knowledge, skills, abilities and other characteristics that an individual must have to successfully perform the job. The most common source of information is the person already in the job. There are limits to the usefulness of this source, however, when the views of the present incumbents differ from those of their supervisors (O'Reilly, 1973). Employees may, for example, exaggerate their duties, especially if the process is associated with a review of remuneration, and it may become necessary to seek out additional information. When the job is a new position or when the incumbent has actually left the organization, further input is usually sought. Under these conditions, for example, it becomes necessary to bring in the views of supervisors or co-workers.

Common methods of data collection include observation, interviews, questionnaires, diaries and critical incident approaches. The choice of the method depends largely on the purpose of the analysis and the nature of the job, and a number of methods are often used together:

☐ *Observation* is useful when the job involves standardized repetitive jobs and manual work: when jobs have actions, observation is a good way to track what needs to be done. More complex positions involving internal thought processing, such as the work of an accountant, are, however, difficult to measure through observation. Similarly, when a job involves irregular work, as, for example, with the role of a manager, observation becomes less useful.

☐ *Interviews* are more appropriate in these situations and overall are one of the most commonly used job analysis data collection methods.

☐ *Diaries* are also helpful when the responsibilities of a job do not form a regular pattern. If diaries are reliably maintained over an extended period, they are especially useful in tracking irregular and infrequent duties.

☐ Finally, critical incident approaches are employed to provide specific explanations for effective and ineffective job performance. This approach is usually used to track what is required and what is to be avoided for the success or failure of the job. The process can be onerous as it requires fairly detailed descriptions of what the employee did during a particular incident and explanations of why the performance was effective or ineffective; for this reason, it is not commonly used across routine tasks.

In addition to these qualitative approaches, quantitative questionnaires such as the position analysis questionnaire provide useful data that can be used to compare information across a range of jobs (Jeanneret and Strong, 2003). These quantitative surveys usually break jobs down into standardized dimensions that are rated; the information obtained can then be used to differentiate jobs with respect to levels of complexity, processing and responsibility.

Despite the usefulness and importance of job analysis, a number of writers have explained that the rational approach described above – which breaks each job down and produces specific job descriptions and specifications – may no longer be viable. As the rate of technology changes and work becomes more knowledge-based, task boundaries created by traditional job classifications are dissipating. Jobs have become more flexible, and their boundaries are vague and dynamic (Brannick et al., 2007).

Stewart and Carson (1997) have argued that, along with the move away from traditional hierarchical structure and control towards flexible, team-based designs, employees have become more than simple components that fit a series of static job descriptions. A key idea is the development of emerging relationships that may create new networks between employees. These emerging networks do not, however, always have a comfortable fit with traditional structures. The more fluid connections mean that what needs to be done and who does it becomes a product of what each person brings into the organization and how they connect with existing staff. Therefore, rather than work roles being planned and fixed, they become indefinite. It is more likely that jobs will develop around individuals rather than the reverse. Therefore, as well as impacting on job content, environmental pressures have led to re-evaluations of who is employed and how the employer–employee relationship is managed.

The following section shifts our discussion away from a review of how HRP is approached, to a broader discussion of managing the strategic issues associated with an over- or undersupply of labour and with attempts to maintain the employee–employer relationship during these periods.

The strategic role of HRP

Restructuring and downsizing

Over the last two decades, technological and market changes have prompted major reviews of organizational processes and structure. During periods of economic uncertainty, firms struggle to find ways to cut costs and become more efficient and effective. Payroll expenses and employee downsizing are often

---

Exercise
When would quantitative approaches to job analysis be more suitable than qualitative approaches?

targeted during periods of recession, for example, as a way to boost company profits (Cascio and Wynn, 2004). Indeed, the Corporate Leadership Council (2008) reported that, by the end of 2008, 20 per cent of Australian and New Zealand firms were preparing for the inevitable downturn in 2009 and had indicated that they might either freeze or downsize their staffing levels in the 6-month period following the financial crisis alert in the October.

The promise of workforce reduction is an immediate reduction of costs, coupled with increased levels of efficiency, productivity and competitiveness (Farrell and Mavondo, 2004; Iverson and Zatzick, 2007). Unfortunately, the expectations of economic benefits following employee reductions are often not realized (Gandolfy, 2008). In an analysis of the financial impact of downsizing, Cascio and Wynn (2004) compared employers adopting a stable position with those who chose to downsize and found no consistent evidence to support the notion that employment downsizing led to an improvement in financial indicators such as return on assets.

The economic premise that profit is driven by either a reduction in costs or an increase in revenues is complicated by the human reactions associated with a reduction in the workforce. Organisations face problems with diminished productivity and loyalty, and loss of critical organizational knowledge. The negative consequences of an organizational downsizing response can include heightened levels of stress, conflict, role ambiguity and job dissatisfaction among employees (Appelbaum et al., 1999).

Downsizing survivors – those employees who remain in the organization – generally find themselves with increased workloads and responsibilities without the necessary training and support. These stresses result in a range of mental and physical illness that impact on the quality of their work. Indeed, Gandolfy (2008), in a review of the research in the area, has shown that the 'victims', or those who are involuntarily downsized out of the job, report more positive outcomes than employees who stay. Victims commonly received transition packages and outplacement services and support, felt lower levels of stress in the job and experienced fewer negative effects than survivors. Such conditions may also encourage talented employees who are already comfortable with mobility to leave organizations that do not offer the appropriate opportunities for development and advancement.

A primary reason given for the negative consequences associated with downsizing is the poor execution and management of these reduction initiatives (Appelbaum et al., 1999). It is possible, however, to strategically manage workforce reductions and tensions during periods of economic stress through effective HRM approaches. Cascio and Wynn (2004) similarly argue that downsizing remains a viable and sometimes necessary response to environmental pressure, but reinforce that how the process is executed is critical (Box 6.2). Specifically, employees' involvement and input are key in creating a sense of psychological control over events that have such major personal consequences. Avoiding rumours by honest, consistent and regular communication from the executive group can also assist in reducing stress levels.

> ## Box 6.2   Clever HRP responses to tough economic conditions
>
> Cascio and Wynn (2004) have argued that pressures to downsize *can* be managed effectively. Staged responses to economic pressure involving pay cuts, reduced working hours and using up outstanding leave can stave off immediate action to downsize.
>
> In response to the global financial crisis, a number of Australian companies avoided immediate wide-scale lay-offs and employed less invasive tactics. Alcoa, the world's largest integrated bauxite mine, froze the wages of its Australian workforce of 6,400 and capped the salary of its managing director for 2 years.
>
> In the banking sector, Ralph Norris, the Commonwealth Bank chief executive, took a 10 per cent pay cut in his base salary, and middle management roles, which were paid more than $100,000 per year, were subject to a 12-month freeze on both base salaries and short-term incentives. The bank also gave a commitment to avoid moving any jobs offshore for the following 3 years and to retain its call centres and operations processing centres in Australia for the next 3 years (*The Australian*, April 21, 2009).
>
> GM Holden also responded to the global downturn by trimming shifts to avoid lay-offs. In May 2009, it moved its Adelaide factory to single-shift operation to avoid job cuts among its production workers (*The Australian*, April 3, 2009).
>
> These companies made it clear that these actions were deliberate attempts to save jobs and maintain viability.

Ethical factors in downsizing

Wilcox and Lowry, in Chapter 5, point out that most, if not all, areas of HRM practice involve ethical considerations, and the following discussion highlights how the area of downsizing, as an HRP initiative, is not a morally neutral event.

The argument can be made that resource munificence, or abundance, may be grounds for judging whether a particular instance of downsizing is morally or socially responsible (Van Buren, 2000). In other words, an organization's resource base can be used to evaluate the extent of its obligations to 'downsized' employees. Based on assumptions made about relationships within the psychological and social contracts between employers and their employees, the expectation is that employment should be stable and secure if firms are doing well. When organizations engage in downsizing merely to increase an already adequate rate of profit, however, they are likely to be held more culpable for such actions than when environmental forces such as technological change or competitive conditions constrain them. Consistent with this, when organizations are characterized by declining resource munificence, downsizing is more ethically justifiable.

Zyglidopoulos (2003) empirically investigated the impact of downsizing on a firm's reputation for corporate social performance (RCSP) and found not only that downsizing had a negative impact on the firm's reputation, but also that firms that experienced higher financial performance prior to downsizing suffered a greater negative impact on their RCSP. The research therefore indicated that, despite the apparent validity of downsizing as a structural response to economic stress, managers have implicit psychological and social contracts with and ethical responsibilities towards their employees, and these are carefully monitored by stakeholders. When these contracts are broken, the impact on the company's reputation can be such that companies that want to re-hire qualified employees after a downsizing cycle may find it more difficult to do so because of the damage done to their RCSP.

Later, Zyglidopoulos (2005) compared downsizing with 'downscoping', in which the structural response is to divest or sell off organizational divisions. Within downscoping, employees swap employers but do not necessarily lose their jobs. A comparison between these approaches revealed that although both restructuring attempts have negative impacts on corporate reputation, downsizing has more damaging ramifications within the market.

A further important ethical consideration within downsizing is how the process is carried out. Issues associated with procedural justice – the fairness and equity of the procedures that are used to make decisions – are critical and have important consequences for employees' behaviours and attitudes. Fair processes encourage organizational citizenship behaviour or discretionary behaviours lying outside the employees' formal roles that support and assist an organization during a period of economic stress rather than work against it. These approaches provide survivors with a reason to stay and, importantly, give future prospective new hires a reason to join (Cascio and Wynn, 2004).

Zatzick and Iverson (2006) reinforce the ongoing impact that careful HRM practices can make during a period of downsizing. They have established that firms that continue to invest in their employees through the use of HRM practices designed to provide employees with skills, information, motivation and latitude can assist in maintaining workforce productivity during periods of reduction in the workforce. The argument is made that investment in these practices lessens perceived contract breaches as employees continue to receive opportunities for skill development as well as reassurance of their value in the workplace.

Meeting HRP challenges through flexibility

The preceding discussion has highlighted the HRP techniques that can be employed to match supply and demand. In reality, however, environmental factors such as economic uncertainty, technological change, demographic changes and shifts in values often pose substantial difficulties that limit the success of the HRP process. HRP approaches that do not build in adaptive labour responses may therefore fail to meet environmental challenges. These realities have led to the emergence of flexible options within HRP as a way of managing fluctuations in the supply and demand of labour.

The concept of the flexible model of the firm was developed by Atkinson (1984) as an alternative to traditional hierarchical structures. The model redefines the organization's workforce into two main segments: the *core* and the *periphery*. The core workforce is made up of permanent, highly skilled workers, and the peripheral workforce is made up of a range of temporary employment arrangements. Flexibility options underpin the management of these labour classifications.

□ *Functional flexibility* involves opportunities for role and task variety and is normally associated with the core workforce. Higher levels of training and development in these core workers mean that they tend to experience higher levels of job security (Burgess, 1997).

□ *Numerical flexibility*, as the name suggests, refers to techniques to vary the quantity of labour on hand, rather than being related to investments in the range and scope of the employee skill base. Internal numerical flexibility refers to the amount and time of labour input required of existing employees; overtime and flex-time are examples of this type of flexibility (Rimmer and Zappala, 1988). Alternatively, external numerical flexibility involves changing the actual number of employees as well as the hours that they work. This latter type of numerical flexibility covers the arrangements made with casual or temporary workers who are called in when needed but do not benefit from a permanent contractual relationship with the employer.

Both functional and numerical flexibility are facilitated by financial and procedural flexibility:

□ *Financial flexibility* refers to the compensation system that builds in variations in wages for different types of worker (Atkinson, 1984). These arrangements allow organizations to reward and therefore encourage skill development in the core workforce.

□ Finally, *procedural flexibility* is critical in that it provides the consultative mechanisms for introducing the other forms of flexibility through changes in both legal and traditional practices covering employment (Boyer, 1988).

The promise of these forms of flexibility to help organizations respond more easily to environmental fluctuations and match labour resources more closely with variations in supply and demand have led to major shifts in the workforce profile. Spain, France, The Netherlands, Finland and Australia are examples of countries that have shown a large growth in the use of temporary employment conditions (Campbell and Burgess, 2001). In the Australian setting in 2003, for example, over a quarter (28 per cent) of all wage and salary earners were employed on a casual basis, and in the period since 1988 more than half of all new jobs created have gone to casual workers (Kryger, 2004). Despite the benefits in terms of flexibility that are offered by alternative forms of work, the arrangements create numerous challenges for both employees and organizations.

For the employee, casual work is closely associated with poor working conditions, including low hourly rates of pay, low and irregular earnings, reduced employment security, lack of access to notice and severance pay, reduced access to unfair dismissal rights, vulnerability to changes in schedules, loss of skill- and age-related pay increments, and lack of representational rights (Pocock et al., 2004). For the employer, although using this category of worker is associated with flexibility and often reduced costs, the arrangement does have potentially negative ramifications (Buultjens, 2001). For example, casual workers are, owing to the transient nature of their terms of employment, less likely to identify strongly with the organization (Hall, 2006); as a result, they may not absorb and display appropriate organizational values and behaviours.

The limited organizational investment in casual workers also means that these employees may have less opportunity to develop the skills necessary for the job, and therefore the contribution that they make may be limited to generic industry tasks rather than adding real value in terms of the specialized tasks expected by some service providers. Lowry's (2001) investigation of the work arrangements for casual employees within the registered club industry in New South Wales indicated that casual workers are employed on a primarily transactional basis and that their employment conditions are characterized by an underinvestment in employee development (Buultjens, 2001; Lowry, 2001). The impact of an underinvestment in HRM activities such as training and feedback has ramifications for the quality of the service delivery provided by these workers. Lowry's (2001) findings, for example, indicated that some employees were so dissatisfied with the lack of feedback and recognition that they made a conscious decision not to improve the quality of their service. This finding is consistent with the previous research by Schneider et al. (1998), who established a relationship between HRM practices, including training and supportive supervision, and the quality of the service.

There is evidence, however, that the move to a greater reliance on non-standard types of worker – those without set hours or the expectation of continued employment – does have benefits for the organization. Ghosh et al. (2009) have established that the greater use of non-standard workers is positively associated with increased financial performance on the part of the firm. As well as having cost-saving benefits, non-standard arrangements allow firms to give workers a trial of employment before assigning them permanent status.

Moreover, Ghosh et al.'s research indicates that non-standard forms of work are associated with a greater financial impact when firms are operating in less uncertain but more competitive environments. Once uncertainty rises, reliance on non-traditional workers becomes less effective, and when uncertainty is high, a permanent workforce becomes more valuable. Permanent staff's high level of task flexibility and knowledge and expertise specific to the firm help an organization to sustain itself at a time when conditions are in flux. The argument is that, during periods of greater uncertainty, the core workforce assist the organization in protecting its technical edge, and consolidate activities that are considered important for organizational success (Ghosh et al., 2009). Although flexible forms of work allow companies to shed workers when they are not needed, the attraction and retention of a talented core workforce remains a priority, and it is this issue that is addressed in the following section (see also Mini Case Study 6.1).

Mini Case Study 6.1
Casual workers at the *BankInfo* Call Centre

BankInfo is a new call centre currently being set up by a small regional bank. The purpose of the call centre is to process a broad range of customer queries ranging from simple account questions to much more complex financial planning matters.

Brad Ellis, the manager of the new centre, is focused on cost minimization and, as people are going to be his major expense, he is considering the use of a primarily casual workforce as a way of keeping costs down. By using more casual workers, he can take people on and off work as he needs them and avoid having a permanent workforce that he has to employ consistently even when demand drops. When the bank introduces new financial products, for example, he will need more staff, but at other times he simply will not require as many people.

Brad thought he should talk about his staffing idea with the human resources manager at head office, Sylvia Waters. He had heard that she was a difficult character who was always going on about how HRM was not involved enough in strategic decisions. But he nevertheless decided to give her a ring and at least hear what she had to say. When he made the phone call, he was surprised by how enthusiastic Sylvia was to hear from him. Sylvia started by saying 'Well, thanks for ringing Brad. I appreciate the opportunity to have some input here – a lot of the managers think that HRM is really just about hiring and firing. What sort of employee profile are you thinking about using?'

Brad outlined his view, and Sylvia seemed to be listening closely. When he had finished, however, he found himself becoming frustrated as she started to warn him about the dangers of relying primarily on a casual workforce, especially for more complex customer interactions. Sylvia made the following comment: 'Think about the ongoing training costs, the problems with retention and the continuous recruitment issues that you are going to face. It may not actually be the best way of keeping costs down in the long run.' At this point, Sylvia had to cut the conversation short to go to an appointment, but she urged Brad to contact her again so that they could come up with a solution.

After the call, Brad could not help thinking that the human resources department sometimes simply got in the way and created more problems than solutions. On the other hand, he felt that Sylvia had made some good points, so perhaps he should set up a meeting with her and try to plan this out more carefully.

Question

1 How can HRP in the call centre be configured to achieve cost-effectiveness but also ensure that more complex customer enquiries are dealt with appropriately?

Talent management

Vaiman and Vance (2008: 3–4) define talent as including 'all of the employed people within an organization who may differ dramatically in levels of knowledge, skill and ability.' Although there will be a variation in the critical strategic nature of this talent within an organization, these authors argue that all employees represent potential sources of valuable knowledge.

Ulrich (2006) provides a more specific definition and characterizes 'talent' in two ways. The first is as competence, or an individual's knowledge, skills and values that are required for both the present and the future. Second, Ulrich specifies that such employees have commitment, as shown through their capacity to work hard, put the time in to do what they are asked to do and give their discretionary energy to the firm's success. Finally, these employees make a real contribution and find meaning and purpose in their work.

The recognition of the value of talent comes at a time when, as indicated above, companies are adopting more flexible work practices and moving away from traditional commitments involving permanent work status. These shifts have been accompanied by a changing psychological contract within the employment relationship such that employees will increasingly look for employability rather than employment and will often want to change jobs (Losey, 2005). Indeed, as pointed out in Chapter 3, these transitions often occur across borders as international employment markets offer advanced opportunities for development. Firms may therefore need to refocus their HRM practices on what employees are looking for in order to attract and retain valuable staff.

Although HRM recognizes the value of people as assets, this does not mean that HRM approaches always adopt an employee focus (Guest, 2002). The unitarist underpinnings of HRM assume that what is good for the organization is also good for its employees (Legge, 2005). In times of economic stress, however, when organizations may constrict employees' conditions and benefits, it may become increasingly difficult for employees to see any evidence of alignment between the employer's and employee's goal. The view of people as a compliant organizational resource is further challenged by an increasingly well-educated workforce and generational shifts in the values of the workforce that now emphasize both challenging work and an acceptable work–life balance (Guest et al., 2003). Uncertain economic conditions may therefore heighten the need to become more employee-focused in order to retain existing talented employees.

Guest (2002) has previously provided some guidance on how to test for employee-focused HRM approaches by exploring the impact of various HRM approaches on employees' reports of work satisfaction. Results indicated that key HRM practices related to work satisfaction included those associated with the high-performance work systems approach discussed by Zatzick and Iverson (2006). Notably, these included efforts to design or make work more interesting and challenging, direct participation and the extensive provision of information. Guest (2002) also identified the importance of a further set of more bureaucratic employee-oriented practices including family-friendly, equal opportunity and anti-harassment initiatives. Pocock (2005) similarly makes the business case for a link between work–life balance and the attraction and retention of a firm's workers. The increase in the number of women in the workforce, coupled with an ageing population base that requires carers, increases the need for companies to support valued employees who have family responsibilities.

Along with these HRM practices, employees' expectations for personal growth, as reported by both Edgar and Geare (2005) and Boxall et al. (2003), are useful in designing employee-focused HRM. Boxall et al. (2003) identified training opportunities as a factor determining employees' decisions to leave their employer. This is consistent with the changing psychological contract that focuses individuals on their own personal development needs (Sheehan et al., 2006). Employees now tend to have a greater appreciation of opportunities to upgrade their knowledge, skills and abilities so that they can remain in demand in the wider employment market (Holland et al., 2007).

Beechler and Woodward (2009) have identified a number of organizations that are implementing new practices to retain valuable employees. Within the accounting profession, where the supply of new talent is well below the anticipated demand and where professional service firms are finding it difficult to retain young associates who are focused on self-development, Deloitte, one of the 'Big Four' global accounting and consulting firms, is engaging in what it calls 'mass career customization'. This programme assists employees to map their careers through a series of interactive exercises and online resources. Other organizations have increased their emphasis on formal training. Goldman Sachs, for example, has set up the Goldman Sachs University. Australia's Macquarie Group, the international investment house, has similarly displayed a commitment to formal training, creating a partnership with INSEAD in 2006 in order to provide the first corporate-specific Masters degree from a top-tier business school. Despite the changing psychological contract and the current tendency for employees to move more freely between organizations, it is clear that many companies are taking quite specific steps to engage and retain talented employees.

International considerations

One of the developments resulting from new forms of work organization as an HRP response has been an increase in the outsourcing of work and the resultant 'offshoring' of tasks to overseas providers. Offshoring refers to work that is not constrained by a need for actual customer contact or local knowledge, meaning that it can therefore be provided remotely or globally (Farrell et al., 2005). The key benefit from offshoring is the economic return of replacing high-wage labour costs with lower costs. Offshoring is also seen as a way of enabling organizations to focus their resources on their core business (Domberger, 1994).

The HRP decision to source labour from international sites is not without its complications. Often, the complexity or idiosyncratic nature of a particular set of tasks makes the move offshore difficult. A further issue is the lack of maturity in the newly developing offshoring market. Middle management skills, for example, may still be under development in the target countries, and services may not meet the expectations of the companies that are choosing to relocate their operations overseas (Farrell et al., 2005). Connected with this is a generalized concern about the suitability of labour to fit with the quality of service demanded by customers. Key suitability factors include problems with language skills, an educational system that does not emphasize interpersonal skills and attitudes towards teamwork, and cultural fit. Tangible savings could be lost if these issues associated with quality and service are not managed (Nash et al., 2004).

These issues require additional monitoring to ensure that quality and service are being delivered in an appropriate manner. Shiu (2004) concludes that the aforementioned issues of culture, language, service integration and maintenance will require time for clients and customers to adjust, and this may not always be an option for a firm that is trying to make strategic headway in a timely manner.

Conclusion

This chapter has provided an overview of technical approaches to HRP as well as a discussion of some of the strategic challenges that are now being incorporated into HRP thinking. HRP has evolved through a series of stages from legal compliance and application as a control mechanism, to more recently being considered as a valuable strategic tool. As a strategic mechanism, HRP is not simply a matter of ensuring that a firm meets swings in the supply and demand of labour, but rather that the process adds real value when addressing the strategic needs of the company. The strategic imperative has been heightened by environmental changes associated with increasing levels of uncertainty and competition.

These forces have alerted companies to the value of the people resource and have led to a rethink of traditional responses to an over- or undersupply or demand for labour. Downsizing to deal with a drop in labour demand, for example, has in the past been adopted as a necessary cost-cutting measure. Although this response is still used, the process is now more likely to factor in the impact on employees and ensure that workers are informed and have some sense of personal control. Such an approach assists in keeping employees engaged in the strategic goals of the company and also enhances the firm's corporate reputation.

Changes in the flexibility of work organization have also been used to deal with variations in the supply and demand of labour, and have resulted in a shift in the expectations of workers in terms of permanent work arrangements. Although this helps companies to deal with changes in demand patterns, it has also raised issues relating to employee loyalty and commitment. Revised expectations on the part of the workforce's employees have led companies to think more carefully about the relationships that they develop with their workers, especially those who provide critical talent resources. Even during periods of a slow-down in labour demand, as was experienced during the 2008–09 global financial crisis, firms have become more mindful of the importance of attracting and retaining talent. Overall, HRP has evolved considerably, and has moved beyond a mere matching of labour needs with output requirements to incorporate a strategic view of the people resource and the impact that can be ultimately made on sustained competitive advantage.

❓ For discussion and revision

1 What are the HRP implications associated with an increase in the services sector?

2 Under what conditions is a qualitative approach to demand forecasting preferable?

3 Do you agree that environmental changes render HRP so problematic that it becomes infeasible? Is there a way to approach HRP under volatile conditions that still adds value?

4 Discuss why some commentators argue that job descriptions have become redundant.

5 How can an organization's resource munificence (abundance) be used to assess whether downsizing is a morally or socially appropriate response?

6 If an organization is committed to retaining talented workers, what sort of HRM initiatives may assist in the retention of valuable workers?

📖 Further reading

Books

Berger, L. A. and Berger, D. R. (2011) *The Talent Management Handbook: Creating a Sustainable Competitive Advantage by Selecting, Developing, and Promoting the Best People, 2.* New York: McGraw-Hill.

Boxall, P. and Purcell, J. (2011) *Strategy and Human Resource Management.* Basingstoke: Palgrave Macmillan.

Caplan, J. (2011) *The Value of Talent: Promoting Talent Management Across the Organization.* London: Kogan Page.

Cascio, W. (2010) *Managing Human Resources: Productivity, Quality of Work Life, Profits.* Boston: McGraw-Hill/Irwin.

Delahaye, B. (2011) *Human Resource Development: Managing Learning and Knowledge Capital.* Prahran: Tilde University Press.

Hartel, C. E. J., Fujimoto, Y., Strybosch, V. E. and Fitzpatrick, K. (2007) *Human Resource Management. Transforming Theory into Innovative Practice.* French's Forest, NSW: Pearson.

Kramar, R., Bartram, T., De Cieri, H., Noe, R., Hollenbeck, J., Gerhart, B. and Wright, P. (2010) *Human Resource Management in Australia* (4th edn). Sydney: McGraw-Hill.

Teicher, J., Holland, P. and Gough, R. (eds) (2006) *Employee Relations Management: Australia in a Global Context* (2nd edn). Frenchs Forest, NSW: Prentice Hall.

Withers, M., Williamson, M. and Reddington, M. (2010) *Transforming HR: Creating Value Through People* (2nd edn). Amsterdam: Butterworth-Heinemann.

Journals

Burgess, J. and Campbell, I. (1998) Casual employment in Australia: growth, characteristics, a bridge or trap? *Economic and Labour Relations Review,* 9(1): 31–54.

Grant, R. (2003) Strategic planning in a turbulent environment: evidence from the oil majors. *Strategic Management Journal,* 24(6): 491–517.

Guest, D. (2004) Flexible employment contracts, the psychological contract and employment outcomes: an analysis and review of the evidence. *International Journal of Management Reviews,* 5/6(1): 1–19.

Lepak, D. and Snell, S. (2002) Examining the human resource architecture: the relationships among human capital, employment and human resource configurations. *Journal of Management,* 28(4): 517–43.

Tsui, A., Pearce, J., Porter, L. and Hite, J. (1995) Alternative approaches to the employee-organizational relationship: does investment in employees pay off? *Academy of Management Journal,* 44: 1089–121.

Case study The Australian Cladding Company

The Australian Cladding Company (ACC) was started in 1998 by Jim Hackett. With a background in engineering, Hackett created a new light-weight, low-cost house cladding product that found a ready market in Australia. The company grew dramatically, and although ACC had located its headquarters in Sydney, the company supplied its product into a number of states, as well as attracting international customers. The cladding product was very popular in major building projects, as well as in home building and extension work.

The general health of the Australian economy and initiatives such as the First Home Owner Grant scheme (a one off payment of $7,000 that was introduced by the government in mid-2000 to offset the effect of the Goods and Services Tax) ensured that the construction industry remained buoyant. ACC had also been involved with the supply and installation of the product in a large number of large building projects in Western Australia, where the mining boom had had a positive flow-on effect to the construction industry.

To staff the venture, Hackett initially used contacts from the building industry, and he hand-picked the members of his management team. This group was very small, and it still consists of just:

☐ Jim Hackett as Managing Director;
☐ Ben Harper, Engineering and design;
☐ Reg Grundy, Marketing and sales;
☐ Arthur Seymour, Financial controller;
☐ Ted Clark, Production manager;
☐ Jill Hackett (Jim's wife), Personnel (wages and salary/personnel admininstration).

The growth of the company was quite remarkable. At first, it employed about 20 crew, but as demand increased the business went from a small operation to a much larger concern employing nearly 150 production staff and a further 25 staff working in support roles such as logistics, engineering, personnel, sales, and accounting and finance.

Despite healthy sales figures, profits during 2007 and into the first part of 2008 were down. At the time, Arthur Seymour explained to Hackett that profit was falling because costs were increasing. The cost management figures were showing increased scrap and wastage rates, and labour costs were rising. Along with these cost increases, there were further issues that were of a concern to Hackett.

First, there were efficiency problems with the production staff: at times, they were waiting around not doing anything, yet at other times they were stressed and working flat out. Second, despite a history of long staff tenure, the company was now having problems with employee retention. This was particularly an issue with the skilled staff on the floor, but several key engineering people had also left, along with an IT specialist who had only been with the company for 6 months.

Finally, the number of workplace accidents was on the rise, and Sandra, one of the machine operators, had approached Jill Hackett to suggest that some of the workers were failing to take enough care around the machinery. She also pointed out that the increasing cohort of female workers at times felt uncomfortable with the way in which some of the men spoke to them, and if the issue was not dealt with appropriately, the company could have a number of sexual harassment cases to deal with.

By mid-2008, Jim Hackett had become so worried about declining performance and the staffing problems that he employed a consultant to find out what was going on. In September, Hackett met with the consultant, Terry Wild. Terry explained that most of the problems seem to be connected with the very quick growth of the company, and, as is often the case with companies that expand at an accelerated rate, the human resources approach had not kept up with the expansion. For example, ACC had not really planned its workforce around peak demand periods. In addition, whether or not Hackett realized it, the workforce that he had in place was quite different from the workforce that he had had years before, when most of the workers were male tradesmen. Jill, who was in charge of hiring new staff, had introduced a large number of women, and these new employees were not prepared to put up with the 'boys club' approach. Terry also observed that there was discontent within the skilled workforce, who felt that they were not receiving enough professional development. Furthermore, all of the senior positions were taken up by the existing management group, and other employees could not see a career path for themselves in the organization.

Hackett took offence at the suggestion that Jill was not managing the personnel issues, and responded to Terry that Jill worked really hard and did a great job. Terry submitted his final report in late October 2008. Hackett briefly read through the executive summary; it seemed to him that Terry was basically pushing for 'a more strategic approach to human resources'. The report sat on Hackett's desk for a while. Then, in late October and early November, news of the international credit crisis hijacked discussions at ACC management level, and Hackett did not get back to reading the rest of the report.

6

As 2009 began, the fall-out from the international economic situation really started to hit ACC. Construction on a number of big projects in Western Australia came to a halt, and orders were cancelled. Furthermore, although the government was dropping interest rates to encourage household spending and the First Home Owners Grant had been increased to $21,000, the construction industry was feeling the impact of the economic downturn. During this time, Arthur Seymour reminded Hackett that one of the major cost blow-outs in 2008 had been associated with labour, and if the company was going to survive it was going to have to cut its labour force – basically, the company was going to have to downsize until economic conditions improved.

Hackett realized the practicality of this suggestion but was still concerned about the impact of such a message, especially in view of the comments that had been made by Terry Wild in late 2008. So Hackett decided to invite Terry to come along to the next management meeting to discuss the company's response to the economic downturn and provide some insights based on Terry's investigation from the previous year.

Hackett rang Terry to ask him if he would attend the management meeting, and Terry was pleased to be involved. Hackett explained that ACC were considering downsizing the workforce, and Terry agreed that this was a reasonable and necessary response. He also made the observation, however, that in light of the staff problems from the previous year, any downsizing approaches would have to be handled extremely carefully. Terry made the comment:

> Prior to the economic downturn, you already had problems with the workforce. The lack of an effective human resources approach that kept up with your expansion was becoming a major problem. You really needed at that time to look at your work flows and how your jobs were designed. You were also losing important staff. Now, if you inform staff that they are going to lose their jobs, existing problems might be made worse. When I come to see you next week, we need to rethink how you are managing some key human resources issues.

As he rang off, Hackett wondered whether getting Terry Wild involved was actually going to be a good idea – it might just complicate matters. He thought to himself that people either wanted to work for the company or they didn't. If they weren't happy at ACC, they would have to find work elsewhere – at least if they went, it would get rid of some of the labour cost problems.

Questions

1 What are the immediate and underlying problems facing ACC?
2 What sort of human resources activities need to be put in place reasonably quickly, and what human resources approaches need to be taken in the longer term to ensure ongoing strategic competitive advantage?

References

Appelbaum, S., Everard, A. and Hung, L. T. S. (1999) Strategic downsizing: critical success factors. *Management Decisions*, 37(7): 535–52.

Atkinson, J. (1984) Manpower strategies for flexible organisations. *Personnel Management*, (August): 28–31.

The Australian (2009) Others To Follow Bank's Executive Pay Cuts. Available from: http://www.theaustralian.com.au/business/news/bank-pay-cuts-set-trend/story-e6frg906-1225700359387 [accessed 21 April 2009].

The Australian (2009) Holden Trims Shifts To Avoid Layoffs. Available from: http://theage.drive.com.au/motor-news/holden-axes-600-jobs-in-adelaide-20070305-140fo.html [accessed 15 August 2011].

Australian Bureau of Statistics (2006) *Yearbook Australia 2006*. Cat. No. 1301.0. Canberra: Australian Bureau of Statistics.

Barney, J. B. and Wright, P. M. (1998) On becoming a strategic partner: the role of human resources in gaining competitive advantage. *Human Resource Management*, 37(1): 31–46.

Beechler, S. and Woodward, I. C. (2009) The global 'war for talent'. *Journal of International Management*, 15(3): 273–85.

Blyton, P. (1989) Working population and employment. In Bean, R. (ed.), *International Labour Statistics*. London: Routledge, pp. 18–51.

Boxall, P., Macky, K. and Rasmussen, E. (2003) Labour turnover and retention in New Zealand: the causes and consequences of leaving and staying with employers. *Asia Pacific Journal of Human Resources*, 41(2): 195–214.

Boyer, R. (1988) *The Search for Labour Market Flexibility: The European Economies in Transition*. Oxford: Clarendon Press.

Brannick, M. T., Levine, E. L. and Morgeson, F. P. (2007) *Job and Work Analysis: Methods, Research, and Applications for Human Resource Management* (2nd edn). Los Angeles: Sage.

Burgess, J. (1997) The flexible firm and growth of non-standard employment. *Labour and Industry*, 7(3): 85–102.

Buultjens, J. (2001) Casual employment: a problematic strategy for the registered clubs sector in New South Wales. *Journal of Industrial Relations*, 43(4): 470–7.

Campbell, I. and Burgess, J. (2001) Casual employment in Australia and temporary employment in Europe: developing a cross-national comparison. *Work, Employment & Society*, 15(1): 171–84.

Cascio, W. and Wynn, P. (2004) Managing a downsizing process. *Human Resource Management*, 43(4): 425–36.

Corporate Leadership Council (2008) *HR Quarterly Trends Report*, Q4 – 2008. Catalogue Number CLC2456755. Arlington, VA: CLC.

Domberger, S. (1994) Public sector contracting: does it work? *Australian Economic Review*, (Third quarter): 91–6.

Edgar, F. and Geare, A. (2005) Employee voice on human resource management. *Asia Pacific Journal of Human Resources*, 43(3): 361–80.

Farrell, D., Laboisseire, M., Pascal, R., Rosenfeld, J., de Segundo, C., Sturze, S. and Umezawa, F. (2005) The Emerging Global Labour Market. Available from: http://www.mckinsey.com/mgi/reports/pdfs/emerginggloballabormarket/Part1/MGI_packagedsoftware_demand_case.pdf [accessed 15 August 2011].

Farrell, M. and Mavondo, F. (2004) The effect of downsizing strategy and reorientation strategy on a learning orientation. *Personnel Review*, 33(4): 383–402.

Gandolfy, F. (2008) Learning from the past – downsizing lessons for managers. *Journal of Management Research*, 8(1): 3–17.

Ghosh, D., Willinger, G. L. and Ghosh, S. (2009) A firm's external environment and the hiring of a non-standard workforce: implications for organisations. *Human Resource Management Journal*, 19(4): 433–51.

Guest, D. (2002) Human resource management, corporate performance and employee wellbeing: building the worker into HRM. *Journal of Industrial Relations*, 44(3): 335–58.

Guest, D., Michie, J., Conway, N. and Sheehan, M. (2003) Human resource management and corporate performance in the UK. *British Journal of Industrial Relations*, 41(2): 291–314.

Hall, R. (2006) Temporary agency work and HRM in Australia: 'Cooperation, specialization and satisfaction for the good of all'? *Personnel Review*, 35(2): 158–74.

Hochschild, A. R. (1983) *The Managed Heart: Commercialization of Human Feeling*. Berkeley, CA: University of California Press.

Holland, P., Sheehan, C. and De Cieri, H. (2007) Attracting and retaining talent: exploring human resources development trends in Australia. *Human Resource Development International*, 10(3): 247–62.

Huselid, M. A. (1993) The impact of environmental volatility on human resource planning and strategic human resource management. *Human Resource Planning*, 16(3): 35–51.

Huselid, M. A. (1995) The impact of human resource management practices on turnover, productivity and corporate financial performance. *Academy of Management Journal*, 38: 635–72.

Iverson, R. D. and Zatzick, D. (2007) High commitment work practices and downsizing harshness in Australian Workplaces. *Industrial Relations*, 46(3): 456–80.

Jeanneret, P. R. and Strong, M. H. (2003) Linking O*NET job analysis information to job requirement predictors: an O*NET application. *Personnel Psychology*, 56: 465–92.

Kalleberg, A. (2000) Nonstandard employment relations: part-time, temporary and contract work. *Annual Review of Sociology*, 26: 341–65.

Kryger, T. (2004) Casual Employment: Trends and Characteristics. Research Note No. 53, 2003–4. Canberra: Statistics Section, Australian Parliamentary Library.

Kulik, C. & Bainbridge, H. T. J. (2006) HR and the line: the distribution of HR activities in Australian organisations. *Asia Pacific Journal of Human Resources*, 44(2): 240–56.

Lam, S. S. and Schaubroeck, J. (1998) Integrating HR planning and organisational strategy. *Human Resource Management Journal*, 8(3): 5–19.

Legge, K. (2005) *Human Resource Management: Rhetorics and Reality*. Basingstoke: Palgrave Macmillan.

Losey, M. (2005) Anticipating change: will there really be a labor shortage? In Losey, M., Meisinger, S. and Ulrich, D. (eds), *The Future of Human Resource Management*. Virginia: John Wiley & Sons, pp. 23–37.

Lowry, D. (2001) The casual management of casual work: casual workers' perceptions of HRM practices in the highly casualised firm. *Asia Pacific Journal of Human Resources*, 39(1): 42–62.

Macdonald, C. L. and Sirianni, C. (eds) (1996) *Working in the Service Society*. Philadelphia: Temple University Press.

Nash, B., Holland, P. J. and Pyman, A. (2004) The role and influence of stakeholders in off-shoring: developing a framework for analysis. *International Employment Relations Review*, 10(2): 20–49.

O'Reilly, A. (1973) Skill requirements: supervisor–subordinate conflict. *Personnel Psychology*, 26: 75–80.

Pocock, B. (2005) Work–life 'balance' in Australia: limited progress, dim prospects. *Asia Pacific Journal of Human Resources*, 43(2): 198–209.

Pocock, B., Buchanan, J. and Campbell, I. (2004) Meeting the challenge of casual work in Australia: evidence, past treatment and future policy. *Australian Bulletin of Labour*, 30(1): 16–32.

Rimmer, M. and Zappala, J. (1988) Labour market flexibility and the second tier. *Australian Bulletin of Labour*, 14(4): 564–91.

6

Rothwell, S. (1995) Human resource planning. In Storey, J. (ed.), *Human Resource Management: A Critical Text*. London: Routledge, pp. 167–201.

Rudd, K., Swan, W., Smith, S. and Wong, P. (2007) *Skilling Australia for the Future: Election 2007 Policy Document*. Canberra: T. Gartrell.

Schneider, B. and Konz, A. M. (1989) Strategic job analysis. *Human Resource Management*, 28(1): 51–63.

Schneider, B., White, S. and Paul, M. (1998) Linking service climate and customer perceptions of service quality: test of a causal model. *Journal of Applied Psychology*, 8(2): 150–63.

Sheehan, C., Holland, P. and De Cieri, H. (2006) Current developments in HRM in Australian organisations. *Asia Pacific Journal of Human Resources*, 44(2): 2–22.

Shiu, K. (2004) Outsourcing: are you sure or offshore? Identifying legal risks in offshoring. *NSW Society for Computers and the Law*, 37(3): 56.

Smith, M. (2005) The incidence of new forms of employment in service activities. In Macdonald, C. and Sirianni, C. (eds), *Working in the Service Society*. Philadelphia: The University Press, pp. 54–73.

Stewart, G. L. and Carson, K. P. (1997) Moving beyond the mechanistic model: an alternative approach to staffing for contemporary organizations. *Human Resource Management Review*, 7(2): 157–84.

Ulrich, D. (1987) Strategic human resource planning: why and how? *Human Resource Planning*, 10(1): 37–56.

Ulrich, D. (2006) The talent trifecta. *Workforce Management*, (September), pp. 32–3.

Vaiman, V. and Vance, C. M. (eds) (2008) *Smart Talent Management*. Cheltenham: Edward Elgar.

Van Buren, H. J. III (2000) The bindingness of social and psychological contracts: toward a theory of social responsibility in downsizing. *Journal of Business Ethics*, 25(3): 205–19.

Van den Heuvel, A. and Wooden, M. (1997) Self-employed contractors and job satisfaction. *Journal of Small Business Management*, 35(3): 11–20.

Wright, P., McMahan, G. and McWilliams, A. (1994) Human resources as a source of sustained competitive advantage. *International Journal of Human Resource Management*, 5: 299–324.

Zatzick, C. and Iverson, R. D. (2006) High-involvement management and workforce reduction: competitive advantage or disadvantage? *Academy of Management Journal*, 49: 281–303.

Zula, K. J. and Chermack, T. J. (2007) Human capital planning: a review of literature and implications for human resource development. *Human Resource Development Review*, 6(3): 245–62.

Zyglidopoulos, S. C. (2003) The impact of downsizing on the corporate reputation for social performance. *Journal of Public Affairs*, 4(1): 11–25.

Zyglidopoulos, S. C. (2005) The impact of downsizing on corporate reputation. *British Academy of Management*, 16: 253–9.

Job and work design

Peter Holland

7

?

After reading this chapter, you should be able to:

☐ Explain the origins of contemporary job and work design

☐ Outline the different theoretical perspectives involved

☐ Describe and analyse the different practical approaches to job and work design

☐ Describe and analyse the job characteristic model

☐ Discuss the changing dynamics of the workplace in the 21st century, exploring contemporary developments in job and work design

Introduction

In this chapter, we will explore the development of job and work design. First, we will examine and review the literature on work organization and design from classical to contemporary perspectives. This will provide a contextual analysis for the development of 'modern' job and work design and explain how it has evolved, and continues to evolve. It will also discuss, from a human resource perspective, how it plays a critical role in the development of sustained competitive advantage within organizations.

Writing in 1998, Parker and Wall noted that:

> These are exciting times for those concerned with job and work design. More than ever before, companies are introducing new forms of work organization, often involving major changes in the nature of people's jobs. The opportunity to create more fulfilling and effective work is considerable; but so too is the danger of making it worse. (Parker and Wall, 1998: ix)

This quote illustrates the dynamic, complex and changing times we live in, and is reflected in the changing nature of job and work organization. In an increasingly deregulated and global work environment, there is immense scope to introduce new patterns of work organization. However, as Parker and Wall note, the danger of making work worse is also a potential outcome.

As advanced market economies (AMEs) move from a manufacturing to a knowledge- and service-based economy, the need to attract and retain employees has attained critical importance. This is because, in this new work environment, the workers own the means of production – knowledge – and have the ability to move their valued skills in the external labour market as they focus their knowledge and skill development on employability rather than employment (Drucker, 1998; Holland et al., 2007). Research shows that what attracts and retains skilled workers is exciting and challenging work that has significant development opportunities (Michaels et al., 2001; Newell et al., 2002). These findings are supported by PricewaterhouseCoopers' (2009: 30) 12th Annual Survey of CEOs (involving 1,124 CEOs from more than 50 countries), which shows that 'ninety-seven percent of CEOs believe that the access to and retention of key talent is critical or important to sustaining growth over the long term'. Therefore, the need for talent management underpinned by quality work has seen a re-emergence of job and work design as critical factors for talent management.

However, in the midst of these new developments, advances in technology have also seen the return of the worst aspects of work organization. Arguably the most significant sector to develop in the past decade has been that of call centres. This sector has gained a mixed reputation, mainly through how jobs have been designed. Call centres have been variously described as the 'workhouses of the 21st century', 'electronic sweatshops', 'dungeons with telephones' and 'assembly lines of the head' (Taylor and Bain, 1999; Kinnie et al., 2000; Deery and Kinnie, 2002), owing to the work, which is characterized as a narrow range of routine telephone operations underpinned by close monitoring and surveillance (Barnes, 2004; Connell and Harvey, 2004). In the midst of this, however, Salesforce, a Melbourne-based call centre, was awarded the 2004 Australian Employer of Choice Award by the Australian Financial Review and Hewitt and Associates, emphasizing the fact that new forms of work do not have to be the same but reflect the dynamic nature of job design.

Before exploring contemporary aspects of job design, it is, however, important to examine the development of modern job and work design so that we can better understand the contemporary nature of work organization.

The classical theory of job and work design – the mechanistic era

The foundations of modern job and work design can be traced to the economic expansion associated with the Industrial Revolution in the 18th century. The increasing scale of production during this period put the traditional craft-based mode of production under pressure to maintain pace. This increasing demand became the catalyst for the development of more efficient and effective work practices (Berg, 1985; Thompson and McHugh, 1995). It was Adam Smith in 1776 (Smith, 1979) who identified that the restructuring of work patterns and practices would be a central factor in increasing organizational efficiency and production. The key features included increased dexterity achieved by one person doing a narrow range of tasks and the application of simple machinery. Through this process of work (re)organization, the monopoly of skilled workers over production was gradually eroded, allowing for the dual effect of falling labour costs and increased productivity.

The deconstructing of work processes and the development of simple machinery continued to reform work patterns and practices (Mathias, 1969). This facilitated the shift from cottage industries to factories in major urban areas, close to markets, sources of power and cheap unskilled and semi-skilled labour (Berg, 1985; Grint, 1991). Significantly, during this period of rapid industrialization, the major changes in work occurred in the organization of the patterns and practices of work, rather than in technology (Hobsbawm, 1968).

Through the 19th century, factories developed in both size and complexity, becoming the dominant mode of production (Hobsbawm, 1968; Grint, 1991). The increased complexity of the machines and organizations that emerged during this period was associated with an almost direct correlation with the reduction in the human skills required (Thompson, 1983). However, in terms of efficiency, effectiveness and organizational performance, the organization of work was still based upon arbitrary decision-making (Merkle, 1980). From this period (and perspective) emerged F. W. Taylor and his concept of scientific management, as described in his seminal books, *Shop Management* (1903) and *The Principles of Scientific Management* (1911).

The techniques of scientific management focused on the elimination of 'rule of thumb' approaches to work organization and on increasing productivity and efficiency by scientific methodology. As Merkle (1980: 15) notes:

the core of Taylorism was clearly an explicit call for reconciliation between capital and labour, on the neutral ground of science and rationality … Science would replace the old tyranny and resistance in industrial society.

The increase in productivity that Taylor described (and demonstrated – see Question 1 in Critical Thinking 7.1, below) during this period of rapid industrialization ensured that these developments in work organization would attract attention. Taylor focused on identifying the optimal relationship between the method of production, the time taken, the tools used and the fatigue generated by the task (Rose, 1988). Although job reconstruction was not a new concept in itself, what was significant with Taylor's methods was the rigorous deconstruction and reconstruction of jobs (eliminating all superfluous actions), 'scientifically – in the one best way', as Nyland (1987) described it.

Despite criticism and resistance (Rose, 1988), scientific management-based job design permeated a wide variety of industries in the first two decades of the 20th century (Chandler, 1977). The significance of scientific management in developing new patterns and practices of work was illustrated by Braverman (1974), who stated:

Modern management came into being on the basis of these principles. It arose as a theoretical construct and as systematic practice, in the very period during which the transformation of labor from processes based on skill to processes based upon science was attaining its most rapid tempo … It was to ensure that as craft declined, the worker would sink to the level of general and undifferentiated labor power, adaptable to a large range of simple tasks. (pp. 120–1)

In the context of working patterns and practices, the development of scientific management varied across industries. However, the underlying theme of 'science' as the neutral arbitrator of work design provided the framework for it to become the dominant paradigm of work organization in the 20th century. The overall effect of scientific management on work organization was the separation of the conception and execution and the 'systemization' of work through the reduction of jobs into narrowly defined, repetitive tasks under strict conditions of (management) decision-making and time (Thompson, 1983; Rose, 1988). As Cole (1988) notes, the key features of job design under this system included:

☐ minimum degrees of job specialization;
☐ minimum levels of skill;
☐ minimum time for completion of the tasks;
☐ minimum learning time;
☐ maximum use of machines;
☐ minimum degree of flexibility or discretion in the job;
☐ minimum number of job tasks.

In appraising the development and prospects of the scientific management system, Taylor concluded that it would require a revolution for it to become accepted (Rose, 1988). This revolution was to come when the principles of scientific management and the process of mass production were combined. Although Taylor provided the framework, it was the American industrialist Henry Ford who realized the true potential of combining these work patterns and processes (Littler and Salamon, 1982).

The combination of scientific management and mass production allowed for standardization, continuity and simplification of the production process and, by implication, of work patterns and practices. The success of this mode of production and its associated patterns of work (through the reduction of labour and production costs, and the pace of production being controlled by the speed of the line), gave competitors the option of adopting these patterns of work organization or surrendering their market share. This allowed Fordism (as it became known) to emerge as the dominant mode of production and work organization through eliminating alternative patterns of work (Thompson, 1983; Lipietz, 1987).

The key feature that distinguished Fordism from scientific management was the control (of pace and intensity) of production. The determinant of this was the technology rather than the 'scientific manager'. As Kelly (1982: 29) notes: 'the degree of the division of labour was taken much further than under Taylorism'. Fordism also had the effect of reversing the dominant relationship between labour and technology (Gorz, 1976; Edwards, 1979). As Littler and Salamon (1982: 75), highlight: 'The model of production worked out by Ford to serve the mass market pre-supposed the major principles of Taylorism, but went further in the transfer of traditional skills to specialist machines.'

Thus, Fordism provided a more intensive form of Taylorist work organization and job design at a time of an expanding (international) market, leading to its dominance as the leading form of work organization in the 20th century (Lipietz, 1987).

Critical Thinking 7.1
The case of Schmidt
In Taylor's most famous experiment, he studied men shovelling pig iron. He noted that one particular man – Schimdt – finished the day's work and jogged home to finish building his own house. Taylor therefore picked Schimdt for his experiment. After restructuring the shovel and how the work was to be undertaken (eliminating all superfluous activity), Taylor told Schimdt when to shovel and when to rest. From this experiment, Taylor was able to demonstrate an increase in production per man from 12 tons to 48 tons a day – a 300 per cent increase in productivity. For this achievement, Schmidt's wages were increased from $1.15 a day to $1.85 a day – a 60 per cent increase.

Questions
1 Identify the ethical issues associated with the choice of Schimdt for this study.
2 Do you agree with Schimdt's wage increasing by 60 per cent compared with the productivity gain of 300 per cent?

The foundations of contemporary theory of job design – the sociotechnical era

The foundation underpinning scientific management-based job design was the concept of rational-economic man (Schein, 1965). The concept is based upon a belief that man will calculate actions that will result in maximum self-benefit (Birchall, 1975). As such, man will be primarily motivated by the economic incentives that provide the greatest gain. In a work context, issues such as working conditions, the environment and relationships are subsidiary to the economic rewards – see Critical Thinking 7.1.

However, a series of British studies into the issues of monotony and the work cycle in the mid-1920s by the Industrial Fatigue Research Board identified a link between social conditions and workers' mental health, productivity and autonomy (Buchanan and Huczynski, 1985; Rose, 1988). Further studies revealed that workers consistently prioritized working conditions and relationships above pay, and there was a relationship between group dynamics and monotony (Brown, 1986). The emerging evidence led this British research group, under the leadership of C. S. Myers, to be increasingly critical of the neglect of human factors in the workplace.

These studies provided the first connection between the human aspects of work and productivity, creating foundations for the ground-breaking work of Elton Mayo's group at the Harvard Business School. In the UK, Myer (1926) had noted the hostility generated among workers by scientific management work practices through their attack on skills and the effects of time and motion studies and speed-ups (Thompson and McHugh, 2002). In the USA, Sward (cited in Braverman, 1974: 148–9) notes on the introduction of these work practices at the Ford car plant that:

> They proved to be increasingly unpopular, more and more it went against the grain. And the men exposed to it began to rebel. They registered their dissatisfaction by walking out in droves … Ford admitted latter that his startling factory innovations had ushered in an outstanding labor crisis.

Rose (1988) highlights two strikes in 1911, one by bricklayers and the second at the federal munitions factory – the Watertown Arsenal – which led to a Special House Committee set up by the American House of Representatives to investigate these (scientific management) work practices in 1912, for which Taylor was a witness. As Parker and Wall (1998: 5), describe: 'The committee failed to completely condemn scientific management, concluding that it was a useful tool, but also noted that it could give managers too much power.'

The Hawthorne studies

The Hawthorne studies provided a paradigm shift in the theory of work design and organization. As Thompson and McHugh (2002) note, the significance of the Hawthorne studies lies in the engagement of social science with industry, with the studies providing the foundations of the *human relations school* of thought and management practice.

The human relations school of management emphasized the sociological and psychological aspects of work and work organization. The Hawthorne studies took place between 1924 and 1932 at the Hawthorne plant of the Western Electric Company in Chicago (Boxes 7.1 and 7.2). The Company was seen as an enlightened employer paying high wages and providing welfare facilities for its workers. However, it should be noted that the Hawthorne studies were conducted in a period when scientific management was the central focus of work organization and industrial efficiency, and they were initially run through this frame of reference exploring optimum working conditions and performance (Pratt and Bennett, 1985).

> **Box 7.1 The telephone relay study**
>
> The telephone relay study was conducted over a 5-year period and explored a variety of working conditions on a group of six women whose job it was to assemble telephone relays. Each relay consisted of around 40 parts, and the employees were paid on a group incentive basis. Changes in working conditions included the incentive scheme, rest breaks, hours of work and refreshments, as well as the withdrawal of the changes (Watson, 1995). In most cases, the employees were consulted before the changes were implemented. As Cole (1988) notes, the focus was on the differing conditions on productivity. There was no deliberate attempt at this stage to examine social relationships or employee attitudes.
>
> Productivity rose throughout the study. On the basis of this study, Mayo identified that, rather than the physical environment being the key variable in productivity, it was in fact the social aspects of the workplace. The close interest taken in the employees and their work by the researchers, the high levels of communication and high social cohesion within the group, the freedom to control and organize their own work and the more democratic style of management/supervision were seen as the critical factors in improving productivity (Pratt and Bennett, 1985; Watson, 1995). From this work, the concept of the 'Hawthorne effect' emerged.

The purpose of the research originally conducted by the company's own research group was to identify the optimum working conditions. The first studies were based on artificial light and productivity. Two groups of workers were set up, one a control group and the second to test the effect of lighting conditions on productivity. Despite varying the light in the test group, productivity increased at a similar rate in both groups (Rose, 1988). Follow-up studies revealed an increase in productivity in both groups even when the lighting level was reduced. At the time, these results greatly puzzled the researchers at Western Electric (Thompson and McHugh, 2002). What the researchers realized was that unidentified factors were at work in determining productivity (Cole, 1988). This led to a request for assistance from Australian Elton Mayo and his colleagues at the Harvard Business School, who led the research from 1927 onwards.

> **Box 7.2 The bank wiring room**
>
> The bank wiring room was the site of the second major investigation associated with the Hawthorne studies; this focused on a group of 14 metal workers separated from the main work group. The most important observation that came from this study was how the group developed its own cohesive rules, value system and dynamics, separate from those of the organization. This value system included restricting production, effectively negating the organization's wage–incentive system and informally sanctioning workers who did not adopt these values (Cole, 1988).
>
> The key outcomes for management from this study were to see individuals and the organizations of work in the context of the work groups, and not in isolation. This reinforced the increasing importance of Schein's social man over economic man in terms of reward systems. As Cole (1988) points out, intrinsic factors such as group membership are more important than extrinsic rewards, and, as such, groups in the workplace exercise a strong influence over employees. These findings reinforced the significance of social aspects of work and, more importantly, the need for management to account for social relationships and to consider these issues when developing work design and organizational practices congruent with organizational goals.

The impact of the Hawthorne studies

Although the Hawthorne studies have been criticized at a variety of levels in terms of their methodology, assumptions and interpretations, these studies, as Thompson and McHugh (2002) identify, occupy a pivotal place in organizational and management theory. The studies recognized the relationship between the social and technical aspects of work organization, and provided the first evidence that productivity was to a large extent dependent on social relationships. They also provided a countercritique of scientific management and economic man and their neglect of human factors in the workplace (Rose, 1988; Thompson and McHugh, 2002). The studies laid the foundations for the human relations school of management and further research on the social and psychological aspects of work (Pratt and Bennett, 1985). In addition, they introduced the concept of social man into the mainstream context of the work relationship, highlighting the power that these relationships had over workers through the development of informal groups establishing their own values and norms outside the formal organization.

These findings provided the basis for management to recognize the importance of these informal groups and look to work with them, by integrating them into organizational goals and strategies. As Thompson and McHugh (2002) argue, this laid the foundations for engaging in participation and communication with employees on workplace issues, and acted as a catalyst for the development of managers with the appropriate skills to manage in such an environment.

Contemporary theory of job and work design – the human relations school

The human relations school began what Parker and Wall (1998) describe as the heyday of job and work design (spanning the 1940s through to the 1980s), in terms of both theory and practice. Building on the work of Mayo and his colleagues, the first of these advances came with the development of the sociotechnical systems approach. The sociotechnical approach originated at the Tavistock Institute of Human Relations in London. The Institute was founded in 1947 as an agency for psychologists to disseminate to industry the expertise they had accumulated during the war (Rose, 1988).

The key features of the sociotechnical approach were that organizations should be viewed as a combination of technical elements and social networks (Warr, 1987). From this perspective, the sociotechnical system approach acts to find the optimum relationship, or what we would term today the 'best fit', between the social and technical components of the organization. This therefore requires both systems to be designed in parallel to take account of each other (Watson, 1995; Parker and Wall, 1998). The importance of this approach lies therefore in its comprehensive overview and joint optimization of the two systems to best attain the organization's goals (Warr, 1987).

It is important to note that, because of the wide range of factors to consider, the sociotechnical approach provides a framework of values to understand the organization, rather than a prescriptive map of how to undertake the organization of these systems (Buchanan and Huczynski, 1985; Warr, 1987). A further critical legacy of the sociotechnical approach is that, in contrast to the previous research on the organization of work and job design, the focus was on teamwork (Parker and Wall, 1998). From this frame of reference, the key innovation was the development of work organization around autonomous and semi-autonomous work groups (Passmore, 1998). This meant that work groups could decide their own methods of work (minimal specification) and handle as many of the operational issues encountered as possible (Parker and Wall, 1998).

Watson (1995) states that the impact of the Tavistock studies into job design were among the most theoretically sophisticated. The two most famous studies of the Tavistock Institute of Human Relations were the Durham mining studies of longwall coal mining in north-east England, and that on the Ahmedabad knitting mills in north-west India (Boxes 7.3 and 7.4).

Box 7.3 The longwall studies

In post-World War II Britain, a nationalization of major industries, including the coal mining sector, was taking place. A major feature of this process was the modernization of these industries. In coal mining, the focus was on implementing modern technological processes to improve productivity. The actual result of the introduction of new technology was decreased productivity and increased disputation, absenteeism and accidents. This was the catalyst for researchers from the Tavistock Institute – Trist and Bamforth – to be invited to help.

Traditional work practices in the coal mine revolved around small (self-selected) teams of up to eight men working a small section of the coal face. The nature of the work required these teams to have a multitude of skills to cut and load the coal and prop the roof (Pratt and Bennett, 1985). This system of work was known as the 'shortwall' method (Cole, 1988). Because of the dangerous conditions, the miners relied extensively on the skills of each group member. Group bonds extended to families: should a group member be injured or killed, his family was often supported (financially and socially) by the group (Pratt and Bennett, 1985). The team also regulated the pace of work, and rewards were group-based (Buchanan and Huczynski, 1985; Cole, 1988).

With technological modernization, the organization of the work in the mine moved from the 'shortwall' to 'longwall' method. In the longwall model of work organization, small groups were replaced by three shifts of miners of between 40 and 80 men working along a coalface up to 150 m in length (Pratt and Bennett, 1985). Each shift concentrated on one specialist task in the production cycle (Buchanan and Huczynski, 1985). As Cole (1988) and Rose (1988), note, the new system was effectively a mass-production system requiring a high degree of job specialization and simplification. The consequences of the new system were the physical, social and psychological isolation of the miners and the breakdown of the highly integrated social structures (developed by the small groups). These changes resulted in a decrease in productivity, an increase in industrial conflict, pay disputes, absenteeism, accidents and the emergence of previously unknown pilfering (Pratt and Bennett, 1985; Cole, 1988).

Trist and Bamforth identified the changes in work organization and job design as the source of the problem (Buchanan and Huczynski, 1985). A 'composite longwall' method was adopted, which maintained the new technology but organized the work around self-selected teams responsible for all the tasks (Pratt and Bennett, 1985). Immediate outcomes included increased productivity, decreased absenteeism and fewer accidents (Argyle, 1989).

> **Box 7.4 The Ahmedabad knitting mills**
>
> The second major study was carried out by A. K. Rice in the Calico knitting mills of Ahmedabad in northern India, where the introduction of automated looms had not increased production. Rice suggested the introduction of small work groups that would be responsible for the productivity of a cluster of looms as well as their maintenance (Sofer, 1972). The workers took up the idea, developing their own scheme based around self-selected groups of seven men responsible for 64 looms.
>
> Results from the study indicated that, as a result of the new work organization, productivity rose by 21 per cent, and the amount of damaged cloth (wastage) was reduced by 59 per cent – both outcomes were reflected in the workers' wages (Argyle, 1989). The reasons put forward for the success of this case study were the development of small cohesive work groups and the increased complexity of the work (Argyle, 1989). As Rice's colleague noted in regard to outside pressure for the workers to conform to the traditional model of work organization:
>
> > The workers stuck to a system that was very largely their own creation and that enabled them to enjoy a quality of work–life as well as a level of income that they had not previously known. (Trist, 1973: 59)

The impact of the sociotechnical research

The Tavistock research demonstrated the importance of the relationship between the social and psychological aspects of work and the technical side, in particular that changes in the organization of work cannot be undertaken without consideration of the social-technical balance. The acceptance of this principle provided a paradigm shift in how work organization and job design should be undertaken at both the individual and the group level (Pratt and Bennett, 1985; Watson, 1995). The key sociotechnical findings were summarised by Buchanan as in Figure 7.1.

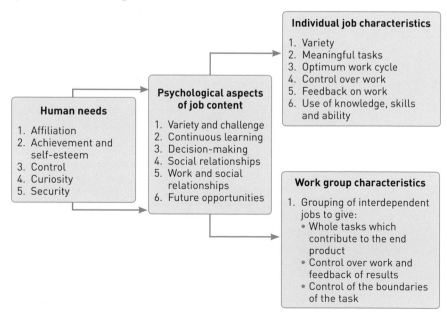

Figure 7.1 The work organization approach to job design
Source: Adapted from Buchanan (1979: 112)

Contemporary theory of job design – the neo-human relations or motivational theorists

The sociotechnical research primarily developing out of the Tavistock Institute provided the foundation for behavioural psychology research in the workplace (also known as the *neo-human relations school*), particularly in the field of motivation (Bendix, 1963; Thompson and McHugh, 2002). The motivational theorists developed the concept of social man, further advocating the model of 'self-actualizing' man (Schein, 1965). In other words, work has to fulfil individuals' inherent needs to use their skills and capacity to realize their own potential (Birchall, 1975).

From a job and work design perspective, the notion of organizing work to release employees' potential became a powerful concept and continued to challenge the mechanistic perspective of designing jobs (Watson, 1995; Thompson and McHugh, 2002). The origin and essence of the 'motivational' perspective can be found in the work of Fredrick Herzberg, Douglas McGregor and Abraham Maslow.

Maslow's hierarchy of needs

Abraham Maslow, an American psychologist, proposed that people need to satisfy a hierarchy of five sets of genetic or instinctive needs (Box 7.5). Maslow argued that when a person satisfies most of one need, he or she moves to seek satisfaction at the next level up. In striving for these needs, the goals are seen as attainable and can therefore prove to be powerful motivators, eventually leading to self-actualization. However, a failure to achieve the next level in the set of needs can result in frustration and pathological symptoms (Rose, 1988).

Box 7.5 Abraham Maslow – the hierarchy of needs

☐ Physiological needs – for survival, such as food and water
☐ Safety needs – shelter and security
☐ Love needs – relationships and affection
☐ Esteem needs – achievement, recognition, reputation and appreciation, based on capability and respect
☐ Self-actualization needs – the development of capabilities to their fullest potential

   In addition, Maslow also identified two further criteria to enhance and maintain self-actualization:

☐ Freedom of inquiry and expression needs – for social conditions that permit free speech and encourage justice and fairness
☐ The need to know and to understand – to gain insight and knowledge to satisfy curiosity and enable continued learning

Source: Adapted from Buchanan and Huczynski (1985: 52)

Obviously, the first two needs – physiological and safety – are required to live, with the second two – love and esteem – providing a sense of usefulness and belonging (Buchanan and Huczynski, 1985). The ultimate step is to reach self-actualization where one achieves one's potential.

Maslow's theory provided an important platform for understanding the motivational drives of individuals. This general theory was adopted by researchers of work organizations and managers, although it was not specifically developed for the workplace, as is often assumed. Maslow qualified this general theory by acknowledging the role and impact of external factors such as the organization and its culture on the individual (Rose, 1988). In addition, Maslow argued that the hierarchy was true for most people but could vary (Pratt and Bennett, 1985).

Subsequent research has been inconclusive regarding the hierarchy. Issues associated with the measurement of satisfaction and the 'tipping point' at which an individual moves to the next stage are unique to each person. In addition, some have suggested that individual needs are so complex and different that the issues of motivation and job satisfaction may be too varied to be generalized (Parker and Wall, 1998). This said, Buchanan and Huczynski (1985) argue that Maslow's theory is a social philosophy in which we can find enough evidence that some individuals pursue this hierarchy of needs. Importantly, the theory draws attention to the different motivations that influence people.

Herzberg's motivation–hygiene theory

Fredrick Herzberg's motivation–hygiene or two-factor theory builds on Maslow's research on intrinsic motivation and, importantly, views this from a workplace perspective. Based on what employees found enjoyable or made them feel good at work and what was bad about work, Herzberg identified two groups of factors, which he coined satisfiers or motivation factors, and hygiene factors. He further refined these paradigms into content- and context-based work issues. The *content-based or motivator* factors were intrinsic job satisfaction issues that gave the employee a sense of well-being; these were:

☐ achievement
☐ autonomy
☐ recognition
☐ responsibility
☐ the work itself.

The *context-based or hygiene factors* were extrinsic issues that could be neutral issues or cause job dissatisfaction, and included:

☐ company policies and administration
☐ supervision
☐ salary
☐ interpersonal relationships
☐ working conditions.

The motivation (intrinsic) factors relate closely to Maslow's higher levels needs, whereas the hygiene factors satisfy only Maslow's lower level needs. From a work perspective, Herzberg's research focused on building facets of motivation into job and work design in order to increase performance. From a practical perspective, this meant that jobs needed to be enlarged and more challenging, as well as to provide a degree of autonomous decision-making (Watson, 1995). Herzberg advocated this as *job enrichment*, in which work and job design deliberately included more complex and more responsible tasks as a way to engage employees' knowledge, skill and abilities (Brown, 1986). This also provided further arguments against the development of scientific management-based job design. Herzberg developed six applications of '*vertical*' loading factors, as these job enrichment features became known:

- ☐ Remove control
- ☐ Increase accountability
- ☐ Create natural work units
- ☐ Provide direct feedback
- ☐ Introduce new tasks
- ☐ Allocate special assignments.

(Buchanan and Huczynski, 1985).

Initially, Herzberg's theory had a positive impact on management thinking and enlightened managers (Brown, 1986). However, the study upon which the research was based has been the focus of criticism. The original study was based on the responses of 203 professional engineers and accountants in Pittsburg, which reflected a very narrow (and privileged) section of US society in the 1950s. Research replicating Herzberg's study using alternate methodologies has failed to confirm the findings of the study, suggesting that the theory is 'method-bound' (Pratt and Bennett, 1985). The main criticism, however, is concerned with Herzberg's assertion that motivation and hygiene factors are mutually exclusive. The situation is today generally seen as being more complex and less clearly delineated. But despite these criticisms, Herzberg's theory is widely credited with directing the focus of research and management practice towards the importance of intrinsic motivation (Pratt and Bennett, 1985).

McGregor's theory X and theory Y

Douglas McGregor's theory X and theory Y is a useful theory to draw together research on the organization of work in the first half of the 20th century. The two assumptions about work reflect the dominant paradigms of the time: the mechanistic system, theory X, and the sociotechnical system, theory Y (Box 7.6).

The assumptions of theory X about employees and how they should be managed reflects the scientific management paradigm that workers need controlling and are focused on extrinsic rewards (Schein's rational-economic man). As Watson (1995) notes, this approach in effect creates the culture and behaviour that management seeks to avoid. In contrast, theory Y was more consistent with the sociological and psychological research of the time, in which employees preferred discretion and autonomy in work that provided more opportunities to be creative (Schein's self-actualizing man).

7

> **Box 7.6** The key features of McGregor's theory X and theory Y
>
> **Theory X**
>
> ☐ Employees have an inherent dislike for work and will avoid it wherever possible
> ☐ Employees must be coerced, directed and threatened with sanctions in order to get them to cooperate
> ☐ Employees are passive, lack initiative and require direction
>
> **Theory Y**
>
> ☐ Work is a natural aspect of life
> ☐ Employees seek opportunities to be creative and assume responsibility
> ☐ Commitment and the achievement of objectives is a function of the intrinsic rewards associated with achievement

Although McGregor's theory was, like many of the theories of the sociotechnical period, influential among managers, he and others have been criticized from a labour process perspective for not challenging the inherent power relationships in the workplace and the inbuilt conflicts between the interests of management and employees. The focus of research from the neo-human relations school was the improvement of work organization and satisfaction only where it enhanced productivity (Brown, 1986). However, the key conclusions that can be drawn from the motivational research is that work needs to be psychologically empowering in order to achieve intrinsic motivation leading to enhanced performance at work and increased productivity (Cordery and Parker, 2007). Underpinning this is work organization designed to satisfy the psychological needs of autonomy, competence and relatedness (Ryan and Deci, 2000).

Parker and Wall (1998) distilled a set of work design criteria from the work of motivational systems research and sociotechnical research, which included the ability to:

☐ arrange work in a way that allows individual employees to influence their own work method and pace;
☐ where possible combine independent tasks into jobs;
☐ group tasks into meaningful jobs that allow for an overview and understanding of the work process as a whole, and as part of the wider organizational objectives;
☐ provide a sufficient variety of tasks within a job, including tasks that offer a degree of employee responsibility, which makes use of the skills and knowledge valued by the individual;
☐ arrange work to enable it to be undertaken in the normal work time allotted, so as not to create work–life balance tensions;
☐ provide opportunities for employees to achieve the (extrinsic or intrinsic) outcomes they value;
☐ ensure feedback is communicated promptly and efficiently to employees on their performance from both a supervisor and a task perspective;
☐ provide internal and external customer feedback directly to employees;
☐ provide employees with the information they need to make decisions.

Hackman and Oldham's job characteristic model

The development of psychological perspectives of work organization, the under-standing of group dynamics and the development of job enrichment by the neo- and human relations school were combined in the theory and framework of Hackman and Oldham's job characteristic model (JCM) and its accompanying measurement instrument – the Job Diagnosis Survey. The model defined five core job characteristics that relate to employee motivation and satisfaction (Parker and Wall, 1998):

1 *Skill variety* – the degree to which the job requires different skills.
2 *Task identity* – the degree to which the job involves completing a whole identi-fiable piece of work rather than simply a part of it.
3 *Task significance* – the extent to which the job has an impact on other people, either inside or outside the organization.
4 *Autonomy* – the extent to which the job allows job-holders to exercise choice and discretion in their work.
5 *Feedback from the job* – the extent to which the job itself (as opposed to other people) – provides job-holders with information on their performance.

The JCM has proved to be the most enduring of the theoretical approaches to job and work design, drawing on key aspects of earlier research (Figure 7.2). However, it is not without its critics. Findings using the JCM have been inconsistent, with the relationship between the core characteristics and the outcome variables often

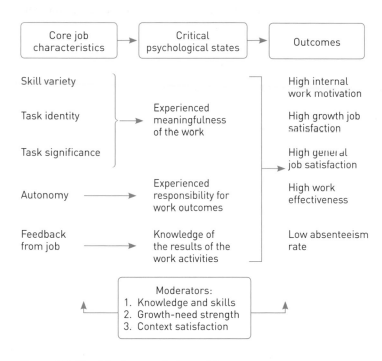

Figure 7.2 The job characteristic model
Source: Oldham (1996)

being cited as difficult to replicate (Parker and Wall, 1998). But, in acknowledging this, Parker and Wall (1998: 14–15) do make the important point that:

> Given the problems, it is clear that all the detailed predictions of the job characteristic model have not stood up to empirical test. Nonetheless, this does not undermine its usefulness … On the whole, the job characteristic model clearly has some concurrent and predictive value, even though it is incorrect in its finer detail.

Theory to practice: job design in the 'long boom'

With the end of World War II and the development of a period of stable economic growth (which became known as the 'long boom'), the developments in understanding employees in the workplace became more important in increasingly 'tight' labour markets. This lack of labour forced employers to seriously address issues of dissatisfaction and alienation in the workplace – in other words, employees' lack of relationship with, and the attachment and self-fulfilment being demanded from, their work.

The first practical attempts at addressing the more oppressive aspects of scientific management work patterns were through job rotation and job enlargement. Job rotation involves moving employees from one job to another at regular intervals. The benefits were seen as increasing the variety of tasks, reducing boredom and increasing the flexibility of the workforce (Parker and Wall, 1998). As with scientific management, the automobile industry was at the vanguard of these new work practices: at Renault's Le Mans factory, employees moved from job to job every hour (Pratt and Bennett, 1985).

Job enlargement involves widening the duties of employees by adding new tasks that broaden the skills required and reduce overspecialization and monotony. In some situations, this can mean the enlargement of tasks to enable the employee to complete the whole job (Parker and Wall, 1998). An example of this was Philips factory in Scotland, which built heaters on a traditional production line. After major disputes and industrial unrest, and in consultation with the trade unions, work was reorganized to allow employees to build complete heaters. Research identified increased job satisfaction, productivity increases of 10 per cent and a reduction in defect rates of 50 per cent (Thornley and Valantine, 1975).

Although both job rotation and job enlargement can be seen to alleviate the worst excesses of mechanistic job design, they have been criticized for the lack of vertical task integration and decision-making, which remains solely in the hands of management. As such, job rotation and job enlargement do not increase the quality or discretion of the work. Indeed, this 'horizontal' loading approach to job design can at best be seen as a short-term measure. As Child (1984: 34) notes:

> To paraphrase Herzberg, adding one Mickey Mouse job to another does not make any more than two Mickey Mouse jobs. In other words, simply adding specialized, repetitive, routine and dreary tasks to one another, or rotating around these, is not likely to create a job that is satisfying or motivating.

Job enrichment developed out of the neo-human relations school of research. In contrast to both job rotation and job enlargement, job enrichment introduces vertical integration into the organization of work. The key aspects of job enrichment are to increase control and discretion into the work environment. This can include how the work is undertaken, quality inspection and maintenance, processes formerly undertaken by front-line supervisors (Child, 1984). Job enrichment emphasizes the redesign of work to increase the individual's satisfaction by focusing on intrinsic needs such as responsibility, recognition and personal growth (Cole, 1988). These critical psychological criteria clearly correlate with Hackman and Oldham's JCM, with its emphasis on meaningful, responsible work with knowledge of its results.

The many examples of job enrichment (both blue collar and white collar) have all emphasized the role of intrinsic satisfaction as a key to job satisfaction (Birchall, 1975; Buchanan and Huczynski, 1985). However, as Child (1984) points out, the focus on the individual needs to be put into the context of the workplace, where jobs are increasingly part of an interdependent cluster forming work groups. As the work of the human relations school has highlighted, the work group can be critical in the determination of successful work design. As such, the design of work needs to be seen in relation to the work group as the platform of work design. Therefore, restructuring work at the group level increasingly becomes the level at which potentially the most effective work redesign will take place.

The work group is also seen as the natural focus for work redesign due to the increased complexity and integration of work. A group approach also offers more scope for individual differences and skills, as well as a natural platform for disseminating knowledge (Wall et al., 1986). In a group context, discretion over a variety of work decisions can fall within the realms of the group – from, for example, decisions about the day-to-day organization of the work, to dealing with buyers and suppliers (Mathews, 1989; Parker and Wall, 1998). This approach also fits with Schein's final development of the individual's motivation – complex man – a person in whom motivation is complex and variable, and changes over time owing to shifting needs, experiences and relationships (Birchall, 1975). The group work environment thus has the potential to provide for these changing needs and the social context in which to achieve individual goals.

Some of the most significant and well-documented studies of work design have emerged out of group-based job design. Of these, the job design carried out by Volvo in the mid-1970s at its then new car manufacturing plant is probably the most famous. Work in the Kalmar plant was designed for groups of 15–20 employees to assemble major car components. Although management determined the output, how the work was conducted was at the discretion of the group (Pratt and Bennett, 1985). Despite initial problems, research by the Swedish government found productivity, quality and job satisfaction to be higher than in traditionally laid out plants (Matthews, 1989).

Similarly, at Air Canada, teams were given the responsibility of determining when and how to replace aircraft windows. Productivity doubled, and supervisory time dropped by 75 per cent (Child, 1984). Other well-documented case studies included Saab, Philips, Shell, ICL, AT&T Xerox and Levi Strauss. However, as noted in the Volvo case, management discretion over work outputs remained.

As Kelly and Clegg (1981) have noted, by the late 1970s and despite the high-profile case studies of Volvo and Saab, the scale, scope and impact of job design had been limited. The lack of impact of job and work design can be linked to a variety of issues including a resistant organizational culture and the development of job design being limited to a particular department or sector of the organization, but not translated to other areas of the organization. This is an important point to note as, for example, Volvo's approach at Kalmar was undertaken at a 'greenfield' site location where no previous culture or work practices existed, so new patterns of work could be far more effectively implemented.

Other factors can be a lack of understanding of the problem, including misdiagnosis, which may lead to the failure of job design. This can be linked to the lack of management skills in understanding, diagnosing and developing appropriate strategies for change management and integrative job design. In addition, the impact of job design may, by its very nature, result in redundancies or redeployment, causing workplace stress and potential trade union resistance. In addition, the simple fact is that job design or redesign is not for all workers. Many workers may simply see work through Schein's lens of rational-economic man and view work as an instrument for other needs. Indeed, Goldthorpe's classic study of affluent workers in the British car industry in the 1950s illustrates exactly this point (see Goldthorpe, 1966).

Possibly the most important factor underpinning all of these points was, however, the continuation of the 'long boom', which provided little incentive to alter practices. But this factor was about to change.

Contemporary theory of job and work design – the concertive era

Concertive work systems are team patterns of work organization that are designed to maximize the employee's effectiveness in pursuing organizational goals (Cordery and Parker, 2007). It was not until the early 1980s that management thinking and commitment to the organization of work significantly changed. As with the implementation of the Fordist mode of work organization, these changes were driven by the issues of sustained competitive advantage (Boxall and Purcell, 2011), as the 'oil shocks' of the 1970s brought to an end the era of the long boom, which was underpinned by certainty in markets and employment.

The emergence of quality as an issue in the late 1970s can be seen as one catalyst for change in the early 1980s, with its links to the success and increasing dominance of Japanese organizations in all the major world markets. Underpinning the competitiveness of these organizations was the high value placed on the management of quality (via quality circles teams) as a key feature of the production process. The irony in the increasing attention given in Anglo-

American countries to quality as a means of competitive advantage was the fact that the concept of quality had had its origins in the USA in the 1920s and was imported to Japan from the USA after World War II, under the guidance of luminaries such as Dr E. W. Deming and, later, Dr Joseph M. Juran (Brewster et al., 2003). Through the concept of total quality management (TQM), quality became an issue for all members of the organization. Echoing the arguments of the sociotechnical and psychological perspectives of work organization, Hill (1991, p. 197) states:

> [TQM] seeks to involve employees from shopfloor to senior management, in a quality improvement culture. It is not just tacked on, so the argument runs, but promises a fundamental overhaul of the labour process.

The fundamental change that TQM brings to organizations is cultural, which Tuckman (1995) asserts can only be achieved with a fundamental review of work patterns and practices. Legge (1995) takes this further by arguing that TQM requires the development of interdepartmental and crossfunctional project teams, and enlisting of the commitment of 'empowered' workers, organized into teams and participating in decision-making.

TQM therefore focuses on the organizational culture, structure and management of human resources to develop team-based work design. At an organizational level, management's focus is on delayering and simplifying the organizational processes, so that decision-making can be pushed down the organization in order to facilitate team-based work and more open communication (Hill, 1995). These tenets are central to empowering employees collectively to become responsible for the quality of their work. Supporting these changes is the need to develop a participative management style based on a relationship of consensus and trust through increased autonomy and self-direction if employees are to embrace these organizational goals (Legge, 1995; Tuckman, 1995; Wilkinson et al., 1998).

With the increasing complexity and pace of work, and the growing volatility in markets since the 'long boom', the focus has continued on developing work organization around highly integrated work teams. Reflecting the underlying philosophy of the sociotechnical theorists, as well as the work of Hackman and Oldham (1976, 1980) and Oldham (1996), at the core of these teams lie the semi-autonomous work groups or 'high-involvement work systems' (HIWSs); advanced developments in work design see these teams becoming 'self-designing' (Hackman, 1987) or 'self-leading' (Manz, 1992).

What is significant about this is that these self-managed teams encompass (vertical) work tasks that would traditionally be seen as functions of supervisors and middle management (Cordery and Parker, 2007). These teams are increasingly having an influence over strategic decisions in terms of what the group actually does and why, rather than just how they undertake the work (Parker and Wall, 1998). Within the team, work is allocated to multiskilled team members as whole tasks. These team members have substantial discretion over how the work is organized (Cordery and Parker, 2007). The components of HIWSs of work design has been articulated by Vanderberg et al. (1999) – see Figure 7.3 – whose work builds on Lawler's (1986) model of high involvement.

This in turn is underpinned by issues associated with the dissemination of power, information, reward and knowledge in the workplace (Boxall and Purcell, 2011).

Figure 7.3 Conceptual model of high-involvement work systems.
Source: Adapted from Vanderberg et al. (1999: 307)

Although evidence of the success of HIWSs has been found in studies of the steelmaking, electronics and automobile industries (Boxall and Purcell, 2011), the development of these work patterns and practices brings with it its own demands. For example, research identifies that the human resource implications of these initiatives are also a critical dimension for success. As Lepak and Snell (1997, 2007) note, human resource systems need to reflect a high-commitment philosophy. In an environment characterized by continuous change and increased competition, where downsizing and offshoring are always options, there needs to be a fit between human resource policies and practices to ensure the development of a relationship of high trust and commitment between employees and management (Brewster et al., 2003).

Middle management can potentially become the strongest advocate of HIWSs. However, the changes that these work practices bring require significant resources to be focused on management training and development in order to ensure a successful transition for these leaders from a role as controller to one as coach or facilitator. Without this, management may resist these changes as they can be seen as a threat associated with a loss of expert power (Marchington, 1995; Wilkinson et al., 1997). Klein (1984) identifies the issues of job security and loss of status as being central to opposition on the part of supervisors to change, as well as, to a lesser extent, a lack of training, resources and belief in their own ability to undertake such a change programme. These findings are also supported by research by Marchington (1995).

In an environment where job insecurity is increasing while promotion opportunities are decreasing, the development of empowerment can lead to increased stress (Delbridge, 2005) and to what Jackson et al. (1996) describe as 'career defense' on the part of lower and middle management. These and industry-specific issues can result in significant variations across industries imple-menting HIWSs (Appleyard and Brown, 2001; Kalleberg et al., 2006). These points are reflected in research indicating that the effects of HIWSs on organizational profitability are still unclear (Cappelli and Neumark, 2001; Way, 2002).

Conclusion

Job and work design in the 21st century – back to the future or forward to the past?

With the emergence of an increasingly complex and competitive global economy, many organizations have embraced new work patterns and practices to sustain their competitiveness. Underpinning these work patterns are the development of sophisticated human resource management strategies. These strategies have the potential to develop high-quality, high-involvement work environments. Conversely, the increasingly deregulated nature of work in AMEs can result in a negative work environment with little opportunity for employees to have a say in the work they do or how they do it. This can create a climate of oppression and control, a situation identified by Guest (1995) as the 'black hole human resource management scenario'.

For example, the archetypal workplaces of the 21st century – call centres – have been variously been described as electronic sweatshops and dungeons with telephones (Kinnie et al., 2000; Deery and Kinnie, 2002). Equally, SalesForce, a call centre based in Melbourne, has been awarded best employer in Australia, which suggests that there is scope for significant opportunities to develop work design policies and practices even in highly structured work environments.

In manufacturing, where traditional scientific management practices of standardization and cost minimization remain highly favoured, industrialists such as Ricardo Semler and his ship component company, Semco, have led the way in job and work design strategies, with high-involvement teams becoming 'self-designing' and 'self-leading'. These teams have the ability to hire and fire their own bosses and peers, set their own budgets and determine how they organize their work and when they do it. These examples and contemporary research reflect the fact that well-thought-out job design strategies can increase employee involvement. As such, it can have a positive impact on organizational performance from an attraction and retention perspective, where highly skilled employees are likely to remain engaged with and committed to the organization for a longer period of time; this will, in turn, be likely to result in enhanced productivity of the organization's key assets – its people.

Returning to the quote at the start of this chapter by Parker and Wall (1998) on the excitement and dangers of developing work organization in a highly deregulated knowledge-based global market, it is worth reflecting, as we acknowledge the 100th anniversary of the first Model T Ford rolling off the first production line in 1908, that although people working in call centres might not see a significant difference in work, the production line has now become mental rather than physical. On the other hand, people working in environment such as that developed by Riccardo Semler at Semco appear to have taken on the ideas of the sociotechnical, motivational and concertive theorists and developed a truly post-Fordist work environment. The next 100 years may provide an increasing number of paradoxical situations in the way work systems are organized.

For discussion and revision

Questions

1 Why has the concept of job design proved to be attractive to both employers and employees?

2 Explain the 'Hawthorne effect'.

3 Despite the criticisms and research, why does the mechanistic approach remain a dominant force in work design today?

4 What are the potential issues that organizations have to deal with when developing HIWSs?

5 How is work design evolving in the early 21st century? Explain some of the key features?

6 Considering what we know today about job satisfaction and work design, do you think it is ethical for employers to continue to develop work patterns and practices along Taylorist/Fordist lines?

Further reading

Books

Boxall, P., Purcell, J. and Wright, P. (2007) *The Oxford Handbook of Human Resource Management: A Critical Text*. Oxford: Oxford University Press.

This book provides an analysis of HIWSs within the context of human resource management policies and practices.

Holman, D., Wall, T., Clegg, C., Sparrow, P. and Howard, A. (2004) *Essentials of the New Workplace*. New York: Wiley.

This book provides a variety of perspectives from which to explore the development of work design.

Parker, S. and Wall, T. (1998) *Job and Work Design: Organizing Work to Promote Well-Being and Effectiveness*. Thousand Oaks, CA: Sage.

A definitive review of the area of work design by two leading experts.

Thompson, P. and McHugh, D. (2002) *Work Organisation: A Critical Introduction* (3rd edn). London: Macmillan Business.

A critical text exploring a variety of issues in the organization of work.

Journals

The following are articles illustrating contemporary aspects of work organization.

Campion, M. A., Mumford, M. M., Morgeson, P. and Nahrgang, D. (2005) Work design, eight obstacles and opportunities. *Human Resource Management*, 44(4): 367–90.

Foss, N. J., Minbaeva, T. P, and Reinholt, M. (2009) Encouraging knowledge sharing among employees: how job design matters. *Human Resource Management*, 48(6): 871–93.

Lantz, A. and Brav, A. (2007) Job design for learning in work groups. *Journal of Workplace Learning*, 19(5): 269–85.

Torraco, R. J. (2005) Work design theory: a review and critique with implications for human resource development. *Human Resource Development Quarterly*, 16(1): 85–109.

7

Case Study Job design at TechCo

The rapid development of the information technology industry has resulted in significant skill shortages in many AMEs. In Australia, the ability to develop and retain key IT staff is a major human resource management issue. The alternative for many organizations is the loss of key staff, intellectual capital and market share. This case study examines human resources policies and practices developed around strategies of innovative work organization and job design to first retain, and second attract key IT staff.

TechCo is a leading supplier of networking IT, providing support applications for the development of e-business and employing over 200 staff in offices in all Australia's major cities . TechCo identified the issue of attracting and retaining its IT staff as a major problem. Whereas the average turnover was high in this sector – at around 10 per cent – TechCo was experiencing a turnover of over 15 per cent. After surveying their staff, the major finding linked to developing and retaining the company's key talent was the understanding that employees required a challenging and stimulating work environment in which to develop their skills.

A clear division emerged from a survey of the requirements of TechCo's IT staff. They were looking to develop their skills as either (internal) project managers or (external) self-employed contractors. The key challenge for TechCo was that, as a small to medium-sized company, it was not able to provide a continuous range of project management roles in house and could not afford to lose employees who wanted to move into contracting. The key paradigm shift for TechCo to address the critical issue was to see itself as part of a network with its customers and suppliers. In doing so, it increased its opportunities to provide its workforce with a variety of work design opportunities.

In response to the project management problem, TechCo developed a partnering programme with its network of distributors and customers. This approach had the dual effect of providing partners with the appropriately skilled staff to project-manage on site, at the same time providing these staff with ongoing (higher order) career and skill development. From an organizational perspective, it also allowed for the growth and retention of knowledge on the part of these core knowledge workers, while enhancing the skills and ability of this critical human resource.

For those employees wanting to become independent contractors, TechCo embraced this by helping them set up autonomously as contractors and then contracting their services back to the organization. The employee is thus guaranteed work, and TechCo enables these employees to remain working for the organization without the on-costs associated with full-time employees. As noted above, the organization restructured its approach to the organization of work in order to facilitate the development of these new work patterns and practices. The success of these work design strategies is reflected in the turnover of IT staff – down from 15 per cent to around 5 per cent.

The achievements of this programme have resulted in the organization including it as a strategy in its recruitment and selection process. Specifically, TechCo identifies people with the appropriate skills in business and management who are looking for knowledge and skill development to enhance their career. In particular, TechCo has identified a series of high-performance competencies that can deliver success at entry-level positions. These include customer service, problem-solving, communication skills, teamworking and project management. In terms of the developmental side of this approach, TechCo has initiated management learning and development programmes that provide more senior IT staff with the skills to advance their career paths into middle- and senior-level management. As one manager noted:

> IT professionals need to have business, communication and leadership skills in order to fully understand their clients' mission statements and the role technology plays in meeting corporate goals and objectives. As an industry, we need to do a better job of teaching our people these skills because they are the fundamental building blocks for successful organizations. Those who ignore them are likely to fail.

Source: Adapted from Holland et al., 2002

Question

1 Critically analyse the case of TechCo, identifying the key features that makes the company's approach to job and work design so successful.

References

Appleyard, M. and Brown, C. (2001) Employment practices and semiconductor manufacturing performance. *Industrial Relations*, 40(3): 436–71.

Argyle, M. (1989) *The Social Psychology of Work*. London: Penguin.

Barnes, A. (2004) Dairies, dunnies and disciple: resistance and accommodation to monitoring in call centres. *Labour and Industry*, 13(3): 127–38.

Bendix, R. (1963) *Work and Authority in Industry*. New York: Harper Row.

Berg, M. (1985) *The Age of Manufactures 1700–1820*. London: Fontana.

Birchall, D. (1975) *Job Design*. Essex: Gower Press.

Boxall, P. and Purcell, J. (2011) *Strategy and Human Resource Management* (3rd edn). Basingstoke: Palgrave Macmillan.

Braverman, H. (1974) *Labor and Monopoly Capital*. New York: Monthly Review Press.

Brewster, C., Carey, L., Dowling, P., Grobler, P., Holland, P. and Warnich, S. (2003) *Contemporary Issues in Human Resource Management: Gaining a Competitive Advantage*. Oxford: Oxford University Press.

Brown, J. A. C. (1986) *The Social Psychology of Industry*. London: Penguin.

Buchanan, D. A. (1979) *The Development of Job Design Theories and Techniques*. Farnborough: Saxon House.

Buchanan, D. A. and Huczynski, A. A. (1985) *Organizational Behaviour*. Upper Saddle River, NJ: Prentice Hall.

Cappelli, P. and Neumark, D. (2001) Do 'high performance' work practices improve established level outcomes? *Industrial and Labor Relations Review*, 54(4): 737–76.

Chandler, A. (1977) *The Visible Hand*. Cambridge, MA: Harvard University Press.

Child, J. (1984) *Organization: A Guide to Problems and Practice* (2nd edn). London: Harper & Row.

Cole, G. A. (1988) *Personnel Management: Theory and Practice*. London: DP Publications.

Connell, J. and Harvey, H. (2004) Call centres and labour turnover: do HRM practices make a difference? *International Employment Relations Review*, 10(2): 49–66.

Cordery, J. and Parker, S. (2007) Work organisation. In Boxall, P. Purcell, J. and Wright, P. (eds), *The Oxford Handbook of Human Resource Management: A Critical Text*. Oxford: Oxford University Press, pp. 187–209.

Deery, S. and Kinnie, N. (2002) Call centres and beyond: a thematic evaluation. *Human Resource Management Journal*, 12(2): 2–13.

Delbridge, R. (2005) Workers under lean manufacturing. In Holman, D., Wall, T., Clegg, C. Sparrow, P. and Howard, A. (eds), *Essentials of the New Workplace*. New York: Wiley, pp. 15–32.

Drucker, P. (1998) *Knowledge Management*. Boston: Harvard Business School Press.

Edwards, P. K. (1979) *Contested Terrain*. London: Heinemann.

Goldthorpe, J. D. (1966) Attitudes and behaviour of car assembly workers: a deviant case and theoretical critique. *British Journal of Sociology*, 17: 227–44.

Gorz, A. (ed.) (1976) *The Division of Labour: The Labour Process and Class-Struggle in Modern Capitalism*. Brighton: Harvester Press.

Grint, K. (1991) *The Sociology of Work*. Cambridge: Polity Press.

Guest, D. (1995) Human resource management, trade unions and industrial relations. In Storey, J. (ed.), *Human Resource Management: A Critical Text*. London: Routledge, pp. 110–41.

Hackman, J. R. (1987) The design of work teams. In Lorsch, J. (ed.), *The Handbook of Organizational Behavior*. Upper Saddle River, NJ: Prentice Hall, pp. 315–42.

Hackman, J. R. and Oldham. G. (1976) Motivation through the design of work. Test of a theory. *Organizational Behavior and Human Performance*, 16: 250–79.

Hackman, J. R and Oldham, G. (1980) *Work Design*. MA: Addison Wesley.

Hill, S. (1991) Why quality circles failed but total quality might succeed. *British Journal of Industrial Relations*, 29(4): 541–69.

Hill, S. (1995) From quality circles to total quality management. In Wilkinson, A. and Wilmott, H. (eds), *Making Quality Critical: Studies in Organisational Change*. London: Routledge, pp. 33–53.

Hobsbawm, E. J. (1968) *Industry and Empire*. Harmondsworth: Pelican.

Holland, P. J., Hecker, R. and Steen, J. (2002) Human resource strategies and organisational structures for managing gold collar workers. *Journal of European Industrial Training*, 26(2): 72–80.

Holland, P. J., Sheehan, C. and DeCieri, H. (2007) Attracting and retaining talent: exploring human resource development trends in Australia. *Human Resources Development International*, 10(3): 247–61.

Jackson, C., Arnold, A., Nicholson, N. and Watts, T. (1996) *Managing Careers in the Year 2000 and Beyond*. Report No. 304. London: Institute of Employment Studies.

Kalleberg, A., Marsden, P., Reynolds, J. and Kooke, D. (2006) Beyond profit? Sectorial differences in high-performance work practices. *Work and Organisation*, 33(3): 271–302.

Kelly, J. and Clegg, C. (1981) *Autonomy and Control at the Workplace*. London: Croom Helm.

Kelly, P. (1982) *Scientific Management, Job Redesign and Work Performance*. London: Academic Press.

Kinnie, N. Hutchinson, S. and Purcell, J. (2000) Fun and surveillance: the paradox of high commitment management in call centre. *Human Resource Management Journal*, 11(5): 967–85.

Klein, J. A. (1984) Why supervisors resist employee involvement. *Harvard Business Review*, (September–October): 87–95.

Lawler, E. E. (1986) *High Involvement Management*. San Francisco: Jossey-Bass.

Legge, K. (1995) *Human Resource Management: Rhetorics and Realities*. London: Macmillan.

Lepak, D. and Snell, S. (1999) The human resource architecture: towards a theory of human capital allocation and development. *Academy of Management Review*, 24(1): 31–48.

Lepak, D. and Snell, S. (2007) Employment subsystems and the 'HR architecture'. In Boxall, P., Purcell, J. and Wright, P. (eds), *The Oxford Handbook of Human Resource Management: A Critical Text*. Oxford: Oxford University Press, pp. 210–30.

Lipietz. A. (1987) *Mirages and Miracles: The Crises of Global Fordism*. Verso: London.

Littler, C. R. and Salaman, G. (1982) Bravermania and beyond: recent theories of the labour process. *Sociology*, 16(2): 251–69.

Manz, C. (1992) Self-leading work teams: moving beyond self-managed myths. *Human Relations*, 45: 1119–40.

Marchington, M. (1995) Fairy tales and magic wands: new employment practices in perspective. *Employee Relations*, 17(1): 51–66.

Mathews, J. (1989) *Tools of Change: New Technology and the Democratisations of Work*. Sydney: Pluto Press.

Mathias, P. (1969) *The First Industrial Nation: An Economic History of Britain 1700–1914*. London: Methuen.

Merkle, J. (1980) *Management and Ideology. The Legacy of the International Scientific Management Movement*. Los Angeles: University of California Press.

Michaels, E., Handfield-Jones, H. and Axelrod, E. (2001) *The War for Talent*. Boston, MA: Harvard Business School Press.

Myers, C. S. (1926) *Industrial Psychology in Great Britain*. London: Jonathan Cape.

Newell, S., Robertson, M., Scarbrough, H. and Swan, J. (2002) *Managing Knowledge Work*. Hampshire: Palgrave.

Nyland, C. (1987) Scientific planning and management. *Capital and Class*, 33: 55–83.

Oldham, G. (1996) Job design. In Cooper, C. L. and Robertson, I. T. (eds), *International Review of Industrial and Organisational Psychology*. New York: John Wiley, 11: 33–60.

Parker, S. and Wall, T. (1998) *Job and Work Design: Organizing Work to Promote Well-being and Effectiveness*. Thousand Oaks, CA: Sage.

Passmore, W. A. (1998) *Designing Effective Organisations: The Sociotechnical Systems Perspective*. New York: Wiley.

Pratt, K. J. and Bennett, S. G. (1985) *Elements of Personnel Management* (2nd edn). London: Van Nostrand Reinhold.

PricewaterhouseCoopers (2009) 12th Annual Global CEO Survey – Future proof Plans. Available from: http://www.pwc.com/ceosurvey [accessed 27 July 2009].

Rose, M. (1988) *Industrial Behaviour* (2nd edn). London: Penguin.

Ryan, R. M. and Deci, E. L. (2000) Self-determination theory and the facilitation of intrinsic motivation, social development and well-being. *American Psychologist*, 55: 68–78.

Schein, E. H. (1965) *Organisational Psychology*. New Jersey: Prentice Hall.

Smith, A. (1979) *The Wealth of Nations*. New York: Penguin Books. (First published 1776.)

Sofer, C. (1972) *Organizations in Theory and Practice*. London: Heinemann Education.

Taylor, F. (1903) *Shop Management*. New York: Harper.

Taylor, F. (1911) *The Principles of Scientific Management*. New York: Harper.

Taylor, P. and Bain, P. (1999) An assembly line in the head: the call centre labour process. *Industrial Relations Journal*, 30(2): 101–17.

Thompson, P. (1983) *The Nature of Work*. London: Macmillian Business.

Thompson, P. and McHugh, D. (1995) *Work Organisation: A Critical Introduction* (2nd edn). London: Macmillian Business.

Thompson, P. and McHugh, D. (2002) *Work Organisation: A Critical Introduction* (3rd edn). London: Macmillian Business.

Thornley, D. and Valantine, G. (1975) *Job Enlargement: Some Implications of Longer Cycle Jobs in Fan Heater Production in Making Work More Satisfying*. London: HMSO.

Tuckman, A. (1995) Ideology, quality and TQM. In Wilkinson, A. and Wilmott, H. (eds), *Making Quality Critical: Studies in Organisational Change*. London: Routledge, pp. 54–81.

Trist, E. (1973) A socio-technical critique of scientific management. In Lockett, M. and Spear, R. (eds), *Organisations as Systems*. Milton Keynes: Open University Press, pp. 58–65.

Vanderberg, R. J., Richardson, H. A. and Eastman, L. J. (1999) The impact of high involvement work process on organizational effectiveness: a second-order latent variable approach. *Group and Organizational Management*, 24(3): 300–39.

Wall, T., Kemp, N., Jackson, P. and Clegg, C. (1986) An outcome evaluation of autonomous work groups: a longitudinal field experiment. *Academy of Management Journal*, 29: 280–304.

Warr, P. (1987) *Psychology at Work*. (3rd edn). London: Penguin.

Watson, T. J. (1995) *Sociology, Work and Industry* (3rd edn). London: Routledge Press.

Way, S. (2002) High performance work systems and intermediate indicators of firm performance with the US small business sector. *Journal of Management*, 28(6): 762–85.

Wilkinson, A., Goffrey, G. and Marchington, M. (1997) Bouquets, brickbats and blinkers: total quality management and employee involvement in practice. *Organizational Studies*, 18(5): 799–819.

Wilkinson, A., Redman, T., Snape, E. and Marchington, M. (1998) *Managing with Total Quality Management: Theory and Practice*. London: Macmillan Business.

Recruitment and selection

Olivia Kyriakidou

8

?

After reading this chapter, you should be able to:

☐ Describe the personnel selection system and its component parts

☐ Understand the role played by the rational and objective staffing technologies, including job analysis and recruitment and selection methods

☐ Critically assess the concern with the selection–performance relationship that underlines the personnel staffing agenda

☐ Come to terms with the fact that employees are not simple 'human resources' that can be selected, recruited, controlled and processed, but are human beings characterized by agency, subjectivity and reflexivity

☐ Consider the international implications of recruitment and selection, analyse the different selection methods for expatriates and develop effective methods for selecting expatriate managers

☐ Understand the necessity of studying recruitment and selection from a critical perspective, exploring, in particular, the ethical dimensions

☐ Identify future theoretical and practical challenges in the field of research into recruitment and selection

Introduction

Recruitment and selection are seminal topics within human resource management (HRM), ensuring that organizations have the necessary human skills, knowledge and capabilities to enable the organization to continue into the future. Recent recognition of the strategic potential of recruitment and selection to enhance organizational performance has placed great emphasis on getting the 'right person' for a post (see also Chapter 2). Selecting the 'right person' means that the personnel recruitment and selection agenda should be dominated by a concern with formalization, enshrined in its language of 'objectivity', 'reliability' and 'validity', with a technology and method that attempt to maximize 'decision-making accuracy', and with the selection–performance relationship.

In most HRM practice, performance is conceptualized in strict economic terms, excluding any consideration of issues of fairness and acceptability for whichever individuals, groups or authorities might take an interest in the selection decisions. Moreover, formalization refers to the use of formal methods that are supposed to aid an objective, fair and rational selection decision, guarding at the same time against inefficiency and discrimination through the use of scientifically validated techniques. This agenda prescribes practices that, if followed properly, should guarantee the 'truth' of selection decisions, producing a better match between the individual and the organization at the point of selection. These practices should also remove any ethical uneasiness from personnel decision-making (see also Chapter 5).

Underpinning this assumption is the idea that the information identified as being central or critical to good selection decisions can be understood as being relatively neutral. 'Neutral' means here that the content of knowledge, skills and ability profiles is treated as largely reflecting the reality of the person's role. However, there is a considerable danger of managers having too much faith in the neutrality and predictive powers of selection techniques and procedures that tend to ignore the amount of human interpretation and intuition involved in all staffing activities. A more critical way of thinking indicates that selection processes should not exclude the broader moral, social and political considerations (Janssens and Steyaert, 2009) that are embedded in a pluralist approach – an approach that stresses the existence of divergent interests within organizations – or the roles of the following in enacting certain types of personnel selection technology:

☐ *human agency* – in other words, employees' capacity to make choices and to impose those choices on their world of work;
☐ *subjectivity* – defined as the ability of the employees to have consciousness and relationships with other entities;
☐ *reflexivity* – the capacity of employees to recognize the impact of forces of organizational socialization on them, and to alter their places in the organization's social structure.

Such a critical way of thinking is further strengthened by research studies exploring the international dimensions of personnel selection. For instance, it has been reported that, consistent with the national culture, organizations in the USA typically have cultures that emphasize individual achievement, competition and rationality (Stone and Stone-Romero, 2004). As a result, the ideal job applicant is one who is individualistic and achievement-oriented (Syed, 2008). In such situations, individuals who come from collectivist societies could be disadvantaged during the processes of recruitment and selection. Similarly, Bevelander (1999) highlights the fact that, in many countries, many monotonous jobs that used to involve low or unskilled labour are increasingly being replaced by jobs that require higher communicative and social abilities, as well as culture-specific social competence and language skills. Such an orientation towards specific social skills that are mainly possessed by those who are native-born may, however, lead to personnel recruitment and selection practices that are not sensitive to the cultural diversity of the labour force.

The structure of this chapter is as follows. In the first section, we will explore the classical theories and current research that underpin the three basic elements of a personnel selection system:

- ☐ studying the job to be performed;
- ☐ recruiting a pool of applicants for the job;
- ☐ selecting the 'best' from the applicant pool.

Such an exploration will be enriched by international considerations and implications for recruitment and selection, with a special focus on expatriate managers.

Finally, we will adopt a critical perspective that tries to reveal the ethical issues underpinning personnel staffing and problematize the currently strong relationship between selection practices and performance.

Stages of recruitment and selection

Most recruitment and selection procedures involve several stages that occur over a period of time. The process usually first includes a job analysis (see Chapter 7) that results in a job description and personnel specification in order to uncover all the qualities that are necessary to perform the job successfully. This analysis also incorporates an initial recognition of the need for new staff (see Chapter 6) and recruitment advertising, followed by pre-screening applicants, and finally the selection decisions and induction of new employees into the organization. This systems view is generally based on the traditional 'predictivist' perspective on selection, which views the job as a given and stable entity into which the most suitable candidate needs to be recruited. Person–job fit is therefore of primary importance. Figure 8.1 illustrates the process and is reasonably self-explanatory in terms of the critical objectives and key activities that are involved at each phase.

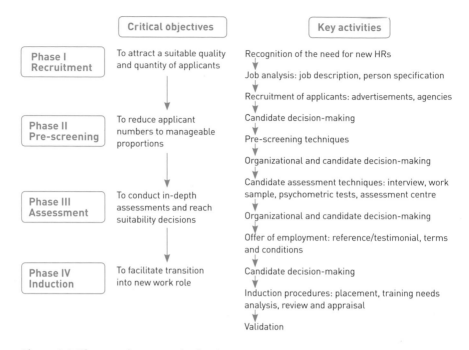

Figure 8.1 The recruitment and selection process.

The advantage of taking such a 'systems view' of selection is that it provides a holistic overview of the entire process underlying two pertinent issues: bilateral decision-making and validation feedback loops. First, decisions are made by both the recruiter and the candidate at several points in the process, supporting the constructivist perspective that both parties consider possible employment options and make decisions over whether to accept a working relationship with each other. Selection therefore serves as an opportunity to exchange information and develop mutual expectations and obligations. Hence, from this perspective, selection aims to ensure not only a person–job fit, but also a person–organization fit (that is, a fit between the applicant's values and organizational culture) and a person–team fit (that is, a fit between the applicant's skills and attitudes and the climate of the immediate working group).

Second, the systems view highlights the importance of the validation feedback loop. In larger scale selection processes, where numerous recruitment decisions are reached over a period of time, the crucial question from the organization's perspective is: 'How accurate are these decisions in selecting individuals who subsequently turn out to be effective job performers?' This question has driven much of the research from the psychometric perspective. Validation feedback loops recycle information on the effectiveness of selection decisions into the selection process at different stages in order to modify and improve the procedure.

Job analysis

The traditional role of job analysis is to provide a fixed starting point for all subsequent steps in the selection process. Job analysis refers to one or more procedures designed to collect information about the tasks people perform and the skills they require to do those jobs effectively. It is a process for describing what is done in any job – not the best way to do it, nor what it is worth to have the job done. Job analysis traditionally seeks the information on the following:

☐ work activities, including both individual behaviours and job outcomes;
☐ the machines, tools, equipment and work aids used;
☐ job-related tangibles and intangibles, such as materials processed and knowledge applied, respectively;
☐ standards of work performance;
☐ job context;
☐ personnel requirements, such as education, experience, aptitudes and so forth.

The end product of job analysis is often a job description, which is a factual statement of the tasks, responsibilities and working conditions involved in a particular job. Box 8.1 presents an example of a job description for a first-level supervisor post. The job description should also include elements of contextual performance as there is still a tendency to focus upon specific, discrete tasks and ignore contextual aspects such as maintaining morale, courtesy and other citizenship behaviours (Viswesvaran and Ones, 2000). There may also be a person specification, which details the knowledge, skills, abilities, experiences and attributes or attitudes required to perform the job effectively.

However, Hough and Oswald (2000) indicate that, in recognition of the increasingly rapid changes that are taking place in the workplace, job analysis should focus on tasks and on the cross-functional skills of workers, including information on personality, cognitive, behavioural and situational variables, rather than on more static aspects of jobs. Moreover, in many selection situations, the need to understand the job is made particularly complex and difficult because the job in question is likely to be radically different, in ways that are very difficult to predict, within as little as 5 or maybe 10 years. Finally, at the managerial/professional level, someone may be employed to fulfil objectives or agendas as opposed to specific tasks. In such instances, Cascio (1995) says that what can often remain is something more 'person-like' than 'job-like' insofar as the job (as a set of objectives or agendas) is defined and enacted in a highly individualized manner.

Box 8.1 Job analysis: First-Level Supervisor – Department of Operations

Performance dimensions and task statements:
Organizing work; assigning work; monitoring work; managing consequences; counselling, efficiency review, and discipline; setting an example; employee development.

Knowledge, skills, abilities and other characteristics (KSAOs) and definitions:
Organizing; analysis and decision-making; planning; communication (oral and written; delegation; work habits; carefulness; interpersonal skill; job knowledge; organizational knowledge; toughness; integrity; development of others; listening.

▷

Predictor measures

☐ Multiple-choice in-basket exercise
   (assume the role of the new supervisor and work through the in-basket on the desk)
☐ Structured panel interview
   (predetermined questions about past experiences relevant to the KSAOs)
☐ Presentation exercise
   (make a presentation to a simulated work group about a change in their working hours)
☐ Writing sample
   (prepare a written reprimand for a fictitious employee)
☐ Training and experience evaluation exercise
   (give examples of training and work achievements relevant to certain KSAOs)

The recruitment process

In most reviews of recruitment research, authors have offered organizing models of the recruitment process (see, for example, Rynes and Cable, 2003). Figure 8.2 presents a model developed by Breaugh et al. (2008). Given the detailed nature of the model, we will not provide a thorough discussion of all of its contents. However, a key part of Figure 8.2, the box labelled 'Intervening job applicant variables', does merit elaboration. Although some of these variables (for example, what makes a position attractive) have received attention, many other variables (such as attracting applicants' attention and applicant self-insight) have received almost no attention from recruitment researchers (Breaugh et al., 2008).

A consideration of the job applicant variables portrayed in Figure 8.2 should play a central role in how an employer plans its recruitment process. For example, if an employer is interested in attracting the attention of individuals who are not currently looking for jobs, many commonly used (and commonly studied) recruitment methods (for example, newspaper advertisements or job fairs) may not be particularly effective. Similarly, if an organization hopes to improve person–job/organization fit by providing realistic information during the recruitment process, applicant self-insight is important to consider – even having received the information, applicants without such insight may not be able to evaluate whether the position described represents a good fit for them. Research (see Rynes and Cable, 2003; Breaugh et al., 2008) has found that many job applicants:

☐ have an incomplete and/or inaccurate understanding of what a job opening involves;
☐ are not sure what they want from a position;
☐ do not have a self-insight with regard to their knowledge, skills and abilities;
☐ cannot accurately predict how they will react to the demands of a new position.

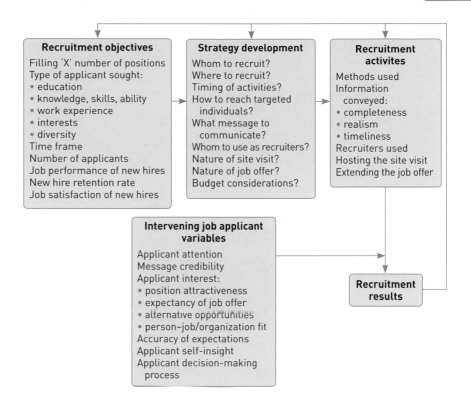

Figure 8.2 A model of the recruitment process.

Recruiting methods

External recruitment

Having done a thorough job analysis and produced an accurate job description, including a realistic person specification, the organization is now ready to start recruiting potential applicants. With regard to the term 'external recruitment', this could be defined as encompassing an employer's actions that are intended to:

☐ bring a job opening to the attention of potential job candidates who do not currently work for the organization;
☐ influence whether these individuals apply for the opening;
☐ affect whether they maintain interest in the position until a job offer is extended;
☐ influence whether a job offer is accepted.

External recruitment sources
The types of recruitment method (Table 8.1) that an employer uses may make a difference to the process here. The two most common explanations for why this might happen (Zottoli and Wanous, 2000) have been labelled the *realistic information hypothesis* and the *individual difference hypothesis*. Simply stated, the realistic information hypothesis suggests that individuals recruited via certain methods

such as employee referrals have a more accurate understanding of what a position involves. The individual difference hypothesis posits that different recruitment methods may bring a job opening to the attention of different types of individual who vary in terms of important attributes (for example, their ability or work ethic).

Table 8.1 External recruitment sources

Employee referrals	Advantages: low-cost, high-quality hires, decreased hiring time, opportunities to strengthen the bond with current employees
	Employees carefully pre-screen applicants due to the activation of a mechanism to protect their reputation: they provide difficult-to-obtain information and coaching, and press their referrals to perform
Job advertisements	Advertisements with more information result in job openings being viewed as more attractive and more credible, increasing applicants' interest and resulting in a better person–organization fit. The inclusion of pictures of minority groups seems to increase the attraction of diverse applicants to the organization
Internet/ employer's website	These sources generate a large number of applicants at a relatively low cost; the effectiveness of these sources depends upon the employer's visibility and reputation, as well as the aesthetics, content and function of the website
	A potential limitation is that a firm may be inundated with applications from individuals who are not good candidates for the positions. As a way to address this issue and given its interactive capability, a website could provide potential applicants with feedback concerning person–job/ organizational fit
Universities, colleges and placement offices	These are a source of people with specialized skills for professional positions. The choice of colleges and universities might depend on past experiences with students at the school, the quality of recent hires, offer acceptance rates and skills, experience and training in the desired areas, ranking of school quality and the costs of recruiting at a particular school
Cooperatives, internships and job fairs	These are part-time working arrangements that allow the organization to obtain services from a part-time employee for a short period of time; they also give the organization an opportunity to assess the person for a full-time position after graduation
Employment agencies and executive search firms	One source of lower level, non-managerial employees is employment agencies. For higher level positions, executive search firms, or 'headhunters', may be used. Care must be exercised in selecting an employment agency for two reasons. First, many agencies might flood the organization with CVs without careful screening. Second, they may misrepresent the organization to the candidate and the candidate to the organization if they are concerned only with a quick placement and pay no regard to the costs of poor future relationships with clients

Recruiter effect

Chapman et al. (2005) found that individuals who viewed a recruiter as having been personable, trustworthy, informative and/or competent were more attracted to a position with the recruiter's organization. Recruiters' behaviour can be very important as the way they treat an applicant may be viewed as a signal of how the person would be treated if hired.

Rynes et al. (1991: 59) have found that recruiters were:

associated with changes in many job seekers' assessment of fit over time – 16 of 41 individuals mentioned recruiters or other corporate representatives as reasons for deciding that an initially favored company was no longer a good fit, whereas an identical number mentioned recruiters as a reason for changing an initial impression of poor fit into a positive one.

Breaugh et al. (2008) underline the importance of different types of recruiters because:

- they vary in the amount of job-related information they possess;
- they differ in terms of their credibility in the eyes of recruits;
- they signal different things to job candidates.

Finally, with regard to the relative importance of recruitment with respect to characteristics associated with the position being offered, conventional wisdom is that position attributes such as pay, job tasks and working hours are more important to job applicants than such recruitment variables as the content of a job advertisement, the design of a company's employment website or a recruiter's behaviour. Comparisons of the relative impact of recruitment variables and position attributes have resulted in some individuals questioning whether the manner in which an employer recruits is important.

In this context, two factors should be considered. First, if an employer does a poor job of recruiting, it may not bring job openings to the attention of the types of people it is seeking to recruit. Second, even if a position is brought to the attention of targeted individuals, poor treatment during the recruitment process may result in individuals withdrawing as job candidates before an employer has even had a chance to present a job offer (Boswell et al., 2003).

Internal recruitment

The objective of the internal recruitment process is to identify and attract applicants from among individuals already holding jobs within the organization (Table 8.2). Many organizations have recognized that careful management of their existing employee base may be a cost-effective way to fill upper-level managerial and professional vacancies.

Table 8.2 Internal recruitment sources

| Job postings | These spell out the duties and requirements of the job and show how applicants can apply. Their content should be based on the job description and should clearly define the knowledge, skills, abilities and other characteristics (KSAOs) needed to perform the job. The main characteristics that lead to high satisfaction on the part of users include the adequacy of job descriptions and job notification procedures, the treatment received during the interview, the helpfulness of counselling and the provision of constructive feedback, and the fairness of the job-posting system |

Intranet and intraplacement	These informs employees quickly about job postings and prospects inside the organization. Some companies include an online career centre where employees can also gain access to information about the KSAOs needed for positions that might interest them
Talent management system	This monitors and tracks the utilization of employees' skills and abilities throughout the organization
Career development centres	These provide employees with opportunities to take interest inventories – self-assessment tools that assess employees' likes and dislikes related to a variety of activities, objects and types of person – assess their personal career goals and have discussions with representatives across the organization. In this way, employees learn about themselves, have a chance to hear about the career options within the organization, and develop methods to structure internal career paths that match their interests
Replacement and succession plans	Succession plans are organized by position and list the skills needed for the prospective position

Realistic job previews

A realistic job preview (RJP; which is provided through work simulations and work tours among other things) requires that employers should provide recruits with candid information concerning the pleasant, and also the unpleasant, aspects of the job as a way to address inaccurate job expectations and decrease turnover.

Three important job applicant-related variables – anchoring and adjustment, the inability to predict how one will react to events in the future, and a lack of self-insight – need to be highlighted in the context of RJPs. Concerning anchoring and adjustment, research in social psychology (Kruglanski and Sleeth-Keppler, 2007) has found that, having formed an initial attitude concerning a topic, individuals typically do not adjust this attitude sufficiently after receiving additional relevant information. This suggests that providing an RJP to an applicant who already has an opinion of what a position with an employer involves may not result in an adequate adjustment of their initial opinion.

Moreover, Dunning (2007) has shown that people who are asked to predict how they will react to a future state of events they have little experience of are typically unable to make accurate predictions. This inability to predict one's reactions means that, even if an organization provides descriptive information about what a job involves, the recipient of an RJP may have difficulty anticipating how he or she will react to various aspects of the new job. This inability to predict one's reactions can be at least partially overcome if an RJP includes information that is both descriptive (that is, factual) and judgemental (that is, addresses the reactions other employees have to the job attributes) (Breaugh et al., 2008).

The effectiveness of an RJP can also be limited by a lack of self-insight on the part of applicants concerning their abilities or what they want in a job. Schmeichel and Vohs (2009) indicate that individuals frequently lack self-insight and typically have an inflated view of their abilities.

Finally, RJPs could be used not only for entry-level hiring, but also for internal recruitment. For example, a study by Caligiuri and Phillips (2003) described how one employer successfully used an RJP to help its current employees make decisions concerning overseas assignments. Templer et al. (2006) also documented the effectiveness of an RJP in facilitating the crosscultural adjustment of employees transferred to non-US assignments.

Personnel selection methods

Application forms, CVs and references

CVs and application forms are used as a straightforward way of giving a standardized synopsis of the applicant's history in order to pre-screen applicants and generate a shortlist of candidates to be invited to the next stage. To facilitate effective pre-screening decision-making, an application form should ideally be designed according to the selection criteria, and a systematic screening process should be adhered to. However, research into graduate recruitment suggests that the typical process is far from systematic (Knights and Raffo, 1990), and this can clearly impact negatively on the selection process in the longer term. Moreover, there is evidence suggesting that the inclusion of competency statements in CVs (for example, 'I am highly motivated with a proven track record in achieving goals and targets') increases the probability of producing an invitation to an interview (Earl et al., 1998). Although application forms are very popular in the UK, there are cultural differences across Europe, with standard application documents being more popular in Germany and CVs being more widely used in Denmark (Shackleton and Newell, 1997).

References involve the assessment of an individual by a third party, for example the applicant's previous employer. The use of references is more common in the UK, Ireland and Belgium than in France, Sweden, The Netherlands and Portugal (Shackleton and Newell, 1997). References may involve either an open-ended format or a structured format with questions developed from selection criteria. References may serve at least two purposes: first, to confirm the accuracy of information provided by the applicant, and second, to obtain information on the applicant's previous work experience and performance.

However, references suffer from problems of restriction of range (as they may provide limited information regarding the areas of interest), low predictive validity, low interrater reliability, low criterion-relatedness (as they are not linked to specific performance areas) and leniency (a bias that occurs when a manager rates an employee too positively), with few applicants being given negative evaluations; this suggests that not too much reliance should be placed upon their content (Shackleton and Newell, 1997). Their validity can be improved when references are sought on a criterion-specific basis (Smith and George, 1992) or by structuring references in the form of systematic ratings of 'personality' (Mount et al., 1994). References are therefore rarely used in the decision-making process, being more likely to be used merely as a final check before any job offer is made.

Selection interviews

The use of interviews as selection technique continues unabated. In organizations around the world, selection interviews continue to be one of the most frequently used methods to assess candidates for employment (Wilk and Cappelli, 2003). McDaniel et al. (1994: 599) define the interview as a 'procedure designed to predict future job performance on the basis of applicants' oral responses to oral enquiries'. Guion (1998), however, cautions against this generic definition because it assumes that interviews are monolithic entities, like tests. Beyond everything else, we should keep in mind that the selection interview is a social interaction where the interviewer and applicant exchange and process information gathered from each other.

The clearest boundary can be drawn between the traditional unstructured (measuring, for example, social skills and aspects of personality) and more structured forms of interview (measuring, for example, cognitive ability and tacit or job knowledge). Traditionally, interviews are used merely to form a global impression about applicants' job suitability, including whether they would 'fit in', rather than asking them job-related questions. By contrast, structured interviews involve a series of job-related questions with predetermined answers consistently applied across all interviews for a particular job (that is, there is a standardization of questions, question sequence, interview length, evaluation and so on). Probably the most consistent finding in interview research is that interviewers' judgements are more predictive of job performance when based on structured rather than unstructured interviews (Dipboye et al., 2004).

The two main ways of structuring interviews are situational interviewing and behaviour description interviewing. The *situational interview* (Latham and Saari, 1984), which assumes that intentions and behaviours are related, tries to elicit from candidates how they would respond to particular work situations. The situational questions can be developed using the critical incident technique of job analysis, which tries to identify the behaviours critical to effective performance on the job. This is then translated into a question about a hypothetical but job-relevant situation. A scoring guide is developed for evaluating an interviewee's response to each question by providing examples of behavioural responses to that question. One such example of a situational interview taken from Latham and Saari (1984) is shown in Box 8.2.

Box 8.2 Example of a situational interview

For the past week you have been consistently getting the jobs that are the most time-consuming (for example, poor handwriting, complex statistical work). You know it's nobody's fault because you have been taking the jobs in priority order. You have just picked your fourth job of the day and it's another 'loser'. What would you do?

Interviewees offer unstructured responses that are then scored against benchmark answers. The benchmark answers for the example question are 1 = Thumb through the pile and take another job (poor); 3 = Complain but do the job anyway (average); 5 = Take the job without complaining and do it (good).

Source: Adapted from Latham and Saari (1984: 571)

The *behavioural description interview* is a variant of the situational interview (Janz, 1982). But where the situational interview invites applicants to respond to questions in light of how they might behave, the behavioural interview requires an examination of how the applicant has actually behaved in the past when encountering similar incidents (with the assumption that past behaviour predicts future behaviour).

Interestingly, *panel interviews*, also referred to as board interviews or team interviews, involving multiple raters for the same set of applicants, are another means of adding structure. Despite their considerably higher administrative costs, they are expected to result in increased reliability and validity over comparably structured one-to-one interviews (Conway et al., 1995). However, the relational demography, which refers to similarity in terms of demographic attributes, and the racial composition of the interview panel may affect judgements in ways that are consistent with similarity–attraction and social identity theories showing same-race biases (McFarland et al., 2004; Buckley et al., 2007). Moreover, Herriott (2003) has suggested that the process of discussion among individual raters can substantially distort the consensual score through conformity and polarization effects, implying that it is perhaps better to obtain individual ratings from panel members before they have a chance to discuss them.

Despite the evidence showing that interviews containing high levels of structure can be valid predictors, surveys show that managers, human resources professionals and organizations use them only infrequently. Most human resources professionals report using interviews with a moderate degree of structure as this affords them more autonomy and ownership over the process (Lievens and De Paepe, 2004). The use of less structured interviews is related to interviewers' concerns about:

- □ having discretion in terms of how the interview is conducted;
- □ losing informal, personal contact with the applicant;
- □ the time demands of developing structured interviews (Lievens and De Paepe, 2004).

There is also a tendency for operational and human resources personnel to use 'satisficing' as opposed to maximizing selection practices. This means that human resources personnel mainly ask themselves 'What must I do at the very minimum to get the best applicants?' instead of asking 'What can I do to most maximize the possibility of getting the best applicants?' Finally, when interviewers are required to justify the procedures they followed in making their ratings – procedure accountability – they are more likely to use structured interview procedures and make better judgements (Brtek and Motowidlo, 2002).

In practice, there is tension between increasing the structure of the interview (to enhance its validity) and avoiding adverse reactions on the part of the applicant. Although the unstructured interview may be charged with being overly personal, the highly structured interview may create an adverse reaction because it is perceived as 'depersonalizing'. Overall, applicants demonstrate a distinct preference for unstructured over structured interviews (Hough and Oswald, 2000). Also, the less structured the interview, the more symbolic opportunity there is for the applicant to get a feel for the organization and its culture (via the interviewer), enabling a more realistic decision to be made on whether to accept any job offer (Anderson, 2001). Mini Case Study 8.1 highlights the dilemmas behind the use of highly structured interview formats.

Applicant factors and characteristics

Recent research has found evidence for the existence of subtle discrimination in interviews. Frazer and Wiersma (2001) found that, 1 week after conducting interviews, interviewers recalled African-American applicants as having given less intelligent answers compared with white applicants. Similarly, Purkiss et al. (2006) observed that those applicants with both an ethnic name and a corresponding accent received the least favourable interviewer ratings, whereas applicants with a Hispanic name but no accent were evaluated most favourably. This result provides support for 'expectancy violation theory' (Jussim et al., 1987): the applicants with Hispanic names were likely to be expected to speak with an accent; when they did not, thus violating expectations, they were viewed more positively.

Finally, there is evidence suggesting an existence of selection bias against overweight applicants, especially when the interviewers perceive the applicants' obesity as being controllable (Kutcher and Bragger, 2004). In addition, Bragger et al. (2002) indicate that pregnancy discrimination claims are the fastest growing type of employment discrimination charge.

Mini Case Study 8.1
Does your company need a highly structured interview format?

David Hill was getting tired. Having sat on Speed's interview panel conducting graduate 'milk round' interviews over the past 5 days at the company's Athens offices, he had become so accustomed to the structured format that he could completely recite the standardized questions asked of all candidates – in reverse order if needs be.

More to the point, his two line management colleagues on the interview panel had needed strict chairing throughout the interviewing process, as both had pronounced tendencies to stray away from the structured format. One in particular, John Oliver, the Director of Speed Production, could not on occasions resist the temptation of asking candidates questions on their personal and family circumstances. This was especially unfortunate, David Hill felt, given that the company had paid a firm of HRM consultants a considerable sum to introduce a highly structured interview format. Still, he mused to himself, only one more candidate to see today and they would be finished. He glanced at the clock – 5.00 pm – settled back into his chair, composed himself and enquired of his fellow panel members whether they were ready for the last interviewee.

Questions:
1 Was David Hill correct to commission a firm of HRM consultants to develop a highly structured interview format?
2 If structure is a 'good thing' in terms of improving the validity and reliability of interviews, could there be situations in which structure would be disadvantageous?
3 How should the chair of an interview panel deal with maverick interviewers who either:
   • deviate from the standardised format; or
   • ask personal or intrusive questions?

Biodata

The use of biodata for employee selection has a long history, and many researchers (for example, Ployhart et al., 2006) have concluded that biodata are one of the best selection devices for predicting employees' performance and turnover.

Biodata forms typically assess factual and sometimes also attitudinal factors that seek biographical information or assess descriptions of individuals' life histories using a retrospective, quasi-longitudinal, self-report format; they should be defined only in terms of an applicant's past behaviour and experience (Mael, 1991). These past behaviours and experiences can reflect events that have occurred in various contexts:

- [ ] a work setting (for example, quitting a job without giving notice);
- [ ] an educational setting (for example, graduating from college);
- [ ] a family environment (for example, travelling widely while growing up);
- [ ] community activities (for example, volunteering for a not-for-profit organization);
- [ ] other domains (for example, activity in local politics and religious activities, or whether the applicant knows people who work for the organization).

Biodata items are often referred to as 'hard' and 'soft' items respectively, in that the former are potentially verifiable whereas the latter are not. Finally, research suggests that biodata scales can be developed so as to be useful in different organizations since the biodata items are relevant to a given job (for example, insurance agent or supervisor) regardless of the organization. Indeed, Dalessio et al. (1996) argue that a biodata scale that has been found to be valid in one country will have value if used in other countries.

A concern that has been raised with using biodata is their adverse impact on members of protected groups (see, for example, Sharf, 1994). Drakeley (1989) also criticizes the model for being derived from work primarily involving a 'classification' of North American university students and thus not being generalizable to other populations. Given some of the items that have been used (for example, age and educational level), this concern seems appropriate. In particular, biodata items that reflect cognitive ability (such as college grade point average) are likely to result in a negative effect. As there is not a lot of research regarding adverse impact, it seems prudent for an organization to examine each biodata item it is considering using. Applicants might also be likely to react negatively to items that are perceived as lacking job-relatedness, are perceived as fakable and are perceived as overly personal in nature.

Psychometric tests

A test can be defined as a standardized measure of aptitude, knowledge, ability or performance that is administered and scored using fixed rules – most of them statistical – and procedures. All psychometric tests are scaled using a finely graded numerical system and a set of statistical formulae to ensure their reliability and validity. Most psychometric tests are also norm-referenced such that the range and distribution of scores obtained from many different types of sample provide group-specific norms against which to compare an individual's score. The scores for a managerial applicant, for example, will be examined with reference to the most closely matching set of norms (that is, managerial).

Reference to norms can also demonstrate whether the test is 'transportable' from one context to another. For example, it has only been fairly recently that

UK norms for the well-known and much-used US-developed 16 Personality Factors Test (16PF) have become available. Finally, there is a variation across Europe in relation to the use of psychometrics, with Britain, Belgium and Portugal making more substantial use of the technique than Germany or Italy (Shackleton and Newell, 1997). Psychometric tests can be divided into two main categories: cognitive ability tests (CATs) and personality tests.

Cognitive ability tests

Since the very earliest research on personnel selection, cognitive ability has been one of the major methods used to attempt to discriminate between candidates and to predict their subsequent performance. CATs can be classified somewhat arbitrarily into:

□ achievement tests
□ specific aptitude tests
□ general mental ability (GMA) tests.

Achievement tests measure skills that have already been acquired and tap current knowledge or ability in a particular ability domain, usually as a function of education or training. *Aptitude tests* look at what one is capable of doing in the future, usually in specific domains such as mechanical aptitude, spatial and perceptual ability, verbal and numerical aptitude and psychomotor ability. *GMA tests* are designed to give an overview of mental capacity indicative of the individual's overall capability for acquiring and using knowledge, passing examinations and succeeding at work.

A variety of questions are included in such tests, including ones relating to vocabulary, analogies, similarities, opposites, arithmetic, number extension and general information. Many meta-analytic studies (see, for example, Schmidt and Hunter, 1998; Salgado et al., 2003) have produced conclusive results not only concerning the validity of cognitive validity, but also showing that the core dimension of cognitive ability (GMA, or 'g') is the key component in providing predictions of subsequent job performance.

The idea of using only an ability test score to select someone is nonetheless highly controversial, underpinned by moral as well as legal debate. For years, it has been consistently argued that ability-testing does not produce differentially unfair predictions for different groups of people. Recently, however, there have been findings suggesting that ability-testing is unfair to minority groups, with over 60 per cent of black individuals likely to be incorrectly rejected for a job (Chung-Yan and Cranshaw, 2002). This finding is set to cast the legal and moral debate into a completely different landscape and has prompted some to develop latent intelligence tests presented as work samples (Klingner and Schuler, 2004). These are, however, potentially costly to develop because they 'sample' work pertinent to particular occupational groups or job, but they may signal one constructive way forward on the issue of how to balance efficiency needs against legal imperatives and psychological concerns.

Moreover, some maintain that many jobs, especially managerial jobs, presuppose 'tacit' knowledge or action-oriented 'know how' rather than ability per se (Sternberg and Wagner, 1995), 'emotional intelligence' (the ability to perceive, understand and manage emotion; Goleman, 1996) and at least some level of commitment (Meyer and Allen, 1997). Reviews, however, show that tests of tacit knowledge, emotional intelligence and 'practical' intelligence do not produce better predictive or incremental validities than CATs (Salgado, 1999), indicating that they are just different ways of referring to 'job knowledge' (Schmidt and Hunter, 1993). Finally, the increased cognitive demands of today's technologically complex, fast-paced, consumer-oriented economic environment underline the fact that GMA might seriously matter to performance.

Personality inventories

Personality measures are increasingly being used by managers and human resource professionals to evaluate the suitability of job applicants for positions across many levels in an organization. There are many different types of personality measure, each assuming a certain number of traits and trait structures. Cattell's (1965) work led to the development of the now-renowned 16PF, one of the most widely used measure of personality in the occupational context. A contrary view is provided by the Eysenck Personality Questionnaire (Eysenck, 1982), which assumes a three-factor personality model: extroversion/introversion, neuroticism/stability and psychoticism.

The contemporary view is that there are five superordinate trait dimensions (the so-called 'big five', or FFM) by which all people can be described (Costa and McCrae, 1990):

- *Extroversion*: the degree to which someone is talkative, sociable, active, aggressive and excitable.
- *Agreeableness*: the degree to which someone is trusting, amiable, generous, tolerant, honest, cooperative and flexible.
- *Conscientiousness*: the degree to which someone is dependable and organized, and conforms and perseveres on tasks.
- *Emotional stability*: the degree to which someone is secure, calm, independent and autonomous.
- *Openness to experience*: the degree to which someone is intellectual, philosophical, insightful, creative, artistic and curious.

Box 8.3 provides some sample items from a personality characteristics inventory.

Box 8.3 Sample items from a personality characteristics inventory

Conscientiousness
I can always be counted on to get the job done
I am a very persistent worker
I almost always plan things in advance of work

Extraversion
Meeting new people is enjoyable to me
I like to stir up excitement if things get boring
I am a 'take-charge' type of person

▷

▷

Agreeableness
I like to help others who are down on their luck
I usually see the good side of people
I forgive others easily

Emotional stability
I can become annoyed at people quite easily (reverse-scored)
At times, I don't care about much of anything (reverse-scored)
My feelings tend to be easily hurt (reverse-scored)

Openness to experience
I like to work with difficult concepts and ideas
I enjoy trying new and different things
I tend to enjoy art, music, or literature

Source: Adapted from Mount and Barrick (1995: 43)

Until quite recently, personality was not a popular method on which to base the selection of personnel. Schmitt et al. (1984) reported very low validities for the relationship between personality and job performance, and Blinkhorn and Johnson (1990) have argued that using personality tests can delude people into assuming that these offer a comprehensive picture of a person, as well as 'overly objectifying' the person. Moreover, few would dispute the conclusion that non-work-related selection tools are relatively poor predictors of job success relative to structured interviews and ability tests and should thus be treated with caution (Robertson and Smith, 2001). However, renewed interest in personality testing and the acceptance of the FFM personality structure has led to a wide-spread belief and confidence that personality can play a significant role in effective personnel selection.

Conscientiousness is considered to be the best predictor of job performance across various performance criteria such as team performance, leadership emergence, task role behaviour, and occupational groups (Schmidt and Hunter, 1998). Ones and Viswesvaran (1998) argue that this finding is not surprising really in that a conscientious person is more likely to spend time on assigned tasks, acquire greater job knowledge, set goals autonomously and persist in achieving them, go beyond role requirements and avoid being counterproductive; however, they advocate the use of some kind of 'social desirability' screening measure in order to minimize the likelihood of distortion.

Apart from conscientiousness, the other FFM dimensions vary in their predictive effects depending on the nature of the performance criterion and the occupational group. For example, agreeableness and openness to experience are related to performance involving interpersonal skills (Nikolaou, 2003), whereas conscientiousness and extraversion predict managerial performance significantly better in jobs categorized as being high in autonomy (Barrick and Mount, 1993). Witt (2002) reported that extraversion was related to job performance when employees were also high in conscientiousness, but with employees low in conscientiousness, extraversion was negatively related to performance. Mol et al. (2005) investigated the relations between expatriate job performance and the FFM personality dimensions, and found that extraversion, emotional stability, agreeableness, and conscientiousness predicted job performance.

Finally, regarding the relationship between FFM and non-standard performance criteria, Williams (2004) found that openness to experience was significantly related to individual creativity, whereas O'Connell et al. (2001) reported a significant correlation between conscientiousness and organizational citizenship behaviours. Lin et al. (2001), investigating the relation between the FFM and customers' ratings of service quality, reported significant relationships between openness to experience and assurance behaviours, conscientiousness and reliability, extraversion and responsiveness, and agreeableness and both empathy and assurance behaviours. In addition, LePine and Van Dyne (2001) found that conscientiousness, extraversion and agreeableness were related more strongly to change-oriented communications and cooperative behaviour than to task performance. Finally, Lievens et al. (2003) found that openness to experience was significantly related to performance during crosscultural training in a sample of European expatriate managers.

The study of the impact of personality on team behaviour and performance is another area that has seen renewed activity in recent years. Overall, extraversion appears to be the best predictor of team performance (Morgeson et al., 2005), group interaction styles (Balthazard et al., 2004), oral communication (Mohammed and Angell, 2003), emerging leadership behaviour (Kickul and Neuman, 2000), task role behaviour (Stewart et al., 2005) and performance in leadership tasks (Mohammed et al., 2002). Moreover, conscientiousness and emotional stability are the two other FFM constructs found to be generally good predictors of team-related behaviour and performance (Halfhill et al., 2005).

Faking and personality assessment

The most pervasive concern that human resources practitioners have regarding the use of personality testing in personnel selection is that applicants may strategically 'fake' their responses and thereby gravely reduce the usefulness of the personality scores. However, most of the research concerning the effects of impression management or intentional or unintentional distortion on the validity of personality assessment has provided results indicating that, in practical terms, there are relatively few problems (see, for example, Barrick and Mount, 1996). Intentional distortion could be minimized if applicants were warned of the consequences of such distortion. Moreover, human resources professionals should also consider incorporating the 'threat of verification' into the faking warning, as applicants may respond more honestly when they believe that their responses will be subject to verification. The threat of verification becomes even more real when accompanied by carefully developed letters of reference that may provide a valid assessment of the applicant's personality.

Finally, it may still be valuable to include 'social desirability' scales in personality instruments, even though there is now considerable evidence that they generally do not improve validity and that elevated scores on typical social desirability scales may be more a function of valid personality differences than of the motivation to fake the results (Ellingson et al., 1999).

Assessment centres

Assessment centres have recently become popular in the business sector for assessing suitability across a whole range of jobs; they mainly measure general intelligence, motivation to achieve, social competence, self-confidence and dominance. In this sense, the primary construct measured relates to the person's GMA. Assessment centres are meant to simulate the job realistically, employ a variety of techniques for eliciting evidence, assess several applicants at once on several criteria and involve several trained assessors. The rationale behind the use of an assessment centre is that an applicant who can perform a sample of the job satisfactorily can probably perform the job itself. How true this is, though, depends on the extent to which the job sample reflects the whole job.

The assessment centre is organized around behavioural dimensions identified through job analysis, and activities are chosen according to their capacity for creating a situation in which these dimensions can be demonstrated. Across Europe, there are wide differences in the use of assessment centres for selection: they are more common, particularly in large organizations, in the UK, Belgium, Denmark and Germany, and less common in France, Switzerland, Spain and Italy (Shackleton and Newell, 1997).

The types of activity involved vary considerably from one assessment centre to another. Individual activities may include psychological tests, biodata inventories and personality tests. Candidates may be asked to perform written and oral communication exercises (such as preparing written and oral reports) and undertake an in-basket exercise. An in-basket exercise requires the candidate to deal with the kind of correspondence that usually accumulates while an executive is on vacation. It contains requests, questions, directives and various pieces of information that must be handled within a specified period of time. Dyadic activities include role-playing exercises, such as how to deal with a troublesome employee or how to interview an applicant for a job, as well as group exercises including the leaderless group discussion, in which candidates work together without any assigned roles on some organizational problem.

However, Zedeck and Cascio (1984) suggest that we should question the assessment centre as a valid selection procedure as many questions have arisen over the validity and reliability of assessing specific competencies. In addition, Lievens and Klimoski (2001) argue for a need to establish the utility and cost-effectiveness of assessment centres. Finally, assessment centres may operate to maintain the status quo in managerial jobs. Individuals who might be successful on the job, yet do not resemble the present employees, can be neglected. Organizational policies and traditions in hiring and promotion may influence who is successful in the organization. If this is the case, basing assessment centres on current employees will amplify these effects.

Work samples

Work samples are said to be one of the most appropriate means of selection because of the 'point-to-point correspondence' between the job and the assessment scenario (Smith and George, 1992). It is an analogous test (as opposed to an analytical test) designed to replicate the key activities of a job. Work samples are relatively easy to construct for manual jobs, clerical jobs (for example, typing) or those involving contact with clients (for example, role-play dealing with a complaint). For more managerial/intellectual jobs, work samples may be built around specific and identifiable concrete tasks (such as writing a report or dealing with the in-basket). These can then be used to assess both performance and 'trainability' potential.

A prime example of a work sample test is the 'in-basket' exercise. One potential problem with the use of in-basket exercises, however, is the organizations' heavy reliance on 'off-the-self' packages. Moreover, just like any other test, a work sample needs to be carefully constructed and validated. The most valid work samples not only correspond with a particular task, but also capture some of its contextual features (Robertson and Kandola, 1982). A basic rule of thumb is to ensure that the work sample is as 'complex' and 'ambiguous' as the task itself; however, the downside here is that the 'sample' cannot be 'transferred' across jobs (unless jobs are similar). On the other hand, the approach provides a good source of RJP for the applicant. Porteous (1997) says that because reliable and valid work samples are time-consuming and costly to construct, administer and score, they are of most value when used in the final stages of a selection process.

Integrity and honesty tests

Integrity and honesty tests are used to predict the likelihood that the individual will engage in counterproductive behaviour such as theft, violence, excessive absenteeism and dishonesty (Hogan and Brinkmeyer, 1997). Integrity tests are more popular in the USA than in most European countries, although both US and French applicants have been found to react somewhat negatively to these tests (Steiner and Gilliland, 1996). There are three types of integrity testing:

□ overt measures of integrity dealing with attitudes towards theft and other forms of dishonesty, including admissions of theft and other illegal activity;
□ personality-oriented methods, which include questions on various dimensions, such as dependability, conscientiousness and social conformity;
□ clinical measures such as the 'galvanic skin response', an indicator of increased physiological arousal.

There are many disagreements about the value of integrity testing, as well as about its ethical status since the construct of integrity is vague and ill-defined, and there is no compelling evidence for its criterion-related validity (Camara and Schneider, 1995). Other concerns include misclassification, high selection thresholds and the adverse impact on applicants screened out by integrity test results, coupled with the fact that anyone can use them. By contrast, Ones et al. (1995) point to good construct and criterion validities suggesting that promising results that should not be ignored.

Recruiting and selecting expatriate managers

For effective performance in overseas work assignments (see also Chapter 3), many researchers have concentrated on how to prepare potential expatriates for overseas transfer. For instance, Lanier (1979) recommends seven steps to be taken in preparing personnel:

1 A well-planned, realistic pre-visit to the site (country) involved.
2 Early language training prior to departure.
3 Intensive study on issues such as history, culture and etiquette.
4 The provision of country-specific handbooks, including useful facts.
5 The efficient, explicit provision of intercompany counselling facilities.
6 Meetings with returnees to hear 'old hand' tips.
7 Notification of the personnel office and spouses' committee on arrival.

Sieveking et al. (1981) stress the importance of orientation programmes prior to expatriation, which aim to do such things as:

☐ develop an understanding of personal and family values so that employees can anticipate and cope with the inevitably unsettling emotions that accompany culture shock;
☐ develop an appreciation of the important ways in which the host culture will differ from the employee's own culture, so that the employee can guide his or her behaviour accordingly;
☐ show the expatriate how he or she can be rewarded in ways in addition to income and travel, such as novelty, challenge and the opportunity to learn new skills;
☐ help expatriates to anticipate and begin to plan for hardships, delays, frustrations, material inconveniences and the consequences of close living and working with others;
☐ help expatriates to anticipate that, although they may have been superior employees in their own culture, they may need to gain greater satisfaction from experiences other than those which are work-related.

In a more considered and thoughtful paper on the selection of personnel for overseas, Tung (1981) outlines a contingency approach and notes four types of factor crucial to success in foreign assignments: (1) technical competence on the job; (2) relational abilities (social skills); (3) an ability to deal with environmental constraints (government, labor issues); (4) and family situation.

Tung offers a contingency approach of coping with the process based on a sensitive selection process. A contingency framework states that there is in practice no one criterion that could be used in all situations. Rather, each assignment should be viewed on its own. In each instance, the selection of the 'right person' to fill the position should be made only after a careful analysis of:

☐ the task (in terms of interaction with the social community);
☐ the country of assignment (in terms of the degree to which it is similar or dissimilar to that of the individual's home country);
☐ the candidate's personality characteristics (in terms of both the candidate's and the spouse's ability to live and work in a different cultural environment) (Tung, 1981).

Mendenhall et al. (1987) indicate that that a number of authors have identified criteria that predict acculturation and productivity in overseas assignments;

these can be summarised as self-orientation, others-orientation and perceptual orientation. Mendenhall et al. suggest that *self-orientation* includes factors such as stress reduction, technical competence, dealing with isolation and alienation. *Others-orientation* includes factors such as relationship skills, willingness to communicate, respect and empathy for others. *Perceptual orientation* includes factors such as flexible attributions, high tolerance for ambiguity and being open-minded and non-judgemental.

Underscoring the importance of personal characteristics, Hailey indicates that the personality and attitude of expatriates is the key to their success, suggesting that:

> those who are outgoing, relaxed, and prepared to work within the local management style are perceived to adapt more successfully, while unsurprisingly those who are inflexible, arrogant, or straight jacketed fail to adapt to the local culture. (1996: 265)

Exercise

The company in this exercise is one of the leading pharmaceutical manufacturers in the UK. Because of the intense competition in the industry and the heightened competition for highly skilled personnel, the company believes that quality of work–life balance is a key factor in achieving competitive advantage. In support of this belief, the company is considering adopting a telecommuting work arrangement for selected jobs.

The job of Public Relations (PR) Specialist has been identified as an appropriate job for telecommuting owing to the fact that its responsibilities are mostly information-related activities that require independent mental effort with no supervisory responsibilities. The current job description for the PR Specialist is shown below; this reflects the primary job activities and qualifications for a full-time, in-office PR Specialist. There is currently only one job incumbent, and that person has just resigned. You have been asked to develop a plan for recruiting and hiring a replacement who will telecommute from home.

- What method of job analysis would you recommend to determine the job requirements and job specifications for a telecommuting job? Is the method you are recommending different from the method you would use if the job were being performed in a traditional office environment?
- What procedures do you recommend for recruiting and hiring a telecommuter? Are the procedures you are recommending different from the procedures you would use if the job were being performed in a traditional office environment?

- What changes would you make to the job description below in order to reflect the telecommuting nature of the job?
- What other recommendations would you make in order to ensure the successful implementation of a telecommuting work arrangement?

Job description

Job title: Public Relations Specialist

Department: Public Relations

Reports to: Director of Public Relations

General summary: Serves as a writer on numerous publications for the firm; coordinates materials; writes, edits and proofs articles, public relations publications and advertising copy using WordPerfect software.

Essential job functions:

1 Writes, edits and proofs public relations articles, newspaper copy and human interest stories.
2 Writes advertising copy in conjunction with the marketing department.
3 Writes, edits and coordinates the printing and layout of the company newsletter.
4 Meets with executives to determine PR needs.
5 Meets with media officials and the public to publicise the firm's accomplishments.
6 Attends information meetings at the main office on an as-needed basis.
7 Gives presentations at meetings and other public events.
8 Performs other related duties as assigned by management.

8

▷

Education and experience required: Degree in Art/ Graphic Design; demonstrated ability to use Windows computer hardware/software; some experience in television or public speaking; considerable knowledge of journalism principles, English grammar and usage; demonstrated ability to write newspaper, news and human interest articles, reports, brochures and advertising copy; demonstrated ability to work and communicate effectively with others.

Critical summary of theories

The above literature review shows an increasing homogenization in the approaches employed to account for the phenomena currently seen in personnel recruitment and selection; these are mainly dominated by a generic focus on improving the efficiency, effectiveness and fairness of personnel management practice and by a concern with the selection–performance relationship. Performance is conceptualized in strict economic terms, thus excluding any broader moral, social and political considerations of selection practice and policy.

Moreover, such approaches (for example, the ones that try to achieve a person–organization fit) assume that all members of an organization have mutual interests and are assimilated into the prevailing socioeconomic order of capitalism. This means that organizations will try to govern the souls of employees and regulate their social behaviour by attempting to persuade them to identify with managerial objectives and the philosophy of individualism as a fundamental way of thinking and behaving in the social and organizational world. The unreflecting adoption of the scientific and rational discourse of 'objectivity', 'validity' and 'reliability' that characterizes recruitment and selection practices reinforces the use of scientific discourse and plays a decisive role in the effective management of employees' performance by persuading them of the objective and rational character of these practices. Such an approach, however, mainly ignores the fact that personnel practices are the outcome of human interpretations, conflicts and generalizations (Watson, 2004), and that employee agency, subjectivity and reflexivity lead employees to many different types of engagement with HRM practices (Zanoni and Janssens, 2007).

Finally, there has been a standardization of employee selection practices and a treatment of certain individual competencies and job characteristics as neutral (that is, as reflecting the reality of the person or the role) rather than as socially constructed or situated. Instead of limiting inequalities, this has paradoxically legitimized gendered employment practices by cloaking them in false objectivity (Özbilgin and Woodward, 2004).

Personnel selection and ethics

Karen Legge (2007) has argued that we need to consider 'moral economy', that is, what moral norms concerning the good and the just should be embodied in and guide choices and action in organizations (see also Chapter 5). Moral economy implies that, instead of being preoccupied with issues of efficiency and performance in strict economic terms, we should include broader moral, social and political considerations related to the practice and policy of recruitment and selection.

First of all, personnel selection should refocus its attention on the employees themselves by considering not only individual variables such as abilities, skills and competencies, but also the political nature of the employment relationship (Janssens and Steyaert, 2009), adopting a pluralist approach to managing the employment relationship. Such an approach criticizes the belief that staffing techniques that lead to high performance are beneficial for employees and for unions that accept them, draws attention to the negative effects of such techniques (such as work intensification) and highlights the existence of continued discrimination against marginalized groups (Knights and McCabe, 1998). Moreover, the complexity of the employment relationship demands an exploration of the impact of a number of issues, such as fear of lay-offs, perceptions of job opportunities, unemployment and labour market positions, on personnel recruitment and selection; however, the interests and perspectives of multiple stakeholders (including employees) must not be ignored.

Furthermore, the quantitative techniques involved in recruitment and selection procedures are methods that create a technical-scientific order in which the technical is superimposed on the moral and constructs a rational, goal-directed image of organizational effectiveness. Consequently, the management of personnel staffing concerns itself with the technical application of techniques even where circumstances may indicate that these might not be the most appropriate responses.

Finally, we need to ensure that the voices of those who tend to be excluded from mainstream analyses are better represented in the theory and practice of recruitment and selection (see also Chapter 4). This includes, but is not limited to, those in non-standard forms of employment, minority workers and those working outside Western industrialized economies.

Critical analysis and discussion

The formalization part of the personnel selection agenda reinforces an image of the work organization as a black-box system that functions more or less well in performance terms according to the neutral, scientific and formal, rational procedures that convert human resource 'inputs' into outputs. Consequently, the objectives pursued by the implementation of such procedures (that is, a maximization of efficiency and effectiveness) should be of benefit to all concerned – managers, employees, government and 'the public' alike. However, it is rare for such 'best practices' to be subjected to any critical analysis of the potential 'operating' costs, the 'unintended consequences' or – more graphically – the 'collateral damage' resulting from their introduction. What is 'good' for business is not necessarily 'best practice' for employees. In this respect, it is important to note that such procedures are never neutral: they always implicate and privilege particular social values, if not also specific socioeconomic interests.

Moreover, the mainstream analysis of personnel selection processes and procedures is based on a unitarist approach – one in which all members of an organization are assumed to have mutual interests. In practice, however, recruitment and selection practices seem to be enacted by both candidates and selectors within organizations. If we take into account concepts such as agency and subjectivity, and recognize employees as human beings capable of reflexive thought and action (Giddens, 1993), there is a possibility that different employees actively engage in different ways with recruitment and selection practices, undermining, delaying or supporting their implementation. On the other hand, selectors do not simply adopt the 'scientific' and rational principles of the practices, but appear to manipulate them according to pre-existing local power relations, since the design of such practices is 'mediated' by managerial interpretation and political manoeuvring (Watson, 2004). One should not ignore the fact that human resources strategies are the outcomes of human interpretations, conflicts, guesses and rationalizations, albeit those of human agency operating within a context of social and political-economic circumstances.

Finally, a significant consequence of the ever-increasing emphasis on the human resources–performance link has been the progressive exclusion of more and more alternative voices, as well as practices that do not necessary promote high commitment and high performance (MacDuffie, 1995). Hence, the problems and issues of personnel selection have largely been ignored in small and medium-sized organizations (see, for example, Taylor, 2004), in various forms of subcontracting designed to increase 'flexibility' through the creation of 'dependent self-employment' (Muehlberger, 2007); there is little specific reference to unionized workplaces or to the increasing problems associated with (and for) immigrant labour, as well as employees in non-Western and so-called developing economies. Similarly, the increasing resort to outsourcing work to countries where labour is cheaper is excluded from the mainstream 'recruitment and selection agenda'. The irony here, of course, is that most of these social practices can be seen as reflecting the 'success' of the globalization project as they can all be seen to be symptoms of the successful deregulation of labour markets, which is a central element of the neo-liberal policy agenda.

Benefits of studying HRM from a critical perspective

A critical perspective is advanced here in order for personnel recruitment and selection practices to be better contextualized within the prevailing socioeconomic, political and cultural factors that shape those practices. In addition, the aim is that the scientific, objective and rational assumptions and language of recruitment and selection may be challenged, and that voices excluded from mainstream personnel selection may be heard. The adoption of a pluralist frame of reference, in which the employment relationship is understood to involve and articulate different interests, has the potential to reintroduce the possible contribution of those 'external' to the organization, such as the state or trade unions, as significant actors in devising selection policies and practices. Such an approach will force selection specialists to consider possible ways of managing the endemic potential conflicts associated with such differential interests.

Moreover, the deconstruction of the natural and neutral language of science, rationality and objectivity that is used to legitimize 'reliable' and 'valid' recruitment and selection procedures might expose the institutionalized power inequalities, as well as the local power relations within organizations that reinforce, but also impede, the implementation of these procedures in practice. A critical perspective directs us towards an analysis of the contextual circumstances in which certain practices are, or are not, adopted by management.

This is perhaps most clearly evident in another aspect of denaturalization: the concern of critical approaches to reveal how the content of knowledge and the individual skills and ability profiles identified as being central or critical to making good selection decisions are understood as relatively neutral and are treated as largely reflecting the reality of the role or the person. Viewing competencies as individual-level attributes deflects attention away from how their meaning is socially constructed in specific contexts. By treating individual skills and job characteristics as neutral rather than as socially constructed or situated, we are in danger of either privileging certain modes of performance or reproducing the idea that different groups are naturally suited to some roles rather than others; this then undermines the chances of achieving equal opportunities. Consequently, recruitment and selection would benefit from the adoption of a critical perspective as it can offer additional insights into how roles, identities and individual competencies are socially constructed and identify the implications of these processes for selection and recruitment.

Finally, a critical perspective will provide a voice for all those marginalized from mainstream personnel recruitment and from research into and the practice of selection. These include, for example, employees of the following: large multinational corporations, non-Western and so-called developing economies, small and medium-sized enterprises, public and third-sector organizations, alternative forms of organization (for example, cooperatives) and non-standard forms of employment. It will also encompass those who are self-employed, subcontractors, part-time and agency workers, and immigrant labour, among others. Such a focus will enhance our understanding of what is happening to employment regulation outside large and multinational corporations.

In short, Boxall et al. (2007) argue that a critical perspective on HRM should be concerned with why management does what it does; with how contextualized processes of HRM work in practice; and with questions of 'for whom and how well' when assessing the outcomes of HRM, taking account of both employee and managerial interests, and laying a basis for theories of wider social consequence.

Conclusion

Employee staffing decisions involving the recruitment and selection of individuals are made every day in work organizations. There has been a tendency for a rational and scientific technology to be applied to these personnel choices. This involves strongly formalized procedures and the heavy use of such devices as psychological tests. Such technology is intended to help select individuals in a way that will be deemed efficient, acceptable and fair.

However, this approach tends to become restrictive and counterproductive. Its use can be associated with a controlling way of thinking about work organizations and people. A more realistic and critical way of thinking indicates that selection processes are highly ambiguous and are dependent on basic human processes of judgement, guesswork, chance-taking, debate and negotiation. Selection processes in general are better seen as parts of broader and more continuous processes of bargaining and adjustment in which both organizational arrangements and human beings themselves change and adapt within the ongoing negotiated order of the organization.

❷ For discussion and revision

1   If you had entered into a joint venture with a foreign company but knew that women were not treated fairly in that culture, would you consider sending a female expatriate to handle the start-up? Why or why not?

2   Evaluation hiring is a procedure in which a job candidate is hired by a staffing company but put to work at another company. After a set period of time (usually 90 days), the company decides whether to hire the person as a permanent employee. Analyse the benefits for the company that arise from using such a procedure. What ethical issues are involved in evaluation hiring?

3   Should applicants be selected primarily on the basis of their ability or on personality/fit? How can fit be assessed?

4   You work for a medium-sized, high-tech firm that faces intense competition on a daily basis. Change seems to be the only constant in your workplace, and each worker's responsibilities shift from project to project. Suppose you have the major responsibility for filling the job openings at your company. How would you go about recruiting and selecting the best people? How would you identify the best people to work in this environment?

5   In many organizations that have worked to a team structure, the team is the principal unit where the work gets done. However, most organizations recruit and hire as though there were one job description and the team did not exist. If there are distinct roles to be played within a team, how would you go about recruiting and hiring for them? The characteristics needed by individual team members depend on the team and the strengths and weaknesses of other team members. How could you include this dynamic and interactive nature in the recruitment and hiring process?

6   One of the strategic staffing choices is whether to pursue workforce diversity actively or passively. First suggest some ethical reasons for an active pursuit of diversity, and then suggest some ethical reasons for a more passive approach. Assume that the type of diversity in question is an increasing representation of women and ethnic minorities in the workforce.

7   Why is it important for the organization to view all components of staffing from the perspective of the job applicant?

8 Assume that the organization you work for practises strict adherence to the rules of objective, scientific and rational recruitment and selection. But beyond that, it seems that 'anything goes' in terms of tolerated staffing practices. What is your assessment of this approach?

9 Do you think that targeted recruitment systems, for example those targeting older workers, women, minority groups or people with the desired skills, are fair? Why or why not?

10 Cognitive ability tests are one of the best predictors of job performance, yet they have a substantial adverse impact on minority groups. Do you think it is fair to use such tests? Why or why not?

11 Do you think it is ethical for employers to select applicants on the basis of questions such as 'Dislike loud music' and 'Enjoy travelling around the world with a backpack' even if the scales that such items measure have been shown to predict job performance? Explain your answer.

12 Given recent changes in the nature of work, especially during the period of economic turbulence, discuss the relative effectiveness of job analysis techniques and suggest how they might be improved.

13 Suppose that you are asked to write a recommendation letter for a friend you like but consider unreliable. Would it be ethical for you to write a positive reference even though you anticipate that your friend will not be a good employee? If not, would it be ethical for you to agree to write the letter knowing that you will not be very positive in your assessment of your friend's abilities?

📖 Further reading

Books

Bolton, S. C. and Houlihan, M. (2007) *Searching for the Human in Human Resource Management*. London: Palgrave Macmillan.

Boxall, P., Purcell, J. and Wright, P. (2007) *The Oxford Handbook of Human Resource Management*. Oxford: Oxford University Press.

Grey, C. and Willmott, H. (2005) *Critical Management Studies: A Reader*. Oxford: Oxford University Press.

Legge, K. (1995) *Human Resource Management: Rhetorics and Realities*. London: Palgrave Macmillan.

Leopold, J., Harris, L. and Watson, T. J. (2005) *The Strategic Management of Human Resources*. London: FT Prentice Hall.

Pinnington, A., Macklin, R. and Campbell, T. (2007) *Human Resource Management: Ethics and Employment*. Oxford: Oxford University Press.

Case Study The design of a new multinational personnel selection system at MobilCom

On Monday morning at 7.30 am, Dr Hans was leaving his apartment, one specifically rented to expatriates, and was heading towards his office in Kuala Lumpur's central business district. On the way, he listened to the voice messages on his mobile phone, one of which was from the assistant of the firm's owner, Frank. The message stated that Hans was expected to call back before his meeting with the human resources (HR) team that he was leading. The team meeting was scheduled in order to bring together Hans and Chinese HR experts to form a crossfunctional project team responsible for the development and implementation of a new personnel process within the context of global restructuring, in order to fill 25 middle management positions in the Australasia region.

According to the in-house global localization policy of the company, MobilCom, 90 per cent of the new management positions were to be filled by individuals originating from the country they would be working in. The affected areas included sales and marketing, purchasing, supply chain management, and finance and accounting, at locations in Hong Kong, Kuala Lumpur, Bangkok, Jakarta, Singapore, Sydney, Oakland and Port Moresby (Papua New Guinea). The new personnel selection system was part of the company's new objective to standardize all HR instruments for selection purposes around the globe. This new personnel selection system had to be developed internally.

When Hans first heard about the above changes, it immediately occurred to him that this would not be easy as personnel selection procedures varied significantly between countries. He also knew that the existing selection instruments were by no means flawless in any specific country. After the application documents had been analysed, structured interviews with the candidates were conducted by a department representative and an HR specialist. If both interviewers came to a positive conclusion on the candidate's qualifications, the top candidates were sent to an individual assessment centre in order to highlight their interpersonal competencies rather than their professional competencies. The approach of the individual assessment centres consisted of biographical questions, case studies on leadership in an international context and participation in a leaderless group discussion. Ultimately, additional references were obtained for each candidate, although different procedures existed in different countries. After the reference checks had been completed, each candidate received written feedback, and a report was generated and added to the successful candidate's personnel file.

For several years now, Hans had been finding faults in the design of the procedures used at the individual assessment centres, but he could not influence possible modifications because the individual assessment centres were run by external consulting firms. In addition, he had been questioning the validity of the information obtained from the centres, as well as the selection system as a whole. He felt there was a need to improve the contents of the structured interviews that were based on the candidate's current situation, as opposed to the candidate's previous work experience. Overall, efforts to improve the current selection systems had only rarely been undertaken owing to limited time and a limit budget allotted for personnel affairs – a fact that Hans had already pointed out to management several times.

The development of a new multinational personnel selection system now posed a huge challenge for Hans and his project team. His team, comprising Australian and Chinese members with HR knowledge as well as HR managers from headquarters, had already been working on the development of the new personnel selection system for 4 months. Over the past few weeks, numerous meetings had been held, yet no significant progress had been made. One reason could be the fact that there was obvious heterogeneity between the opinions of the Australian and Asian team members regarding the new personnel selection system. This created a tense atmosphere and dissent with respect to sharing the workload. The goal of today's meeting was to come to a consensus on several important issues:

☐ what individual modules the new personnel selection system should contain;
☐ whether country-specific adaptations were necessary and feasible for each module;
☐ the implementation process of the new personnel instrument at each location.

When Hans arrived at his office, one of the three Chinese secretaries reminded him that Frank was waiting for him to return his call. She avoided eye contact by looking down to the floor, but with a big smile and gestures that appeared submissive as she perpetually nodded her head. Hans rang Frank, and Frank began speaking:

Dr Hans, you know how much I appreciate your dedication to the company, but I have concerns about the current international selection procedures. We need something that is going to work, and work immediately! And don't you dare try to offer me this empirical or validity stuff. I don't give a damn. You have a whole department with highly qualified people. I assume you are capable of filling these vacant management positions. We also need a selection system that works everywhere. We cannot afford to apply different procedures in every country. What we need are consistent procedures, something applicable crossnationally and crossregionally. You, as a cosmopolitan man, should know exactly what I mean. I also expect everything to be documented in complete detail.

Although Hans shared Frank's enthusiasm for an improved personnel selection system, there were many complications that could arise; Frank seemed completely unaware of these, and Hans tried to inform him about the possible problems. Hans argued that although a multinational selection system would have its advantages, these advantages might become costly if they could not easily be implemented in each region. Each country has its own unique economic and education situations, which would undoubtedly cause difficulties when creating a universal personnel selection system. With respect to cultural difference, he argued that a standardized personnel selection system would also ignore cultural differences and culture-specific circumstances. This would affect not only individual modules in the system, but also the basic job requirements, the adaptation of modules to specific countries, and the use of specific selection methods. Hans also expressed his concern with Frank's lack of interest in testing the validity of the new selection procedures.

Of course, that wasn't exactly what Frank wanted to hear:

Don't tell me about problems; I want solutions. And you should not forget that this is what I pay you and your team to do. You have until the end of this week to deliver the final and written conclusions on this matter. If not, I will reduce your team in Kuala Lumpur by half, and I will delegate the development of this new system to global headquarters. Either you come up with something useful by the end of this week, or central headquarters will do the job. End of discussion.

The team meeting
At the meeting, Hans informed everyone about the current situation with Frank, set the objectives of the meeting and asked for the detailed recording of everything they discussed. The Chinese colleagues agreed by nodding their heads uniformly, a behaviour that was always expected when there was an order

from a member with higher hierarchical status, whereas the Australian colleagues openly disapproved the detailed recording of the discussions.

During the meeting, there was an apparent disagreement between a Chinese HR employee and the Australian economist regarding the definitions of the job requirements and their profiles. Yu wanted to include 15 dimensions – five components that tested the candidate's professional competencies and 10 dimensions that evaluated social competencies. However, Andreas openly disagreed with this proposition, stating: 'I have told you many times that the acquisition of 15 dimensions is simply impossible. It is important to define clearly distinguishable job requirements that are measurable, describable and equally relevant in all countries in the region'.

Yu, intimidated by her Australian colleague's manner, blushed and looked down towards the floor, signalling that she did not dare to say anything further. She often found it difficult to cope with negative feedback, particularly when it occurred in front of her colleagues. There had been several times already when she had not been able to stand up to Andreas, which seemed to affect her more and more each time. She had once spoken to Hans about her difficulties communicating with Andreas; however, Hans was quickly irritated by the complaint and asked her to wait and hope for an improvement in the situation. Yu never discussed the situation with Hans again.

The German in-house psychologist intervened in the discussion and proposed the inclusion of six competencies – technical and vocational skills, social competencies, leadership competencies, communicative competencies, flexibility, and adaptability – that showed great validity and reliability. There was disagreement from some Chinese members, who proposed the inclusion of several more and different competencies, which ended with them feeling irritated and intimidated. Andreas proposed that, due to the time pressure, they should bring a majority vote with respect to the skills, but the Chinese HR member argued: 'No, a majority vote is not the solution. It may lead to good decisions not succeeding because certain team members follow the uniform opinion of the majority. We should try to reach a consensus on this issue.' The dispute was solved by Hans, who decided which would be the final job requirements for selecting the managers, and who adopted the six dimensions proposed by the German team members.

The next important issue on the agenda was to define the modules and the job requirements for each module. For this issue, there was agreement that a multinational selection system should be two-tiered. The first tier would consist of three modules: viewing the candidates' application documents, a telephone conference with the applicants that should be conducted in an unstructured manner, and obtaining three references from former employers. Unlike the current procedures, references should not only be used to verify the past employment and duration of employment, but also include a statement regarding the candidate's personality. Four modules would follow in the second tier – a panel interview, a biography-oriented in-depth interview, a simulated group exercise and testing procedures. All the modules were described in great detail, and emphasis was placed on including standardized tests in order to increase the validity of the entire process, even though there is evidence that intelligence and personality tests are not generally highly accepted and that cultural problems exist.

Towards the end of the long and detailed presentation of the modules, Hans's colleague Anne, who held a MBA degree from one of the major Australian business schools, interrupted: 'I don't want to be rude, but isn't it important to take the candidate's perspective into consideration, as well?' But Andreas countered: 'Unfortunately, nobody cares about the candidate's perspective. We are interested in choosing the right person, certainly not in satisfying the applicants – these never-ending discussions on fairness and acceptance. Reality differs significantly from the ideal procedures we are taught in university.'

Now, Angela jumped into the discussion:

But let's not forget that management is not just a technical matter, and sometimes, if you find someone generally useful, then you could adapt the job to fit the person. The selection process is always a sort of negotiation between the potential employee and the potential employer. We, as recruiters, cannot really know what any of these people are really going to be like if you take them on. Therefore, we need to deploy the basic human skills of eliciting helpful responses from people and judging the likelihood of one person being a better bet for the organization than another. In this sense, there is no 'right person', there is only 'the better bet'. Some of the most important determinants of how well someone does the job are ones that arise after the appointment of the individual.

Hans could not stand any further disputes at the time and took the initiative to terminate the long meeting, which had at least achieved the first step towards specifying the modules in terms of content and procedures. However, they had not been able to specify the adaptations for each target country and the ways of implementing those modules. Hans thought that he should make the decisions himself and then include them in the report to be handed to Frank.

Right after the meeting, Hans went straight to his office and did not come out again for the rest of the afternoon. As soon as he had received the minutes of the meeting, he wrote his final report for Frank. He later received a short notice sent by Frank, informing him that important basic conditions and necessary adaptations had not sufficiently been taken into consideration in the new multinational personnel selection system; therefore, he had handed the case over to global headquarters. Finally, he stated that there would be staff-related consequences for Hans's department in Kuala Lumpur.

Questions

1 Describe in detail all the modules included in the two-tiered selection system proposed by the team.

2 What is the critical analysis of the case study?

References

Anderson, N. (2001) Towards a theory of socialization impact: selection as pre-entry socialization. *International Journal of Selection and Assessment*, 9(1/2): 84–91.

Balthazard, P., Potter, R. E. and Warren, J. (2004) Expertise, extraversion and group interaction styles as performance indicators in virtual teams. *Database for Advances in Information Systems*, 35(1): 41–64.

Barrick, M. R. and Mount, M. K. (1993) Autonomy as a moderator of the relationship between the Big Five personality dimensions and job performance. *Journal of Applied Psychology*, 78(1): 111–18.

Barrick, M. R., and Mount, M. K. (1996) Effects of impression management and self-deception on the predictive validity of personality constructs. *Journal of Applied Psychology*, 81: 261–72.

Bevelander, P. (1999) The employment integration of migrants in Sweden. *Journal of Ethnic and Migration Studies*, 25(3): 445–68.

Blinkhorn, S. and Johnson, C. (1990) The insignificance of personality testing. *Nature*, 348: 671–2.

Boswell, W. R., Roehling, M. V., LePine, M. A. and Moynihan, L.M (2003) Individual job-choice decisions and the impact of job attributes and recruitment practices: a longitudinal field study. *Human Resource Management*, 42: 23–37.

Boxall, P., Purcell, J. and Wright, P. (2007) Human resource management: scope, analysis, and significance. In Boxall, P., Purcell, J. and Wright, P. (eds), *The Oxford Handbook of Human Resource Management*. Oxford: Oxford University Press, pp. 1–16.

Bragger, J. D., Kutcher, E., Morgan, J. and Firth, P. (2002) The effects of the structured interview on reducing biases against pregnant job applicants. *Sex Roles*, 46: 215–26.

Breaugh, J. A., Macan, T. H. and Grambow, D. M. (2008) Employee recruitment: current knowledge and directions for future research. In Hodgkinson, G. P. and Ford, J. K. (eds), *International Review of Industrial and Organizational Psychology*, Vol. 23. New York: John Wiley & Sons, pp. 45–82.

Brtek, M. D. and Motowidlo, S. J. (2002) Effects of procedure and outcome accountability on interview validity. *Journal of Applied Psychology*, 87(1): 185–91.

Buckley, M. R., Jackson, K. A., Bolino, M. C., Veres, J. G. III and Field, H. S. (2007) The influence of relational demography on panel interview ratings: a field experiment. *Personnel Psychology*, 60: 627–46.

Caligiuri, P. M., and Phillips, J. M. (2003) An application of self-assessment realistic job previews to expatriate assignments. *International Journal of Human Resource Management*, 14: 1102–16.

Camara, W. J. and Schneider, D. L. (1995) Questions of construct breadth and openness of research in integrity testing. *American Psychologist*, 50: 459–60.

Cascio, W. F. (1995) Whither industrial and organizational psychology in a changing world of work. *American Psychologist*, 50(11). 928–39.

Cattell, R. B. (1965) *The Scientific Analysis of Personality*. Harmondsworth: Penguin.

Chapman, D. S., Uggerslev, K. L., Carroll, S. A., Piasentin, K. A. and Jones, D. A. (2005) Applicant attraction to organizations and job choice: a meta-analytic review of the correlates of recruiting outcomes. *Journal of Applied Psychology*, 90: 928–44.

Chung-Yan, G. A. and Cranshaw, S. F. (2002) A critical re-examination and analysis of cognitive ability tests using the Thorndike model of fairness. *Journal of Occupational and Organisational Psychology*, 75(4): 489–509.

Conway, J. M., Jako, R. A. and Goodman, D. F. (1995) A meta-analysis of interrater and internal consistency reliability of selection interviews. *Journal of Applied Psychology*, 80: 565–79.

Costa, P. T. Jr and McCrae, R. R. (1990) *The NEO Personality Inventory Manual*. Odessa, FL: Psychological Assessment Resources.

Dalessio, A. T., Crosby, M. and McManus, M. A. (1996) Stability of biodata keys and dimensions across English-speaking countries: a test of the cross-situational hypothesis. *Journal of Business and Psychology*, 10: 289–96.

Dipboye, R. L., Wooten, K. and Halverson, S. K. (2004) Behavioral and situational interviews. In Thomas, J. C. (ed.), *Comprehensive Handbook of Psychological Assessment*, Vol. 4, *Industrial and Organizational Assessment*. Hoboken, NJ: John Wiley & Sons, pp. 297–316.

Drakeley, R. J. (1989) Biographical data. In Herriot, P. (ed.) *Handbook of Assessment in Organizations*. Chichester: Wiley, pp. 439–53.

Dunning, D. (2007) Prediction: the inside view. In Kruglanski, A.W. and Higgins, E. T. (eds), *Social Psychology: A Handbook of Basic Principles*. New York: Guilford Press, pp. 69–90.

Earl, J., Bright, J. E. and Adams, A. (1998) 'In my opinion': what gets graduates resumes short-listed? *Australian Journal of Career Development*, 7: 15–10.

Ellingson, J. E., Sackett, P. R. and Hough, L. M. (1999) Social desirability corrections in personality measurement: issues of applicant comparison and construct validity. *Journal of Applied Psychology*, 84: 155–66.

Eysenck, M. W. (1982) *Attention and Arousal*. New York: Springer-Verlag.

Frazer, R. A. and Wiersma, U. J. (2001) Prejudice versus discrimination in the employment interview: we may hire equally, but our memories harbour prejudices. *Human Relations*, 54: 173–91.

Giddens, A. (1993) *The Constitution of Society: Outline of the Theory of Structuration*. Cambridge: Polity Press.

Goleman, D. (1996) *Emotional Intelligence*. New York: Bantam Books.

Guion, R. M. (1998) *Assessment, Measurement and Prediction for Personnel Decisions*. Mahwah, NJ: Lawrence Erlbaum.

Hailey, J. (1996) The expatriate myth: cross-cultural perceptions of expatriate managers. *International Executive*, 38(2): 255–71.

Halfhill, T., Nielsen, T. M., Sundstrom, E. and Weilbaecher, A. (2005) Group personality composition and performance in military service teams. *Military Psychology*, 17(1): 41–54.

Herriott, P. (2003) Assessment by groups: can value be added? *European Journal of Work and Organizational Psychology*, 12(2): 131–45.

Hogan, J. and Brinkmeyer, K. (1997) Bridging the gap between overt and personality-based integrity tests. *Personnel Psychology*, 50: 587–600.

Hough, L. A. and Oswald, F. L. (2000) Personnel selection: looking toward the future – remembering the past. *Annual Review of Psychology*, 51: 631–64.

Janssens, M. and Steyaert, C. (2009) HRM and performance: a plea for reflexivity in HRM studies. *Journal of Management Studies*, 46(1): 143–55.

8

Janz, T. (1982) Initial comparisons of patterned behaviour description interviews versus unstructured interviews. *Journal of Applied Psychology*, 67: 577–80.

Jussim, L., Coleman, L. M. and Learch, L. (1987) The nature of stereotypes: a comparison and integration of three theories. *Journal of Personality and Social Psychology*, 52: 536–46.

Kickul, J. and Neuman, G. (2000) Emergent leadership behaviors: the function of personality and cognitive ability in determining teamwork performance and KSAs. *Journal of Business and Psychology*, 15(1): 27–51.

Klingner, Y. and Schuler, H. (2004) Improving participants' evaluations while maintaining validity by a work sample-intelligence test hybrid. *International Journal of Selection and Assessment*, 12(1–2): 120–34.

Knights, D. and McCabe, D. (1998) The times they are a changin'? Transformative organizational innovations in financial services in the UK. *International Journal of Human Resource Management*, 9: 168–84.

Knights, D. and Raffo, C. (1990) Milk round professionalism in personnel recruitment: myth or reality? *Personnel Review*, 19: 28–37.

Kruglanski, A. W. and Sleeth-Keppler, D. (2007) The principles of social judgment. In Kruglanski, A. W. and Higgings, E. T. (eds), *Social Psychology: A Handbook of Basic Principles*. New York: Guilford Press, pp. 116–37.

Kutcher, E. J. and Bragger, J. D. (2004) Selection interviews of overweight job applicants: can structure reduce the bias? *Journal of Applied Social Psychology*, 34: 1993–2022.

Lanier, A. R. (1979) Selecting and preparing personnel for overseas transfer. *Personnel Journal*, 58: 160–3.

Latham, G. P. and Saari, L. M. (1984) Do people do what they say? Further studies on the situational interview. *Journal of Applied Psychology*, 69: 569–73.

Legge, K. (2007) Putting the missing H into HRM: the case of the flexible organisation. In Bolton, S. C. and Houlihan, M. (eds), *Searching for the Human in Human Resource Management*. London: Palgrave Macmillan, pp 115–36.

LePine, J. A. and Van Dyne, L. (2001) Voice and cooperative behavior as contrasting forms of contextual performance: evidence of differential relationships with big five personality characteristics and cognitive ability. *Journal of Applied Psychology*, 86(2): 326–36.

Lievens, F. and De Paepe, A. (2004) An empirical investigation of interviewer-related factors that discourage the use of high structure interviews. *Journal of Organizational Behavior*, 25: 29–46.

Lievens, F. and Klimoski, R. J. (2001) Understanding the assessment centre process: where are we now? *International Review of Industrial and Organizational Psychology*, 16: 245–86.

Lievens, F., Harris, M. M., Van Keer, E. and Bisqueret, C. (2003) Predicting cross-cultural training performance: the validity of personality, cognitive ability, and dimensions measured by an assessment center and a behavior description interview. *Journal of Applied Psychology*, 88(3): 476–86.

Lin, N.-P., Chiu, H.-C. and Hsieh, Y.-C. (2001) Investigating the relationship between service providers' personality and customers' perceptions of service quality across gender. *Total Quality Management*, 12(1): 57–67.

McDaniel, M. A., Whetzel, D. L., Schmidt, F. L. and Maurer, S. (1994) The validity of employment interviews: a comprehensive review and meta-analysis. *Journal of Applied Psychology*, 79: 599–616.

MacDuffie, J. P. (1995) Human resource bundles and manufacturing performance: organizational logic and flexible production systems in the world auto industry. *Industrial and Labor Relations Review*, 48(2): 197–221.

McFarland, L. A., Ryan, A. M., Sacco, J. M. and Krista, S. D. (2004) Examination of structured interview ratings across time: the effects of applicant race, rater race, and panel composition. *Journal of Management*, 30: 435–52.

Mael, F. A. (1991) A conceptual rationale for the domain and attributes of biodata items. *Personnel Psychology*, 44: 763–92.

Mendenhall, M., Dunbar, E. and Oddu, G. (1987) Expatriate selection, training and career pathing: a review critique. *Human Resource Management*, 26(3): 331–45.

Meyer, J. P. and Allen, N. J. (1997) *Commitment in the Workplace: Theory, Research and Application*. Thousand Oaks, CA: Sage.

Mohammed, S. and Angell, L. C. (2003) Personality heterogeneity in teams: which differences make a difference for team performance? *Small Group Research*, 34(6): 651–77.

Mohammed, S., Mathieu, J. E. and Bartlett, A. L. (2002) Technical–administrative task performance, leadership task performance, and contextual performance: considering the influence of team- and task-related composition variables. *Journal of Organizational Behavior*, 23(7): 795–814.

Mol, S. T., Born, M. P., Willemsen, M. E. and Van Der Molen, H. T. (2005) Predicting expatriate job performance for selection purposes: a quantitative review. *Journal of Cross-Cultural Psychology*, 36(5): 590–620.

Morgeson, F. P., Reider, M. H. and Campion, M. A. (2005) Selecting individuals in team settings: the importance of social skills, personality characteristics, and team work knowledge. *Personnel Psychology*, 58(3): 583–611.

Mount, M. K. and Barrick, M. R. (1995) *Manual for Personal Characteristics Inventory*. Livertyvill: Wonderlic Personnel Test.

Mount, M. K., Barrick, M. R. and Strauss, J. P. (1994) The joint relationship of conscientiousness and ability with performance: test of the interaction hypothesis. *Journal of Management*, 25: 707–21.

Muehlberger, U. (2007) *Dependent Self-employment: Workers on the Border Between Employment and Self-employment*. Basingstoke: Palgrave Macmillan.

Nikolaou, I. (2003) Fitting the person to the organisation: examining the personality – job performance relationship from a new perspective. *Journal of Managerial Psychology*, 18(7/8): 639–48.

O'Connell, M. S., Doverspike, D., Norris-Watts, C. and Hattrup, K. (2001) Predictors of organizational citizenship behavior among Mexican retail salespeople. *International Journal of Organizational Analysis*, 9(3): 272–80.

Ones, D. S. and Viswesvaran, C. (1998) The effects of social desirability and faking on personality and integrity assessment for personnel selection. *Human Performance*, 11: 245–69.

Ones, D. S., Viswesvaran, C. and Schmidt, F. L. (1995) Integrity tests: overlooked facts, resolved issues, and remaining questions. *American Psychologist*, 50(6): 456–57.

Özbilgin, M. and Woodward, D. (2004) Belonging and otherness: sex equality in banking in Turkey and Britain. *Gender, Work and Organization*, 11(6): 668–88.

Ployhart, R. E., Schneider, B. and Schmitt, N. (2006) *Staffing Organizations: Contemporary Practice and Theory* (3rd edn). Mahwah, NJ: Lawrence Erlbaum.

Porteous, M. (1997) *Occupational Psychology*. London: Prentice Hall.

Purkiss, S. L., Segrest, W. L., Perrewe, P. L., Gillespie, T. L., Mayes, B. T. and Ferris, G. R. (2006) Implicit sources of bias in employment interview judgments and decisions. *Organizational Behavior and Human Decision Processes*, 101: 152–67.

Robertson, I. T. and Kandola, R. S. (1982). Work sample tests: validity, adverse impact, and applicant reaction. *Journal of Occupational Psychology*, 55: 171–83.

Robertson, I. T. and Smith, M. (2001) Personnel selection. *Journal of Occupational and Organizational Psychology*, 74: 441–72.

Rynes, S. L. and Cable, D. M. (2003) Recruitment research in the twenty-first century. In Borman, W. C., Ilgen, D. R. and Klimoski, R. J. (eds), *Handbook of Psychology: Industrial and Organizational Psychology*, Vol. 12. Hoboken, NJ: John Wiley & Sons, pp. 55–76.

Rynes, S. L., Bretz, R. D. Jr and Gerhart, B. (1991) The importance of recruitment in job choice: a different way of looking. *Personnel Psychology*, 44: 487–521.

Salgado, J. F. (1999) Personnel selection methods. In Cooper, C. L. and Robertson, I. T. (eds), *International Review of Industrial and Organizational Psychology*, Vol. 14. Chichester: Wiley, pp. 1–54.

Salgado, J. F., Anderson, N., Moscoso, S., Bertua, C., De Fruyt, F. and Rolland, J. P. (2003) A meta-analytic study of general mental ability validity for different occupations in the European Community. *Journal of Applied Psychology*, 88(6): 176–84.

Schmeichel, B. J. and Vohs, K. D. (2009) Self-affirmation and self-control: affirming core values counteracts ego depletion. *Journal of Personality and Social Psychology*, 96(4): 770–82.

Schmidt, F.L. and Hunter, J.E. (1993) Development of causal models of processes determining job performance. *Current Directions in Psychological Science*, 1: 89–92.

Schmidt, F. L. and Hunter, J. E. (1998) The validity and utility of selection methods in personnel psychology: practice and theoretical implications of 85 years of research findings. *Psychological Bulletin*, 124(2): 262–74.

Schmitt, N., Gooding, R. Z., Noe, R. A. and Kirsch, M. (1984) Meta-analyses of validity studies. *Journal of Applied Psychology*, 70: 280–9.

Shackleton, V. and Newell, S. (1997) International assessment and selection. In Anderson, N. and Herriot, P. (eds), *International Handbook of Selection and Assessment*. Chichester: Wiley, pp. 81–95.

Sharf, J. C. (1994) The impact of legal and equal employment opportunity issues on personal history inquiries. In Stokes, G. A., Mumford, M. D. and Owens, W. A. (eds), *Biodata Handbook*. Palo Alto, CA: Consulting Psychologists Press, pp. 351–90.

Sieveking, N., Anchor, B. and Marston, R. (1981) Selecting and preparing expatriate employees. *Personnel Journal*, 18: 197–202.

Smith, M. and George, D. (1992) Selection methods. In Cooper, C. L. and Robertson, I. T. (eds), *International Review of Industrial and Organizational Psychology*, Vol. 7. Chichester: Wiley, pp. 55–97.

Steiner, D. D. and Gilliland, S. W. (1996) Fairness reactions to personnel selection techniques in France and the United States. *Journal of Applied Psychology*, 81: 134–41.

Sternberg, R. J. and Wagner, R. K. (1995) *Practical Intelligence in Everyday Life*. Cambridge: Cambridge University Press.

Stewart, G. L., Fulmer, I. S. and Barrick, M. R. (2005) An exploration of member roles as a multilevel linking mechanism for individual traits and team outcomes. *Personnel Psychology*, 58(2): 343–65.

Stone, D. L. and Stone-Romero, E. F. (2004) The influence of culture on role-taking in culturally diverse organizations. In Stockdale, M. S. and Crosby, F. J. (eds), *The Psychology and Management of Workplace Diversity*. Malden, MA: Blackwell Publishing, pp. 78–99.

Syed, J. (2008) Employment prospects for skilled immigrants: a relational perspective. *Human Resource Management Review*, 18: 28–45.

Taylor, S. (2004) Hunting the snark: a critical analysis of human resource management discourses in relation to managing labour in smaller organizations. In Marlow, S., Patton, D. and Ram, M. (eds), *Managing Labour in Small Firms*. London: Routledge, pp. 18–42.

Templer, K. J., Tay, C. and Chandrasekar, N. A. (2006) Motivational cultural intelligence, realistic job preview, realistic living condition preview, and cross-cultural adjustment. *Group and Organization Management*, 31: 154–73.

Tung, R. L. (1981) Selection and training of personnel for overseas assignments. *Columbia Journal of World Business*, 16(1): 68–78.

Viswesvaran, C. and Ones, D. S. (2000) Perspectives of models of job performance. *International Journal of Selection and Assessment*, 8: 216–25.

Watson, T. (2004) HRM and critical social science analysis. *Journal of Management Studies*, 41: 447–67.

Wilk, S. L. and Cappelli, P. (2003) Understanding the determinants of employer use of selection methods. *Personnel Psychology*, 56: 103–24.

Williams, S. D. (2004) Personality, attitude, and leader influences on divergent thinking and creativity in organizations. *European Journal of Innovation Management*, 7(3): 187–204.

Witt, L. A. (2002) The interactive effects of extraversion and conscientiousness on performance. *Journal of Management*, 28(6): 835–51.

Zanoni, P. and Janssens, M. (2007) Minority employees engaging with (diversity) management: an analysis of control, agency and micro-emancipation. *Journal of Management Studies*, 44: 1371–97.

Zedeck, S. and Cascio, W. F. (1984) Psychological issues in personnel decisions. *Annual Review of Psychology*, 35: 461–518.

Zottoli, M. A. and Wanous, J. P. (2000) Recruitment source research: current status and future directions. *Human Resource Management Review*, 10: 353–83.

Performance management

Jane Maley

9

?

After reading this chapter, you should be able to:

- ☐ Understand the strategic importance of a performance management system in a global context
- ☐ Explain the purpose, criteria and ethics of an effective global performance management system
- ☐ Identify the main approaches to performance appraisal
- ☐ Critically reflect on the most effective sources for performance management
- ☐ Recognize strategies to improve performance

Introduction

This chapter looks at one of the most critical procedures within a multinational corporation (MNC) – the international performance management system. Performance management is the process by which organizations set goals, determine standards, assign and evaluate work, and distribute rewards. These systems are now widely and routinely used for many employees. Their use increased through the 1990s as a result of the pressures of globalization, increased competition and a greater analysis of all the characteristics of employee performance (Varma et al., 2008). Performance management systems were originally used for managers, professionals and technical employees, but today they are frequently used to appraise staff at all levels in many parts of the world.

Measuring the performance of individuals and teams has become an important tool to ensure good organizational performance, and is critical to identifying possible gaps between job expectations and the organization's strategic intent. Hence performance management is considered to be a central element of strategic human resource management (HRM), and it is argued that a successful performance management system is vital if an organization wants to implement strategy into employee action. If the process is conducted appropriately, it can provide a huge benefit for a firm, its supervisors and its employees. An effective performance management system can help to create a sustainable competitive advantage for the firm that is not easy for others to replicate (Hanson et al., 2005).

Nonetheless, performance management is viewed by many managers around the world as a pointless annual ritual, and the use of, and satisfaction with, performance appraisal systems has a history of being problematic (Nankervis and Compton, 2006). As with everything else in the global arena, managing performance in an international context is a lot more complex than is the case with a one-dimensional national structure.

There are a number of reasons for the complications arising in the cross-border context. First, culture profoundly influences management practices. For example, the purpose of performance management, employees' acceptance of the system, and the cultural value dimensions that affect performance management vary immensely across borders (Claus and Briscoe, 2009). The unique norms, values and beliefs inherent in different cultures affect the way employees are controlled as well as their perceptions of equity, expectations and justice. Consequently, a performance management system developed in one country may not be suitable in another (Chiang and Birtch, 2010).

Second, organizations must be cognizant of the potential influence of other institutional and economic factors that may influence performance management (Chiang and Birtch, 2010). Third, international human resources managers in MNCs face a major dilemma in terms of reconciling whether performance management should be a single, standard practice throughout the organization, or a divergent system that can be used to reflect local culture and local management practices.

Finally, the performance management of international employees presents particular challenges. In addition to the special case of the expatriate manager, who has been the focus of much research over the past two decades, other international employees need attention too. For instance, employees in an MNC's subsidiary who are nationals of the country in which they are working have been found to be neglected in international performance management studies (Dowling et al., 2008). For example, the manager of the subsidiary has been found to require particular consideration. These managers are usually isolated from their supervisor, and it has been found (Maley and Kramar, 2007) that they may experience difficulties in the conduct of their own performance appraisal.

In other words, the dilemma of both geographical distance and cultural distance must be considered when a company operates across different countries and continents (Harzing and Noordhaven, 2005). The performance management system cannot be one-dimensional, and human resources managers need systems that can be applied to a range of cultural values.

The structure of this chapter is as follows. It begins with a review of the strategic importance of the performance management system in a global context. This is followed by an examination of the various characteristics that underpin a performance management system, which includes the purpose, criteria and ethics of performance management. Subsequently, the key approaches and the value of multiple sources in a crosscultural setting are considered. This section includes various suggestions to help improve the performance management process. Next there is an overview of performance management in an international context. Finally, there is a summary of the chapter that incorporates a critical evaluation and the future direction of performance management, and outlines the benefits of studying performance management from a critical perspective.

The strategic importance of performance management in a global context

In order to understand the strategic significance of performance management in a global setting, it is important to recognize that the purpose and approach of performance management changes as the MNC expands and subsidiaries develop. These changes have been attributed to the staffing structures and strategies of human resources (Birkinshaw and Morrison, 1995). Evidence suggests that it is these structures and strategies that determine the types of employee who will be employed in an international setting (Dowling et al., 2008), as well as the importance placed on the purpose and approach of performance management (Maley, 2011).

Three key types of international employee have been identified:

☐ Parent country nationals (PCNs). These employees are from the parent country; expatriates are always PCNs.

☐ Host country national (HCNs). These employees work in their host subsidiary.

☐ Third country nationals (TCNs). These employees are not from the parent office and do not work in their host country.

For example, the US MNC General Electric employs Australian citizens in its Australian operations (HCNs), often sends US citizens (PCNs) to Asia-Pacific countries on assignment, and may send some of its UK employees on an assignment to its Japanese subsidiary (TCNs). The nationality of the employee has been found to be a major factor in determining the person's category.

The employees in its subsidiaries (HCNs, TCNs) become increasingly more important to the success of the MNC as the globalization strategy advances and the subsidiary takes a central role in the success of the MNC. For that reason, the international performance management process must consider not only the employees from the parent country (HCNs), but also these new forms of employee (Milliman et al., 2002). In Chapter 3, the concept of the 'global professional' was introduced. In this chapter, this idea will be extended to illustrate three distinct category of global employee. What is more, as the MNC continues to expand, there will be an increasingly larger percentage of the organization that is both geographically and culturally distant from the parent MNC (Harzing and Noordhaven, 2005). This widening cultural distance has been found to have a major effect on the purpose, criteria, acceptance and ethics of performance management (Fenwick, 2005). Consequently, the international performance management process needs to adopt a broader cultural perspective with an appreciation of cultural diversity.

Characteristics of performance management

Performance management and performance appraisal

'Performance management' is the general term for a number of human resources functions that are concerned with managing performance. It is the systematic process that involves employees, as individuals and members of a group, in improving organizational effectiveness to accomplish the firm's mission and goals. Employee performance management (Figure 9.1) includes:

☐ planning work and setting expectations;
☐ continually monitoring performance;
☐ developing the capacity to perform;
☐ periodically appraising performance;
☐ rewarding good performance.

It is important to reiterate here that these numerous functions are much more complex to administer in an international setting.

The aspects of the performance management cycle are magnified and become more complex when a firm globalizes. When a company internationalizes its operations, the human resources manager needs to become familiar with the aspects of performance management that may be influenced by the political, economic, legal and cultural feature of the countries in which the MNC is operating. In addition, the human resources manager must be aware of the various stages of evolution of the subsidiary and how these stages may impact on the individual functions of the performance management system. The appraisal is therefore just one component of the performance management system, albeit a major component. Along with the other important functions, it forms part of the umbrella of performance management. The cycle can form a structure for the design of a performance management system in diverse cultures; its particular form and method of implementation may, however, vary between different cultures.

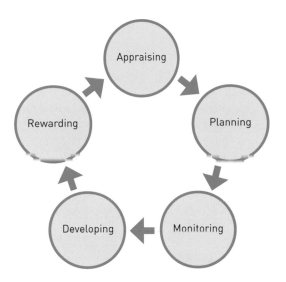

Figure 9.1 The performance management cycle.

The purpose

The purpose of the international performance management system, in particular the performance appraisal, has been the focus of recent debate and discussion by academic scholars and practitioners; this has indicated that employees often have little idea why their supervisor is conducting a performance appraisal (Chiang and Birtch, 2010). Because its purposes are not always well understood, the performance management systems tend to be poorly implemented in many countries (Claus and Briscoe, 2009). Three key aspects of purpose in the global context will be considered in this chapter – first, what influences the purpose; second, the implications of the purpose; and third, the purposes themselves – and these elements will now be considered in turn.

What influences the purpose?

The strategic human resources literature (Wright and McMahan, 1992; Delery and Doty, 1996; Ulrich, 1997) and international HRM literature (De Cieri and Dowling, 1998; Ghoshal and Bartlett, 1998; Harvey et al., 2002) have established that strategic alignment and internationalization have an enormous influence on the purpose of performance management. Claus and Briscoe (2009) argue that context-specific issues need to be taken into account when executing performance management activities, and that multiple contextual elements are critical to understanding the universality and purpose of performance management practices. Similarly, Milliman et al. (2002) propose that contextual factors direct the purpose of the performance appraisal: for example, the firm's strategy, structure, industry, culture (both national and organizational) and local regulations may influence the type and selection of performance management purposes (Figure 9.2).

Implications of the purpose

In turn, the purpose of the performance management has been found to affect the associated level of accountability (Harris et al., 1995; Mero and Motowildo, 1995), the feedback (Aguinis, 2008), the relationship with the supervisor (Maley and Kramar, 2007), and the level and accuracy of observation and recall (Cleveland and Murphy, 1992; Farr and Jacobs, 2006).

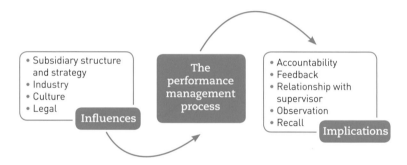

Figure 9.2 The purpose of performance management: the influences and implications.

The purpose of performance management in MNCs

Milliman et al. (2002) contend that the purpose of performance management is based on a similar fundamental premise in most countries – to control individuals in firms to maximize the MNC's financial performance. This view is shared by Cardy and Dobbins (1994) and Ouchi (1982). Milliman et al. (2002) add that although performance management is based on similar fundamental ideas in many countries, its specific purpose and practice may vary slightly between nations. Performance management is also seen as an important way to identify employee strengths and weaknesses, evaluate training needs, set plans for further development and provide motivation by ascertaining rewards and career advancement (Cardy and Dobbins, 1994). Lansbury and Quince (1988) proposed that one of the first steps in establishing a performance management scheme should be to determine what the scheme is supposed to achieve.

A pragmatic depiction of performance management purpose is offered by De Cieri and Kramar (2010), who describe the purpose as threefold:

☐ as a strategic link to the firm's goals;
☐ to supply data for administrative use;
☐ for developmental purposes.

Milliman et al. (2002) expand this viewpoint by describing five main purposes: documentation, development, administrative purposes involving pay and promotion, and subordinate expression.

Box 9.1 The cultural context of performance appraisal

Chiang and Birtch (2010) recently investigated the effects of culture on the purposes of performance appraisal in the banking industry in seven countries across Europe, Asia and North America. They found that the effects of power distance, collectivism, masculinity and uncertainty avoidance (see Hofstede, 1980) should not be understated, nor are they straightforward. Multinational organizations must be cognizant of the potential influence that a range of other organizational, institutional and economic factors may wield on appraisal.

These findings hold significant implications for the theoretical underpinnings of appraisal, a management tool largely rooted in the values and traditions of US equity, expectancy and procedural justice (see below). Chiang and Birtch conclude that not only is the transferability of appraisal and its operationalization affected by interactions with divergent cultures and contextual settings, but new hybrid appraisal architectures are also emerging that demand further research.

Moreover, subordinate expression is an important addition and highlights the significance of feedback in the appraisal (Cardy and Dobbins, 1994; Cascio, 2000, 2003; DeNisi and Pritchard, 2006). Milliman et al. (2002) found that cultures characterized by high individualism (Hofstede, 1980), in particular that of Australia, place an enormous emphasis on subordinate expression and feedback, and view this as a crucial part of the appraisal purpose.

It appears that the purpose of the performance appraisal may vary between cultures and change as the subsidiary evolves through various structures and strategies. Murphy and Cleveland (1995) claim that whereas over 85 per cent of US MNCs use appraisals for administrative purposes, in particular salary decisions, performance management is less frequently used for training and development purposes. They also expressed a key concern that information from performance appraisals is used by raters, ratees and firms for many purposes, and that the goals pursued by the rater and ratees are not necessarily the same as those pursued by the firm.

However, Murphy and Cleveland (1991) suggested in an earlier study that too many purposes could be conflicting, and that one or two purposes tend to dominate and cancel out the others. This argument was also advanced by Milliman et al. (2002), who proposed that expectations might be high in relation to what could be realistically achieved, and that firms needed to devote more time and effort to the appraisal process. Furthermore, they concluded that the purpose of appraisal had fallen short not only in the USA, but also in 10 other countries they sampled. A simple definition of the purpose of performance management has been proposed by DeNisi and Pritchard (2006). They propose that the purpose is to accurately diagnose individual and group performance in order to be able to reward good performance and remedy poor performance so that, in the aggregate, overall organizational performance will be enhanced.

In sum, the evidence in the literature points to the fact that an MNC's purpose in conducting appraisals will be shaped by several contextual factors (see also Box 9.1). In addition, the purpose may influence various aspects of the appraisal process and outcome. It is for these reasons that the purpose needs to be clearly communicated by the firm or at least understood by all its international employees. In other words, not only should the subordinate and supervisor's expectations be aligned, but both also need to be congruent with the MNC's rationale for using a performance management system (Milliman et al., 2002). The literature on the purpose of performance management indicates that the purpose is vitally important, having widespread and pervasive implications that impinge on many aspects of the MNC's operations.

The criteria of an effective performance management system

Just as it is important to have a clearly defined purpose for conducting the performance management process, particularly in an international context, it is also fundamental to have a set of clear criteria by which to measure employees' performance. All too often, employees do not fully understand the particular criteria according to which they are being measured.

Research has focused on whether culture affects the performance criteria used in performance appraisal. Lam et al. (1999) found that criteria were treated differently across different cultures, indicating that there are emic (culturally specific) and etic (universal) dimensions in the perception of performance criteria. In additional, national differences in power distance also played an important role in defining the criteria (Lam et al., 1999). Another study found that there were culturally related and culturally neutral performance dimensions for retail managers in Singapore and Australia, and that the importance attached to the criteria varied significantly, showing the mediating effect of culture (Campbell and Zarkada-Fraser, 2000).

An effective international performance management system needs in particular to identify performance criteria that are important to the MNC and related to the job at hand (Arvey and Murphy, 1998). There are several different opinions on which external criteria should be used to evaluate performance. A recent standpoint (Kramar and Bartram, 2010) advocates five clear criteria: strategic alignment, validity, reliability, specificity and acceptability. These recommendations are unequivocal and, importantly, encompass all the important areas, including acceptability and strategic congruence – the latter being the term used to define the alignment of HRM strategy with the overall business strategy. Each criterion will now be discussed in relation to the performance appraisal.

Strategic alignment

Strategic alignment is the degree to which the employee's individual performance management system matches or fits with the organization's global business plan. In other words, the employee's performance objectives should be aligned with those of the supervisor, and the supervisor's plan should be aligned with the manager's performance objectives, and so forth up to the objectives of the CEO and the board of directors. It has been proposed that performance criteria include the individual's aspirations, and that the individual's best possible performance criteria need to be identified and fitted with the firm's conceptual criteria (Borman, 1994). More recently, the system of the balanced scorecard (BSC), developed by Kaplan and Norton (1992), has become a popular method of developing strategic congruence by linking the firm's long-term goals to its employees' short-term actions.

Validity

Validity and reliability are statistical terms (and concepts) that lie at the centre of most research into the various aspects of performance appraisal. They get to the heart of concerns over biases inherent in the performance appraisal process – reducing these biases increases the effectiveness of the performance management system.

Validity refers to fact that people are being measured on areas that are truly important to the firm's objectives, and refers to the extent to which a performance measure assesses all the relevant aspects of the job (De Cieri and Kramar, 2010). If a performance management process lacks validity, it does not measure all aspects of the employee's performance.

Failure of validity is a very common phenomenon in performance management. A recent study of the performance management systems of national managers from MNCs of British, European and USA origin found that 80 per cent of performance appraisal lacked validity and did not measure important aspects of the national manager's job (Maley and Kramar, 2007). Validity has been found to be particularly important to many employees, and has been found to be a major contributor of poor employee acceptability of the system. Both validity and reliability are also important in recruitment and selection, and it is therefore well worth understanding these scientific terms and their relevance in international HRM.

Reliability

Reliability refers to uniformity of performance and to freedom from random error. There are several types of reliability that are pertinent to the performance appraisal. The most important is *interrater reliability*; this refers to the level of consistency among the supervisors who are appraising the employees. Evidence indicates that many supervisors are subjective, and therefore their appraisal of employees will be low in reliability.

Another important and relevant form of reliability in performance measurement is the reliability and constancy of measures over time. This is particularly important in a seasonal business. Take, for example, sales people who work in real estate. The real estate market in most Western countries typically picks up in late winter and reaches a peak in late summer. Louis Evangelidis, a real estate proprietor in Sydney, Australia, has stated that, in order to accurately assess a new salesperson, their sales performance needs to be assessed over a complete year. If, for example, a salesperson starts with the firm in early autumn and is first reviewed at the end of their first 6 months in late winter, their sales will be evaluated over a period where sales are predictably slow. This will most likely compare unfavourably with the results of another salesperson who has worked and been assessed over the previous 6 months (the high season). Many businesses exhibit such seasonal fluctuations, and these must be considered in order to improve appraisal reliability.

It is extremely challenging in the workplace to obtain good reliability in performance appraisal, but it is a challenge that human resources managers and supervisors must strive to meet. Scholars have researched and written copious amounts of data on the reliability of performance appraisal, but there is little evidence of a quick fix. The whole culture of a firm often needs to change in order to achieve high reliability in performance appraisals.

Acceptability

The behavioural criterion of acceptability of the performance appraisal is a fairly recent addition to the field, and research literature on acceptability from the perspective of the employee is limited. An exception is a recent study conducted in China (Taormina and Goa, 2009) that found acceptability of performance appraisal to be paramount and to relate to the way in which the performance appraisal process was executed. In the same way, acceptability of ratee appraisal in an international context has been found to increase when the ratee has regular communication and a positive relationship with the rater (Milliman et al., 2002).

From the perspective of the appraisees, acceptability is more likely to occur when they perceive the appraisal to be fair (Taylor et al., 1998; Bradley and Ashkanasy, 2001) and when the feedback they receive from the appraiser is timely and accurate (Milliman et al., 2000; Sully De Luque and Sommer, 2007). Moreover, where a subordinate and a supervisor are geographically distant, regular feedback has been found to be particularly important (Cascio, 2000; Milliman et al., 2002; Harzing and Noordhaven, 2005; Sully De Luque and Sommer, 2007). Hedge and Teachout (2000) have claimed that acceptability may be the critical criterion for determining the success of the performance management process.

In the international setting, a vital aspect of the acceptability of the performance appraisal process on the part of both the supervisor and the employee has been found to be attributed back to how clear the purpose of the appraisal is (Lindholm et al., 1999; Milliman et al., 2002; Maley, 2009). The acceptability and purpose of performance management emerge from the literature as both paramount and interdependent. Evidence suggests that, from an employee's perspective, the performance management process needs to have a clear purpose in order for it to be acceptable, and that purpose also has to be acceptable.

The relationship between purpose and acceptability reinforces the need for the performance appraisal to be embedded in a performance management system rather than to stand alone as a human resources event. For example, if appraisal is part of a fully fledged performance management system, it is more likely that the appraisal will be linked to the organization's strategy, and that both compensation and training and development needs will be achieved. Under these conditions, the appraisal is more likely to be acceptable to the ratee.

Construct theories and acceptability

Construct theories may help to explain the phenomenon of the acceptability of performance management. For example, a psychological explanation for people's resistance to performance evaluation could be that a negative evaluation can represent a threat to one's self-efficacy. Consequently, it might be expected that these feelings could be to some extent reduced if the appraisal criteria were acceptable and the purpose was clear to the person receiving the appraisal. The threat to self-efficacy that may occur in a dysfunctional appraisal could have a knock-on effect on many psychological aspects of the employee–employer relationship.

Cognitive dissonance theory (Festinger, 1957) is a theory on the basis of which aspects of performance appraisal may be interpreted. From the perspective of cognitive dissonance theory, a negative evaluation from another person would be inconsistent with the individual's generally upbeat perception of him- or herself as a capable person. Such conflicting cognitions would possibly affect the spirit of the individual's relationship with the MNC, that is the psychological contract with the organization.

Organizational justice (Colquitt et al., 2001) is another theoretical construct with which performance appraisal acceptability may be viewed. A dysfunctional performance appraisal system may affect the employee's perception of organizational justice. This construct may help to explain employees' attitudinal and behavioural reactions to both performance appraisal and organizational commitment (Masterson et al., 2000).

Because the appraisal has implications for individual reward, employees' perceptions of justice are especially significant. Erdogan (2002) claims that organizational justice has two subjective perceptions: *procedural justice* (fairness of procedures) and *distributive justice* (fairness of outcome). For example, when employees feel unfairly treated in their appraisal, they are likely to react negatively. Distributive justice is concerned with the perceived fairness of the outcomes or allocations received. In appraisal, in order to reach a perception of distributive justice, individuals compare their efforts with the rating they receive and the fairness of that rating (Erdogan, 2002).

On the basis of the two construct theories described above, an appraisal is unlikely to be perceived as acceptable unless those involved in the process perceive it to be unbiased (that is, from the perspective of cognitive dissonance theory) and fair (that is, from the perspective of MNC justice theory). It is reasonable to expect that, if employees believe they are being treated unfairly by the organization, this will in turn impact on their perception of their relationship with the organization. Thus, cognitive dissonance theory and organizational justice theory assist in understanding the acceptability of the performance management process.

The important point here is that the additional complexity of geographical distance and cultural distance in the global setting makes achieving the criterion of acceptability of the performance management system increasingly challenging to achieve. It is therefore essential that international human resources managers be mindful of the various contrasts influencing the acceptability of a performance management system within the MNC.

Ethics in performance management

For a performance appraisal to be acceptable, it must be ethical. One of the key intentions of an ethical performance appraisal should be to provide an honest assessment of performance. Although some supervisors are competent and lawful in reviewing an employee's performance, evidence suggests that there is an inconsistency in the approach to the ethics of performance management when a firm goes global, one which may cause employees to become frustrated, cynical, and withdrawn (Murphy, 1993).

Survey results in one large study (Aydinlik et al., 2008), examined the ways in which the largest private sector organizations in Sweden and Turkey communicated the intent of their codes of ethics to their employees. The research identified some interesting findings showing that the small group of companies in Turkey that have a code may appear to be more 'advanced' in their handling of ethics than Sweden. Such a conclusion is counterintuitive as one would have expected a developed nation like Sweden to be more advanced in these measures than a developing nation such as Turkey. Culture may play a large role in the implementation of ethics in corporations and could be a major reason for this difference. Moreover, it has been reported that, in performance appraisals, factors not related to performance (for example, race) are one of the top 10 serious ethical considerations for human resources managers in MNCs. It is, therefore, paramount that firms ensure that their performance management processes are conducted to a high ethical standard.

The climate in some organizations does not encourage people to think through ethical considerations because of an overwhelming focus on the bottom line (Maley and Kramar, 2007). The pressure from the parent company to meet unrealistic performance objectives may encourage managers to cut corners or act in an unethical manner. A case in point can be found in the history of Enron (see Mini Case Study 6.1): managers at Enron were given unrealistic performance objectives that resulted in dysfunctional and unethical behaviour.

In a crosscultural setting, supervisors must take extra precautions to ensure that the performance management process maintains equality, equity and justice. Stakeholder theory states that 'the MNC and its managers are responsible for the effects of activities on others' and that 'the MNC should be managed for the benefit of the stakeholders'. This theory supports utilitarian ethics. In performance management, this relates to equity, procedural and distributive justice, autonomy, respect and safety in the workplace. As a rule, these principles are to some degree understood by many cultures.

Notwithstanding, basic rights in a performance management process also include principles that are not easily translated across all cultures. These principles include feedback, openness and consultation, which are not usual traits of collectivist, high-power-distance cultures. The international human resources manager must be alert to the sensitivities of the ideals of these cultures within the four key dimensions of cultures (Hofstede, 1980). International research evidence indicates that, if the firm's purpose for doing the performance appraisal is clearly communicated throughout the organization, and the criteria of strategic congruence, validity, reliability and acceptability are upheld to a high ethical standard, the performance management process is more likely to be successful.

Mini Case Study 9.1
Ethics: performance appraisal at Travelscence

In 2004, Keith Gavin became financial controller and a member of the executive committee of Travelscence, a medium-sized, family-owned travel agency in the Hunter valley, 2 hours' drive north of Sydney, Australia. Keith sold his home in Sydney and relocated to the Hunter valley with his wife and two young children aged 8 and 10 to take up the position. He was the first person from outside the family running the company to hold a senior position in it or to be included on the executive committee, and he took the job despite sensing that some members of the family were concerned about his ability to fit in with the company culture.

One year after Keith had commenced work at Travelscence, the company decided to downsize. This was a response to huge changes never before seen in the travel business industry. Keith, who had been through this before when he was a financial controller in the healthcare industry, agreed this was good for the long-term health of the 35-year-old company. He decided not to be anxious that the dynasty members of Travelscence seemed more concerned about short-term profits.

The MD, Max Murphy, was relying on Keith to help him determine how to downsize in an ethical manner – Max said he trusted Keith more on this than he did Sonia Foley, the human resources manager. On Keith's recommendation, the company decided to make its lay-off decisions based on the annual performance appraisal ratings of the employees. Each department manager would submit a list of employees ranked by the average score of their last three appraisals. At some point, Keith and the executive committee would decide who would be made redundant. This decision would be based on the employees with the poorest performance.

When Keith received the evaluations, he was confused. Six employees did not appear to have been appraised. However, their names were highlighted for redundancy. When he asked the relevant managers to explain, they told him that these employees had been with the company for many years. When performance appraisals had been introduced 10 years earlier, Max had agreed to a request from this group of loyal employees that they would not have to endure formal performance appraisal, which they felt was unnecessary. The managers told Keith they had questioned this decision, and Max reassured them that it would only be temporary and that in the interim he would evaluate them himself.

When Keith discussed this matter with the Max, he

▷ said that he had never had the time to conduct the appraisals. He also said that it was less important because these particular six employees were all very near retirement age. He added that the firm had been good to them and that they had received more than enough retirement superannuation. In addition, Australian legislation required Travelscence to pay them a generous redundancy package. Max believed that the right thing to do was to keep the jobs for the younger guys, the breadwinners with families. Max reassured Keith that the six employees would never dream of causing a disruption or taking Travelscence to court. Keith enquired whether they were actually performing satisfactorily, and Max said he was uncertain.

As Keith left the office, Max told him that he was doing a tremendous job and that he had made a big impact on the executive committee. Max confirmed that Keith was right to let the six old-timers go, and added that although Travelscence was a caring company, that they could not keep 'dead wood' for ever. Keith left Max's office knowing that he had some principled and ethical decisions to make.

Questions

1 How would you describe the management of the human resources function at Travelscence?
2 What are the ethical issues in this case?
3 What are the personal and professional dilemmas for Keith Gavin, and what do you believe is the right action for him to take?

Source: Case based on a personal interview with the informant, June 2009

Main approaches to performance appraisal

Informal

Performance appraisal may be either informal or formal. An informal approach to performance appraisal was once commonplace and still occurs in some small to medium-sized organizations. An informal approach usually involves giving an employee some degree of guidance and feedback. Bernadette Harris, for example, is the owner and manager of a small estate agency in North Yorkshire, UK, and manages her employees with an informal performance appraisal process. Bernadette has five staff members – three salespeople, a receptionist and a customer service assistant; she considers that she gives her staff regular feedback and guidance, but she does not formally document the process. Bernadette believes that her company is small enough to manage with an informal performance appraisal system.

Although this method may be satisfactory for small businesses, it can become cumbersome and unmanageable in larger organizations. Once a firm has more than about a dozen employees, it is recommended that a more formal system be introduced. According to Chiang and Birtch (2010), informal performance appraisal is more commonly found in individualistic cultures.

Formal

A formal system of performance appraisal involves a formal documented interview with the employee and is the process typically employed in MNCs. There are several types of formal appraisal system. When choosing the type of performance appraisal system that the company should use, the human resources manager needs to consider the compatibility of the system with the strategic business objectives of the organization, as well as specific purposes of the performance evaluation. The major types of appraisal methods will now be reviewed.

Major types of performance appraisal systems

In this section, we will explore the various approaches to measuring and managing performance. Today, most firms, certainly most MNCs, use a behavioural type of performance appraisal combined with an objective goal-based method such as management by objectives (MBO) or key performance indicators. Essays and critical incidents are rarely used these days, except perhaps in a very small number of small to medium-sized enterprises. In the past, some firms conducted closed or blind performance appraisal systems. In a closed system, the employee did not participate in the process and was unaware what was written about them (see Box 9.2).

Box 9.2 Appraisals at Atomic Energy

The former UK Atomic Energy Authority was one of the first government agencies to be privatized by then British Prime Minister Margaret Thatcher in 1981. The newly formed company was named Amersham International. This new organization continued with the old system of performance appraisal, which utilized a closed appraisal method for all employees. Not surprisingly, this process resulted in a degree of mistrust between the management and employees. A more transparent process that involved employee participation was introduced in the mid-1980s. Following the introduction of an open, transparent performance management system, the company's profits started to increased dramatically after a 5-year decline.

Source: Interview with the Chief Operating Officer, Amersham International, May 2000

Major types of performance appraisal are outlined in Table 9.1 and will now be discussed.

Ranking

Ranking compares each person's performance, with the manager ranking all subordinates from 'best' to 'worst'. Typically, 10 per cent of ratings are required to be poor or excellent. Ranking forces the rater to distribute the ratings evenly across a broader range of results. This is similar to scaling requirements in university examinations. Ranking can occur independently without any other system being involved, but this raw ranking method is rarely used nowadays.

The General Electric Company, however, gave forced ranking a degree of respectability. It is argued that forced ranking avoids problems of manager bias and, in particular, leniency. On the other hand, forced ranking was believed to be one of the major factors contributing to the dysfunctional behavior of employees that triggered the downfall of Enron.

Behaviour observation scales

Behaviour observation scales (BOSs) use critical incidents to develop a list of the desired behaviours needed to perform a specific job successfully. This method has recently gained in popularity and is used by many large MNCs.

Medtronic Incorporated is a Fortune 500 company that makes medical and surgical devices. Its US headquarters is in Minneapolis, but the company operates in 120 countries around the world. Medtronic uses a BOS appraisal-based system for its 38,000 employees. Tziner and Kopelman (2002) collated the results of four separate studies with samples in two nations (Israel and Canada) and lent support to the proposition that performance appraisal and review based on BOSs may be superior to other appraisal methods as it may yield more favourable attitudinal effects.

Goal setting

Employee motivation and performance are improved if employees clearly understand and are challenged by what is to be achieved. If performance management is to have a developmental purpose, it ought to focus on the process of getting results, and that process must be considered in terms of the job-related behaviours over which the individual employee has control.

There has been much support for MBO among HRM scholars. For example, Wright and Snell (1998) believe that MBO is a flexible process and that this flexibility means that it can be used across a large range of jobs. Although MBO was originally intended for use as a stand-alone process, it has in practice been found to be used alongside traditional methods of appraisal such as behavioural methods, in a belt-and-braces style of approach. MBO has been found to be acceptable method of appraisal in individualistic cultures. This could be because of its emphasis on goals and measurement, as well as employees' involvement and collaborative efforts, which are integrated into the MBO philosophy. Dinesh and Palmer (1998) argue that performance management systems incorporating MBO appear to offer significant advantages, such as good validity, reliability, strong specificity in terms of results, high acceptability and a very good opportunity for strategic congruence.

In contrast, however, some scholars are not in favour of MBO. For example, it has been argued that MBO may destroy teamwork (Deming, 1982), and there may be conflict with total quality management initiatives (Levinson, 1991; Castellano and Harper, 2001). Furthermore, MBO can lack comparability and therefore have limitations with regards to their administration, particularly if the administration requires valid comparisons, such as promotion and salary awards (Bernardin and Beatty, 1984; Wood and Marshall, 1993). Importantly, the concept of individual objectives does not fit with the ideals of teamwork found in a collectivist society (Hofstede and Hofstede, 2005), and therefore MBO-type objectives may have crosscultural limitations.

The BSC is a performance management framework that became popular during the early 1990s. Kaplan and Norton (1992) presented the BSC as an integrative device that would encourage and facilitate the use of non-financial information by senior managers in organizations, with the choice of non-financial measure being driven primarily by 'strategic' considerations. They argued that, when equipped with this better information, managers would be able to deliver improved strategic performance. As a consequence, BSC has attracted considerable interest among organizations seeking to improve the implementation of their strategies (Lawrie, 2004).

On the other hand, Othmana et al. (2006) raise questions about the effectiveness of BSCs and argue that their effective implementation may be more difficult to develop in Malaysian organizations. Other researchers argue that there are inherent weaknesses in the concept of the BSC itself, and that these weaknesses will limit its usefulness.

Table 9.1 Summary of performance appraisal approaches

Method	Description	Positive features	Drawbacks
Ranking	Employees ranked from best to worst	Reduces bias	Disliked by both individualistic and collectivist cultures
Behaviour observation scales	Use critical incidents to develop a list of the desired behaviours	High acceptability Reliable Valid	Can be complicated and costly to set up, particularly for global operations
Management of objectives/key performance indicators	Manager and employee set goals	High acceptability	May not fit a collective culture Destroys teamwork Lacks comparability

Multisource feedback

The supervisor as a source

So far, this chapter has assumed that the sole arbiter of performance is the supervisor, and that information from other sources is indirect and filtered through him or her. In many MNCs, this is the case, but there is evidence that this may not always be the best practice. It is apparent from human resources research that one of the key problems for the supervisor in evaluating subordinates' performance is that it is extremely difficult to observe employees' behaviour directly. Supervisors often complain that they do not always have time to fully observe the performance of their employees.

This is particularly evident in MNCs where supervisors may be managing employees across national borders. Murphy and Cleveland (1995) argue that supervisors are one of the groups least able to assess behaviour, and contend that much of what the supervisor knows about employees is probably the result of secondary data or indirect data rather than direct observation. For this reason, people other than the supervisor may be better placed to evaluate employees' performance, as they may have more opportunity to directly observe them. As a result, direct supervisors, peers, customers and employees themselves can all provide information on the employee's performance.

Moreover, the requirement for superior objectivity, the increased use of teams and the accent on customer service and quality have created awareness in using multiple sources to evaluate employees' performance (Eichinger and Lombardo, 2003; Levy and Williams, 2004; see also Box 9.3). A study conducted by the Corporate Leadership Council (2006) revealed that 90 per cent of Fortune 1000 firms had implemented some degree of multisource feedback. The same study revealed that the presence of multisource feedback increased individual performance by 8.1 per cent.

Box 9.3 Multisource assessment at Peace Corps

The Peace Corps, a government initiative created by President John F. Kennedy, implemented the use of self-appraisal tests, based on the premise that individuals would adapt better to cultural change if they had a better understanding of themselves.

In 1970, Robert Dorn, who worked in Peace Corps leadership training, joined the Center for Creative Leadership and introduced the practice of self-appraisal. Years later, Robert Bailey, an economist who had worked for Dorn, had the idea of including others in the assessment process and initiated the multisource assessment process.

Source: Justo (2009)

Subordinates as sources

Murphy and Cleveland (1995) argue that subordinates may be a strong source of information for the employee, especially in relation to interpersonal behaviours and results. The subordinate may not fully understand all aspects of the manager's job, but he or she will directly witness interpersonal behaviours that the supervisor or peer assessor may miss. The subordinate usually has day-to-day contact with the employee and would therefore usually have a reasonable view of his or her behaviours. Feedback from a subordinate is a valuable resource for the employee, as one of the keys to effective performance as a manager is the ability to get good work from one's subordinates (Mintzberg, 1973; Ilgen and Feldman, 1990).

Even though subordinates may be the optimal source for behavioural information, they cannot usually assess all tasks or technical skills (Murphy and Cleveland, 1995), and subordinate assessment, which turns the normal hierarchy on its head, may be uncomfortable for both the subordinate and the boss (Carroll and Schneier, 1982). This has been suggested as the principle reason that not all MNCs have adopted this system, despite the merits it has to offer for assessing behaviours (Eichinger and Lombardo, 2003). The idea of reversing the hierarchy does not translate well into a collectivist society with a low individuality or a high power-distance dimension. These cultures acknowledge a leader's power and do not like to reveal or ask too much personal information.

Self as source

Self-assessment – the facility of employees to assess their own performance – has become routine over the past decade. Ashford et al. (2003) found that self-assessment offered the qualities of self-trust, reliability, availability and trustworthiness. She found that, in order to perform self-assessment, an individual must perform three tasks: establish a standard, decide which feedback cues to use, and correctly interpret those cues. She also stressed that decoding cues was the most vital aspect but the most neglected. Many of the employee's cues from supervisors may come indirectly by e-mail, or by telephone, and, according to Cascio (2000), these indirect cues could be more susceptible to encoding problems. According to Ashford et al. (2003), when decoding cues, the individual needs to maintain self-preservation as a self-confident performer.

There is evidence from the USA that self-rating is more lenient than ratings obtained from supervisors (Eichinger and Lombardo, 2003). In contrast, self-ratings were examined in China by Yu and Murphy (1993), showing that Chinese workers would self-rate themselves lower than their peers or supervisors. This is not surprising considering that China is a high-power-distance, collectivist society where modesty and humility are highly respected.

Evidence, therefore, points to self-appraisal offering a degree of reliability, validity and acceptability to the employee. Moreover, in turbulent times, when such events as mergers and restructuring occur with increasing frequency, the pressing reality of having to survive in such a setting makes the self-assessment process an important area of inquiry for the employee.

Peers as sources

It has been argued that peers are in closer proximity to ratees than supervisors, and are therefore more able to give accurate assessments (Borman, 1994). This is particularly evident in teams. However, research indicates that effective peer appraisals require a great degree of trust among team workers, a non-competitive reward system, and frequent opportunities for colleagues to observe each other. There is evidence, however, that peers tend to give harsh evaluations (Saavedra and Kwun, 1993). Peer evaluations are often not acceptable in collectivist cultures and have been found to be unacceptable in China, Korea and Japan (Gillespie, 2006).

Multisource feedback (360-degree appraisal)

The process of multisource feedback (360-degree appraisal) involves obtaining feedback from subordinates, peers, supervisor, self and customers. This gives everyone more information about a ratee's behaviours, thus enhancing the potential for improvement. In recent years, multisource feedback has received a deal of research and management attention, the general findings suggesting that multisource feedback results in more accurate ratings (Palmer and Loveland, 2008). There is sometimes disagreement among the various sources used (Eichinger and Lombardo, 2003), yet if all the ratings produced the same findings, there would probably be little value in obtaining information from all sources – each of the rating sources appears to have its own inherent advantages and disadvantages.

On the one hand, experienced supervisors usually have good norms because they have seen several employees working on the job; this can result in well-calibrated views of different performance levels, and supervisor rating is acceptable across most cultures. Peers are often in closer proximity to the work being done. Self-ratings, however, have the advantage that there is a large amount of information conveniently available. In addition, other forms of feedback have been found to be invaluable when managing employees who are geographically distant and whose supervisor may not be there to witness the majority of their behaviours. Moreover, it is argued (Kaplan and Palus, 1994) that all sources should be used if an accurate and comprehensive assessment is to be achieved. On the other hand, peers and subordinates are often inexperienced in making rater and task judgements, and may be aware of only a small portion of a manager's performance; self-ratings can be distorted because of an inflated perception of one's own performance.

In an international context, multisource feedback has been found to be particularly challenging, and recent evidence suggests that multisource feedback is not transferable across all cultures. For example, Varela and Premeaux (2008) investigated the effect of crosscultural values on multisource feedback with managers from Venezuela and Colombia, two collectivistic and high-power-distance countries. The results of their study indicated that cultural values distort the evaluations involved in multisource systems. Specifically, unlike reports of studies conducted in individualistic and low-power-distance environments, Varela and Premeaux found that peers were the least discrepant source of information, that subordinates tended to provide the highest evaluations across all the feedback sources, and that there was an excessive emphasis on people-oriented behaviours. Likewise, Gillespie (2006) addressed whether multisource feedback ratings made by subordinates were equivalent across national cultures in Great Britain, Hong Kong, Japan and the USA. These results emphasize the need for MNCs to use caution when transporting multisource feedback to international locations.

Identifying strategies to improve international performance

In many cases, the appraisal interview will provide the foundation for noting inadequacies in employees' performance and for making improvements – unless these inadequacies are brought to the employee's notice, they are likely to become critical. Poor employee performance is most likely to be due to one or more of three conditions. For example, if an employee's performance is not up to standard, it could be caused by either:

☐ a lack of skill;
☐ a lack of knowledge;
☐ a lack of motivation.

For satisfactory performance to occur, an employee usually requires certain skills, knowledge and motivation suited to the job. In addition, the supervisor needs to be able to detect these three important traits, which can be challenging when the supervisor and employee are from different cultures.

The first step in managing unsatisfactory performance is to detect and determine the reason behind it. This almost certainly requires the supervisor to be trained to conduct a professional performance appraisal interview. Once the source of the problem is known, a course of action can be planned. For instance, if the performance issues are due to a lack of skills or knowledge, the solution may lie in providing training and development in an effort to improve the employee's deficiency of skills and knowledge. Poor motivation may have a devastating effect on performance, but it is often difficult to diagnose and is frequently a multifaceted, complex matter; this may be particularly difficult to detect in another culture. Nonetheless, it is essential that employees with low levels of motivation are identified during the appraisal interview. These employees in particular need to be given enough time to express their views through an adequate feedback session.

Politics

It has also been found that politics, combined with power, plays a fundamental role in the appraisal process. Longnecker (1994) found that increased power on the part of the rater may make the rater more critical and more likely to rate the employee harshly. It is therefore necessary for the human resources manager to carefully monitor the performance appraisal process and ensure that the appraisal system is fair, and that politics are kept to a minimum.

Trust

A low level of trust between either the employee and the company, or the employee and the supervisor, has been found to have a detrimental effect on the outcome of the appraisal. Murphy and Cleveland (1995) noted that trust between an individual and the organization reduces the need for appraisal to be used as a control mechanism. In addition, they reported that as trust increases, it is likely that the appraisal will be future-oriented, focused on developmental processes generally used in a productive manner and, above all, fair. It is essential, therefore, that the supervisor and employee meet regularly in an attempt to build trust.

Fairness

The employee's perception of the supervisor's trustworthiness has been found to be related to the interpersonal atmosphere, helpfulness and perceived fairness of the session (Bradley and Ashkanasy, 2001). Kramar and Bartam (2010) contend that, for a performance appraisal system to be fair, several criteria must be met:

☐ the employee must have adequate notice;

- the employee must fully understand the purpose, criteria and standards of the system;
- the employee must be given a fair hearing;
- the rater must apply performance standards with consistency across all employees.

A fair appraisal system has been found to increase the level of trust and acceptability (Juncaj, 2002), which makes fairness a crucial component of the appraisal system.

Feedback

Feedback has been identified as essential for a satisfactory performance appraisal. In spite of this, most employees do not get adequate feedback from their supervisors (Longnecker and Gioia, 1988; Juncaj, 2002; Milliman et al., 2002; Cascio, 2003; Maley, 2009). It is necessary, therefore, for the supervisor to ensure that there is adequate time during the appraisal interview for feedback and employee expression. Gosselin et al. (1997) established that employees preferred receiving formal appraisals at least twice per year, with ongoing informal feedback throughout the year. A study conducted by the Corporate Leadership Council (2006) revealed that feedback and that fairness and accuracy of informal feedback increased staff performance by 39.1 per cent.

Performance management in an international context

Performance management has been shown to be susceptible to many problems when a firm globalizes its operations. All HRM processes have been identified as becoming more complex due to the geographical and cultural distance between the subsidiary and the head office (Shen, 2004; Harzing and Noordhaven, 2005; Sully De Luque and Sommer, 2007; Taormina and Goa, 2009). The end result is that international employees are often found to be predominantly despondent about their performance management (Fenwick, 2004; Maley and Kramar, 2007; Taormina and Goa, 2009).

The cultural impact of performance management

Performance appraisal is an area that experiences a great deal of difficulty when translated into different cultural environments (Hempel, 2001; Shen, 2004). For example, ratee bias (Tziner et al., 1998), work practice (Dowling et al., 1999), productivity (Harvey et al., 2002; Milliman et al., 2002), interpretation (Milliman et al., 2000), perception of status (Chong, 2008) and the need for feedback and acceptance of the appraisal system (Bradley and Ashkanasy, 2001, Chong, 2008; Milliman et al., 2002) have all been found to be influenced and shaped by culture.

Tziner et al. (1998) found that, although there was some consistency in appraisals across cultural settings, cultural attitudes and beliefs could influence ratee discrimination. They found that confidence in the international performance appraisal was strongly influenced by culture. For example, they argued that raters

Mini Case Study 9.2
Point of view: unfair performance management in schools in England

Tom O'Malley, a geography teacher in southern England, has this to say about performance management:

When performance management first came in, it was seen as an initiative aimed at tightening control on the profession. Performance management would ensure teachers set annual targets that were deemed appropriate by the establishment, agreed by the schools and overseen by local authority inspectors and OFSTED (the Office for Standards in Education). Targets were to be agreed between the individual being assessed and an assigned performance management mentor. Targets were usually, although not always, at least in part tied closely to measurable academic standards. Teachers who were deemed to have successfully completed the set targets by their line managers and performance management mentors, as well as by the head teacher, were often eligible for rewards in the way of promotion and salary increase.

The whole system is hampered by the practical difficulties of finding the time for meetings between key staff to complete the process, and for verification of progress through lesson observation, etc., not to mention agreeing recorded outcomes. Establishing what constitutes 'progress' in the world of education and understanding what this looks like for any given child or class or cohort, and then agreeing how best this can be measured, is fraught with difficulty. In practice, successful annual performance management depends as much or more on a positive relationship with a teacher's assessor than on any real 'progress' in relation to the actual or perceived needs and progress of the children being educated. Consequently, performance management is becoming increasingly viewed as an unfair game one needs to play and, in terms of improving schools, is gradually diminishing

Question

1 Is this another disgruntled teacher, or is there evidence of more widespread performance management problems in the British school system?

in international settings were more susceptible than domestic raters to distorting and inflating their subordinate's performance appraisal ratings.

Dowling et al. (2008) state that culture is one of the most significant constraints that must be considered when evaluating employees in a foreign subsidiary. They argue that variations in work practices between the parent MNC and the subsidiary need to be recognized. For example, one does not fire a Mexican manager just because worker productivity in Mexico is half the US average. In Mexico, this would mean that a manager working to US criteria would be working three or four times harder than the average Mexican manager. Dowling et al. argue that international appraisals require relevant comparative data rather than absolute numbers; the harassed Mexican manager in the above example has to live within Mexican constraints, not European or North American ones, which can be very different. Additionally, Harvey et al. (2002) and Milliman et al. (2002) found that the way MNCs measure worker productivity is often similar, but the results appear different because of cultural nuances.

Interpretation of the performance appraisal incorporates the issue of cultural applicability (Milliman et al., 2000). In different cultures, for example, the performance appraisal can be interpreted as a signal of distrust or even as an insult. In Japan, for instance, it is important to enable one to 'save face' by avoiding direct confrontation and, according to Dowling et al. (1999), this influences the way in which performance appraisal is conducted. A Japanese manager cannot point out a work-related problem or error committed by a subordinate. He would explain the consequences of a mistake without pointing out the actual mistake.

A study involving 10 leading Chinese MNCs (Shen, 2004) found that there were commonalities in the procedures and criteria of international performance appraisal between Chinese and Western MNCs. However, Shen (2004) found that the purpose of performance appraisal in Chinese MNCs was largely to decide how much to pay rather than for the organizational development, as it was more concerned with short-term business achievement. He also found performance appraisals in Chinese MNCs to be low in feedback and less transparent. In addition, it has been established that different forms of multisource assessment other than the traditional supervisory appraisal are virtually non-existent in China and Hong Kong (Entrekin and Chung, 2001; Shen, 2004). Research from Hong Kong (Snape et al., 1998) revealed that Hong Kong respondents had a preference for group-based appraisal, and that appraisals were more directive and less participative. The appraisals in Hong Kong companies were found to have been modified to suit the cultural collectivist characteristics of the society

In Indian firms, Varma et al. (2005) found that interpersonal relations and performance levels had an effect, and that performance level had a significant effect, on performance ratings, and that supervisors inflated the ratings of low performers, suggesting local that cultural norms might be operating as a moderator.

Acceptance of the performance appraisal by both the rater and the ratee has been argued to be essential for a successful appraisal (Bradley and Ashkanasy, 2001). In the international setting, acceptance of performance appraisal has been found to vary widely across different cultures (Milliman et al., 2002; see also Box 9.4). For instance, Japanese employees have been found to be less accepting of the appraisal process than USA employees.

Box 9.4 **Performance appraisals at Chinese multinationals**

In a recent large study (Shen, 2004), Chinese multinationals were found to adopt different approaches towards different groups, particularly different nationalities and those of managerial status. The Chinese international performance appraisals were found to be a mix of home and local appraisal systems, and of traditional Chinese personnel management and modern Western human resources concepts. Moreover, Chinese international performance appraisal policies and practices were found to be affected by various host-contextual and firm-specific factors, and there was also an interplay between international performance and other international HRM activities.

The divergence–convergence question

One of the most perplexing questions on the cultural impact of appraisal concerns whether performance appraisal systems designed in parent MNCs should be transferred to other countries (Harvey, 1997). On the one hand, Dowling et al. (2008) hold that this is possible providing the manager conducting the performance appraisal is sensitive to foreign values. On the other hand, Hempel (2001) and Vance (2006) argue that it is doubtful that traditional principles guiding the design and management of appraisal in Western countries can be successfully transferred to other countries. Vance (2006) found that cultural management styles may translate into distinct differences in the optimal management of performance, raising important doubts about how traditional performance appraisal principles can be transferred across boundaries. Hempel (2001) presented both theoretical arguments and exploratory results suggesting that Western-style performance appraisals need to be extensively modified in order to work with Chinese employees. He argues that until more is known in this area, there should be strong reservations about the direct applicability of the performance appraisal practices typically implemented by US and European MNCs.

International legislation

It is important for the international human resources manager to understand that industrial relations governing performance management will most likely differ across national boundaries (Harzing and Ruysseveldt, 2005). It is essential to acknowledge that, in the industrial relations field, no industrial relations system can be understood without appreciating the way in which rules are established and implemented, and decisions are made, in the society concerned. It is usually necessary to have some appreciation of the historical origin of the country's performance appraisal legislation.

Conclusion

This chapter has addressed the crucial issue of performance evaluation. It has discussed the contentious nature of performance management and its implications for the organization and its employees. Recommendations to improve performance management are nothing new. Improvements to the system have been recommended since the inception of performance appraisal over 50 years ago. There has been a plethora of ideas to improve the basic concept of managing employee performance. Fifty years later, this area still arouses controversy, and if we make predictions on the future based on the past, we can expect even more change.

The further use and refinement of behavioural methods (BOS) will be a major step in the development of performance appraisal systems. Behavioural methods possess good validity and reliability and are presently widely used in MNCs. BOSs will soon become cost-effective and accessible for smaller and medium-sized enterprises.

A weakness in many performance appraisal programmes is that managers and supervisors are not trained to give appraisals. This means that these managers may give inadequate appraisals; they particularly make rater errors and are less likely to give sufficient feedback to their subordinates. Arvey and Murphy (1998) proposed that rater training showed some promise in improving the effectiveness of performance ratings and that the systematic errors, particularly leniency and the halo effect – a classic finding in social psychology in which initial evaluations of a person carry over into judgements about their specific traits – were found to be reduced with rater training. It is envisaged that there will be more emphasis on training managers to give effective performance appraisal and manage the overall performance management process.

The area of culture in the MNC presents many challenges, and firms will need to consider the acceptability of performance appraisal and performance management in different cultures, and recognize that 'one performance management system may not fit' (Chong, 2008). Research has revealed that only scant attention has been paid to the performance management of international employees (Harvey, 1997; Maley and Kramar, 2007; Claus and Briscoe, 2009). MNCs, therefore, should consider their international employees and need to think about tailoring the performance management system to fit the norms and beliefs of the various national cultures they work with.

The virtual office presents difficulties for performance management. Online performance management systems are now widespread. Unfortunately, firms often introduce elaborate and expensive performance management systems but fail to ensure that employees know how to use them adequately. It has even been suggested that managers tend to give more negative ratings using online appraisals compared with those given on an old-fashioned paper form (Kurzberg et al., 2005). There is little doubt that technology has impacted the way in which firms manage performance management, and this is an area that will continue to witness enormous change. For example, the impact of the speed of communication and social network sites could have a major influence on the politics of performance management.

Performance management is a human relations process and needs trust between the supervisor and the employee in order to work well. Although progressive contemporary technology has removed the burden of many tedious administrative tasks in the office, it must be considered that, for a performance management process to work effectively across a diversity of cultures, there need to be three vital activities between the supervisor and the subordinate that cannot be substituted by a computer:

☐ regular face-to-face contact;
☐ repeated opportunity for feedback;
☐ follow-up of performance appraisal.

In other words, looking towards the future, the MNC's performance appraisal must be embedded in a performance management system that transcends all cultures.

Benefits of studying performance management from a critical perspective

Studying performance management in organizations from a critical outlook permits future international managers to acquire a better perception of the numerous perspectives of their different employees. This involves under-standing cultural divergence and the structural and strategic inconsistency of human resources. Interpreting both cultural and structural differences and their effect on performance management will allow future international managers to weigh up situations, identify problems and determine suitable solutions to the multifaceted issue of international performance management.

International performance management, although not new, has not yet matured. Some significant studies have been carried out, but they have provided conflicting results, and a complete body of knowledge is some time away. Never-theless, there is little doubt that, in some form, performance management and its main activity – performance appraisal – are preferred to the alternative of doing nothing. It is therefore critical that we not only continue to refine and perfect the process, but also gain a better insight into the process in an interna-tional context. It is only by studying the process that we will be able to redefine and improve it.

Finally, international performance management research will be substan-tially strengthened by an effective collaboration between university scholars and industry practitioners (Perkmann and Walsh, 2007). As the complexity of international management issues and the velocity of change in international business increases, such collaborations may become essential if research is to make any real difference to an academic understanding of the issues surrounding international performance management.

❷ For discussion and revision

Questions

1   How has globalization changed the nature of the performance appraisal?

2   How does performance appraisal differ from performance feedback?

3   What are the challenges involved in giving feedback to employees from a different culture?

4   How can leaders influence the creation of a performance-based culture in a MNC?

Exercise

1   Go to the University of Massachusetts (UMASS) website at http://www.umass.edu/humres/library/PMPGuide.pdf and review the information on the performance management process for academic staff.

  • Assess the procedure and criteria used at UMASS and suggest the strengths and weaknesses of the system.

  • Compare and contrast performance management at UMASS with that of the multinational healthcare company Medtronic after looking at their website: http://www.medtronic.com/2010CitizenshipReport/total-employee/global-learning.html

Further reading

Books

Brewster, C., Carey, L., Dowling, P., Grobbler, P., Holland, P. and Warnich, S. (2007) *Contemporary Issues in Human Resource Management* (2nd edn). Cape Town: Oxford University Press Southern Africa.

Briscoe, D., Randall, S. and Clauss, L. (2009) *International Human Resource Management: Policies and Practice for Multinational Enterprises* (3rd edn). London: Routledge.

Casio, W. (2006) Global performance management systems. In Stahl, G. K. and Bjorkman, J. (eds) *Handbook of Research in International Human Resource Management*. Cheltenham: Edward Elgar, pp. 176–96.

Dowling, P., Festing, M. and Engle, S. (2008) *International Human Resource Management*. Melbourne: Cengage Learning.

Harzing, A. W. and Van Ruysseveldt, J. (2005) *International Human Resource Management*. London: Sage.

Kramar, R. and Bartam, T. (2010) *Human Resource Management in Australia: Strategy, People and Performance* (5th edn). Sidney: McGraw-Hill.

Nankervis, A., Comptom, R. and Baird, M. (2007) *Strategic Human Resource Management* (6th edn). Melbourne: Cengage Learning.

Stone, R. J. (2008) *Human Resource Management* (6th edn). Milton, Queensland: John Wiley.

Case Study Performance appraisals in the not-for-profit sector

The Foundation, founded in the USA in 1960, is an international evangelical relief and development organization whose stated goal is 'to work with the poor and oppressed to promote human transformation, seek justice and bear witness to the good news of the Kingdom of God'. Working on six continents, The Foundation is a large relief and development organization that in 2009 had a $1.5 billion budget. In that same year, the group's total revenue, including grants, products and foreign donations, was $2.6 billion.

William Webster was a senior aid manager for The Foundation. William, a US citizen, had joined The Foundation's Boston office with excellent references following 10 years of global experience in international aid management, including working in Haiti, Mexico and India. Thirty-five-year-old William had an accounting degree from the University of New York and an International MBA from Columbia Business School. He had been working for The Foundation for 2 years when he gave the following account of his performance management experience there:

'Originally I was hired as the senior program manager for all of The Foundation's programmes worldwide. When I arrived for duty, the position had been split between me and a woman who had been at The Foundation for 5 years. She insisted on keeping India and Pakistan and would not cooperate in my redesign of the regional offices. This came as a great shock. I felt this was crazy as I had actually been on the ground in India for 2 years and felt I had a good understanding of the culture and people.

'This woman appeared to me to be very close to the director. They shared a love of the theatre and, as far as I can gather, were really good friends and frequently visited the theatre, opera and ballet together. This part of the arts is, I'm afraid, something I know very little about. While I enjoy a West End production, I am more a ball game kind of guy. To cut to the chase, in the end she and I didn't get along very well. After 2 years, the tsunami hit Asia and I told the chief operating officer (whom I reported to) that I would rather work on a special project, such as the tsunami-affected areas, and start a new programme in Indonesia. The chief operating officer took over my responsibilities. I told him that we needed one person in the role of senior program manager.

'After a few months, they hired a very capable Vice President of Programs, and I reported to her. We went out for lunch, and the topic of the Myers–Briggs personality test came up. She told me that she was an ENTJ (I am an INFP – the direct opposite). I went back to the office after lunch and looked up ENTJ. One of the famous quotes of a typical ENTJ is, 'I'm so sorry you have to die', so I knew I was in trouble. She came into the company like a bulldozer and ruffled a lot of feathers.

'I had been trying to raise funds for the tsunami and had $1 million to work with. I put together several proposals and started the programme in Indonesia. My assistant was a very power-hungry, ambitious recent graduate from graduate school, and her room-mate was best friends with the new VP of Programs. I assured her that we would raise the funds, but it took longer than I expected. Part of the problem was that there were no clear objectives for me and I had the office politics stacked against me.

'One Friday afternoon, a meeting was scheduled for my assistant Mary and me to meet with the VP of Programs. The VP then said that there was no need for Mary to join the meeting. I walked into the conference room and found the head of human resources and the chief operating officer in the room. The human resources manager proceeded to tell me that they were going to let me go but gave no reason. One of the most surprising things was that I had been given a very good performance appraisal a month earlier. Nothing negative had been raised, and all the top boxes had been ticked. The human resources manager, whom I had only met briefly once or twice before, asked me if I had anything to say. I told her I didn't know what to say. The three of them got up and left the room and closed the door. I remember sitting there crying alone.

'A week after I was let go, the American Red Cross granted the Foundation a $10 million grant for the tsunami programme – the proposal I had written and submitted. The chief operating officer resigned from his post a month later, and the VP resigned from hers within a year.'

Questions

1. Describe the major HRM issues at The Foundation?
2. If you were the head of human resources at The Foundation, how would you have handled this situation?
3. Describe the role of objectives and feedback in this case.
4. Discuss the process you might implement to strengthen the performance management process at The Foundation.

Source: This case is based on a personal interview with the informant. The name of the organization and employee have been changed for confidentiality

9

References

Aguinis, H. (2008) Enhancing the relevance of organizational behaviour by embracing performance management research. *Journal of Organizational Behavior*, 9: 139–45.

Arvey, R. and Murphy, K. (1998). Performance evaluations in work settings. *Annual Review of Psychology*, 49: 141–68.

Ashford, S. J., Blatt, R. and Vande Walle, D. (2003) Reflections on the looking glass: a review of search on feedback-seeking behavior in organizations. *Journal of Management*, 29(6): 773–90.

Aydinlik, D., Arzu, D. and Ulgen, G. (2008) Communicating the ethos of codes of ethics within the organization: a comparison of the largest private sector organizations in Sweden and Turkey. *Journal of Management Development*, 27(7): 778–95.

Bernardin, H. and Beatty, R. (1984) *Performance Appraisal: Assessing Human Behaviour at Work*. Boston: Kent.

Birkinshaw, J. and Morrison, A. (1995) Configurations of strategy and structure in subsidiaries of MNCs. *International Business Studies*, 26(4): 729–40.

Borman, W. C. (1994) *Performance Evaluation in Organisations*: Farnham, Surrey: International Library of Management.

Bradley, L. and Ashkanasy, N. (2001) Performance appraisal interview: can they really be objective and are they useful anyway? *Asian Pacific Journal of Human Resources*, 39(2): 83–97.

Campbell, F. and Zarkada-Fraser, A. (2000) Measuring the performance of retail managers in Australia and Singapore. *International Journal of Retail and Distribution Management*, 28(6): 228–43.

Cardy, R. L. and Dobbins, G. H. (1994) *PA: Alternative Perspectives*. Cincinnati, OH: South-Western College Publishing.

Carroll, S. and Schneier, C. E. (1982) *Performance Appraisal and Review Systems: The Identification, Measurement and Development of Performance in Organisations*. Glenview, IL: Scott, Foresman.

Cascio, W. F. (2000) Managing a virtual work place. *Academy of Management Executive*, 12(3): 81–91.

Cascio, W. F. (2003) *Managing Human Resources: Productivity, Quality of Work Life, Profits* (8th edn). New York: McGraw-Hill.

Castellano, J. and Harper, R. (2001) The problems with MBO. *Quality Process*, 34(3): 39–49.

Chiang, F. T. and Birtch, T. (2010) Appraising performance across borders: an empirical examination of the purpose and practices of performance appraisal in a multi-country context. *Journal of Management Studies*, 47(7): 1365–92.

Chong, E. (2008) Managerial competency appraisal: a cross-cultural study of American and East Asian Managers. *Journal of Business Research*, 61(3): 191–200.

Claus, L. and Briscoe, D. (2009) Employee performance management across borders: a review of the relevant literature. *International Journal of Management Reviews*, 11(2): 175–96.

Cleveland, J. and Murphy, K. (1992) Analysing performance appraisal as goal-directed behaviour. In Ferris, G., Rowland, K. R. (eds) *Research in Personnel and Human Resource Management* (Vol. 10). Greenwich, CT: JAI Press, pp. 121–85.

Colquitt, J. A., Kossek, E. E. and Raymond, A. (2001) Care giving decisions, well-beings, and performance: the effects of place and provider as a function of dependent type and work-family climates. *Academy of Management Journal*, 44(1): 29–44.

Corporate Leadership Council (2006) *Considerations for Implementing 360-Degree Reviews: Secondary Research Findings*. Washington, DC: Corporate Executive Board.

De Cieri, H. and Dowling, P. (1998) *The Tortuous Evolution of Strategic Human Resources in Multinational Enterprises*. Department of Management, Working Paper in Human Resource Management and Industrial Relations No. 5. Melbourne: University of Melbourne.

De Cieri, H. and Kramar, R. (2010) *Human Resource Management in Australia* (3rd edn). North Ryde, NSW: McGraw-Hill.

Delery, J. and Doty, D. H. (1996) Modes of theorising in strategic human resource management: tests of universalistic, contingency and configurational performance predictions. *Academy of Management Journal*, 39(4): 802–22.

Deming, W. E. (1982) *Quality Productivity and Competitive Position*. Cambridge, MA: Massachusetts Institute of Technology Press.

DeNisi, A. S. and Pritchard, R. D. (2006) Performance appraisal, performance management and improving individual performance: a motivational framework. *Management and Organization Review*, 2: 253–77.

Dinesh, D. and Palmer, E. (1998) MBO and the balanced scorecard: will Rome fall again? *Management Decisions*, 36(6): 363–9.

Dowling, P., Welch, D. and Schuler, R. (1999) *International Dimensions of Human Resources*. Cincinnati, OH: South-Western College Publishing.

Dowling, P., Festing, M. and Engle, S. (2008) *International Human Resource Management* (5th edn). Melbourne: Cengage Learning.

Eichinger, R. and Lombardo, M. (2003) Knowledge 360-degree theory. *Human Resource Planning*, 26(4): 34–45.

Entrekin, L. V. and Chung, J. K. (2001) The attitudes toward different sources of executive appraisal: a comparison of Hong Kong Chinese and American managers in Hong Kong. *International Journal of Human Resource Management*, 12(6): 965–87.

Erdogan, B. (2002) Antecedents and consequences of justice perceptions in performance appraisals. *Human Resource Management Review*, (12): 555–78.

Farr, J. and Jacobs, R. (2006) The criterion problem today and into the 21st century. In Bennett, W., Lance, C. E. and Woehr, D. J. (eds) *Performance Measurement: Current Perspectives and Future Challenges*. Mahwah, NJ: Lawrence Erlbaum, pp. 321–38.

Fenwick, M. (2004) International assignments and expatriation. *Asian Pacific Journal of Human Resources*, 42(3): 365–77.

Fenwick, M. (2005) International compensation and performance management. In Harzing, A. W. and Ruysseveldt, J. (eds) *International human resource management*. London: Sage, Chapter 12.

Festinger, L. (1957) *A Theory of Cognitive Dissonance*. Stanford, CA: Stanford University Press.

Ghoshal, S. and Bartlett, C. (1998) *Managing Across Borders: The Transnational Solution*. London: Random House Business.

Gillespie, T. (2006) Internationalizing 360-degree feedback: are subordinate ratings comparable? *Journal of Business and Psychology*, 19(3): 361–82.

Gosselin, A., Werner, J. M. and Halle, N. (1997) Ratee preference and appraisal. *Human Resource Development Quarterly*, 8(4): 315–33.

Hanson, D., Dowling, P. J., Hitt, M. A., Ireland, D. R. and Hoskisson, R. E. (2005) *Strategic Management: Competitiveness and Globalisation* (2nd edn). Victoria, Australia: Thomson Learning Australia.

Harris, R., Smith, D. E. and Champagne, D. (1995) A field study of PA purpose research vs administrative based ratings. *Personnel Psychology*, 48(1): 151–60.

Harvey, M. (1997) Focusing on international performance appraisal process. *Human Resources Development*, 8(1): 41–62.

Harvey, M., Speier, C. and Novicevic, M. (2002) The evolution of SHRM systems and their application in a foreign subsidiary context. *Asian Pacific Journal of Human Resources*, 40(3): 284–300.

Harzing, A.W. and Noordhaven, N. (2005) Geographical distance and the role of management of the subsidiaries: the case of subsidiaries down under. *Asian Pacific Journal of Management*, 23: 167–85.

Harzing, A.W. and Ruysseveldt, J. (2005) *International Human Resource Management*. London: Sage.

Hedge, J. W. and Teachout, M. S. (2000) Exploring the concepts of acceptability as a criterion for evaluating performance measures. *Group and Organisation Management*, 25(1): 22–44.

Hempel, P. (2001) Differences between Chinese and Western managerial views of performance. *Personnel Review*, 30(2): 203–26.

Hofstede, G. (1980) *Culture's Consequences: International Differences in Work Related Values*. Beverly Hills, CA: Sage.

Hofstede, G. and Hofstede, G. J. (2005) *Cultures and Organisations: Software of the Mind*. London: McGraw-Hill.

IIgen, D. and Feldman, J. M. (1990) Performance appraisal: a process focus. In Cummings, L. and Staw, B. (eds) *Evaluation and Employment in Organisations*. Greenwich, CT: JAI Press.

Juncaj, T. (2002) Do performance appraisals work? *Quality Progress*, 35(11): 45–9.

Justo, A. (2009) The Effective Implementation of Multi-source Feedback Processes. Available from: http://armandojusto.blogspot.com/2009/09/effective-implementation-of-multi.html [accessed 14 October 2011].

Kaplan, R. S. and Norton, P. (1992) The balanced scorecard – measures that drive performance. *Harvard Business Review*, 70(1): 71–5.

Kaplan, R. and Palus, C. J. (1994) *Enhancing 360-Degree Feedback for Senior Executives*. Greensboro, NC: Center for Creative Leadership.

Kramar, R. and Bartram, T. (2010) *Human Resource Management in Australia*. Australia: McGraw-Hill.

Kurzberg, T., Naquin, C. and Belkin, Y. (2005) The effects of email communication on peer ratings in actual and simulated environments. *Organizational Behavior and Human Decision Processes*, 98(2): 216–226.

Lam, S., Hui C. and Law, K. (1999) Job-analysis; organizational-behavior; supervision-of-employees; cultural-differences. *Journal of Applied Psychology*, 84(4): 594–601.

Lansbury, R. D. and Quince, A. (1988) Performance appraisal: a critical review of its role in HRM. In Palmer, G (ed.) *Australian Personnel Management: A Reader*. Melbourne: Macmillan.

Lawrie, G. (2004) Third-generation balanced scorecard: evolution of an effective strategic control tool. *International Journal of Productivity and Performance Management*, 53(7): 611–30.

Levinson, H. (1991) Management by whose objectives. *Harvard Business Review*, 69(92): 176–90.

Levy, P. and Williams, J. (2004) The social context of performance appraisal: a review and framework for the future. *Journal of International Management*, 30(6): 881–905.

Lindholm, N., Tahvanainen, M. and Bjorkman, I. (1999) Performance appraisal of host country employees: Western MNEs in China. In Brewster, C. and Harris, H. (eds) *International HRM: Contemporary Issues in Europe*. London: Routledge, pp. 143–59.

Longnecker, C. O. (1994) The paradoxes of political appraisal: tales from the dark side. Paper presented at the Society for Organisational and Industrial Psychology Conference, September 1994, Nashville, TN, USA.

Longnecker, C. O. and Gioia, D. A. (1988) Neglected at the top: executives talk about appraisals. *Sloan Management Review*, 21: 183–93.

Maley, J. (2009) The impact of the performance appraisal on the psychological contract of the remote subsidiary manager. *South African Journal of Human Resource Management*, (2): 63–73.

Maley, J. (2011) The influence of various human resource management strategies on the performance management of subsidiary managers. *Asia Pacific Journal of Business*, 3(1): 2.

Maley, J. and Kramar, R. (2007) International performance appraisal: policies, practices and processes in Australian subsidiaries of healthcare MNCs. *Research and Practice in Human Resource Management*, 15(2): 21–41.

Masterson, S., Lewis, K., Goldman, B. and Taylor, M. (2000) Integrating justice and social exchange: the differing effects of fair procedures and treatment on work relationships. *Academy of Management Journal*, 43: 738–48.

Mero, N. P. and Motowidlo, S. J. (1995) Effects of rater accountability on the accuracy and the favourability of performance ratings. *Journal of Applied Psychology*, 80(4): 517–24.

Milliman, J., Taylor, S. and Czaplewski, A. (2000) Performance feedback in MNC: opportunities for organizational learning. *Human Resource Planning*, 25(3): 29–44.

Milliman, J., Nason, S., Zhu, C. and De Cieri, H. (2002) An exploratory assessment of the purpose of PA in North and Central America and the Pacific Rim. *Asian Pacific Journal of Human Resources*, 40(1): 78–101.

Mintzberg, H. (1973) *The Nature of Managerial Work*. New York: Harper & Row.

Murphy, K. (1993) *Honesty in the Workplace*. Belmont, CA: Wadsworth.

Murphy, K. and Cleveland, J. (1991) *Performance Appraisal: An Organisational Perspective*. Boston: Allyn & Bacon.

Murphy, K. and Cleveland, J. (1995) *Understanding Performance Appraisal*. London: Sage.

Nankervis, A. and Compton, R. (2006) Performance management: theory in practice. *Asian Pacific Journal of Human Resources*, 44(1): 83–101.

Othmana, R., Domil, A., Senik, Z., Abdullah, A. and Hamzah, H. (2006) A case study of balanced scorecard implementation in a Malaysian company. *Journal of Asia-Pacific Business*, 7(2): 55–72.

Ouchi, W. (1982) *Theory Z*. New York: Addison-Wesley.

Palmer, J. and Loveland, J. (2008) The influence of group discussion on performance judgment accuracy, contrast effects and halo. *Journal of Psychology: Interdisciplinary and Applied*, 142(2): 117–30.

Perkmann, M. and Walsh, K. (2007) University–industry relationships and open innovation: towards a research agenda. *International Journal of Management Reviews*, 9(4): 259–80.

Saavedra, R. and Kwun, S. K. (1993) Peer evaluation in self-managing work groups. *Journal of Applied Psychology*, 78(3): 450–62.

Shen, J. (2004) International performance appraisals: policies, practices and determinants in the case of Chinese multinational companies. *International Journal of Management*, 25(6): 547–63.

Snape, E., Thompson, D., Yan, F. and Redman, T. (1998) Performance appraisal and culture: practice and attitudes in Hong Kong and Great Britain. *International Journal of Human Resource Management*, (5): 842–61.

Sully De Luque, M. and Sommer, S. (2007) The impact of culture on feedback seeking behaviour: an integrated model and propositions. *Academy of Management Review,* 25(4): 829–49.

Taormina, R. and Gao, J. (2009) Identifying acceptable performance appraisal criteria: an international perspective. *Asia Pacific Journal of Human Resource Management*, 47(1): 102–24.

Taylor, S., Masterson, S., Renard, M. and Tracy, K. (1998) Managers reactions to procedurally just management systems. *Academy of Management Journal*, 41(5): 568–79.

Tziner, A. and. Kopelman, R. (2002) Is there a preferred performance rating format? A non-psychometric perspective. *Applied Psychology*, 51: 479–503.

Tziner, A., Murphy, K. and Cleveland, J. (1998) Relationships between attitudes towards organisations and performance appraisal systems and rating behaviour: a multinational study. Paper presented at the 24th International Congress of Applied Psychology, May 1988, San Francisco, USA.

Ulrich, D. (1997) *Human Resource Champions*. Boston: Harvard Business School Press.

Vance, C. M. (2006) Strategic upstream and downstream considerations for effective global performance management. *International Journal of Cross Cultural Management*, 6(1): 37–56.

Varela, O. and Premeaux, S. (2008) Cross-cultural values affect multisource feedback dynamics? The case of high power distance and collectivism in two Latin American countries. *International Journal of Selection and Assessment*, 16(2): 134–42.

Varma, A., Pichler, S. and Srinivas, E. (2005) The role of interpersonal affect in performance appraisal: evidence from two samples – the US and India. *International Journal of Human Resource Management*, 16(11): 2030–43.

Varma, A., Budhwar, P. and De Nisi, A. (2008) *Performance Management Systems: A Global Perspective*. New York: Routledge.

Wood, R. and Marshall, V. (1993) Performance appraisal: practice, problems and issues. Paper presented at the Private Pay for Public Work conference, May 1993, Paris, France.

Wright, P. M. and McMahan, G. C. (1992) Theoretical perspectives for strategic human resource management. *Journal of Management*, 18: 295–320.

Wright, P. and Snell, S. (1998) Toward a unifying framework for exploring fit and flexibility in strategic human resource management. *Academy of Management Review*, 23(4): 756–72.

Yu, J. and Murphy, K. (1993) Modesty bias in self-ratings of performance: a test of the cultural relativity hypothesis. *Personnel Psychology*, (46): 357–63.

Reward management

John Shields

10

?

After reading this chapter, you should be able to:

☐ Appreciate the value of a constructively critical (pluralist) approach to understanding the theory and practice of reward management, particularly taking an employee-centred perspective

☐ Understand how reward strategies, programmes and policies are structured in both domestic and international contexts

☐ Demonstrate a detailed awareness of the variety of financial and non-financial reward practices and of the different motivational and behavioural assumptions associated with particular types of reward

☐ Recognize the concepts, methods and techniques associated with managing employee reward in both domestic and international contexts

☐ Demonstrate a detailed understanding of the differences and complementarities between each of the three main components of monetary reward for employees: base pay, benefits and performance pay

☐ Understand the options and challenges involved in the application of theories, concepts and practices related to reward

☐ Appreciate how social and cultural factors affect employees' perceptions of pay fairness, and how these perceptions affect the design and effectiveness of pay programmes

☐ Formulate practical solutions to the challenges of designing and implementing reward strategies, programmes and policies that will support the organization's needs to attract, retain, motivate and develop domestic and international employees

Q

Introduction

Reward management is one of the most important yet most problematic of all human resource management (HRM) functions. Reward management is not only one of the most technically demanding facets of HRM, but also one of the most complex and controversial in terms of the assumptions and debates surrounding the drivers of human motivation and work behaviour. Rewards are a 'red button' issue in the domain of people management.

As experienced human resources professionals know, reward management is very easy to do badly – but difficult to do well. An effective reward system has to be not only soundly designed and integrated, but also carefully implemented, communicated and monitored. The telltale signs of reward mismanagement include perceived reward inequity (or unfairness), low motivation and effort on the part of employees, low job satisfaction, reduced commitment to the organization, higher intention to leave and increased staff turnover: in short, poor 'engagement' of employees with their job, their managers, their peers, their organization and its customers.

This chapter presents an overview of the controversies, concepts and practices associated with the reward management function. In doing this, it offers a constructively critical perspective on the main theories, tools and techniques for configuring effective reward systems for both domestic and international employees. First, we will consider the basic nature and purpose of remuneration and other rewards. We then proceed to explore one of the central debates in the field – that surrounding the relative merits of extrinsic and intrinsic rewards. Next, we will consider the value of seeking to understand reward management from a constructively critical (pluralist) perspective, particularly in relation to acknowledging that employees are not simply 'resource' objects but, rather, are organizational stakeholders with their own distinct needs, expectations and rights, as well as their own responsibilities and contractual obligations to their employer.

Attention then turns to the three main elements of monetary reward or remuneration – base pay, benefits and performance-related rewards – and the types of pay plan associated with each of these. We will consider the general strengths and weaknesses of each major pay plan type, along with debates concerning both the effectiveness and the fairness of incentive plans and other performance-related reward practices.

As reward effectiveness is not simply a matter of system design, but also a function of how clearly and consistently the system's principles and practices are communicated to the employees concerned, the penultimate section of the chapter will examine both reward communications and the cognate and highly controversial matter of reward secrecy and transparency.

Finally, we will explore the special challenges associate with managing employee rewards in international contexts, noting the differences between 'home', 'host' and 'regional' approaches to reward configuration. This section also sets the stage for the chapter's major case study, which describes the additional challenges and options associated with the management of reward systems in an international context. Specifically, this case study of the reward strategies and practices of Chinese multinational corporations (MNCs) invites us to reflect on the complexities of reward management for line employees and expatriate reward management in host country contexts. As we shall see, the case highlights the dual approach to international reward practice favoured by firms headquartered in this rapidly emerging economic superpower.

However, before immersing ourselves in the details of domestic and international reward practice, it is important that we address the nature and purpose of rewards in general.

Employee rewards: nature and purpose

A reward may be anything tangible (for example, pay) or intangible (for example, praise) that an organization offers to its employees in exchange for their belonging to the organization and for contributing work behaviours and results of the type that the organization needs from its people in order to meet its strategic objectives, however these might be defined.

A reward system has four primary objectives:

☐ To attract (or 'buy') the right people at the right time for the right jobs, tasks or roles.
☐ To retain the best people by satisfying their work-related needs and aspirations, and recognizing and rewarding their contribution.
☐ To develop (or 'build') the required workforce capabilities by recognizing and rewarding employees' actions to enhance their knowledge, skill and ability.
☐ To motivate employees to contribute to the best of their capability by recognizing and rewarding high individual and group contributions towards meeting the organization's strategic objectives.

At the same time, a well-designed and administered reward system has a number of important secondary objectives. In particular, it should seek to be the following:

☐ *Needs-fulfilling*: the rewards should be of value to employees in satisfying their relevant human needs.
☐ *Equitable or 'felt-fair'*: reward levels should be seen to be both commensurate with individual contributions and appropriate in comparison with the reward levels received by others.
☐ *Legal*: rewards should comply with relevant legal requirements regarding employees' rights and entitlements, including standards for mandatory minimum pay and benefits.
☐ *Affordable*: the rewards allocated, and any associated on-costs, should fall within the organization's financial means.
☐ *Cost-effective*: there should be an appropriate 'return on investment' from total reward outlays.
☐ *Strategically aligned*: the reward system should be configured so as to support the organization's strategic objectives.

There is, however, considerable potential for conflict between these objec-tives. For instance, tensions may arise between the goals of cost-containment and of offering rewards that are sufficient to attract and retain the right type and number of employees. From an organizational perspective, the optimal approach is not necessarily the cheapest. Rather, the optimal approach is the one that will maximize the returns to the organization in comparison with the outlay made – and this takes us back to the vital matter of strategic reward management.

Exercise
- What would you say are the three most important functions of any system of employee reward, and why do you think these are the most important overall?

Intrinsic versus extrinsic rewards: which are more motivating?

Rewards can be divided into two broad categories: 'extrinsic' and 'intrinsic'.

Extrinsic rewards arise from factors associated with but external to the job that the employee does, that is, from the job context. Extrinsic rewards are of three main types:

- □ financial rewards
- □ developmental rewards
- □ social rewards.

Financial rewards – also referred to as 'pay', 'remuneration' or 'compensation' – are also of three main types:

- □ base pay (the fixed component of the total remuneration);
- □ benefits, such as the employer's contributions to superannuation and personal health insurance;
- □ performance-related pay plans, including 'incentives', which vary with the performance measured.

Although pay may be the most obvious form of extrinsic reward, it is not the only form of reward, nor is it necessarily the most important in terms of influ-encing employees' attitudes, behaviour and effort. *Developmental rewards* cover those rewards associated with personal learning, development and career growth, such as skills training and performance and leadership coaching. *Social rewards* are those associated with seniority and other forms of social esteem or status, a positive organizational climate, support for performance, quality of supervision, work-group affinity, and opportunities for enhanced work–life balance, such as flexible working time arrangements, staff sabbaticals, fitness and wellness programmes, and so on. In some cultures, developmental and social rewards may be more highly prized than rewards of a monetary nature. As the example in Box 10.1 suggests, employees in India may respond much more positively to having access to a clear career pathway than to being offered performance-related pay.

Intrinsic rewards arise from the content of the job itself, including the interest and challenge that it provides, task variety and autonomy, the degree of feedback, and the meaning and significance attributed to the job. One of the most important determinants of the level of intrinsic rewards in any organiza-

> **Box 10.1 For Indian employees, money isn't everything**
>
> Globe Ground India (GGI), a subsidiary of the German airline Lufthansa, operates passenger and cargo handling for Lufthansa, as well as ground and ramp activities in Delhi, Mumbai and a number of other Indian cities. In 2006, facing serious staff turnover and motivation problems, GGI conducted focus interviews with staff with a view to identifying ways in which the firm's reward system could be strengthened to improve staff retention and motivation.
>
> The initial plan was to use the information gathered to develop a long-term incentive plan on top of the yearly bonus. However, one of the interview questions asked staff to nominate the 'highest incentive for you to increase your motivation', and the results were both unexpected and revealing. Staff rated 'money/higher wages' as third behind 'career/status' and 'job pleasure/enjoyment'. Clearly, intrinsic rewards and developmental opportunities were most salient for GGI's staff. Other studies confirm that career management, job design, benefits entitlements and consistent salary adjustment are particularly important to employees in India.
>
> After analysing the results, GGI developed and introduced a new 'total rewards' approach focusing not on long-term incentives but on meeting employees' developmental and job interest needs, and on offering career pathways and prospects. This approach was then set out clearly and comprehensively in a new human resources manual.
>
> This is not to suggest that money does not matter at all. As employees often queried the prior mode of salary adjustment and argued for seniority-based adjustment, the manual explains that salary increases are based on individual contribution and not on time of service alone.
>
> *Source:* Adapted from Lang (2008)

tion is thus the way in which its jobs are designed. One of the longstanding and animated debates in contemporary theory and practice in reward management concerns the relative merits of intrinsic and extrinsic rewards. Many commentators contend that extrinsic rewards in general, and performance-related pay in particular, are the most powerful motivators (see, for example, Deci and Ryan, 1985; Kohn, 1993a, 1993b). Others argue that intrinsic rewards provide the best basis for superior motivation and performance (see, for example, Gupta and Mitra, 1998; Gerhart et al., 2009).

Arguments that support incentive-based rewards derive either explicitly or implicitly from one or other of the main 'process' theories of work motivation. These theories, which include agency theory, reinforcement theory, expectancy theory, goal-setting theory and equity theory, all emphasize the centrality of employees' cognitive processes in understanding and managing the relationship between rewards and task motivation (Shields, 2007):

☐ *Agency theory*, which assumes a potential conflict of interest between 'principals' (that is, owners) and self-seeking 'agents' (that is, hired employees), holds that performance-contingent pay is the most effective means of aligning employees' economic interests with those of employers/owners.

☐ *Reinforcement theory* posits that a timely reward for a given desired action will motivate employees to repeat the rewarded action, whereas punishment in the form of non-reward will extinguish any misbehaviour.

10

☐ *Expectancy theory* holds that an incentive is likely to motivate higher work effort if: (1) employees see the promised reward as personally valuable; (2) they expect that they can achieve the required level of performance; and (3) they trust the employer to deliver the reward in exchange for the achieved performance.

☐ *Goal-setting theory* suggests that employees will be motivated more strongly by performance targets that are specific, agreed and challenging, and by feedback that is precise and instantaneous.

A further common rationale for performance-related rewards is that they operationalize the 'equity' norm of distributive justice. *Equity theory* proposes, in part, that reward satisfaction stems from making employee reward outcomes (including pay level) commensurate with employees' individual inputs (Shields, 2007). In short, high performers should be paid more than low performers, with the inequality of the reward being proportional to the difference in individual performance. This is a common justification for performance-related pay. However, some motivation theorists question the claimed efficacy of extrinsic rewards and propose that rewards that are intrinsic to the job are the only true motivators.

Exponents of cognitive evaluation theory go further still, contending that the use of extrinsic rewards (and punishments) may destroy the intrinsic motivation that flows from inherent interest in the job. Also known as intrinsic motivation theory, *cognitive evaluation theory* posits that people are much more likely to act first and only evaluate, rationalize and ascribe meaning and motive to what they have done after the event. The tendency is to confer motivational meaning on the behaviour – that is, to attribute meaning and purpose to it – only in retrospect. People are more likely to ask, 'Why *have* I done this?' than 'Why *should* I do this?' Cognitive evaluation theory suggests that individuals who have been deriving high intrinsic rewards for their work tasks may radically revise their self-attributed motives for doing the work once a financial incentive is offered to them.

The point here is that the initial motivation to do something is likely to be implicit and intrinsic rather than premeditated and driven by the pursuit of some extrinsic reward. For this reason, Deci and Ryan (1985) argue that extrinsic rewards should not be applied to task performance because these may very well dissipate the intrinsic motivation that may initially have driven the employee's performance. The perception of being 'controlled' extrinsically is assumed to be demotivating, a point embraced with some passion by several prominent opponents of performance incentives (Kohn, 1993a).

Nevertheless, cognitive evaluation theory is also open to challenge. As suggested in Box 10.2, it is by no means clear that intrinsic and extrinsic motivation are opposites; indeed, as critics suggest, the weight of evidence indicates that the two are, if anything, mutually reinforcing (Rynes et al., 2005). Furthermore, it is questionable whether most work behaviour is impulsive rather than premeditated, experience suggesting that both play a part in work behaviour. On the practical side, although cognitive evaluation theory may be quite appropriate for jobs and roles that are intrinsically motivating in the first instance, not all jobs will be intrinsically rewarding. In such cases, it will be necessary either to enrich the job content or to offer more in the way of pay or other extrinsic rewards.

Box 10.2 Intrinsic versus extrinsic rewards – which are best?

The assumption that extrinsic and intrinsic factors are dichotomous rather than complementary is open to challenge. Some research suggests that extrinsic and intrinsic rewards can make a joint contribution to job satisfaction and other desired work attitudes and behaviour. Cameron and Pierce (1997) used a meta-analysis of a hundred studies of reward–performance effects to argue that intrinsic and extrinsic motivation combine in an additive way to produce an overall motivational force. They found that people generally enjoyed performing a task more rather than less when they received an extrinsic verbal or tangible reward. In particular, Cameron and Pierce highlighted that praise led to greater task interest and performance. The negative effects of extrinsic rewards, they suggested, were limited and easily prevented.

Exponents of the intrinsic rewards approach assume that it is possible to enrich all jobs when, in reality, this is not always so. For better or worse, many manufacturing and service organizations succeed quite effectively with job assignments that have limited skill content, a narrow task range and low autonomy.

Taking a critical perspective on reward management

The debate over the relative influence of intrinsic and extrinsic motivational drivers and rewards also illustrates the value of adopting a constructively critical approach to the theory and practice of reward management. An ill-conceived reward system may not only fail to elicit the desired behaviour, but may instead also encourage behaviour that is dysfunctional, deceptive or even destructive; that is, it may give rise to endemic organizational misbehaviour. A critical approach to reward management may help to avert such problems.

A critical approach to reward management requires us to both question our assumptions about what employees may find rewarding and motivating, and also to seek to interpret reward management from a multi-stakeholder (or 'pluralist') perspective – one acknowledging that employees have rights, interests and expectations that are not wholly congruent with those of the employing organization. As such, a critical approach moves away from the 'unitarist' or 'managerialist' assumption that the only relevant stakeholder interest is that of the employer, and that employees are merely 'human resource' objects serving employer-determined ends (Watson, 2004). It also reminds us of the ethical importance and analytical value of adopting an employee-centred approach to understanding the nature and impact of reward management practice (Grant and Shields, 2006). What is a cost to the employer is income and economic security for employees and their dependents; what is a competitive level of pay to the employer may be seen as inequitable by the employee.

Building on these points, a critical pluralist approach also requires consideration to be given to the nature and significance of employees' 'voice', 'say' or 'representation' in determining rewards. How much influence do employees have, either collectively or individually, over the processes by which their monetary rewards are determined? In developed economies, trade unions have traditionally been seen as the chief vehicles of the collective voice in determining pay and conditions of employment, particularly by means of collective bargaining at industry or enterprise level. In 'coordinated' market economies of the type typical of the northern and western Member States of the European Union, the unions' influence in setting pay has traditionally been paralleled by government intervention and regulation designed both to protect low-paid workers and moderate pay increases for employees with greater bargaining power.

However, in developed economies, recent decades have witnessed a decline in union membership and union influence via collective bargaining, particularly in the private sector, along with a retreat from direct government intervention in pay regulation, and this has been accompanied by significant changes in employee voice. Such changes are sometimes taken as signifying the erosion of the employee's voice and a strengthening of 'managerial prerogative' in pay determination.

An alternative interpretation is that employee 'say in pay' has assumed new forms rather than necessarily diminishing. According to Lindrop (2009), new outlets for collective and individual employee voice have emerged. In countries such as the UK and Australia, the vacuum created by the decline in union collective bargaining has been filled, in part, by the rise of new institutions to determine pay, including occupational pay review bodies and tribunals changed with determining 'fair pay' standards for low-paid workers.

At an organizational level, suggests Lindrop (2009), the new voice mechanisms include collective mechanisms such as joint management–employee consultative committees and individually focused direct communication practices, for example direct employee attitude surveys; these are designed in part to inform improvements in reward system design and hence to strengthen employees' satisfaction with rewards, as well as their motivation and commitment to the organization. As we shall see, various forms of 'financial participation' on the part of employees, such as employee share ownership and profit-sharing, may also be vehicles for employee voice and involvement. Yet the extent to which these new mechanisms do in fact support a genuine voice and influence, and a critical pluralist perspective, requires their consequences to be examined from the employees' frame of reference rather than simply from that of the employing organization.

A critical approach also reminds us that the language of reward management – the 'discourse' or 'talk and text' – serves to influence ('construct') employees' and management's perceptions of themselves, each other, the nature of the employment relationship, organizational power inequalities and, indeed, organizational 'reality' itself.

Drawing on the work of French philosopher and historian, Michel Foucault, Barbara Townley (1993a, 1993b, 1994, 1998, 1999) argues that managers simultaneously empower themselves and subjugate those whom they are managing. They do this by means of discourses and practices that individualize, objectify and discipline workers and shape their subjectivity and concept of self and work reality by means of complex regimes of classification, ordering and measurement. As such, the language associated with reward practices such as job evaluation, performance-related pay and competency-based pay can be understood as serving to shape employees' perceptions that differences in reward levels are natural, appropriate and objectively determined.

For our purposes, the key point here is that reward management is concerned with shaping employees' identities, attitudes and behaviour through both language and practice. From a critical perspective, then, it is important that we appreciate the centrality of reward concepts, how these are communicated to employees by managers, and the meanings that employees attribute to these discursive concepts (Grant and Shields, 2006).

Base pay

Base pay is the foundational or 'fixed' component of remuneration and, for most employees, typically comprises the largest single component of total remuneration, with benefits and performance pay making up the remainder. In many countries, legislatures or tribunals have prescribed the payment of guaranteed minimum wage or salary levels. Base pay is generally regarded as the pay type best suited to addressing the objectives of attracting and retaining staff. Providing each employee with a guaranteed level of base pay demonstrates the employer's commitment to the employee, which in turn means that the employee is more likely to reciprocate. Base pay is also the pay component most closely involved in the setting and enforcement of minimum pay standards.

Although base pay systems can be very diverse, there are two broad approaches to building base pay:

☐ job-based pay;
☐ person-based pay.

As well as making different assumptions about what base pay can contribute to an organization and how it can do so, these two approaches to configuring base pay entail distinct types of pay structure (that is, the formal 'architecture' of the base pay system) as well as different modes of evaluation (that is, the pricing of jobs and/or job-holders) and distinct modes of pay progression (that is, the 'rules' determining how each person's base pay level adjusts over time). Table 10.1 highlights the main points of difference between the job-based and person-based approaches, while Table 10.2 summarises the two main base pay options, including the structures, evaluation techniques and modes of progression associated with each.

Table 10.1 Job-based versus person-based base pay

Job-based base pay	Person-based base pay
Jobs add value	Individuals add value
Pay for job's worth	Pay for individual's worth
Pay for the 'size' of the job occupied	Pay for each individual's capacity to perform (that is, their KSAs)
Standard rate for the job, irrespective of KSA differences between job-holders	Different rates of pay depending on assessed capacity (KSAs)
Time-based payment according to time on the job	Time-based payment according to KSA levels
Direct external market pricing	Indirect external market pricing (disaggregated job pay rates)
Evaluation method: job evaluation	Evaluation methods: skill and/or competency assessment
Pay progression and promotion are based on seniority or merit	Pay progression is based on KSA development
Reinforces the promotional hierarchy	Reinforces KSA development

KSA, knowledge, skill and ability.

Table 10.2 Options for base pay

	Structures	Evaluation techniques	Modes of pay progression
Job-based pay	Pay ladders Narrow grades	Market surveys and/or job evaluation	Seniority and/or 'merit'-based increments and promotion
Person-base pay	Broad grades or job families Broadband systems	Skill assessment Competency assessment	Skill sets Competency zones or levels

Job-based base pay

The traditional practice has been to fix base pay according to the 'size' or 'value' of the *job* or *position* occupied. Jobs of larger 'size' – that is, with a greater content of tasks, duties and responsibilities – attract higher levels of base pay, and employees can increase their base pay chiefly by ascending a hierarchy of job-related pay steps incorporated into either a ladder-like pay scale or a stairway of narrow job grades.

A pay scale typically consists of a hierarchy of position-specific pay levels, each comprising a sequence of flat pay rates, steps or points. Traditionally, step-wise pay increments within each level were based on seniority or service, with the increase occurring automatically after each year of service.

A narrow grade (also known as a 'job grade') houses a group of jobs of similar size/value to the organization, and specifies a pay range for these jobs rather than a scale step or spot rate. Each grade will cover a group of jobs regarded as being of similar value to the organization and therefore worthy of roughly the same range of base pay. Unlike simple pay scales, each grade allows for some variance in pay level based on the 'merit' of the individual job holder, but the range over which pay can vary is usually quite narrow, typically no more than 30 per cent, with the midpoint of the range serving as the pay rate for acceptable proficiency in the job (Shields, 2007; Perkins and White, 2008).

In job-based systems, there are two main techniques for pricing each job or position: market surveys and job evaluation.

Market surveys involve setting pay rates for particular jobs according to what other employers are paying for the same or similar jobs in external labour markets. Regular market surveys also allow organizations to monitor changes in market rates and adjust their own pay rates accordingly. As such, the approach emphasizes 'external competitiveness' in determining the rate for the job. The organization ascertains the range of amounts that other organizations are paying for jobs similar to its own, and then makes a strategic choice about where it will position itself relative to its competitors. For this purpose, the market range for each position is commonly expressed as either percentile or quartile means (Shields, 2007). Rather than undertaking the data-gathering themselves, many organizations use the market data provided by consulting firms specializing in remuneration.

Job evaluation, which is frequently seen as an alternative to reliance on market data, involves determining relative pay rates by relating them to the importance or relative value of the job to the organization. This is achieved by comparing jobs on a number of factors thought to be important in determining job value, such as skill, effort, responsibility or working conditions. The end result of job evaluation is a hierarchy of jobs in which all jobs of similar value to the organization, no matter how different they might be in other respects, are placed at the same level in the job-based pay hierarchy. As such, job evaluation emphasizes 'internal equity' in setting job-based pay rates rather than 'external competitiveness' per se (Shields, 2007; Perkins and White, 2008).

Job evaluation is thus a means of establishing and maintaining equitable differences in base pay between jobs within the organization, particularly between jobs at different organizational levels. The degree of difference in pay level between jobs at the top and the bottom of an organizational hierarchy is also known as 'vertical pay dispersion', and there is considerable debate over whether a high degree of dispersion is preferable to a low degree of dispersion or vice versa. Critical Thinking 10.1 challenges you to frame your views about this important aspect of base pay structure.

Critical Thinking 10.1
Pay dispersion
The term 'pay dispersion' refers to the degree of inequality in pay levels between jobs at the same organizational level (also called 'horizontal pay dispersion') and between jobs at different levels in the organization (also known a 'vertical pay dispersion') (Gerhart and Rynes, 2003).

Questions
1 Is it better for an organization to have a high degree of vertical pay dispersion or a low degree of vertical dispersion?
2 How might the appropriateness of high variability differ according to the company's social and cultural context?

The most widely used approach to systematic job evaluation is the points factor method. A points factor system typically has four main elements:

1 *'Compensable' factors*: job inputs (such as skill, knowledge, education, training and experience), job reqirements (such as mental effort, physical effort, decision-making and supervision), job outputs (such as product accuracy, consequences of error, and responsibility for cash and assets) and job conditions (work environment, hazards, and so on).

2 *Points-based rating scales* for these factors based how much of each factor is present.

3 *Factor weightings* reflecting the 'value-adding' importance of each factor for the organization.

4 Assigning a monetary value to the total number of points assigned to each job.

As a means of valuing jobs and developing job-based pay structures, the points factor approach has much to commend it. It can introduce order, rationality, strategic focus and consistency into potentially arbitrary pay structures by using transparent and clearly defined measures of job size, and by offering a consistent means of measuring the relative size or value of the jobs involved. Furthermore, the points factor approach can also help to identify and eliminate inequities in the existing pay structure, as well as provide a rational basis for setting pay rates for new or changed jobs.

However, the points factor approach also has some weaknesses and drawbacks. In focusing on relative comparisons of job contents and on generic job content factors, it may downplay or even ignore critical strategic success factors related to the market, a point actually conceded by commentators who assert the continuing relevance of the approach to contemporary reward practice. According to Lawler (1988, 1990), points factor methods highlight job size over job-holder contribution, emphasize internal equity over external competitiveness, and reinforce bureaucracy and hierarchy. In practice, a well-managed system of job-based pay requires simultaneous attention to both internal equity and external competitiveness (Heneman and LeBlanc, 2002)

Job evaluation is sometimes seen as a means of correcting the gender-based pay inequality and distributive injustice (that is, unfairness in terms of reward outcome) evident in the wider labour market. Yet whether organizationally specific job evaluation can do much to further pay equity is a moot point. Indeed, some have argued that badly designed and badly implemented job evaluation may be a cause of continuing gender pay inequality rather than a reliable remedy (England and Kilbourne, 1991; Gupta and Jenkins, 1991).

> **Exercise**
> - When it comes to pricing jobs, what are the three main advantages of focusing on 'internal equity' considerations via the use of job evaluation?
> - What are the three main disadvantages of such an approach to job pricing?

Person-based base pay

More recently, the trend has been to configure base pay around the skills and competencies of the person rather than the 'size' of the job occupied, and to couple this to very different base pay structures. Person-based pay can be configured according to the ('hard') technical knowledge and skills possessed by the individual employee, according to underlying ('soft') personal abilities or competencies, or in terms of a combination of both 'hard' and 'soft' attributes.

By recognizing and rewarding the acquisition of technical skills and job-related knowledge, skill-based pay is said to facilitate functional flexibility through multiskilling and teamworking. Multiskilling allows employees to be redeployed quickly without delays for retraining and minimizes the down-time arising from a lack of the required skills. By breaking down rigid job demarcations, it can in addition enable a more flexible utilization of the workforce as employees acquire a breadth and depth of relevant skills. Skill-based pay also lends itself to employees' involvement in system design and administration (Barrett, 1991; Ledford, 1991a, 1991b; Ledford and Heneman, 1999; Shields, 2007).

The basic building block for a skill-based system is the *skill set*. A skill set consists of a bundle of related tasks and activities – or 'skill elements' – the mastery of which constitutes a finite and verifiable unit of learning that can be used to develop and deliver training. Each skill set becomes a training module that must be completed successfully in order to warrant a further increase in the amount of base pay. In order to determine pay, associated skill sets are commonly housed in structures known as 'broad grades'. The pay range for each broad grade is typically 40–60 per cent, that is, some two to three times that of a narrow grade. Monetary values are attached to each skill set according to the estimated learning time required (Ledford, 1991b; Shields, 2007).

The combination of broad grades and skill-based pay is especially appropriate for roles with significant technical knowledge and skill requirements, such as process work, technical or paraprofessional roles, maintenance work and administration. In such roles, technical skills are relatively easy to identify, impart, assess and reward.

Some commentators suggest that a better means of configuring person-based base pay is to focus on assessing and rewarding deeply embedded abilities or 'competencies' such as leadership ability, motivation to achieve goals, persistence, composure, problem-solving ability, and so on. The appeal of the competencies approach lies chiefly in its focus on those personal attributes that are seen to be the most important and reliable drivers of high individual performance. As such, the suggestion that competency assessment should apply not only to performance management and development, but also to employee reward has intuitive appeal. Likewise, the competencies model is applicable to staff at all levels of the organization and not just to skilled manual workers (Armstrong and Brown, 1998; Shields, 2007).

The defining features of competency-based pay are:

☐ a system of competency assessment;
☐ a 'broadbanded' pay structure.

Broadbanding (also known as 'career banding') involves doing away with a large number of narrow jobs arranged in a steep hierarchy in favour of a much smaller number of job bands. Pay ranges are substantially wider – frequently 100–300 per cent – and the mode of pay progression is linked to either competency assessment or a combination of competency development and performance outcomes. A typical broadbanded structure will have between five and 10 bands.

Progression within a given broadband may be linked either to competency assessment alone (that is, competency-*based* broadbanding) or to a combination of competency assessment and individual performance outcomes (that is, competency-*related* broadbanding). The latter approach is also known as 'contribution-related pay'. In purely competency-based systems, each broadband is divided into a small number of competency 'zones', each representing a successively deeper level of competency development. Pay increments are not automatic, and progression to the upper zones is not guaranteed. In fact, both in-zone and between-zone progression becomes increasingly difficult as competency requirements become more demanding (Rosen and Turetsky, 2002; Shields, 2007; Perkins and White, 2008).

Competency-based broadbanding promises employers an unprecedented degree of flexibility in determining individual base pay levels. Broadbanding has many potential advantages over traditional graded structures. By flattening job hierarchies, it can redirect employees' attention away from competition for jobs and promotion, and towards individual and group contributions to organizational success. Uncoupling promotion from individual career development and base pay progression redefines career 'success' from a vertical to a horizontal trajectory. This means that individuals no longer have to aspire to a managerial role in order to further their careers and base pay. By linking career development and pay progression to capability and achievement in terms of individual performance, broadbanding also supports a more strategic approach to reward management. For these reasons, the competencies model is also especially applicable to high-performance knowledge work, managerial and executive roles. It is also applicable to service work roles (Shields, 2007).

Despite their promise, person-based approaches have a number of potential drawbacks (Murray and Gerhart, 2000; Shields, 2007; Canavan, 2008; Ledford, 2008):

☐ Paying for skills and competencies does not guarantee that the employee will apply them effectively.

☐ Skill and competency assessment is administratively complex and costly.

☐ Labour market values are still determined mainly by job 'size' rather than by the skills and competencies of individual job holders, so valuation remains problematic.

☐ 'Topping out': once employees have acquired all the skills or demonstrated all of the required competencies, their base pay will plateau. They may therefore lose task motivation and organizational commitment unless additional rewards, such as performance incentives, are made available.

☐ Obsolescence of skills and competencies: employees whose skills or competencies are no longer needed, for example because of changes to the product range or in terms of technology, may be exposed to a pay reduction or even redundancy.

☐ The wider pay ranges characteristic of person-based systems may create unrealistic expectations of opportunities for pay rises, and this can cause feelings of pay inequity, especially if these expectations remain unfulfilled.

For these reasons, the enthusiasm initially associated with skills- and competency-related pay has, in recent years, been replaced by a healthy degree of caution (Hofrichter and McGovern, 2001; Heneman and LeBlanc, 2003).

Benefits plans

Employee benefits are financial rewards that directly supplement the cash base pay and are generally focused on addressing the well-being and long-term security needs of employees and their dependants. As such, benefits are an increasingly heterogeneous phenomenon, ranging from employers' contributions to employee superannuation (that is, retirement savings) planning, health and medical insurance and paid holiday leave, to various work-related 'fringe benefits' such as employer-funded mobile technology and travel.

Voluntary benefits

Although employers in most countries are obliged by law to make certain benefits available to employees (that is, 'mandatory benefits'), it is also open to employers to offer employees additional benefits as part of a strategic approach to reward management (that is, 'voluntary benefits'). In many developed countries, benefits comprise a growing proportion of total remuneration costs (Shields, 2007; Wright, 2009). Depending on the country involved, mandatory benefits may include employer-funded superannuation savings, life, health and disability insurance, worker compensation, various forms of paid leave (for example, annual, long-service, sickness, parental or carer leave) and severance pay.

Voluntary benefits can enhance the organization's ability to attract and retain high-value employees and enable it to offer employees a more appealing 'value proposition'. As the workforce becomes more diverse and as the employees' level of education and expectation of reward rises, voluntary benefits are likely to assume an increasingly critical role in the ability of the reward management system to attract, retain and motivate high-potential and high-performing employees.

Voluntary benefits include a wide range of rewards known collectively as 'fringe benefits', such as discount company loans, housing or mortgage subsidies, product or service discounts, company cars and/or free parking, self-education expenses, and the like. In addition to fringe benefits of a financial nature, many organizations now offer a range of voluntary non-monetary benefits carefully targeted at enhancing employees' work–life balance and well-being. These benefits include, among others, wellness programmes of various types. Examples include free medical check-ups, in-house gyms or subsidised gym membership, personal trainers, aerobics, yoga, pilates and t'ai chi classes, in-office massages, stress reduction and relaxation sessions, ergonomic consultations, meditation rooms, staff health food canteens, nutrition seminars, weight control programmes and quit smoking programmes. As well as being inherently beneficial to employees themselves, health and fitness initiatives such as these can make a significant contribution to reducing absenteeism and raising productivity (Shields, 2007). In part, these non-monetary plans are also targeted at reducing the costs associated with compulsory financial benefits, including statutory sick leave and stress leave entitlements.

Flexible benefits

The content of benefits packages may be either 'fixed' or 'flexible.' They may have a standard content, with the composition being determined by legal requirements and employer choice. Alternatively, they may be flexible in content, with employees having a degree of choice in how best to configure their package within a range of options made available voluntarily by the employer. The latter are also known as 'flexible' or 'cafeteria' benefits plans. The logic of flexible packages is that one size does not fit all. Differences in age, family responsibilities, financial circumstances and life-style preferences mean that different employees will have different benefit needs, and the needs of any one employee will change considerably over time (Long, 2006; Shields, 2007).

Exercise
- Why do the reward systems of some organizations place such a strong emphasis on voluntary benefits?

Performance-related reward plans

Performance-related reward plans, including incentives, cover rewards given on the basis of performance (that is, desired behaviour or results) delivered by employees either individually or collectively. An 'incentive' is a payment made on the basis of past performance in order to reinforce and enhance future performance. Performance pay is usually an overlay to base pay, and it varies according to the level of measured or assessed performance. In short, perform-ance pay is contingent or 'at risk', rather than fixed or guaranteed.

Although there are many types of performance-related rewards, these can be classified according to four key variables: the *performance unit* involved (indi-vidual, work group or whole organization); the *performance criteria* used (behav-iour, results or both); the *time frame* over which performance is measured (short term or long term); and the *form of reward* (monetary, non-monetary or company share equity) (Shields, 2007). Using these dimensions, we can identify three main categories of performance-related rewards:

- □ individual performance-related reward plans;
- □ collective short-term cash incentive plans;
- □ collective long-term equity-based incentive plans.

Table 10.3 summarises the specific reward practices within each of these three broad categories, and each of these practices will be examined in more detail below.

Individual performance plans

Schemes that reward individuals on the basis of formal performance appraisal scores are known generically as *merit pay* plans. In traditional merit pay plans, payments take the form of cumulative additions to base pay. These additions

Table 10.3 Performance-related reward options

Who? (= performance entity or unit) and when (= time frame for payout)	How? (= behaviour)	How much? (= results)
Individual performance reward plans	Merit raises or increments Merit bonuses	Piece rates Sales commissions Goal-based bonuses
	Discretionary bonuses Individual non-cash recognition awards	
Collective/group short-term incentives		Profit-sharing Gain-sharing Goal-sharing Team incentives Team non-cash recognition awards
Organization-wide long-term incentives		Share grant plans Share purchase plans Share option plans Executive long-term incentive plans

are termed 'merit raises' or 'merit increments.' These reward employees for appraised performance in a previous time period – typically 1 year – by raising their base pay to a higher level in the relevant job-based pay range.

From an organizational perspective, merit increments have a number of potential advantages. Since pay increments are linked to the individual performance achieved, the risk of the employer receiving no return on a pay increase is less than would be the case where pay is not directly performance-related, as in a traditional structure involving seniority-based pay scales. Because they are a permanent addition to base pay, merit increments can also reinforce the attraction and retention of staff.

On the other hand, because merit increments combine performance pay and base pay, employees may fail to see a clear and objective 'line of sight' between performance and pay outcomes. Since each merit increment is a permanent addition to base pay, the resulting compound increase in base pay can over time compromise the cost-effectiveness of the pay system. The emphasis on individualism may also be problematic in national cultural contexts that place a high value on collectivism, as is the case throughout much of South-East Asia and Latin America.

An alternative approach is the *merit bonus* method, in which the appraisal-based payment does not roll into base pay but instead stands apart from it and does not become an ongoing entitlement (Shields, 2007). The critical difference between this approach and traditional merit increments is that the payments made are conditional rather than cumulative. To be retained, the bonus must be must be re-earned. Motivation is driven by both the prospect of a higher bonus and the risk of loss of the bonus. Although this may be appropriate in many Western contexts, at-risk bonuses may be quite incompatible with cultures high on 'uncertainty avoidance' (see Chapter 1), such as those in Latin America, Eastern Europe and Japan (Hofstede, 1984).

A simpler form of cash recognition is the discretionary bonus. These are irregular 'lump sum' awards for outstanding performance made at the discretion of the supervisor and/or senior management. Discretionary lump sum payments, being highly visible, can communicate a strong performance message. By the same token, the absence of formal performance assessment means that award allocation may be seen as being arbitrary and as having little clear link between performance and reward.

Incentives geared to measured individual results, or individual 'payment-by-results' plans, are among the oldest and most enduring of all performance pay plans. A major attraction of results-based plans for employers is that they offer greater certainty, immediacy and objectivity in the pay–performance relationship than are offered by other pay plans. Included in this category are piece rates, sales commissions and bonus payments to individuals for goal achievement.

Piece rates were developed primarily for labour-intensive manufacturing jobs and had their heyday in the early to mid-20th century, when they lay at the forefront of innovation in reward theory and practice in industrialized economies. However, interest in individual output-based incentives of this type has waned with the relative decline in manufacturing activity in Western economies. Instead, sales commissions remain widely used in such sectors as consumer retailing, finance, insurance and real estate, and goal-based individual reward plans have become an increasingly important feature of white-collar professional and managerial work. For these reasons, we shall focus here on commissions and goal-based bonuses.

In general, *commissions* have the attraction of being simple to set and measure. They institute automatic task clarity and provide instant feedback and reinforcement. However, they may also encourage aggressive, deceptive or negligent selling practices, foster excessive competition among sales workers working for the same firm, and encourage sales staff to neglect important tasks, such as good record-keeping, after-sales follow-up and the training of new sales workers (Shields, 2007). Clearly, commissions are only applicable in sales roles.

Goal-based bonus plans, however, are capable of being adapted to virtually any role. In essence, these plans entail annual or quarterly bonus payments linked directly to individual goal setting. If the goals are financial in nature, such plans are self-funding, which means that they avoid one of the major shortcomings of traditional merit pay plans – budget underfunding. Even so, goal setting can be problematic. Where goals are either too loose/easy or too tight/hard, too few or too many, a goal-based bonus plan is unlikely to be effective. Rewarding only the hard, measurable results may encourage employees to ignore equally important but less quantifiable aspects of the job or role. For these reasons, individual results-based incentive plans tend to be of measure a range of parameters and often built around a 'balanced scorecard' of weighted indicators and goals (Shields, 2007).

Many organizations now use recognition of a non-monetary nature to reward individual performance. Non-cash rewards range from merchandise, shopping vouchers and retailer-specific debit cards to symbolic awards in the form of plaques, 'thank you' notes, pins, watches, pens and desk-sets, and the like. Such rewards are said to have the advantage of being personalized, immediate and more enduring than cash (Nelson, 1994; McAdams, 1999). McAdams (1999: 245–51) asserts: 'It is easier and more effective to promote the excitement of a non-cash award than its cash equivalent. Non-cash awards have built-in excitement and recognition factors that cash simply doesn't have.' They are also likely to be less costly than cash. Conversely, non-cash recognition plans may create an atmosphere of 'winners' and 'losers' (when the same few employees repeatedly get the award) or, alternatively, of 'everyone a winner' (where everyone takes a turn at receiving recognition). They may also be demotivating where employees feel that the reward is tokenistic (Shields, 2007).

☑

Exercise
- When it comes to recognizing and rewarding individual performance, what are the three main advantages and three chief disadvantages of using non-cash recognition plans?

Collective performance plans

In certain contexts, rewarding group results may have decided advantages over individual performance rewards. The latter may be quite dysfunctional in organizations where work is organized on interdependent and cross-functional lines and where results are founded on a high degree of interemployee cooperation. Interdependence of this type is one of the hallmarks of teamworking and high-involvement management.

In such organizations, it may be neither possible nor logical to attribute performance to specific individuals, since what counts is collective effort and contribution. Collective incentives may encourage employees to work collaboratively to achieve goals that require teamwork and cooperation. Accordingly, collective incentive schemes are more likely to elicit a greater degree of organizational citizenship behaviour than are schemes of an individual nature. Collective incentives may also be more appropriate in national cultural contexts where collectivism is valued above individualism, such as in most Asian countries and in Latin America (Hofstede, 1984). Workplace-wide collective plans are also likely to encounter less opposition from trade unions than are individual incentive plans. Table 10.4 summarises the main advantages and disadvantages of collective incentives generally.

Table 10.4 Collective incentives – pros and cons

Advantages	Disadvantages
Provide an incentive for improving group performance	Employees may feel that group reward undervalues individual contributions
Self-funding; total labour costs vary with organizational 'capacity to pay'	The bigger the group, the weaker the 'line of sight'
Can increase employees' understanding of the business	'Free-riding'/'social loafing'
Self-monitoring reduces supervision costs	Conflict over peer surveillance and peer pressure
Peer pressure on underperformers	Perverse sorting: everyone will want to belong to the group that gets the highest rewards
Encourage organizational commitment and citizenship behaviour	May encounter resistance from middle managers

This is not to suggest that collective incentive plans are necessarily incompatible with individual performance pay plans. With careful planning, it is possible to combine the two approaches in such a way that they are mutually reinforcing. For instance, while the funding of a performance pay pool might be based on measures of an improvement in collective results, the distribution of payments from the pool could be based on an assessment of individual contribution (Heneman and Von Hipple, 1995; Merriman, 2009).

Most collective incentive plans fall into one or other of three plan types:

☐ profit-sharing
☐ gain-sharing
☐ goal-sharing.

Profit-sharing

A profit-sharing plan typically involves a formal arrangement under which bonus payments are made to eligible employees on a regular (usually annual) basis, based on a formula that links the size of the total bonus pool to an accounting measure of periodic (typically annual) profit, such as net profit (total income less operating costs) or net profit after tax. By allowing overall labour costs to be varied automatically according to the employer's 'capacity to pay', profit-sharing is seen as providing a form of organizational insurance against external contingencies, particularly fluctuations in demand and prices in the product market. As such, profit-sharing is wholly self-funding. It may also increase employees' identification with and understanding of the organization's financial circumstances, enhance citizenship behaviour and reduce industrial conflict.

Conversely, because profitability is influenced by many variables that are beyond the employees' collective control, the line of sight between individual performance and reward is likely to be weak; that is, the 'instrumentality' (cause-and-effect) link between effort and reward, as prescribed by expectancy theory (see above), is at best very weak. For the same reason, profit-sharing may give rise to 'free-riding' or 'social loafing', especially where payments are allocated on an equal basis irrespective of individual contribution (Shields, 2007).

Gain-sharing

Gain-sharing is a form of collective performance-related pay in which management shares with all its employees in a particular production plant or business unit the financial gains associated with specific measures of improvement in the results achieved by that work group, as measured against a historical benchmark of the group's performance. Traditional gain-share plans emphasize 'hard' single-factor performance measures such as reductions in labour cost or improvement in labour productivity.

Like profit-sharing, such plans are self-funding, but gain-sharing also has a number of advantages over profit-sharing. Such schemes can be targeted to particular plants, departments or divisions, or to discrete business units in the wider organization. This compares with profit-sharing, which is generally organization-wide. Unlike profit-sharing, this approach can be applied in public sector and other non-profit organizations. It also seeks to reward only those results that are within the group's control. It can support a high-involvement culture through employee involvement programmes and devolution of decision-making. In addition, it is compatible with a unionized workforce and collective bargaining (Kim and Voos, 1997; Dalton, 1998).

The emphasis on continuous improvement means that gain-sharing is well suited to competitive strategies emphasizing either cost containment, quality improvement or both. However, traditional gain-share plans are a poor fit for highly dynamic contexts since each change in technology, work organization and product type will require a recalibration of historical performance benchmarks. Cost-focused plans also ignore non-financial or 'soft' aspects of group performance, such as worksite safety, environmental compliance and customer satisfaction (Shields, 2007).

Goal-sharing

Goal-sharing is the collective equivalent of individual goal-based bonuses (discussed above) and, like the latter, draws on the technique of goal setting. While goal-sharing resembles gain-sharing, it has several major differences. Goal-sharing is future-oriented, whereas gain-sharing is tied to retrospective performance benchmarks. This makes goal-sharing simpler to develop and more flexible, as well as wider in application and better placed to accommodate rapid changes in technology and product or service type. Goal-sharing generally includes both 'soft' performance factors, such as customer satisfaction and product quality, and financial targets. However, this means that goal-sharing is generally not self-funding, which in turn gives rise to the possibility of under-funding and of bonus payments that may not be seen as being commensurate with the group's achievements (Shields, 2007).

Employee share plans

Organization-wide, long-term incentive plans – more commonly known as employee share (or 'stock' or 'equity') plans, or ESOPs – allow eligible employees access to share ownership in the organization that employs them and reward employees for improvements over time in the employing firm's share market performance (via an appreciation in share price) and operating performance (via share dividends and special bonus share issues).

As such, share plans are seen as having a long-term benefit by reinforcing employees' commitment to the success of the organization. Because they stand to foster an 'ownership' mentality among employees, broadly based share plans (that is, plans in which many or most employees are eligible to participate) are particularly appropriate for organizations that embrace a high degree of employee involvement and participation (Kaarsemaker and Poutsma, 2006). Depending on how they are configured, share plans may also give employee-owners a genuine voice in management of the business and perhaps in managing other elements of the firm's reward system. However, the precise attitudinal and behavioural outcomes will depend on, among other things, the extent of employee eligibility and take-up, and on the particular plan or plans involved.

Although share employee plans come in a wide variety of forms, most fall into one of three main types:

☐ share grant plans
☐ share purchase plans
☐ option plans.

Share grant plans

With share grant plans, employees receive a gift of fully paid shares in the firm. In some cases, the shares granted can be traded immediately, which means that the grant is technically 'unrestricted'. However, it has become increasingly common for share grants to have certain limitations attached, which generally means that ownership does not transfer ('vest') immediately and/or that the shares cannot be tradable immediately in the same way as 'common stock' (that is, ordinary shares held by external investors). Conditional share grants of this type are known as 'restricted' share plans: while employees are not required to outlay any of their own money, they usually cannot sell their shares until a specified minimum period has elapsed. For the company, share grants may encourage long-term employee commitment and membership behaviour, particularly where restricted shares and trust arrangements are involved.

From the employee's perspective, regular share grants can serve as a convenient means for employees to supplement their retirement savings, although employee shareholders may well have a far higher risk exposure than external shareholders since the latter are more likely to have a diversified share portfolio covering a range of sectors, industries and firms (Shields, 2007).

Share purchase plans

With share purchase plans, employees have the opportunity to purchase part or all of a specified quota of shares in the company. Employees typically pay a small deposit on the full share purchase price, with the balance of the purchase price repayable over a specified term. The plan typically includes favourable purchase terms, such as a purchase price that is set below the prevailing market value and/or a low- or zero-interest loan from the company to fund the purchase. Some schemes allow the share purchase loan to be repaid from dividends so that the repayment period is open-ended and there is no employee outlay from personal savings. Other schemes allow employees to fund their acquisition in a tax-effective way by means of a 'salary sacrifice', which allows the employees to quarantine the outlay from their taxable income. Some schemes involve employee savings plans and pay deductions to fund the purchase. Legal ownership of the shares vests to the employee over time as the loan is paid off.

As share purchases funded by a company loan mean that employees are indebted to the company for the duration of the loan, employees may thus be more accommodating of management initiatives. Also, where employees have had to pay for the shares, their motivation in terms of 'ownership' is likely to be considerably stronger and more enduring than would be the case where shares have been received as a gift. This helps to explain why organizations in countries such as Australia tend to favour share purchase plans over share grant plans, a preference highlighted by the examples provided Box 10.3.

Box 10.3 Varieties of equity ownership in Australian firms

While only around 6 per cent of Australian employees receive shares as an employment benefit, some of the country's largest companies have broadly based share plans in place, and these come in a wide variety of forms.

At property development firm Lean Lease, employees own almost 8 per cent of the company. At communications giant Telstra, the employee share scheme is run by a trustee subsidiary, employees are offered interest free loans to acquire shares, and some employees are also eligible for extra shares and loyalty shares as a result of participating in the plan.

OneSteel offers tax-deferred and tax-exempt plans enabling employees to buy shares each month by means of salary sacrifice contributions, with those participating in the tax-exempt plan receiving fully paid shares to the value of $125 per year. Under this plan, shares must be held for a minimum of 3 years while the employee remains with the firm.

Furniture retailer Fantastic Holdings offers employees 11 matching shares for every 100 shares they purchase, with one in four employees participating in the plan.

At listed metals miner Perilya, employees own around 2 per cent of the firm through a share purchase plan, with 60 per cent of employees participating by means of salary sacrifice. The scheme grants shares to the value of 10 per cent of the employee's salary and then matches dollar for dollar any further contributions made.

Share plans are also used by private (that is, unlisted) companies. For example, food and energy firm Gardner Smith operates four schemes for its workforce in Australia and New Zealand. Employees with more than 12 months' service are eligible to participate, and just under 10 per cent of the firm's issues capital is targeted for employee ownership.

At advertising agency Clemenger, the employees own 53 per cent of the firm, with around one-third of its local employees participating.

Source: Adapted from Gettler (2010: 30–2)

By the same token, share purchase plans entail a greater risk all round than is the case with share grants. In particular, by their very nature, share purchase plans expose employees to greater financial risk. Employees committed to repaying the principal on a company loan at a fixed purchase price will experience severe financial difficulties if the share price collapses and the debt is not renegotiated or forgiven (Shields, 2007).

Employee option plans

A third type of share plan – employee option plans – gives employees the option of acquiring a specified quantity of company shares at a particular price on or after a designated future date. An option plan is a variant of share purchase in which the earliest date of purchase is set some time in the future. Such plans give the employee the right to buy a specified number of company shares at a predetermined price on a specified future date, such as the third anniversary of the option grant date. The price payable to exercise the option to acquire some or all of the shares – the 'strike price' – is commonly set at or below the market value of the shares at the time the option is granted.

Since the granting of an option does not confer an immediate ownership of equity, there will be no 'ownership' effect on motivation unless and until the option has been exercised. Until the options are exercisable, the main behavioural effects will be twofold. First, the restriction on exercising the options will reinforce staff retention, since the options are likely to be forfeited if the option-holder leaves the company. Second, during the holding period, the incentive effect will be largely extrinsic; that is, the holder will be motivated to improve the company's performance in order to strengthen market perceptions and increase the market share price, with a view to maximizing any capital gain when it becomes possible for the employee to exercise the option to buy and sell the shares involved.

However, with option plans, the line of sight between the employee's effort and the financial reward is even more remote than is the case with share bonus and purchase plans, since there is a significant delay in realizing any market-related rewards . In 'bull' share market conditions, in which most companies are experiencing share price appreciation, options may confer unearned ('windfall') gains on some option-holders. As with all equity plans, options are 'fair-weather' reward instruments: they may work well in times of share price growth, but can also compound a firm's problems if the share price falls, say in a declining ('bear') share market, and the market price falls below the option strike price. Option plans may also encourage a speculative outlook among employees rather than an ownership mentality (Shields, 2007).

Criticisms of performance-related rewards

Performance-related rewards are among the most controversial facets of contemporary HRM practice, with some critics contending that they are doomed to fail because they rest on invalid assumptions about employee motivation. Others similarly argue that they are inherently unfair.

Those who argue that performance pay is dysfunctional tend to base their case on the premises underlying cognitive evaluation theory, discussed above, that extrinsic performance-related rewards are inimical to intrinsic motivation. One proponent of this view, US social psychologist Alfie Kohn (1993a, 1993b), asserts that incentive pay plans fail because they:

☐ undermine intrinsic interest in the job;
☐ motivate people to pursue the reward rather than do a good job;
☐ are instruments of behavioural manipulation and punishment;
☐ rupture cooperative work relationships;
☐ ignore or mask the reasons underlying work problems;
☐ discourage sensible risk-taking.

Although well-publicised instances of failing incentive plans lend support to such arguments (see, for example, Beer and Cannon, 2004), these criticisms are themselves open to challenge on both theoretical and empirical grounds (see, for instance, Gupta and Mitra, 1998; Gupta and Shaw, 1998). Research shows that, under certain conditions (such as those prescribed by expectancy theory), incentives can exert a positive influence on performance, at least in certain organizational and cultural contexts (Gerhart and Rynes, 2003; Gerhart et al., 2009).

As we have seen, the assumption that extrinsic and intrinsic factors are dichotomous rather than complementary is also open to empirical challenge (see, for example, Cameron and Pierce, 1997). Overall, the evidence for a positive incentive effect is stronger for results-based plans than for plans based on behavioural assessment. Citing US examples, Gerhart and Rynes (2003: 170–1, 175) note that there are 'compelling examples of the effectiveness of results-oriented plans' and that there is 'ample evidence that results-based incentive plans can greatly increase performance'. Furthermore, they suggest (2003: 195) that strong individual results-based incentives have not only a positive incentive effect, but also a potentially powerful 'job-sorting' effect, whereby poor performers are actively 'managed out' while high performing individuals actively seek out positions that offer high reward for high effort.

A further criticism of Kohn's case is that he underplays the distinction between individual and collective incentives (Bennett Stewart et al., 1993; Cumming, 1994; Evans et al., 1995). Kohn overlooks that fact that group incentives are consciously directed towards encouraging the very attitudinal, behavioural and cultural characteristics that Kohn himself appears to endorse: teamwork, cooperation, shared effort and employee participation. Again, there is some evidence that appropriately designed group incentives can work (Gerhart et al., 2009) – what remains at issue empirically is the magnitude of the relationship.

So far we have only considered the arguments and evidence relating to the effectiveness of performance-related rewards in delivering the results and behaviours desired by the organization, that is, to whether such plans can and do 'work'. From the employees' perspective, however, an equally important – if not more important – consideration is whether such plans are fair.

One of the most common rationales for performance-related pay is that it operationalizes the 'equity' norm of distributive justice. To reiterate: equity theory proposes, in part, that reward satisfaction stems from establishing a good fit between an employee's inputs and outcomes. Reward relative to contribution – what could possibly be fairer? Yet there are those who argue that performance-related rewards can violate both distributive and procedural justice requirements. For instance, Heery (1996) argues that performance-related pay poses a threat to employee well-being because it contradicts employees' need for a stable and secure income, a need that is both economic and psychological. Without some level of guaranteed income, workers are likely to overwork and experience work-related stress and anxiety. Heery also suggests that performance-related pay tends to expose employees' pay to disproportionate risks. Shareholders may take calculated risks to reap a return, but employees have very different stakeholder needs, motives and expectations (Heery, 1996).

Critics also suggest that performance pay may also be procedurally unjust. According to Heery, such plans typically leave little scope for any independent representation of employees' interests, or 'voice'. Performance pay has also been questioned on the grounds that it may be especially disadvantageous to women employees. For instance, Rubery (1995) argues that women are likely to be worse off under performance-related pay, particularly where it takes the form of individual merit pay. In the context of the greater discretion available to line managers, the subjectivity inherent in behavioural assessment is likely to disadvantage women relative to men, especially in service work, where supervisory positions tend to be male-dominated. Furthermore, where individual incentives apply, the individualization of the employment relationship stands to weaken women's bargaining power further still. At least with job-based pay and job evaluation, the prospects for evening up the gender gap in pay and earnings are somewhat greater, partly because the process of pay determination is relatively open, transparent and amenable to collective bargaining (Rubery, 1995).

So the question remains: 'What proportion of an employee's total pay should be "at risk" against – or vary with – the performance?' Critical Thinking 10.2 invites you to formulate a considered position on the issue of 'pay variability'.

Critical Thinking 10.2
Pay variability
The term 'pay variability' refers to the degree to which pay outcomes for any given job or any given set of job-holders will vary by performance rather than being fixed or guaranteed (Gerhart and Rynes, 2003).

Questions
1 Is it better for an organization to have a high or a low level of pay variability?
2 How might the appropriateness of high variability differ according to the social and cultural context?

Perhaps the most meaningful conclusion to draw from these debates on the efficacy and fairness of performance pay is that such plans may have the potential to improve individual and group performance, but that the effectiveness and felt-fairness of any such plan will be contingent on several factors: the mode of application, particularly the manner in which the pay–performance linkage is configured; how effectively this linkage is communicated and accepted; and how appropriate it is for the organizational context involved. In this respect, differences in social and cultural values are likely to be highly salient.

Reward communication

Creating and maintaining employees' understanding and acceptance of the way in which they are rewarded is one of the most challenging yet important aspects of contemporary organizational communication. In a recent survey of UK reward professionals (Cotton and Chapman, 2010), poor rewards communication was ranked as the single greatest risk to the effectiveness of a reward system. Evidence suggests that reward communications practice looms as a potentially powerful but underutilized human resource tool (Shields et al., 2009). Even the most elegantly designed and contextually appropriate reward system will fail to attract, retain and motivate employees unless it is understood and accepted by the managers and employees affected.

Clear communication of the philosophy and details underlying the reward system stands to increase employees' acceptance of the composition, structure and level of the rewards, as well as to sharpen employees' line of sight between what they contribute and how they are rewarded. Two-way communication also has great potential here. Given the centrality of reward practice to achieving strong employee engagement, giving employees a say in how they are rewarded may be an effective outlet for both the individual and the collective voice. Regular attitude surveys are one way in which employees can be given a 'say in pay'. Other possibilities here include focus groups and employee participation in job evaluation teams.

The other key stakeholder group in this respect comprises line managers. Without their 'buy-in', the line of communication between reward professionals and ordinary employees will be weak and unreliable. Given that such managers will also be pivotal to the administration and maintenance of the system, it is advisable that they are involved in the designing the reward process (Brown and Purcell, 2007).

However, reward communication does not necessarily equate with reward openness. The amount of pay information that should be shared with employees is a matter of longstanding debate, and a range of competing arguments have been advanced for both pay transparency and pay secrecy. The case for transparency rests on the proposition that unless employees understand the pay system and how their individual rewards are determined, the system cannot contribute to the strategic goals of the firm or gain the trust of employees. Conversely, opponents argue that employee privacy must be respected since a knowledge of how others are being paid can foster jealousy, cause performance problems and engender a cycle of 'catch-up' claims.

In determining the policy and practice of rewards communication, what, then, is the appropriate balance between disclosure and secrecy? Certainly, a policy of high transparency and regular employee attitude surveys would be more appropriate where a high-involvement management approach applied. Even here, though, it may be best to focus communication on the reward system 'rules' rather than on the details of pay outcomes for individual employees. Try your hand at addressing the issue of reward openness/secrecy by formulating responses to the questions posed in Critical Thinking 10.3.

Critical Thinking 10.3
Reward secrecy and transparency
One approach to reward communication suggests that withholding from each employee details of the pay received by their fellow employees may restrain their demands for pay increases. In other words, revealing all may just encourage pay 'racheting', that is, employees in the same job or role demanding the same level of pay as that received by the highest paid employees in that role. The alternative approach proposes that pay secrecy of this type stands to violate the right of the employee to be treated with dignity and

▷ respect. Moreover, revealing more detail on reward levels, it is suggested, stands to reduce potentially counterproductive rumour and speculation about who has received what and why this might be so.

Questions

1 In what circumstances might pay secrecy be appropriate or justified?
2 Can an organization have too much pay transparency?
3 When and how should reward information be communicated to employees?

Employment relations and reward management

Although the main focus of decisions relating to reward system configuration may be the individual organization or its constituent business units, determination of reward in general, and pay structure and level in particular, is also influenced by the context or contexts within which the organization operates. These contextual factors include:

☐ the nature of the relevant product and labour markets;
☐ sociocultural norms and standards;
☐ the nature of government intervention and regulation;
☐ the contours of the prevailing employment relations system.

Key elements of the employment relations system include the nature of organization and institutional power of the union and employer, the mode of industry-, regional- and national-level bargaining, and the nature and extent of the government's regulation of pay and conditions of employment. As noted earlier in the chapter, the employment relations context also shapes the opportunities for and mechanisms of employee voice in the process of reward determination. Likewise, it can widen or constrain management choices regarding organizational pay structure and level.

Governments can have a major influence on reward processes and outcomes via a direct regulation of pay levels, equal pay legislation, industrial tribunals, pay review bodies, fair/minimum/low-pay bodies, centralized wage indexation, mandatory provision for works councils, and the like. However, the degree of government influence over setting pay varies significantly over time and between countries and sectors.

The nature of national- and industry-level bargaining systems may also exert a strong influence on reward practice at the organizational level. Traditionally, the mode and level of pay have been central issues in unions' collective bargaining at all levels: national, industry, occupational, and organizational. As we have seen, trade unions generally prefer some types of pay plan over others – job-based pay over person-based pay, fixed pay over variable pay, group incentives over individual incentives, for example (Long and Shields, 2009). The general decline of union influence in developed economies has undoubtedly influenced pay practices and levels. However, according to Katz and Darbishire (2000, cited in Perkins and Vartiainen, 2010: 179), the pattern of change in the European context has been non-uniform: within both the union and non-union sectors, the degree of variation in pay levels and practices has increased in recent decades.

The impact of changes in the level of government intervention and collective bargaining within the European Union is illustrative of these wider contextual influences on determining reward. As noted by Perkins and Vartiainen (2010: 178):

> Across much of the European continent – and featuring explicitly in the taxonomy adopted by the European Union – an attempt has been made to socialize employment relations using the existence of intermediaries between employers and employees to act as a mechanism for regulating the pay issue and to attempt to codify working practices that employers may be able to adopt to secure a return on the payments that agree to make to employees, as laid down in statutory provisions resulting from collective bargaining.

This regime of 'social partnership' and reward regulation dates back many decades and includes a wide range of mandatory provisions. The Equal Pay Directive of 1975 required member countries of the then European Economic Community to adhere to and enforce the principle of 'equal pay for work of equal value', a requirement reiterated under the Treaty of Amsterdam, effective from 1999. In practice, this has been taken to mean that job evaluation systems should be free from discrimination.

Wage indexation is another characteristic feature of European employment relations systems. Indexation aims to preserve the real value of wages by adjusting them automatically for price inflation. Works councils and joint consultative committees, coupled with multi-employer collective bargaining, have also been prominent features of the European approach to pay determination. In addition, there have been a number of initiatives at the level of the European Union to encourage employee share ownership and other forms of financial participation such as profit-sharing. In the late 1990s, the proportion of business units with 200 or more employees that had broad-based share plans averaged 16 per cent, and in the decade that followed, Belgium, France, Germany, The Netherlands and the UK all legislated to encourage greater share ownership on the part of employees (Pendleton, 2009).

However, there are now clear signs that these pillars of the model of the European 'coordinated' market economy are beginning to fragment. Although several countries still use indexation, a number (Denmark, France, Italy, The Netherlands and Spain) have now abandoned this form of pay regulation out of a fear that indexation will actually fuel inflation (Robinson and Winning, 2011).

Pre-existing pay disparities between Eastern European countries and European Union countries also poses a pay equity dilemma for the European Commission itself. With workers from Poland and the Baltic States flocking to take up more highly paid administrative jobs in the Commission's headquarters in Brussels, the earnings of these employees far exceeds the pay levels available to even the most senior office-holders in their countries of origin. The Commission has come under pressure to peg salaries to the pay structure in these countries. However, doing so would mean that some Commission employees would be doing the same work as fellow workers but for vastly different rates of pay (Castle, 2011).

Trade liberalization and exposure to international markets are also beginning to erode multi-employer collective bargaining within even the strongest coordinated economies in the European Union. The recent global crisis has impacted no less severely on the German employment model – until recently the exemplar of a 'coordinated market economy' and social partnership – than on those of less coordinated economies. Outcomes have included outsourcing, the rise of precarious employment, a growing low-wage sector, and the emergence of two-tier wage agreements under which unions agree to accept lower pay rates for non-union workers in exchange for the prospect of organizing the latter and coopting them onto works councils (Lehndorff et al., 2009; Haipeter, 2011).

In sum, as the European Union experience demonstrates, the changing nature of employment relations institutions and bargaining processes can exercise a powerful sway over pay structure and pay levels at the level of the individual organization.

International reward management

Most of the reward concepts and tools that we have discussed so far have emerged in Western business contexts and are thus informed by Western assumptions about the nature of the employment 'deal'. Yet whether they are engaged in international joint venture operations with host country partners, or in direct investment in subsidiaries in one or more host countries, firms with an international or multinational business focus – that is, MNCs – have to meet reward challenges that are often very different from those applicable to domestic employees.

These cross-border differences are relevant to three main groups of employee:

☐ host country nationals (HCNs) hired to work in the MNC's operations in the host country;
☐ home country employees sent abroad (that is, 'expatriated') for periods of time to manage or work in operations in host countries;
☐ employees from other countries – third country nationals (TCNs) – hired to work in either the home or host country operations.

Given the particular social, cultural, legal-institutional, economic and political context within which they live and their boundaries, HCN employees may have very different reward expectations from those in the firm's home base, as well as from expatriates and TCNs. For instance, in some countries such as India and Indonesia, employees have a strong cultural respect for hierarchy and equally strong attachments to a stable, long-term employment relationship and to customary allowances and benefits. Managing base pay and benefits for HCN employees thus requires that the conditions and traditions of the host country be carefully taken into account.

In order to maintain reward consistency, some MNCs export the main elements of their home country reward practice to their subsidiary operations in other countries (an 'exporter' or 'ethnocentric' approach). Others seek to adapt to local or regional conditions (an 'adaptor' or 'polycentric' approach), while still others apply a blend of home and host practices at either a national level (a 'geocentric approach') or a regional level (a 'regiocentric' approach). This means not only being aware of the reward expectations and entitlements of HCNs, but also having to make careful choices about how to reward local employees in order to establish and maintain a positive employment relationship (Bloom et al., 2003; Dowling et al., 2008).

Likewise, in configuring reward packages for expatriates, the MNC must decide whether it wishes to benchmark the level and mix of its rewards against parent country standards, host country standards or a blend of home and host or home and regional standards.

On this basis, we can identify three broad approaches towards configuring expatriate rewards:

☐ the home-based or 'balance sheet' approach;
☐ the host-based or 'going rate' approach;
☐ the region-based approach.

Home-based approach

This approach, which remains the preferred approach in Western MNCs, aims to maintain a relativity of rewards against those of home country employees while providing a beneficial inducement to compensate for the employee's foreign assignment. In essence, the approach links the expatriate reward level to the home country pay structure and seeks to preserve home country purchasing power and living standards by means of a 'balance sheet' of compensatory financial adjustments.

The approach typically covers four main reward components:

☐ *Base salary*: the main component that serves as a benchmark for other components.
☐ A *foreign service inducement, relocation or 'hardship' premium*: to attract home country employees to accept an expatriate assignment, or to compensate them for any hardship associated with a foreign assignment.
☐ *Allowances*: to compensate for any potential diminution in living standards relative to home standards, including cost of goods and services, housing expenses and differences in income tax liabilities.
☐ *Benefits*: including pension/superannuation contributions, health and medical insurance, social security, education expenses and paid leave entitlements (Dowling et al., 2008).

While the balance sheet approach preserves an equitable relationship between expatriate reward levels and those remaining in the parent entity, the approach may create a considerable pay discrepancy between expatriates and HCNs performing similar roles. In low-pay countries, such as India and China, this may trigger internal perceptions of inequity/distributive injustice among HCNs (Watson and Singh, 2005; Dowling et al., 2008).

Host-based approach

Here, the base salary is linked to salary levels in the host country, partly with a view to maintaining an equitable relationship in reward levels between the parent firm and HCNs. In general, if prevailing pay rates in the host country are high by international standards, the firm may have little choice but to match the local market. Conversely, if local pay levels are low by international standards, as is the case in most developing countries, the firm will typically augment its employees' base pay with additional allowances and benefits in order to attract home country and third country expatriates (Dowling et al., 2008).

The 'going rate approach' is relatively uncomplicated, sets a common standard for expatriates from both the parent country and third countries, reinforces expatriates' identification with the host country, and institutes a degree of equality with HCN salaries. Conversely, a strict adherence to the going rate approach will make it difficult to attract expatriates to low-pay locations, while the prospect of major variations in pay level from one posting to the next may be equally damaging.

Region-based approach

In essence, this is the remuneration approach typical of a geocentric staffing strategy and is especially well suited to a staffing strategy emphasizing labour mobility on a regional or a global scale, and selection of the best person for the position, irrespective of nationality. With such an approach, remuneration levels will need to be expressed in a major global currency, such as the US dollar, or a regional currency such as the Euro. The global approach also relies on the MNC developing a set of reward principles, policies and practices that fit its global strategy, structure and culture. The chief tenet of this approach is the marriage of competitiveness and flexibility of rewards at the local or regional scale, especially by allowing subsidiary managers the autonomy to configure the base pay, benefits and incentives in line with local standards. There must also be consistency in the worldwide application of a set of 'core' reward principles, including, for instance, performance-based recognition and reward differentiation (Bloom et al., 2003; Watson and Singh, 2005).

Exercise
- What are the three main differences between an 'exporter' and an 'adaptor' approach to managing the rewards of host country employees?

Conclusion

For many organizations operating within and between countries, employee rewards constitute the single largest operating expense. How – and how well – an employee reward system is designed, implemented, communicated and maintained can make the difference between the success and failure of the organization. Reward management is difficult to do well and easy to mismanage. The efficacy and fairness of reward practice is also the subject of an ongoing and robust debate.

This chapter has explored employee reward management from three perspectives: the critical, the applied and the international. Each perspective invokes different assumptions regarding the role of rewards in the employment relationship; each also carries different implications regarding the efficacy and fairness of rewards.

The *critical approach* alerts us to the dangers of 'unitarist' assumptions about the nature, meaning and influence of employee rewards. In essence, we have argued for a pluralist, or multi-stakeholder, framework for both understanding and 'managing' rewards. What is a cost to the organization is income and economic security to the employee, and what is valued by the organization may have little meaning or value for its employees.

In this sense, our exploration of the debate on the relative merits of extrinsic and intrinsic rewards serves to highlight the indeterminate nature of the relationship between the rewards on offer and the employees' reactions. Just as it is unsafe to assume that monetary rewards are invariably the primary motivator, so is it problematic to suppose that every employee is galvanized by the prospect of work that is inherently challenging and task-diverse. The key point here is that employees are not simply 'resource' objects but, rather, are organizational stakeholders with their own distinct needs, expectations and rights, as well as responsibilities and contractual obligations to their employer.

A critical pluralist perspective also alerts us to the changing nature and significance of the employees' voice in how rewards are determined. As we have seen, this 'say in pay' may take various forms: individual or collective; union or non-union; formal or informal; direct or indirect. Indeed, it is erroneous to think of the structure, type and level of rewards as being free of employee influence – that is, as being an artefact of unconstrained managerial discretion. Employee voice and agency continue to have an important bearing on setting pay, whether directly and collectively via the unions' collective bargaining activity, indirectly via minimum pay bodies and industrial tribunals, or by means of individual employees' choices about the worth and equity of the rewards on offer.

The *applied approach* draws attention to the vast variety of reward practices – and to the factors that should be taken into account in choosing between them. Here we have focused on the distinction between job- and person-based base pay, between fixed and flexible benefits plans, between individual and group performance pay plans, and between cash, non-cash and equity-based plans. We have also considered the general strengths and weaknesses of each major pay plan type, as well as examining debates on both the effectiveness and fairness of incentive plans and other performance-related reward practices. In essence, the chapter argues for an applied approach to reward management that favours 'best fit' over 'best practice'. In other words, the choice of plan type and structure of rewards, including horizontal and vertical pay dispersion and pay variability, should reflect the organization's particular strategy, structure and environmental circumstances rather than any supposed 'one best way' to configure the reward system.

The *international approach* draws attention to the wider context and the additional challenges and options associated with the management of reward systems in cross-border contexts. What works well in one country may be highly problematic in another country and national culture. Equally, however, this itself poses a major strategic challenge to MNCs based in home countries with strong national cultures: should their approach to international reward management simply reflect the home country practice, or should they seek to adapt to the practices of the host country and culture? Like the USA and Japan before it, China is now the archetypal instance of a strong home country culture. The end-of-chapter case study on the reward strategies and practices of Chinese MNCs accentuates the complexities of reward management for managing line employees' and expatriates' rewards in host country contexts that vary markedly from that of the parent entity's home country.

In sum, managing pay and other forms of reward is one of the most challenging and sensitive facets of contemporary HRM, while reward management itself is one of the most controversial areas of human resource practice. Perhaps more than with any other human resources process, it also allows human resources strategists to demonstrate their worth in terms of organizational effectiveness. Equally, effective reward management demands high-order competencies in organizational and behavioural analysis, as well as solid abilities in strategic decision-making, communication and human resource leadership. For these reasons, it can also be immensely rewarding in its own right.

❓ For discussion and revision

Questions

1 Why should a firm use base pay at all?
2 Why does the gender pay gap persist, who is responsible for it, and what (if anything) can be done about it?
3 What makes for an effective employee share plan?
4 What are the telltale signs of failure of a performance and reward system?

Exercises

1 Break the class into pairs and allocate the following pay practices to a specific pair of students. Have each pair consider the pros and cons of their assigned pay practice as a means of furthering pay equity between the genders, and then have each pair report back to the full group. The practices are:
   • points factor job evaluation
   • skill-based pay
   • competency-based broadbanding
   • flexible benefits
   • merit raises
   • discretionary bonuses.

2 As the human resources director of an MNC with a subsidiary operation in Indonesia, you have been asked to design a comprehensive reward system for the subsidiary's HCNs. What reward practices would you use?

3 Your UK-based organization is planning to open a major facility (eventually employing 5,000 people) in Thailand, for which your team will be responsible. Senior management has asked you to assess the impact that cultural values will have on using traditional UK reward practices for the

HCNs there, and to propose a comprehensive reward system for the new facility. Specifically, you are required to address the following issues:

- the pros and cons of replicating in the Thai context the large pay differences between more senior executives, mid-level managers and the hourly workforce that apply in the UK context;
- the possibility of using incentive pay programmes driven by individual performance;
- identification of the benefits that employees will place a high value on, and those they will place a low value on;
- identification of work rules or traditions that may be different from those in the UK.

In making your assessment, you should refer to Hofstede's cultural dimension scores for the parent and host countries, which are available at: http://www.geert-hofstede.com/hofstede_dimensions.php

ⓜ Further reading

Books

Armstrong, M. and Brown, D. (2006) *Strategic Reward. How Organisations Add Value Through Reward*. London: Kogan Page.

A UK text with an applied focus and practical examples of innovative reward practices.

Armstrong, M. and Murlis, H. (2007) *Reward Management. A Handbook of Remuneration Strategy and Practice* (revd 5th edn). London: Kogan Page & Hay Group.

The standard UK practitioner text in the rewards field, taking an applied rather than critical focus.

Gerhart, B. and Rynes, S. (2003) *Compensation. Theory, Evidence, and Strategic Implications*. London: Sage.

A US text offering an excellent coverage of research and concepts related to reward management.

Gomez-Mejia, L. R. and Werner, S. (eds) (2008) *Global Compensation. Foundations and Perspectives*. London: Routledge.

Contains several solid chapters on the theory and practice of international rewards.

Greene, R. J. (2010) *Rewarding Performance. Guiding Principles; Custom Strategies*. New York: Routledge.

Provides an insightful and practical coverage of performance pay practices.

Guthrie, J. P. (2007) Remuneration: pay effects at work. In Boxall, P., Purcell, J. and Wright, P. (eds) *The Oxford Handbook of Human Resource Management*. Oxford: Oxford University Press, pp. 344–69.

An illuminating overview of theories and evidence on the effects of reward plans.

10

Henderson, R. I. (2006) *Compensation Management in a Knowledge-based World* (10th edn). Upper Saddle River, NJ: Prentice Hall.

A US text offering a solid coverage of applied aspects of reward management.

Long, R. (2006) *Strategic Compensation in Canada* (3rd edn). Toronto: Thomson Nelson.

Provides both a solid coverage of Canadian reward practice and a clear and persuasive discussion of the relationship between reward practices and organizational strategy, structure and management culture.

Martocchio, J. J. (2009) *Strategic Compensation: A Human Resource Management Approach* (5th edn). Upper Saddle River, NJ: Pearson/Prentice Hall.

A US text offering a solid coverage of applied aspects of reward management.

Milkovich, G. and Newman, J. (2007) *Compensation* (9th edn). New York: McGraw-Hill Irwin.

A leading US text in the rewards management field.

Perkins, S. and White, G. (2008) *Employee Reward. Alternatives, Consequences and Contexts*. London: Chartered Institute for Personnel and Development.

Offers a fresh and an insightful treatment of reward theory and practice from a UK perspective.

Rynes, S. L. and Gerhart, B. (eds) (2000) *Compensation in Organisations. Current Research and Practice*. San Francisco: Jossey Bass.

A multiauthor text offering a detailed and sophisticated coverage of the strategic and psychological dimensions of employee rewards. Retains value despite its publication date.

Shields, J. (2007) *Managing Employee Performance and Reward: Concepts, Practices, Strategies*. Melbourne: Cambridge University Press.

Offers an integrated coverage of performance and reward management from a 'best fit' perspective.

White, G. and Drucker, J. (eds) (2009) *Reward Management. A Critical Text* (2nd edn). London: Routledge.

The second edition of a multiauthor text with chapters covering all key aspects of reward practice from various critical perspectives.

WorldatWork (2007) *The WorldatWork Handbook of Compensation, Benefits and Total Rewards*. New York: Wiley.

Offers an encyclopaedic coverage of rewards practices for line employees and executives. The text is informed by a unitarist rather than a critical perspective. WorldatWork is the leading US body representing reward professionals.

Wright, A. (2004) *Reward Management in Context*. London: Chartered Institute of Personnel and Development.

Another useful UK text.

Journals

Gerhart, B., Rynes, S. and Fulmer, I. (2009) Pay and performance: individuals, groups, and executives. *Academy of Management Annals*, 3(1): 251–315.

Provides a provocative but circumspect and evidence-based argument in support of incentive plans for executives and line employees.

Werner, S. and Ward, S. (2004) Recent compensation research: an eclectic review. *Human Resource Management Review*, 14: 201–27.

A meticulous and high-level survey of rewards research and conceptual models for explaining the configuration and influence of reward systems. Particularly useful for framing research topics and models in the rewards field.

Other resources

Chartered Institute for Personnel and Development. Reward Management. Available from: http://www.cipd.co.uk/subjects/pay/default.htm

A UK professional body website carrying information on rewards practices and strategies, including survey data.

E-Reward UK. About e-reward. Available from: http://www.e-reward.co.uk/about.asp

A UK proprietary research organization website providing information on reward practices, strategies and case studies.

WorldatWork. Available from: http://www.worldatwork.org/waw/home/html/home.jsp

A US professional body website carrying information on rewards practices and strategies, including survey data.

10

Case Study The strategy and practice of rewards in Chinese MNCs

The People's Republic of China now plays a central role in global economic growth and development, and Chinese state-owned enterprises and private firms are rapidly internationalizing their operations in both developed and developing economies. China is a global economic power and yet a country that is still 'developing' rather than 'developed'.

Transition in Chinese domestic reward practices

Under China's old planned economy, Chinese domestic employment practices were based on long-term job security, lifelong social security, pay structures characterized by low dispersion/egalitarianism and group-based rather than individual incentives. The principal pay system was the national wage scales, which were determined by central legislation and regional government agencies and were configured differently for blue- and white-collar employees. Pay differences between low-skilled workers, skilled workers and managers were minimal, and wage increases were infrequent and primarily took the form of nationwide grade promotions for all employees (Dowling et al., 2008). The combination of egalitarian pay structures and the 'iron rice bowl' model, which addressed workers' basic needs through free housing, schooling and medical care, gave employees few extrinsic incentives to improve their performance or pursue promotion.

Since the 1980s, however, government controls have eased and firms have been given more autonomy to configure their own reward systems, albeit still within government guidelines. Job size has replaced age/seniority as the main determinant of reward level, and rising education levels have begun to influence pay differences. A performance-related reward approach in the form of an efficiency-based bonus has also been introduced to replace the grade-based system. Despite these changes, seniority and egalitarianism remain key characteristics of Chinese domestic reward practice, pay dispersion remains low, and enterprises tend to favour group bonuses over those of an individual nature.

International reward management in Chinese MNCs: a 10-company case study

How, then, do Chinese MNCs approach international reward management? Do they seek to export domestic practices or are they more adaptive and innovative in their cross-border approach? Does their approach emulate that of Western MNCs or do they take a different and perhaps uniquely Chinese path?

One of the few studies to date to have examined the reward practices of Chinese MNCs, that by Shen (2004), provided revealing evidence on these and related questions. Shen's study used a semi-structured, interview-based survey to collect data from 10 Chinese MNCs with subsidiaries in the UK. Of these case study companies, seven were state-owned enterprises covering a variety of industries – from banking and technology importing to airlines and shipping – while the remaining three were share-issuing companies in the electronics and health products fields.

Shen's study found that the pattern of reward practice in the case organizations was company-specific rather than simply being a reflection of national or industry factors. On the basis of the evidence generated, Shen identified four different approaches to international reward management in the companies studied:

- ☐ host-based;
- ☐ home salary plus host-based;
- ☐ contract-based;
- ☐ diplomat-based.

Rewards for host country nationals

All 10 companies used the host-based approach for non-executive HCNs and a contract-based approach for HCN executives, with pay levels for HCNs commonly set quite high by UK standards. For HCN non-executives, the pay package generally included a fixed salary contract plus an individual merit bonus, typically of 2–3 months' additional salary based on an individual performance appraisal. The contract-based system applied to HCN executives differed from both home- and host-based practices in that the pay package was negotiated directly between the individual manager and the firm's headquarters, with payment based on a combination of individual capability, project importance and divisional performance.

Expatriate rewards

For Chinese employees expatriated to a UK subsidiary, Shen's study identified three distinct reward approaches. In two firms, expatriates received a host-based salary plus their old home salary. One company adopted a negotiable contact-based approach identical to that applied to HCN executives; this emphasized individual capability, how important the project was and the assignment location.

The other seven companies used a post-based approach for their expatriates, with the pay package including a fixed position-based salary, a post-based individual performance bonus and a range of additional payments. The fixed component was much higher than for home-based employees. Bonuses were linked to divisional or departmental performance or to the status of the managerial post. This post-based approach, which accentuates hierarchy, originally used by the Chinese Foreign Ministry for international postings and now widely used by Chinese MNCs, is also commonly known as the 'diplomat-based' approach. In all cases, a uniform approach was applied to expatriate reward throughout all divisions within the subsidiary.

The Chinese dual model: the best of both worlds?

This heterogeneity is very different from the situation with domestic operations in Chinese enterprises, where companies tend to adopt a uniform approach to reward management. The contract and home-plus-host approaches are negotiable and based chiefly on individual capability and performance, compared with domestic reward practice under which pay is position-based and essentially non-negotiable. On this basis, Shen concluded that 'Chinese [international HRM] is more progressive than domestic HRM in adopting modern Western HRM concepts' (Shen, 2004: 23).

However, Shen's study showed in addition that this process of adaption also had uniquely Chinese characteristics, such that the firms involved could be seen as pursuing a 'dual' approach to international reward management. Even though the approaches taken were noticeably different from home-based reward practices, they also differed from the three standard approaches typically specified in the Western literature – host-based, home-based and region-based. The firms involved adopted a 'best fit' approach that took account of both firm- and employee-specific factors, with reward practices tailored to employees' nationalities and their position in the organizational hierarchy. Under the dual model, HCN reward was either host-based or contract-based, whereas expatriate reward varied substantially from firm to firm. According to Shen (2004), the dual model reflected the 'dilemma' of Chinese MNCs wanting both to embrace international practices, in order to encourage an international transfer of talent, while at the same time maintaining close control over reward practices in their subsidiaries so as to limit the discrepancy between domestic practices and expatriate experience.

Factors influencing reward strategy and practice in Chinese MNCs

The study also showed that the reward strategies and practices adopted were influenced more strongly by some firm-level and contextual factors than by others. Reward strategies were shaped chiefly by the firm's international competitive strategy, its degree of reliance on international markets, and senior management's perception of the efficacy and appropriateness of the Chinese domestic reward system. However, interfirm differences in actual reward practices, including reward structures and levels, were determined by a combination of three main contextual factors – legal, economic and sociocultural – and by several firm-specific factors, most notably the industry in which the firm is involved.

Turning first to contextual factors, pay levels were generous by both Chinese and UK standards in order to attract high-quality home and host country managers and professionals. The firms studied also placed much weight on conformity to host country mandatory requirements, including minimum pay rates and paid leave entitlements. In a significant departure from home country practice, all companies also offered expatriates paid holiday leave, although, as Shen suggests (2004), the relatively high levels of base pay and benefits for HCNs need to be weighed against the fact that the firms studied offered HCNs almost no opportunity for development, promotion or transfer to the parent entity.

The dual approach to host- and home-sourced employees also reflected the cultural differences between China and the UK. Chinese practice is that the salary is non-negotiable, set according to position, level, seniority and the firm's overall performance, and not specified in the employment contract. However, with UK HNCs, the need to negotiate pay packages that would attract, retain and motivate local talent meant that this dual approach was embraced uniformly by all of the case companies, as was the use of individual performance bonuses. This host-based approach was also applied selectively to some expatriates, although egalitarianism remained the dominant consideration in relation to this group.

The study also highlighted the influence of a number of firm-specific factors. Regarding the impact of international HRM strategy generally, while two companies embraced a universal host-based approach to rewarding both HCN and expatriate employees, the majority of companies sought to retain control over expatriate reward expectations by means of diplomat- and contract-based approaches. Companies pursuing a polycentric approach to staffing were more likely to favour host-based reward practices, whereas those favouring ethnocentric staffing tended to adopt the diplomat-based approach.

The attitudes of senior management to home and host reward models were also influential. All firms judged the Chinese model to be unsuitable for HCN employees. However, there were differences in perceptions of the transferability of the Chinese model to expatriates, with some companies opting for a host-plus-home-based approach, and others preferring a more cautious contract-based solution. The nature of the industry itself also had an impact, with individual performance pay more likely to be applied to employees in trading enterprises and sales offices than elsewhere. In addition, reliance on and exposure to international markets was an important factor: firms with a relatively low reliance on international markets were more likely to prioritize egalitarianism over pay competitiveness, chiefly via the diplomat-based approach. Conversely, firms with a high reliance on international markets were more inclined to favour host-based standards.

Interestingly, Shen's study suggests that a range of firm-specific factors commonly assumed to influence reward practices – factors such as organizational structure, organizational culture, international experience and the size of international operations – appeared to have little impact in this sample of firms.

In sum, Shen's 10-firm case study highlights the dual approach to international reward management taken by these Chinese firms, the character-istically Chinese approach to the adaptor or 'host' strategy, the tension between the objectives of egalitarianism and competitiveness in reward practice, and the complex array of home country, host country and firm-specific factors that serve to shape strategies and practices related to international rewards. Although it remains to be seen whether further internationalization will weaken the preference of Chinese MNC for a dual approach to international reward management, it is very likely that China's rapidly rising importance in the global economy will mean that Chinese firms will exercise far greater influence over global rewards in the decades to come.

Questions

1 Do you think that the 'dual' approach to international reward management preferred by Chinese MNCs is sustainable over the longer term as Chinese firms become progressively more integrated into the global economy?

2 If Chinese MNCs are to make greater use of HCNs in their staffing, how might they best modify their reward practices to support this change?

3 As China consolidates its position as an economic superpower, how might the reward practices preferred by Chinese MNCs influence trends in international reward management?

References

Armstrong M. and Brown D. (1998) Relating competencies to pay: the UK experience. *Compensation and Benefits Review*, (May–June): 28–39.

Barrett, G. V. (1991) Comparison of skill-based pay with traditional job evaluation techniques. *Human Resource Management Review*, 1: 97–105.

Beer, M. and Cannon, M. D. (2004) Promise and peril in implementing pay-for-performance. *Human Resource Management*, 43(1): 3–20; critical commentaries 21–50.

Bennett Stewart, G. III, Applebaum, E., Beer, M., Lebby, A. M, Amabile, T. M., McAdams, J., Kozlowski L. D., Baker, G. P. III and Wolters, D. S. (1993) Rethinking rewards. *Harvard Business Review*, 71(6): 37–49.

Bloom, M., Milkovich, G. and Mitra, A. (2003) International compensation: learning from how managers respond to variations in local host contexts. *International Journal of Human Resource Management*, (December): 1350–67.

Brown, D. and Purcell, J. (2007) Reward management: on the line. *Compensation and Benefits Review*, 39(3): 28–34.

Cameron, J. and Pierce, D. (1997) Rewards, interest and performance: an evaluation of experimental findings. *ACA Journal/WorldatWork Journal*, 6(4): 6–15.

Canavan, J. (2008) Overcoming the challenge of aligning skill-based pay levels to the external market. *WorldatWork Journal*, 17(1): 18–25.

Castle, S. (2011) European Union salaries a haven for Eastern Europeans. *New York Times*, 8 March. Available from: http://www.nytimes.com/2011/03/09/world/europe/09latvia.html?_r=1 [accessed 20 March 2011].

Cotton, C. and Chapman, J. (2010) Rewards in the U.K. top 10 risks. *Workspan*, 53(1): 53–7.

Cumming, C. (1994) Incentives that really do motivate. *Compensation and Benefits Review*, (May–June): 38–40.

Dalton, G. (1998) The glass wall: shattering the myth that alternative rewards won't work with unions. *Compensation and Benefits Review*, 30(6): 38–45.

Deci, E. L. and Ryan, R. M. (1985) *Intrinsic Motivation and Self-determination in Human Behavior*. New York: Plenum Press.

Dowling, P. J., Welch, D. E. and Schuler, R. S. (2008) *International Human Resource Management: Managing People in a Multinational Context* (5th edn). Melbourne: Cengage Learning.

England, P. and Kilbourne, B. (1991) Using job evaluation to achieve pay equity. *International Journal of Public Administration*, 14(5): 823–43.

Evans, E., Hillins, J. F., McNally, K. A., Zingheim, P. K., Bahner, R. R. and Wilson, T. B. (1995) A series of essays about how rewards can succeed. *ACA Journal*, 4(2): 20–35.

Gerhart, B. and Rynes, S. (2003) *Compensation. Theory, Evidence, and Strategic Implications*. Thousand Oaks, CA: Sage.

Gerhart, B., Rynes, S. and Fulmer, I. S. (2009) Pay and performance: individuals, groups, and executives. *Academy of Management Annals*, 3(1): 251–315.

Gettler, L. (2010) Shares and share alike. *HR Monthly*, (March): 29–33.

Grant, D. and Shields, J. (2006) Identifying the subject: worker identity as discursively contested terrain. In Hearn, M. and Michelson, G. (eds) *Rethinking Work: Time, Space and Discourse*. Melbourne: Cambridge University Press, pp. 285–307.

Gupta, N. and Jenkins, G. D. (1991) Practical problems in using job evaluation systems to determine compensation. *Human Resource Management Review*, 1(2): 133–44.

Gupta, N. and Mitra, A. (1998) The value of financial incentives: myths and empirical realities. *ACA Journal/WorldatWork Journal*, 7(3): 58–66.

Gupta, N. and Shaw J. (1998) Let the evidence speak: financial incentives are effective!! *Compensation and Benefits Review*, 30(2): 26, 28–32.

Haipeter, T. (2011) Works councils as actors in collective bargaining: derogations and the development of codetermination in the German chemical and metalworking industries. *Economic and Industrial Democracy*. epub 22 February 2011, doi: 10.1177/0143831X10393039.

Heery, E. (1996) Risk, representation and the 'new pay'. *Personnel Review*, 25(6): 54–65.

Heneman, R. L. and LeBlanc, P. (2002) Developing a more relevant and competitive approach for valuing knowledge work. *Compensation and Benefits Review*, 34(4): 43–7.

Heneman, R. L. and LeBlanc P. (2003) Work valuation addresses shortcomings of both job evaluation and market pricing. *Compensation and Benefits Review*, 35(1): 7–11.

Heneman, R. L. and Von Hipple C. (1995) Balancing group and individual rewards: rewarding individual contributions to the team. *Compensation and Benefits Review*, 27(4): 63–8.

Hofrichter, D. and McGovern, T. (2001) People, competencies and performance: clarifying means and ends. *Compensation and Benefits Review*, 33(4): 34–8.

Hofstede, G. (1984) *Culture's Consequences*. London: Sage.

Kaarsemaker, E. and Poutsma, E. (2006) The fit of employee ownership with other human resource management practices: theoretical and empirical suggestions regarding the existence of an ownership high-performance work system. *Economic and Industrial Democracy*, 27(4): 669–85.

Kim, D.-O. and Voos, P. (1997) Unionization, union involvement, and the performance of gainsharing programs. *Industrial Relations/Relations Industrielles*, 52(2): 304–32.

Kohn, A. (1993a) *Punished by Rewards*. Boston: Houghton Mifflin.

Kohn, A. (1993b) Why incentive plans cannot work. *Harvard Business Review*, 71(5): 54–63.

Lang, J. M. (2008) Human resources in India: retaining and motivating staff in a Lufthansa subsidiary. *Compensation and Benefits Review*, 40: 56–62.

Lawler, E. E. (1988) What's wrong with pointfactor job evaluation. *Compensation and Benefits Review*, 18(2): 20–8.

Lawler, E. E. (1990) *Strategic Pay: Aligning Organizational Strategies and Pay Systems*. San Francisco: Jossey-Bass.

Ledford, G. E. (1991a) Three case studies on skill-based pay: an overview. *Compensation and Benefits Review*, 23(2): 11–23.

Ledford, G. E. (1991b) The design of skill-based pay plans. In Rock, M. and Berger, L. (eds) *The Compensation Handbook: A State of the Art Guide to Compensation Strategy and Design* (3rd edn). New York: McGraw-Hill, pp. 199–217.

Ledford, G. E. (2008) Factors affecting the long-term success of skill-based pay. *WorldatWork Journal*, 17(1): 6–17.

Ledford, G. E. and Heneman, R. L. (1999). Pay for skills, knowledge and competencies. In Berger, L. A. and Berger, D. R. (eds) *The Compensation Handbook. A State-of-the-Art Guide to Compensation Strategy and Design* (4th edn). McGraw-Hill, pp. 143–56.

Lehndorff, S., Bosch, G., Haipeter, T. and Latniak, E. (2009) The vulnerability of an export champion: upheaval in the German employment model. Paper presented at the Annual Congress of the International Industrial Relations Association (IIRA), Sydney, Australia, August.

Lindrop, E. (2009) Employee voice in pay determination. In White, G. and Drucker, J. (eds) *Reward Management. A Critical Text* (2nd edn). London: Routledge, pp. 41–5.

Long, R. (2006) *Strategic Compensation in Canada* (3rd edn). Scarborough, ON: Thomson Nelson, pp. 187–213.

Long, R. and Shields, J. (2009) Do unions affect pay methods of Canadian firms? A longitudinal study. *Relations Industrielles/Industrial Relations*, 64(3): 442–65.

McAdams, J. L. (1999) Non-monetary rewards: cash equivalents and tangible awards. In Berger, L. A. and Berger, D. R. (eds) *The Compensation Handbook: A State-of-the-Art Guide to Compensation Strategy and Design* (4th edn). New York: McGraw-Hill, pp. 241–60.

Merriman, K. K. (2009) On the folly of rewarding team performance, while hoping for teamwork. *Compensation and Benefits Review*, 41(1): 61–6.

Murray, B. and Gerhart, B. (2000) Skill-based pay and skill seeking. *Human Resource Management Review*, 10(3): 271–87.

Nelson, B. (1994) *1001 Ways to Reward Employees*. New York: Workman Publishing.

Pendleton, A. (2009) Employee share ownership in Europe. In White, G. and Drucker, J. (eds) *Reward Management. A Critical Text* (2nd edn). London: Routledge, pp. 224–44.

Perkins, S. J. and Vartiainen, M. (2010) European reward management? Introducing the special issue. *Thunderbird International Business Review*, 52(3): 175–87.

Perkins, S. J. and White, G. (2008) *Employee Reward. Alternatives, Consequences and Contexts*. London: Chartered Institute of Personnel and Development.

Robinson, F. and Winning, N. (2011) EU nations may only get stay of execution on indexation. *Wall Street Journal* (7 March). Available from: http://online.wsj.com/article/BT-CO-20110307-710793.html [accessed 20 March 2011].

Rosen, A. S. and Turetsky, D. (2002) Broadbanding: the construction of a career management framework. *WorldatWork Journal*, 11(4): 45–55.

Rubery, J. (1995) Performance-related pay and the prospects for gender pay equity. *Journal of Management Studies*, 32(5): 637–53.

Rynes, S. L., Gerhart B. and Park, L. (2005) Personnel psychology: performance evaluation and pay for performance. *Annual Review of Psychology*, 56: 571–600.

Shen, J. (2004) Compensation in Chinese multinationals. *Compensation and Benefits Review*, 36: 15–25.

Shields, J. (2007) *Managing Employee Performance and Reward: Concepts, Practices, Strategies*. Melbourne: Cambridge University Press.

Shields, J., Scott, D., Sperling, R. and Higgins, T. (2009) Rewards communication in Australia: a survey of policies and programs. *Compensation and Benefits Review*, 41(6): 14–26.

Townley, B. (1993a) Foucault, power/knowledge, and its relevance for human resource management. *Academy of Management Review*, 18(3): 518–45.

Townley, B. (1993b) Performance appraisal and the emergence of management. *Journal of Management Studies*, 31(2): 221–38.

Townley, B. (1994) *Reframing Human Resource Management. Power, Ethics and the Subject at Work*. London: Sage.

Townley, B. (1998) Beyond good and evil: depth and division in the management of human resources. In McKinlay, A. and Starkey, K. (eds) *Foucault, Management and Organization Theory*. London: Sage, pp. 191–210.

Townley, B. (1999) Nietzsche, competencies and Übermensch: reflections on human and inhuman resource management. *Organization*, 6(2): 285–306.

Watson, T. (2004) HRM and critical social science analysis. *Journal of Management Studies*, 41(3): 447–67.

Watson, B. W. and Singh, G. (2005) Global pay systems: compensation in support of a multinational strategy. *Compensation and Benefits Review*, (January/February): 33–6.

Wright, A. (2009) Benefits. In White, G. and Druker, J. (eds) *Reward Management. A Critical Text* (2nd edn). London: Routledge, pp. 174–91.

Training, development and learning

Peter A. Murray

11

?

After reading this chapter, students should be able to:

- ☐ Understand the differences between training and learning
- ☐ Distinguish between the more classical approaches to training and more contemporary training and learning strategies
- ☐ Explore needs and person assessments in relation to building the human capital pool of an organization
- ☐ Reflect on individual differences in training, development and learning and explore various training methods
- ☐ Link the organization's needs with performance capability matched to broader organizational strategies
- ☐ Analyse the relationship between knowledge and learning and ways to implement knowledge-sharing strategies
- ☐ Explore different narratives in learning and their influence on performance
- ☐ Relate to various international issues of training and learning and to context-specific problems
- ☐ Specify how to solve training problems by analysing case study material

Introduction

Training, development and learning concepts

Remaking history: from training to learning

Learning for international environments

Conclusion

For discussion and revision

Further reading

Case study: Sanyo

References

Introduction

This chapter discusses and explores a number of critical issues related to training, development and learning (TDL). It does this by highlighting the differences between the terms, reflecting on older, more classical approaches to training versus more contemporary and recent trends that are more situation- or context-specific. Such context-specificity means that the older approaches to training, although useful, have to be rethought. More recent trends in global organizations such as technological advances, human expectations of what constitutes a valuable job, organizational expectations related to capabilities that match strategic business needs, and increased social interaction, have meant that the older approaches are now less valuable.

The discussion here explores the nuances and differences between individual and organizational learning including, but not limited to, developing versus recruiting workers, needs assessments linked to issues of training design and performance, various training and learning methods, the link between learning and knowledge, and critical issues within an international context. The chapter is designed to take readers from the existing normative and traditional views of TDL to a more critical creative viewpoint that is context-specific.

Training, development and learning concepts

First, there are differences between 'training', 'development' and 'learning' that should be noted. *Training* can be thought of as a kind of formal learning process provided in the workplace that might include training for a discrete job or role (Gibb, 2003). As we discuss later, however, training does not always lead to learning (Antonacopoulou, 1999), or to learning that can be applied in the workplace (Cortese, 2005).

Development is tied to training since organizations want to increase the capabilities and skills of their workers or 'develop' them in such a way that skill levels increase. The notion of development then extends to changing the whole person by helping people to grow (Gibb, 2003). However, this is not necessarily confined to skill enhancement. In fact, the original idea of human resources development originated from the behavioural school of management in the 1930s and 40s (Fulop et al., 1992). This was associated with a refocusing away from the more efficiency-driven approach of managing people at work (essentially seeing people at work as machines) to an approach developed in the 1920s by Elton Mayo (a Harvard Business School professor) that helped people excel in their workplace through better human relations and by recognizing the power of social factors (Rose, 1975).

Learning is about a demonstrated change in the level of knowledge displayed by individuals (Gibb, 2008). However, it is also about recognizing that individuals have different learning styles such that people 'learn' in different ways and at a different rate from other learners (Honey and Mumford, 1986, cited in Allinson and Hayes, 1996). For the purposes of this chapter, 'learning' will closely follow what Antonacopoulou (2001: 328) describes as 'the liberation of knowledge through self-reflection and questioning' by developing a space through which common language and experiences can be observed. The nuances between the terms in TDL should be noted, but the important point is that one aspect cannot be useful without the others.

Remaking history: from training to learning

Contrasting classical views of training

Think of imperatives or needs for training. Most countries have had similar needs for training within business enterprises, but the path and history of their experiences has been different. It is not the purpose of this section to trace the history of training country by country in a chronological way. However, it is useful to reflect on why the traditional, more standardized approaches to training that are common to different countries have had far-reaching implications for modern-day or contemporary training methods. We can do this by contrasting the classical and contemporary views of training by exploring four different themes.

In the first theme, we will examine the variation in training experiences between the UK and Australia. Although many differences are present, both countries have seen a similar evolution in terms of training, and similar systems of governance. Although the discussion is limited to two countries, training methods as a means of increasing resources and capabilities are remarkably similar across all countries, meaning that training methods are somewhat universal in application: they may not be applied in exactly the same way, yet the foundations for training are almost identical. The development of the strategic human capital pool, for instance, is a worldwide phenomenon (Wright et al., 2001; Clardy, 2008; Boxall and Macky, 2009) in which training plays a key role.

In the second theme, we will analyse the external and internal organizational factors that drive training and learning and are common to all organizations irrespective of their geographical location. The factors that drive organizational change are for the most part the same factors that drive training agendas. Although the topics covered by the chapters in this book are integrated, job design and redesign are organizational factors that generally lead to a training needs analysis (TNA), suggesting that, in a world of fast-changing contexts, the stated intentions of training should be matched to the strategic needs of the business.

In the third theme, we will look at more recent research findings that influence training outcomes. We are particularly interested in organizational training consistent with the chapter's purpose of understanding what organizations should be doing with respect to TDL.

For the fourth theme, we will explore and contrast classical and contemporary training methods. Some questions to ask of this theme concern individual differences, social interaction and the generation of knowledge. That is, to what extent do the two approaches – classical and contemporary – contribute to a learner's ability to capture and share knowledge?

Classical views

Let's look at the first theme. From the early 1900s, the emphasis was mainly on establishing apprenticeships, meeting the skills requirements for all kinds of occupational persuasion from mechanical and building skills to engineering and architectural skills. The former, more 'blue-collar' occupations were typically confined to trade halls and institutional colleges around the globe, such as technical schools in the UK and technical and further education colleges in Australia. In comparison, training and teaching for professionals was always the domain of the universities. Many of the latter in the UK were established by counties, whereas in Australia, these were Commonwealth institutions run by university councils and academic boards.

For technical training, priority was given to supervisory and technical staff, and most teaching occurred at night. It is useful here to point out that, for most of the 20th century, training has been mostly focused on teaching a sell-and-tell, systematic and highly structured approach (Antonacopoulou, 1999). While the classical approaches will be outlined more clearly in theme four, training was typically thought of in terms of classroom instruction (university or technical), on-the-job (supervisor to worker) or off-the-job (attending a training course) learning. Training also occurred through vocational training or occupational or professional training for individuals (not always in a university but, for example, in a vocational college), and action learning (such as employees working in a cross-functional team). Out of these, classroom instruction was the most common.

Technical training did not extend to ordinary workers. Training for the latter depended on the organizational imperative for training, that is, the connection between business growth and training (Jones, 2004). Early approaches to skills were focused on just three skill types: technical, conceptual and people. Generally, it was commonly thought that workers needed only technical skills, whereas managers required thinking ability related to conceptual and people skills. In terms of learning, with its simplistic attachment to skills, it is understandable why organizations advanced slowly in relation to connecting skills development with learning outcomes that matched organizational needs.

As an aside, the training that occurred in organizations across much of the world through to the 1960s was very much efficiency-driven and, as discussed earlier, focused more on occupational than individual needs (Fulop et al., 1992). In recognition of the latter, both the UK and Australia established a training system based on a national vocational qualification framework that has played an important role in increased skill development. This involves gaining nationally recognized qualifications that may or may not meet an organization's needs (De Ceiri and Kramar, 2008); principally however, these national vocations systems have been designed to help people find work.

In terms of our first theme, the notion of training for ordinary workers was not really part of the earlier technical approaches, and tailored training for individual differences was not even considered. Training for the professions was mainly the domain of universities, where a qualification was more careers-focused. For individual learning, the earlier approaches were systematic and ad hoc (Antonacopoulou, 2006). In fact, technical-type instruction was generally considered poor (Chartered Institute of Personnel and Development, 2009), and organizations considered this to be more of a cost than an investment (Smith, 2003).

In Australia, for instance, it was not until 1989 that a training reform agenda was established via a National Training Board, together with a new competency-based training system. These initiatives led to the training guarantee scheme in which enterprises with payroll costs in excess of A\$200,000 were required to spend at least 1.5 per cent of their payroll on 'structured' training for their workers (Smith, 2003). These schemes have now been abandoned, and it is a matter of conjecture whether employing organizations spend enough on training. Recent research by Sheehan et al. (2006) of 1,372 senior human resources professionals found that only 54 per cent of managers felt that organizations were placing enough emphasis on developing training policies and practices to attract and retain talent.

In contrast, in the UK, some of these initiatives occurred much earlier through the Industry Training Act of 1964 and various training schemes. However, not dissimilar to the situation in Australia, industry training boards were replaced by enterprise councils, which in turn were replaced by sector skills councils (Chartered Institute of Personnel and Development, 2009). In both countries, and indeed in much of the developed world, a benchmark or yardstick is often used to measure how much one country lags behind another in terms of its skills and the education of its workforce, including manufactured outputs. Here, both the UK and Australia show similar experiences, systems of reforms and relative failures in educational investment. For a discussion on training in smaller firms, see Chapter 16.

Taken together, these older classical approaches and ideas for training remain dominant. Within the context of this chapter, they need to be contrasted with contemporary practices that are both critical and more reflective. Importantly, however, it is questionable whether the classical approaches are still relevant for the workers of today, who need greater flexibility and more socially interactive approaches to systems of instruction.

Overall, the classical approaches remain quite rigid, very systematic, highly structured and inflexible in terms of their scope and type of learning (Beckett and Murray, 2000). Even for most universities, it is questionable whether existing lecture theatres and halls familiar to baby-boomer and generation X professors are suitable for predominately generation Y learners who favour e-learning techniques and familiar discussion forums in which their peers participate (Chartered Institute of Personnel and Development, 2008; Conway and Monks, 2008; Khanna and New, 2008). What this indicates for modern learners is that instructional preference has most probably shifted to a variety of training techniques that facilitate deeper learning and knowledge acquisition (see theme four below).

Needs assessment and discontinuous change

In moving to theme two, one can contrast the old classical approach to work and training needs with discontinuous markets. From earlier 20th-century and post-War priorities for training, dramatic changes in the design of work became evident. This meant that training and learning changed fundamentally from about midway through the 1960s, moving from a more structured approach to a more holistic and flexible approach that valued workers' input into the actual design of programmes.

There are important lessons for trainers and managers to be learned from earlier failures. For the most part, older production failures point to inadequate needs assessments that were poorly articulated into training strategies. Understanding organizational and job needs is equally as important as understanding work design and redesign (see Chapter 7). Training and learning should be matched to strategic goals in such a way that training makes a real difference to learning outcomes. The strategic aspect of training is about structuring work in such a way that managers get the best out of their people (Wright et al., 2001; Antonacopoulou, 2006). In relation to these earlier approaches, it is useful to ask how structured learning was complemented by critical and creative thinking. To make training and learning really count, more efficient job design approaches focus on finding out about what is required for a job in the form of person, task and *organizational needs assessments* (Nankervis et al., 2008).

Before training can be articulated into training methods, some type of job analysis needs to occur. This requires trainers/managers to collect information related to a job description (lists of tasks, duties and responsibilities), position descriptions related to work behaviours, work conditions and job characteristics, all linked to some way of measuring an employee's performance at a later date. For instance, graphic rating scales are used to measure performance (rating attributes from, for example, poor = 1 to distinguished performance = 5) for each employee; behavioural ranked scales (defined behaviours exhibited) can also be used, as can some mixture of these methods. Generally, an organization uses a standardized graphic and behavioural scale to measure all employee performance. Performance outcomes are a critical part of training in the sense that training should be linked to performance in order to determine whether workers have transferred training knowledge into demonstrated skills (Khanna and New, 2008).

But, getting back to job assessment, a position analysis questionnaire (PAQ) analysis is critical:

> The job analyst is asked to determine whether each item (*such as those on a position description*) applies to the job being analysed. The analyst then rates the item on six scales: extent of use, amount of time, importance to the job, possibility of occurrence, applicability and special code (special rating scales used with a particular item). These ratings are submitted to the PAQ headquarters where a computer program generates a report regarding the job's scores on the job dimensions. (De Ceiri and Kramar, 2008: 193; emphasis added)

But before human resources managers or any other managers can develop people at work, they require a clear idea of what is expected of each worker. This generally refers to a *training needs analysis* (TNA). Note that the latter is different from a job analysis or position needs assessment. Whereas a PAQ, for instance, ascertains what skills, attitudes and behaviours are required for each job, it is then the task of the trainer to assess whether existing workers can adequately demonstrate these.

In one sense, TNA is about the systematic gathering of data to highlight gaps in the existing skill levels, knowledge and abilities of workers (Chartered Institute of Personnel and Development, 2009; Nankervis et al., 2008). These gaps are then matched to changed job requirements that job analysts need to assess. That is, as organizations increasingly compete through discontinuous information, technological and process and manufacturing changes, job requirements/ position descriptions alter in such a way that trainers/managers have to assess the gaps and train workers to close them. Thus, old skills and abilities need to be rematched with the new skills and abilities needed for new job functions and processes. TNA could extend to the whole organization (providing the right capabilities to meet organizational strategies) for a specific project (new ways of working or reorganization) or just to individuals (tying personal development and individual capabilities to those of the business) (Wright et al., 2001; Chartered Institute of Personnel and Development, 2009). Table 11.1 encapsulates the discussion here. Human resources managers also have to grapple with estimating the size and focus of the human capital pool given that workers will leave and that training methods need to be sufficient to replace the skills lost.

Training in practice

For theme three, trends and the evidence from training outcomes in Australia are mixed. In the mid-1990s, a study of senior human resources managers was conducted by Kramar and Lake (1997). This study of 331 organizations, investigating the nature of human resources policies, found that in the organizations whose training expenditure was known, about 50 per cent of employees received internal or external training and another 20 per cent received some form of training. That is, according to data from the Australian Bureau of Statistics, approximately 80 per cent per cent of Australian workers received some form of training from their employer (Smith, 2003).

In research conducted in 2001, the amounts spent on training as a proportion of total salaries and wages had increased in most countries, for example in the UK (3.6 per cent) and Singapore (3.1 per cent), followed by Denmark and The Netherlands (3.0 per cent and 2.8 per cent, respectively). Australia was ranked fifth (2.5 per cent) and, interestingly, the USA sixth (1.9 per cent; Brown et al., 2001). In comparison, however, a more recent survey conducted by Deloitte and the Australian Industry Group of 500 CEOs in businesses of all sizes found that, as a consequence of the 2008/09 global downturn, the overall expenditure on training was reduced by 4.1 per cent in 2009/10 (Australian Industry Group, 2009). In this survey, a third of businesses planned to cut their training budgets, with four in five reducing their training expenditure by up to 20 per cent. At the employee entry level, 36.8 per cent of companies employing apprentices expected to reduce the number of apprentices they would train during 2009/10.

This is in stark contrast to the situation in large manufacturers, who have been attracted to new business opportunities in emerging markets such as China and India. In a global survey of 446 executives from manufacturing companies headquartered in 31 different countries, 63 per cent of executives stated that training was an important talent management strategy in emerging markets (Deloitte, 2007). Yet in a US survey of 325 employees of companies with an annual revenue of $500 million or more, only 32 per cent stated that training and retention were a top talent priority (Deloitte, 2009).

Table 11.1 Position analysis and training needs assessment for a production controller

Job requirements using PAQ, January 2010	Job analysis using PAQ, July 2011	Gap analysis from PAQ, August 2011	Training needs analysis and training methods to use
1. Information: how does this worker get information 2. Mental processes: reasoning, decision-making, planning and information processes 3. Job context: mixture of physical and social contexts	1. Reports directly to manufacturing manager and purchasing manager 2. High-level thinking, regular planning meetings; communicates processes to other factory workers 3. Must show skills lying between technical requirements and individual consideration/people in factory	1. Now reports only to purchasing. More knowledge of purchasing required 2. High-level thinking; planning meetings with assistant; now trains workers in safety; must conduct quality meetings 3. Requires a statement of the impact on workers of new roll-out process technology	1. On the job. Issue report 12b to production controller 2. Should attend safety training; needs updates on quality control and legislation changes. Off-the-job training 3. On the job. Issue report 21c to controller on process technology. Needs to attend training course on new technology. Team training necessary
Desired behaviours 1. Performs in a cooperative manner 2. Is a team player 3. Makes clear decisions linked to goals 4. Assigns production tasks in a timely way 5. Understands and implements quality features 6. Focuses on achieving controlling tasks 7. Identifies and fixes control barriers	Note: from performance appraisal (PAP), December: 1. PAP high 2. Team skills average 3. Tends to work by herself 4. Very good 5. Quality control high 6. Very task-oriented 7. Some new goals need to be set	Gap analysis extracted from behavioural ranked scales in PAP: Main concern is team skills. Leadership gaps appear in instructional techniques and some social skill is lacking concerning other managers	Should attend a leadership course run externally Cross-functional team training is recommended, as well as attending an off-the-job team training seminar Would also benefit from reflective instructional techniques, learning from workers and increased social interaction

PAQ, position analysis questionnaire.

So what do these mixed survey results indicate? To a large extent, they suggest that the amount expended on training is context-specific from one country to the next, and that in times of global crisis, companies tend to slash their training budgets to save costs. The results also suggest that training is very much tied to strategic business goals. For instance, in the 2007 Deloitte global survey, approximately one-quarter of the executives surveyed found it difficult to attract qualified workers in China, India, Latin America and Eastern Europe.

Perhaps another way to interpret the results is by speculating on the type of training. Almost uniformly, surveys reflect training metrics for traditional forms of instruction such as in-house and external training, yet they seldom include learning from social forms of interaction and networking, story-telling and recalling narratives based on experience, self-reflection and electronic learning.

Apart from poor management practices, another reason why training outcomes do not translate into practice is the shift from an employee-centred focus to a strategic focus on the part of human resource management professionals. Modern human resources professionals work with management to analyse and devise solutions for organizational problems (Brown et al., 2009). Increasing pressure and an emphasis on strategic goals has meant a shift away from personnel managers – who focused more on the employee – towards human resource management professionals, who focus more on matching human capital to strategic goals.

Many researchers now talk more about human resources professionals building the human capital stock in such a way that it adds to the business's strategic advantage (Wright et al., 2001; Boxall and Macky, 2009). For some commentators, this has created a conflict between the ability of human resources professionals to see the world from the workers' perspective and the need to build customer and shareholder value from the employer's perspective (Peterson, 2004; Ulrich and Brockbank, 2005; Brown et al., 2009). Although the study by Brown et al. found that human resources professionals simply incorporated the older personnel functions into their strategic roles, this does not discount the reality that a great majority spent less than a third of their time on employee-centred activities (Brown et al., 2009), including training (Australian Industry Group, 2009).

In comparison, the governments of both the UK and Australia have changed their perspectives on the value of internal training matched to external pressures. Public sector reforms have been based on three driving forces. The first of these concerns the reshaping of organizational structure and management through a better control of finances and the monitoring of performance (Rainbird and Munro, 2003). The second is that most federal, state and local governments (boroughs and counties in the UK) now tender contracts on a competitive basis, leading to a third driving force: the need to mimic the competitive pressures of the private sector. In both the UK and Australia, the establishment of quite complex training registers is common, and competency or skill ladders consisting of a training matrix for worker progression (Table 11.2) are well known in both the public and the private sector. In the National Health Service in the UK, for example, people from a relatively low skills base can move up and across a skills escalator through training and development, which provides an impetus for innovative approaches to 'growing your own staff' (Rainbird and Munro, 2003: 31).

Table 11.2 Career skills ladder for a bank manager

Levels	Leadership	Budgeting/ finance	Team skills	Customer relations
Branch manager	Leads the entire team in the branch	Competencies within the entire branch reporting	Can design, implement and grow teams	Designs customer programmes
Relationship manager	Leads the sales and marketing team	Can complete full budgets and reports	Can develop full team and skill enhancement	Demonstrates superior customer skills
Support manager lending	Leads several groups by demonstrating strong leadership skills	Completes reports and analyses results	Practises team analytical skills	Principles of marketing course
Assistant support manager, lending	Leads one small group and demonstrates performance	Can complete budgetary documentation	Analyse team behaviour	Advanced customer programme
Front desk 2	Leadership course 2	Financial planning course	Team development course	Customer programme
Front desk 1	Leadership course 1	Learn budgeting techniques	How to act in a team setting	How to deal with customers

From classical to contemporary training methods

Questioning the logic of learning

Earlier, we briefly highlighted typical training and learning methods common in human resources development, including formal classroom training, on-the-job and off-the-job instruction, and others. Figure 11.1 highlights the various forms of traditional and mechanistic training methods. The most common are on-the-job, off-the-job and the traditional classroom instruction that many learners experience in school classrooms. The point is that traditional methods of instruction perpetuate the myth that these approaches are good for learning. As Bratton and Gold (2007) suggest, though, 'good for whom?'

Traditional methods conform to a 'one best way' approach and propagate the conflict between labour and capital (Rainbird and Munro, 2003) in which work-place learning is related to managerial strategies of labour control from one perspective and workers' resistance from another. This is not to say that these forms of training are outdated. Traditional or classical views still dominate learning in almost every university and college across the globe. However, it is becoming increasingly challenging for professors and organizational trainers to construct classroom learning in a way that young learners (generation Y) find interesting. So this begs the question of whether new learning should be chal-lenging and much more reflective, as Bratton and Gold suggest:

> It is increasingly being recognised that, rather than seeing organizations as single, unified and stable entities, a more pluralist and dynamic view needs to be adopted, composed of a set of ongoing activities and processes. It is within such activities and processes that people make sense of what they do

and how work should occur, including what should and should not be learned ... *a learner may become aware that learning [from] a restructuring* has a cost and could undermine her or his collective relations with other employees. Employees may realise that the learning agenda belongs to management and that talk of corporate values, strategy and competencies is not neutral but rests on a dominant management ideology ... learning is about enhancing the ability of individuals and groups to learn. (2007: 337; emphasis added)

The flow of learning

Before we can explore different contemporary learning methods common to our fourth theme, let us for a moment note the difference between individual, group and organizational learning, as well as the idea that every organization has a culture for learning that reflects the dominant values and ideologies that we will call here the *learning climate*. Previous literature suggests that learning flows between different levels within the organization (Crossan and Berdrow, 2003). A learning climate is the flow of beliefs between the individual, the group and the organizational level. Individuals pass on their learning to teams, who in turn pass it on to the organization (Crossan and Berdrow, 2003). In its turn, the organization embeds the knowledge in its systems, processes and procedures before passing it back to new employees – and so the cycle of learning continues.

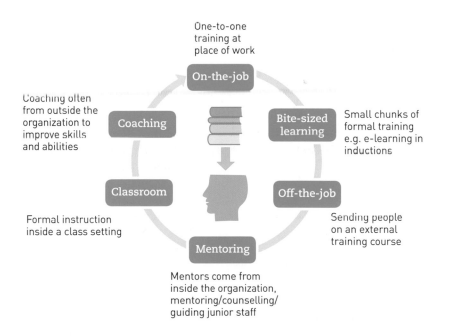

Figure 11.1 Typical traditional training methods.

First, let's examine individual-level learning. According to Argyris and Schön (1978), individuals learn by engaging in a discover–choose–act cycle often called single-loop learning: they make choices from what they discover and then act on them. The problem here, however, is that no new learning occurs that challenges past assumptions. Think of a merchandising procedure within a retail store where the manager does all the training and possesses most of the knowledge. This may be satisfactory until he or she leaves and takes that knowledge away. The discovery process here might perhaps concern what other types of training are necessary to ensure that the knowledge is retained. The choice might be the manager passing on information in a traditional classroom setting. Several procedures and processes included in the training might, however, be challenged at a later date by other individuals, managers or teams questioning the training methods and even the type of training conducted. This could lead to simple merchandising charts relating to particular merchandise that could be pasted onto the shop wall. This latter approach is one of double-loop learning. That is, individuals should be given the opportunity in the workplace to challenge, question and test the assumptions that drive most of the decisions they face. They do this by challenging a dominant or existent view, by questioning related assumptions and by testing the old assumptions in a new conceptual model (Hedberg, 1981; Kim, 1993; Espedal, 2008) (see the learning flows in Figure 11.2).

Another complementary idea is that individual learning is both a methodical and an emergent practice. Learning becomes standardized in organizational systems, methods and procedures, leading to *method-based* learning, that is, behaviour that enables a firm to constantly exploit its existing capabilities (Miller, 1996; March, 2006). This is lower-order learning associated with improving practices that are already known (Espedal, 2008). Conversely, the idea behind better learning is *emergent* learning, that is, higher-order learning associated with 'the changing of a logic of action that is known and experimentation with what is not known but might become known' (Espedal, 2008: 366). The latter is an extension of double-loop learning except that it has shifted to a more complex context, such as questioning existing decisions related to market development, for example, and whether these old decisions stand the test of time and competitive pressures in changing markets.

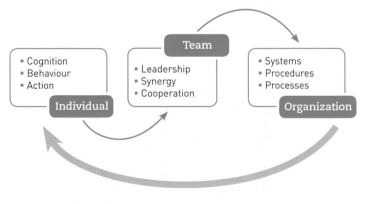

Figure 11.2 Flow of learning.
Source: Adapted from Crossan et al. (1999: 524)

So from one perspective, individuals can be trained to think in double-loop terms, but so too can organizations through teamwork. Team members will most likely need training to understand how past decisions can be a stumbling block to new decisions that a team might have to negotiate. Organizations are only entities and of themselves do not learn; therefore they rely on individuals and teams to pass on learning in the form of existing knowledge or new knowledge learned.

Cognition and behaviour

Early theories of organizational learning fail adequately to address the relationship between cognitive structures (human thought processes) and the behavioural actions they give rise to (Hedberg, 1981). Many scholars suggest, for example, that changes in behaviour may occur without any cognitive development (Fiol and Lyles, 1985; Cortese, 2005; Antonacopoulou, 2006); conversely, the acquisition of knowledge – such as knowledge from a training course – may be gained without any accompanying change in behaviour (action that results from knowledge). This interplay between knowledge and behaviour means one of two things. That is, people might acquire knowledge but might not have the means to implement it; organizations might train people, for instance, but may not have the right workplace procedures available for people to practise the knowledge. Conversely, people might learn behaviours on the job but may not understand the reason why these behaviours are necessary, meaning that they will lack the knowledge to explain their actions. Creating change may be creating the illusion of learning such that management appears to be in control (Hedberg, 1981). Similarly, major behavioural change does not lead to a dramatic change in cognitive development. The creation of change may not be brought about by cognitive growth but merely by a need to do something (Hedberg, 1981; Antonacopoulou, 2001).

Carl Jung was one of the first theorists to try to make this connection by developing the idea of archetypes or cognitive patterns that structure thought and hence give order to the world (Jung, 1968; Morgan, 1997). Morgan explains how archetypes shape the way we 'meet ourselves' in encounters with the external world and are crucial for understanding links between conscious and unconscious aspects of the human psyche. Jung distinguished between two ways of perceiving reality (sensation and intuition) and two ways of judging (thinking and feeling):

- □ *Sensing–thinking* individuals tend, according to Jung, to make judgements and interpretations on the basis of 'hard facts' and logical analysis.
- □ *Sensing–feeling* individuals pay a great deal of attention to data derived from the senses, but arrive at judgements in terms of 'what feels right' rather than in terms of analysis.
- □ *Intuition–thinking* individuals tend to work their way through problems by thinking about the possibilities inherent in a situation. Their actions are guided by a combination of insight and feelings.
- □ *Intuition–feeling* individuals pay much more attention to values than to facts (Jung, in Morgan, 1997: 240–1).

The archetype patterns that guide thinking and action partly explain why managers find it difficult to link cognitive change with behavioural change. Managers often speak of frustration, for example, when trying to convert knowledge into action (Antonacopoulos, 2001). In trying to examine the archetypes from a workplace perspective, one can see that sensing–thinking individuals would be mainly concerned about the 'here and now' as hard facts would drive their decisions, whereas intuition–feeling individuals would relate more to concerns about the values and ideologies related to a problem.

A production manager who needs to meet targets knows exactly what she needs to do with her largely multicultural workers. However, a human resources manager who receives complaints about workplace conflict will want to analyse the problem based on values and individual differences. Whereas a production manager might solve the problem by 'getting on with it', the human resources manager wants to sit people down and talk about the problems. If a religious person is required to pray six times a day because of her religious practices, a sensor and pragmatist may say that this is not allowed and that all workers are only allowed three breaks in an 8-hour shift. A thinking–feeling manager, however, might see the logic in making a separate room available and allowing the worker to make up the time lost at a later date.

Honey and Mumford (cited in Allinson and Hayes, 1996) also suggest a complementary archetype system based on activists, reflectors, theorists and pragmatists:

- Similarly to Jung's classification, *activists* learn best when they use trial and error to discover something.
- *Reflectors*, however, learn best when given adequate time to digest, consider and prepare.
- *Theorists*, on the other, hand prefer a sound structure and a pattern or purpose, responding well to complex ideas that stretch their current thinking.
- Lastly, *pragmatists* learn best when given real-life practical issues to discuss.

Once again, the connection between cognition and behaviour should be noted. A manager may have several groups with different learning styles, and some groups will clearly learn more quickly than others. This is because the make-up of one group may consist of predominately sensors and pragmatists who want to make quick decisions based on 'facts'. However, this group may arrive at a decision prematurely without questioning the facts and assumptions. Another group, by comparison, may consist of both activists and theorists or some combination lying in between, allowing the group to question past actions and arrive at a better decision.

Kolb (1984) mixes the styles by suggesting a process loop in which concrete experience involves learning from the past. Learners then reflect on and observe their experiences, drawing from many perspectives (reflective observation) before integrating their thoughts into logically sound theories (abstract conceptualization). Finally, they actively experiment with their decisions in light of the thinking process (active experimentation) (Rylatt, 1994; Bratton and Gold, 2007). Interestingly, in a class setting, have you ever wondered why some groups finish far earlier than others?

Knowledge management

Organizations have difficulty in dealing with knowledge-sharing and knowledge conversion (Nonaka and Takeuchi, 1995) or even understanding what knowledge actually is and how it should be defined (Cook and Brown, 1999). Knowledge accumulation, knowledge-sharing and knowledge conversion are key resources in an organization's capacity to turn capabilities into skills that make a difference in knowledge dissemination (Byosiere and Luethge, 2008; Eisenhardt and Martin, 2000). It is one thing to capture and store knowledge (Bassi, 1999) but quite another thing to share it so that its practical application is more evident throughout the organization. While explicit and tacit knowledge is possessed by people, knowing is not about possession but about 'practice' and about interacting with the components of the social and physical world (Vera and Crossan, 2003: 126). As we discussed earlier, learning is valuable when the knowledge gained can be practised.

At the organizational level, knowledge is retained in systems, procedures and policies by facilitating the formal articulation and codification of ideas (Arthur and Huntley, 2005). Learning behaviours will be required in practice to allow individuals and teams to express the 'know-what' and the 'know-how' by converting their knowledge into practice (Brown and Duguid, 1991; Arthur and Huntley, 2005). One question is whether double-loop learning is evident in actions that allow individuals to convert the 'know-what' into 'know-how'. A second question concerns whether individuals themselves have acquired the right type of knowledge to make a significant contribution to the organization. For knowledge to be useful for the organization, individuals need to transform and challenge existing knowledge, often in groundbreaking ways that allow them to radically change and alter decisions (Miller, 1996; Crossan and Berdrow, 2003). Although learning is needed for knowledge conversion to occur, simple or basic training may not be enough to facilitate the knowledge conversion process (Byosiere and Luethge, 2008).

The knowledge conversion process can become a problem when not enough skills are in place through traditional training to convert knowledge into practice. For example, the conversion of tacit knowledge into explicit knowledge (externalization), tacit knowledge into tacit knowledge (socialization), explicit knowledge into tacit knowledge (internalization) and explicit knowledge into explicit knowledge (combination) will require an approach to learning that may not be based on traditional learning practices. Rather, managers will need to reflect on how people learn, and to develop a range of learning methods that will allow knowledge-sharing to occur. To externalize what they have learnt, there has to be some way for both individuals and teams to convert tacit knowledge into explicit knowledge. This might be achieved by many joint activities, face-to-face interactions over time and 'managing by walking around' (Byosiere and Luethge, 2008). For example, knowledge communities or communities of practice (COPs) are a way of connecting experts or groups of people who have ideas to be shared. Typically, COPs acknowledge that learning is mostly informal and improvisational or situated within a context.

Building on earlier work by Lave and Wenger (1991), Brown and Duguid (1991) outline how COPs make a distinction between canonical and non-canonical practice, the former referring to what is supposed to be learned (as in traditional training), and the latter to what is actually learned (Bratton and Gold, 2007). At its most basic, a COP is organized as informal and self-organizing around the needs of a situation, which is another form of conversion from knowledge into practice. It can be suggested that these conversion strategies are needed in far greater quantities in organizational contexts involving difficult strategic decisions. In a context of constant change, such as the computer industry, people will benefit from a variety of learning or multi-learning methods that enable tacit knowledge to be shared, or external knowledge (such as knowledge in a system) to be taught in such a way that workers relate to it. For externalization, what is understood intuitively needs to be translated into a form that can be understood. Although traditional learning is clearly invoked where one learns the knowledge to the point at which it becomes second nature (Byosiere and Luethge, 2008), different behaviour through the use of metaphor, dialogues or analogies will be more useful for externalization. This brings us to some other contemporary ideas for theme four related to learning in the workplace.

Learning from narrative and reflection

One can see from the flow of learning that explicit knowledge or knowledge communicated in some written form or spoken word can be independent of the individual so that it becomes organizational knowledge (Cortese, 2005). So an individual as described earlier as a learner who expresses a point of view of 'self' is only one agent of learning, and the self is always subjected to learning by others. Other agents could be students, instructors, mentors, experts, groups or collective 'others'. For example, acquiring knowledge through concrete experiences (see Kolb's learning cycle) is only one medium from which a distinct learning style might emerge. In reality, a learner learns from multiple sources.

If managers, for example, always see learning as objectified, that is, what the learner learns must be right in his or her frame of mind, or what the organization or teacher teaches must be 'real', large gaps in knowledge may occur. Objectified learning is based on a realist assumption, blinding learners to one reality (either their own or someone else's) by restricting learning from multiple realities (Gergen, 1994; Ramsey, 2005). One can criticize Kolb's cycle for restricting learning to a closed lens – knowledge gained by an individual is also a communal joint production; experiences are not only constructed by one's self, but by others. This means that an objectivist approach should be supplemented by a subjectivist or social constructionist approach (Gergen, 1991; Hosking, 1999) in which a learner such as a worker is tied to various ongoing relations or experiences at work that enrich the learner's knowledge (see Mini Case Study 11.1).

Mini Case Study 11.1
Learning from narratives and experience

Suzy Pakston had strong ideas from what she had learned in her marketing degree about how to build value into a products brand (branding). She often recounted her professor's words: 'Brands are built from capabilities by adding advantage to the product, by augmenting the product.' All her strategies related to this. This led to an objectivist state in which Suzy's own experiences dictated her view of the world.

But things changed when Jose was also hired as a brand manager – he had a conciliatory approach to building ideas related to a brand. He valued people's viewpoints and challenged his own on a consistent basis. Their two learning styles clashed dramatically. Suzy became frustrated by Jose's lack of clarity, while Jose viewed Suzy's views as one of many. This led to a major showdown in the general manager's office.

The general manager himself was sympathetic to Suzy's views, recounting his own experience as a product manager years earlier. He suggested that 'Jose get on with the job of management and leave managing people to the human resources department'. This greatly pleased Suzy, who left the meeting with a big grin. Jose, on the other hand, felt somewhat bemused and reflective, questioning his own methods.

On his way back to the office, he stepped in to see the marketing manager and had a quick chat. He began to explain his narrative of the meeting only to learn that Suzy had done the same 15 minutes earlier. Jose left a quarter of an hour later having heard the marketing manager's view that the answer lay somewhere in the middle. Jose later began to value the thought that collective others had influenced his ideas related to managing a brand. But there was still the problem of what to do with Suzy …

Questions

1 What approach would you take with Suzy if you were Jose?
2 Could Suzy learn anything from Jose? Or Jose anything from Suzy?

One way of understanding this is by linking the 'text' (such as a gesture, word or action, mannerism, acclamation or direction) to the context (the actual place, background or situation in which the text has occurred). If three workers are sent from the sales department to the factory floor to gain an appreciation of the factory's processes, it is highly likely that each will return with a different story based on the text–context relations. The first worker's narrative of his experiences retold later to, say, a manager is capable of communicating just as meaningfully but in a different way from that of the second or third worker, who expresses the narrative in a dissimilar way. Importantly, if all three sit down and retell their experiences, one worker will learn something from the others as their interpretations are different. Together, ongoing and regular social relations have the potential to lead to a more enriched collective learning experience in which the perspectives of reality are treated as an ongoing social performance in which knowing becomes simply a relational premise:

> What all these different language tools do is to tie the knower into ongoing relations. From a relational perspective, text cannot be separated from context, act cannot be separated from supplement and self cannot be separated from other. These relational language tools invite a reflector to avoid being tied down to one particular account as if true. They prompt us to treat what people claim to know as saying as much about them as a situation. (Ramsey, 2005: 222)

With story-telling, understanding occurs not only in how the story is told, but also in how it is received and interpreted, meaning that story-telling is a communal and not an individual activity. Our narratives are influenced by other narratives, which in turn reflect 'local realities' (see Mini Case Study 11.1). Stories will be coordinated based on the context of what is occurring in practice, so although different managers will have different views about how goods are delivered once produced by the factory, communal stories will lead to joint action to ensure that customers are happy with the delivery process. What is interesting about Antonacopoulous's (2006) accounts of stories of learning in the banking industry is that many managers believed that training was learning, yet later, in accounts to the researcher about the effectiveness of training, most managers reported text–context relations explaining why the training had not been effective: multiple realities reduced the ability of the learner to practise what he or she had learned.

Similarly, Cortese (2005), in a study of 24 middle and top managers about learning in their working life, collected 282 stories that described learning episodes. Out of these, 85 per cent of managers suggested that learning increased through the experience of others, through either observation, listening or experimentation. For example, in support of a relational or highly interactive process, the teacher's own learning benefited from observation when a pupil pointed out a mistake in the teacher's demonstration. This led the teacher to question her own professional practice by adapting and rewriting her own internal manual of what she 'thought' she was demonstrating. Learning occurs by understanding that 'the other is different from me because I am different from him or her, in other words one succeeds in stepping back and observing oneself through the eyes of others' (Cortese, 2005: 102).

Corporate social responsibility

For training and development purposes, corporate social responsibility (CSR) concerns two things:

☐ the demand for and supply of labour over a long period of time;
☐ socially responsible behaviour.

For example, in the hospital system in most countries, CSR is related to ensuring the survival of public health services in such a way that current generations will have the right type of health services available, and that enough funding and provisions are made to ensure the survival of the health system for future generations. The latter goal extends to the lack of workers that would be available to fulfil these services if organizations did not make enough funds available for training and development purposes. As hospital services grow, governments need to ensure that enough funding is available to increase the number of workers (supply) to meet the demand of tomorrow's hospital systems. This takes us back to our earlier discussions on training. The question relates to whether organizations are spending enough on training to ensure the continued growth of their organization.

The second point about CSR is global and local citizenship. This means that organizations should not emulate the circumstances leading to the collapse of energy company Enron and other similar corporations by not being responsible with shareholder funds. The situations of organizations who maintain a commitment to CSR on the one hand yet spend little in relation to TDL is an oxymoron. That is, one cannot advance the ethics of being socially responsible, socially sustainable in the supply of labour, if one does very little in terms of TDL.

Learning for international environments

In their study of the Swedish telecommunications giant Ericsson, Hocking et al. (2007) found that expatriate workers had no pressing need to be bound to their host country sources for knowledge applications, even though generally they were more likely to access their own expanded international networks in their home country. As we shall see, there are mixed realities surrounding this statement because it suggests that the source of most knowledge for individuals on international assignments may well reside in the home country. In striving for greater knowledge, however, a kind of double-loop learning process enables individuals to expand their own (and others') knowledge, suggesting that expatriates will regularly consult individuals with diverse backgrounds.

In terms of Kolb's learning cycles, expatriates' experiential learning is heavily influenced by local knowledge such as local personal networks and local culture. Drawing from the earlier point of narrative and reflection, learning from collective others' and different narratives and tales from the field is an important source of learning. Learning stems from observation, narratives, listening and other opinions that challenge one's own worldview. This contrasts strongly with the approach that knowledge and learning is fundamentally an imperial and universal application of home country knowledge (Bartlett and Ghoshal, 1988) in which the application of knowledge in the host country is heavily influenced in advance of action. As we shall discuss below, social networks are important in dealing with significant cultural and social challenges.

It is not enough to send expatriates abroad only for them to rely on knowledge networks in their home country, or only for them to learn from or form networks only in their host country. The issue here is that many employees may not cope with or be able to adjust to the local network in the host country, much less learn from local colleagues. For instance, Tarique and Caligiuri (2009) suggest that crosscultural adjustment does not always follow from crosscultural training. In circumstances of poor adjustment, this may lead to early termination, lost business opportunities, low morale, anxiety and even depression.

Another issue is the type of training. Large companies appear to rely more on the classical training approaches (such as pre-departure training) and one-off training events designed to 'equip' the expatriate with the cultural knowledge required. Although crosscultural training, for example, has the potential to lead to better crosscultural adjustment, recent research has been inconclusive (Littrell and Salas, 2005; Waxin and Panaccio, 2005): some researchers contend that it is impossible to take as definitive the general consensus that such training is effective (Kealey and Protheroe, 1996). That is, many programmes are poorly designed and criticized for lacking theoretical justification.

Research by Tarique and Caligiuri (2009) found that knowledge (for example, cultural and procedural knowledge) should be established over time by expanding on the stock of existing knowledge. This approach to international training is based on absorptive capacity, where memory development or the ability to put information into memory is self-reinforcing (Cohen and Levinthal, 1990). This means that accumulated prior knowledge, such as knowledge about objects, patterns or concepts, is necessary for new knowledge to be recognized, assimilated and utilized (see Bower and Hilgard, 1981; Cohen and Levinthal, 1990).

For instance, many researchers have found that, compared with pre-departure training, more frequent in-country crosscultural training is likely to be more effective since expatriates increase their experiences and exposure to the host country's culture, beliefs and values over time. The basis of absorptive capacity here is that the ability of an individual to adjust will depend on the magnitude of prior accumulated cultural knowledge. The more cultural knowledge that has accumulated, the more likely it is that new cultural knowledge will be learned, leading to enhanced cultural adjustment.

Note that the importance of cultural adjustment is similar to the earlier point that training should be linked to performance outcomes to determine whether a worker has transferred training knowledge into demonstrated skill (Khanna and New, 2008). So the point of absorptive capacity relates to the sequencing and timing of training. It suggests that how knowledge is accumulated and applied in the host country will depend on *different types of training activity* conducted at *different times* along an expatriates' journey.

The notion of absorptive capacity becomes more salient with the rise of international and multinational corporations. The importance of transferring knowledge and maximizing learning outcomes has become more critical in the face of the global financial crisis and increasing competition, and the challenge for training and development within this context has never been more focused. There are many issues here related to learning and knowledge, such as how to provide access to knowledge, different knowledge applications and communication, as well as experiential learning (Hocking et al., 2007). The host country in which foreign nationals are to work will need to rely on the home country's stock of corporate knowledge, but host country nationals also have a habit of relying on their own experiences for local adaptation. The balance between global and local knowledge application, knowledge access, communication and experiential learning will be important here (Figure 11.3).

For the expatriate, knowledge application in the host country relies heavily on the headquarters and other global units. Here, expatriate managers access the deep stores of knowledge of organizational learning, as outlined in Figure 11.3. Expatriates, however, learn from local knowledge. As discussed, although crosscultural training may be useful for expatriates, research suggests that context-generic knowledge gained by individuals is valuable when sourced from globally dispersed units (Hocking et al., 2007). As our previous description of the flow of learning indicates, corporate or organizational knowledge will also be enriched and embedded by adding more diversified knowledge, in this case from the host country and local managers.

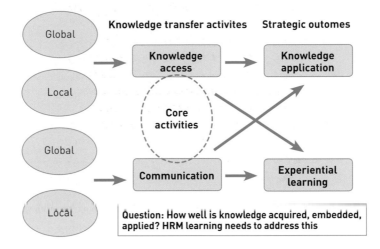

Figure 11.3 Making sense of knowledge transfer and outcomes. HRM, human resource management.
Source: Adapted from Hocking et al. (2007: 527)

In relation to Figure 11.3, the key for human resources practitioners is to balance global needs with local ones. Although corporate knowledge networks are critical for continued expatriate learning, local experiential learning and communication challenges corporate knowledge by balancing corporate needs with local contexts (see Chapter 3 for a detailed discussion of this).

In more recent times, research has not only focused on expatriates and how they learn, how they share knowledge and how they accumulate it. Instead, multinational companies in particular are beginning to understand the value of social capital and social ties in building networks of relationships that enhance both individual and organizational knowledge in international assignments. Individuals, for example, build social ties and networks through short-term assignments. Social ties provide access to information, reduce the costs associated with expatriation, enhance cross-border mobility and multilateral ties, and improve individual decision-making that can be used later to solve difficult international (see Mini Case Study 11.2).

Social ties can be explained by the weak ties theory (Granovetter, 1973). This theory holds that distant and infrequent relationships (weak ties) are efficient for knowledge-sharing as they provide access to novel information, whereas strong ties defined by the frequency of contact often lead to redundant information because they occur among smaller groups of actors. Strong ties may accordingly lead to redundant information since everyone knows what the others know (Van den Bossche et al., 2010). Recent research by Bozkurt and Mohr, for

Mini Case Study 11.2
Social ties as means of problem-solving
Jawad Gronich was quite frequently sent on short-term assignments to China and other countries to develop knowledge about local furniture manufacturing capabilities in those countries. In doing this, he developed social ties with a large number of people whom he would refer to or contact on a fairly infrequent basis. The visits were in direct contrast to the experience of expatriates who were sent abroad by the company to establish local factories making furniture for the local market.

Expatriates would often experience difficulty with local manufacturing laws, staff training and cultural experiences related to communication even though they had many contacts. By comparison, Jawad's disparate network of social ties (for example, with government agents in China) helped him solve many issues related to local customs and laws, hiring staff and transport issues. This was because his contacts were not only limited to home country knowledge. Instead, he had built up quite a sophisticated network of local manufacturers and secondary organizations, including contacts with officials, that helped him to achieve his objectives.

Consequently, in training and development, human resources managers decided to include short-term assignments as a means of training and equipping managers for international assignments. This prompted Jawad's company to completely revisit the benefits of expatriate training and its policy on expatriation.

Questions
1 What kinds of social tie could be enhanced through short-term assignments?
2 Combining social ties theory with what we know about expatriation (such as absorptive capacity), create a flowchart outlining a training programme for managers about to be sent on an international assignment.

example, found that 'short-term assignments and business travel helped initiate cross-unit ties in large number of locations and with large numbers of partners' (2010: 150), confirming the value of social ties.

For organizations, however, challenges relate to mobility and to allowing individuals to accumulate a more superficial level of knowledge over a wider range of locations through business travel. Figure 11.3 might well be expanded by adding in a box related to social ties as a means of increasing social capital. The latter is also consistent with learning from narrative and reflection in which social ties expand narratives in ways that help managers to solve difficult problems.

Conclusion

This chapter has set out many issues related to TLD. The classical learning approaches were mainly concerned with training in classroom settings and short-course-type orientations. Common to these methods was that training was learning. Yet more recent contemporary research would suggest that training does not always lead to know-how or an application of learning in practice. Training might lead to an increase in cognitive knowledge, but only for a while. Without other learning experiences, knowledge will be forgotten. The key here is that knowledge learned must be practised so that cognition and behaviour work together.

The difference between individual and organizational learning is as pronounced as the difference between cognitive styles, learning styles and how people 'actually' learn. The learning cycle put forward by Kolb is useful in advancing the notion of self-reflection, concrete experience and learning from abstract conceptualization in practice. However, as we discussed, this view of learning is restricted by the 'self'. Individualized accounts suggest that individuals can be objective about their personal reflection, yet individuals are only one agent of learning. Here, we discussed how multiple agents and realities potentially influence what a person learns and how she or he actually learns, the latter being related more to subjective or socially constructed learning, learning from narratives and observation in practice. Unique styles and cognitions of learning need to be considered by managers. Whether individuals reflect one or two archetypes or cognitive patterns in the way people see reality should be considered. The chapter highlighted examples related to how sensing–thinking might act differently from sensing–feeling archetypes in practice.

One overriding theme to consider is the difference between single-loop and double-loop learning. It seems probable that organizations would consider multi-method learning in practice to allow workers and individuals to question and challenge long-held traditions so that new learning could be framed. Readers should also note the difference between learning and knowledge. Whereas learning typically describes 'flow', knowledge is embedded in systems and structures. Learning flows ultimately help learners to repudiate and challenge embedded knowledge. Accordingly, in developing the individual, learning plays a key role, not only in terms of what is learned, but also by how the learning actually occurs; TDL should not occur in isolation from other human resources practices. For example, for needs and assessment purposes, TDL should be closely tied to performance management and to position and job descriptions. This is to ensure that TDL adopts an integrated approach to avoid the inevitable conflicts between general managers and human resources personnel over whether training is no more than a function needed for a specific time and place, but no longer.

Specific recommendations for learning ultimately depend on the organization in its context. That is, text–context is a viable learning consideration, suggesting that a variety of texts should also be matched to the context. A case in point in the chapter is learning in the international environment, given that learners need to hear multiple voices and perspectives in order to expand their own. Although the traditional forms of learning should be noted, these are a form of text–context pattern that will work in some situations but not others.

❓ For discussion and review

Questions

1 Contrast and compare traditional forms of learning with more contemporary forms. From a management perspective, what are the strengths and weaknesses and issues for reflection?

2 Think of any organization whose text–context learning pattern could be influenced. In taking a narrative perspective, describe how text–context knowledge may change over time.

3 Collect at least 10 articles of research related to multi-methods of learning. Using this approach, discuss how organizational knowledge could be challenged and updated over time for an automotive firm such as a car retailer or manufacturer.

Exercises

1 Design a fictitious merchandising organization that produces T-shirts and related apparel that has one factory outlet and a head office. The total size of the company should be 100 people, with generally one manager for every eight workers. The company is approximately 10 years old but is facing stiff competition in terms of better designs and merchandising, including electronic merchandising and selling. Sales have dropped by 15 per cent during the year, and workers are starting to fear for their jobs. Annual turnover has peaked at $10 million. Staff complaints are common, and the organization relies on the design skills of two or three workers. Competencies and skills are often not matched to position statements, and there is no internal training/learning policy.

In outlining your design for the company, include a list of jobs and job functions most likely to be practised. Concentrate only on the managers. Perform a needs analysis followed by a position description and training plan. The latter should be focused on how the company can solve its immediate problems by concentrating on new management skills. Take about an hour in total for this exercise.

2 Organize the class into two broad groups. Imagine that one group learns only through traditional training, whereas the other learns through multi-method training and access to a variety of text–context learning forms. Initiate a class debate on the following topic 'Traditional learning is far more valuable in practice than multi-method learning', with one group arguing in support of the statement, and the other against it.

3 Using your laptop or a class-based computer, log on to http://www. brainboxx.co.uk/A2_LEARNSTYLES/pages/roughandready.htm

On this webpage, you will find a sample of Honey and Mumford's learning styles inventory. Go through the exercise (activist, pragmatist, theorist, reflector) in your tutorial or at home and bring your answers to share in class.

Further reading

Journals

Abma, T. A. (2003) Learning by telling: storytelling workshops as an organizational learning intervention. *Management Learning*, 34: 221–40.

Bozkurt, O. and Mohr, A. T. (2010) Forms of cross-border mobility and social capital in multinational enterprises. *Human Resource Management Journal*, 21(2): 138–55.

Galagan, P. (2010) Disappearing act: the vanishing corporate classroom. *Training and Development*, 64(3): 29–31.

Reynolds, M. and Trehan, K. (2003) Learning from difference. *Management Learning*, 34: 163–80.

Tarique, I. and Caligiuri, P. (2009) The role of cross-cultural absorptive capacity in the effectiveness of in-county cross-cultural training. *International Journal of Training and Development*, 13(3): 148–64.

Van den Booooho, R., Segers, M. and Jansen, N. (2010) Transfer of training: the role of feedback in supportive social networks. *International Journal of Training and Development*, 14(2): 81–94.

Case Study Sanyo

When Tomoyo Nonaka took over Sanyo, the struggling Japanese electronics maker, in June 2005, she already had one strike against her: Nonaka was a female CEO in a business culture that was overwhelmingly male. A more timid executive would have charted a cautious course, focusing on slashing costs at a company that had lost $1.6 billion in its 2005 fiscal year. But Nonaka, a former TV journalist, instead announced a bold plan to transform Sanyo into a leader in the area of environmentally friendly products. 'The 21st century is about turning away from oil to alternate forms of energy,' Nonaka, aged 52, told *Time* shortly after her appointment as Sanyo CEO and chairwoman. 'It's about sustainability, and Sanyo will be the solution provider for this new world.'

But it turned out that the old world wasn't ready for Nonaka's vision, and Sanyo's losses continued to mount. Nonaka lost the CEO title last year, and she resigned as chairwoman in March. Her radical program, dubbed *Think Gaia*, 'was a very good strategy,' says Yasuyuki Onishi, a Tokyo-based financial journalist who wrote a recent book on Sanyo's woes. 'But it wasn't the right time to think Gaia. Sanyo had to think for itself.'

Nonaka's failed turnaround shows that although going green may save the world, it may not save your business. With climate change and high oil prices in the headlines, corporations everywhere are rushing to show off their green credentials. But the demand for environmentally friendly products – niche-market successes such as the Toyota Prius hybrid car notwithstanding – has yet to reach critical mass. This is because the economics of green products still do not make sense for many items. Take solar power, in which Sanyo is a significant competitor. Although numerous start-ups in the USA, China and Taiwan have been investing in the technology over the past 2 years, generating electricity from solar panels is still at least twice as expensive as buying it from the fossil fuel-reliant USA utility grid. Experts say that the solar power industry will need support from government subsidies and incentives for years to come.

Nonaka also underestimated the difficulty of selling her plan internally within the organization. She reorganized Sanyo's 300 subsidiaries into three divisions – environment, energy and lifestyle – and began marketing new products such as a battery that could be recharged with a solar panel and a washing machine that recycled water. These moves were a hard sell in a proud manufacturing company like Sanyo, which had started by making bicycle lamps in 1947 and was best known for its refrigerators and batteries. 'Talking about the environment doesn't send a good message to the old-timers who made Sanyo what it is,' says Hideyo Waki, a business professor at Tokyo Denki University. It was even harder to persuade investors such as Goldman Sachs and Daiwa Securities, which had sunk billions of dollars into a Sanyo turnaround, to be patient. Saddled with $3.4 billion in long-term debt, Sanyo only had the resources to restructure, not revolutionize.

With Nonaka gone, analysts expect Sanyo to sell losing divisions while focusing on its best product: rechargeable batteries. But even her critics say that Nonaka may simply have been ahead of her time. Better-financed companies are now attempting the same kind of corporate reinvention with more success. The US food-processing giant Archer Daniels Midland has become a hot stock-market play as America's largest producer of ethanol, an alternative fuel. 'The direction toward environmental issues is the right one,' says Tatsuya Mizuno, an analyst with Fitch Ratings. 'But it's too soon for some CEOs to bet that going green will get them out of the red,' says Yuki Oda, Toko Sekiguchi/Tokyo.

Source: Adapted from *Time Magazine*, April 20, 2007

Postscript

Analysts and other industry experts were bemused by the fact that Sanyo's bold strategy never worked. After all, interpreting environmental events is part of a good strategy. Internally, Nonaka concentrated on the shared values of the new vision, and teams seemed to catch on to the vision. But interpreting and integrating did not seem to work in this case, and industry analysts wondered why. It appears that other senior managers and investors had other ideas and beliefs that derailed the vision related to thoughts and actions. Still, to industry experts, Nonaka was ideally equipped to transform status quo views to her own. On the surface, everyone shared the learning values.

After joining Sanyo, Nonaka quickly set about developing team behaviour to tackle novel and opportunistic environmental patterns. She concentrated on critical relationships and systematic ways to identify new possibilities. Similarly, connecting departments and people in crossfunctional teams was consistent with implicit learning in which members bargained and traded with each other. Interaction was important to Nonaka. At the same time, other senior managers in her team alerted her to the quite structured view related to careful and rational analysis. Older 'hard heads' particu-

▷

▷ larly favoured strong analysis, yet Nonaka tempered these views with intuition. The behavioural views she instilled institutionalized behaviour in such a way that Sanyo was able to develop the new innovative products, yet older strategies already institutionalized as knowledge were often also influential in the decision process.

Nonaka and her senior team, it appeared, felt somewhat invincible about exploring the new opportunities. So what went wrong? To this day, analysts are scratching their heads in disbelief over why a positive learning culture did not materialize into success and why a continuous approach to change went so wrong.

Questions

1 To what extent did Sanyo's activities fall into the area of experiential learning?

2 It could be argued that experiential learning only went so far. What went wrong?

3 Is there evidence of a 'social constructionist' approach to knowledge here? If so, what evidence is this?

4 In relation to the previous question, was this approach successful or not? What does the case indicate about 'other' voices?

5 To what extent was the double-loop learning process adopted? What does the case indicate about organizational learning?

6 In terms of learning and knowledge, what other approach might have worked better for Nonaka? Give examples.

Make reasonable assumptions in giving your answers to the above questions.

References

Allinson, C. W. and Hayes, J. (1996) The cognitive style index: a measure of intuition-analysis for organisational research. *Journal of Management Studies*, 33(1), 119–35.

Antonacopoulou, E. P. (1999) Training does not imply learning: the individual's perspective. *International Journal of Training and Development*, 3(1): 14–32.

Antonacopoulou, E. P. (2001) The paradoxical nature of the relationship between training and learning. *Journal of Management Studies*, 38(3): 327–50.

Antonacopoulou, E. P. (2006) The relationship between individual and organizational learning: new evidence from managerial learning practices. *Management Learning*, 37: 455–72.

Argyris, C. and Schön, D. A. (1978) *Organizational Learning*. Reading, MA: Addison-Wesley.

Arthur, J. B. and Huntley, C.L. (2005) Ramping up the organizational learning curve: assessing the impact of deliberate learning on organizational performance under gain sharing. *Academy of Management Journal*, 48(6): 1159–70.

Australian Industry Group (2009) Business working hard to keep skilled workforce during downturn. Media Release, Corporate Affairs, Sydney.

Bartlett, C. A. and Ghoshal, S. (1988) *Transnational Management. Text, Cases, and Reading in Cross-Border Management*. Chicago: Richard D. Irwin.

Bassi, L. (1999) Harnessing the power of intellectual capital. In Cortada, J. and Woods, J. (eds) *The Knowledge Management Yearbook 1999–2000*. Boston, MA: Butterworth Heinemann, pp. 422–31.

Beckett, R. and Murray, P. (2000) Learning by auditing. *TQM Magazine*, 12(2): 125–36.

Bower, G. and Hilgard, E. (1981) *Theories of Learning*. Englewood Cliffs, NJ: Prentice Hall.

Boxall, P. and Macky, K. (2009) Research and theory on high-performance work systems: progressing the high-involvement stream. *Human Resource Management Journal*, 19(1): 3–23.

Bozkurt, O. and Mohr, A. T. (2010) Forms of cross-border mobility and social capital in multinational enterprises. *Human Resource Management Journal*, 21(2): 138–55.

Bratton, J. and Gold, J. (2007) *Human Resource Management, Theory and Practice* (4th edn). Hampshire: Palgrave Macmillan.

Brown, J. S. and Duguid, P. (1991) Organizational learning and communities-of-practice: toward a unified view of working, learning and innovation. *Organization Science*, 2(1): 40–7.

Brown, M., Metz, I., Cregan, C. and Kulik, C. T. (2009) Irreconcilable differences? Strategic human resource management and employee well-being. *Asia Pacific Journal of Human Resources*, 47: 270–94.

Brown, P. A., Green, A. and Lauder, H. (2001) *High Skills: Globalization, Competitiveness and Skills Formation*. Oxford: Oxford University Press.

Byosiere, P. and Luethge, D. J. (2008) Knowledge domains and knowledge conversion: an empirical investigation. *Journal of Knowledge Management*, 12(2): 67–78.

Chartered Institute of Personnel and Development (2008) *Training: A Measured Response*. London: CIPD.

11

Chartered Institute of Personnel and Development (2009) *Training: A Short History*. London: CIPD.

Clardy, A. (2008) Human resource development and the resource-based model of core competencies: methods for diagnosis and assessment. *Human Resource Development Review*, 7(4): 387–407.

Cohen, W. and Levinthal, D. (1990) Absorptive capacity: a new perspective on learning and innovations. *Administrative Science Quarterly*, 35: 128–52.

Conway, E. and Monks, K. (2008) HR practices and commitment to change: an employee-level analysis. *Human Resource Management Journal*, 18(1): 72–89.

Cook, S. and Brown, J. S. (1999) Bridging epistemologies: the generative dance between organizational knowledge and organizational knowing. *Organizational Science*, 10: 381–400.

Cortese, C. G. (2005) Learning through teaching. *Management Learning*, 36: 87–115.

Crossan, M. and Berdrow, I. (2003) Organizational learning and strategic renewal. *Strategic Management Journal*, 24: 1087–105.

Crossan, M. M., Lane, H. W. and White, R. E. (1999) An organizational learning framework: from intuition to institution. *Academy of Management Review*, 24: 522–37.

De Cieri, H. and Kramar, R. (2008) *Human Resource Management in Australia* (3rd edn). Sydney: McGraw-Hill.

Deloitte (2007) *Innovation in Emerging Markets*. Annual Survey. Sydney: Deloitte's Global Manufacturing Industry Group.

Deloitte (2009) Corporate Leaders Pre-emptively Leaning into the Recovery. Press release, 16 November, Sydney.

Eisenhardt, K .M. and Martin. J. A. (2000) Dynamic capabilities: what are they? *Strategic Management Journal*, 21: 1105–21.

Espedal, B. (2008) In the pursuit of understanding how to balance lower and higher order learning in organizations. *Journal of Applied Behavioural Science*, 44(3): 365–90.

Fiol, C. M. and Lyles, M. A. (1985) Organizational learning. *Academy of Management Review*, 10(4): 803–13.

Fulop, L., Frith, F. and Hayward, H. (1992) *Management for Australian Business: A Critical Text*. Melbourne: Macmillan.

Gergen, K. J. (1991) *The Saturated Self*. New York: Basic Books.

Gergen, K. J. (1994) *Realities and Relationships*. Cambridge, MA: Harvard University Press.

Gibb, S. (2003) Line manager involvement in learning and development: small beer or big deal? *Employee Relations*, 25(3): 281–93.

Gibb, S. (2008) *Human Resource Development: Process, Practices and Perspectives* (2nd edn). Basingstoke: Palgrave Macmillan.

Granovetter, M.S. (1973) The strength of weak ties. *American Journal of Sociology*, 78(6): 1360–80.

Hedberg, B. (1981) How organizations learn and unlearn. In Nystrom, P. C. and Starbuck, W. H. (eds) *Handbook of Organisational Design*. London: Oxford University Press, pp. 8–27.

Hocking, B., Brown, M. and Harzing, A. W. (2007) Balancing global and local strategic contexts: expatriate knowledge transfer, applications and learning within a transnational organization. *Human Resource Management*, 46(4): 513–33.

Hosking, D. M. (1999) Social construction as process: some new possibilities for research and development. *Concepts and Transformations*, 4(2): 117–32.

Jones, J. (2004) Training and development, and business growth: a study of Australian manufacturing small-medium sized enterprises. *Asia Pacific Journal of Human Resources*, 42: 96–121.

Jung, C. (1968) *The Archetypes and the Collective Unconscious*. Princeton, NJ: Bollingen.

Kealey, D. and Protheroe, D. (1996) The effectiveness of cross-cultural training for expatriates: an assessment of the literature on the issue. *International Journal of Intercultural Relations*, 20: 141–65.

Khanna, S. and New, J. R. (2008) Revolutionizing the workplace: a case study of the future of work program at capital one. *Human Resource Management*, 47(4): 795–808.

Kim, D. H. (1993) The link between individual and organizational learning. *Sloan Management Review*, (Fall): 37–50.

Kolb, D. (1984) *Experiential Learning*. Englewood Cliffs, NJ: Prentice Hall.

Kramar, R. and Lake, N. (1997) *Price Waterhouse Cranfield Project on International Strategic Human Resource Management*. Sydney: Macquarie University.

Lave, J. and Wenger, E. (1991) *Situated Learning*. Cambridge: Cambridge University Press.

Littrell, L. and Salas, E. (2005) A review of cross-cultural training: best practices, guidelines, and research needs. *Human Resource Development Review*, 4(3): 305–34.

March, J. G. (2006) Rationality, foolishness, and adaptive intelligence. *Strategic Management Journal*, 27: 201–14.

Miller, D. (1996) A preliminary typology of organizational learning: synthesizing the literature. *Journal of Management*, 22(3): 485–505.

Morgan, G. (1997) *Images of Organization*. London: Sage.

Nankervis, A., Compton, R. and Baird, M. (2008) *Human Resource Management: Strategies and Processes* (6th edn). Melbourne: Cengage Learning.

Nonaka, I. and Takeuchi, H. (1995) *The Knowledge-creating Company*. Oxford: Oxford University Press.

Peterson, R. B. (2004) A call for testing our assumptions. *Journal of Management Inquiry*, 13(3): 192–202.

Rainbird, H. and Munro, A. (2003) Workplace learning and the employment relationship in the public sector. *Human Resource Management Journal*, 13(2): 30–44.

Ramsey, C. M. (2005) Narrative: from learning in reflection to learning in performance. *Management Learning*, 36(2): 219–35.

Rose, M. (1975) *Industrial Behaviour: Theoretical Development Since Taylor*. Harmondsworth: Penguin.

Rylatt, A. (1994) *Learning Unlimited*. Chatswood, Sydney: Business and Professional Publishing.

Sheehan, C., Holland, P. and De Cieri, H. (2006) Current developments in HRM in Australian organisations. *Asia Pacific Journal of Human Resources*, 44: 132–52.

Smith, A. (2003) Recent trends in Australian training and development. *Asia Pacific Journal of Human Resources*, 41: 231–44.

Tarique, I. and Caligiuri, P. (2009) The role of cross-cultural absorptive capacity in the effectiveness of in-county cross-cultural training. *International Journal of Training and Development*, 13(3): 148–64.

Ulrich, D. and Brockbank, W. (2005) *The HR Value Proposition*. Boston, MA: Harvard Business School Press.

Van den Bossche, P., Segers, M. and Jansen, N. (2010) Transfer of training: the role of feedback in supportive social networks. *International Journal of Training and Development*, 14(2): 81–94.

Vera, D. and Crossan, M. (2003) Organizational learning and knowledge management: toward an integrative framework. In Easterby-Smith, M. and Lyles, M. (eds) *The Blackwell Handbook of Organizational Learning and Knowledge Management*. London: Blackwell, pp. 123–30.

Waxin, M. and Panaccio, A. (2005) Cross-cultural training to facilitate expatriate adjustment: it works. *Personnel Review*, 34: 51–67.

Wright, P., Dunford, B. and Snell, S. (2001) Human resources and the resource based view of the firm. *Journal of Management*, 27: 701–21.

11

Part 3
Human resource management and contemporary issues

Change management and human resource management

Christina Kirsch and Julia Connell

12

?

After reading this chapter, you should be able to:

☐ Discuss four eras relating to the management of organizational change

☐ Define the various approaches, drivers and change measurements utilized in each era

☐ Explain some of the key roles associated with change agents and human resource managers that are concerned with the implementation of organizational change

☐ Analyse two case studies depicting different change management approaches and identify the key issues associated with each case

Introduction

In recent years, the increasing globalization of industries and markets has resulted in a highly turbulent and unpredictable environment. Economic rationalism, increased environmental dynamics and technological change mean that companies, more than ever before, need to be highly flexible and adaptable to 'survive and thrive'. Consequently, change has become part of life for most managers in today's business world, and it is now seen as a continuous process of adaptation to constantly changing external circumstances. These changes in the global and domestic external environment, along with changing role expectations, have led to different demands from human resources specialists (Boston Consulting Group, 2008). It is evident that, in a world economy increasingly shaped by the emergence of China and India as major powers, the challenges in human resource management (HRM) relate to complex work environments.

Factors related to organizational change have been conceptualized, studied and analysed in a range of different ways as researchers seek to understand how organizations and the behaviour of people within them can deal with change (Dibella, 2007). As Daft (2001) points out, many of the changes in today's world are being driven by advances in computer and information technology as organizations use technology to improve their productivity, customer service and competitiveness. This requires organizational leaders to undergo constant evaluation, initiate system upgrades, adopt new ways of doing business and provide new skills for employees in order to ensure that internal changes keep pace with what is happening in the external environment.

Several recognized 'change experts', such as Kotter (1996) and Kanter et al. (1992), suggest various 'recipes' for dealing with organizational change that include factors such as creating a vision, communicating the change and mobilizing commitment. Such advice led, in past decades, to the belief that organizational change generally involved a short period of upheaval, or 'unfreezing', after which the system was left to operate at a new equilibrium (see Lewin, 1948). Change was considered to be a discontinuous process of incremental changes and stepwise improvements. It tended to be a slow process that left ample time for people to adjust to the new situation. In the 21st century, for many organizations, change has, however, become a continuous process with multiple projects affecting various aspects of the organization simultaneously. As a result, the 'refreezing' of organizational structures and processes is rare as before one process ends, others begin. This means that employees need to cope in an environment that is in constant flux in order to adapt to highly volatile external contingencies.

Moreover, Kotter (1996) has suggested that change will happen at a more rapid pace in the business environment in the future. He argues that the rate of environmental movement will increase and pressures on organizations to transform themselves will grow over the next few decades. Given this scenario, Kotter suggests that the only rational solution is to learn more about what creates successful change. This chapter intends to support that process.

Since the first attempts at increasing organizational effectiveness and improving productivity were introduced, they have been applied, tested, verified and overturned. Each change approach has resulted in characteristic dilemmas – 'black spots' that have demonstrated a mismatch between theory and reality and resulted in a further evolution of the organizational change management approach. It has been proposed that management and change are synonymous, and that the management of change is a complex, dynamic and challenging process rather than a set of recipes to be followed. Moreover, change is generally not a choice between addressing technological, structural or people-focused interventions but instead involves integrated combinations of all three (Paton and McCalman, 2001). That said, it is technology that has assisted in the process of globalizing organizations and enabling structural changes such as the growth in virtual teams. However, we argue here that the key to effectiveness in bringing about such changes is the mobilization of human resources. Thus, some key questions have challenged managers over the years such as:

☐ What is the best way to manage people?
☐ What systems could be put in place to support the effective management of human resources?

These and other questions will be addressed in this chapter. The authors will ask three key questions:

1 Where has it been?
2 Where is it now?
3 Where is it going?

First to be addressed is *Where has it been?* – this section involves the introduction of four eras of change management. Next, critical analysis is applied to various change paradigms.

Where is it now? involves further discussion of the complex adaptive systems (CAS) approach. This approach is aligned with the advent of increasingly complex organizational structures – such as virtual organizations and network industries – and increasing changes in environmental and change dynamics. Such factors mean that new approaches have been needed that could deal with the emerging and non-linear nature of organizational change.

The next section examines change and HRM, introducing the Warwick model as a lens through which these factors can be examined. Various change strategies, human resources activities and their associated advantages and disadvantages are examined before the discussion moves to that of change agents and organizational development (OD). A case study in this section and an end-of-chapter case study outline quite different sectors and change situations. One of the authors of this chapter visited both organizations – one a food factory in rural Australia, the other a television network organization in the Middle East. Readers are asked to reflect on the various change strategies described in each case study organization.

Finally, the authors attempt to address the question *Where is change going?* In this section, conclusions are drawn and implications for managers and the human resources function are discussed.

Change management in review

Where has it been?

This section begins by analysing four key eras relating to the management of change since the Industrial Revolution began, outlining the various underlying paradigms and dilemmas.

At the beginning of the 19th century, a series of major developments in agriculture, manufacturing and transport facilitated the unprecedented economic development that became known as the Industrial Revolution. New inventions, production processes, tools and technologies resulted in increasingly complex products and production processes. The small production units of the pre-industrial era grew into factories, whereby the subsequent increase in size and complexity precluded any one individual from being able to oversee and coordinate the whole production process. This resulted in the rise of a new profession – the manager – with its related sciences and academic schools of thought. Since the earliest times, such managers have faced the dual challenge of getting the immediate job done and managing change to improve effectiveness in the future. The complexity of their task has increased as the nature of 'organization' itself has changed. With the increases in organizational size came a rise in the levels of centralization and bureaucratization until market forces and environmental dynamics forced companies to develop new organizational structures that could more easily adapt to external contingencies.

As companies and products proliferated, markets became increasingly competitive, and companies and their managers needed to find ways of gaining competitive advantage. This launched a process of ongoing growth and innovation in product, technologies, production processes and methods. Product cycles were getting shorter and shorter, and companies were caught in a process of accelerating transformation and continuous change.

In the early days of the Industrial Revolution, managers tended to focus on isolated aspects of the work system as they started to tackle the issue of efficiency. Labour was divided into planning and execution, and thus began the division and fragmentation of work. The resulting fragmented and repetitive work design led to a backlash from workers and unions. New management tools – mainly surveys developed for the selection of troops during World War II – led to a shift in focus towards the human aspects of work design, and considerations regarding the quality of labour and the job/work itself increased in importance (see Burgess and Connell, 2008 for a further discussion on quality work).

As competition increased, the need for change and improvement grew, and management sciences started to concentrate less on managing the status quo and more on managing change. The result was an explosion of management theories, such as lean production, business process re-engineering, total quality management, total quality control, Kaizen, Six Sigma, management by objectives, management by walking around and similar. The underlying assumption was that there was 'one best way' of managing the production system, and that the manager's task was to find that 'best way' and ensure that the production system followed it.

Although some organizations (such as fast food chain McDonald's) still adopt scientific management systems, this approach has largely been abandoned in recent years as the increasing globalization of industries and markets has resulted in a highly turbulent and unpredictable environment. Increasing environmental dynamics and technological changes mean that companies more than ever before need to be highly flexible and adaptable to 'survive and thrive' (Szamosi and Duxbury, 2002). In addition, the number of factors that managers need to take into consideration during a change process has expanded exponentially. The complexity of change projects has increased from the early 'Tayloristic' projects that focused on isolated factors, for example time and motion studies, to the complex, multidimensional, multi-method analyses that have become the norm in current organizational change projects. Change has become a part of life for most managers in today's business world, and it is now seen as a continuous process of adaptation to constantly changing external contingencies.

As a result, organizational change projects have in many cases evolved in the following ways:

☐ from simple to complex – these increases in complexity have led to change processes being beyond the comprehension of a single individual;
☐ from tangible/visible (task-focused) to more intangible (people-focused) areas;
☐ from slow, incremental and discontinuous to fast and continuous;
☐ from a focus on measurement to scenario-planning and forecasting;
☐ from imposed solutions to employee involvement and a participative approach.

These five ways generally refer to the degree of change and whether it is considered to be largely superficial (and thus barely noticeable) or substantive, affecting many areas and people within an organization. Dibella (2007) argues that the various categories of change have been refined by various researchers demarcating further distinctions that represent finer and finer levels of detail. Furthermore, he provides examples of three types of transformational change, ranging from the revitalization of an existing business to a fundamental re-evaluation of the industry an organization may be part of.

That said, as organizational change itself is evolving, new approaches to the management of organizational change are needed that effectively deal with the issues arising under these new conditions as the change management advice of the past is ill-suited to the new dynamic environment. Moreover, evidence indicates that change frequently takes longer than expected, costs more and achieves less than expected (Box 12.1). This is reflected in the lack of success of organizational change projects, reported by Balogun and Hailey (2004) to be approximately 70 per cent of all change programmes.

12

> **Box 12.1** Change frequently takes longer than expected, costs more and achieves less
>
> Despite what are generally good intentions, change implementation tends to take longer, cost more and achieve less than planned. A study conducted by the Boston Consulting Group revealed that only 52 per cent of the 100 companies analysed reported achieving their business goals, and only 37 per cent could point to a tangible financial impact from their change projects (Anton et al., 2003). A study conducted by Oxford University found that only 16 per cent of IT projects actually ran on budget and on time, and that the average overrun on budget was 18 per cent and on schedule was 23 per cent; in addition, underachievement on functionality was 7 per cent (Sauer and Cuthbertson, 2003).
>
> The leading cause of failure is not frequently found to be related to the technical factors; instead, it tends to be associated with poor management, miscommunication and a lack of training or other factors related to the social and organizational aspects of the system. As highlighted by Dunphy and Stace (1993), the competencies needed to manage change are different from those needed to manage the 'day-to-day' business of organizations. The exercise below assists in illustrating some of the issues related to managing change.

Exercise

In small groups of three or four, discuss and then give feedback on your responses to the whole group on the following questions:
- What do you believe an effective change manager spends his or her time doing?
- What skills or qualities do you believe that an effective change leader should possess?
- How do you believe that effective change managers get the best from the people who work for them?

Critique – four eras of organizational change management

This chapter distinguishes four main eras of organizational change. Other authors have put forward different versions of the history of change interventions (see, for example, Mathews, 1993; Dunphy and Griffiths, 1994; Cummings and Worley, 2005; Mumford, 2006). Yet, as with any categorization, this is by no means a complete list of all the authors, researchers and various approaches to organizational change. Each new era evolved as a result of the dilemmas and problems encountered in an earlier era – but instead of simply being replaced by a new school of thought, each theory of and approach to change coexists and evolves, creating a multitude of hybrid approaches and variations. One of the aims of this chapter is to provide an understanding of where change is now in terms of theoretical developments and which challenges and dilemmas change agents are facing today; it also aims to take a step forward in overcoming the challenges of working with CAS.

In the following section, the four main eras of organizational change – scientific management, human relations, sociotechnical systems and CAS – are briefly analysed. We advance the notion that theories of organizational change have evolved and increased in complexity and dimensionality in line with changes in the dominant scientific paradigm (Table 12.1):

☐ The *scientific management* era was all about achieving the change, no matter what; there was no concern for any implication that the change – generally increased standardization and fragmentation of labour – might have for other system components, such as the employees.

☐ During the *human relations* era, the focus shifted towards achieving the change and getting people on side, involved and engaged to make the change sustainable.

☐ The *sociotechnical systems* approach focused on the 'joint optimization' of technological and social subsystems and took into account the complex interactions within the system.

☐ The *CAS* approach attempted, through the use of enabling technologies, to find answers about how best to change while change took place, achieving the change in a more holistic way, thus making it easier to achieve and more sustainable.

Table 12.1 Four eras in the management of organizational change

Approach	Proponents	Focus	Complexity	Pace	Measurement
Scientific management	Taylor, Gilbreth	Tangible Work, task, tools, time and motion studies	Very low Few objective, observable variables	Slow Only isolated aspects of the system	Simple Basic variables, simple measures before and after
Human relations	Mayo, Maslow, McGregor Herzberg, Argyris, Hackman and Oldham	Intangible Human, social relations, emotions, attitudes	Low Measures include 'intangible' variables	Stop–start Strong focus on people	Low Statistical analysis, paper-and pencil-based
Sociotechnical systems	Tavistock Institute Trist, Emery, Thorsrud, Bamforth	System Social and technical systems, joint optimization	Medium Concurrent interactions between various aspects of the system	Medium Change process still incremental	Medium Systemic interactions, increased complexity of statistics
Complex adaptive systems	Napoli, Dunphy, Parry	Process Complex adaptive processes	High Complex multi-dimensional data	High Change a continuous process	Complex Complex computer models and simulation

Theories on the management of change emerge from an intricate web of applied theory and 'communities of practice' (Wenger, 1998). These theories are influenced by the particular paradigm that determines the worldview at that point in time. The underlying paradigm also influences the scientific perspective and the aspects or 'variables' that are measured and recorded.

Each of the four main eras of organizational change is characterized by a specific paradigm as well as a related concept of human beings, their role and function within the work system, and a methodological approach to the analysis and redesign of the work system. The fact that each of those eras tends to focus on certain characteristics of the change process at the expense of others resulted in specific dilemmas that could be explained away for a period of time until mounting evidence of the insufficiency of the theoretical perspective and paradigm led to a fundamental shift in the underlying paradigm and advances in the underlying theory of organizational change.

Each of the methodological approaches led to certain factors being the focus of attention while other important aspects were neglected. The resulting inconsistencies in the empirical data led to paradigmatic changes and advances in the underlying theory of organizational change. Each new theoretical approach showed an increase in complexity and resolved the dilemma originating from the limitations of the earlier theoretical approach and its related methodologies.

Scientific management and change: 'achieving the change, there is one best way'

The late 19th century saw the emergence of 'scientific management', now often referred to as 'Taylorism'. Ford's assembly line was the culmination of the attempt to mechanistically standardize and fragment human labour within the confines of the production process. The worker was part of the process of a complex production 'machine' (Figure 12.1).

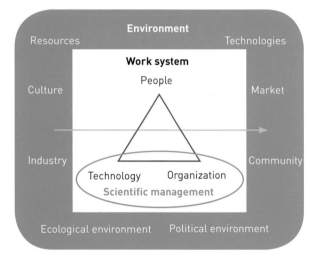

Figure 12.1 The analytical focus of the scientific management approach.

☑

Exercise

In small groups of two or three, consider some of the reasons why employees may resist change. These are likely to be linked to their perceptions of the positives and negatives related to change. The table below shows some examples to start you off. Also consider how the negatives may be addressed.

Positives and negatives related to change

Change positives	Change negatives
More opportunities	Stress and uncertainty
Improvements to processes	Fear of the unknown

This resulted in routine, repetitive work with little autonomy for workers and no involvement in the decision-making process. Organizational change was imposed from the top down by factory owners or the new emerging breed of 'managers'. The design of jobs was fragmented, repetitive and lacking in variety and challenge – causing alienation, boredom and apathy, which in turn led to increased absenteeism, increased turnover and finally resistance from workers and increasing demands by unions for a change in work design and conditions.

The principles of scientific management saw a continuation of the various methods aimed at optimizing work processes by focusing on the technical and technological aspects, such as corporate re-engineering, business process re-engineering (Hammer and Champy, 1993) and total quality management (Gluckman and Reynolds Roome, 1990). The main elements of the scientific management approach are summarised in Table 12.2.

Table 12.2 Key elements of the scientific management approach

Paradigm	Mechanistic, Newtonian; based on core principles of reductionism, determinism and equilibrium The underlying metaphor is the organization as 'machine', with the ideal being efficient, repetitive, fragmented, standardized tasks with predictable outcomes
Methodology	Time and motion studies, observation, task-based structural analysis (hierarchy, position status, delegation, rules and job descriptions), comparison of pre- versus post-implementation measures of productivity or output
Theory of man	Economic beings (*Homo economicus*)
Change approach	Authoritative, top-down conducted by an expert
Dilemma	Reductionism neglects systemic aspects and complex interactions; the fact that the system is more than just a sum of its parts is ignored; neglect of the 'human aspect' – attitudes, feelings, social relations at work, group processes, and so on

The human relations era

In the early 1930s, it became increasingly evident that there were important variables – social relations, employee attitudes and group processes – that had been neglected in the previous era, and a series of experiments led to the advent of the human relations era and a change in focus from mechanistic task design to social networks and relations between employees (Box 12.2). Suddenly, the employees – formerly treated as a simple, mechanical part of an overall production 'machine' and analysed only in terms of their output and efficiency – became the focus of the analysis. With regard to organizational change, the focus shifted from the utilitarian aspect of productivity improvement to a focus on the social and psychological factors that led workers to accept and support or resist change initiated by management. It became widely accepted that, in order to increase productivity, organizations needed to address employee motivation and morale.

The human relations school evolved into the OD school in the USA and the 'quality of working life' movement in Europe. The common denominator for these was a strong focus on the human element and a humanistic orientation that emphasized the importance of humane work design and the provision of jobs that addressed and fulfilled human needs. Organizational change and redesign was now aimed not solely at increasing profitability, but at increasing employee morale and satisfaction. The underlying assumption was that organi-

> **Box 12.2** Lewin's 'action research' as an iterative cycle of planning, action and evaluation
>
> Elton Mayo (1933) pointed to the importance of group relations and team cohesion, factors that continued to be studied by Kurt Lewin in his work on group dynamics and sensitivity training (Lewin, 1946). Lewin also pioneered 'action research' as an iterative cycle of planning, action and evaluation. The new focus on employee attitudes saw the emergence of employee surveys as a tool for organizational analysis, spearheaded by researchers such as Likert (1970).

zations and people needed each other, and that a good 'fit' between employee and job would result in increased productivity and satisfaction.

Organizational change was an inclusive process of mutual influence and negotiated outcomes with a strong focus on employee morale and organizational culture. The change itself generally was incremental and directed at the lower levels of the organizational hierarchy, with the change agent in the role of the 'facilitator' rather than the 'technical expert'. The dilemma of the human relations era was that it neglected other aspects that influenced organizational performance and productivity, such as technical systems, organizational structures and processes, and environmental contingencies. It also obscured the fact that employee morale was used as a utilitarian approach to increase profit for the employer. It treated organizational change as a discontinuous process of 'unfreeze–change–freeze' (see Lewin, 1946).

The human relations era expanded the scientific management perspective and included 'subjective', introspective data. However, managers found it difficult to determine priorities using this method. It was ineffective at promoting rapid change, and the results were often based on compromise (Lindblom, 1959). Elton Mayo was criticized for being simplistic and providing a 'garbage can model' full of easy answers, as well as for an overly idealistic perception of the workers themselves (March and Simon, 1958).

With increasing technological advances, it became obvious that technology as much as people had a tremendous effect on the efficiency of the work system. The sociotechnical system approach aimed to address and resolve these issues. Figure 12.2 illustrates the analytical focus of the human relations era, and Table 12.3 outlines the key elements of the human relations approach.

Table 12.3 Key elements of the human relations approach

Paradigm	'Organic', focus on individual and groups
Methodology	Person-focused analysis of the social system; employee surveys, employee motivation and satisfaction, participative self-diagnosis, job redesign, team development, interpersonal skills
Theory of man	Social beings: *Homo sociologicus* (Dahrendorf, 1973)
Change approach	Incremental change at lower levels of the organizational hierarchy; participation and involvement of employees
Dilemma	Neglect of the technical system and ongoing aspects of change

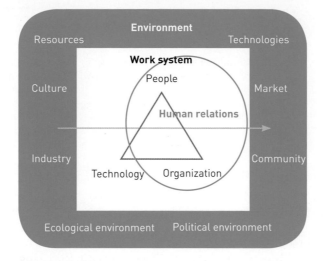

Figure 12.2 The analytical focus of the human relations era.

The sociotechnical systems era: a systemic and participative approach to organizational change

In the 1970s, with the evolution of systems theory, the focus shifted from isolated aspects of the system to the complex interactions between the various systems components. The sociotechnical systems approach emerged during the post-War period and is generally traced back to the Tavistock Institute in London. Here, a group of therapists, researchers and consultants, disappointed with the deterioration of working life in the wake of Taylorism and inspired by earlier encounters with proponents of the human relations school, decided to work towards improving the design of work systems and organizations (Mumford, 2006). Inspired by von Bertalanffy's work on general systems theory (1950), Emery devised the 'open systems approach' (Trist, 1981), arguing that organizations were 'open systems' consisting of a technical and a social component, and were in constant exchange with their environment (Emery, 1960). Figure 12.3 outlines the analytical focus of the sociotechnical systems era.

The sociotechnical systems approach encompassed strong ideals of humane work design, self-determination, industrial democracy and participation, autonomy, purpose and meaning for all at work. With a greater understanding of the process of how systems interact, and using enabling technologies to facilitate a wide range of points of view and democracy, it was possible for the wider workforce to get more actively involved in decision-making about change while change was itself taking place. The sociotechnical consultant (change agent) was generally seen in the role of the outside expert with process facilitation skills, who would teach the workers how to analyse and investigate the work system and aid them in coming up with solutions (Chisholm and Elden, 1993).

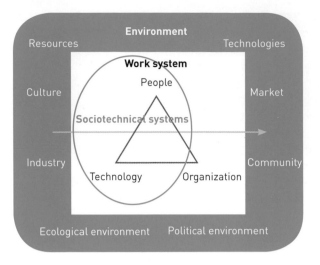

Figure 12.3 The analytical focus of the sociotechnical systems era.

Another issue is the assumption that employee involvement and participation are a prerequisite for successful organizational change (Ulich et al., 1991; Ulich, 2005). Not all organizational change projects that aim to implement new technologies allow project management to follow a 'work-oriented' basis, with the technology adapted to suit the needs of the employee and the work design. Other initiatives, for example large-scale mergers, or the outsourcing of certain services and departments, may be imposed 'top down' by senior management with little involvement of the actual site management. The focus in the sociotechnical systems approach was on the characteristics of the work system, but the characteristics of the change intervention itself were overlooked. Table 12.4 summarises the key aspects of the sociotechnical systems approach to change.

Table 12.4 Sociotechnical systems approach to change

Paradigm	Holistic system; linear system dynamics; systems reverting to a 'natural' state of equilibrium
Methodology	Sociotechnical systems analysis, participatory design
Theory of man	Self-actualizing beings
Change approach	The change agent is seen as an 'external' expert (process design, generic) who cooperates with the 'internal' expert (company, specific); facilitator with an expertocratic, participative action research approach; job redesign based on sociotechnical principles; 'work-oriented' design principles; best practice model often encompassing 'semi-autonomous teams'; deductive process
Dilemma	Neglect of the dynamic aspect and the fact that change is a continuous process of ongoing adaptation to ever-changing external contingencies

A further dilemma of the sociotechnical systems approach was that it accepted the theory of 'homeostasis', which assumes that systems evolve but eventually settle into a steady state having accommodated the organizational change (Davies and Taylor, 1972). Nowadays, it is generally agreed that stability is an elusive concept for 'open systems' and that systems become increasingly chaotic as they progress from one state to another. It is recognized in complex systems theory that stability and chaos are not mutually exclusive states in an organization, as both linear and non-linear dynamics operate in different aspects of the organization simultaneously. The challenge in managing change projects, especially within a complex global environment, is how to roll out major change projects within a short time frame on a global scale while managing widespread and often unexpected effects on the various system components.

During the late 1980s, the sociotechnical systems approach and the successful 'humanization of work' programmes started to fade as companies came under increasing pressure due to mounting international competition. Cost-cutting exercises became the norm in an era of 'lean production' (Womack et al., 1991), and increasing levels of automation and computerization dominated the industrial landscape. The streamlined work design of the lean enterprise (Levinson and Rerick, 2002) was characterized by limited teamwork and growing levels of intensification and stress at work (Steward, 1996). In the 1990s, after this 'dark age' of what Niepce and Molleman (1998) refer to as 'neo-Taylorism', new holistic approaches to organizational design started to emerge, expanding on the original sociotechnical systems approach. Other researchers also began to develop discursive methods for making sense of the highly politicized character of organizational change (McLoughlin and Badham, 2005), and to focus on its dynamic characteristics (see Dawson, 2003).

> **Exercise**
>
> Change management is usually perceived to be a top-down, management-driven approach.
> - Is it possible for an employee to introduce change management to her or his supervisors?
> - In what circumstances and how could this be possible, and what could be its possible implications for the employee and the organization?

Where is it now?

We suggest that change management is now on the brink of a new era, one in which it will be necessary to expand the focus beyond the limitations of the organization as system and take into account its integration into the larger economic, social and environmental system. This requires an expanded systems perspective and complex forecasting and modelling of the larger systems in order to achieve sustainable change in a complex global environment.

Dibella (2007) maintains that as the interpretive or cognitive view of organizational phenomena has become stronger, the focus of many researchers has become how organizational reality and change itself are viewed or perceived. Specifically, this means that the success of a change process is not determined by how change is explained or understood by scholars, but instead (and perhaps more understandably) by how change is experienced and what it means to those who are directly affected by it.

The fourth era of change management: complex adaptive systems

In this view, transformation is viewed as a continuous process of adaptation to changing circumstances.

With the advent of increasingly complex new organizational structures – such as virtual organizations and network industries – and increasing environmental and change dynamics, a new approach was needed that could deal with the emerging and non-linear nature of organizational change. The advent of chaos theory (Dooley et al., 1995), 'chaotic dynamics' (Tushman and Romanelli, 1986) and 'dissipative systems' (Prigogine and Stengers, 1984) has greatly influenced contemporary researchers at the beginning of the 21st century and led to the CAS theory of management and organizational change (Dooley, 1997). CAS (Gell-Mann, 1994) refers to organizations that are not only open, holistic and in constant exchange with the environment, but also contain stable and potentially chaotic dimensions at the same time, continuously evolving and adapting to ever-changing external circumstances, as illustrated in Figure 12.4.

Organizational change as a random, unpredictable, uncertain and non-linear process of iterative cycles of adaptation

In CAS, order is emergent, which means that it is not a characteristic inherent to any of the system components, but emerges as a result of the interaction between system components. The state of the system is generally unpredictable and irreversible. Change happens when the system moves away from equilibrium (Stacey, 1992) towards a point where it needs to reorganize itself into a new state or mode of behaviour, determined by 'attractors' within a chaotic 'space sphere'. Thus, organizational change is considered random, unpredictable, uncertain and a non-linear process of iterative cycles (Cheng and Van der Ven, 1996).

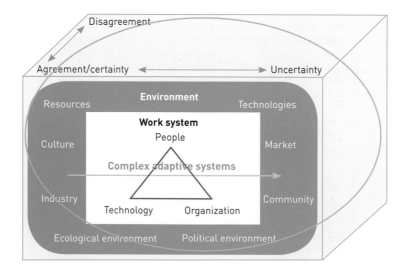

Figure 12.4 The analytical focus in the complex adaptive systems era.

Proponents of the CAS approach argue that, owing to the fact that the external environment is continuously progressing, there are 'no rules, regulations or structures' derived from the past that can be successfully applied to provide guidance for the future, and that the change needs to instead focus on 'mission, vision and values' (Napoli et al., 2007). An 'internal locus of control' is needed to generate stability in the midst of chaos, rather than being dependent on external factors that can rapidly change. According to Napoli et al. (2007), companies need to learn to operate at 'the edge of chaos'. This implies that companies need to empower and train their employees in order to increase flexibility by allocating authority and power as close as possible to where it needs to be enacted.

The situation is further exacerbated by the fact that organizational change projects are often affected by factors beyond the control of the change manager – an organization's culture and politics, for example. Complexity theory (see Anderson, 1999) focuses on how CAS exhibit predictable behaviour, and offers new insights that can enable change project managers to work more effectively in this environment (Brown and Eisenhardt, 1997).

One of the key findings is that self-reflectivity is the key for change in CAS (Napoli et al., 2007). In order to change an organization, proponents of CAS suggest that the primary focus needs to be the process of 'collective sense-making' and the development of a shared understanding of the current situation and vision for the future (Stacey, 1992). The recent popularity of story-telling as a way of managing organizational change has arisen as a means of synthesizing these complexities (Heracleous and Barrett, 2001). The use of intuition, myths, values, images and symbols integrates high degrees of complexity and allows meaning to be derived and communicated across all levels of the organization. The individual's perception of the work system needs to be altered by improving communication and increasing the available feedback (Goldstein, 1994). The individual can understand the story being played out and his or her individual role as the story unfolds. This creates an awareness of the gap between the perceived and the desired state of the work system. At the same time, it increases the level of agreement among 'agents', which moves the system further from equilibrium towards a point of 'bifurcation' where change becomes inevitable.

Managing change

The approach to managing change in CAS (Table 12.5) is shifting from one in which employees are involved and consulted in a process that is facilitated and often dominated by an external 'change expert' who generally has the final say, to a 'reflexive' methodology that restrains the change agent to the role of being a pure facilitator of dialogue between the various stakeholders involved in and affected by the change (Moldaschl and Brödner, 2002). The focus has shifted from the outcome of change to the process of change itself and the need to equip companies with the skills and flexibility to continue to change indefinitely.

The key in managing change in CAS is to be able to predict and model the effect of possible interventions. It is not enough to measure, as used to be done in previous eras, what has happened in the past, as often the 'problems of today

12

are an outcome of solutions of the past'. Looking in the rear-view mirror is not adequate to steer projects towards better future performance. The limitation of the CAS approach to date has been its inability to find ways to measure and model the actuality of what is happening across simultaneous dimensions in organizations. Although story-telling allows complexity to be communicated, it does not put facts on the table for making decisions. It is difficult for managers who are used to measuring and counting as a way of life, and can create a polarization between 'believers' and 'non-believers' in the change journey.

In the wake of increasingly sophisticated multidimensional computerized scaling methods (Young, 1985), analytical techniques are moving from post hoc evaluations of organizational change to predictive analysis, aiming to forecast and model possible futures, simulate possible scenarios and allow managers to determine the appropriate actions that will optimize their journey towards high performance.

One of the problems that scientists analysing organizational change are facing is the fact that organizational change rarely happens within the controllable confines of the research laboratory. Theories on organizational change are primarily derived from 'action research' and based on the interaction between agents of change and the organizations that have become their experimental field. The need to analyse 'theory in action' – actual interventions in a complex organizational environment – implies that a rigorous empirical test of causality

Table 12.5 Complex adaptive systems approach

Paradigm	Complex, adaptive system, characterized by linear and non-linear dynamics operating at the same time, self-renewal and self-ordering; non-linear flows of information and resources, self-reflectivity, paradoxical nature of 'dynamic stability'
Methodology	Systemic inquiry; multi-method approach combining quantitative and qualitative methods from story-telling to complex statistical analysis methods and modelling of complex relationships; methods that support self-reflectivity, provision of relevant, real-time feedback on system performance and advanced predictive analytics
Theory of man	Self-reflective beings
Change approach	High levels of employee involvement; employees enabled to become change agents; reflexive methodology; emergent and open process; process design criteria; facilitator is seen as a process expert, establishes and develops groups, moderation, conflict management, cyclical evaluation, predictive modelling; systems are pushed to the 'edge of chaos' (or 'far from equilibrium') in order to reach a 'bifurcation point'
Dilemma	With increasing community expectations (corporate social responsibility and sustainability), the broader external environment is neglected as the main focus is still the company; the impact on global systems – for example, environment, community, broader political and socioeconomic environment and so on – is neglected, which leads to issues of organizational sustainability; growth and profit focus unchallenged

is impossible. The old approach used to be the measurement of certain variables before and after an intervention.

Within the CAS approach, the focus has shifted towards the actual process characteristics of organizational change. Systemic aspects have come to the foreground of the analysis. This has resulted in an increased use of reflective data and story-telling as a means to access the complex reality of change. Systemic inquiry is used to investigate the multidimensional reality of work systems. The purpose of data collection has changed from a 'post hoc' evaluation of the change initiative, to the provision of ongoing feedback and predictive analysis that can fine-tune the intervention and manage the chaotic dynamics of the process itself.

Change and HRM

The four eras of change management can be considered from the perspective of the Warwick model of change and HRM (Hendry and Pettigrew, 1990). The Warwick model (Hendry and Pettigrew, 1990) extended the Harvard model of HRM, emphasizing an analytical approach to HRM while recognizing the impact of the role of the human resources function on the human resource strategy content. This model considers the outer context of an organization through a strategy similar to that of a 'PESTLE' lens, recognizing that the political, economic, socioeconomic, technological, legal and environmental contexts influence the inner context of the organization with regard to an organization's culture, structure, leadership, technology and business results (see Figure 1.1). The model identifies strategic change as both a dynamic and an iterative process while taking into account the role of contextual factors in shaping strategic decisions over time (Huczynski and Buchanan, 2007).

According to the Warwick model, the inner context influences, and is influenced by, the HRM content. This refers to the way in which an organization defines the role and structure of the HRM function and the outputs expected of it. Human resources policies are, of course, considered to be dependent on organizational strategy. It is suggested that strategic alignment of HRM systems should be implemented externally and internally for an organization (Hendry and Pettigrew, 1990). The requirement for HRM policy to support business strategy indicates that HRM is moving towards an organization-wide responsibility with greater commitment and involvement on the part of all levels of management (Sheehan et al., 2006).

Strategic management offers firms a systematic framework for managing their internal and external environments, affecting both short- and long-term organizational decision-making and competitive advantage. Gaining competitive advantage through strategic action has become an important focus of research and analysis in the HRM field (Delery and Shaw, 2001; Wright et al., 2001).

A basic principle underlying the concept of strategic intention is that firms cope with external environmental changes through the choice and application of appropriate strategies. In order to build competitive advantage, an organization needs to align its capabilities and resources with the opportunities and

12

challenges occurring within the external environment. This refers to the matching of organizational competencies (that is, resources and skills) with strategic capability (that is, the ability to develop and implement strategies that will achieve sustained competitive advantage.

By shifting the emphasis in the strategy literature from external factors (that is, industry) to the internal resources of the firm as a source of competitive advantage (Barney, 2001), the resource-based view of a firm provides a foundation for stressing that it is the strategic importance of people *within* organizations that makes the difference in gaining competitive advantage. Alterations to the strategic direction and activity of an organization may necessitate changes to its structures, systems, culture, managerial approach and technology. This brings into focus the role of human resource personnel in the change process as the use of human resources strategies is integrally linked to change management. Some of the key change strategies adopted in organizations are outlined in Table 12.6, in conjunction with associated human resources activities and their potential advantages and disadvantages.

Few planned change efforts run as smoothly as managers would like them to, primarily because many run into resistance. This should be anticipated and expected, although resistance to change can, of course, depend on one's particular perspective (Nord and Jermier, 1994). For example, Casey (1993) maintains that organizations are defined as resistant to change only by those who are trying to change them, and Collins (1999) argues that the term 'resistance' is illuminating since it seems to imply that those who resist change are setting themselves to struggle against the inevitable when they would do better to come to terms with it. Experienced managers may be well aware that various forms of resistance can be manifest as immediate criticism, malicious compliance, sabotage, insincere agreement, silence, deflection and defiance (Hellriegel and Slocum, 2002). Some resistance to change can be useful, however, as employees may operate as a 'check and balance' mechanism to ensure that management plans thoroughly to implement change.

Exercise
Few planned change efforts run as smoothly as managers would like them to, primarily because many run into resistance.
- What are some possible sources of or reasons for resistance?
- How may managers best tackle such resistance to change?

Casey (1993) states that people are not by nature resistant to change and neither are organizations; on the contrary, they are frequently open to change. It is all a question of where the change comes from: if it is imposed from outside, it can feel like a threat, because it is unknown and outside one's own control. It should be no surprise that people (and organizations) are defensive in the face of perceived threat – we are all absolutely right to be defensive when threatened, and indeed it is irresponsible not to defend against threat. But it is not *change* that we resist, but the *threat* that fills us with fear. As resistance to change is fundamentally an emotional reaction, one which is often alogical or even illogical (Werther, 2003), contemporary business leaders have to relate to their followers not only at the cognitive level, but also at an emotional level in order to enable effective strategic change. Thus, when change is considered by those it is likely to affect, it will be filtered through individual preferences and accepted

Table 12.6 Change strategies, associated human resources (HR) activities, advantages and disadvantages

Change strategy	HR activities	Advantages	Disadvantages
Education and employee involvement	Management development Employee training Joint consultation Team briefings and other forms of employee communication Performance management Employee counselling	Greater sense of employee ownership of change – more likely to achieve 'buy-in' New ideas introduced More opportunity to discover potential problems with proposed change Longer lasting change	Time-consuming Expensive Change implementers may not have the effective skill mix necessary to educate and involve employees May be resistance spillover through negative attitudes towards change
Changes in staffing	Severance Redundancy programmes Recruitment and selection Secondments	Speed Can cut payroll costs Bring about change in corporate culture through the exit and entry of new staff Can buy in skills, new behaviours	Can lead to survivor syndrome – that is, a negative impact on those workers left behind after redundancy Can be expensive May find have lost important tacit knowledge/relationship capital when employees leave
Changes to structures and systems	Changes to organizational structures including employee accountabilities Changes to reward systems Changes to performance management Changes to career management Changes to employee relations structures (that is, consultation and bargaining)	Longer lasting change Regeneration of employees' knowledge and skill Regeneration of tired systems Employee 'buy-in' through improved career pathing/performance management	Can be slow to have an impact May be difficult to establish a causal link between changes to structures and systems and organizational change May be viewed negatively by some employees, that is, changes from seniority-based to performance-based pay

Source: Adapted from Thornhill et al. (2000)

or resisted accordingly, also related to whether it is considered to be consistent with personal values or self-interest (Dibella, 2007).

Many other issues influence how organizational change may occur, for example the level and breadth of change – is it to be organization-wide or just concentrated within one department? Will it be fast or incremental? In order to assist with these and other change questions, many organizations turn to change agents, either external or internal to an organization, or even to both working together.

The role of the change agent

Change classifications such as scale, causes of change, temporal factors and consultant roles are usually standard topics in most texts that refer to change management as the authors seek to explain organizational change. Those who write on OD topics, such as French and Bell (1998), tend to advocate that the greater the number of participants who are involved in the change process, the more attractive the change will tend to be. Others, such as Senior and Fleming (2006), maintain that the effectiveness of the OD approach to change is dependent upon the qualities and capabilities of those who act as the facilitators of change.

Change agents can be the leaders and managers of an organization, human resources personnel, consultants or internally recruited employees. The literature referring to change agents is categorized under the OD approach. Others have argued that established strategies for managing change have largely proved inadequate, and that the existing literature has been of little help as it predominantly addresses incremental change drawing on the OD paradigm (Patrickson et al., 1995). This paradigm is criticized as it indicates that change should be incremental and employee involvement in the implementation of the change should be widely encouraged. This may be an 'ideal state' change situation, but Dunphy and Stace (1993) propose there has been a move away from change being associated with organizational growth to change occurring due to a downturn in economic activity or in response to unexpected events affecting the organization.

Exercise

Consider some of the potential advantages and disadvantages of utilizing internal/external change agents. Each box contains some examples to start you off. Working in small groups, add two or three more items to each box and discuss your findings.

	Internal change agents	External change agents
Advantages	Know the company	Are unbiased
Disadvantages	Might have own agenda	Can walk away when change implementation has been completed

In the 1990s, the Australian Best Practice Demonstration Program (ABPP) was introduced as a AU$41 million initiative of the federal Labor government that was designed to reform Australian workplaces. A micro-economic reform initiative, the goal of the ABPP was to encourage organizations to improve their performance to internationally competitive levels through the adoption of certain 'leading-edge' workplace practices; these practices would then be diffused among other Australian businesses. To achieve this objective, the government of the day established Australian Best Practice Centres in regional and metropolitan areas to educate business leaders and trade union officials on the merits of the best practice programme. Typically, management consultants from these Australian Best Practice Centres would also be used to facilitate best practice change programmes.

A common criticism of this approach was that these consultants would often advocate a common model of organizational change allied to conventional workplace practices, regardless of the unique problems or issues faced by individual organizations. These 'practices' included flattened hierarchies, teamworking, quality management techniques and similar. However, the change agents introduced the practices as recipes that had to be followed with 'no ingredients left out'. The organization outlined below was visited by Connell, who was part of a team contracted to assess the effectiveness of the ABBP programme. Connell interviewed 18 managers and employees and later wrote the short case study here (Mini Case Study 12.1) on 'how not to manage change'. The name of the organization has been disguised in order for it to remain anonymous.

Mini Case Study 12.1
Foodco: a short case in how *not* to introduce change

Change was in the air at Foodco. Senior management had recently contracted consultants who had advocated changing the culture of the workplace through teamwork in which individuals would take on responsibility by being empowered and contributing to decision-making. Senior management took the advice of the management consultants literally by downsizing all the middle managers and supervisors on one day without warning. This stunned not only those who were retrenched, but also those who were left behind. In a close-knit country town where everybody knew everybody else, the remaining employees had to encounter the bosses they had worked with for many years in shops, in clubs and in the street. Worst of all, in a workplace where empowerment was previously unknown, the remaining employees found it difficult to be productive with no one there to tell them what to do. As a team member commented:

> Prior to the change programme, we weren't allowed to do anything – we weren't even allowed to touch the buttons on the machines. Then, after the redundancies, we came in the next day and looked at each other and said 'How do we switch the machines on?' We pressed a button, and if that didn't work we pressed another one until we worked out what to do

Following the middle management redundancies, productivity slumped until employees worked out how they could function as a team and how the machinery operated. Four years later, Foodco was taken over and significant investments were made in updating the plant and machinery and in employee training. These investments made a huge difference to employee morale as the downturn in productivity had led to an overriding perception that Foodco would be shut down and the remaining jobs threatened.

Subsequent to the updating of plant and machinery, Foodco began 6 months of intensive training for employees in a new diagnostic method of working. Employees found that this method allowed them to work out where problems were occurring in the plant and to measure and predict productivity. This tool provided employees with a great deal of empowerment as they gained extensive control over their work function. As a result, morale was reputedly higher than it had been for many years previously. In contrast to the earlier quote, a team coordinator observed, 'If I walked out of here today, my team could still function as every member has been trained.' The experience of Foodco highlights the importance of the appropriate implementation of change programmes and the significance of employees' 'ownership' of change processes.

Questions

1 Which of the four eras of change described here is this organization most closely associated with and why?
2 Utilizing Table 12.6, explain the key change strategies that took place in Foodco and the resulting advantages and disadvantages.
2 How could the change agents and Foodco management have undertaken a different change approach, and what do you think the potential results of this approach would have been?

With an increasing focus on corporate social responsibility (CSR) in the workplaces of the 21st century, it is increasingly unlikely that the events outlined in the Foodco case would be enacted today. Strandberg (2009) argues that as HRM influences many of the key systems and business processes underpinning effective delivery, it is well positioned to foster a CSR ethic and achieve a high-performance CSR culture so that CSR can become 'the way we do things around here'. Furthermore, Strandberg maintains that human resources can be the key organizational partner to ensure that what the organization is saying publicly aligns with how people are treated within the organization. A CSR approach was taken by many organizations during the recent global financial crisis whereby, instead of downsizing employee numbers when undertaking cost-cutting exercises, they instead encouraged all employees to take a pay cut until the situation had improved (Chafetz et al., 2009). This had the effect of ensuring that key skills and competencies were not lost when the organization began hiring again, and helped to avoid 'survivor syndrome' among those employees left behind.

Conclusion

Where is change going?

The report *Developing the Global Leader of Tomorrow* (Gitsham, 2008: 10) observed that:

> a range of human resource levers are important for developing [CSR] organizational capabilities: building knowledge and skills through leadership development programs, career development planning, succession planning, performance management and incentive systems and competency frameworks, and seeking these knowledge and skills when recruiting new talent into the organization.

Thus, human resource managers and personnel have many challenges and opportunities ahead that will require competencies in change management (see Box 12.3). These include the need to develop strategic approaches to change management due to ageing workforces, the challenges of increasingly diverse workplaces, the need to address work–life balance and moves towards the outsourcing of various operations (including some relating to human resources) and addressing sustainability.

These challenges will also increase as community expectations focus on CSR and the expectation that companies will encompass environmental aspects, community issues, the broader social system implications, ethical expectations and similar issues. System boundaries between what is inside and outside the organization are dissolving, especially with new organizational forms – virtual organizations and network industries.

We have proposed in this chapter that the nature of organizational change itself has evolved from simply achieving the change – no matter what – to the need for scenario-planning among other change strategies within CAS. Thus, managers at the cutting edge of change need greater capabilities to deal with the dynamic factors occurring in external organizational environments in a useful and action-oriented way. Stakeholder perceptions of change can serve as indicators of the relative success or progress of change implementation. This means that when change initiatives are evaluated, it is important to consider the perspective of the change participants in order to develop a richer understanding of the change experience and the effectiveness of the various strategies utilized. Thus, the evolution of change management is based on advances

> **Box 12.3** The advent of a new era of organizational change management
>
> It appears that we are witnessing the advent of a new era of organizational change management, one in which complexity is increasing to incorporate the broader impacts and implications into the larger ecological and economic environment on a global level. As our industries are facing increasing ecological problems, ranging from overpopulation to global warming, there is a growing awareness in academic (Dunphy et al., 2003) and industrial (Business Roundtable for Sustainable Development, 2003) circles that the perspective needs to shift from the survival of the organization to the survival of the overall (eco-)system. Only a concerted approach that optimizes the different system components will succeed, and that is where complex computer-based modelling tools can provide support for policy-makers and change agents. The focus of organizational change is expanding towards broader system dynamics and complex interrelationships with external institutions and the environment at large.
>
> It is ostensibly necessary to expand the change focus beyond the limitations of the organization as a system and take into account its integration into the larger economic, social and environmental system. This requires an expanded perspective and the forecasting and modelling of larger systems in order to achieve sustainable change in a complex global environment.
>
> Organizations all around the world are confronted with an increasingly volatile and unpredictable environment. In the past, organizational change used to be a journey towards a new state of homeostasis, but those times of alternating stages of chaos and peace are over. Escalating environmental dynamics are creating unprecedented pressures for organizations to continuously evolve and adapt to ever-changing external circumstances. In order to survive 'at the edge of chaos', companies need to remain adaptable. Change has become the only continuum, and companies are in a state of 'punctuated equilibrium' (Gersick, 1991), with unpredictable change dynamics occurring whenever the system reaches a threshold that forces it into a new mode of operation and behaviour.

in the techniques and methodologies used to measure, analyse and evaluate change processes. A further illustration of 'change in action' can be found in the end-of-chapter case study on TV Middle East.

The important focus of this chapter is that although organizational change is inevitable, can be painful and is not always successful, it can also be challenging and rewarding. There are a number of interventions, concepts and models that can assist with the passage of change, and when these are utilized effectively, there is more likelihood that change initiatives will succeed – these are the enduring challenges for anyone involved in organizational change and, it is argued, will remain so for the foreseeable future.

❓ For discussion and revision

Questions

1   Resistance to change is normal and should be expected when organizational change is introduced. Give two reasons why an employee

might resist change, and two strategies outlining how that resistance might be addressed.

2 Choose one 'era' outlined in this chapter and identify the key theories, concepts and models that are associated with that era. Then consider whether those theories, concepts and models are still being used today, and if so, whether you consider them to be effective.

3 'Resistance to change is inevitable.' Consider this statement and discuss whether or not you agree with it, and why.

4 Contemporary organizations are characterized by unrelenting change. Drawing on some of the key concepts in this chapter, discuss how managerial actions can assist effective change processes.

Further reading

Books

Bridges, W. (1991) *Managing Transitions: Making the Most of Change*. Reading, MA: Wesley Publishing Company.

Covey, S. (1989) *The 7 Habits of Highly Effective People: Powerful Lessons of Personal Change*. Melbourne: Business Library.

Kotter, J. (1996) *Leading Change*. Boston, MA: Harvard Business School Press.

Senior, B. and Fleming, J. (2006) *Organisational Change*. Harlow: Pearson Education.

Journals

Worren, N. A. M., Ruddle, K. and Moore, K. (1999) From organizational development to change management: the emergence of a new profession. *Journal of Applied Behavioral Science*, 35(3): 273–86.

Case Study Change management in TV Middle East

In 2007, the new company TV Middle East was launched. This involved rebranding and, in particular, the setting up of four new channels. The new channels were planned to provide TV and show a leap in subscribers just before the football season started in August 2007. However, the TV Middle East management team was not complacent. Their competitors – the 'free to air' stations – could pose more of a threat in the future due to the fast-changing nature of the industry. Competition in this sector is high as competitors learn from each other very quickly. For example, if TV Middle East develops something new, it frequently sees its competitors doing the same thing just 1 week later.

Prior to the launch, organizational changes were widespread throughout TV Middle East. These began in earnest in 2006. The first high-level change began when the TV President and CEO stepped down and a new CEO and President was appointed.

How and why did TV Middle East need to change?

According to TV Middle East's OD manager, the organization had previously been in an 'entrepreneurial mode'. Specifically, it had grown sporadically over the years and, as a result, lacked a clear picture of where it needed to go in the future. The company also needed to 'grow up' in terms of its processes and systems. Lines of decision-making needed to be clear, as did lines of accountability. Hence, he stated that changes were necessary to enable business survival.

To bring about the necessary changes, there needed to be transformations in the organization's culture and the way in which employees were operating. The first stages in the change process involved a restructuring whereby the management team was reduced from nine to five people and 60 job roles were made redundant (although 30 people were subsequently redeployed into other roles in the company). This brought the number of employees to 700 people in 2007. The changes were perceived as non-negotiable as they were introduced by the new management team in a fairly directive manner. The CEO and chief operations officer first came into the organization and initially just listened to what employees had to say. This strategy assisted their decision-making regarding the restructuring processes that subsequently took place.

Next, the OD manager worked with the leadership team in a coaching role and held development sessions on the management of change. Simultaneously, he introduced a range of behavioural competencies and recruitment and development strategies. These included assessment centres, the development of a leadership programme and succession planning processes that were also put in place.

McKinsey's Seven S principles (see Peters and Waterman, 1983) were adopted as a guide for the change process. One of the 'S's – structure – involved large-scale changes. Even though the organization had previously been quite flat in terms of structure, these new structural changes involved the removal of blockages in decision-making and improved interdepartmental communication. Strategies also focused on encouraging new teams to develop, particularly moving to the 'performing' stages of the team development cycle. Project teams also worked within matrix structures whereby team members met together more frequently than they would previously have done – for example, working on strategies such as advancing 'customer first' processes.

The OD manager indicated that some of the change processes had been traumatic as where there was resistance to change, it was often because staff needed to 'let go of the past'. However, it is evident that the new style of leadership has now been effective. This was particularly noticed by some employees who had left the organization during the advent of the change processes but had since returned, commenting that it seemed as if it were a totally new organization.

Although the leadership style towards change was initially directive, later in the process control and decision-making authority was delegated. Prior to the changes taking place, decision-making authority went up the hierarchical levels. Following the change, information was shared more readily internally. For example, following the change, employees were able to track progress on customer abandonment calls, sales and management reports on the Internet.

In attempts to 'bed down' the changes and reward desired behaviour, the OD manager introduced a new reward and recognition policy. This ranged from having dinner with the CEO to a flight package. Rewards were allocated as a result of performance management processes, line manager suggestions or direct commissions for the sales staff. In addition, 'mini 360-degree' feedback meetings were held at TV Middle East that involved two or three people giving feedback on a particular person.

Employee performance was not, however, all quantitatively focused as there was also an emphasis on behaviours whereby competencies, including strategic thinking, were encouraged at every level in the organization. For example, a person who works in the warehouse may be required to adopt strategic thinking processes with regard to how warehouse space might be utilized more effectively than before, rather than just working on storage issues.

Moreover, TV Middle East has a number of what are referred to as 'business-critical roles'. These are defined as meaning that if the holder left the organization tomorrow, the impact on the customer relationship would be strong. That is why there is a need for succession planning and talent management in addition to developing knowledge management processes that need to be integrated into the organization.

In summary, the change processes have been very effective so far, but the OD manager indicated that the trauma from such changes was felt for some time after they were introduced. The changes will not, however, be stopping, and the impact will be measured to some extent through a staff survey that is conducted every 2 years. In the future, surveys will take place more regularly and speedily through on-line polls that are likely to be related to specific projects.

So at TV Middle East, it appears that, at least for the foreseeable future, that the only constant will be change!

Questions

1 What were some of the problems associated with TV Middle East before the new CEO headed up the organization?
2 What approach to organizational change was adopted, and what were the key outcomes?
3 How did the organizational development manager attempt to 'anchor change' in the organization?

References

Anderson, P. (1999) Complexity theory and organization science. *Organization Science*, 10(3): 216–32.

Anton, J., Petouhoff, N. L. and Schwartz, L. M. (2003) *Integrating, People, Process and Technology*. Santa Maria, CA: Anton Press.

Balogun, J. and Hailey, V. H. (2004) *Exploring Strategic Change* (2nd edn). London: Prentice Hall.

Barney, J. B. (2001) Is the resource based 'view' a useful perspective for strategic management research? Yes. *Academy of Management Journal*, 26(1): 41–56.

Boston Consulting Group (2008) Creating People Advantage. How to Address Global Challenges Worldwide Through 2015. Executive Summary. Available from: http://www.thebostonconsultinggroup.es/documents/file8905.pdf [accessed 12 January 2009].

Brown, S. L. and Eisenhardt, K. M. (1997) The art of continuous change: linking complexity theory and time-paced evolution in relentlessly shifting organizations. *Administrative Science Quarterly*, 42: 1–34.

Burgess, J. and Connell, J. (2008) Quality jobs – the implications for HRM. *International Journal of HRM*, 19(3): 407–18.

Business Roundtable for Sustainable Development (2003) A Vision of a Sustainable Australia from a Business Perspective. Available from: http://www.ret.gov.au/Documents/VisionOfSustainableAustralia20060405144137.pdf [accessed 2008].

Casey, A. (1993) *The Path of Most Resistance: Reflections on Lessons Learned from New Futures*. Baltimore, MD: Annie E. Casey Foundation.

Chafetz, B., Erickson, R. A. and Ensell, J. (2009) Where Did Our Employees Go? Examining the Rise in Voluntary Turnover During Economic Recoveries. Deloitte Review. Available from: Browse-by-Content-Type/deloitte-review/f506d5ce78ea2210VgnVCM200000bb42f00aRCRD.htm [accessed 11 September 2011].

Cheng, Y. T. and Van der Ven, A. (1996) Learning the innovation journey: order out of chaos? *Organization Science*, 7(6): 593–664.

Chisholm, R. F. and Elden, M. (1993) Features of emerging action research. *Human Relations*, 46(2): 275–98.

Collins, D. (1999) *Organisational Change, Sociological Perspectives*. London: Routledge.

Cummings, T. G. and Worley, C. G. (2005) *Organization Development and Change* (8th edn). Mason, OH: Thomson/South-Western.

Daft, R. (2001), *Organization Theory and Design*. Cincinnati, OH: South-Western.

Dahrendorf, R. (1973) *Homo Sociologicus*. London: Routledge & Kegan Paul.

Davies, L. E. and Taylor, J. C. (1972) *The Design of Jobs*. Harmondsworth: Penguin.

Dawson, P. (2003) *Reshaping Change: A Processual Perspective*. London: Routledge.

Delery, J. E. and Shaw, J. D. (2001) The strategic management of people in work organisations: review, synthesis and extension. *Research in Personnel and Human Resources Management*, 20: 165–97.

Dibella, A. J. (2007) Critical perceptions of organisational change. *Journal of Change Management*, 7(3–4): 231–41.

Dooley, K. (1997) A complex adaptive systems model of organization change. *Nonlinear Dynamics, Psychology, and Life Sciences*, 1(1): 69–97.

Dooley, K., Johnson, T. and Bush, D. (1995) TQM, chaos and complexity. *Human Systems Management*, 14: 297–302.

Dunphy, D. and Griffiths, A. (1994) *Theories of Organizational Change as Models for Intervention*. Sydney: Centre for Corporate Change Publications, Australian Graduate School of Management.

Dunphy, D. and Stace, D. A. (1993) The strategic management of corporate change. *Human Relations*, 46(8): 905–21.

Dunphy, D., Griffiths, A. and Benn, S. (2003) *Organisational Change for Corporate Sustainability: A Guide for Leaders and Change Agents of the Future*. London: Routledge.

Emery, F. E. (1960) *Systems Thinking*. Harmondsworth: Penguin.

French, W. and Bell, C. (1998) *Organization Development and Transformation: Managing Effective Change*. Englewood Cliffs, NJ: Prentice Hall.

Gell-Mann, M. (1994) *The Quark and the Jaguar*. New York: Freeman.

Gersick, C. J. G. (1991) Revolutionary change theories: a multilevel exploration of the punctuated equilibrium paradigm. *Academy of Management Review*, 16(1): 10–36.

Gitsham, M. (2008) *Developing the Global Leader of Tomorrow*. Berkhamsted, Hertfordshire: Ashridge.

Gluckman, P. and Reynolds Roome, D. (1990) *Everyday Heroes: From Taylor to Deming: The Journey to Higher Productivity*. Knoxville, TN: SPC Press.

Goldstein, J. (1994) *The Unshackled Organization*. Portland, OR: Productivity Press.

Hammer, M. and Champy, J. (1993) *Reengineering the Corporation*. New York: Harper Business.

Hellriegel, D. and Slocum, J. W. (2002) *Organizational Behaviour* (10th edn). Cincinnati, OH: South-Western.

Hendry, C. and Pettigrew, A. (1990) Human resource management: an agenda for the 1990s. *International Journal of Human Resource Management*, 1(1): 17–43.

Heracleous, L. and Barrett, M. (2001) Organizational change as discourse: communicative actions and deep structures in the context of information technology implementation. *Academy of Management Journal*, 44(4): 755–78.

Huczynski, A. A. and Buchanan, D. A. (2007) *Organizational Behaviour* (6th edn). Harlow, Essex: Prentice Hall.

Kanter, R. M., Stein, B. and Jick, T. D. (1992) *The Challenge of Organizational Change: How Companies Experience it and Leaders Guide it*. New York: Free Press.

Kotter, J. P. (1996) *Leading Change*, Boston, MA: Harvard Business School Press.

Levinson, W. A. and Rerick, R. (2002) *Lean Enterprise: A Synergistic Approach to Minimizing Waste*. Milwaukee, WI: ASQ Quality Press.

Lewin, K. (1946) Action research and minority problems. *Journal of Social Issues*, 2(4): 34–46.

Lewin, K. (1948) *Resolving Social Conflicts: Selected Papers on Group Dynamics*. New York: Harper & Row.

Likert, R. (1970) A technique for the measurement of attitudes. In Summers, G. F. (ed.) *Attitude Measurement*. Chicago: Rand McNally, pp. 149–58.

Lindblom, C. (1959) The science of muddling through. *Public Administration Review*, 19: 79–88.

McLoughlin, I. and Badham, R. (2005) Political process perspectives on organization and technological change. *Human Relations*, 58: 827–43.

March, J. G. and Simon, H. A. (1958) *Organizations*. New York: John Wiley.

Mathews, J. (1993) *Competing Paradigms of Productive Efficiency – Industrial Relations and Organisational Change*. Sydney: Centre for Corporate Change Publications, Australian Graduate School of Management.

Mayo, E. (1933) *The Human Problems of an Industrial Civilization*. New York: Macmillan.

Moldaschl, M. and Brödner, P. (2002) A reflexive methodology of intervention. In Docherty, P., Forslin, J. and Shani, R. (eds) *Creating Sustainable Work Systems: Emerging Perspectives and Practices*. London: Routledge, pp. 180–90.

Mumford, E. (2006) The story of socio-technical design: reflections on its successes, failures and potential. *Info Systems Journal*, 16: 317–42.

Napoli, D., Whitley, A. and Johansen, K. (2007) *Organizational Jazz. Extraordinary Performance through Extraordinary Leadership*. Sydney: Content Management.

Niepce, W. and Molleman, E. (1998) Work design issues in lean production from a sociotechnical systems perspective: neo-Taylorism or the next step in sociotechnical design? *Human Relations*, 51(3): 259–87.

Nord, W. R. and Jermier, J. M. (1994) Overcoming resistance to resistance: insights from a study of the Shadows. *Public Administration Quarterly*, 17(4): 396–409.

Paton, R. A. and McCalman, J. (2001) *Change Management: A Guide to Effective Implementation*. London: Sage.

Patrickson, M., Bamber, V. and Bamber, G. (1995) *Organisational Change Strategies: Case Studies of Human Resource and Industrial Relations Issues*. Melbourne: Longman Australia.

Peters, T. J. and Waterman, R. H. (1983). *In Search of Excellence: Lessons from America's Best-run Companies*. New York: Harper Business Essentials.

Prigogine, I. and Stengers, I. (1984) *Order Out of Chaos*. New York: Bantam Books.

12

Sauer, C. and Cuthbertson, C. (2003) *The State of IT Project Management in the UK 2002–2003*. Oxford: Templeton College.

Senior, B. and Fleming, J. (2006) *Organisational Change*. Harlow: Pearson Education.

Sheehan, C. R., Holland, P. J. and De Cieri, H. (2006) Current developments in HRM in Australian organisations. *Asia Pacific Journal of Human Resources*, 44(2): 132–52.

Stacey, R. (1992) *Managing the Unknowable*. San Francisco: Jossey-Bass.

Steward, P. (1996) *Beyond Japanese Management. The End of Modern Times*. London: Routledge.

Strandberg, C. (2009) The role of human resource management in corporate social responsibility. Issue Brief and Roadmap, Report for Industry Canada. Available from: http://www.corostrandberg.com/pdfs/CSR_and_HR_Management1.pdfstrandberg consulting [accessed 30 January 2010].

Szamosi, L. T. and Duxbury, L. (2002) Development of a measure to assess organizational change. *Journal of Organizational Change Management*, 5(2): 184–201.

Thornhill, A., Lewis, P., Millmore, M. and Saunders, M. (2000) *Managing Change: A Human Resource Strategy Approach*. Harlow: Prentice Hall.

Trist, E. L. (1981) *The Evolution of Socio-technical Systems. Issues in the Quality of Working Life*. Occasional Paper No. 2. Toronto: Ontario Quality of Working Life Centre.

Tushman, M. L. and Romanelli, E. (1986) Convergence and upheaval: managing the unsteady pace of organizational evolution. *California Management Review*, 29(1): 29–44.

Ulich, E. (2005) *Arbeitspsychologie*. Stuttgart: Schäffer-Poeschel, pp. 83–94.

Ulich, E., Rauterberg, M., Moll, T., Greutmann, T. and Strohm, O. (1991) Task orientation and user-oriented dialog design. *International Journal of Human-Computer Interaction*, 3(2): 117–44.

Von Bertalanffy, L. (1950) The theory of open systems in physics and biology. *Science*, 3: 23–9.

Wenger, E. (1998) *Communities of Practice: Learning, Meaning, and Identity*. Cambridge: Cambridge University Press.

Werther, W. B. (2003) Strategic change and leader-follower alignment. *Organisational Dynamics*, 32(1): 32–45.

Womack, J. P., Jones, D. T. and Roos, D. (1991) *The Machine That Changed the World: The Story of Lean Production*. New York: Harper Perennial.

Wright, P. M., Dunford, B. B. and Snell, S. A. (2001) Human resources and the resource based view of the firm. *Journal of Management*, 27(6): 701–21.

Young, F. W. (1985) Multidimensional scaling. In Kotz, S. and Johnson, N. L. (eds) *Encyclopedia of Statistical Sciences*, Vol. 5. New York: John Wiley.

Human resource management, productivity and employee involvement

Amanda Pyman

13

?

After reading this chapter, you should be able to:

- ☐ Explain the link between strategic human resource management and employee involvement, and why productivity is a better measure of the impact of human resource management practices than profitability
- ☐ Define employee involvement and identify the different channels used to facilitate employee involvement
- ☐ Distinguish between employee involvement and employee participation
- ☐ Identify the major trends in employee involvement in Anglo-American and European countries and the major drivers of these trends
- ☐ Identify and critically discuss the objectives and effectiveness of employee involvement
- ☐ Identify good practices in employee involvement and participation for organizations, managers, employees and policy-makers

🔍

Introduction

The term 'employee voice' has been used to cover a variety of processes and structures that enable, and at times empower, employees, both directly and indirectly, to contribute to and/or participate in a firm's decision-making (Boxall and Purcell, 2003). Within the strategic human resource management (SHRM) literature, employee involvement is afforded a central role in high-commitment and high-performance work systems approaches, with such models advocating that high levels of involvement, among other bundles of human resources practices, are linked to the improved productivity and profitability of the firm, adding value to organizational goals (Marchington, 2007; Richardson et al., 2010) (see also Chapter 16). This assumption is based on the notion that employees are a major source of competitive advantage, and thus employee involvement practices increase the stock of ideas and enhance employee commitment and cooperative, high-trust relations, as employees want to contribute to organizational success (Marchington, 2007).

The aim of this chapter is to critically evaluate the relationship between human resource management (HRM), productivity and employee involvement. The chapter begins by considering the link between SHRM and employee involvement. This is followed by a review of the theories and concepts of employee involvement, distinguishing four types. The distinction between the different types of employee involvement is followed by a consideration of the relationship between employee involvement and productivity, and a critical analysis of the utility of different forms of employee involvement.

Employee involvement is then discussed in a global context, emphasizing the importance of situating involvement in a broader political, social and legislative framework. Students are directed to consider a comparative analysis of employee involvement in Australia and Britain, and then have the opportunity to apply this knowledge by considering the importance of the regulation of employee involvement in Australia and Britain. A case study of employee involvement in a British site of a multinational corporation (MNC) follows. The chapter concludes with a critical analysis and summary of employee involvement, identifying the benefits to managers of studying HRM from a critical perspective. Good practice and recommendations for organizations, managers, employees and policy-makers are identified.

SHRM and employee involvement

The rise of the SHRM field has led to a focus on the way in which human resources practices are linked with, and impact upon, organizational performance and productivity. As Kaplan and Norton (1992) identify, human resource variables such as employees' skills, commitment and satisfaction levels are performance-drivers in all firms. However, profit and labour productivity are also core elements of the causal chain within an organization and are influenced by human resources strategies.

Boxall and Purcell (2003) argue that HRM ought to be concerned with three goal domains that contribute to a firm's viability:

☐ productivity
☐ flexibility
☐ legitimacy.

Superior performance equates to the attainment of successful outcomes across all three domains. For organizations, the key concern is adopting a cost-effective set of human resources practices that underpin profitable and productive relations in the firm, while simultaneously achieving flexibility and legitimacy (Boxall and Purcell, 2003). In strategy terms, this would normally include a blend of human resources practices concerned with hiring and developing employee skills, motivating appropriate performance and providing leadership and opportunities for employees to be involved and participate in organizational decision-making. This blend of human resources practices is commonly referred to as the abilities (A), motivations (M) and opportunities (O) – AMO – model (Boxall and Macky, 2009). Similarly, the resource-based view identifies employee skills, knowledge and technical systems as competencies of the organization (Leonard, 1998).

Boxall and Purcell (2003) argue that labour productivity is a better measure of HRM in firms than is profitability, as labour productivity is solely concerned with the management of people. Labour productivity is defined as the value of labour outputs proportional to the cost of labour inputs, the objective being that HRM will be cost-effective (Boxall and Purcell, 2003). Cost-effectiveness is a core requirement of the overarching HRM system and strategy within a firm. All firms need to assess what human resources practices are needed to ensure cost-effectiveness within the given context in which they operate. Employee involvement has been advocated as one human resources practice, among others, that can enhance labour productivity.

Theories and concepts of employee involvement

This chapter analyses direct and indirect means of employee involvement, which can take a wide variety of forms. Employee involvement is management-initiated and management-led, and has a number of objectives, some of which are summarised in Box 13.1; it should be noted that these objectives are not mutually exclusive. Therefore, management may introduce employee involvement for a variety of reasons, with an overarching objective of improving labour productivity and organizational competitiveness.

Box 13.1 The objectives of employee involvement

☐ To enhance employees' abilities, skills and motivation
☐ To enhance the meaning of work for employees, and their job satisfaction and morale
☐ To enhance employees' commitment and loyalty

13

▷
☐ To enhance employees' performance
☐ To enhance employees' cooperation and engagement
☐ To create networks among employees
☐ To allow employees to express complaints or grievances to management and reduce industrial conflict
☐ To tap into and release employees' skills, creativity, knowledge and ideas, and to incorporate these contributions into the company's decision-making
☐ To permit employees to exercise discretion, control and autonomy, and to encourage discretionary behaviour among employees
☐ To enhance organizational operations and performance

Source: Boxall and Purcell (2003), Marchington (2007), Richardson et al. (2010)

Employee involvement systems became more prominent in the 1980s as external environmental changes exacerbated the need for organizational flexibility and the proactive management of human resources. Prior to the 1980s, involvement was framed in broader terms under the umbrellas of employee participation and industrial democracy (see, for example, Brewster et al., 2007; Marchington, 2007). The differences in terminology are in part related to the decline of trade unions and representative forms of participation, and to the rise of direct, management-led forms of involvement, which have become the norm. These trends will be further discussed later in the chapter.

Leopold (2004) defines employee involvement as management-initiated, inspired structures designed to secure the direct involvement and contributions of individual employees in decision-making, in an attempt to secure employees' commitment, motivation and loyalty (see also Chapter 1). The purpose of employee involvement is to contribute to the achievement of organizational goals and objectives of increased efficiency, productivity and customer service, as part of a larger strategy to achieve and sustain a competitive advantage. Employee involvement therefore has a strong impact on the psychological contract (see also Chapter 6). Examples of channels of employee involvement include:

☐ regular meetings;
☐ suggestion schemes;
☐ employee attitude surveys;
☐ quality circles;
☐ task forces;
☐ semi-autonomous work groups/self-managed teams;
☐ off-line teams;
☐ joint consultative committees (JCCs);
☐ financial involvement;
☐ team briefings;
☐ grievance procedures.

Employee involvement is based on a unitarist frame of reference, that is, one that assumes an identity of interest between employers and employees (Boxall and Purcell, 2003). Employee involvement takes place within the context of a strict management agenda, and therefore the incidence of employee involvement varies, dependent upon managerial choices and the organizational context, with individual circumstances and contingencies within the given firm acting as determinants. Dundon and Gollan (2007) categorize the micro-organizational dimensions that impact upon employees' voice as follows:

☐ management strategies towards trade unions;
☐ occupational identity and group solidarity;
☐ autonomy;
☐ trust;
☐ power and influence.

Marchington and Wilkinson (2002) identify four categories of employee involvement: *downward communication*, *upward problem-solving*, *task participation* and *financial involvement*. These categories are summarised in Table 13.1.

> **Exercise**
> • Choose one of the micro-organizational dimensions that impact on employee voice as specified by Dundon and Gollan (2007). Use an example of a company you know of to explain how this dimension could affect employee involvement.

Table 13.1 Categories of employee involvement

Objectives	Potential problems
Downward communication	
1 Informs and educates employees directly on management's plans 2 Formal or informal 3 Regular or irregular	1 A lack of commitment to implement employee involvement mechanisms in practice 2 A lack of line management skills and/or cynicism and suspicion among employees (Townley, 1994; Leopold, 2004) 3 Acts as a threat to or may marginalize unionized mechanisms of communication in the workplace (Fiorito, 2001; Leopold, 2004; Wood and Fenton-O'Creevy, 2005)
Upward problem-solving	
1 Allows management to draw on employees' knowledge, skills and expertise within their jobs, for example with respect to diversity (see also Chapter 4) 2 Individual or group level 3 Increases the stock of ideas in an organization to encourage cooperative relationships and legitimate change. Examples include suggestion schemes, off-line teams, quality circles, two-way briefings and total quality management systems (see also Chapters 11 and 15) 4 Improves quality and customer service within the organization	1 Employee competence is a precondition for effective decision-making (Marchington, 2007) 2 Employees may not see the added value of such schemes and/or may be resentful of the level of involvement required relative to the potential gains 3 May lead to work intensification for employees (Godard, 2001; Green, 2004) 4 Supervisors and/or line managers may feel threatened by employees' ideas and the practice of sharing information. This may lead to feelings of resentment or marginalization in the managerial chain of command (Marchington, 2007) 5 Rewarding staff through upward problem-solving initiatives undermines the assumption that continuous improvement should be an objective for all staff and for the organization (Leopold, 2004). Upward problem-solving may also increase organizational performance without a commensurate increase in employees' rewards 6 Upward problem-solving may be used to achieve improvements in productivity that will result in job losses (Marchington, 2007)

13

Objectives	Potential problems
Task participation	
1 Encourages employees' to extend the range and types of tasks they undertake. Examples include job restructuring (job enrichment, job redesign) and teamworking 2 Counteracts alienation among employees 3 Increases employees' commitment and satisfaction and their responsiveness to change (see also Chapter 11) 4 Improves levels of quality, productivity and customer service, and therefore enhances the organization's competitive advantage (see also Chapter 15) 5 Horizontal or vertical	1 Work intensification for employees, or perceptions of increased control by employers over the labour process 2 An actual increase in managerial control and the subsequent dilution of employees' autonomy (Marchington, 2007)
Financial involvement	
1 Links individual employees' rewards to the success of a department/unit of the larger organization. Examples include profit-sharing, share/incentive plans, employee share ownership schemes and employee share ownership plans (see also Chapter 10)	1 Financial involvement exposes employees to the vagaries of the share market 2 In times of financial difficulty, and in extreme cases of corporate collapse, organizations may be unable to provide employees with rewards, undermining the whole premise of this mechanism and violating notions of fairness and legitimacy 3 Employees can free-ride: if they only care about their personal pay-offs, group-based incentive schemes can be rendered ineffective (Kalmi et al., 2005)

Sources: Marchington (1992, 2007) and Marchington and Wilkinson (2002)

The typology shown in Table 13.1 is just one example of classifying employee involvement, and a range of different typologies are advocated in the HRM literature (see, for example, Dundon et al., 2004; Leopold, 2004; Marchington, 2007). Nevertheless, key dimensions of employee involvement can be identified across all the existing typologies (Cox et al., 2006; Brewster et al., 2007). These include the following:

☐ *Level of involvement*: the level at which employees are involved, for example the individual, work group/team or organizational level.

☐ *Scope of involvement*: the workplace subjects or issues in which employees are involved, for example task-/job-related issues, operational issues and/or strategic organizational issues (see, for example, Knudsen, 1995).

☐ *Breadth of involvement*: the number of mechanisms (employee involvement channels) operating in the workplace (Marchington, 2007).

☐ *Depth of involvement*: the frequency of meetings, the opportunities employees have to raise issues with managers and the degree of influence employees feel they have over decisions (Marchington, 2007).

The key learning points from the discussion of the objectives and categories of employee involvement are summarised in Box 13.2.

Exercise

Consider your own experiences of employee involvement within an organization.
- Using Marchington and Wilkinson's (2002) typology, how were you involved?
- What channels of involvement did you find most effective? Why?

> **Box 13.2** Key learning points: the objectives and categories of employee involvement
>
> ☐ The scope, level and nature of employee involvement varies across organizations
> ☐ Employee involvement can take place over task-/job-related issues and/or strategic issues
> ☐ Employee involvement can take place over decisions at the corporate/organizational level, the plant level, the team level or the individual level. The location at which decisions take place can be distinguished in terms of power-centred decisions, ownership-centred decisions and task-centred decisions (Marchington and Wilkinson, 2002)
> ☐ The level at which employee involvement takes place will be linked to the objectives of employee involvement within the organization and the organizational setting itself
> ☐ Employee involvement can coexist with or replace employee participation in an organization. The extent to which the two are used simultaneously will be related to management's objectives and to the strength and level of employee participation in the organization
> ☐ Employee involvement will have different degrees of influence within organizations. The extent to which employees believe that their views are listened to and that they have a genuine influence on decision-making will be important in determining employees' overall evaluations and judgements of the effectiveness and fairness of employee involvement mechanisms within the organization, and of management in general (Boxall and Purcell, 2003)

Employee involvement and productivity: examples from Europe

While organizations adopt employee involvement schemes for many different reasons, one of the main drivers is increased productivity. This notion of increased productivity is derived from the resource-based view of the firm, which focuses on the relationship between 'bundles' of HRM practices and organizational performance outcomes (Poutsma et al., 2003, 2006). Employee involvement is one such HRM practice that can be linked to improved productivity and organizational performance. For example, direct involvement schemes such as upward problem-solving and task participation may be used to improve communication and cooperation between management and workers, to coordinate employees' tasks without supervision and/or to facilitate joint problem-solving. These objectives can lead to increased employee commitment, trust and information flows, organizational learning and efficiency, and in turn reduced turnover (Hardy and Adnett, 2006; Poutsma et al., 2006; Wheeler, 2008). Financial involvement may also be used to align employees' interests to the organization, by linking rewards to organizational outcomes, thus engendering greater employee commitment, reduced absenteeism and improved productivity (Kalmi et al., 2005; Poutsma et al., 2006). However, as Hardy and Adnett (2006) note, there is a trade-off between increased employee involvement that can provide greater information and innovation, and the costs of delay and lower short-term employment growth that may result from increased employee involvement.

13

The literature suggests that different forms of employee involvement and participation can complement each other, further enhancing organizational performance effects (Kalmi et al., 2005; Poutsma et al., 2006). For example, financial participation can provide an incentive for employees to share information, complementing direct involvement schemes that encourage a cooperative corporate culture and thereby contributing to the effectiveness of work teams and quality circles (Poutsma et al., 2006). Recent research evidence indicates that financial participation does have increased beneficial impacts on performance when other forms of participation are present, although there is also some evidence to the contrary (see Poutsma et al., 2006). Poutsma et al. (2006) suggest that evidence on the coexistence of different forms of employee involvement, irrespective of performance outcomes, is more balanced; however, drawing on data collected from listed companies in Finland, Germany, The Netherlands and the UK, they find little evidence of a complementarity between financial participation and other forms of involvement.

There has been increased interest in the global phenomenon of financial participation and the growing use of profit-based pay and employee share ownership plans in many European economies (Poutsma et al., 2003; Kalmi et al., 2005). In Western Europe, financial participation has been part of the social policy agenda of the European Community (Wheeler, 2008) and is central to the Lisbon and European Employment Strategies, which seek to transform the performance of the European economy to create the most competitive and knowledge-based economy in the world (European Commission, 2001). While European labour laws introduced since the 1970s have sought to strengthen employers' consultation with the workforce, workplace democracy has returned to the fore of the European Social Policy Agenda (Hardy and Adnett, 2006).

A study by the European Foundation for the Improvement of Living and Working Conditions conducted between 1999 and 2004 reported active engagement with financial participation across Europe. According to this study, financial participation had become increasingly common among large European companies and had the potential to deliver tangible benefits for employees, organizations and national economies alike (European Foundation for the Improvement of Living and Working Conditions, 2005). In particular, this study found the following (p. 1):

□ Profit-sharing was the most prevalent form of financial participation, but there was variation between countries.
□ Worker ownership via share ownership plans was common in countries with legislation and tax breaks that supported such schemes.
□ Small and medium-sized enterprises confronted significant difficulties in adopting share ownership plans due to the high costs and administrative detail involved.
□ Companies that had share ownership plans in place, compared with those that did not, tended to communicate better with their employees.

Diversity in employee share ownership and profit-sharing schemes is also supported by Poutsma and de Nijs (2003). They found that the spread of different forms of financial participation in European countries was strongly linked with promotional measures taken by governments. Where macroeconomic policy explicitly encouraged incentives and financial advantages, systems of financial participation were stronger (Poutsma and de Nijs, 2003). The data also revealed that financial participation was more commonly found in dynamic workplaces with participative work structures; in addition, contextual factors, including national institutional patterns, were more important than company-specific characteristics in shaping the spread and use of financial participation schemes (Poutsma and de Nijs, 2003) (see also the section on macroenvironmental influences below). Drawing on data from listed firms in four EU countries, Poutsma et al. (2006) also found clear differences between the types of financial participation used within organizations.

Recent survey evidence from 151 organizations in France, Germany, Spain, The Netherlands, Finland and the UK further identifies considerable variation across European Member States (Poutsma, 2006). In fact, while 32 per cent of firms had share acquisition plans for all or most of their employees, such plans were most common in Germany (40 per cent), France (54 per cent) and the UK (91 per cent), and were relatively rare in Spain (16 per cent), The Netherlands (14 per cent) and Finland (12 per cent) (Poutsma, 2006). With respect to profit-sharing, 37 per cent of firms overall used such schemes for all or most of their employees, but stock options were generally limited to managerial employees (Poutsma, 2006). Participation rates were approximately 80 per cent in profit-sharing plans, but only 60–65 per cent in share plans (Poutsma, 2006). The incidence of profit-sharing plans also varied considerably between countries, being most common in France (52 per cent), Finland (52 per cent) and The Netherlands (45 per cent) (Poutsma, 2006). Important conclusions identified from Poutsma's (2006) study included that:

☐ profit-sharing plans and share-related plans were broadly based in those organizations where they existed, had varied participation rates and were more common in participative organizations;

☐ the main objectives of financial participation were to increase employees' motivation and demonstrate that employees were valued by the organization;

☐ the main obstacles to financial participation were restrictive and complicated legal frameworks, as well as insufficient tax breaks.

Critical summary of employee involvement

The utility of different forms of employee involvement and participation have increasingly attracted widespread attention within the academic literature (see, for example, Wood and Fenton-O'Creevy, 2005; Brewster et al., 2007; Charlwood and Terry, 2007). The literature often distinguishes between direct and indirect (representative-based) approaches to employee voice. Direct channels of consultative voice are defined as two-way mechanisms of employee communication and involvement, such as team briefings, quality circles and suggestion schemes (Marginson et al., 2010). Indirect consultative voice (involvement and participation) is achieved through representative arrangements, which may include union structures, JCCs (union or non-union based) or non-union structures (company councils/associations).

Trends in employee involvement and participation have been one of the drivers underlying increased interest in the utility of different forms of employee voice. In most Anglo-American economies, the decline of trade union membership and representation, increasing globalization and the rise of neo-liberal economic policies focused on labour market flexibility, individualism and decollectivization have spawned the growth of employee involvement, and at the same time a decline in participatory mechanisms (through elected union representatives particularly) (see, for example, Boxall and Purcell, 2003; Gollan, 2006; Brewster et al., 2007; Dundon and Gollan, 2007; Purcell and Georgiadis, 2007; Wood and Wall, 2007). Indeed, the use of employee involvement by employers became the dominant approach in the latter decades of the 20th century, illustrating the impact of broader macroeconomic factors, beliefs and values on the structures of HRM. Nevertheless, in some instances, employee involvement coexists with employee participation.

Despite the common assumption that employee involvement substitutes for union representation, a growing body of empirical literature reveals that a combination of employee involvement and participation is most effective for employers and employees (see, for example, Bryson, 2004; Wood and Fenton-O'Creevy, 2005; Gollan, 2006; Charlwood and Terry, 2007). For instance, Sako (1998), in a study of the impact of employee voice in the European car components industry, found that a combination of direct and indirect forms had the strongest effect on performance in this sector.

These findings have been reinforced by a large-scale European survey of participation in the mid-1990s, which found that the greater number of participatory forms that were used, the more likely managers were to report benefits from increased output and declining absenteeism (Boxall and Purcell, 2003). In Australia, Pyman et al. (2006) also found that the combination of direct and indirect voice mechanisms was a stronger predictor of employees' perceived control over their jobs and their influence over job rewards than was a single voice channel alone. Despite favourable evidence for the complementarity or coexistence of direct and indirect voice channels, the decision of an employer to utilize direct or indirect mechanisms will be strongly influenced by the environment in which the firm operates and the nature of its operations (Brewster et al., 2007).

Employee involvement in a global context: macroenvironmental influences

Previous sections of this chapter have identified the importance of internal, organizational and workplace factors in shaping employee involvement mechanisms. Although there is an evident link between human resources practices, performance and labour productivity, it is important to understand the strategic goals and impact of HRM and employee involvement in a broader sense, because employee involvement relates to a range of stakeholder interests (Marchington, 2007). Boxall and Purcell (2003) refer to this as the 'social legitimacy' element of the causal chain, and this chain identifies the human resources practices that are required to underpin legal, ethical and socially responsible employment relationships in the firm, addressing issues such as minimum employment standards and human rights.

Social legitimacy is a necessary feature of SHRM, and should not be understated (Boxall and Purcell, 2003). Therefore, it is important to examine employee involvement through the lens of social legitimacy and ethics, and not just performance and productivity, because as Hyman (2005) argues, voice mechanisms are bound by other systemic social and economic features. Similarly, Marchington (2007) argues that voice is the area of HRM in which tensions between organizational and employees' goals, and between shareholder and stakeholder interests, are most apparent, because it connects with the question of managerial prerogative and social legitimacy.

Employee involvement is one human resources practice that is directly shaped by industry and by societal, legal and political forces (Boxall and Purcell, 2003). More specifically, Dundon and Gollan (2007) and Marchington (2007) identify the following macroenvironmental factors that, together with the organizational and workplace factors previously identified, shape voice:

☐ market influences (product and labour markets, industrial relations and competitive pressures);
☐ technology, skills and staffing levels;
☐ structural influences (organizational size, sector and nationality or ownership);
☐ the regulatory or policy environment and financial system (including legislation and the national business system).

These forces impact on managerial decision-making at the level of the organization, and will be shaped by the origin and structure of industrial relations systems and wider social institutions, as well as by their pathways of evolution in different countries. For example, the UK, a liberal market economy, is often criticized on the basis that weaker labour market regulation allows employers more freedom and choice over their management of the employment relationship. In the case of employee involvement, this has led to a preoccupation with task-based structures that fail to challenge managerial dominance or enable genuine empowerment; this is also known as the low-road or low-commitment approach to SHRM (Wood and Fenton-O'Creevy, 2005; Brewster et al., 2007).

Therefore, as Boxall and Purcell (2003) note, although legislation can dictate the form taken by some involvement and participation systems, it can never specify how organizations manage or deal with such structures in practice. It is always the case that if management does not wish to engage in a meaningful dialogue with its employees and their representatives, it can render legislatively imposed systems of involvement and participation largely insignificant. Organizations and managers retain discretion, even in the presence of legislation; therefore involvement can range from a strategic, organizational-wide, embedded initiative, to the rendering of employee involvement as a trivial nuisance or 'bolt-on' that becomes an additional burden or simply a means of perfunctory compliance for line managers (Boxall and Purcell, 2003). Legislation, in order to be effective, must have a catalytic effect on beliefs and values, especially on those who are required to share power and be accountable to their subordinates within organizations (Boxall and Purcell, 2003).

Employee involvement systems that are 'empty shells' (Noon and Hoque, 2004), that is, disconnected from organizational life and decision-making, will have a short lifespan and will fail to provide effective or meaningful channels for employee influence and empowerment (Marchington, 2007). For employee involvement to be effective and meaningful, the 'social contract' (Walton et al., 1994) must be centred upon commitment and cooperation, with employee involvement being legitimate and actively encouraged and promoted by managers and employees in practice. The beliefs and values of the society in which organizations, managers and employees operate are a crucial added dimension.

Box 13.3 Employee involvement in Australia

Within Australian workplaces, a majority of respondents to the Australian Worker Representation and Participation Survey 2004 reported having access to one or more forms of direct employee involvement arrangements. The key results from the survey included the following:

- ☐ 83 per cent of respondents agreed that their workplace had an open door policy enabling the discussion of problems with supervisors or senior management.
- ☐ 60.1 per cent of respondents reported the occurrence of regular staff meetings.
- ☐ 48.1 per cent reported the presence of a human resources or personnel department or person.
- ☐ 35.8 per cent of workplaces reported the existence of formal employee involvement programmes such as quality circles.
- ☐ 50.3 per cent of respondents reported the presence of JCCs, often identified as a means of employee participation. The majority of these committees, however, consisted of employees chosen by a method other than by a union or staff association. These committees were also rated as very effective by respondents: 79.9 per cent indicated that these committees were broadly representative of employees' views.
- ☐ Organizational size and perceived managerial attitudes towards unions were found to be significantly related to the presence of employee involvement. A full-time human resources or personnel department or person was more common in larger organizations and organizations where unions were present.
- ☐ Regular staff meetings and a committee of employees were also more common in larger organizations.
- ☐ Employees who perceived that their managers were opposed to unions were less likely to agree that they had an open door policy, regular meetings or a committee of employees in their workplace.

Source: Adapted from Teicher et al. (2007)

Practical examples of the differences in employee involvement across countries arising from the influence of both macro and micro determinants can be seen in *What Workers Say: Employee Voice in the Anglo-American Workplace* (Freeman et al., 2007). This book was based upon an international comparison of employees' voice in six countries: the USA, Canada, Britain, Ireland, Australia and New Zealand. The country researchers adopted a common methodology: a set of surveys based upon the 1994–1995 Worker Representation and Participation Survey in the USA (Freeman and Rogers, 1999) and the 2001 British Worker Representation and Participation Survey (Diamond and Freeman, 2001).

Practical examples of the level and nature of employee involvement in Australia and Britain can be seen in Boxes 13.3 and 13.4.

Box 13.4 Employee involvement in Britain

Within British workplaces, there has been a dramatic growth in direct communication between employees and management. Bryson and Freeman (2007), analysing employees' needs and the problems they faced in their workplace, found the following:

☐ Non-union channels of employee involvement, including an open door policy and JCCs, reduced the number of needs reported by employees.

☐ There has been an increase in the proportion of workplaces running problem-solving groups involving non-managerial employees, but a decline in the proportion of workplaces with JCCs and higher level consultative forums.

☐ The above findings are supported by the Workplace Employment Relations Survey (1998) in the UK, which suggests that regular meetings with management and the presence of quality circles reduce the number of workplace needs.

☐ The 2004 Workplace Employment Relations Survey data reveal an increase in direct communication and a decline in workplaces covered by a JCC. With respect to direct employee involvement: 91 per cent of all workplaces used meetings with the entire workforce or team briefings; 61 per cent of all workplaces made systematic use of the management chain; 45 per cent of all workplaces circulated regular newsletters; 74 per cent of all workplaces used notice boards; 38 per cent of all workplaces used direct e-mail communication; 34 per cent of all workplaces made use of an intranet; 30 per cent of all workplaces employed suggestion schemes; and 42 per cent of all workplaces ran employee surveys. The survey results reinforce the fact that a high proportion of UK workplaces use direct employee involvement, but there was also evidence that some workplaces employ a combination of direct and indirect consultative voice (Kersley et al., 2005).

Source: Adapted from Bryson and Freeman (2007)

It is interesting to further explore employee involvement in a global context, as well as the important influence that regulation and national origin have on employee involvement mechanisms in practice – the European Union (EU), for example, provides a different picture from Australia and Britain. As previously noted, attempts to regulate employee participation and industrial democracy in Europe have been on the EU agenda since the early 1990s (Waddington, 2003; Hall, 2005). In 2002, representing one of the most significant interventions with regard to employee representation, the EU Information and Consultation Directive came into effect. This Directive established a general framework of minimum requirements for employees' rights to information and consultation. The Directive (Gollan and Wilkinson, 2007: 1146) requires organizations in all Member States to:

☐ Share information on the recent and probable development of the undertaking's or the establishment's activities and economic situation;

☐ Inform and consult on the situation, structure and probable development of employment and on any anticipatory measures envisaged, in particular where there is a threat to employment; and

☐ Inform and consult, with a view to reaching an agreement, on decisions likely to lead to substantial changes in work organization or in contractual relations. Information means the provision of data on the business to employees and/or their representatives, whether over workplace or strategic issues, with a view to allow employees to participate in dialogue. Consultation is defined as the exchange of views between employers and employees, with a view to the establishment of dialogue, yet, management ultimately retain decision making power.

The impact of the EU Directive on Information and Consultation has been varied across Member States owing to the different statutory systems and national influences that exist (Gollan and Wilkinson, 2007; Marginson et al., 2010). This variation is consistent with evidence of variation in financial participation schemes in Europe. Differences in information and consultation can be illustrated by recent research undertaken by Marginson et al. (2010), which shows that MNCs have distinct preferences regarding the structures for employee representation and the form that arrangements for employees' voice take, based on the different countries of origin in which they are based. This research is summarised in Box 13.5 (see also Mini Case Study 13.1).

Box 13.5 **Employee representation and consultative voice in MNCs operating in Britain**

The research by Marginson et al. (2010) was based on a survey of employment practices and a structured interview with a senior human resources executive in 302 MNCs in the UK. Focusing on the results for indirect and consultative voice mechanisms, the findings showed that:

☐ meetings of senior management and the entire workforce were used in 76 per cent of MNCs;
☐ team (briefing) groups were used in 76 per cent of MNCs;
☐ problem-solving or continuous improvement groups were used in 77 per cent of MNCs;
☐ formally designated teams with delegated responsibility were used in 73 per cent of MNCs;
☐ in summary, 99 per cent of MNCs had one or more direct consultative voice mechanism in operation.

In terms of differences between the MNCs' consultative voice policies, the research revealed the following:

☐ Japanese-based MNCs were significantly more likely than US MNCs to emphasize indirect forms of consultation, as were those MNCs based in the rest of Europe.
☐ MNCs from the UK did not significantly differ from US MNCs regarding their consultative voice policy: both emphasized direct forms.

▷

▷

□ Sector had an influence on the practices of MNCs, with service sector MNCs, in comparison with MNCs involved in manufacturing, emphasizing direct rather than indirect channels.

□ MNCs that had been operating in the UK only over the past 5 years were less likely to emphasize direct channels compared with longer established companies.

□ MNCs that had grown by acquisition emphasized direct over indirect channels.

In summary, Marginson et al. (2010) concluded that there was evidence for country of origin influences on the patterns of employee representation and consultative voice in MNCs, but that these influences were also shaped by other factors, including sector and method of growth.

Mini Case Study 13.1
A comparative analysis between Australia and Britain

Compare the legislative and political environments in Australia and Britain to consider the importance of the regulation of employee involvement, and the subsequent implications for the parties involved in the employment relationship and for HRM.

Australia

The election of a federal Labor government in 2008 brought about a significant change in industrial relations and HRM in Australia. Replacing a hostile, conservative neo-liberal government that had been seen to tip the balance of industrial relations regulation in favour of the employers (Cooper and Ellem, 2008), the Labor government introduced the Fair Work Act (Cth) in 2009. This new Act has the capacity to significantly change industrial relations in Australia, and is likely to have an impact on employee involvement and participation. The major object of the Fair Work Act 2009 (Cth) (Division 2, Section 3) is to provide a balanced framework for cooperative and productive relations that promotes national economic prosperity and social inclusion for all Australians by:

- providing workplace relations laws that are fair, are flexible for businesses and promote productivity and economic growth;
- ensuring a guaranteed safety net of fair, relevant and enforceable minimum terms and conditions;
- ensuring that the above conditions cannot be undermined by individual employment agreements;
- assisting employees to balance their work and family responsibilities;
- enabling fairness and representation at work and the

prevention of discrimination, providing protection against unfair treatment and discrimination, providing access to effective procedures to resolve grievances and disputes, and providing effective compliance mechanisms;

- achieving productivity and fairness through a focus on enterprise-level bargaining underpinned by good faith obligations and clear rules;
- acknowledging the special circumstances of small and medium-sized businesses.

Case questions

In light of the objectives of the Fair Work Australia Act 2009 (Cth), consider the following questions:

1 How can you relate the objectives of the new legislation to the objectives of employee involvement as described by theory?

2 What are the likely future outcomes for employee involvement in Australia given the new legislation introduced in 2009?

UK

The Information and Consultation of Employees Regulations (ICE) in the UK establish a general statutory framework giving employees a right to be informed and consulted by their employers over a range of business, employment and restructuring issues (Hall, 2005). The legislation was established in 2005, was implemented over 3 years, and stems from the EU Information and Consultation Directive introduced in 2002. The legislation has applied since April 2005 to large undertakings (with at least 150 employees), since April 2007 to those undertakings with at least 100 employees, and since April 2008 to companies with at least 50 employees. The

13

▷

▷
Regulations diverge from the EU Information and Consultation Directive (2002) by providing considerable flexibility for employers in their response, and therefore enabling the adoption of information and consultation arrangements that are organization-specific. There has been an increase in research evaluating the impact of the Regulations and of management's approach to information and consultation in the UK (see, for example, Hall, 2005; Hall et al., 2007, 2009; Gollan and Wilkinson, 2007; Wilkinson et al., 2007).

Case questions
In light of the introduction of the ICE Regulations (2005) in the UK, consider the following questions:
1 Why might employees value information and consultation that is imposed by legislation?
2 What are the benefits for organizations of informing and consulting employees?
3 What factors are likely to influence a company's strategy for information and consultation in the workplace?

A critical analysis of employee involvement

Employee involvement is management-initiated and management-driven. The shortcomings of management-controlled employee involvement, oriented toward management goals, are manifold.

First, there is potential for contradictory and competing objectives and initiatives between senior and line managers. For example, where line managers play a critical role in the delivery and implementation of employee involvement with frontline staff, it is possible that line managers may prioritize operational production and service issues over and above investment in employee involvement initiatives (Boxall and Purcell, 2003). Anglo-American models of corporate governance, which promote short-termism, management-driven capitalism and returns to shareholders at all costs, may also serve to undermine longer term investment in potentially costly employee involvement initiatives (see, for example, Brewster et al., 2007). Line managers may also lack adequate training in employee involvement or lack an understanding of why investing in such initiatives is important and/or may benefit the organization.

Any contradictions between senior and line management, or between espoused and actual employee involvement policies and initiatives within an organization, will be noticed by employees. Such contradictions will mean that the penetration of employee involvement will be weak, and may therefore have adverse consequences for employees' job satisfaction, commitment and loyalty (Boxall and Purcell, 2003). In order to facilitate employee involvement, line managers and senior managers must create a strong and supportive environment by exhibiting trust, encouraging development and the sharing of concerns, communicating, listening, acting in a genuine manner, and being transparent, honest and open with their employees. Managers must collectively demonstrate enthusiasm and respect employees' views by asking them what matters and by devolving autonomy (Robertson, 2010a, 2010b).

Second, the very notion of employee involvement, from a theoretical perspective of unitarism, assumes that there is an identity of interest between employers and employees. However, the very purpose and objective of employee involvement is to create commitment and loyalty, meaning that, in practice, a common identity of interest between employers and employees may simply be a fallacy (Boxall and Purcell, 2003). Ultimately, as Boxall and Purcell (2003) note, the justification for employee involvement is an end value in its own right. As such, it is always contentious and subject to reinterpretation, as employers and employees in the organization and the wider political system have to deal with changing industrial and ethical problems (Boxall and Purcell, 2003).

The constantly changing and contradictory nature of employee involvement therefore underscores the importance of trust between employers and employees, and the maintenance and sustainability of trust over time. For example, Kessler and Purcell (1996), in a study of joint working practices, found that the level of trust between employers and employees markedly increased when employees and/or their representatives were involved in all stages of a change process overseen by a joint working party. Management also reported greater benefits to the organization when such employee involvement took place.

Third, the presence of employee involvement initiatives is not in itself enough to secure favourable outcomes for the employee and employer. It is not the mere presence of employee involvement that guarantees quality or favourable outcomes. Rather, it is the systems, processes, values and degree of embeddedness of employee involvement initiatives that determines their success in practice, suggesting the need for complementary human resources practices alongside employee involvement (see, for example, Dundon et al., 2004; Marchington, 2005, 2007; Cox et al., 2006; Gollan, 2006; Wilkinson et al., 2007; Brown et al., 2009; Richardson et al., 2010). Indeed, research evidence shows that where employee voice arrangements are established by law and are socially embedded, they are more successful and durable over time (Boxall and Purcell, 2003; Richardson et al., 2010).

However, although legislation can dictate the forms that employee involvement or employee participation can take, it can never specify how organizations manage or deal with these structures at an organizational level. As a result, the contextual factors within the individual firm and the strategic choices of the individual company are critical in shaping and driving employee involvement and participation. As Boxall and Purcell (2003) note, it is always the case that if management does not wish to engage in a meaningful dialogue with employees and/or their representatives, it can render legislatively imposed voice systems largely trivial.

It is likely, therefore, that the solutions and means to achieve employee involvement are different for each firm, influenced by institutional, societal, sectoral, industrial and organizational factors. For instance, evidence shows marked differences in the strategies of small firms, which favour informal and direct employee involvement, compared with the more formalized processes of employee involvement in larger firms (Wilkinson et al., 2007; see also Chapter 16). Employers are more likely to adopt sophisticated methods of employee involvement where:

☐ they are competing in a sector that requires innovative investment in human resources due to capital-intensive production systems;
☐ they are using sophisticated technology;

13

☐ there is a clear pay-off to the employees and the firm of doing this, with regard to employees' skills, abilities, motivation and training (Boxall and Purcell, 2003).

Finally, despite the assumed benefits of employee involvément for organizational productivity and performance, there are numerous difficulties in substantiating the performance effects of employee involvement systems in practice (see, for example, Boxall and Purcell, 2003; Dundon and Gollan, 2007; Richardson et al., 2010). One key problem arises due to the individual contingencies and context of the firm acting as a determinant of employee involvement initiatives, meaning that a vast array of different schemes are used in practice. It is therefore very difficult to tease out the impact of individual practices across different contexts (Boxall and Purcell, 2003). In addition, empirical research tends to be cross-sectional rather than longitudinal, meaning that causation cannot be determined. Much of the research also relies on managers' interpretations of the perceived impact of employee involvement on performance, thus ignoring employees' perceptions (Dundon and Gollan, 2007; Marchington, 2007; Richardson et al., 2010).

Related to the issue of causation is the difficulty of measuring the embeddedness of employee involvement initiatives and how they shape and change behaviours (Boxall and Purcell, 2003). More longitudinal research is needed to evaluate the embeddedness of employee involvement and how this influences and changes the behaviour of employers and employees over time. Despite the difficulty of proving the performance- and productivity-enhancing effects of employee involvement, there is also substantial empirical evidence to support the notion that employee involvement can have benefits for employees and the organization, particularly in terms of increasing employees' job satisfaction, loyalty and commitment (see, for example, Cox et al., 2006; Pyman et al., 2010; Holland et al., 2011).

Exercise
• What behaviours should managers employ to facilitate employee involvement in the workplace?

Benefits of studying HRM from a critical perspective for managers

It is important to study employee involvement, as part of HRM, from a critical perspective, because it allows practising managers to evaluate both employers' and employees' perceptions and judgements of the operation and the effectiveness of employee involvement initiatives. This is fundamental, given that both parties will have different interests and will therefore utilize different effectiveness criteria. It is the goal of practising human resources managers to maximize both parties' interests and outcomes, in order to generate favourable outcomes for both the individual and the organization.

Being aware of and understanding the different interests of employers and employees is also critical for human resources managers, in order to appreciate the importance of the nature and quality of the underlying relationship between the parties, and in particular the levels of trust between them. It is the understanding and management of trust by human resources practitioners that is key to ensuring a genuine and beneficial exchange for employers and employees, in both an economic and a psychological sense. With respect to employee involvement, trust needs to be carefully managed by human resources practitioners over the long term, as trust and justice are potential outcomes of employee involvement and are also likely to influence the way in which employee involvement develops internally (Cox et al., 2006).

Given evidence suggesting that it is the degree to which employee involvement mechanisms are embedded within the organization that will determine the success and durability of involvement initiatives (see, for example, Dundon et al., 2004), management of trust in the implementation and operation of employee involvement over time is critical. As Gollan (2006) argues, only by establishing mechanisms that enable employees to have a legitimate voice and allow differences to emerge will managers be able to channel such differences into more productive outcomes.

Conclusion

Employee involvement is argued to be a core ingredient in high-performance work systems that can subsequently lead to improvements in the organization's performance and productivity by enhancing employees' contributions, satisfaction and commitment (see also Chapter 16). This in turn leads to a sustainable competitive advantage. The level and scope of employee involvement systems varies enormously, with decisions ranging from those on task-based issues to those related to strategic, power-centred issues. The locus of decision-making will influence the type and scope of employee involvement systems adopted, as will the organizational and national context. Since the 1980s, there has been an evident shift away from indirect, union-based forms of involvement and participation, to the increased use of direct, task-based forms of involvement such as regular meetings, suggestion schemes and team briefings; this shift has been visible in most advanced market economies.

The development of employee involvement systems granting employees access to, and participation in, managerial decision-making has been heralded as a means of empowerment and mutual gain. However, empowerment and mutual gains are not guaranteed by the presence of an employee involvement system – it is how employee involvement systems operate in practice that will determine the outcomes for employers and employees. Although legislation remains an important influence on employee involvement and participatory systems, particularly the degree to which they are viewed as legitimate, it is the process of managing people and how this is undertaken at the level of the organization that remains an ethical and social choice for managers. The choices that managers make fundamentally shape the outcomes gained from employee involvement systems, and organizational and managerial empowerment initiatives must be situated and integrated within the larger work environment, because isolated initiatives will not achieve their intended outcomes (Leopold, 2004).

13

As Gallie and White (1993) further note, involvement is of fundamental importance in shaping employees' attitudes to the organization in which they work. It is strongly related to the way they respond to changes in work organization and to their perception of the overall quality of the relationship between management and employees. Employee involvement systems must therefore be integrated, meaningful and effective in the eyes of employees in order to have tangible effects on job satisfaction, organizational commitment and discretion and, in turn, favourable impacts on organizational performance and labour productivity. A central debate within the literature therefore centres on the degree to which employee involvement systems are illustrative of a passing fad or, alternatively, represent socially embedded structures that enable more cooperative and effective ways of managing people and attaining good organizational performance.

The degree to which employee involvement systems are socially embedded within an organization is critically dependent on senior and line managers and the degree of importance and purpose they attach to such systems, in addition to the means and extent to which they support and activate them. Just because employee involvement is present does not mean that it will be effective. Therefore, where employee involvement systems are embedded, legitimate and morally accepted activities, strongly supported and activated by managers in practice, they will produce positive, sustainable, win–win outcomes for the company and its employees. A supportive organizational climate and culture of involvement, and high levels of trust between employers and employees, are seminal design elements allowing employee involvement to take root and prosper in an organization in practice (Boxall and Purcell, 2003). Positive outcomes in terms of performance and labour productivity are multidimensional for employers and employees, reinforcing how important it is to address both parties' evaluations and perceptions of the effectiveness of employee involvement systems.

The key learning points from this chapter, areas of good practice and recommendations for key stakeholders are summarised in Box 13.6.

Box 13.6 Key learning points: good practice and recommendations for employers, employees and policy-makers

☐ Employee involvement varies according to institutional, organizational and workplace contexts. In this respect, the ideologies of policy-makers, employers and employees will shape the nature and success of such mechanisms

☐ Managers need to consider the rationale for employee involvement, the implementation of employee involvement, the influence of broader social systems and employees' expectations

☐ For employees, changes at the work group level can make a significant difference within the organization and to their experience of work

☐ Employee involvement needs to be embedded within the workplace as much depends on how employee involvement is implemented and sustained. The regularity and thoroughness with which employee involvement practices are applied

$\triangleright$

▷ can have a significant impact on their quality. To be effective, employee involvement must operate in a strong, supportive organizational climate, and be underpinned by the principles of consistency, fairness and legitimacy. The lifespan of employee involvement mechanisms will also determine their quality and effectiveness. Employee involvement mechanisms that are deeply embedded within the workplace, are legitimized as valued aspects of organizational routines and cover a wide range of employees will be more effective for managers and employees and will have a more positive impact on employees' perceptions

☐ The effectiveness of employee involvement mechanisms also depends on whether they are used individually or in isolation. Combinations of direct (employee involvement) and indirect (participation) mechanisms have the strongest relationship with workers' commitment, satisfaction and discretion. Employee involvement mechanisms must link with other components of HRM. The greater the degree of 'fit' between employee involvement and the rest of the human resources system, the more meaningful its impact will be

☐ Most research focuses on intended employee involvement practices within a workplace, rather than on those experienced by employees themselves. Research must be sensitive to the complexities of voice and examine employees' experiences in greater detail

☐ The impact of employee involvement mechanisms on bottom line performance and labour productivity is contested. Employers always retain some degree of choice over whether or not they implement employee involvement and other voice systems. Employee involvement will have a positive impact on performance and labour productivity if the relevant channels are embedded within the workplace

(See, for example, Pyman et al., 2006; Marchington, 2007; Richardson et al., 2010)

For discussion and revision

1 How does employee involvement link to SHRM?

2 Why is labour productivity a better measure of the impact of human resources practices than profitability?

3 Distinguish between three categories of employee involvement.

4 Discuss the differences between direct and indirect consultative voice.

5 Identify two major trends in employee involvement since the 1980s. What have been the implications of these trends for managers, employees and trade unions?

6 What are the limits of legislated employee involvement systems?

7 Why is it important for employee involvement systems to be socially embedded within an organization?

8 How can an organization achieve socially embedded employee involvement systems?

9 Why is it difficult to establish a causal link between employee involvement systems and performance and productivity?

13

📖 Further reading

Journals

Boxall, P. and Macky, K. (2007) High-performance work systems and organisational performance: bridging theory and practice. *Asia Pacific Journal of Human Resources*, 45(3): 261–70.

This paper explores the meaning and significance of high-performance work systems, in which work reforms designed to increase employee involvement are seen as a core underpinning. This paper argues that practices such as employee involvement need to be adapted to industry and occupational conditions, and considers the managerial and governance processes in which they are embedded. The paper concludes by reaffirming the value of evaluating both management practices and employee responses to organizational outcomes, as a means to bridge the gap between theory and practice.

Boxall, P. and Macky, K. (2009) Research and theory on high-performance work systems: progressing the high involvement stream. *Human Resource Management Journal*, 19(1): 3–23.

This paper critically analyses the notion of a high-performance work system and its companion terminology: high-involvement work systems and high-commitment management. The major models proposed in the literature are reviewed, and it is argued that research should be dedicated to examining the processes that underpin employees' experiences of high-involvement management systems and their subsequent links to employee and operational outcomes. The paper is useful in critiquing the existing HRM literature and theory which assumes that employee involvement is a core component of a high-performance/high-commitment and/or high-involvement work system. The paper also makes robust recommendations for advancing theory in this field.

Brown, M., Geddes, A. and Heywood, J. S. (2009) The determinants of employee-involvement schemes: private sector Australian evidence. *Economic and Industrial Democracy*, 28(2): 259–91.

This paper utilizes data from the Australian Workplace Industrial Relations Survey to examine the determinants of four different types of employee involvement scheme: autonomous groups, quality circles, JCCs and task forces. The authors found that employee involvement is associated with employees who are expected to stay in their jobs for longer and with higher attachment to the labour force. Complementary human resources practices such as formal training and incentive pay are also associated with the increased use of employee involvement, as are unionization, workplace size and the extent of competition. The paper is useful in providing an up-to-date perspective on the nature and scope of employee involvement systems in private sector organizations in Australia.

Budd, J., Gollan, P. and Wilkinson, A. (2010) New approaches to employee voice and participation in organizations. *Human Relations*, 63(3, Special Issue).

This special issue of *Human Relations* extends existing knowledge on employee voice and participation by capturing a variety of different contemporary streams of research on the topic, including institutional, behavioural and strategic approaches. The articles extend our current knowledge and understanding by examining new organizational forms and the practices and processes affecting the nature and structure of employee voice and participation within organizations.

Holland, P., Pyman, A., Cooper, B. and Teicher, J. (2011) Employee voice and job satisfaction in Australia: the centrality of direct voice. *Human Resource Management*, 50(1): 95–111.

This paper examines the relationship between employee voice and job satisfaction, utilizing data from the Australian Worker Representation and Participation Survey (2007). Regression analyses suggest that direct voice appears to be central in underpinning employees' job satisfaction. This paper is useful for considering the design of direct employee involvement schemes with the objective of enhancing employees' job satisfaction.

Pyman, A., Holland, P., Teicher, J. and Cooper, B. (2010) Industrial relations climate, employee voice and managerial attitudes to unions: an Australian study. *British Journal of Industrial Relations*, 48(2): 460–80.

Using data from the Australian Worker Representation and Participation Survey (2007), this paper examines how employee voice arrangements and managerial attitudes to unions shape employees' perceptions of the industrial relations climate. Regression analyses demonstrate that employees' perceptions of the industrial relations climate are more likely to be favourable if they have access to direct-only voice arrangements. Where management is perceived by employees to oppose unions (in unionized workplaces), the industrial relations climate is more likely to be reported as poor.

13

Case Study Employee involvement at Paper Co

Paper Co is a large, multisite manufacturing organization that is a joint venture between two blue-chip MNCs (Swedish and Anglo-American). Paper Co supplies recycled newsprint paper to regional and national publishers and printers in Western Europe and the USA. The company employs a total of 370 staff, two-thirds of whom are manual shift workers. The company is unionized, with a union density of approximately 40 per cent, but this density has been declining on an annual basis.

Paper Co operates 24 hours a day, 7 days a week, 365 days a year. The production process is highly automated, and two paper machines produce 400,000 tonnes of paper per annum. Its annual turnover is approximately £130 million. Operations at Paper Co have, however, not escaped the effects of globalization and the economic downturn. Increased global competition and rising energy prices have continued to threaten the profitability and competitiveness of the UK paper-making industry, an industry that collectively employs over 10,000 workers across 60 mills (Carley, 2007) . Over the last decade, paper production has fallen by over a quarter, with the closure of over 35 paper mills across the UK (Confederation of Paper Industries, 2008). The domestic market for paper, including newsprint, has contracted, but the collection of recovered paper has continued to rise. The industry has thus witnessed a rapid expansion in the export of recovered paper to the Far East and Europe. In October 2008, due to rising costs and a decline in profits, Paper Co announced 37 redundancies below management level.

Notable features of the company's culture are its longstanding commitment to health and safety, product quality and communication and consultation, in which employee voice comprises union and non-union (direct and indirect) channels. Union voice within the company, and the paper-making industry in general, is a longstanding feature, and industry-wide bargaining arrangements continue to set pay, terms and conditions. In May 2007, the national agreement was modernized through the launch of a national partnership agreement between the Confederation of Paper Industry, Amicus, the Transport and General Workers Union and the GMB (Carley, 2007). Similar to the partnership agreement found in the printing industry, the 'Papermaking Partnership' encourages stakeholders to 'work together, grow together, and stay together' in order to improve the industry's competitiveness.

Despite the continuation of national collective bargaining, the locus of consultation and negotiation at Paper Co is mainly at plant level. Consultation occurs through an elected 'Operating Council' that was established in 1994, which represents all production workers for the purposes of information and consultation. The formal purpose of the Operating Council is to promote the efficient and profitable development of Paper Co and all its employees, the safety, education and welfare of operations personnel, and the quality of communication and cooperation within the operations.

Critical incident: the establishment of a new employee involvement channel

Alongside union voice within Paper Co, a Joint Consultation Forum (JCF) was established in early 2005. This forum extended consultation rights to the non-manual workforce. The JCF operates in parallel with the Operating Council. The JCF and the Operating Council are supplemented by a variety of other direct involvement and communication channels, including monthly team briefings, a quarterly magazine, a company intranet and notice boards.

The establishment of the JCF within Paper Co was management-driven at the level of the organization. The rationale for establishing the JCF was twofold:

☐ to pre-empt the ICE Regulations, which came into effect on the April 6, 2005 and legally mandated the provision of information and consultation in UK workplaces;
☐ on the basis that the human resources manager deemed information and consultation to be an indicator of best practice, particularly in light of the history and successful involvement of the Operating Council in the paper mill's operational issues.

Therefore, the establishment of the JCF was important in order to ensure the equal treatment of non-manual workers.

The structure and implementation of the JCF

A consultation committee, comprising a cross-section of managers and supervisors and four employee representatives (from the non-manual workforce), was charged with developing the JCF. These employee representatives were management-appointed rather than elected, based on who the human resources manager felt could meaningfully contribute to the consultation exercise. Three consultation meetings followed to determine the structure, the constituency, that is, the body of employees to be covered, the method of selecting employee representatives and the scope of the forum. The consultation committee also drafted the

▷

JCF constitution. The structure of the forum dominated the committee's discussions, and a number of possibilities were considered, including the extension of the Operating Council to cover non-unionized employees. However, the consultation committee decided that the most appropriate course of action was to form a separate body, the JCF, that would sit alongside the Operating Council.

During the consultation process, employee representatives had very little input into the structure and content of the constitution, since it was management that decided to implement the JCF. For the most part, human resources developed the constitution with reference to the formal provisions of the ICE Regulations and in light of the constitution of the Operating Council. The objectives of the JCF emphasized the business case for involvement and were to promote the efficient and profitable development of [Paper Co] ... and the safety and development of its employees. A formal election process, including a secret ballot, was used to fill the representative positions on the JCF and was supervised by the consultation committee. Non-manual staff employed on a permanent or temporary contract of employment were eligible to stand as representatives. Once the elections had been concluded, the constitution was signed by management and the JCF representatives during a joint meeting between the consultation committee and the JCF members. The consultation committee was subsequently abandoned.

On the JCF, provision is made for the appointment of five employee representatives from the non-manual workforce, who tend to be office-based. The average representative load is 30 employees per representative. Representatives serve a 2-year term and are allowed to stand for re-election; there is no limit on the number of terms that a representative may serve. On the management side, the finance director is the chair of the JCF, and the operations director is a permanent member of the JCF. The senior human resources advisor is the JCF secretary. UNITE (as the representative union) has not been assigned a formal seat on the JCF, but rather an observational role. In practice, however, union representatives participate in JCF discussions. Non-union representatives on the JCF are sceptical of the presence of union representatives and question whether they add any value to the consultation process. For example, union representatives do not always attend meetings owing to their shift patterns being inconsistent with the timing and dates of JCF meetings, and it is felt that union representatives tend to raise issues that relate only to their members.

The scope of the JCF is fairly broad. As Box 1 shows, issues relating to the workplace, the economic situation, employment prospects and work organization all fall within the ambit of the forum. However, the constitution is vague in terms of what information and consultation entails in practice: these terms are not formally defined. There is also no reference to the timing of consultation, or the extent to which managers involve employees in the issues listed in Box 1.

Box 1 The scope of the JCF at Paper Co

Issues included:

☐ The workplace
☐ The economic situation of the business
☐ Employment prospects within the business
☐ Training and development
☐ Decisions likely to lead to substantial changes in work organization or contractual relations
☐ Social and welfare facilities

Issues excluded:

☐ Matters related to pay, terms and conditions of employment, and individual employee issues beyond the scope of the JCF

The constitution provides for quarterly meetings to be conducted in a positive and constructive atmosphere, where individual contributions are to be encouraged and respected, and considered in terms of the effect on all parts of the business. Parties to the JCF are reminded that some subjects may be highly sensitive and should thus be treated as private and confidential. However, although no confidentiality agreements exist, management has also not provided representatives with any information that they have asked to be kept confidential in practice. Rights to time off and training are addressed within the constitution. Representatives are given 'reasonable' time to carry out their representative duties and the right to attend any training felt necessary for their development. The training of representatives so far has been conducted by the Involvement and Participation Association (IPA). The IPA facilitated a 1-day training session for all management and employee representatives at the inception stage of the JCF, and additional training took place 2 years later for those representatives who had joined the forum within this period.

The operation of the JCF

The senior human resources advisor is responsible for compiling the JCF agenda and e-mails representatives 2 weeks in advance of each meeting for suggestions. Employee representatives rely on e-mail and informal interaction in their search for agenda items. In practice, however, few employees put forward suggestions to their representatives.

Networking between the representatives is fairly formalized. Although the constitution does not provide for formal pre-meetings of representatives, with management's consent, non-union employee representatives meet formally before the agenda is finalized. These meetings are used by the representatives to clarify any issues that employees propose to the JCF, and to discuss what information the representatives should seek from management at the next meeting. The finance director and senior human resources advisor also meet once a week before JCF meetings to discuss the agenda. After each meeting, the minutes of the JCF are posted on the intranet and on office notice boards. However, employee representatives do not formally report back to employees what happened at the JCF, either face to face or as a collective group.

Issues raised and impact on decision-making

All parties to the JCF are content with the frequency of meetings and the relaxed manner in which these are conducted. Nevertheless, a general sentiment among the human resources manager, senior human resources advisor and employee representatives is that the nature of the JCF is to provide information rather than being for consultation. The agenda is also seen as one-way, weighted towards employee-initiated rather than management-initiated issues. Issues voiced by representatives are largely 'office-based' and concern organizational welfare issues rather than strategic matters applicable to the larger mill. Examples of employees' suggestions made to the JCF have encompassed dress-down Fridays, on-site maintenance and transport, car parking, showers, site access cards, health and safety and canteen facilities.

Despite the preoccupation of the JCF with welfare issues, the scope of issues considered has broadened, particularly since the IPA's second training session in 2007. This development of the JCF has heightened employees' confidence in, and expectations for, information and consultation. Examples of higher level issues considered by the JCF since 2007 include flexible working practices and individual performance-related pay for non-manual employees. Some representatives do, however, feel that the potential impact of IPA training, in terms of advancing the scope of the JCF, has been weakened by the lack of participation of management and existing representatives.

Despite the fact that higher level issues have been raised by the JCF, employees have also reported that these were not discussed or considered in depth by management. For example, the prospect of introducing performance-related pay for non-manual employees was rejected outright, generating scepticism and distrust among employees regarding the level of employee involvement provided in practice.

The representatives' perceptions of how management treats employees' suggestions and ideas (the extent of management buy-in) varied. On the positive side, there was a sentiment that meetings were conducted in a relaxed and sociable manner, and that management were genuine in their efforts to discuss matters raised within the JCF. Tangible changes have also resulted from the issues raised on the JCF. Examples include the cycle to work scheme, a health care plan and changes to the inside and exterior of the mill. Nevertheless, there was a conception among representatives that the finance director was reluctant in his role as chair of the JCF, and that management were not fully engaged, evidenced by the fact that they were selective in the information they provided to employees, particularly regarding Paper Co's future plans. Nevertheless, at each meeting, management provides an overview that includes the company's financial situation, sales figures, news items and a summary of the issues raised at the previous meeting. Some employees feel, however, that this does not provide added value over and above the information already available on the intranet.

The JCF has been used for consultation. Examples include the implementation of policies regarding bullying and harassment, smoking legislation, the company pension scheme and redundancies. Separate subcommittees were established to handle these issues individually, yet the ability of employees to influence management's final decision was limited, demonstrating a reactive approach to consultation by management. Management's reluctance to share decision-making power has been largely evidenced by the stage at which consultation has taken place. The human resources manager and the majority of representatives perceived that consultation has tended to happen too late in the decision-making process. The JCF is therefore seen as a 'toothless beast'. One example was during a redundancy process in which management was seen to pay lip service to employees' suggestions for alternative ways in which management could reduce costs, in order to subsequently reduce the number of redundancies.

▷

Impact and effectiveness of the JCF

Senior managers and employee representatives believe that the JCF is a good initiative within the company, despite some cynicism that the scope and influence of the JCF are trivial. For managers and employee representatives, the JCF is perceived as an important upward communication tool, enabling employees to understand the progress and situation of the company, in addition to providing a channel to raise issues of concern. This then allows management to take advantage of employees' initiatives and ideas and to develop better solutions and make better, more informed decisions. For employees, the beneficial outcomes include increased levels of trust, involvement and engagement.

Despite these common views, the scope and impact of the JCF, in terms of delivering genuine employee involvement and acting as a driver of change, is less clear. This lack of impact is illustrated by the wider lack of interest in the JCF among employees which acts as a source of frustration for representatives. It is also important to note that Paper Co has not reviewed the effectiveness of the JCF since its introduction. Nevertheless, the JCF is seen as an effective mechanism operating alongside the Operating Council, particularly with regard to organization-wide issues such as redundancies.

Despite the successful co-existence of union and non-union voice mechanisms in Paper Co, albeit for different sections of the workforce and different areas of the business, there is a sentiment among employees that communication from senior and line management has deteriorated as company profitability has fallen, prompting a suggestion that management inform and consult only in the 'good times'. A new CEO has also been seen to lack visibility and presence among the employees, particularly at the lower organizational levels. These perceptions reinforce among employees their view of a lack of leadership, varied management styles and the selective distribution of information. Employees have also reported that interdepartmental communication has been lacking. Regardless of these criticisms of leadership and communication, employees have also reported that Paper Co is a good place to work, due to the existence of close working and social relationships, good working conditions, varied shift patterns, staff development opportunities, a family feel and a strong culture of safety.

Source: Dr Elaine Bull, Kingston University

Questions

1 Utilising Marchington and Wilkinson's (2002) typology, how would you classify the JCF at Paper Co?

2 What are the strengths and weaknesses of the JCF in Paper Co?

3 To what extent do management at Paper Co exhibit a lack of buy-in or commitment to employee involvement?

4 Employee representatives on the JCF reported a lack of interest among employees. What factors might explain the indifference of employees to the JCF?

5 The CEO of Paper Co has asked you to strategically advise on how the JCF can be developed in order to be more effective in the future. Identify and justify your recommendations for the improvement of the JCF.

References

Boxall, P. and Macky, K. (2009) Research and theory on high-performance work systems: progressing the high-involvement stream. *Human Resource Management Journal*, 19(1): 3–23.

Boxall, P. and Purcell, J. (2003) *Strategy and Human Resource Management*. Basingstoke: Palgrave Macmillan.

Brewster, C., Croucher, R., Wood, G. and Brookes, M. (2007) Collective and individual voice: convergence in Europe? *International Journal of Human Resource Management*, 18(7): 1246–62.

Brown, M., Geddes, L. A. and Heywood, J. S. (2009) The determinants of employee-involvement schemes: private sector Australian evidence. *Economic and Industrial Democracy*, 28(2): 259–91.

Bryson, A. (2004) Managerial responsiveness to union and nonunion worker voice in Britain. *Industrial Relations*, 43(1): 213–41.

Bryson, A. and Freeman, R. B. (2007) What voice do British workers want? In Freeman, R.B., Boxall P. and Haynes, P. (eds) *What Workers Say: Employee Voice in the Anglo-American Workplace*. Ithaca, NY: Cornell University Press, pp. 72–96.

Carley, M. (2007) Partnership deal agreed in papermaking industry. *European Industrial Relations Observatory*. Available from: http://www.eurofound.europa.eu/eiro/2007/08/articles/uk0708019i.htm [accessed 18 October 2008].

13

Charlwood, A. and Terry, M. (2007) 21st-century models of employee representation: structures, processes and outcomes. *Industrial Relations Journal*, 38(4): 320–37.

Confederation of Paper Industries (2008) 2008 Annual Review. Confederation of Paper Industries. Available from: http://www.paper.org.uk/information/annualreviews/2008review.pdf [accessed 10 September 2011].

Cooper, R. and Ellem, B. (2008) The neoliberal state, trade unions and collective bargaining in Australia. *British Journal of Industrial Relations*, 46(3): 532–54.

Cox, A., Zagelmeyer, S. and Marchington, M. (2006) Embedding employee involvement and participation at work. *Human Resource Management Journal*, 16(3): 250–67.

Diamond, W. and Freeman, R. B. (2001) *What Workers Want from Workplace Organizations: A Report to the TUC's Promoting Trade Unionism Task Group*. London: Trades Union Congress.

Dundon, T. and Gollan, P. (2007) Re-conceptualizing voice in the non-union workplace. *International Journal of Human Resource Management*, 18(7): 1182–98.

Dundon, T., Wilkinson, A., Marchington, M. and Ackers, P. (2004) The meanings and purpose of employee voice. *International Journal of Human Resource Management*, 15(6): 1150–71.

European Commission (2001) *EU Employment and Social Policy 1999–2001: Jobs, Cohesion, Productivity*. Luxembourg: Office for Official Publications of the European Communities.

European Foundation for the Improvement of Living and Working Conditions (2005) *Employee Financial Participation in the European Union*. Dublin: European Foundation for the Improvement of Living and Working Conditions.

Fiorito, J. (2001) Human resource management practices and worker desires for union representation. *Journal of Labor Research*, 22(2): 335–54.

Freeman, R. B. and Rogers, J. (1999) *What Workers Want*. Ithaca, NY: Cornell University Press.

Freeman, R. B., Boxall, P. and Haynes, P. (2007) *What Workers Say: Employee Voice in the Anglo-American Workplace*. Ithaca, NY: Cornell University Press.

Gallie, D. and White, M. (1993) *Employee Commitment and the Skills Revolution*. London: Policy Studies Institute.

Godard, J. (2001) High-performance and the transformation of work? The implications of alternative work practices for the experience and outcomes of work. *Industrial and Labor Relations Review*, 54: 776–805.

Gollan, P. (2006) Editorial: Consultation and non-union employee representation. *Industrial Relations Journal*, 37(5): 428–37.

Gollan, P. and Wilkinson, A. (2007) Implications of the EU Information and Consultation Directive and the regulations in the UK: prospects for the future of employee representation. *International Journal of Human Resource Management*, 18(7): 1145–58.

Green, F. (2004) Why has work effort become more intense? *Industrial Relations*, 43(4): 709–41.

Hall, M. (2005) Assessing the information and consultation of employees regulations. *Industrial Law Journal*, 34(2): 103–26.

Hall, M., Hutchinson, S., Parker, J., Purcell, J. and Terry, M. (2007) *Implementing Information and Consultation: Early Experience under the ICE Regulations*. Department for Business, Enterprise and Regulatory Reform, Employment Relations Research Series No. 88. London: Department for Business Enterprise and Regulatory Reform/CIPD/ACAS.

Hall, M., Hutchinson, S., Purcell, J., Terry, M. and Parker, J. (2009) *Implementing Information and Consultation: Evidence from Longitudinal Case Studies with 150 or More Employees*. Department for Business Innovation and Skills, Employment Relations Research Series No. 105. London: Department for Business Innovation and Skills.

Hardy, S. and Adnett, N. (2006) 'Breaking the ICE': workplace democracy in a modernized social Europe. *International Journal of Human Resource Management*, 17(6): 1021–31.

Holland, P., Pyman, A., Cooper, B. and Teicher, J. (2011) Employee voice and job satisfaction in Australia: the centrality of direct voice. *Human Resource Management*, 50(1): 95–111.

Hyman, R. (2005) Whose (social) partnership? In Stuart, M. and Martinez Lucio, M. (eds.) *Partnership and Modernisation in Employment Relations*. Oxford: Routledge, pp. 251–65.

Kalmi, P., Pendleton, A. and Poutsma, E. (2005) Financial participation and performance in Europe. *Human Resource Management Journal*, 15(4): 54–67.

Kaplan, R. S. and Norton, D. P. (1992) The Balanced Scorecard – measures that drive performance. *Harvard Business Review*, (January – February): 71–9.

Kersley, B., Alpin, C., Forth, J. et al. (2005) Inside the Workplace: First Findings from the 2004 Workplace Employment Relations Survey (WERS 2004). Available from: http://cw.routledge.com/textbooks/0415378133/firstfindings/report.asp [accessed 6 September 2011].

Kessler, I. and Purcell, J. (1996) The value of joint working parties. *Work, Employment and Society*, 10(4): 663–82.

Knudsen, H. (1995) *Employee Participation in Europe*. London: Sage.

Leonard, D. (1998) *Wellsprings of Knowledge: Building and Sustaining the Sources of Innovation*. Boston, MA: Harvard Business School Press.

Leopold, J. (2004) Employee participation, involvement and communications. In Leopold, J., Harris L. and Watson T. (eds) *The Strategic Managing of Human Resources*. Harlow: Pearson Education, pp. 434–60.

Marchington, M. (1992) *Managing the Team*. Oxford: Blackwell.

Marchington, M. (2005) Employee involvement: patterns and explanations. In Harley, B., Hyman J. and

Thompson P. (eds) *Participation and Democracy at Work: Essays in Honour of Harvie Ramsay*. Basingstoke: Palgrave Macmillan: pp. 20–37.

Marchington, M. (2007) Employee voice systems. In Boxall, P., Purcell, J. and Wright, P. M. (eds) *The Oxford Handbook of Human Resource Management*. Oxford: Oxford University Press, pp. 231–50.

Marchington, M. and Wilkinson, A. (2002) *People Management and Development: Human Resource Management at Work* (2nd edn). London: Chartered Institute of Personnel and Development.

Marginson, P., Edwards, P., Edwards, T., Ferner, A. and Tregaskis, O. (2010) Employee representation and consultative voice in multinational companies operating in Britain. *British Journal of Industrial Relations*, 48(1): 151–80.

Noon, M. and Hoque, K. (2004) Equal opportunities policy and practice in Britain: evaluating the 'empty shell' hypothesis. *Work, Employment and Society*, 18(3): 481–506.

Poutsma, E. (2006) *Changing Patterns of Employee Financial Participation in Europe*. Nijmegen: Nijmegen School of Management.

Poutsma, E. and de Nijs, W. (2003) Broad-based employee financial participation in the European Union. *International Journal of Human Resource Management*, 14(6): 863–92.

Poutsma, E., de Nijs, W. and Poole, M. (2003) The global phenomenon of employee financial participation. *International Journal of Human Resource Management*, 14(6): 855–62.

Poutsma, E., Kalmi, P. and Pendleton, A. (2006) The relationship between financial participation and other forms of employee participation: new survey evidence from Europe. *Economic and Industrial Democracy*, 27(4): 637–67.

Purcell, J. and Georgiadis, K. (2007) Why should employers bother with worker voice? In Freeman, R. B., Boxall, P. and Haynes, P. (eds) *What Workers Say: Employee Voice in the Anglo-American Workplace*. Ithaca, NY: Cornell University Press, pp. 181–97.

Pyman, A., Cooper, B., Teicher, J. and Holland, P. (2006) A comparison of the effectiveness of employee voice arrangements in Australia. *Industrial Relations Journal*, 37(5): 543–59.

Pyman, A., Holland, P., Teicher, J. and Cooper, B. (2010) Industrial relations climate, employee voice and managerial attitudes to unions: an Australian study. *British Journal of Industrial Relations* 48(2): 460–80.

Richardson, M., Danford, A., Stewart, P. and Pulignano, V. (2010) Employee participation and involvement: experiences of aerospace and automobile workers in the UK and Italy. *European Journal of Industrial Relations*, 16(1): 21–37.

Robertson, R. (2010a) Employee. *Stakeholder Magazine*, (February): 24–7.

Robertson, R. (2010b) Workforce 2010. Employee section. *Stakeholder Magazine*, (May): 24–7.

Sako, M. (1998) The nature and impact of employee 'voice' in the European car components industry. *Human Resource Management Journal*, 8(2): 6–13.

Teicher, J., Holland, P., Pyman, A. and Cooper, B. (2007) Australian workers: finding their voice? In Freeman, R.B., Boxall, P. and Haynes, P. (eds) *What Workers Say: Employee Voice in the Anglo-American Workplace*. Ithaca, NY: Cornell University Press, pp. 125–44.

Townley, B. (1994) Communicating with employees. In Sisson, K. (ed.) *Personnel Management: A Comprehensive Guide to Theory and Practice in Britain* (2nd edn). Oxford: Blackwell, pp. 595–633.

Waddington, J. (2003) What do representatives think of the practices of European works councils? Views from six countries. *European Journal of Industrial Relations*, 9(3): 303–25.

Walton, R. E., Cutcher-Gurshenfeld, J. E. and McKersie, R. B. (1994) *Strategic Negotiations: A Theory of Change in Labor–Management Relations*. Boston, MA: Harvard Business School Press.

Wheeler, H. N. (2008) A new frontier for Labor: collect action by worker owners. *Labor Studies Journal*, 33(2): 163–78.

Wilkinson, A., Dundon, T. and Grugulis, I. (2007) Information and consultation: exploring employee involvement in SMEs. *International Journal of Human Resource Management*, 18(7): 1279–97.

Wood, S. J. and Fenton-O'Creevy, M. P. (2005) Direct involvement, representation and employee voice in UK multinationals in Europe. *European Journal of Industrial Relations*, 11(1): 27–50.

Wood, S. J. and Wall, T. D. (2007) Work enrichment and employee voice in human resource management performance studies. *International Journal of Human Resource Management*, 18(7): 1335–72.

13

Work–life balance in the 21st century

Nicolina Kamenou

14

?

After reading this chapter, you should be able to:

- ☐ Understand the changing nature of the workplace and its effects on work–life balance in a global context
- ☐ Review the changing nature of employment in relation to issues of work–life balance for different social groups, focusing on gender, age, disability, ethnicity, religion and sexuality
- ☐ Outline the range of work–life balance initiatives and flexible working practices
- ☐ Outline the legislative context for work and family balance, as well as key equality legislation
- ☐ Evaluate the societal and economic benefits and costs in relation to balancing work and life
- ☐ Outline key current debates on work–life balance issues in a global context
- ☐ Acknowledge, and engage in debates relating to, cultural specificity and variation across countries and regions in terms of issues of work–life balance
- ☐ Critically engage with key work–life balance issues through examples, questions and an end-of-chapter case study

🔍

Introduction

Globalization, increased competition, a long-hours working culture, people living longer, changes in family structures and evolving legal provisions related to employment and working conditions have a direct effect not only on individuals' workplace experiences, but also on their private and social life experiences.

This chapter engages in key debates on work–life balance (WLB) by taking a global perspective, acknowledging national and cultural differences in how WLB is perceived and how flexible working arrangements are negotiated, and noting diverse legal frameworks and workplace practices dealing with work and employment, rights for parents, carers, and so on. The experiences of social groups, including among others women, older workers and ethnic minority groups, in relation to WLB issues are also explored. A range of WLB organizational initiatives and flexible working types are presented, together with the legal protection associated with these practices. A discussion on the social and economic benefits of a healthy, fulfilled workforce is presented, as is an evaluation of the costs of inaction on the part of organizations and the government, such as the costs of high absenteeism and work-related stress. Key concepts will be evaluated and examples and exercises will be provided throughout the chapter, along with an end-of-chapter case study, in order to help readers engage with critical issues and debates on WLB in varied contexts.

Changing demographics such as the ageing population trend experienced in most developed economies, the increasing number of women in the labour market, renegotiated social roles, the rise in single-parent families and an increased awareness of diversity and legislative changes have had an impact on WLB and governmental and organizational initiatives related to WLB. The increased importance placed on the public image of organizations and the drive to engage in corporate social responsibility initiatives indicate an understanding from the employers' view of the need to engage with well-being and WLB initiatives. Coupled with legal regulation and an acknowledgment of the business case argument – that is, the argument that treating employees with respect, providing flexible working arrangements and acknowledging external-to-work responsibilities can be linked to increased productivity and commitment – this makes a compelling case for treating WLB initiatives as key to organizational success. The Sunday Times 100 Best Companies to Work For, a large-scale survey that focuses on best practice initiatives in relation to people management, includes as some of its key areas 'well-being', which relates to WLB, and 'giving something back', which focuses on whether the organization contributes to its local community and society (http://www.bestcompanies.co.uk, as cited in Bolton and Wibberley, 2007).

It should be noted at this point that the term 'balance' is often deceiving as it implies distinct lives that can be experienced as finite and separate from each other. A central critique, therefore, of discussions on WLB surrounds the problematic notion that a well-balanced approach between paid work and life outside work is assumed to be feasible (Sparrow and Cooper, 2003). The term 'balance' assumes a trade off between work and life, whereas in reality there is

14

great overlap between these two worlds, with 'no clear-cut distinction between the world of work and the work of family, friends and social networks and community' (Taylor, 2002: 17).

Despite this critique, as well as discussions on wide-ranging issues in WLB, most debates in the area have typically assumed a naive view of the 'life' aspect of the WLB equation (Kamenou, 2008). The focus has typically been placed on working mothers and family-friendly policies, but more recently the experiences of fathers and their 'contribution to the home' have been gaining increasing attention (see, for example, Featherstone, 2003; Clarke and O'Brien, 2003). Discussions on juggling work and personal demands have typically ignored issues faced by other groups, for example disabled or older workers or the carers of older or disabled people (Equal Opportunities Commission, n.d.; Gardiner et al., 2007). With few exceptions (see, for example, Rana et al., 1998; Healy et al., 2004; Bradley et al., 2005; Dale, 2005; Kamenou, 2008), issues around ethnicity, culture and religion have also been absent from the majority of discussions around WLB debates and initiatives.

One cannot assume that employment experiences are universal across the world or, indeed, universal within a country or region. Economic, sociopolitical and cultural factors, education systems and family structures will have an effect on individuals' experiences in the workplace, on the centrality of work in people's lives, on how work and family responsibilities are negotiated and on how childcare responsibilities are divided.

The following sections will engage with key issues in relation to work and life, and will critically review changing trends in employment in relation to a number of social groups who have been historically disadvantaged in the labour market. Key equality legislation for the protection of each group will also be cited. Readers are advised to refer to Chapter 4 on 'Diversity Management' for a more detailed discussion of diversity issues and equality approaches.

The changing face of employment

Gender

The number of women entering employment has been steadily increasing since World War II, with the male participation rate slowly falling. From 1971 to 2008, the female participation rate increased from 56 per cent to 70 per cent. Within the same period, the male participation rate fell from 92 per cent in 1970 to 79 per cent in 2008 (Office for National Statistics, 2008). This trend is predicted to continue, and some argue that the number of women in the labour market will be higher than that of their male counterparts in the next decade. This has been stated as a key driver for WLB and family-friendly policies in organizations (Kodz et al., 2002; Torrington et al., 2008).

There has also been a rise in the number of single-parent families, with most of these families being headed by women rather than men. The number of dual-career couples is increasing, and this trend makes the effort to 'balance' work and personal life more challenging. It is argued that today's fathers are more 'hands-on' than their own fathers and grandfathers were, and are more willing to share childcare responsibilities. Interestingly, some recent research has indicated that, in dual-career households where women earn the same as or more than their male counterparts, men are willing to help with childcare but are reluctant to support their partners with domestic work (Crompton and Lyonette, 2009). Research indicates that women typically do three-quarters of the domestic work even when they are in paid employment: they do an average of 18.5 hours a week, whereas their male counterparts typically undertake 6 hours a week of domestic work (Kan, 2001).

As stated earlier, the majority of discussions on WLB have focused on women, mainly working mothers. Although this should be acknowledged as a shortcoming in the literature as the experiences of other social groups have, in the majority, been absent, it has to be recognized that gender is a key component of WLB debates – women in the workplace still face disadvantage in employment and career progression, and are still subjected to stereotypical gendered assumptions.

Some seminal research in the UK in the 1990s brought to the forefront the shortcomings of existing organizational cultures in relation to family-friendly policies and WLB issues. Lewis (1997) and Liff and Cameron (1997) argued that there is an underlying assumption that women are not as committed to work and to their careers as their male counterparts, and women are often seen as 'the problem' (Liff and Cameron, 1997). The writers have argued that notions of commitment are therefore gendered, commitment being assessed on male standards such as hours of work and a linear career path with no career breaks. This ignores the unequal distribution of domestic and childcare responsibilities and focuses on inputs (that is, hours at work) rather than outputs (that is, productivity and end results). Moreover, Lewis (1997) argued that two main barriers to effective family-friendly policies are a low sense of entitlement to these policies by employees who do not feel they can utilize them, and organizational discourses of time, which:

> obscure the advantages of alternative ways of working, for the organization as well as for individual employees and their families, and perpetuate organizational structures which interfere with family life, and help to maintain gender inequalities. (Lewis, 1997: 21)

In the UK, a statutory Gender Equality Duty had been enforced from 2007, which required all British public authorities to actively promote gender equality and to eliminate unlawful discrimination and harassment. As discussed in Chapter 4, recent developments, such as the UK Equality Act 2010, combine previous equality legislation, including the Sex Discrimination Act 1975.

It has been argued that some countries have made further progress in renegotiating traditional gender roles. Scandinavian countries are often cited as best-practice examples of employment practices, welfare systems and initiatives on well-being. For example, Lamb (2009) contends that gender roles have successfully changed at work and home in Sweden. Swedish social policies presume that couples adopt the dual breadwinner model, which then places the

14

onus on the government and organizations to enable both men and women to be part of the labour force. Through a number of cultural or societal changes, Lamb argues that Sweden has redefined the notion of a 'good father' by emphasizing the need for men to be involved in their children's care. Critical Thinking 14.1 explores some key issues in relation to WLB and fathers in Britain in some more detail, including some questions for readers to consider.

Critical Thinking 14.1
Fathers and WLB
An Equality and Human Rights Commission (EHRC) Report has highlighted the tensions that British fathers experience in attempting to balance work and family. It touches on the lack of confidence of many fathers to request flexible working as they fear this would have a negative effect on their career as they could be perceived to be less committed to their organization. The report also states that 45 per cent of men fail to take 2 weeks' paternity leave after their child is born, citing financial reasons for not taking advantage of this policy.

Andrea Murray, Acting Group Director of Strategy from the EHRC has stated:

Two-thirds of fathers see flexible working as an important benefit when looking for a new job. This highlights an opportunity for British businesses to use flexible working as an incentive for attracting and retaining the most talented of employees. [Such policies have been associated with] increased productivity, reduction in staff turnover, reduced training costs and an ability to respond better to customer requirements.
Source: Equality and Human Rights Commission (2009)

Questions
1 What are the longer term implications of fathers not spending time with their children? Think of the impact this situation can have for both home life and organizations.
2 Imagine you are an human resources manager. Your organization has well-developed policies on WLB initiatives and flexible working arrangements, but you are aware that the 'take-up' of these initiatives is much lower for male than female staff. You will head a group meeting to discuss ways to encourage all staff who might benefit from these initiatives to utilize them. What would be your main recommendations? What barriers could you envisage facing?

Age

WLB is central to all individuals and should not always be equated with balancing work with family or childcare demands. As discussed earlier in the chapter, developing economies are faced with an ageing population, and this has a profound effect on issues to do with care, retirement and pensions. In the UK, the proportion of people over the age of 65 to people of working age is 21 to 100 (Torrington et al., 2008). It is also predicted that by 2030 more than a quarter of the population will be over 65 (Torrington et al., 2008).

With the age structure of the population changing, the competition for young employees can intensify, and the increase in the group of 35-year-olds and older will increase demand for WLB policies as men and women in this group are likely to have family commitments (Bunting, 2004). With the removal of the compulsory retirement age, the proportion of people over 60 who stay economically active will also increase, and Bunting (2004) argues that this group includes individuals who are disillusioned with work and experience low job satisfaction:

Meanwhile, those at the beginning of their working lives will increasingly have to consider how they can maintain the intensity of work over the long haul; retirement no longer beckons at sixty, but at seventy or even beyond. (Bunting, 2004: 305)

There are age-related stereotypes labelling older workers as less able to learn and adapt to technology, and younger workers as unmotivated and not experienced. Torrington et al. (2008) argue, however, that, in relation to older workers, there is evidence that people over the age of 50 can perform well and be highly motivated if the appropriate systems and support structures are in place. It is argued that the availability of flexible working arrangements, training, clear performance targets and proactive avoidance of discriminatory practices are central factors in older workers having a positive employment experience, accompanied by job satisfaction and high productivity. Platman (2002)'s study investigated the adoption of 'portfolio' careers as a means in retaining older workers in organizations. The research investigated portfolio careers in the media industry for people over the age of 50, the findings suggesting that this type of career is seen as attractive to this age group as it provides high flexibility in terms of hours and type of work, and does not impose a retirement threshold.

There is legal protection against age discrimination in the European community through the European Union's (EU) Framework Directive for Equal Treatment in Employment and Occupation (2000). This was adopted in the UK in 2006 as the Employment Equality (Age) Regulations. These Regulations cover workers of all ages and all employers, encompassing employment and vocational training, flexible working, retirement, redundancy and pay. Through this legislation, there is now no official retirement age in the UK. The 'standard' or 'default' age is 65, but this is not mandatory. The EU Directive, and subsequently the UK legislation, is seen as a response to the trend of an ageing population and therefore as capitalizing on the available pool of candidates, as well as addressing concerns about labour shortages and about age discrimination in the labour market. Interestingly, protection for age discrimination in the USA, through the Age Discrimination in Employment Act (1967) only protects individuals who are 40 years of age or older. Box 14.1 presents some good practice examples of British organizations that have actively attempted to recruit and develop employees of diverse ages.

Box 14.1 Age-positive British organizations

☐ A recent staff survey at supermarket chain Somerfield showed that 80 per cent of employees over the age of 50 felt strongly committed to the company, compared with 62 per cent overall. Similarly, older workers were more likely than others to say they were proud to work for the company.

☐ Home improvement company B&Q experienced 39 per cent less short-term absenteeism after employing older workers at one of their locations.

Source: Department for Work and Pensions (2007)

Disability

Despite extensive policies and initiatives in the UK focusing on disability, mainly developed under the Labour government, discrimination and disadvantage are still faced by people with disabilities. A lack of understanding and engagement with the varied forms of disability has been exacerbating the marginalization of disabled people. People who have a disability are a highly disparate group in that their disability can vary in terms of its severity, stability and type (Wood-hams and Danieli, 2000) and also include mental health issues, learning difficulties and sensory impairments.

Legal protection against disability discrimination was formalized in the UK with the Disability Discrimination Act in 1995 (extended in 2005), which placed the onus on employers to have to make 'reasonable adjustments' to the workplace environment and working arrangements in order to accommodate people with disabilities. Since 2006, the public sector has had specific responsibilities through the Disability Equality Duty. This duty requires employers in public sector organizations to proactively promote equality for disabled people and to carry out equality impact assessments on their policies. Disability discrimination is now covered as part of the New Equality Act 2010, mentioned above.

In terms of the need to balance work and personal life demands, it is important for employers to recognize the needs of staff with a disability or impairment. Staff who have health problems, especially long-term illnesses, are 'in particular need of working practices that facilitate a balance between work demands and life needs' (Hogarth et al., 2001: 253).

Sexual orientation

Falling outside the heterosexual (and male, white, able-bodied) norm is still a challenging situation for lesbian, gay, bisexual and transgender (LGBT) people in employment and society. Discrimination based on sexual orientation is often difficult to identify and challenge as members of the LGBT community may not disclose their sexuality due to fear of exclusion and discrimination. There is legal protection for EU Member States, and the UK's sexual orientation regulations give effect to the requirement in the Equal Treatment Framework Directive through the Employment Equality (Sexual Orientation) Regulations 2003.

The USA does not have federal legislation in place to protect lesbian, gay and bisexual people on sexual orientation grounds (Sargeant, 2009), despite a long-running campaign for national legislation. States and municipalities had the option to enforce legislation at that level, but they also had the option not to; 15 states actually have anti-gay partnership laws in place (Howenstine, 2006).

Sargeant (2009: 639) argues that lesbians, gay men, bisexuals and transgender people are placed in one category mainly for convenience in terms of identifying 'the discriminatory treatment that they jointly suffer as a result of not conforming to the expectations of a heterosexist society'. The author argues that the life experiences and discrimination faced by the 'LGBT group' are not identical and that there is a distinction in law between lesbians, gay men and bisexuals as a group and transgender people as a separate group. Sargeant's

(2009) paper explores issues of LGBT elders from a UK and a US perspective. There is very limited research on LGBT elders, and this paper argues that this group experience particular discrimination that is unique and different from the experiences of elders in general and heterosexual elders in particular.

There is little academic research on lesbian and gay parents and their experiences in the workplace and society. A report by the American Psychological Association (2005) cited research comparing the children of lesbian and gay parents with the children of heterosexual parents, and indicated that common stereotypes of the effect of gay parenting on children's sexuality and development were not supported. Early studies focused on middle-class, well-educated families, but recent research has acknowledged differences in terms of ethnicity, socioeconomic statues and regions (American Psychological Association, 2005).

Race, ethnicity, culture and religion

Protection from race discrimination in the UK came in the form of the Race Relations Act 1976 and the Race Relations (Amendment) Act 2000, and there is now protection through the Equality Act 2010. The UK public sector also has specific responsibilities through the Race Equality Duty. In terms of religion or belief, the EU's Employment Equality (Religion or Belief) Regulations 2003 provide protection for groups or individuals on the grounds of their religion or belief. An important effect of this legislation is the fact that religious groups who do not share a common ethnicity are now protected from discrimination.

As mentioned earlier in this chapter, when engaging in debates on WLB, an understanding of the diversity of forms of life and life experiences is crucial. Factors such as race, religion and culture may have an effect on how individuals conceptualize and experience key issues in terms of both their work and their personal life. Issues such as religious responsibilities, caring for extended families, and priorities in different regions and countries in relation to WLB are very important to consider. At the same time, one should not generalize and assume that specific ethnic or religious groups would behave in a specific way – the main point is that diversity should be acknowledged both within and across groups.

An area that has been receiving more attention in recent years is the impact of the interaction of gender with race, culture and religion on work and societal experiences. This section will present some key literature and key arguments in relation to ethnic minority women, focusing on their experiences in terms of work and life.

In relation to domestic labour and household structures, Gardiner (1997) has proposed that there are different experiences across racial and ethnic groups. Carby (1982) argued, for example, that the experiences of African-American and Black Caribbean women were shaped by the history of slavery and colonialism. Gardiner (1997) also contended that full-time motherhood was never dominant for this group of women as there was a necessity to work full time to support their families. More recent data support these views, with Duncan and Irwin (2004: 394) suggesting that Caribbean mothers are more likely to see 'substantial hours in employments as a built-in component of good mothering' and to

14

accept that they have the primary responsibility for childcare and domestic responsibilities as well as taking the necessity to work for granted.

Bhopal (1997: 4) contended that South Asian women's experiences may be different from those from African and Caribbean communities in that 'the specific cultural norms and standards of South Asian families may be reinforced through different forms of patriarchy experienced by women'. In addition, South Asian women may experience oppression 'by the form of marriage they participate in, the giving of dowries, participating in domestic labour and the degree of control they have in domestic finance'. She argued that although South Asian communities are diverse, there are similarities that place them in a different setting from white communities: 'there is the primacy of family over the individual … with emphasis on child rearing and family interaction patterns for both males and females' (Bhopal, 1997: 7).

Research supports the contention that a major factor of stress for ethnic minority women is their perception of living two separate lives (Bell, 1986; Denton, 1990; Davidson, 1997; Kamenou, 2008). Thomas and Aldefer (1989: 135) define this as 'bicultural stress': 'the set of emotional and physical upheavals produced by a bicultural existence'. Bell et al. (1993: 118–19) have argued that 'circumstances often dictate that, for women of colour to be successful managers, they must adopt a new identity and abandon commitment to their old culture [of racial or ethnic community]'. The bicultural stress can be intensified by the fact that the ethnic minority women's own communities may perceive them as 'traitors' when they try to fit in the white dominant culture of their organizations (Bell et al., 1993).

It is important, therefore, to acknowledge the diversity of experiences when focusing on work and life debates as placing all women – and men – in predetermined groups, regardless of their ethnicity, socioeconomic status, age or other factors, which assumes a naive understanding of the different societal and work experiences. Acknowledging different forms of life is crucial in order to engage in a realistic analysis that can inform organizational policy and practice (Kamenou, 2008).

Critical Thinking 14.2 engages in a key discussion on the interaction between choice and structural constraints in the context of employment and career development.

Critical Thinking 14.2
All about choice?
There have been ongoing debates on the importance of agency and the strategies that women and other social groups employ in determining their own career path. Hakim (1991, 1995, 2004) has argued that agency is central to women's choices in terms of decisions on whether they focus on their job or career, or whether they choose to focus on their family. Hakim has been heavily criticized for assuming that everyone can make free choices without acknowledging structural constraints (Devine, 1994; Ginn et al., 1996; McRae, 2003).

On the other side of the debate, some writers analysing women's position in the labour market have focused on the limitations imposed by structures for women's opportunities and advancement (see, for example, Walby, 1983, 1986; Bhopal, 1997). Walby's

▷ theory of patriarchy (1983, 1986) has been criticized for its indifference to the practices and motivation of individuals. As Collinson et al. (1990: 48) have argued, Walby is 'unable to explain how these social structures are constituted, and this inevitably results in a theory of patriarchy which is heavily deterministic as well as economistic'.

A number of writers have argued that an acknowledgement of the interaction of structure and agency, as well as culture, is needed when examining the impact of gender on employment (see, for example, Devine, 1994; Evetts, 2000) and of ethnicity and gender on career development (see, for instance, Kamenou, 2002, 2008).

Questions

1 In the context of the agency versus structure debate, reflect on key issues discussed in this chapter in relation to WLB. How important to do you think women's and men's choices are in relation to balancing work and life?

2 What would you consider to be the key constraints in taking up flexible working and other WLB initiatives offered in organizations?

3 Do you think there are issues or concerns that may affect some social groups more than others? Extend your discussions beyond a focus on gender, to include other groups such as ethnic minority or disabled groups.

Work–life balance initiatives and flexible working arrangements

The chapter now turns to a review of a number of WLB initiatives and flexible working arrangements.

The majority of WLB initiatives focus on arrangements to help parents or carers with children or older and disabled family members. These initiatives typically include a number of flexible working arrangements, as discussed below, as well as the possibility of on-site crèche facilities and childcare allowances. There is, however, a trend, mainly for larger organizations, to provide programmes that can benefit all of their employees; these typically centre around well-being, reducing stress and providing support. Free or subsidized health club memberships are now common in larger organizations, as are health insurance provisions. Some organizations also provide opportunities for counselling for staff who may be facing work and also personal problems. There is a wide range of flexible working arrangements, the most common being:

- part-time work;
- flexible hours;
- job-sharing;
- career breaks;
- working from home/working remotely (teleworking);
- seasonal hours;
- term-time work;
- shift-swapping;
- compressed working time;
- unpaid leave/unpaid sabbatical.

Box 14.2 provides an insight into some key WLB policies at IBM Corporation.

Dieckhoff and Gallie (2007) cite flexible working arrangements as being high on the EU agenda of economic inclusion and adaptability. The UK government policy on flexible working focuses on the business case argument; that is, the

14

> **Box 14.2 WLB policies at IBM**
>
> IBM is a multinational computer, technology and IT consulting corporation with its headquarters in New York, USA. It is a company often cited for its progressive WLB policies and flexible work initiatives. Some of the more innovative policies at IBM include:
>
> ☐ **The Self Funded Leave policy**: as stated on the IBM website, this 'policy provides scope for employees to "purchase" one to four weeks additional leave in a calendar year. This … is in addition to normal annual entitlements. All participants in the program need to take their annual leave entitlements as well as this additional leave.'
> ☐ **Men@Work:** the Men@Work program is a 2-day program allowing men to address issues such as balancing work and family issues, physical and psychological concerns, discussions on relationships, and so on.
> ☐ **Work Life Essentials:** this online portal assists IBM staff in sourcing information to help manage their work and life. The portal offers access to a wide variety of information on childcare, eldercare, multimedia resources, useful readings, seminars and educational resources, divided into three sections: Caring for the Family, Caring for Me and Caring for My Employees.
>
> *Source:* IBM website, Work Life Flexibility Programs; http://www-07.ibm.com/au/diversity/work_life_balance_programs.html (accessed April 2010)

focus is on the benefits to employers and business. Policy and practice in relation to WLB and flexible working in EU countries have in the main focused on the parents of young children, but as discussed earlier in the chapter, there has been more attention recently on other groups, such as older workers and carers.

'Flexible work' is typically seen as work outside the 'standard' arrangements of permanent, fixed daytime work of between 30 and 48 hours a week and working 'on site' (Tomlinson and Gardiner, 2009). Booth and Frank (2005), as cited in Tomlinson and Gardiner (2009), found that only two-fifths of male and female employees have 'standard' jobs in the UK. As a number of writers have argued (see, for example, Lewis, 1997; Liff and Cameron, 1997), the notion of 'standard' work assumes a male model of work characterized by continuous employment with no career breaks. There is, however, a gender dimension as research indicates that women are less likely to have this linear career model and more likely to work on a casual basis or in part-time contracts, to have career breaks and to work from home. Tomlinson and Gardiner (2009) also argue that there are gender differences in terms of the requests for flexible working. Men typically request 'flexi-time', while women more often request a reduction in hours, be it permanent or temporary.

Existing research alerts us to the dangers of flexible working arrangements as they often reinforce gendered working patterns rather than challenge them. The rhetoric, therefore, of flexible working assuming more engagement from a wider talent pool, and consequently increased productivity and commitment, may be conflated by the reality of employers using arrangements that suit them and their business, with no real impact on the gendered culture of organizations.

Guest's (1987, 1989) normative model of human resource management (HRM), based on four key dimensions (strategic integration, commitment, flexibility –

numerical and functional – and quality) has been criticized in relation to equality. HRM appears to promote equality as the emphasis is on attracting, retaining and fostering the commitment of the 'best people' for the job, regardless of irrelevant characteristics such as gender or race. The critique focuses on the argument that, in reality, HRM may be a barrier to equality as individuals may foster their own interests, there are power relations at play, and there may be a desire to maintain the status quo of inequality in order to utilize people for the benefit of the organization. For example, organizations may benefit from a system in which peripheral labour is cheaper and available on demand, with fewer benefits for individuals working at lower levels of the organization or on casual or fixed-term contracts. Such a system reinforces existing inequalities and horizontal and vertical segregation.

> **Exercise**
> - What issues do women – and men – face in employment today in relation to balancing work and personal life commitments?
> - There may be additional concerns for other social groups (that is, ethnic minority groups, people with disabilities and so on) in relation to balancing work and life. Discuss.

The legal framework

The legal framework has been developing in the area of employment and work practices, and legislation has been a key driver for developing organizational policies on family-friendly policies and, more widely, on WLB. UK legislation has been mostly driven by EU Directives, and a number of legal provisions were significantly extended in April 2003. The UK government introduced a 10-year strategy for childcare in 2004, which included proposals to extend existing statutory provisions on maternity and paternity leave. These provisions resulted in the Work and Families Act 2006 (Box 14.3), mostly effective from April 2007 onwards.

> **Box 14.3 Provisions of the UK Work and Families Act 2006**
>
> ☐ Annual leave: all staff are entitled to a minimum of 28 days' paid annual holiday, and from April 2009 Bank Holidays could be counted towards this.
> ☐ Working time: this is limited to 48 hours, unless 'opted out'. The Working Time Regulations provide for minimum rest periods and have provisions for night work.
> ☐ Parental leave: there is a right to 13 weeks' unpaid parental leave for men and women at any time up to their child's fifth birthday.
> ☐ Time off for dependant care (for family emergencies, elderly dependants, children, etc.) can be granted.
> ☐ Maternity leave: all women are entitled to 9 months' paid leave with the option of an 3 additional months on an unpaid basis. In terms of paternity leave, fathers under this Act were initially entitled to 2 weeks' paid paternity leave. In April 2010 it was announced that Additional Paternity Leave and Pay (APL&P) would enable eligible fathers to take up to 26 weeks' additional paternity leave. The leave may be paid if taken during the mother or partner's Statutory Maternity Pay period, Maternity Allowance period or Statutory Adoption Pay period, but leave taken after this period has ended will be unpaid. (http://www.bis.gov.uk/policies/employment-matters/strategies/paternity-leave)

> ☐ Adoption leave: there is entitlement to 26 weeks' ordinary adoption leave and 26 weeks' additional adoption leave.
> ☐ Right to request flexible working: employees with children under the age of 17 (under the age 18 if child is disabled) and those with caring responsibilities for adults can request a change to their working arrangements. The employer can refuse such a request on business grounds but needs to follow procedures to do so.
> ☐ Part-time work: part-timers are entitled to the same hourly rate of pay and have the same entitlements to annual leave and maternity/parental leave as full-timers on a pro-rata basis. There is the same entitlement to sick pay and the same treatment in terms of access to training.
> ☐ Detriment: an employer cannot subject an employee to a detriment because he or she has attempted to exercise the rights mentioned above. This can be taken to an employment tribunal.
>
> *Source:* Chartered Institute of Personnel and Development. Work–Life Balance Factsheet; http://www.cipd.co.uk/subjects/health/worklifebalance/worklifeba [accessed March 2010]

Continental Europe provides more comprehensive and equitable childcare arrangements than the UK. France, Denmark and Sweden offer publicly funded childcare, which has an effect in increasing female participation rates. The provision of parental leave is higher than in Britain, with 3 years offered in France, Sweden and Denmark, and with higher levels of pay. In Norway, a component of parental leave is only available to fathers in order to encourage men to take it up. Bunting (2004) cites a remarkable rise in the take-up rate of this, which increased from a mere 2 per cent in 1990 to 85 per cent in 2000. The author also cites examples from Italy, Spain and Belgium, where parents have the flexibility to spread out parental leave over a number of years.

Employee well-being and health

The implications of a long-hours culture in which commitment is often linked to inputs rather than outputs can have a negative effect on employees. As Noon and Blyton (1997) have argued, individual working hours do not always equate to an organization's operating hours, and more flexibility is demanded to serve a '24/7 society'. There is wide evidence of work intensification over the last couple of decades and of increased levels of stress. Stress is now seen as a common phenomenon in the workplace, with wide-ranging negative implications for both workers and employers. Studies have indicated that individuals in employment have been suffering from anxiety and have been experiencing work overload, loss of control and insufficient personal time (Holbeche and McCartney, 2002).

Other writers have argued that employers will occur 'costs of inaction' (see, for example, Liff and Cameron, 1997; Sparrow and Cooper, 2003) if they do not attempt to challenge the long-hours, input-driven work cultures. Some of these costs include poor health, overwork resulting in stress and stress-related illnesses, dissatisfaction, family conflicts, higher absenteeism, lower productivity and high staff turnover. Existing work cultures implicitly demand that work takes priority over everything else, including family. Bunting (2004), in her book *Willing Slaves: How the Overwork culture is Ruling our Lives*, warns about the dangers of the British overwork culture (Box 14.4) and its negative effects on our own health and the health of our children, as well as the negative impact on relationships between parents and their children.

Box 14.4 Working hours: overly committed or overly stretched?

Coats (2007) argues that the UK government may need to adopt an interventionist stance and reconsider its position in relation to the EU Working Time Directive (1993) and the UK's Working Time Regulations 1998. Coats contends that the UK government should consider a phased approach to the removal of the opt-out from the 48-hour maximum working week that the EU Working Time Directive advocates. He argues that this initiative was adopted in the Republic of Ireland with no adverse impact on economic growth or employment.

Bunting (2004: 304) argues that, in many European countries, long hours at work are considered as 'a sign of inefficiency or incompetence, rather than of commitment as it is in overwork cultures'. A number of the UK's neighbours, such as Austria, Finland, Spain and Sweden, have limits of 39- or 40-hour weeks.

Bunting also cites Australia and New Zealand as countries with an 'overwork culture' and states this is mainly due to the deregulation of the labour market: 'the number of male employees working more than eleven hours a day jumped from one in eighteen to one in eight between 1974 and 1997' (2004: 302).

International and contextual considerations in work–life balance debates

Throughout the chapter, examples were cited in countries outside the UK, mainly in Europe and in the USA, in relation to their involvement with work and life issues. This section will provide further discussion and some illustrations of key issues in different contexts, including non-Western societies such as Africa, India and Japan, as well as issues facing employees, including expatriates, in multinational corporations (MNCs) around the world.

Within international HRM research, issues are intertwined with the theories and practices of cross-cultural management and diversity management. As Özbilgin (2005: 164) argues 'the international level, by definition, embodies a greater level of diversity than the national level'. At the international level, Stephens and Black (1991), as cited in Özbilgin (2005), noted the significance of WLB issues in a study on 67 American expatriate managers and argued that recognizing the career aspirations of the expatriates' spouses and partners was an important area to consider within international HRM.

Shaffer et al. (2001) explored the impact of perceived organizational support and of work–family conflict on the psychological withdrawal of expatriates, and identified that both these factors have a direct effect on their decision to quit international assignments. These two studies highlight the importance of a better understanding of work–family issues and of the needs of family members

14

accompanying expatriates on international assignments. This understanding of and sensitivity to key issues can provide organizations with an important insight into the issues faced by international staff, and in turn to higher chances of the international assignments being successfully completed.

De Cieri and Bardoel (2008), in their study of 13 MNCs, identified key tensions in relation to the management of work–life issues. Participants in their research, mainly human resources and diversity managers, contended that WLB was important for talent management and for developing a high-performing workforce. As the authors state (p. 31): 'Managers and employees are beginning to recognize the strategic role of global work–life policies and practices in managing a global workforce; this presents several challenges for the [human resources] function in MNCs.'

As stated earlier in the chapter, it is important, when engaging with debates on balancing work and personal life, to recognize the diversity of experience in terms of regions, culture and nationality. Lewis et al. (2007) argue, however, that the WLB concept originated in a Western, neo-liberal context, particularly in the USA and the UK. This is not to argue that issues and tensions in balancing work and family/personal lives are not universal concerns. However, the context in which one operates should be kept in mind when attempting to understand these concerns as a model based on a Westernized, developed economy setting, with a reliance on market forces, may not be applicable to a developing, non-Westernized emerging economy. In the latter situation, other issues, such as rapid industrialization, security and efforts to maintain traditional family structures may be at play (Box 14.5). Recent work on the negotiated self and work identities of Indian call-centre workers has highlighted WLB tensions and stress for these workers, in the context of global outsourcing (see, for example, Aryee et al., 2005; D'Cruz and Noronha, 2008).

Box 14.5 **WLB in non-Western economies**

Lewis et al.'s (2007) study of WLB tensions involved interviews with participants in seven countries, including India, South Africa and Japan. They argue that work intensification is becoming a global phenomenon, in which long hours are equated with commitment in the context of a 'new economy'. The authors cite a participant in a South African country meeting as stating: 'You work long hours, and then you are seen as really making a difference.' An Indian management consultant is also cited as arguing that the long-hours culture 'has become so entrenched ... especially in the new economy ... we've got to work hard and ... literally give up our personal lives' (Lewis et al., 2007: 366). There is increasing attention to work–life balance challenges in Japan, partly due to the context of very low birth rates, and there are ongoing debates on how to further engage men in domestic and childcare work. One female participant argued however that:

> There is a two-tier workforce in Japan. One, which is very highly career orientated, which is described as full-time work and is largely dominated by men. The second is part-time work, which lacks any of the benefits associated with full-time work and is largely dominated by women. [Men] are seen as the breadwinners and they are desperate to get jobs that enable them to provide economically for current or future families. (p. 364)

Conclusion

This chapter has critically reviewed key WLB theories, debates and pertinent issues. It has been argued that most WLB debates have assumed a naive view of the 'life' aspect, and this chapter has attempted to provide a more balanced perspective on key issues. It has engaged with changing trends in the workplace, acknowledging the diversity of experiences across social groups and across regions. It has been highlighted throughout that both researchers and managers should be sensitive to this diversity and should not attempt to prescribe a 'one-size-fits-all' approach when offering suggestions and solutions to balancing work and personal life demands.

Some areas emerging through the discussions have focused on the dangers of equating commitment and productivity with a long-hours culture, where input is considered as more important than output. The Work Foundation (Chartered Institute of Personnel and Development, 2003) contends that managers need to shift the way they measure staff, focusing on performance and outputs. A shake-up of the existing organizational cultures and a shift to a more supportive environment, where all individuals are valued irrespective of characteristics such as gender, race and age, is crucial. In addition, the involvement of human resources as well as line managers in supporting this change and leading by example cannot be overestimated.

Glynn et al. (2002) suggest a range of management skills needed in promoting and managing flexibility, including planning, delegating fairly, understanding the capacity and skills of their staff, and being able to resist pressure from other parts of their organization when demands are deemed unrealistic. In addition to these skills, there is a need to identify a business case for WLB initiatives as this should provide organizations and staff with a clear rationale for the benefits to themselves and, in the latter case, their employers. Adapting policies to operational needs, monitoring progress and highlighting success stories are also positive steps that organizations can take in the quest for a better balance between work and life (whatever form that life may take).

As indicated through international examples, managers should be aware of differences in terms of priorities and perspectives in different regions across the world. An understanding of socioeconomic, political and cultural settings is fundamental in devising and implementing appropriate WLB policies that employers and employees can embrace and benefit from.

❓ For discussion and revision

1 What areas do WLB debates seem to be focusing on?

2 Would you consider this to be limiting? If so, in what way?

3 What can be the costs of an 'overwork' culture to both employees and organizations?

4 What key legislation can you cite which protects social groups from discrimination?

14

5   What legislation can you cite in relation to employment and work and life?

6   Highlight key differences in how employers and employees may be dealing with WLB in different regions. Think of examples in the Western, developed economies and also in non-Western, emerging markets.

7   If you were a senior human resources manager in an MNC who has been transferred to the Chinese office, how would you attempt to implement the flexible working arrangements and family-friendly policies designed at the parent company? What issues would you need to consider?

Further reading

Books

Burke, R. J and Cooper, C. L. (2008) *The Long Hours Culture: Causes, Consequences and Choices*. Bingley: Emerald Group.

An edited collection of chapters on key issues of WLB, divided into three sections of causes, consequences and choices.

Chartered Institute of Personnel and Development (2000) *Getting the Right Work–life Balance*. London: CIPD.

This research report by M. Coussey from the University of Cambridge engages with a number of real-life case studies focusing on work and life and family-friendly practices.

Felstead, A. and Jewson, N. (1999) *Global Trends in Flexible Labour*. London: Macmillan Business.

An edited book with chapters from numerous authors on flexible work and non-standard forms of employment. It includes discussions and research from European countries, such as Germany, Spain, Sweden and the UK.

Heery, E. and Salmon, J. (2000) *The Insecure Workforce*. London: Routledge.

An edited collection of chapters focusing on the 'insecurity thesis' and looking at this in a variety of contexts, such as the public sector, 'gendered employment', the psychological contract, trade unions and so on.

Houston, D. M. (2005) *Work–Life Balance in the 21st Century*. Basingstoke: Palgrave Macmillan.

An edited collection of chapters on a wide range of WLB issues including gender, careers, fatherhood, job insecurity, ethnicity and organizational cultures.

Other resources

Readers are also encouraged to utilize the following relevant websites that provide numerous articles, statistics and information on WLB issues:

☐ The Chartered Institute of Personnel and Development (CIPD): www.cipd.co.uk
☐ The Equality and Human Rights Commission (EHRC): http://www.equalityhumanrights.com/
☐ The HRM guide: http://www.hrmguide.co.uk/

Case Study Balancing work and life in a non-Western economy

Adesuwa woke up at 5:15 am to start getting ready for her job as a human resources manager in a large Nigerian bank in the busy city of Lagos. If she wanted to avoid the hectic Lagos traffic jam, she would need to leave the house by 6 am. At this time, it would only take her 20 minutes to reach the office, but if she set off any later, it could take more than 2 hours to cover the short distance. She was already dreading another long day; the return journey would be quicker if she stayed at work till about 7 pm. Her husband, Osagie, was also up and getting ready for a similar day.

Their two daughters were still peacefully asleep. They were growing up so fast: Itohan was 2 and Egie was 4 years old. She was very thankful to her parents, especially her mother, for all their help and support with the girls. Her mother and father were staying with her and Osagie, and were often relied upon to help with the kids. She couldn't help feeling guilty, though, for missing out on her children's everyday life. She wasn't sure her mum was aware of it, but she would make comments that made Adesuwa feel like a bad parent. She would often say, as Adesuwa came through the front door after a hard day at work, 'Oh, you are home ... the girls kept crying and asking for you all day.' But her mum would never say anything similar to Osagie. Comments from both her parents that she never has the time to fulfil her home responsibilities didn't help the tension she constantly felt when she was in the office.

When she arrived at work to start another day in the bank, her boss, Mr Adebayo, was standing by her desk with a large pile of staff appraisals that she need to review and countersign. They were needed by lunchtime, he mentioned on his way out. After the consolidation of Nigerian banks a few years before, competition had increased in the industry, and senior managers in her bank kept reminding staff 'how lucky' they were to have a job. This didn't really help the already tense situation, and there was a feeling of insecurity and competitiveness. The old culture of support and encouragement, which she had encountered before the consolidation, was no longer present, and Adesuwa felt that everyone was out for themselves and wanted to showcase their own individual achievements.

Adesuwa had been working as a human resources manager in this bank for 2 years, but she didn't feel she connected with her colleagues: everyone was always so busy and focused on their work. She could see, however, that staff were not necessarily productive, although they were very keen to be 'seen to be working'. Her relationship with her boss, although always courteous and professional, was sometimes strained as she felt he was not willing to listen to anything critical about the company or its processes or procedures. They had been working together for the 2 years Adesuwa had been at the bank, but he had never asked her any questions about her personal circumstances. He probably didn't even know she had young children, he never asked where she lived, whether she was driving into work or anything to do with her life outside her work. It was clear to all of his staff that he just expected everyone, men and women, to be committed to the organization, and he would often be overheard saying 'we need to put the company first'. Adesuwa knew that Mr Adebayo had teenage sons and that his wife never worked but took care of the home.

She didn't like complaining about how stressed and guilty she often felt, though, as she thought it made her sound selfish. She had a good job, security and a good enough salary. She knew of other friends and colleagues who were really struggling to make ends meet, and some had lost their jobs. She craved, however, for an organization that would at least acknowledge staff's non-work responsibilities and demands. Flexibility or flexible policies were never discussed as an option at the bank. When you were hired, it was assumed you would work full time – although it often felt like she working two days in one, from 6:30 am to 7:30 pm. There was never any acknowledgment or explicit appreciation of her hard work and the long hours she put in.

Her husband was starting to get frustrated with the demands Adesuwa's job was placing on her. He kept mentioning that he had married her and not her mother. Her mum, he would say, was the one taking care of their children and the home. Adesuwa felt Osagie didn't appreciate that this was not a clear-cut choice for her; it wasn't as if she didn't want to spend more time with her children or even just have time to rest and unwind. She sometimes contemplated looking for another job with more flexibility, but from her preliminary investigations, she knew the salary would not be as good – and they needed the money.

Adesuwa was almost half way through the appraisal forms. It was 10:30 am and she was already exhausted. She had four meetings scheduled in the afternoon and still had to prepare for two of them, but her mind was elsewhere. Her mum had

14

▷

told her the previous night that she and her father were 'too old to be full-time parents for the second time'. Adesuwa didn't know what to do. She had been talking to another female human resources manager, Grace, who had been facing similar issues, but neither of them could find a way round their problems and recurring guilt. Adesuwa enjoyed her job, she knew she was good at it, and she prided herself in being known as conscientious and reliable. She had ambitions to progress further, but she also felt she was missing out on so much at home. Her husband had mentioned a couple of times recently that if he started making more money, she could stop working, but she didn't want that. It was now 12 pm and she had finished countersigning all the forms. She had about 15 minutes for a quick early lunch, and then she would need to go straight into her meetings.

Her boss was still at work when she started getting ready to leave at 7:15 that evening. He had another couple of hours of work to get through before he could leave. Adesuwa looked exhausted when he saw her leaving. She was a hard worker and he valued her contribution to his team. He knew she was struggling with the long hours at work and with having two young girls at home. A few times he thought of chatting to her about it and telling her that she was working 'over and above the call of duty', but he was unsure about acknowledging this openly. He didn't want her to start thinking that she could get a better job elsewhere as this would mean losing one of his best employees.

Adesuwa opened the front door to her home at 8 that evening. Her mum had managed to keep the girls awake so she could at least hold them and play with them for the next 20 minutes or so. They were tired though, so they were fast asleep by 9. Her husband walked in as her mum was laying the table for them to eat. Adesuwa could hardly hold a conversation as she was eating her dinner. She could feel her mum's disapproving stare on her, but she chose not to acknowledge it or say anything. She and Osagie got up, said goodnight to her parents and went to bed exhausted, knowing that the next day would be very similar to the one they had just had.

Some background/context for guidance

A consolidation exercise of Nigerian banks took place in 2005, and a number of banks merged at that point. The case study uses this background as the relevant context in order to acknowledge tensions, job insecurities and increased competition that might have developed following this change.

Some key issues to be considered relate to the culture of the organization and the hesitation experienced by Adesuwa's boss, Mr Adebayo, in acknowledging the demands of Adesuwa's life outside work. It seems that his situation is different as he has a wife at home and older children, and he may be lacking an understanding of the demands on a dual-career couple. His views with regard to recognizing his employees' hard work is also a concern as this management style can create alienation, resentment and eventually a higher turnover, which is what Adesuwa's boss is trying to avoid. There are no flexible policies in the organization, and students should discuss this as well as the culture of the organization, where 'presenteeism' seems to equate to commitment.

In the home, Adesuwa is expected to 'take care of the home', and both her husband and parents seem – implicitly or explicitly – to have that expectation. Her work is not considered to be as important as her home demands, and although she receives much practical support, mainly from her mum, this does not always alleviate the tension and guilt she is feeling.

Students should engage with both work and personal life experiences, discuss the context/background to the case study, and acknowledge potential cultural differences in terms of the region/country in which this case study is situated. They should suggest organizational developments, such as the development of flexible work and/or family-friendly policies in the organization. There is no 'one solution' to the problems presented here, but instead a critical engagement, using material, literature and examples from the chapter, should guide students in answering the questions below.

Questions

1 What are the key issues Adesuwa is facing at work and at home?

2 Is she receiving support from her organization? What is her relationship with her manager?

3 What areas could be improved at work to help her better balance her work and personal life demands?

4 Is she receiving support from her family? What is the form of this support? Could her husband and parents further support her in order to alleviate her stress?

5 Could the long work hours that both Adesuwa and Osagie experience have an impact on their relationship with their daughters? In what ways?

6 Could there be any cultural elements that readers need to be sensitive in when offering their suggestions?

▷

Guided reading

Ituma, A. and Simpson, R. (2007) Moving beyond Schein's typology: individual career anchors in the context of Nigeria. *Personnel Review*, 36(6): 978–95.

Lewis, S., Gambles, R. and Rapoport, R. (2007) The constraints of a work–life balance approach: an international perspective. *International Journal of Human Resource Management*, 18(3): 360–73.

Kamenou, N. (2008) Reconsidering work–life balance debates: challenging limited understandings of the 'life' component in the context of ethnic minority women's experiences. Special Issue on Gender in Management: new theoretical perspectives. *British Journal of Management*, 19(S1): S99–109.

References

American Psychological Association (2005) *Lesbian and Gay Parenting.* Washington: APA.

Aryee, S., Srinivas, E. S. and Tan, H. H. (2005) Rhythms of life: antecedents and outcomes of work–family balance in employed parents. *Journal of Applied Psychology*, 90(1): 132–46.

Bell, E. L. (1986) The power within: bicultural life structures and stress among black women. Unpublished PhD dissertation, Case Western Reserve University.

Bell, E. L., Denton, T., C. and Nkomo, S. (1993) Women of color in management: towards an inclusive analysis. In Larwood, L. and Gutek, B. (eds), *Women in Management: Trends, Issues, and Challenges in Managerial Diversity.* California: Sage.

Bhopal, K. (1997) *Gender, 'Race' and Patriarchy: A Study of South Asian Women.* Farnham: Ashgate.

Bolton, S. C. and Wibberley, G. (2007) Best companies, best practice and dignity at work. In Bolton, S. C. (ed.), *Dimensions of Dignity at Work.* Burlington: Butterworth-Heinemann, pp. 134–53.

Booth, A. L. and Frank, J. (2005) Gender and work–life flexibility in the labour market. In Houston, D. M. (ed.), *Work–life Balance in the 21st Century.* Basingstoke: Palgrave Macmillan, pp. 11–28.

Bradley, H., Healy, G. and Mukherjee, N. (2005) Multiple burdens: problems of work–life balance for ethnic minority trade union activist women. In Houston, D. (ed.), *Work–life Balance in the 21st Century.* Basingstoke: Palgrave Macmillan, pp. 211–29.

Bunting, M. (2004) *Willing Slaves: How the Overwork Culture is Ruling Our Lives.* London: HarperCollins.

Carby, H. V. (1982) White women listen! Black feminism and the boundaries of sisterhood. In Centre for Contemporary Cultural Studies. *The Empire Strikes Back: Race and Racism in 70s Britain.* London: Hutchinson, pp. 212–35.

Chartered Institute of Personnel and Development (2003) Managers obstruct flexibility. *People Management*, 9(18): 9.

Clarke, L. and O'Brien, M. (2003) Father involvement in Britain: the research and policy evidence. In Day, R. and Lamb, M. (eds), *Reconceptualising and Measuring Fatherhood.* Mahwah, NJ: Lawrence Erlbaum, pp. 34–52.

Coats, D. (2007) Respect at work: just how good are British workplaces? In Bolton, S. C. (ed.), *Dimensions of Dignity at Work.* Burlington: Butterworth-Heinemann, pp. 53–70.

Collinson, D., Knights, D. and Collinson, M. (1990) *Managing to Discriminate.* London: Routledge.

Crompton, R. and Lyonnette, C. (2009) Partners' Relative Earnings and the Domestic Division of Labour. Paper presented at the Gender Inequalities in the 21st Century, Queen's College, Cambridge, 26–27 March.

Dale, A. (2005) Combining family and employment: evidence from Pakistani and Bangladeshi women. In Houston, D. (ed.), *Work–Life Balance in the 21st Century.* Basingstoke: Palgrave Macmillan, pp. 230–45.

Davidson, M. J. (1997) *The Black and Ethnic Minority Woman Manager: Cracking the Concrete Ceiling.* London: Paul Chapman.

D'Cruz, P. and Noronha, E. (2008) Doing emotional labour: the experiences of Indian call centre agents. *Global Business Review*, 9: 131–47.

De Cieri, H. and Bardoel, E. A. (2008) Tensions for HR: Who Takes Responsibility for Work–Life Management in Multinational Corporations? Final Report to the Society for Human Resource Management (SHRM) Research Foundation. Based on a paper presented to the Academy of International Business Annual Conference, June 30 – July 4, Milan, Italy.

Denton, T. C. (1990) Bonding and supportive relationships among black professional women: rituals of restoration. *Journal of Organizational Behavior*, 11: 447–57.

Department for Work and Pensions (2007) Flexible Retirement and Retirement: Age Positive Guide. Available from: http://www.dwp.gov.uk/docs/AP_Retirement_Guide.pdf [accessed 9 September 2011].

14

Devine, F. (1994) Segregation and supply: preferences and plans among 'self-made' women. *Gender, Work and Organization*, 1(2): 94–109.

Dieckhoff, M. and Gallie, D. (2007) The renewed Lisbon strategy and social inclusion policy. *Industrial Relations Journal*, 38(6): 480–502.

Duncan, S. and Irwin, S. (2004) The social patterning of values and rationalities: mothers' choices in combining caring and employment. *Social Policy and Society*, 3(4): 391–9.

Equality and Human Rights Commission (2009) Fathers Struggling to Balance Work and Family: Working Dads Want More Time with Their Children. Available from: http://www.equalityhumanrights.com/media-centre/october-2009/fathers-struggling-to-balance-work-and-family/ [accessed 9 September 2011]

Equal Opportunities Commission (n.d.) Policy Statement: Carers and Work–Life Balance. Available from:http://www.eoc.org.uk/Default.aspx?page=15440 [accessed August 2006].

Evetts, J. (2000) Analysing change in women's careers: culture, structure and action dimensions. *Gender, Work and Organization*, 7(1): 57–67.

Featherstone, B. (2003) Taking fathers seriously. *British Journal of Social Work*, 33: 239–54.

Gardiner, J. (1997) *Gender, Care and Economics*, Basingstoke: Macmillan.

Gardiner, J., Stuart, M., Forde, C., Greenwood, I., MacKenzie, R. and Perrett, R. (2007) Work–life balance and older workers: employees' perspectives on retirement transitions following redundancy. *International Journal of Human Resource Management*, 18(3): 476–89.

Ginn, J., Arber, S., Brannen, J., Dale, A., Dex, S., Elias, P., et al. (1996) Feminist fallacies: a reply to Hakim on women's employment. *British Journal of Sociology*, 47(1): 167–74.

Glynn, C., Steinberg, I. and McCartney, C. (2002) *Work–Life Balance: The Role of the Manager*. Horsham: Roffey Park Institute.

Guest, D. E. (1987) Human resource management and industrial relations. *Journal of Management Studies*, 24(5): 503–21.

Guest, D. E. (1989) Personnel and HRM: can you tell the difference? *Personnel Management*, (January): 48–51.

Hakim, C. (1991) Grateful slaves and self-made women: fact and fantasy in women's work orientations. *European Social Review*, 7(2): 102–21.

Hakim, C. (1995) Five feminist myths about women's employment. *British Journal of Sociology*, 46(3): 429–55.

Hakim, C. (2004) *Key Issues in Women's Work: Female Diversity and the Polarisation of Women's Employment*. London: Glass House Press.

Healy, G., Bradley, J. and Mukherjee, N. (2004) Inspiring Union women – black and minority ethnic women in trade unions. In Healy, G., Heery, E., Taylor, P. and Brown, W. (eds), *The Future of Worker Representation*. London: Palgrave, pp. 103–26.

Hogarth, T., Hasluck, C., Pierre, G. Winterbotham, M. and Vivian, D. (2001) *Work–Life Balance 2000: Results from the Baseline Study*. Norwich: Department of Education and Employment Institute for Employment Research with IFF Research.

Holbeche, L. and McCartney, C. (2002) *The Roffey Park Management Agenda*. Horsham: Roffey Part Institute.

Howenstine, D. W. (2006) Beyond rational relations: the constitutional infirmities of anti-gay partnership laws under the equal protection clause. *Washington Law Review*, 81(2): 417–46.

Kamenou, N. (2002) Ethnic minority women in English organisations: career experiences and opportunities. Unpublished PhD thesis, Leeds University Business School, University of Leeds.

Kamenou, N. (2008) Reconsidering work–life balance debates: challenging limited understandings of the 'life' component in the context of ethnic minority women's experiences. Special Issue on Gender in Management: New Theoretical Perspectives. *British Journal of Management*, 19(S1): S99–109.

Kan, M. (2001) *Gender Asymmetry in the Division of Domestic Labour. Who Does the Housework? Report*. Colchester: University of Essex Institute for Social and Economic Research.

Kodz, J., Harper, H. and Dench, S. (2002) *Work–Life Balance: Beyond the Rhetoric*. Institute for Employment Studies Report No. 384. Brighton: Institute for Employment Studies.

Lamb, M. (2009) Mothers, Fathers, or Parents at Home and at Work. Paper presented at Gender Inequalities in the 21st Century, Queen's College, Cambridge, 26–27 March.

Lewis, S. (1997) 'Family friendly' employment policies: a route to changing organizational cultures or playing about at the margins? *Gender, Work and Organization*, 4(1): 13–23.

Lewis, S., Gambles, R. and Rapoport, R. (2007) The constraints of a work–life balance approach: an international perspective. *International Journal of Human Resource Management*, 18(3): 360–73.

Liff, S. and Cameron, I. (1997) Changing equality cultures to move beyond 'women's problems'. *Gender, Work and Organization*, 4(1): 35–46.

McRae, S. (2003) Choice and constraints in mothers' employment careers: McRae replies to Hakim. *British Journal of Sociology*, 54(4): 585–92.

Noon, M. and Blyton, P. (1997) *The Realities of Work*. London: Macmillan Business.

Office for National Statistics (2008) Working Lives: Employment Rates Higher for Men, ONS focus on gender. Available from: http://www.sigmascan.org/Live/Source/ViewSource.aspx?SourceId=7373 [accessed 15 September 2011].

Özbilgin, M. (2005) *International Human Resource Management: Theory and Practice*. London: Palgrave Macmillan.

Platman, K. (2002) Matured assets. *People Management*, 8(24): 40–2.

Rana, B. K., Kagan, C., Lewis, S. and Rout, U. (1998) British South Asian women managers and professionals: experiences of work and family. *Women in Management Review*, 13(6): 221–32.

Sargeant, M. (2009) Age discrimination, sexual orientation and gender identity: UK/US perspectives. *Equal Opportunities International*, 28(8): 634–45.

Shaffer, M. A., Harrison, D. A., Gilley, K. M. and Luk, D. M. (2001) Struggling for balance amid turbulence on international assignments: work–family conflict, support and commitment. *Journal of Management*, 27(1): 99–121.

Sparrow, P. R. and Cooper, C. L. (2003) *The Employment Relationship: Key Challenges for HR*. Oxford: Butterworth-Heinemann.

Stephens, G. K. and Black, S. (1991) The impact of spouse's career orientation on managers during international transfers. *Journal of Management Studies*, 28: 417–28.

Taylor, R. (2002) *The Future of Work–Life Balance*. Swindon: Economic and Social Research Council.

Thomas, D. A. and Aldefer, C. P. (1989) The influence of race on career dynamics: theory and research on minority career experiences. In Arthur, M., Hall, D. T. and Lawrence, B. S. (eds), *Handbook of Career Theory*. Port Hope, ON: Cambridge University Press , pp. 133–58.

Tomlinson, J. and Gardiner, J. (2009) Organisational approaches to flexible working: perspectives of equality and diversity managers in the UK. *Equal Opportunities International*, 28(8): 671–86.

Torrington, D., Hall, L. and Taylor, S. (2008) *Human Resource Management*. Harlow: Prentice Hall.

Walby, S. (1983) Patriarchal structures: the case of unemployment. In Gamarnikow, E., Morgan, D., Purvis, J. and Taylorson, D. (eds), *Gender, Class and Work*. London: Heinemann.

Walby, S. (1986) *Patriarchy at Work*. Oxford: Polity Press.

Woodhams, C. and Danieli, A. (2000) Disability and diversity – a different too far? *Personnel Review*, 29(3): 402–17.

Managing human resources and quality

Ebrahim Soltani

15

?

After reading this chapter, you should be able to:

☐ Understand the nature and definitions of total quality and human resource management practices

☐ Examine the underlying assumptions of total quality management and the key elements of the human resource management cycle

☐ Analyse the linkages between total quality and human resource management

☐ Discusses how human resource practices support the successful implementation of quality management programmes

☐ Reassess the vital role of human resource practices in the success of quality management programmes

Introduction

The aim of this chapter is to discuss the link between total quality management (TQM) and human resource management (HRM). By reviewing the relevant literature, it is possible to make out a case for compatibility between the two concepts. In doing this, the frequently cited elements of the 'HRM cycle' have been used to discuss the vital role of human resources in enhancing quality and organizational productivity. To provide empirical verification for the link, we base our arguments on inference from a range of theoretical and previously published research in the two domains of quality and HRM.

The chapter is organized as follows. The first section begins by defining TQM and HRM and their underlying precepts. The second section examines the linkages between TQM and HRM and the role of human factors in the successful implementation of quality programmes. In order to explain this link, HRM practices are grouped into four functional areas: work organization, staffing and planning, training and development, and performance appraisal and remuneration. The third and final section reassesses the vital role of HRM practices in the success of TQM programmes.

TQM and HRM: definitions and underlying assumptions

A review of the literature on TQM reveals that TQM has a rather imprecise nature (see Deming, 1986; Hill and Wilkinson, 1995; Wilkinson et al., 1998; Oakland, 2004; Dale et al., 2007; Soltani et al., 2008b). TQM encompasses a vast spectrum of definitions, topics and approaches. For example, the British Quality Association defines TQM in terms of 'hard' and 'soft' aspects of quality management practices. The systematic measurement and control of work, setting standards of performance and using statistical procedures to assess quality are examples of hard TQM. Customer orientation, a culture of excellence, the removal of performance barriers, teamwork, training and employee participation are considered to constitute the 'soft' qualitative characteristics of TQM (**see** Wilkinson et al., 1998; Rahman and Sohal, 2002).

Such an integration of hard and soft approaches to quality is characterized by three features (Wilkinson, 1992; Wilkinson et al., 1998): an obsession with quality, the need for a scientific approach, and the view that all employees are to be involved in this process (see Summers, 2005; Fotopoulos and Psomas, 2009). Most advocates of TQM, for example Oakland (2004), are more influenced by a mixture of both soft and hard aspects of TQM practices and propose a definition of this mode as follows:

> TQM is an approach to improving the effectiveness and flexibility of business as a whole, meeting customer requirements both external and internal to the organization. It is an integrated effort, aiming at organizing and involving the whole organization, every department, every single person at every level. (Crosby, 1979; Sila and Ebrahimpour, 2005; Reid and Sanders, 2009)

15

Despite the fact that a great deal of confusion has surrounded definitions of and approaches to TQM over the past three decades, there is now reasonable agreement on what TQM actually comprises as a generic approach to the management of organization. Based on insights from the writings of TQM gurus (see, for example, Feigenbaum, 1961; Crosby, 1979; Deming, 1986), Zaire (1991) sites his account of TQM approaches in terms of three important aspects: continuous improvement, value-added management, and employee involvement. Price and Gaskill (1990) have identified three dimensions of TQM: the product and service dimension, the people dimension, and the process dimension. Similarly, Flynes' (1999) review of empirical studies of quality management practices highlights seven key quality practices:

- □ top management support;
- □ process management;
- □ product design;
- □ workforce management;
- □ quality information;
- □ supplier involvement
- □ customer involvement.

(For further detail, see Powell, 1995; Bank, 2000; Sousa and Voss, 2002; Sila and Ebrahimpour, 2005; Soltani et al., 2005). In the interest of clarity, Box 15.1 lists the major features of TQM proposed by some of the leading theorists of quality management.

TQM is therefore seen as a holistic and organizational-wide approach based on three fundamental precepts (Hill and Wilkinson, 1995):

- □ customer focus (that is, considering both internal employees and end customers);
- □ process orientation;
- □ continuous improvement.

These three precepts and other versions of TQM (see Box 15.1) fundamentally represent two quite different perspectives on TQM (Torrington and Hall, 1998): the 'hard' statistical approach versus the 'soft', people-based approach. Of these, the latter, which relates to the theory and practice of HRM, constitutes the primary aim of this chapter.

Unlike TQM theory, HRM has had a longer history with its own different definitions, theoretical perspectives, models and frameworks (Syed, 2006; see also Chapter 2). HRM is a synthesis of themes and concepts drawn from a long history of work practice, more recent management theories and social science research (Price, 2007). Similarly to TQM, advocates of HRM have found the concept to be rather vague and elusive, not least because it is an elastic term that encompasses a range of applications. For example, Boxall and Purcell (2003: 1) view HRM as 'all those activities associated with the management of the employment relationship in the firm'. For others (for example, Bach, 2005), such a definition places a heavy emphasis on management practices and therefore undermines the interests of employees. As a result of these different definitions and understandings of the concept, different approaches to HRM have emerged

Box 15.1 Popular perspectives on TQM

Deming's 14 points
1 Consistency of purpose
2 Adopt the philosophy
3 Do not rely on mass inspection
4 Do not award business on price
5 Constant improvement
6 Training
7 Leadership
8 Drive out fear
9 Break down barriers
10 Eliminate slogans and exhortations
11 Eliminate quotas
12 Pride of workmanship
13 Education and retraining
14 Plan of action

The Juran trilogy
I Quality planning
  -Set goals
  -Identify customers and their needs
  -Develop products and processes
II Quality control
  -Evaluate performance
  -Compare with goals and adapt
III Quality improvement
  -Establish infrastructure
  -Identify projects and teams
  -Provide resources and training
  -Establish controls

Crosby's 14 quality steps
1 Management commitment
2 Quality improvement teams
3 Quality measurement
4 Cost of quality evaluation
5 Quality awareness
6 Corrective action
7 Zero-defects committee
8 Supervisor training
9 Zero-defects day
10 Goal-setting
11 Error cause removal
12 Recognition
13 Quality councils
14 Do it over again

Oakland's 13 quality steps
1 Understanding of quality
2 Commitment to quality
3 Policy on quality
4 Organization for quality
5 Measurement cost of quality
6 Planning for quality
7 Design for quality
8 System for quality
9 Control of quality
10 Teamwork for quality
11 Capability for quality
12 Training for quality
13 Implementation of quality

Conway's 6 tools for quality improvement
1 Human relation skills
2 Statistical surveys
3 Simple statistical techniques
4 Statistical process control
5 Imagineering
6 Industrial engineering

Source: Deming (1986), Juran (1989), Crosby (1979), Oakland (2004); Reid and Sanders (2009)

over the past few decades (see Storey and Sisson, 1993; Marchington and Wilkinson, 2000; Storey, 2000; Redman and Wilkinson, 2009; Storey et al., 2009).

In this respect, a common key discussion of most of authorities on HRM appears to relate to a difference between hard and soft HRM. For Price (2007), hard HRM focuses on the resource side of human resources and costs in the form of 'head counts' and places control firmly in the hands of management (see Critical Thinking 15.1). Their role is to manage numbers effectively, keeping the workforce closely matched with requirements in terms of both bodies and behaviours. On the contrary, soft HRM, which stresses the 'human' aspects of managing people, has concerns related to communication and motivation. People are led rather than managed; they are involved in determining and realizing strategic objectives. Among some of the best-known HRM models are Beer et al.'s (1984) Harvard model, Guest's (1987) UK model, the Michigan model developed by Fombrun et al. (1984), Storey's (1992) HRM versus personnel management model, and Brewster and Bournois' (1991) European environment model. Guest has been particularly influential in developing the distinction between 'hard' and 'soft' HRM (Morgan, 2000).

Despite differences in the nature of and approaches to TQM and HRM, both concepts share the paramount importance of people-focused organizational contexts – as opposed to merely hard-oriented TQM or HRM practices. Such a common characteristic of both concepts suggests a resurgence of the value attached to managing human resources. It also reflects the heightened pressures faced by all types of organization, particularly TQM-driven ones, in designing compatible TQM HRM systems that serve the common interests of both the organization and its employees (Hill and Wilkinson, 1995; Rees, 1995; Simmons et al., 1995; Snape et al., 1996; McElwee and Warren, 2000; Prajogo and McDermott, 2005; Summers, 2005).

Critical Thinking 15.1
Is TQM a control mechanism for management?

Despite a surge of interest in designing HRM practices to incorporate the precepts of TQM, many critics of TQM view it as a means of tightening managerial control over the workforce – as opposed to improving work processes. Thus, the significance of any shift from controlling the workforce to developing the workforce in the name of TQM should not be overestimated. A review of the literature pertinent to HRM and industrial relations indicates that managing TQM organizations is mainly concerned with control and that, in order to achieve a balance between control and employee consent, an element of disguise is necessary: 'process control' – which is central to TQM. So 'TQM … in practice, may be seen as resulting in high levels of control' and 'the aim of initiatives such as TQM is to maximize the surplus value of labour through increased control over the workforce' (Legge, 1995: 246; see also Godfrey et al., 1997: 571).

Although direct control of the workforce is not an aim of TQM, TQM consists of an increasing set of tasks that are closely monitored and strictly controlled. (For further detail, see Delbridge et al., 1992; Oliver and Wilkinson, 1992; Legge, 1995; Godfrey et al., 1997; Soltani et al., 2008a).

Questions

1 Given that TQM may result in an increased control of the workforce in order to maximize labour productivity, what ethical implications must be considered when designing and implementing TQM in an organization?
2 How can organizations achieve a balance between employees' consent and control over employees?

TQM and HRM: an integrated perspective

A common theme that emerges from most recent writings on managing organizations highlights an ongoing fundamental change or transformation in the traditional methods of managing people (see Storey, 1989, 2007; Sisson, 1994; Legge, 2005; Bach, 2005; Torrington and Hall, 2005; Beardwell and Claydon, 2007; Redman and Wilkinson, 2009). Traditionally, management policies and practices were characterized by mass-production methods in which a high proportion of machinery and energy (in relation to workers) was used, ensuring lower labour costs, a faster rate of production and finally lower cost per unit. Such capital-intensive manufacturing processes have their origins in the system initially developed by Taylor, which was subsequently advanced fully by Henry Ford when he founded the Ford Motor Company during the late 18th and early 19th centuries (Taylor, 1911; Aitken, 1985; Sisson, 1994).

Sisson's (1994) analysis of the so-called 'Taylorist' or 'Fordist' methods elucidated three underlying features: hierarchy, bureaucracy and specialization. She further recognized the reasons for the dysfunctionality of traditional methods as being primarily associated with the changing context of business, particularly at a global level. In this respect, Sisson (1994) identified two developments that are deemed to have fundamentally changed the nature and scope of how organizational practices and policies were traditionally managed:

☐ the rise of manufacturers in low labour-cost countries that were able to take advantage of modern technology and challenge the established producer countries;

☐ Japanese companies' growing dominance of markets in global manufacturing industries through the successful application of 'lean production' systems involving new working methods such as 'just-in-time', Kaizen or continuous improvement, and the direct participation of the workforce.

In order to counteract the problems associated with traditional management practices and the emerging developments in the global market, Sisson (1994) and most authorities on HRM and TQM (see, for example, Hill and Wilkinson, 1995; Snape et al., 1996; Wilkinson et al., 1998; Summers, 2005; Dale et al., 2007) recommend an integration of 'TQM and HRM' practices. With respect to TQM, there is a need on the part of the management to switch from mass production to 'flexible organization'; in this way, they can get much closer to customers in order to establish their desires, they can institutionalize continuous improvement through the whole organization, and they can make quality the responsibility of everyone from the top of the company down to the shopfloor. In terms of HRM, the onus is on the management to design a 'flexible organization', to 'empower the whole organization', to 'promote a learning culture' and to view employees as human capital – as opposed to human cost (for further detail, see Wilkinson et al., 1992, 1993; Sisson, 1994; Willmott, 1994).

So, for HRM (to quote Ellig, 1997: 91) 'to be optimally effective [in terms of managing, supporting and developing employee working in organizations], its function must be both an employee advocate and a business partner'. Accordingly, for TQM practices to be planned and successfully implemented, they need to focus on a systematic and careful approach to the recruitment of employees, the use of teamwork and group problem-solving, egalitarian work structures, commitment to training, and performance and reward systems (Flynn et al., 1994; Waldman, 1994a).

Despite the centrality of human resources to the successful implementation of both the HRM and TQM functions and their close linkage and interaction, some commentators have suggested that quality management faces its biggest problem in 'soft' areas such as workforce management (see, for example, Wilkinson, 1994). To add to the vital role of HRM functions in improving TQM, Flynes (1999) asserts that the absence of HRM practices in environments practising TQM can be a major obstacle to a quality involvement programme. Thus,

15

'TQM requires a particular approach to human resource strategy if it is to be implemented successfully' (Wilkinson et al., 1998: 41). Accordingly, whereas much of the early research in this area concentrated on quality circles, more recent empirical studies in the HRM literature studying the interaction between HRM issues and quality management have focused on practices that improve quality performance. Wilkinson et al. (1998), for instance, analysed various elements of HRM that should fit together as coherent whole, using the 'HRM cycle' initially presented by Devanna et al. (1984), and then talked in terms of the 'formation of a quality culture' by HRM practices (Figure 15.1).

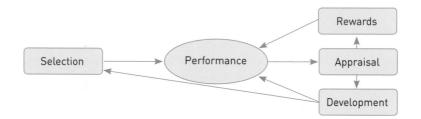

Figure 15.1 The human resource management cycle.
Source: Adapted from Devanna et al. (1984: 41) and Wilkinson et al. (1998: 42)

As Figure 15.1 shows, the journey towards a quality culture begins with staff selection and induction, with the purpose of selecting employees with the required qualifications, that is, attitudinal and behavioural features; this is then followed by inducting them into the quality culture. Having selected the employees and integrated them into the organization, the HRM cycle then focuses on performance through evaluation, remuneration and development.

In fact, TQM as a management system is designed as an integrated, customer-focused approach to improving the quality of an organization's processes, products and services through human resources; more specifically, it is everyone's responsibility. Palmer and Saunders' (1992) definition of TQM, for example, is consistent with this argument since they view TQM as a process that emphasizes a continuous improvement in the customer-oriented quality of processes, goods and services. Such a definition is generic and captures the strategic intent of TQM to focus internally (processes) and externally on the beneficiaries of the organization. Therefore, it highlights the more specific relationships that exist between TQM and HRM – that is, various customer groups (see Saunders and Preston, 1995). Sisson (1994) characterizes HRM as a holistic process, integrating all the functions of personnel management into business strategy and planning. Thus, both TQM and HRM are underwritten by an organization-wide approach. Strategic HRM proponents such as Guest (1989) suggest that individual policies and practices should be linked to the overall management strategy. The same is also true of TQM (see Deming, 1986).

All quality systems, such as EFQM (formerly known as the European Foundation for Quality Management), the Malcolm Baldrige National Quality Award

(USA), the Deming Prize (Japan) and the International Organization for Standardization quality management standards, strongly support the integration of TQM and HRM practices (see EFQM, 1999). To appreciate such a vital link and achieve excellence on the basis of the link between TQM and the role of human factors, the following five elements have been emphasized (Incomes Data Services, 1990; Smyth and Scullion, 1996):

- *Identifying the customer*: one primary element of TQM requires all employees to be aware of their customers, that is, both internal and external, and in turn to identify their requirements.
- *A TQM organization*: TQM must be applied across the whole organization, directed and maintained by a structure of quality 'bodies'. This requires the commitment of the chief executive and senior management, with the full involvement of all the company's employees.
- *Continuous problem-solving activity*: problem-solving is a purposeful technique used as an integral part of any TQM programme that allows people the opportunity to view problems from all angles.
- *Measurement*: measuring and monitoring is a continuous process within any TQM programme. Benchmarking is one common method commonly used as a systematic mechanism of evaluating companies recognized as industry leaders. This concept decides business and work processes that represent 'best practices' and establishes rational performance goals.
- *Training*: training has been identifying as the single most significant factor in improving quality (Oakland, 2004). Effective training programmes must be planned systematically and objectively.

Hence, a highly effective and successful TQM organization arises from both centralizing its own strategic TQM elements as well as creating the kind of organizational environment that allows sufficient latitude for employees to fulfil their specific personal needs (Simmons et al., 1995; see also Wilkinson et al., 1998; Summers, 2005). To this end, HRM practices appear to be implicit in their attention to internal customers, teams and training, with a reference to quality skills. So without compromising this internal focus, the organization of TQM also needs to make sure that (internal) organizational behaviour ultimately serves the interests of the company's external customers. Such an external focus, in turn, is akin to the operating paradigm of HRM.

In order to provide a stronger case for the intersection of HRM with elements of TQM, and consistent with previous research (for example, Simmons et al., 1995) on integrating TQM and HRM, the four oft-cited HRM cycle practices – selection, appraisal, reward and development – will be grouped into four functional areas as follows (see Bratton and Gold, 1999):

- work organization;
- training and development;
- staffing and planning;
- performance appraisal and remuneration.

Each of these elements will be discussed below through the lens of the assumptions underlying TQM.

TQM and work organization

Both team-based work organization and flexible work practices constitute an integral part of an effective HRM system. Although some evidence exists to show that human resources practices have lagged behind this movement over the past few decades (see, for example, O'Neil et al., 1992), other recent surveys consistently reveal that organizations ranging in size from large to small businesses are using teams to accomplish their work (for example, Manz and Sims, 1993; Hackman, 2002; Smith, 2002; Katzenbach and Smith, 2003).

Overall, there are several reasons why different organizations embrace the team concept (Reilly and McGourty, 1998: 245):

☐ The pressure on businesses to respond to increased competition makes organizations search for new ways to work more efficiently and effectively.
☐ Competitive pressures have also led to wholesale organizational change such as downsizing and flattening of organizations. Smaller, flatter organizations, as Lawler et al. (1992) point out, require employees to be more flexible and to play a greater role in deciding how work gets done. In this respect, self-directed work teams have been seen to gain wider usage and increasingly popular over the past two decades.
☐ The increasing complexity of many jobs makes it difficult for one person to perform them, leading to the use of teams as the basic work unit.

Gross's (1995) study also identifies the top three reasons for adopting team-based work practices: (1) to improve customer satisfaction, (2) to improve products and services, and (3) to increase productivity.

Proponents of TQM (Deming, 1986; Juran, 1989; Crosby, 1999; Feigenbaum, 2004) also strongly value the importance of teamwork and flexibility as the preferred way to organize and accomplish good quality work (see also Cordery, 1996; Wilkinson et al., 1997; Bacon and Blyton, 2000; Harman et al., 2002). Here the primary focus is on workflow analysis and precisely measuring all aspects of the work process. As a result, there are close similarities between TQM and HRM regarding work organization, including how they deal with job analysis and redesign. On the one hand, TQM requires that job design serve the purpose of providing long-term benefits to a range of beneficiaries (Saunders and Preston, 1995). On the other hand, a future-oriented job analysis seems to be central to effective HRM because job-related information needs to be gathered in order to facilitate informed decision-making on future work arrangements (Rothwell and Kazanas, 1989). A future orientation to job analysis clearly resembles process analysis within TQM as it aims to scrutinize job content and work systems to identify where improvements can be made (Simmons et al., 1995).

Standards-based measuring systems place a heavy emphasis on job control and standardization – as opposed to teamwork and a flexible working environment (Albrecht, 1990) – so standards-based measuring systems do not support flexibility and loosely coupled work arrangements (Berggren, 1992). However, teamwork and flexibility can be incorporated into the work design through other initiatives, such as job rotation within the group and a multiskilling work environment (Simmons et al., 1995). In other words, although job standardization is important and necessary for work improvement, it is not sufficient. A balance between measurement and control on the one hand and flexibility and autonomy on the other hand can, in the end, be maintained.

To clarify this complexity, Simmons and colleagues provide an example of service-oriented operations where a degree of flexibility and variation can co-exist in terms of process analysis and how jobs are performed. For example, a careful examination of work processes (referred to as workflow analysis) can result in a minimum of three desirable outcomes: identifying the unnecessary tasks or procedures that need to be abandoned; reducing employees' workload without removing the flexibility that is present in their work activities; and granting employees greater freedom over their work since less time needs to be spent on its unnecessary components (Simmons et al., 1995; see also Chapter 7).

In short, despite widespread awareness of the positive ramifications of teamwork for both employee productivity and organizational performance, and evidence that the movement to team-based work has been attracting many businesses in recent years (Benson, 1994; Lawler et al., 1995; Cordery, 1996; Harman et al., 2002; Cooney and Sohal, 2004), 'It is undeniable that the management of teams will be a major issue facing organizations for some time', as will team performance measurement (Reilly and McGourty, 1998: 245).

TQM and training

There is a growing appreciation of training, development and the retention of talent as the key to organizational survival (Squires and Adler, 1998). This is particularly true in any continuous improvement context such as TQM in which organizations have to anticipate the skill requirements for future work and prepare their workforce. One explanation for this is that well-trained and skilful employees can perform quality activities precisely and consistently as planned; as a result, they are deemed essential to the successful implementation of TQM. Although it is possible to evaluate the extent to which an employee already has the skills that will be required next year and to take action to ameliorate any deficiencies before they affect future performance, 'effective performance in last year's environment may not be strongly predictive of next year's performance if the environment changes significantly' (Squires and Adler, 1998: 445). An ongoing, organization-wide human resources development programme is therefore needed to guide future performance, leverage existing strengths and address skill deficiencies so that both employees and managers will be provided with sufficient skills to implement TQM successfully.

A review of the writings of TQM gurus (Crosby, 1979; Deming, 1986; Feigenbaum, 2004) and their advocates (see, for example, Waldman, 1994a, 1994b; Hackman and Wageman, 1995; Knights and McCabe, 1997, 1998, 1999; Wilkinson et al., 1997; Waldman et al., 1998; Yong and Wilkinson, 1999; Oakland, 2004; Dale et al., 2007; Soltani and Wilkinson, 2010) indicates that adopting TQM practices will result in the empowerment of non-managerial employees as problem-

solvers, decision-makers and the real implementers of improvement initiatives. Such delegation of authority in TQM is largely realized through helping
and indeed enabling employees' participation in the improvement process.
Enabling employees to decide on their own training and development needs is
a prerequisite for the successful implementation of TQM, not least because
TQM uses data-driven problem analysis as a method for improvement – an
indication of not only a need for specific TQM training, but also an ongoing
alteration in the skills demanded of employees and managers (Simmons et al.,
1995; see also Shadur and Bamber, 1994; Dale, 2003; Oakland, 2004). In this
respect, Clinton et al. (1994) give a very useful account of the dimensions of
training and development required by employees in the TQM process in the
form of three basic issues:

☐ instruction in the philosophy and principles of TQM;
☐ specific skills training, such as the use of statistical process control;
☐ interpersonal skills training to improve team problem-solving abilities.

As the use of cross-functional teams to achieve the organization's cross-
functional aims is central to, and indeed an integral part of, implementing TQM,
employees are required to possess a broad base of skills that cover several
different jobs across different functions and levels (Simmons et al., 1995).
Furthermore, as a result of employee empowerment and labelling managers'
jobs as advisor or facilitator, leadership and management training also needs to
be part of the overall training and development programme in order to ease the
transition (Shadur and Bamber, 1994); this is made even more important
because of the increasing stress encountered at middle and supervisory levels
of management. This is the position taken by Wilkinson et al. (1998: 43), who
assert that:

> TQM also has implications for management development, particularly given
> the likely impact on management style, with an emphasis on interpersonal
> skills and leadership …, and in the longer term for career development paths
> … due to reducing the scope for hierarchical career progression.

In short, TQM organizations cannot benefit from advances in training, development and subsequent learning outcomes unless they create a continuous
training and development programme – as opposed to conventional one-off
training and development schemes – from top to bottom in the company. Such
quality-driven training programmes clearly need to thoughtfully incorporate
quality management precepts into all elements of the HRM cycle on an ongoing
daily rather than annual basis (see Oakland, 2004; Dale et al., 2007).

TQM and recruitment

The training and development of both managerial and non-managerial
employees is only one of HRM's responsibilities in supporting the implementation of TQM: HRM must also take the lead in attracting, retaining and motivating a high-quality workforce (Greene, 1991). In order for HRM practices to be
updated and revised, Nankervis et al. (1992) recognize the place of HRM in a

wider organizational context and emphasize the development of human resources in light of organizational strategy. Here the primary aim is to take a strategic view of the firm's future human resources needs across all its activities from recruitment to training, career development, succession planning and employee exit. In order to ensure close conformance and harmony with the organizational strategy, employee recruitment and selection policies then need to be further developed and adjusted to fit any emerging changes (see Simmons et al., 1995).

Viewing human resources recruitment in the frame of quality management, it is evident that human resources planning plays a vital role in the successful implementation of quality management programmes. In doing this, recruitment and selection policies must provide the organization with employees who are familiar with the organization's mission, who are aware of the intended TQM objectives, who understand the goals and values of TQM and, more importantly, who can work effectively as a team towards achieving the goals and values of TQM. Clinton et al. (1994) follow a very similar line of argument, explaining that the successful recruitment and selection of employees with the proper knowledge, skills, abilities and attitudes compatible with a TQM philosophy can be a driving and enabling force supporting the programme's continued effectiveness. Having reviewed the related literature on the qualities of candidates that should be targeted in recruiting and selection, Clinton et al. have elucidated several key qualities that are deemed essential if TQM is to succeed and sustain:

□ a willingness to receive new training and to expand job roles;
□ a willingness to try new ideas and problem-solving techniques;
□ a willingness to work patiently in teams within and across departments;
□ being enough of a team player to be evaluated and rewarded on a team basis.

Wilkinson et al. (1998) provide some proof that these requirements are important for selecting employees with the required attitudinal and behavioural characteristics to fit into the organization's quality culture , and also highlight the paramount importance of issues such as:

□ effective recruitment advertising;
□ realistic job previews;
□ involving members of the work team in the selection process;
□ the use of psychometric testing and assessment centres.

Thus, as the first step towards developing a quality culture based on the HRM cycle, the selection and induction of staff needs to be given appropriate attention and weight on the management agenda.

TQM and performance appraisal

Another important interface between HRM and TQM relates to a need for an effective performance appraisal and reward system that can reinforce and improve employees' performance in achieving the intended objectives of TQM (see Clinton et al., 1994; Soltani et al., 2005, 2006). The importance of perform-

15

ance appraisal for organizations in general (see Boice and Kleiner, 1997; Longenecker and Fink, 1999) and TQM companies in particular (see Bowman, 1994; Waldman, 1994a, 1994b; Ghorpade et al., 1995; Cardy, 1998; Wilkinson et al., 1998), has been highlighted by many scholars and practitioners of quality and human resources.

However, some proponents of TQM explicitly argue against the adoption of performance appraisal, for a range of individual and organizational reasons (see, for example, Deming, 1986). Put simply, the main difficulties with traditional performance appraisal systems are as follows (see, for further detail, Deming, 1986; Hemmings, 1992; Scholtes, 1993, 1995; Randell, 1994; Waldman, 1994a; Ghorpade et al., 1995; Cardy and Dobbins, 1996; Cardy, 1998; Smither, 1998; Wilkinson et al., 1998; Seddon, 2001):

☐ a focus on the past;
☐ a use of quantifiable measures;
☐ the view that traits are inputs to work, not outputs from it;
☐ traits being subjective;
☐ a conservative use of performance evaluation rating scales;
☐ pay awards being 'unrelated' to performance evaluation;
☐ annual performance evaluation emphasizing formal procedures;
☐ the limits of having only two performance evaluation views;
☐ the fact that performance evaluation forms can impede wider discussion;
☐ performance evaluation objectives not always being measurable.

Deming (1986), one of the most notable quality management advocates, lists 'evaluation of performance, merit rating and annual review' as the third of his 'seven deadly diseases'. Deming states that the effects of this disease are devastating American industries. This attack on human resources performance appraisal has also been spearheaded by others (for example, Scholtes, 1993) following the lead of W. Edwards Deming (1986).

In contrast, other TQM and HRM researchers (for example, Carson et al., 1991; Glover, 1993; Waldman, 1994a; Boice and Kleiner, 1997; Cardy, 1998; Wilkinson et al., 1998; Soltani et al., 2005, 2006) would hasten to say that much can be done, through integrating TQM assumptions into employee performance appraisals, to make the system more effective. Given that there is more room to improve employees' performance in positively contributing to the TQM process, Clinton et al. (1994) suggest that performance appraisal, or in more general terms HRM practices, can be integrated into the fundamental tenets of a TQM culture in order to promote the notion of customer satisfaction. In doing this, HRM can exert a great deal of influence over developing promotion policies that are consistent with the overall goals of both the TQM programmes and the organization itself. In an attempt to make performance appraisal more effective and congruent with the TQM context, Wilkinson et al. (1998) have described the following main factors regarded as being central to a TQM-focused performance appraisal:

☐ the inclusion of customers (both internal and external) in the evaluation process;

☐ peer review as a source of evaluation;

☐ the establishment of a link between individuals' personal objectives and their training and development needs.

Commentators advocating the integration of TQM precepts into human resources performance appraisal have also argued that a well-designed performance appraisal system that is compatible with TQM requirements may result in the acceptance and successful implementation of quality programmes. In addition to measures such as customer focus, peer review and a link between individuals' personal objectives and training needs (see Wilkinson et al., 1998), other elements of such a quality-oriented performance appraisal system could be as follows (Clinton et al., 1994: 10):

☐ identify and recognize the quality of inputs and processes and not just outputs

☐ focus on the achievements of the individual, team and enterprise

☐ improve future performance through performance planning, coaching and the counselling

☐ reward personal improvement and not just rating performance relative to peers

☐ provide qualitative feedback to employees.

Given the aforementioned dimensions of quality-driven performance appraisal, the HRM department can help to design the performance appraisal system. In rewarding team efforts for quality improvement, human resources managers can also keep both management and employees informed about TQM achievements, so that opportunities to feature the outstanding accomplishments of team members who deserve recognition and rewards can be identified. Accordingly, quality improvement teams would conduct performance appraisals on each another, interview and select team members, schedule the team's work and set performance goals (Clinton et al., 1994).

The literature abounds with strong evidence showing that most organizations have some form of performance appraisal in place, and there is also sufficient evidence supporting the positive effects of performance appraisal on productivity and quality (see, for example, Shadur and Bamber, 1994). As Cardy (1998: 132) puts it: 'there is no doubt that performance appraisal can be difficult and error-ridden. However, it is important to both the organizational and individual perspectives that the task still be done as effectively as possible'. Perhaps the best that can be stated is that 'a growing number of organizations are adopting TQM, but most, instead of eliminating performance evaluation, have attempted to make it more compatible with quality management' (Bowman, 1994: 131; see also, Carson et al., 1991). Thus, the way to consistency is 'to listen to the customers of the process [both internal and external] and to work toward improvement' (Cardy, 1998: 133) (see also Critical Thinking 15.2).

15

The majority of today's organizations have made progress towards delivering a good-quality product or service via the adoption of different quality management approaches, some of which have become popular through recognizing a variety of quality awards. However, their human resources performance appraisal systems continue to focus on individual differences in the management of performance rather than emphasizing the system factors and system improvements needed, and finally removing the system's barriers to good performance.

This focus is not only insufficient, but is also in sharp contrast to the approach taken by TQM. The most notable quality management guru W. Edwards Deming argues that system factors account for up to 95 per cent of organizations' variance in performance. Although this figure is not based on any empirical evidence, the emphasis in TQM is on removing system barriers to performance in order to provide an opportunity for the natural motivation of workers to be expressed. Hence, many current performance appraisal systems in human resources may need to be modified in order to meet TQM requirements. In the case of a TQM-based company, the powerful implication of TQM and HRM is that the focus of human resources performance appraisal should become one of the corporate strategic objectives linking to an employee's personal aspirations and developmental needs; in turn, this should lead to continual review, to a development of human resources performance appraisal and to an improvement in employees' performance and potential (see Soltani et al., 2004).

Questions
1 Is it possible to reconcile HRM's focus on individual performance with TQM's focus on system improvement?
2 What possible changes in performance appraisal are likely after the implementing TQM in an organization?

Integrating TQM and HRM

Environmental pressures to change have left organizations little choice but to introduce new approaches to HRM, TQM and the management of change initiatives (Smyth and Scullion, 1996). Having analysed the profound and notable transformation in the organizational context, Smyth and Scullion (1996) identify the following important changes in today's organizations:

- from centralized to decentralized units;
- from functional structures to functional semi-autonomous units;
- flatter organizations.

As a result of ongoing changes in the areas of communication, workplace organization and reward systems linked to pay, Smyth and Scullion (1996) further recognize new methods of managerial control and investing in people at work that are practised widely throughout different organizations. Among these methods are teamworking, quality circles, single status, lean production, customer care training, performance-related pay, profit-related pay, profit-sharing and share options. These schemes in turn link the general thrust involved in implementing programmes of HRM and TQM.

Given these improvements in managing human resources and their role in enhancing quality, a number of studies have been carried out over the past decade to further demonstrate the vital role of HRM in TQM (see, for example, Clinton et al., 1994; Wilkinson et al., 1993, 1998). In addition to this, Clinton et al.

differentiate between the focuses of responsibility for quality improvements in the past (which were the sole responsibility of specialists such as quality engineers, product designers and process designers) and today, illustrating that developing quality across the entire organization can be an important function of the HRM department in today's organizations. Failure on the part of HRM to recognize this opportunity and act on it may, however, result in the loss of responsibilities for TQM implementation to other departments with less expertise in training and development.

Clinton et al. (1994, p. 11) also talk in terms of HRM as a role model for TQM by arguing that 'HRM can jumpstart the TQM process by becoming a role model'. By role model, they define two specific tasks for human resources:

☐ serving customers, that is, viewing other departments in the firm as their customer groups and trying to satisfy these internal customers, who indirectly provide ultimate satisfaction to external customers;
☐ making a significant contribution to running the business through demonstrating a commitment to the principles of TQM by soliciting feedback from internal groups or current human resources services.

Innovations such as 'right first time', 'zero defects', 'plan–do–check–action' and 'fitness for use' are buzzwords associated with TQM, and are in turn extensively used, linking employers' emphasis on quality to a wider industrial relations approach (Smyth and Scullion, 1996). Although recent years have witnessed a great enthusiasm for clarifying the link between HRM and TQM, few studies have so far provided evidence of their close relationship. Of these few but impressive studies, Wilkinson et al. (1993) present a thorough model for the role of the personnel function in TQM. As Figure 15.2 indicates, their discussion is succinct when considering the measurement of HRM involvement and related indicators, as well as the various roles of human resources in TQM.

Figure 15.2 The role of human resources in quality management
Source: Adapted from Wilkinson et al. (1993: 34)

Moreover, Wilkinson et al. take the argument further and illustrate the contribution of the human resources function to quality management in terms of its breadth and depth of involvement. As Table 15.1 shows, breadth refers to the range of TQM-related activities to which the human resources function makes a contribution, and depth is a measure of how well these activities have integrated into the organizations. Wilkinson et al.'s main findings were that the HRM function has made a greater contribution to TQM than they envisaged at the outset of their research, and that this role is increasing in significance.

Table 15.1 The breadth and depth of human resource (HR) involvement in total quality management (TQM)

Type of activities to assess the breadth of HR's involvement in TQM	Types of indicators to measure the depth of HR's involvement in TQM
• Recruiting and selecting high calibre personnel • Designing and running induction courses related to quality • Training for various quality initiatives and teams • Developing training programmes which result in empowered employees • Help to set up and facilitate teams and organising communication • Working with trade union representatives on quality-related issues • Dealing with grievances which can affect the process • Designing pay and appraisal system to recognize and reward quality work • Shaping organization structures which help to assist and support TQM • Ensuing of alignment of HR strategy with TQM strategy • Setting up management development programmes to stress TQM • Manager as a coach or facilitator to support the operating staff	• Perception of managing director and senior management team of HR contribution to TQM • The number of employees trained on quality-related issues by HR department • The number of quality teams which have been facilitated by HR • The amount of TQM training material developed by HR • The number of quality team leaders and team mentors counselled by HR • The amount of money spent on HR issues connected with TQM • The input made by HR functions to the TQM steering group/quality councils • The closeness of any links between the HR and quality management functions • The degree to which TQM principles are practised by HR personnel • The number of local service level agreements developed by the HR function with its own internal customers and assessment of performance against such agreements

Source: Wilkinson et al. (1993: 32)

Smyth and Scullion (1996: 105) also provide a very useful account of this relationship, saying: 'the elements involved in HRM and TQM are closely associated'. As Table 15.2 shows, their study also displays the vital role of the HRM department as being central to the success of a total quality approach. As can be seen from Table 15.2, the nature of TQM offers the HRM function several opportunities to contribute, ranging from designing and conducting to evaluating the underlying TQM philosophy. Indeed, 'TQM and HRM are in pursuit of the same goals that is, productivity, profitability, a customer-oriented firm and a motivated workforce' (Smyth and Scullion, 1996: 91).

In a similar vein, Blackburn and Rosen's (1993) study of Baldrige Award-winning companies in the USA indicates that these companies have developed portfolios of HRM policies to complement their strategic TQM objectives. The

Table 15.2 The relationship between human resource management (HRM) and total quality management (TQM)

Factors to be managed	HRM responsibilities	Elements of TQM
Interpretation of corporate strategy	Manpower and future planning	Identifying manpower needs highlighted in the corporate strategy
Establishing a structure to support the strategy	Organizational design and development	Involvement in identifying what is right for the business and what will enable it to achieve its goals
Management style	Impact on management behaviour, skills and attitudes Modification of these where they inhibit the successful introduction of TQM	Identification of management/ employee styles and attitudes
Skills	Analysis of training and development needs, skills requirements and gaps	Meeting demands
Human resources	Appropriate recruitment, career development and remuneration policies	Effective policies and procedures
Shared values	Ability to identify attitudes, improve motivation and morale	Shared values are pertinent in a TQM programme. The HRM and communication department can make a major contribution in this area

Source: Adapted from *Personnel Manager Factbook* (1994) by Smyth and Scullion (1996: 91)

findings indicated that an appropriate alignment of human resource practices with quality initiatives required revolutionary changes in the way the organizations selected, trained, empowered, evaluated and rewarded both individuals and teams. However, the revolution was far from over, and even among the organizations recognized for their TQM achievements, there was still a need for continuous improvement with respect to human resources practices governing the selection, promotion and development of future leaders. Table 15.3 contrasts traditional HRM policies with those policies in companies recognized for successfully implementing a total quality effort.

In addition to the evolution from traditional HRM practices to new HRM policies, Table 15.3 also illustrates the evolving role of HRM from a support function to a leadership function in the firm. In traditional organizations, HRM functions identify, prepare, direct and reward organizational actors to follow rather narrow organizational and job scripts. In TQM organization, HRM units develop policies and procedures to ensure that employees can perform multiple roles (as the result of cross-training and membership on crossfunctional work teams), improvise when necessary and direct themselves in the continuous improvement of product quality and customer service. Such evidence led Blackburn and Rosen to hypothesize that Award-winning organizations have not only applied a

Table 15.3 The evolution of a total quality human resources (HR) paradigm

	Traditional paradigm	Total quality paradigm
Corporate context dimension		
Corporate culture	Individualism Differentiation Autocratic leadership Profits Productivity	Collective efforts Crossfunctional work Coaching/enabling Customer satisfaction Quality
Human resources characteristics		
Communications	Top-down Horizontal, lateral Multidirectional	Top-down
Voice and involvement	Employment-at-will Suggestion systems	Due process Quality circles Attitude surveys
Job design	Efficiency Productivity Standard procedures Narrow span of control Specific job description	Quality Customization Innovation Wide span of control Autonomous work teams Empowerment
Training	Job-related skills Functional, technical	Broad range of skills Crossfunctional Diagnostic, problem solving Productivity and quality
Performance measurement and evaluation	Individual goals Supervisory review Emphasise financial performance	Team goals Customer, peer, and supervisory review Emphasise quality and service
Rewards	Competition for individual merit increases and benefits	Team/group-based rewards Financial rewards, financial and non-financial recognition
Health and safety	Treat problems	Prevent problems Safety problems Wellness programs Employee assistance
Selection/promotion Career development	Selected by manager Narrow job skills Promotion based on individual accomplishment Linear career path	Selected by peers Problem-solving skills Promotion based on group facilitation Horizontal career path

Source: Blackburn and Rosen (1993: 51)

highly reliable quality system, but would also show portfolios of HRM policies to complement strategic TQM objectives and consequently the effective integration of TQM and HRM practices. Blackburn and Rosen's further in-depth analysis of the information yielded a checklist of what they saw as an 'ideal' profile of human resources strategies in support of TQM (Box 15.2).

> **Box 15.2** Ideal profile of human resources strategies in support of TQM
>
> 1 Top management is responsible for initiating and supporting a vision of a total quality culture.
> 2 This vision is clarified and communicated to the remainder of the firm in a variety of ways.
> 3 Systems that allow upward and lateral communications are developed, implemented, and reinforced.
> 4 TQM training is provided to all employees, and top management shows active support for such training.
> 5 Employee involvement or participation programme are in place.
> 6 Autonomous work groups are not required, but processes that bring multiple perspectives to bear on quality issues are imperative.
> 7 Employees are empowered to make quality-based decisions at their discretion. Job design should make this apparent.
> 8 Performance reviews are refocused from an evaluation of past performance only, to an emphasis on what management can do to assist employees in their future job-related quality efforts.
> 9 Compensation systems reflect team-related quality contributions, including mastery of additional skills
> 10 Non-financial recognition systems at both the individual and work group levels reinforce both small wins and big victories in the quest for total quality.
> 11 Systems allow employees at all levels of the organization to make known their concerns, ideas, and reactions to quality initiatives. These systems might include suggestion opportunities with rapid response, open-door policies, attitude surveys, and so on.
> 12 Safety and health issues are addressed proactively not reactively. Employee participation in the development of programmes in both areas improves acceptance of these programmes.
> 13 Employee recruitment, selection, promotion, and career development programmes reflect the new realities of managing and working in a TQM environment.
> 14 While assisting others to implement processes in support of TQM, the HR professional does not lose sight of the necessity to manage the HR function under the same precepts.
>
> *Source:* Adapted from Blackburn and Rosen (1993: 64)

It is therefore evident that quality and HRM have many implications for each other. Although there appears to be some conflict between these two approaches (for example, in terms of performance appraisal), any conflict can be resolved by tailoring HRM to fit into the context of quality management (see Wilkinson et al., 1998; Soltani et al., 2003, 2004, 2005, 2006).

Conclusion

This chapter has made an attempt to void the 'apples and oranges' problems of previous research by providing a more credible case for the complementarity of TQM and HRM practices. It has presented the view that there exist both incompatibility and congruence between TQM and HRM. With respect to incompatibility, the presence of various barriers facing HRM at both the individual and the organizational level in fulfilling the specific needs of TQM does not dilute its vital support of the human resources function. Rather, it has the particular benefit of highlighting areas where the design of HRM practices may need strengthening. For example, although the conventional individual-based performance appraisal of HRM is said to be dysfunctional to a TQM context, it is still a vital necessity in the quality management context – but it needs revisiting and researching in important ways that are likely to work better where they are in line with the quality management context.

Clearly, as Cardy (1998) has pointed out, there is no easy recipe for a perfect performance appraisal system that fits all aspects and requirements of TQM. However, a more compatible performance appraisal could be achieved by the following:

- □ with TQM underlying any assumptions made, an adequate understanding of both TQM and the rationale for using performance appraisal;
- □ the inclusion of expectations of both internal and external customers in the dimensions and standards of performance that are appraised;
- □ using performance appraisal as a driver for developing empowerment and trust in the workforce;
- □ using performance appraisal results not as a control approach to perform-ance but as a mechanism to help employees improve their performance and develop their interpersonal skills;
- □ the use of multi-rater feedback and self-appraisal;
- □ finally, the inclusion of situational or systems-level factors as a set of explicit performance measures to assess employees (see Waldman and Kenett, 1990; Carson, 1992; Graber et al., 1992; Blackburn and Rosen, 1993; Waldman, 1994b; Ghorpade et al., 1995; Cardy, 1998; Wilkinson et al., 1998).

Despite some incongruence, particularly with regard to the essentially indi-vidual-based performance appraisal of HRM, the paramount role of HRM is evident and therefore central to the success of quality programmes. Therefore, HRM's responsibility in implementing TQM should extend beyond appraising employee performance. In doing this, other elements of the HRM function could also play a vital role in implementing and maintaining a TQM process. Referring to the HRM cycle, human resource managers are responsible for recruiting high-quality employees, for the continual training and development of those employees, and for creating and maintaining reward systems (Clinton et al., 1994). Furthermore, HRM must take the lead in attracting, retaining and moti-vating a high-quality workforce.

All these contributions reflect the fact that quality can no longer be viewed as being the responsibility of just one department. Instead, it is a company-wide activity that must permeate all departments and all levels. The often-cited TQM notion of 'quality as the responsibility of everyone' clearly implies that the key element of any quality and productivity improvement programme centres on the employees. Because of its fundamental employee orientation, HRM should seek the responsibility for implementing TQM programmes rather than risk losing its influence over the key element of TQM: the employee.

In closing, this chapter suggests a resurgence in the value attached to HRM as being complementary to TQM, reflecting the heightened pressures faced by all types of organization, particularly TQM organizations, in designing effective HRM systems to fulfil the needs of both the TQM organization and its employees (see Murphy and Cleveland, 1991; Ghorpade et al., 1995). A TQM approach to managing human resources, inspired in detail by TQM gurus and their advocates, appears to be shifting towards a more balanced outlook in which all people in any organizational position will be responsible for quality – but there is still a long way to go.

❓ For discussion and revision

Questions

1 Define TQM and HRM. Discuss the popular perspectives on TQM and HRM.

2 How do TQM practices support HRM to take the lead in retaining and motivating a high-quality workforce?

3 What are the fundamental differences between TQM and HRM with regard to appraising and rewarding employee performance?

4 Using the four key elements of the HRM cycle, discuss how TQM can contribute to achieving the intended objectives of each of these elements?

Exercises

1 Quality can mean different things to a customer and an employee. In a role-play, consider yourself a customer and one of your friends as an employee, and debate your different perceptions of quality.

2 As a human resource manager, list all the changes that you would wish to include in a performance management system consistent with TQM.

3 Study TQM in a local company. Ask the human resources manager and the quality manager separately about their perceptions of each other's departments. Are there any differences in their perceptions? What could be the possible reasons for such differences?

📖 Further reading

Books

Armstrong, M. and Baron, A. (2007) *Performance Management: The New Realities.* London: Institute of Personnel and Development.

Bach, B. (2000) From performance appraisal to performance management. In Bach, S. and Sisson, K. (eds) *Personnel Management: A Comprehensive Guide to Theory and Practice* (3rd edn). Oxford: Blackwell Publishers, pp. 241–63.

Bach, B. (2005) New directions in performance management. In Bach, S. (ed.) *Managing Human Resources: Personnel Management in Transition*. Oxford: Blackwell, pp. 289–316.

Bernardin, H. J., Hagan, C. M., Kane, J. S. and Villanova, P. (1998) Effective performance management: a focus on precision, customers, and situational constraints. In Smither, J. W. (ed.) *Performance Appraisal: State of the Art in Practice*. San Francisco: Jossey-Bass, pp. 3–47.

Deming, W. E. (1986) *Out of Crisis*. Cambridge, MA: MIT Centre for Advanced Engineering Study.

Dundon, T. and Wilkinson, A. (eds) (2011) *Case Studies in People Management, Strategy and Innovation*. Australia: Tide University Press.

Latham, G., Sulsky, L. and Macdonald, H. (2007) Performance management. In Boxall, P., Purcell, J. and Wright, P. (eds) *The Oxford Handbook of Human Resource Management*. Oxford: Oxford University Press, pp. 364–84.

Marchington, M. and Wilkinson, A. (2008) *People Management and Development* (4th edn). London: Chartered Institute of Personnel and Development.

Murphy, K. R. and Cleveland, J. N. (1995) *Understanding Performance Appraisal: Social, Organisational, and Goal-Based Perspectives*. Thousand Oaks, CA: Sage.

Prince, J. B. (1996) Building performance appraisal systems consistent with TQM practices. In Knouse, S. B. (ed.) *Human Resources Management Perspectives on TQM, Concepts and Practices*. Milwaukee: ASQC Quality Press, pp. 43–56.

Redman, T. (2009) Appraisal. In Redman T. and Wilkinson A. (eds) *Contemporary Human Resource Management*. Harlow: FT Prentice Hall, pp. 175–206.

Journals

Beer, M. (2003) Why total quality management programs do not persist: the role of management quality and implications for leading a TQM transformation. *Decision Sciences*, 34(4): 623–42.

Ghorpade, J. (2000) Managing five paradoxes of 360-degree feedback. *Academy of Management Executive*, 14(1): 140–50.

Haines, V. Y., St-Onge, S. and Marcoux, A. (2004) Performance management design and effectiveness in quality-driven organizations. *Canadian Journal of Administrative Sciences*, 21(2): 146–61.

Jimenez-Jimenez, D. and Martinez-Costa, M. (2009) The performance effect of HRM and TQM: a study in Spanish organizations. *International Journal of Operations and Production Management*, 29(12): 1266–89.

Masterson, S. and Taylor, M. (1996) Total quality management and performance appraisal: an integrative perspective. *Journal of Quality Management*, 1(1): 67–89.

Case Study ABC

ABC, founded in the 1960s, is a large engineering organization based in Seoul, which manufactures auto parts for a wide range of applications in the auto industry. It makes both make-to-stock and make-to-order auto parts so that it can meet both the general and the more specific requirements of a wide range of customers. The majority of ABC's customers are car and tractor manufacturing companies based in Europe and North America. ABC's value statement is 'quality, productivity, perfection'.

A review of the firm's performance over the past two decades indicates that it has experienced successful operations in both domestic and international markets. ABC's success can be attributed to many factors, as the vice-president of quality has explained:

If you review our internal working processes in any function, you can easily identify how congruent and consistent we are with regard to our working processes, functions and employees. Again, such internal consistency follows a more important factor: conformance to our customers' specific needs.

A review of ABC's archival evidence shows that the company adopted TQM as a business strategy in late 1980s. Senior managers of the company were sent to some leading auto manufacturing companies in Japan and the USA to learn about their knowledge and experiences in TQM. These managers in turn imparted this knowledge to second- and third-tier supervisors in order to introduce and implement the TQM culture in the organization. Quality is now the responsibility of every individual and every department.

As a result of adopting and implementing TQM, extensive changes were made in other functional units so that a shared and common objective was established across the entire company. One of the functions that underwent extensive change was the HRM department. For example, before the adoption of TQM practices, there was a sole focus on individual performance. Training programmes were on more of a one-off basis and focused on a few functional areas such as the manufacturing department; they were also particularly limited to production-line supervisors. In addition, there was a close association between pay and performance. In other words, tangible and monetary rewards were seen to be the major driver for and appreciation of employee performance.

However, since the TQM practices were adopted and implemented, employees, through self-directed teams, are now playing a vital role in making their own working decisions and achieving TQM-intended objectives; in addition, supervisors exercise less power and control over employees, not least because they are expected to facilitate employees' work performance. Employee loyalty and retention are high on the management agenda, so that the training and development of employees are seen to constitute a key element of their organizational life. Finally, the company's employee performance evaluation system aims to enhance employees' performance and develop their interpersonal and work-related skills so that they can make a more meaningful contribution to the overall objectives of the organization.

Kim Ong, ABC's Human Resources Manager, while appreciating the positive impact of TQM on employee morale, also notes the blurring lines of responsibility between TQM and HRM. In particular, she feels that it is difficult to evaluate employees' individual performances given that an entire team is usually involved in decision-making and its implementation in each department. The vice-president of quality, however, has ignored the human resources manager's concern by stating that TQM is system-oriented instead of individual-oriented, and that a closer coordination between human resources and line managers could in due course result in improvement to the overall system.

Questions

1 What are the main challenges or problems facing organizations that decide to adopt TQM practices? How can such problems be overcome?
2 What do you think are the advantages of adopting TQM for (1) the HRM department and (2) the employees?
3 To what extent is HRM focused on individual performance instead of system improvement? How can TQM help HRM to enhance its overall focus?
4 How does the concept of TQM apply to a service organization such as a university, hospital or bank? What differences does it make for the managers and service employees involved in back-office and front-office operations?

References

Aitken, H. G. J. (1985) *Scientific Management in Action: Taylorism at Watertown Arsenal, 1908–1915*. Princeton: Princeton University Press.

Albrecht, K. (1990) *Service Within: Solving the Middle Management Leadership Crisis*. Homewood, IL: Dow Jones–Irwin.

Bach, S. (2005) *Managing Human Resources: Personnel Management in Transition*. Oxford: Blackwell.

Bacon, N. and Blyton, P. (2000) High road and low road teamworking: perceptions of management rationales and organizational and human resource outcomes. *Human Relations*, 53: 1425–58.

Bank, J. (2000) *The Essence of Total Quality Management* (2nd edn). Hemel Hempstead: Prentice Hall.

Beardwell, J. and Claydon, T. (2007) *Human Resource Management: A Contemporary Approach*. Harlow: Prentice Hall.

Beer, M., Spector, B., Lawrence, P. R., Quinn-Mills, D. and Walton, R. E. (1984) *Managing Human Assets*. New York: Free Press.

Berggren, C. (1992) *Alternatives to Lean Production*. New York: ILR Press.

Blackburn, R. and Rosen, B. (1993) Total quality and human resource management: lessons learned from Baldrige Award-winning companies. *Academy of Management Executive*, 7(3): 49–66.

Boice, D. F. and Kleiner, B. H. (1997) Designing effective performance appraisal system. *Work Study*, 46(6): 197–201.

Bowman, J. S. (1994) At last, an alternative to performance appraisal: total quality management. *Public Administration Review*, 45(2): 129–36.

Boxall, P. and Purcell, J. (2003) *Strategy and Human Resource Management*. Basingstoke: Palgrave Macmillan.

Bratton, J. and Gold, J. (1999) *Human Resource Management: Theory and Practice* (2nd edn). London: Macmillan.

Brewster, C. and Bournois, F. (1991) Human resource management: a European perspective. *Personnel Review*, 20(6): 4–13.

Cardy, R. L. (1998) Performance appraisal in a quality context: a new look at an old problem. In Smither, J. W. (ed.) *Performance Appraisal: State of the Art in Practice*. San Francisco: Jossey-Bass, pp. 133–61.

Cardy, R. L. and Dobbins, G. H. (1996) Human resource management in a total quality management environment: shifting from a traditional to a TQHRM approach. *Journal of Quality Management*, 1(1): 5–20.

Carson, K. P. (1992) Upgrade the employee evaluation process. *HR Magazine*, 37(11): 88–92.

Carson, K. P., Cardy, R. and Dobbins, G. H. (1991) Upgrade the employee evaluation process. *Survey of Business*, 29(1): 29–33.

Clinton, R., Williamson, S. and Bethke, A. L. (1994) Implementing total quality management: the role of human resource management. *SAM Advanced Management Journal*, 59(2): 10–16.

Cooney, R. and Sohal, A. (2004) Teamwork and total quality management: a durable partnership. *Total Quality Management and Business Excellence*, 15(8): 1131–42.

Cordery, J. L. (1996) Autonomous work groups and quality circles. In West, M. A. (ed.) *Handbook of Work Group Psychology*. New York: John Wiley, pp. 225–46.

Crosby, P. (1979) *Quality Is Free: The Art of Making Quality Certain*. New York: McGraw Hill.

Crosby, P. B. (1999) *Quality and Me: Lessons from an Evolving Life*. San Francisco: Jossey-Bass.

Dale, B. G. (2003) *Managing Quality* (4th edn). Oxford: Blackwell Publishers.

Dale, B., van der Wiele, T. and van Iwaarden, J. (2007) *Managing Quality* (5th edn). Oxford: Blackwell.

Delbridge, R., Turnbull, P. and Wilkinson, B. (1992) Pushing back the frontiers: management control and work intensification under JIT/TQM factory regime. *New Technology, Work and Employment*, 7(2): 97–106.

Deming, W. E. (1986) *Out of Crisis*. Cambridge, MA: MIT Centre for Advanced Engineering Study.

Devanna, M. A., Fombrun, C. J. and Tichy, N. M. (1984) A framework for strategic human resource management. In Fombrun, C. J., Tichy, N. M. and Devanna M. A. (eds) *Strategic Human Resource Management*. New York: John Wiley & Sons, pp. 33–51.

EFQM. Homepage. Available from: http://www.efqm.org/en/ [accessed 17 July 2010].

Ellig, B. R. (1997) Is the human resource function neglecting the employees? *Human Resource Management*, 5(1): 91–5.

Feigenbaum, A. V. (1961) *Total Quality Control* (3rd edn). New York: McGraw-Hill.

Feigenbaum, A.V. (2004) *Total Quality Control* (4th edn). New York: McGraw-Hill.

Feigenbaum, A.V. (2007) The international growth of quality. *Quality Progress*, 40(2): 36–40.

Flynes, B. (1999) Quality management practices: a review of the literature. *Irish Business and Administration Research*, 19/20(2): 113–38.

Flynn, B. B., Schroeder, R. G. and Sakakibara, S. (1994) A framework for quality management research and an associated measurement instrument. *Journal of Operations Management*, 11(4): 339–66.

Fombrun, C., Tichy, N. and Devanna, M. (1984) *Strategic Human Resource Management*. New York: John Wiley.

Fotopoulos, Ch. and Psomas, E. (2009) The impact of 'soft' and 'hard' TQM elements on quality management results. *International Journal of Quality and Reliability Management*, 26(2): 150–63.

Ghorpade, J., Chen, M. M. and Caggiano, J. (1995) Creating quality-driven performance appraisal systems. *Academy of Management Executive*, 9(1): 32–40.

Glover, J. (1993) Achieving the organisational change necessary for successful TQM. *International Journal of Quality and Reliability Management*, 10(6): 47–64.

Godfrey, G., Dale, B. G., Marchington, M. and Wilkinson, A. (1997) Control: a contested concept in TQM research. *International Journal of Operations and Production Management*, 17(6): 558–73.

Graber, J. M., Breisch, R. E. and Breisch, W. (1992) Performance appraisals and Deming: a misunderstanding? *Quality Progress*, (June): 59–62.

Greene, R. J. (1991) A 90's model for performance management. *HR Magazine*, 1 (April): 62.

Gross, S. J. (1995) *Compensation for Teams: How To Design and Implement Team-based Reward Programs*. New York: American Management Association.

Guest, D. E. (1987) Human resource management and industrial relations. *Journal of Management Studies*, 24(5): 503–21.

Guest, D. E. (1989) Human resource management: its implications for industrial relations and trade unions. In Storey, J. (ed.) *New Perspectives on Human Resource Management*. London: Routledge, pp. 41–55.

Hackman, J. R. (2002) *Leading Teams: Setting the Stage for Great Performances*. Boston: Harvard Business Press.

Hackman, J. and Wageman, R. (1995) Total quality management: empirical, conceptual and practical issues. *Administrative Science Quarterly*, 40: 309–42.

Harman, R., Golhar, D. and Deshpande, S. (2002) Lessons learned in work teams. *Production Planning and Control*, 13(4): 362–9.

Hemmings, B. (1992) Appraisal development. *TQM Magazine*, 4(5): 309–12.

Hill, S. and Wilkinson, A. (1995) In search of TQM. *Employee Relations*, 17(3): 8–25.

Incomes Data Services 1990. *Total Quality Management*. IDS Study No. 457. London: IDS.

Juran, J. M. (1989) *Juran on Leadership for Quality: An Executive Handbook*. New York: Free Press.

Katzenbach, J. R. and Smith, D. K. (2003) *The Wisdom of Teams: Creating the High-performance Organization*. New York: Collins Business Essentials.

Knights, D. and McCabe, D. (1997) How would you measure something like that?: quality in a retail bank. *Journal of Management Studies*, 34(3): 371–88.

Knights, D. and McCabe, D. (1998) Dreams and designs on strategy: a critical analysis of TQM and management control. *Work, Employment and Society*, 12(3): 433–56.

Knights, D. and McCabe, D. (1999) Are there no limits to authority? TQM and organisational power. *Organization Studies*, 20(2): 197–224.

Lawler, E. E. III, Mohrman, S. A. and Ledford, G. E. J. (1992) *Employee Involvement and Total Quality Management: Practices and Results in Fortune 1000 Companies*. San Francisco: Jossey-Bass.

Lawler, E. E., Mohrman, S.A. and Ledford, G.E., Jr (1995) *Creating High Performance Organizations*. San Francisco: Jossey-Bass.

Legge, K. (1995) Human resource management: a critical analysis. In Storey, J. (ed.) *New Perspectives on Human Resource Management*. London: Routledge, pp. 19–40.

Legge, K. (2005) *Human Resource Management: Rhetorics and Realities*. Hampshire: Palgrave Macmillan.

Longenecker, C. O. and Fink, L. S. (1999) Creating effective performance appraisal. *Industrial Management*, 41(5): 18–23.

McElwee, G. and Warren, L. (2000) TQM and HRM in growing organisations. *Journal of Strategic Change*, 9(7): 427–35.

Manz, C. C. and Sims, H. P. J. (1993) *Business Without Bosses: How Self-managing Teams Are Building High Performance Companies*. New York: Wiley.

Marchington, M. and Wilkinson, A. (2000) *Core Personnel and Development*. London: Chartered Institute of Personnel and Development.

Morgan, P. (2000) Paradigms lost and paradigms regained? Recent developments and new directions for HRM/OB in the UK and USA. *International Journal of Human Resource Management*, 11(4): 853–66.

Murphy, K. R. and Cleveland, J. N. (1991) *Performance Appraisal: An Organisational Perspective*. Boston, MA: Allyn & Bacon.

Nankervis, A. R., Compton, R. L. and McCathy, T. E. (1992) *Strategic Human Resource Management*. Melbourne: Thomas Nelson.

Oakland, J. S. (2004) *Oakland on Quality Management*. Boston: Elsevier Butterworth-Heinemann.

Oliver, N. and Wilkinson, B. (1992) *The Japanisation of British Industry* (2nd edn). Oxford: Blackwell.

O'Neil, H. F., Baker, E. L. and Kazlauskas, E. J. (1992) Assessment of team performance. In Swezey, R. W. and Salas, E. (eds) *Teams: Their training and performance*. Norwood, NJ: Albex, pp. 3–29.

Palmer, G. and Saunders, I. (1992) TQM and HRM: comparisons and contrasts. *Asia Pacific Journal of Human Resource Management*, 30(2): 67–78.

Powell, T. C. (1995) Total quality management as competitive advantage: a review and empirical study. *Strategic Management Journal*, 16(1): 15–37.

Prajogo, D. I. and McDermott, C .M. (2005) The relationship between total quality management practices and organizational culture. *International Journal of Operations and Production Management*, 25(11): 1101–22.

Price, A. (2007) *Human Resource Management in a Business Context* (3rd edn). London: Thomson/Cengage Learning.

Price, R. C. and Gaskill, G. P. (1990) Total quality management in research: philosophy and practice of total quality management. *Proceedings of 3rd International Conference*. London: IFS/Springer-Verlag, pp. 77–87.

Rahman, S. and Sohal, A. S. (2002) A review and classification of total quality management research in Australia and an agenda for future research.

15

International Journal of Quality and Reliability Management, 19(1): 46–66.

Randell, G. A. (1994) Employee appraisal. In Sisson, K. (ed.) *Personnel Management: A Comprehensive Guide to Theory & Practice in Britain*. Oxford: Blackwell Publishers Ltd, pp. 221–52.

Redman, T. and Wilkinson, A. (2009) *Contemporary Human Resource Management: Text and Cases*. London: Pearson Education.

Rees, C. (1995) Quality management and HRM in the service industry: some case study evidence. *Employee Relations*, 17(3): 99–109.

Reid, R. D. and Sanders, N. R. (2009). *Operations Management* (4th edn). John Wiley.

Reilly, R. and McGourty, J. (1998) Performance appraisal in team settings. In Smither, J. W. (ed.) *Performance Appraisal: State of the Art in Practice*. San Francisco: Jossey-Bass, pp. 244–77.

Rothwell, W. J. and Kazanas, H. C. (1989) *Strategic Human Resource Development*. Englewood Cliffs, NJ: Prentice Hall.

Saunders, I. and Preston, A. (1995) A model and a research agenda for total quality management. *Total Quality Management*, 5(4): 185–202.

Scholtes, P. R. (1993) Total quality or performance appraisal: choose one. *National Productivity Review*, 12(3): 349–63.

Scholtes, P. R. (1995) Performance appraisal: obsolete and harmful. *Quality Magazine*, (October): 66–70.

Seddon, J. (2001) Performance a Miracle: Praise the Workers. *The Observer*, 11 March. Available from: http://www.lean-service.com [accessed April 2003].

Sexton, C. (1994) Self managed work teams: TQM technology at the employee level. *Journal of Organizational Change Management*, 7(2): 45–52.

Shadur, M. A. and Bamber, G. J. (1994) Toward lean management? International transferability of Japanese management strategies to Australia. *International Executive*, 36(3): 343–64.

Sila, I. and Ebrahimpour, M. (2005) Critical linkages among TQM factors and business results. *International Journal of Operations and Production Management*, 25(11): 1123–55.

Simmons, D. E., Shadur, M. A. and Preston, A. P. (1995) Integrating TQM and HRM. *Employee Relation*, 17(3): 75–86.

Sisson, K. (ed.) (1994) *Personnel Management: A Comprehensive Guide to Theory and Practice in Britain*. Oxford: Blackwell.

Smith, M. R. (2002) High performance work organisations in theory and practice. *Global Business and Economics Review*, 4(2): 187–204.

Smither, J. W. (1998) Lessons learned: research implications for performance appraisal and management practice. In Smither, J. W. (ed.) *Performance Appraisal: State of the Art in Practice*. San Francisco: Jossey-Bass Publishers, pp. 537–48.

Smyth, H. and Scullion, G. (1996) HRM and TQM linkages: a comparative case analysis. *International Journal of Manpower*, 17(6): 89–105.

Snape, E., Wilkinson, A. and Redman, T. (1996) Cashing in on quality? Pay incentives and the quality culture. *Human Resource Management Journal*, 6(4): 5–17.

Soltani, E. and Wilkinson, A. (2010) Stuck in the middle with you: the effects of incongruency of senior and middle managers' orientations on TQM programmes. *International Journal of Operations and Production Management*, 30(4): 365–97.

Soltani, E., van der Meer, R. B., Gennard, J. and Williams, T. (2003) A TQM approach to HR performance evaluation: a questionnaire survey. *European Management Journal*, 21(3): 323–37.

Soltani, E., van der Meer, R. B., Gennard, J. and Williams, T. (2004) HR performance evaluation in quality management context: a review of the literature. *International Journal of Quality and Reliability Management*, 21(4): 377–96.

Soltani, E., van der Meer, R. B. and Williams, T. M. (2005) A contrast of HRM and TQM approaches to performance management: a survey. *British Journal of Management*, 16: 211–30.

Soltani, E., van der Meer, R. B., Williams, T. M. and Lai, P. (2006) The compatibility of performance appraisal systems with TQM principles – evidence from current practice. *International Journal of Operations and Production Management*, 26(1): 92–112.

Soltani, E., Lai, P. and Phillips, P. (2008a) A new look at factors influencing total quality management failure: work process control or workforce control? *New Technology, Work and Employment*, 23(1–2): 125–42.

Soltani, E., Sayed Javadin, R. and Lai, P. (2008b) A review of the theory and practice of quality management: an integrative framework. *Total Quality Management and Business Excellence*, 19(8): 461–79.

Sousa, R. and Voss, C. A. (2002) Quality management re-visited: a reflective review and agenda for future research. *Journal of Operation Management*, 20(1): 91–109.

Squires, P. and Adler, S. (1998) Linking appraisals to individual development and training. In Smither, J. W. (ed.) *Performance Appraisal: State of the Art in Practice*. San Francisco: Jossey-Bass Publishers, pp. 443–95.

Storey, J. (ed.) (1989) *New Perspectives on Human Resource Management*. London: International Thomson.

Storey, J. (1992) *Developments in the Management of Human Resources*. Oxford: Blackwell.

Storey, J. (2000) *Human Resource Management: A Critical Text* (2nd edn). London: International Thomson.

Storey, J. (ed.) (2007) *Human Resource Management: A Critical Text* (3rd edn). London: International Thomson.

Storey, J, and Sisson, K. (1993) *Managing Human Resources and Industrial Relations*. Buckingham: Open University Press.

Storey, J., Wright, P. M. and Ulrich, D. (2009) *The Routledge Companion to Strategic Human Resource Management*. Abingdon: Routledge.

Summers, D. C. (2005) *Quality Management: Creating and Sustaining Organization Effectiveness*. New Jersey: Pearson Education.

Syed, J. (ed.) (2006) *Instructor's Manual: Contemporary Issues in Management and Organisational Behaviour*. Melbourne: Thomson Learning.

Taylor, F. W. (1911) *The Principles of Scientific Management*. New York: Harper Bros.

Torrington, D. and Hall, L. (1998) *Human Resource Management* (4th edn). London: Prentice Hall.

Torrington, D. and Hall, L. (2005) *Human Resource Management* (6th edn) London: Prentice Hall.

Waldman, D. A. (1994a) Designing performance management system for total quality implementation. *Journal of Organisational Change Management*, 7(2): 31–44.

Waldman, D. A. (1994b) The contributions of total quality management to a theory of work performance. *Academy of Management Review*, 19(3): 510–36.

Waldman, D. A. and Kenett, R. S. (1990) Improve performance by appraisal. *HR Magazine*, 35(7): 66–9.

Waldman, D. A., Lituchy, T., Gopalakrishnan, M., Laframboise, K., Galperin, B. and Kaltsounakis, Z. (1998) A qualitative analysis of leadership and quality improvement. *Leadership Quarterly*, 9(2): 177–201.

Wilkinson, A. (1992) The other side of quality: soft issues and the human resource dimension. *Total Quality Management*, 3(3): 323–9.

Wilkinson, A. (1994) Managing human resource for quality. In Dale, B. G. (ed.) *Managing Quality* (2nd edn). Hemel Hempstead: Prentice Hall, pp. 273–91.

Wilkinson, A. and Marchington, M. (1994) Total quality management – instant pudding for the personnel function? *Human Resource Management Journal*, 1(1): 33–49.

Wilkinson, A., Marchington, M., Goodman, J. and Ackers, P. (1992) Total quality management and employee involvement. *Human Resource Management Journal*, 2(4): 1–20.

Wilkinson, A., Marchington, M. and Dale, B. G. (1993) Human resource's function. *TQM Magazine*, 5(3): 31–5.

Wilkinson, A., Godfrey, G. and Marchington, M. (1997) Bouquets, brickbats and blinkers: total quality management and employee involvement in practice. *Organisation Studies*, 18(5): 799–819.

Wilkinson, A., Redman, T., Snape, E. and Marchington, M. (1998) *Managing with Total Quality Management: Theory and Practice*. London: Macmillan.

Willmott, H. (1994) Management education. Provocations to a debate. *Management Learning*, 25(1): 105–36.

Yong, J. and Wilkinson, A. (1999) The state of total quality management: a review. *International Journal of Human Resource Management*, 10(1): 137–61.

Zairi, M. (1991) *Total Quality Management for Engineers*. Cambridge: Woodhead.

Human resource management in small to medium-sized enterprises

S. O. Raby and M. W. Gilman

16

?

After reading this chapter, you should be able to:

☐ Understand how to define and differentiate between micro, small and medium-sized enterprises (SMEs)

☐ Discuss why SMEs are an important component of a healthy economy

☐ Critically assess the nature of the employment relationship within SMEs

☐ Understand the role that HRM plays within SMEs and how it impacts on organizational performance

Introduction

With small to medium-sized enterprises (SMEs) accounting for the vast majority of all businesses worldwide (Small Business Service, 2004), their importance to the international economy is not in doubt – but how to promote improved productivity, efficiency and overall long-term sustainable growth within SMEs is. Little is known about how SMEs achieve success, and even less is known about the practices and processes involved in the sustainability and growth of businesses. Although academic information on the area is expanding, the actual processes by which SMEs digest, understand and utilize such practices for improvement and growth are limited.

Such understanding is vital when one considers that some economies perform better than others. Recent comparative statistics highlight the existence of a productivity gap, with the UK lagging behind Italy, France and the USA with regard to gross domestic product, both per worker and per hour worked. Indeed, the USA outperforms the UK by 32 per cent per worker and 21 per cent per hour worked (Office for National Statistics, 2009). In the past, the primary cause for this productivity gap has focused on the underinvestment and under participation in workforce development. For instance, the mindset of UK manufacturing SMEs, and more widely reported 'Anglo-Saxon' management styles, have tended to focus on tangible investment such as technological advancements in machinery rather than employees.

The role that SMEs can play in enhancing economic performance has been driven by a somewhat simplistic view of small company relations as being 'harmonious'. More recent research has, however, challenged this notion on several grounds, not least of which is the fact that one cannot assume that the SME sector is homogeneous. Greater complexity and contradiction surrounds the management of SMEs than has been historically presumed.

This chapter aims to critically assess the role of employees in SMEs, and in doing so will explore the following: how SMEs are defined; the importance and contribution of SMEs to national economies; the employment relations environment within SMEs; and the role of human resource management (HRM) and its influence on performance within SMEs.

Defining SMEs

The definition of an SME has long been a topic of confusion, with research labelling firms by size of organization (number of employees), sales turnover and net worth (their balance sheet). In the UK, the complexity of formulating a suitable definition for what constitutes an SME became increasingly apparent during an inquiry into small firms by the Bolton Committee in the early 1970s. Objective measures alone were not considered to be appropriate as they were unable to take into account the idiosyncrasies of the small firm sector; therefore, the committee proposed specific 'economic' measures. Firms were classified as 'small' if they satisfied the following criteria:

Firstly, in economic terms a small firm is one that has a relatively small share of its market. Secondly, an essential characteristic of a small firm is that it is managed by its owners or part-owners in a personalised way, and not through the medium of formalised management structure. Thirdly, it is also independent in the sense that it does not form part of a larger enterprise and that the owner-managers should be free from outside control in taking their principal decisions. (Bolton, 1971: 1)

In addition, the Committee developed 'statistical' measures that related to the contribution of smaller firms to the economy, affording an opportunity to draw international comparisons. These measures led the Committee to dissect smaller firms into distinct sectors, and to select firms using an assortment of characteristics ranging from size by employee and sales turnover to asset size (Table 16.1).

A number of criticisms were levelled at the Committee's conclusion on the definition of a small firm, not least because it did not allow for a direct comparison within sectors. In addition, although the Committee suggested that a small firm would be managed in a personalized way, the definition of a manufacturing firm was deemed too large to meet this criterion as a firm with over 200 employees would normally require a formalized management structure (Storey, 1994).

Table 16.1 Definitions of a 'small firm' as proposed by the Bolton Committee

Sector	Definition
Manufacturing	200 employees or less
Construction	25 employees or less
Mining and quarrying	25 employees or less
Retailing	Turnover of £50,000 or less
Miscellaneous	Turnover of £50,000 or less
Services	Turnover of £50,000 or less
Motor trades	Turnover of £100,000 or less
Wholesale trades	Turnover of £200,000 or less
Road transport	Five vehicles or less
Catering	All excluding multiples and brewery-managed houses

Source: Bolton (1971: 3)

The lack of a clear definition of what constitutes an SME has led scholars to adopt a range of definitions when investigating smaller firms. These definitions vary from those organizations with fewer than 19 employees (Kotey and Sheridan, 2004) to those with over 500 employees (Golhar and Deshpande, 1997), with a range of categories in between. For instance, Hornsby and Kuratko (1990), in their study of 247 small firms in Midwest America, classified a small firm as one that had up to 150 employees. MacMahon (1996) included only those firms of under 100 employees in her study of 269 small Irish manufacturers. Nguyen and Bryant (2004), in their study of 89 Vietnamese small firms, included any firms with under 200 employees. Indeed, the literature even draws attention to studies that do not differentiate between small, medium or large firms (Cardon and Stevens, 2004), and those studies which purport to investigate SMEs but actually focus on medium-sized enterprises within their sample (see, for example, Harney and Dundon, 2006).

This is problematic not only because firms of varying sizes will have very different management and organizational needs, but because comparing studies is inherently difficult. This debate has led to size warranting undue attention, with research being 'concerned more with prescribing what small business ought to be than analysing what it actually is' (Goss, 1991a: 24). More recently, the European Commission (EC) has sought to rectify this through a new recommendation that came into effect in early 2005 with the launch of the first common definition for SMEs (European Commission, 2005). These EC thresholds take account of three elements – staff head count, annual turnover and annual balance sheet – leading to a classification of SMEs as outlined in Table 16.2.

Table 16.2 The new thresholds for small to medium-sized enterprises

Enterprise category	Head count	Annual turnover	Annual balance sheet total
Medium-sized	<250	≤ €50 million	≤ €43 million
Small	<50	≤ €10 million	≤ €10 million
Micro	<10	≤ €2 million	≤ €2 million

Source: European Commission (2005: 3)

In updating the definition of an SME, the EC has sought to raise the profile of micro enterprises, a previously undefined area. It was hoped that this would improve access to capital, research and development, and promote innovation among SMEs, thus ensuring that 'only those enterprises that genuinely require support are targeted by public schemes' (European Commission, 2005: 3).

Despite this, a recent report highlighted that several countries are still using different size categories. The report also reports that statistics are made all the more difficult by the 'informal' or 'grey economy', defined as a 'set of economic activities concerned with the production of goods and services which are legal in themselves but whose generation entails illegal or extra-legal activity' (Edwards and Ram, 2006a: 2; see also Edwards and Ram, 2006b). In addition, although European definitions have, to an extent, become standardized, the USA remains committed to size standards that make reference to individual industry codes. The resultant effect is an employment size band for SMEs that range from below 500 employees to below 1,500 employees depending on sector (US Small Business Administration, 2010).

The importance of SMEs

How important are SMEs to national and global economies? The resounding conclusion is 'very', when one considers that of the four million businesses regarded as being active within the UK economy, over 99 per cent are accounted for by SMEs (Small Business Service, 2004). As Table 16.3 illustrates, SMEs account for 59 per cent of the employed workforce, a figure of over 13 million employees, demonstrating the substantial role that SMEs play as a source of employment and taxable revenue.

Table 16.3 The contribution of small to medium-sized enterprises (SMEs) to the UK economy

Enterprise category	No. of enterprises	Employment	Turnover (£billion)
All industry	4,484,535	22,514,000	3.2
SMEs (0–249 employees)	4,478,595	13,316,000	1.56
Large organizations (250 or more employees)	5,940	9,198,000	1.65

Source: Data taken from Department for Business, Innovation and Skills (2011)

The significance of SMEs to the wider European Union (EU) is also clear, with SMEs representing 99.8 per cent of all enterprises, 67.4 per cent all employment and 58 per cent of value added. The UK SME sector is ranked fifth by number employed (behind Italy, France, Spain and Denmark), and second behind Denmark in terms of added value (European Commission, 2009). In the EU, SME employment rates vary from 70 per cent or more in The Netherlands (77.0%), Denmark (75.7%), Sweden (72.2%) and Austria (71.6%) to those up to ten percentage point below the Lisbon target, including Malta (54.9%), Hungary, (55.4%), Italy (57.5%), Romania (58.6%), Poland (59.3%) and Spain (European Commission, 2010). It is also interesting to note that although the USA is often portrayed as offering the ideal environment for small businesses to develop, 'by every measure of small business employment, the United States has among the world's smallest small-business sector (as a proportion of national employment)' (Schmitt and Lane, 2009: 1).

The contribution that small firms could make to the economy was initially explored in a paper by David Birch in the late 1970s, in his analysis of Dun and Bradstreet data on businesses in the USA. Birch (1979) demonstrated that SMEs could be associated with higher proportions of job creation, findings that would later be seen to play an influential role in setting the Thatcher government's approach towards SMEs (Storey, 1994; Bamber et al., 2004). The UK supported these findings, using them as justification for a subsequent array of policy initiatives and support for the SME sector, focusing on finance, legislation and administration, and information and advice (Goss, 1991a). Since the 1970s, the growth of industrial districts in countries such as Italy and Germany has often been seen as a model for other countries to follow. The prospect of SMEs working together to produce 'high-tech–high-skill' products and processes further promoted the SME superlative. However, this should be balanced against the challenges that smaller firms face in keeping pace with change given that they have increasingly found themselves exposed to international competition (Edwards and Ram, 2006b).

Although scholars initially upheld SMEs as exemplars of job creation through the early studies of Birch (1979), latterly these calculations have been proven to be by no means conclusive. SMEs may create new jobs when compared with their share of the employment base, but they do not have a demonstratable effect when compared with the economy as a whole (Davidsson et al., 1998). Indeed, studies even demonstrate that the contribution of the SME sector to job creation has not increased since the 1960s (Harrison, 1996) and that although SMEs may create more jobs than large firms, they also contribute greater to job losses (Davis et al., 1996).

Despite this, successive governments have remained committed supporters of SMEs in the economy, identifying the key role that SMEs play in the generation of employment, value and innovation in the UK, Europe (European Commission, 2005; Department for Business Enterprise and Regulatory Reform, 2008) and beyond:

> Small businesses will lead the way to prosperity in today's challenging economic environment … Our Nation's success depends on America's small businesses and entrepreneurs. (President Barack Obama on May 15, 2009; cited in Schmitt and Lane, 2009: 3).

Not only does the attention afforded to SMEs by national governments complement a political and economic philosophy, but, crucially, it is believed that SMEs avoid the complex employment relations issues and conflicts inherent in large firms whose poor management had such a damaging effect on the economy in the 1970s (Marlow and Patton, 1993). Indeed, the conclusions drawn by the Bolton inquiry attributed low levels of industrial action within SMEs to their more harmonious, flexible working conditions:

> In many respects the small firms provides a better environment for the employee than is possible in most large firms. Although physical working conditions many sometimes be inferior in small firms, most people prefer to work in a small group where communication presents fewer problems: the employee in a small firm can more easily see the relation between what he is doing and the objectives and performance of the firm as a whole … No doubt mainly as a result of this, the turnover of staff in small firms is very low and strikes and other kinds of industrial disputes are relatively infrequent. (Bolton, 1971: 21)

The findings of the Bolton Committee, coupled with other influential studies (see, for example, Ingham, 1970), supported a 'harmony thesis', proposing that employees were in fact drawn towards working in the small firm sector as a result of their inherently rewarding working environment. These findings reinforced the government's hostile stance in countries such as the UK towards collective employment relations.

The emphasis implied through the above review is that the importance of SMEs to all economies has increased dramatically over recent decades. Consequently, scholars seek a better understanding of how SMEs function and the nature of the work environment. In order to broaden our understanding, the next section will aim to delve further into the particularities of small businesses employment relations.

A critical analysis of employment relations in SMEs

Although some see SMEs as an avenue for employment for those workers made redundant by larger firms (Storey, 1994), others hold the view that workers become snared in the trappings of SMEs, finding it difficult to break out. In the latter case, the workers' fate is seen to be sealed through their inability to work in large firms due to unattainable skill levels (Scase, 1995) or family ties (Ram, 1994). Indeed, Ram's (1994) study of ethnic minority workplaces found that Asian workers ended up working in smaller firms in the clothing sector because few other employment opportunities presented themselves.

Given the ways in which workers enter employment within SMEs and the findings presented within the previous section, a number of crucial questions present themselves, and we will now turn our attention to these:

- ☐ Are harmonious working relationships a true representation of the employee relations environment of SMEs?
- ☐ What are the dominant proprietorial management styles?
- ☐ What other factors influence the employment relations environment of SMEs?

A workplace characterized by harmony: dispelling the myth?

The positive stance portrayed by the Bolton Committee is not surprising when one considers that the inquiry did not directly address employment relations issues, failing to pursue any research at the employee level. Since the Bolton inquiry reached its verdict, a number of studies have set out to investigate whether worker relations in SMEs are indeed harmonious. Subsequently, a range of conflicting evidence has since presented itself that contrasts with this idea of 'small is beautiful'.

The adeptly named 'bleak house', or 'small is brutal', images were formed by academics who found evidence of poor working conditions, low wage rates and low standards of health in SMEs (Rainnie, 1989). Indeed a review of the literature undertaken by Storey (1994) contrasted large firms with their SME counterparts in terms of seven job 'quality' dimensions. Storey identified that workers in SMEs are more likely to have lower wages, are less likely to be in receipt of fringe benefits, experience lower levels of formal training, work longer hours and have a higher chance of being injured while at work. Low levels of unionization were also evident among SMEs, although this was attributed to incompatible structures for trade unions and a preference for informal communication (Storey, 1994). Low levels of pay in conjunction with high levels of employee turnover were also found in a study of 269 small Irish manufacturers (MacMahon, 1996). MacMahon attributed this employee outcome to the working environment of the SME and the strict management styles employed.

In contrast, evidence has been found that service firms may better represent the harmony thesis, with a lack of promotional opportunities being outweighed by the ability to recognize their (employees') contributions to the business (Barrett, 1999), as well as by employees' preference for personal autonomy (Scase, 2003).

Mini Case Study 16.1
A window of opportunity for staff: the effects of poor human relations practice on productivity in a medium-sized manufacturer

This case example draws upon detailed action research undertaken during a 2-year Knowledge Transfer Partnership (KTP) programme. KTP is a UK government scheme that creates a strategic partnership between a company and a knowledge base (for example, universities) in order to transfer and develop the latest in management thinking. The programme is typically led by an 'associate' recruited to the partnership.

Window Co. is a manufacturer and installer of UPVC windows located in Kent, UK. The firm was founded in 1980 following a growing need to provide refurbishment construction services to housing authorities, councils, defence establishments and schools. At the time of the investigation, the company employed 132 employees in total. This case focuses on the manufacturing activities of the company, and on the 60 employees working on the shop floor.

Window Co. has been relatively successful and has grown considerably since its formation in 1980. The firm had a turnover of £11.7 million at time of the investigation, and had grown substantially in turnover in the 4 years prior to this. This increase in company turnover and head count was not, however, matched by an increase in profit. In fact, the opposite was happening.

Following an investment of £1.2 million in state-of-the art machinery, Window Co. was yet to realize its full available manufacturing capacity. The managing director had little understanding of why this was the case but saw the company's outdated production flow and layout as principal problem areas. On investigation, however, the university partner quickly noted that the emphasis lay with employee relations and, more importantly, with how the managing director was dealing with such issues:

He [the managing director] had little respect for employees, considering them to be lazy and ignorant. He also made decisions within the firm in a very authoritative manner. Often they were made in isolation from each other, and other managers/departments had a clear lack of understanding as to what they were meant to be achieving. (Knowledge-base Supervisor)

Within the first month of the study, the data that were collated demonstrated high levels of staff absenteeism and turnover, with the manufacturing unit exhibiting a turnover of 95 per cent. In real terms, this meant that the plant had to recruit 57 new employees each year to sustain the 60 employees needed on the shop floor. To highlight the severity of the problem, the industry average for staff turnover among craft/manual workers is 12.1 per cent (Chartered Institute of Personnel and Development, 2009). Turnover was found to be most likely to occur within 1 month of employment, with 44 per cent of leavers separating within 1 month and a 74 per cent separating within 1–3 months.

An interesting characteristic of high levels of turnover and absenteeism was that the factory could never reach the required staffing level. This resulted in the production facilities being permanently understaffed by, on average, 26 per cent per day. This placed added pressure on existing staffing resources, and produced a consistent emphasis on recruitment. Indeed, it was common to find the production manager working on the shop floor in the drive to meet numerical targets and to compensate for the managing director's autocratic management style and controlling approach. This was often at the expense of good management practice.

Questions
1 If you were placed as the associate in this company, which human resources practices would you concentrate on, and why?
2 How would you gain the commitment of the managing director to allow you and other staff to place a greater emphasis on human resources?

As debates between 'small is beautiful' and 'bleak house' have continued, scholars have criticized the dichotomous nature of such comparisons, postulating that they are too simplistic and require a more detailed examination of the complex issues involved (Scase, 1995; Wilkinson, 1999). Since these early studies, a range of typologies have been formed against which SMEs can be aligned, affording an opportunity to better identify the characteristics that have influenced the way in which management approaches employment relations (see also Mini Case Study 16.1). These frameworks investigate the role of large firms (Rainnie, 1989) and the proprietor (Scase and Goffee, 1987), and bring to the fore notions of power and control (Goss, 1991a).

Acting in response to the demands of large firms?

Rainnie's (1989) typology depicts SMEs according to their relationship with large firms, and proposes four models of firms: dependent, dominated, isolated and innovative:

- □ *Dependent* SMEs are entirely reliant on large firms and are, as a result, driven to orient their operations (for example, finance, working practices and so on) towards the requests of these large firms.
- □ *Dominated* firms compete against large firms and in many respects are subservient to their large counterparts who define the rules of the market and as a result drive the behaviour of SMEs.
- □ *Isolated* SMEs exist within specific niches that are not viable for large firms to enter owing to the low profitability. These niches are typified by the existence of sweatshops.
- □ Finally, *innovative* SMEs develop distinctive products or services, often with high risk attached, that they may later gain commitment from large firms to grow.

Other academics acknowledge that SMEs can provide flexibility to large firms in the delivery of their product or service, or may even be reduced to a 'web of dependency' (Scase, 2003).

Despite academics criticizing Rainnie's typology for possessing Marxist and deterministic qualities (Goss, 1991b), Rainnie highlights the ability of the framework to take account of the differences between SMEs and move away from the dominant role of management. Indeed, Barrett and Rainnie (2002) conjecture that little progress has actually been made into understanding the influences that guide SME employment relations since Rainnie's original paper was written.

In response, Ram and Edwards (2003) argue that research on employee relations in SMEs is 'alive and well'. They support this view through a review of articles reporting a range of external and internal factors, including social aspects such as family and community, that have been found to impact on worker relations in SMEs. Furthermore, the authors draw on their own prior work and that of a 'dominated firm' that developed a strategic orientation towards its environment instead of succumbing to the supremacy of the large firm.

Having investigated the impact of large firms, we will now turn our attention to the role of the proprietor in employment relations in SMEs.

The all-powerful proprietor? Styles for 'managing' employee relations

Stanworth and Curran (1981) provide context to the mindset of the proprietor through three entrepreneurial 'latent social identities': the 'artisan', who assumes most reward from autonomy and status; the 'classical entrepreneur', whose behaviour is motivated by the bottom line; and the 'manager', who seeks acknowledgment for the way he or she works with those internal and external to the business. Goss (1991a) expands on the above typology by contrasting two distinct characteristics of the proprietor, namely 'managerial orientation' and 'vocational attachment'. Goss uses these to elucidate on four specific proprietorial styles: 'traditional', which is akin to Stanworth and Curran's (1981) 'artisan'; 'technocentric', resulting in high levels of both managerial and vocational attachment; 'marketeers', analogous to the 'classical entrepreneur'; and 'isolationists', who maintain the business for their own personal lifestyle. Although the above descriptors act as a useful background to proprietorial motivation, they provide little understanding of how relations with workers might play out in practice.

Scase and Goffee (1987) provide a context to employment relationship in SMEs by taking account of the role that the proprietor holds within the firm, thus accounting for changes in size. They do this by identifying four distinct proprietorial roles: self-employed, small employers, owner-controllers and owner-directors:

- ☐ The *self-employed* are in essence sole-traders who do not have access to paid subordinate labour, but may draw upon family ties for support.
- ☐ *Small employers* take managerial responsibility for the firm while continuing to support their employees in an administrative capacity, an approach that often results in an uncertain employee relations environment.
- ☐ *Owner-controllers* take a managerially oriented role, focusing on financial and supervisory roles.
- ☐ Finally, *owner-directors* use more formal mechanisms for management and control and may vary between personal or more bureaucratic approaches depending on individual desires.

As Goss (1991a: 28) concludes, these proprietorial roles 'identify that there is likely to be some degree of 'fit' between the meanings, definitions and abilities of proprietors and workers'.

Goss (1991a) elaborates further by focusing attention on two related concepts – power and control – acted out through 'the dependence of the employer upon particular employees and vice versa; and the power of workers individually or collectively to resist the exercise of proprietorial control' (p. 73). This leads Goss to define four distinct proprietorial styles: fraternalism, paternalism, benevolent autocracy and sweating (Figure 16.1). Each of these employer control strategies is reflective on the one hand of employees' ability 'to resist proprietorial prerogative' and on the other of the employer's ability to define the employment relationship. Employers who exhibit a fraternal approach afford employees greater discretion and autonomy in their roles, in contrast to benevolent autocracy and sweating, in which employees' skills are easily available with the labour market, and hence the employer makes few concessions for employees.

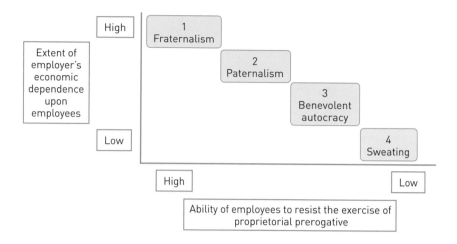

Figure 16.1 Types of employer control in small to medium-sized enterprises
Source: Goss (1991a: 73)

In his longitudinal study of clothing manufacturers in the UK's West Midlands, Ram (1994) identifies that power and control are constantly changing phenomena, played out in a 'negotiation of order' best described as 'negotiated paternalism'. Indeed, Ram notes that:

> Workers were not passive in the face of authoritarian managements; they would endeavour to alter the terms of the effort bargain if they felt that they were not 'fairly' rewarded ... the stockpiling of work and 'modifying' the role of supervisor ... cannot be regarded as deliberate strategies of resistance. Rather, they were opportunistic and pragmatic actions by workers attempting to secure a degree of stability over their earnings. (Ram, 1994: 123)

The findings of Moule (1998) are analogous to those from this study. Moule provides further insight into the world of small manufacturers in the clothing industry through a detailed case study, that of Button Co. The author uncovers evidence of particular strategies used by employees to facilitate workers' negotiations with management. The work environment also afforded opportunities for work avoidance, so-called 'workplace fiddles', which were tolerated by management and demonstrate the notion of 'leeway'.

Further confirmation of the influence that employees can have on the way in which SMEs are managed is also evident in information-intensive service firms through a study of computing and training firms in the West Midlands (Ram, 1999). Ram notes that there was clear opportunity for discretion and autonomy in an employee's role, and that this approach reduced the need for direct supervision. These findings are reinforced by those of Scase (2003), who notes that employees are essentially the intellectual property of businesses that exist within information-intensive industries, and as such command greater respect.

Latterly, the literature has developed through frameworks that draw attention to the range of internal and external influences shaping employment relations behaviours in SMEs. These include size, labour market power, customer and supplier relationships, the role of the family and kinship relations, and institutional context (Edwards and Ram, 2006a). In the process, scholars have communicated more lucidly on the role of institutions and on how firms are embedded within their wide social context. Academics highlight that SMEs are not a homogenous group, that employers and employees do not necessarily share common interests, and that the employee relations environment is subject to significant heterogeneity and hence complexity. Early assumptions of 'small is beautiful' or 'bleak house' are therefore unwarranted, and indeed too simplistic (Scase, 1995), with employees seen to play a significant role in workplace bargaining.

Despite the inherent complexities and contradictions embedded within the employment relationship outlined above, recent debates have tried to reinstate the view that SMEs can indeed be treated as a homogeneous group. This approach highlights SMEs as potential incubators for the development of HRM practices that result in superior performance, and it is this that we will explore next.

A critical analysis of HRM and high performance: an SME phenomenon?

Growth in SMEs

Although growth theories draw our attention to some of the key development requirements that a business should consider, they have been highly contested on the basis that no one model or theory can adequately explain the growth of small business (Gibb and Davies, 1990). Not all SMEs aspire to be large, nor do they pass through predefined stages in a linear fashion. Growth is a complex process involving an interrelated range of factors occurring in differing amounts and at different times, and hence having differing effects (Smallbone et al., 1992). Such critiques, however, appear not to have led to better research but to limiting further research in this area, which is unfortunate because it represents the type of knowledge that small business managers typically need and demand (Davidsson et al., 2005).

Growth models highlight key barriers and constraints to business growth. These can be viewed both internally, in terms of the strategic choices of the owner/manager and the organization's ability to make structural adaptations as it grows, and externally, in terms of the structural characteristics of the external market, such as competition, market, regulation, finance, labour and legislation. Interestingly, studies have recognized that although SMEs face a number of external barriers to growth, it is more often the internal factors that determine their growth (Arthur Anderson and Binder Hamlyn, 1996). Such studies have found that 'a company's attitude to growth ... as well as the structure, skills and age profile of management ... dominates its ability to grow' (Smith and Whitaker, 1998: 179).

Research is beginning to develop an understanding of some of the key drivers, including the environment (Starbuck, 1976; Dess and Beard, 1984; O'Gorman, 2001), strategic choice (Porter, 1985; O'Gorman, 2001) and competitive advantage (Porter, 1985; Jonash, 2005; O'Gorman, 2001; Simpson et al., 2004; Gentle and Contri, 2005). These concepts involve a high level of human capital and have therefore more recently moved the boundaries of the growth and performance debate towards theories of HRM (see also Chapters 1–3).

HRM and performance

Although there is a growing body of evidence that certain types of human resources practices are associated with high performance, the lists of effective practices vary widely and even contradict one another (Hiltrop, 1996). The early and rather rudimentary descriptions of HRM are based on the 'hard' and 'soft' dichotomies (Forster and Whipp, 1995). To confuse matters, as was highlighted in Chapter 2, there are also various models of HRM (Hiltrop, 1996). The 'universal' or 'best practice' model proposes that a similar set of human resources policies and practices applies for all occasions (Schuster, 1986: Pfeffer, 1994; Jayoram et al., 1999). The 'contingency' or 'best fit' approach implies that the success of HRM practice is reliant on their interaction and alignment with other variables (e.g. systems, strategy and the environment) (Guest, 1997). The 'multiple stake-holder' perspective (for example see Beer et al., 1984; Hendry and Pettigrew, 1990) suggests that the needs of a range of individuals (e.g. employees, share-holders, etc.) must be taken into account, and the 'resource-based' perspective denotes that that competitive advantage – a competitive advantage that can arise even from a firm's technical and/or social complexity (Eddleston et al., 2008) – can only be achieved through human resource capabilities that are valu-able, rare, imperfectly imitable and imperfectly substitutable (Barney, 1991; Kearns and Lederer, 2003; Lavie, 2006; Wilkinson and Brouthers, 2006).

More recently, scholars have endeavoured to define a package of HRM prac-tices that a firm can adopt to achieve high performance. The so-called high-performance work system (HPWS) has been approached from a range of theoretical perspectives despite Paauwe's (2004) argument that HPWSs mainly fall into the 'universalistic' approach. HPWSs are conceptualized as a set of distinct but interrelated HRM practices that together select, develop, retain and motivate a workforce (Way, 2002; de Menezes and Wood, 2006) in a completely superior manner (Kerr et al., 2007). They are generally characterized by a set of managerial practices that serve to enhance the involvement, commitment and competencies of the employees (Osterman, 2006) by transforming them from merely being workers into being partners with their employers in realizing the company's goals (Caspersz, 2006).

Such practices are argued to occur in three 'bundles', although the components of the bundles differ from author to author (Sung and Ashton, 2005; Shih et al., 2006; Angelis and Thompson, 2007): high employee involvement practices, human resource practices, and reward and commitment practices represent dominant components (see the following for individual practices: Osterman, 2006; Blasi and Kruse, 2006; Denton, 2006; Drummond and Stone, 2007; see also Chapters 1–3). Although there are a common set of variables, evidence shows that it is the use of comprehensive systems of work practices in firms that is the key to higher productivity and stronger financial performance (Denton, 2006). It is even argued that concepts such as the HPWS may be more applicable at the level of SMEs rather than large businesses. The success of HPWS in SMEs is supposedly based on them being more innovative, informal, flexible and in touch with their employees (Bacon et al., 1996) – an off-shoot of the 'harmony' perspective.

Table 16.4 provides some examples of the required features and their problematic nature within SMEs, and raises questions over the degree to which these alleged characteristics of small businesses exist. At the heart of the debate is the acute shortage of research identifying and validating HRM practices in SMEs, let alone the relationship between strategy, HRM practices and performance (Andrews and Welbourne, 2000; Chandler et al., 2000; Paauwe, 2004).

Table 16.4 Features and problems of high-performance work systems in small to medium-sized enterprises (SMEs)

Required feature	Problems
Managerial vision	Small firms rarely have any coherent strategy, let alone one aimed at developing employees' flexibility, commitment and trust
	Convincing the owner to get on board with such ideas is problematic
	There is a limited ability to understand the sources of sustained competitive advantage
	There is a lack of capabilities to develop HRM practice
HRM expertise	The costs of hiring a full-time human resources specialist are highly prohibitive to SMEs
Integration with other systems, for example quality	Small firms very rarely have any coherent quality strategy for quality issues
Skill development and encouragement of innovation	Innovation is inconceivable without accurate information, but SMEs generally have fewer information sources despite having a greater need for them
	The external competitive environment (globalization, foreign competition, and so on) plays a role in the incidence of work innovations, whereas SMEs work mainly on a local basis
	There is a lack of finance and knowledge

HRM, human resources management.

Source: Scott et al. (1989); Marlow and Patton (1993); Andrick (1998); Van der Wiele and Brown (1998); Wilkes and Dale (1998); Bacon and Hoque (2005); Bryson et al. (2005); Blasi and Kruse (2006); Denton (2006); Lado et al. (2006); Angelis and Thompson (2007); Kerr et al. (2007)

Is a small business 'a little big business?'

As we have alluded to, there has been much debate on how SMEs conceptualize and adopt HRM. This has not been helped by the tendency for studies to place a greater emphasis on the practices of large firms. Indeed, early studies that could have shed further light on small workplaces (for example, the Workplace Industrial [now 'Employment'] Relations Survey – WERS) were seen to show a preoccupation with the functioning of unionized workplaces (Sisson, 1993). Sisson's early assessment of the WERS3 dataset argued that HRM should be given more attention, with a call for data to be gathered on planning and resourcing, recruitment and selection, reward and evaluation, and training and development.

Early studies drew attention to the fact that small businesses are not 'little big businesses' (Welsh and White, 1981). Attention was drawn to the 'resource poverty' of SMEs (Miner, 1973), arguing that SMEs are less likely to adopt a sophisticated range of practices (Hornsby and Kuratko, 1990; Pearson et al., 2006) or have a full-time individual responsible for human resources (Little, 1986). With the costs of hiring a human resources specialist on a full-time basis being highly prohibitive for SMEs, responsibility for human resources issues is more likely to rest on the shoulders of line management (Harney and Dundon, 2007).

This evidence must be contrasted to those studies which have uncovered little difference between the HRM environment in small and large firms (Way, 2002). A study by Barrett (1999) on the Australian information industry found that size did not vary the approach taken towards employment relations matters. Similarly, Harney and Dundon's (2007) study of small and medium-sized firms noted that 'two of the firms with the lowest number of HRM initiatives … were among the three largest firms, each with over 200 employees' (p. 147). These results are analogous with those of others (Way and Thacker, 2004) who find that size is not an antecedent of the presence of a human resources manager or a range of issues including growth, efficiency and conforming to regulatory pressures (Kerr et al., 2007). Critical Thinking 16.1 highlights the effect of the international context.

Critical Thinking 16.1
Comparative study of employment relations in SMEs across 17 European countries

Edwards and Ram (2006b) have highlighted that the average pay of employees in SMEs is typically between 70 and 80 per cent of national average pay, with some clear differences spread across sector as well as country. Workers in SMEs experienced longer working hours in all countries when compared with the employees of large firms. Training provision by SMEs was also inconsistent, with the formality of training policy argued to be higher in France than elsewhere, which would appear to reflect the statutory nature of training.

Although the collection of data on HRM practices on a comparative basis is typically problematic, the study in general found a low take-up of HRM practice, especially for practices such as teamwork, appraisal and career development. While greater consistency was found among pay practices, the same was not true for representation arrangements. The UK demonstrated one of the weakest networks of representative institutions, whereas countries such as Austria, Belgium, Denmark, France and Italy had much stronger forms of representation (for example, through the use of employers' associations). A similar picture emerged in terms of collective bargaining, trade union and voice arrangements.

Questions
1 To what extent does national context affect employment relations in SMEs?
2 Which elements of the macronational context are most relevant in shaping the nature of employment relations in SMEs?
3 Compare and discuss the differences in employee management in SMEs in two or more countries.

This small versus large debate has led to undue weight being attached to the role of formality within SMEs. A large body of research notes the informal nature of HRM in SMEs (for performance appraisal, see Wagar; 1998; for training, see de Kok and Uhlaner, 2001; and in general, see Kaman et al., 2001; Bartram, 2005). A study by MacMahon (1996) of 269 small Irish manufacturers noted high levels of informality with regard to communication. Similarly, a paper by Matlay (1999: 292) contrasting micro businesses and SMEs discovered a preference for an informal approach 'which facilitated open communication and resolution of complex and occasionally acrimonious work-related situations'; these results led Matlay to proclaim that 'informality rules' in SMEs, although continued tensions between formality and informality are apparent (Gilman and Edwards, 2008).

Although some academics deem informality to be problematic for SMEs, for instance in hampering their ability to appreciate employees' roles when aligned with the needs of the firm (Mayson and Barrett, 2006), others point to the uncritical and simplistic nature of HRM research (Marlow, 2006), the harmful effect of formality on SMEs (Kaman et al., 2001) and the fact that informality may actually be a competitive advantage (Bacon et al., 1996). Informality is seen to afford SMEs a degree of flexibility they otherwise would not have, increasing their responsiveness and their ability to deal with uncertainty (Marlow, 2006). Academics are, however, critical that size has preoccupied the debate on small-firm HRM (see, for example, Marlow et al., 2010), with comparisons against large firm being neither appropriate nor warranted (Tansky and Heneman, 2004):

> HRM is considered by many to be a large company phenomenon ... bureaucracy, policies, procedures, and paperwork ... that does not sound very important for a fast moving entrepreneurial firm. (Katz et al., 2000: 8)

In addressing this bias, research has unearthed the changing human resources needs of SMEs over time (Kotey and Sheridan, 2004). A range of conditional internal promoters, including the skills mix of workers and management, and the importance placed on human resources issues by the proprietor, drive SMEs to adopt more sophisticated HRM practice, as do a range of contingent external influences such as the product market, trade unions and customers or suppliers.

Conclusion

This chapter has acknowledged the important role that SMEs play in the global economy. Although early studies drew naive conclusions that SME employment relations were largely harmonious – a notion of 'small is beautiful' – it is now widely accepted that these early visions were unwarranted and indeed too simplistic (Scase, 1995); employer prerogative does not rule without challenge (Ram, 1994).

Mini Case Study 16.2
Keeping things personal: human resources in a high-growth financial services firm

Mortgage Co is an independent mortgage provider for buy-to-let, development finance and residential and commercial mortgages. Their head office is located in Sevenoaks, just outside London, and they also have a regional office in Manchester that is supported for marketing, IT, human resources and payroll functions. Mortgage Co can be classed as a medium-sized enterprise, with a sales turnover of £6.7 million and 58 employees. Its regional office contributes £1.5 million to turnover and has five employees.

Established in 1990, the firm did not grow significantly until 2001, 11 years after the business's initial conception. On average, over the last 5 years, the company has grown year on year in turnover by 26 per cent, in net profit by 16 per cent and in number of employees by 9 per cent. Within the firm's early phase of growth, financial management and defining the business model were seen as key to affording a solid foundation upon which to build. Latterly, the company has focused attention on a number developments to support growth, including a move to new premises, marketing and brand value, management structure, delegation and human resources, operational procedures and IT systems and resources.

These developments have subsequently allowed the company to take a more professional approach to the management of clients and employees. Indeed, the managing director has been able to relinquish control over the business, thereby allowing greater time to be spent on the company's vision and strategic direction. Time was not, however, the only reason for placing an emphasis on strategy: the availability of accurate industry data provided the opportunity to track the impact of a particular strategy, which in turn drove a deep analytical approach to all business matters.

The ability to achieve a balance between formality and informality as the company grew was seen to be a particular challenge. As the managing director said:

I think it was when we went from eight or nine others and we drove it up into the 30s very quickly. I wished to hold onto cultural values but implement a structure … of course most of the guys who come out of banks, the last thing they want to do is go back into a structure, so it was a case of getting the values right as to why we wanted a structure without it being seen as a tool with which management would beat the staff. It is fairly subtly done.

Mortgage Co sought to provide a balance between operational processes and the most appropriate human resources practices. This led to the integration of operations and human resources improvement roles so as not to make the company overly bureaucratic. The company saw structured human resources policies and practices as an important aspect of the business, and was observed to be using a range of formal practices, including multiskilling, staff induction, employee appraisal, internal promotion, formal pay systems, performance/profit-related pay, job security, teamwork, a culture change programme, and formal recruitment and selection procedures. In addition, 10 per cent of the firm was owned by the staff, with the company having made a commitment to pass more ownership to employees through an employee share option scheme, increasing this to 20 per cent over the coming years.

As is not uncommon in high-growth firms, Mortgage Co has placed an emphasis on recruitment practices in order to respond to growth need. All new starters pass through a well-structured recruitment, selection, induction and probationary review process, as one would expect in a large firm. The difference here was that the process was seen as a 'light touch', and contact with the managing director at this early stage was seen to be important in order to instil the company's history and future vision into new recruits.

Questions

1 How important was the introduction of HRM to Mortgage Co's recent performance?
2 Critically assess what other developments occurred and the nature of the relationships between them.

In recognizing the heterogeneous nature of the SME sector, scholars have begun to uncover the rich and complex tapestries of the employment relations environment. Although some issues, such as resources and financing, may be common the world over, it is apparent that there are more differences than similarities. To propose that the SME sector and large firms are simply dichotomous is misleading. Such a view appears to have inhibited the development of more critical investigations of what HRM actually means to SMEs and how it influences performance – knowledge that SMEs desperately need.

More recently, academics have begun to utilize notions of embeddedness, purporting that this is a more fruitful avenue to follow rather than size per se. The concept of embeddedness allows for SMEs to operate across different 'domains' (Whittington, 1994). It is also necessary to examine the ways in which behaviour in SMEs is shaped by institutional contexts (DiMaggio and Powell, 1991; Rubery, 1997; Gilman et al., 2002; see also Mini Case Study 16.2). The resource-based view of the firm is important within this context as it identifies distinct sets of resources that small businesses can deploy (Chua et al., 2003; Sirmon and Hitt, 2003). This kind of explanatory approach embraces a more dynamic analysis by paying attention to history and context, and placing an emphasis on the limits of economic models (Edwards, 2003).

❓ For discussion and revision

Questions

1 What role do SMEs play in employment and in the growth of an economy?
2 Critically examine the nature of employment relations in SMEs.
3 Why is the formality of HRM practices seen as a contentious issue for SMEs?
4 In what ways are SMEs different from large firms with regard to HRM?

Exercises

1 Study HRM in a local SME. Ask the human resources manager how HRM in SMEs is different from HRM in large public or private sector organizations.
2 In a local newspaper, identify some job advertisements posted by SMEs and large organizations. What visible differences can you identify in job adverts from SMEs and large organizations? What could be the possible reasons for this?

📖 Further reading

Journals

Brand, M. J. and Bax, E. H. (2002) Strategic HRM for SMEs: implications for firms and policy. *Education and Training*, 44(8/9): 451–63.

Harney, B. and Dundon, T. (2006) Capturing complexity: developing an integrated approach to analysing HRM in SMEs. *Human Resource Management Journal*, 16(1): 48–73.

Harney, B. and Dundon, T. (2007) An emergent theory of HRM: a theoretical and empirical exploration of determinants of HRM among Irish small-to medium-sized enterprises (SMEs). *Advances in Industrial and Labor Relations*, 15: 109–59.

Hornsby, J. S. and Kuratko, D. F. (1990) Human resource management in small business: critical issues for the 1990's. *Journal of Small Business Management*, 28(3): 9–18.

Case Study HPWSs in a European context

This case study draws upon a comparative study of the HRM practices of SMEs based in Northern France and South East England. In particular, the study sought to investigate the nature of HPWSs in SMEs by examining wider management practices including strategy, HRM practices, communication mechanisms, training and skills methods and performance measurement systems.

Although scholars differ in the practices that they include in a HPWS, a broad definition of an HPWS covers three main categories: high employee involvement practices, human resource practices and reward and commitment practices (Ashton and Sung, 2002; Thompson, 2002; Sung and Ashton, 2005). These broad areas are often referred to as components of high-performance work practices (HPWPs) and cover up to 38 different work practices within this study (see Table 3 below).

Adoption of practices associated with a high-performance approach

Table 1 reports the uptake of HRM practices associated with a high-performance approach. As can be seen, UK SMEs were found to use a greater number of HPWPs than their French counterparts. Even so, only 15 per cent of UK firms and 5 per cent of French firms utilized more than 20–30 or more practices. This highlights the fact that very few of the SMEs studied appeared to utilize a comprehensive set of practices.

The evidence displayed in Table 2 further illustrates the low levels of uptake in each of the HPWS components by UK and French firms, reflecting the scope for SMEs to adopt greater levels of HRM/HPWPs (Way, 2002; Sels et al., 2006). Despite such

Table 1 The distribution of HPWP adoption

Number of practices	Percentage of workplaces	
	UK	France
Under 10	42	71
10 to <20	42	24
20 to <30	15	5
30 or more	1	0

low levels of HPWP usage, the research highlighted how significant differences were found in the level of uptake, with British firms using greater levels of human resources practices and of reward and commitment practices. These results were cognisant with that fact that British firms displayed greater levels of HPWP across all categories (see Table 2). Higher rates of uptake were found among the manufacturing and hotel and restaurant sectors for British firms, and among the manufacturing and wholesale and retail sectors for French firms.

The nature of HPWPs within the UK and France

In investigating the individual practices that made up the components within Table 2, it was found that UK and French employers were both more likely to communicate through face-to-face meetings such as team briefings, but that French firms were more likely to involve employees through a teamwork approach.

French firms were also more likely to invite employees to participate in quality-related matters through quality circles, a trend that continued through higher levels of works council and trade

Table 2 The distribution of HPWP adoption by country

Practice	Setting	Total practices	Mean	Uptake (%)	Difference
High involvement	British	13	3.0	23	0.512
	French	13	2.9	22	
	All	13	3.0	23	
Human resources	British	15	5.3	35	0.00***
	French	15	2.8	19	
	All	15	4.4	29	
Reward and commitment	British	10	3.6	36	0.00***
	French	10	2.5	25	
	All	10	3.2	32	

*** Significant to 0.01, ** Significant to 0.05, * Significant to 0.10.

union representation. Written forms of communication, including suggestion schemes and attitude surveys, were less prevalent in both UK and French firms. Certainly, downward communication methods appeared to be relatively dominant among UK employers, who were more likely to communicate through managers and by e-mail.

Clear differences were also observed with regard to the distinct human resources practices used by firms, with UK employers more likely to use all of the practices listed in the human resources practice component. Anticipated disparities between employees' working hours were apparent, with three-fifths of employees in French firms experiencing a 35-hour working week, in contrast to a fifth of UK firms. Overall, it was highlighted that UK employees were more likely to work much longer hours, although productivity was generally higher within French firms. In addition, French firms were four times as likely to be a member of an employment association, and twice as common to seek advice from this source.

Training and skills development in general appeared to be of greater importance to UK employers. There were clear differences in the types of training provided to employees, British firms being more likely to run training in job-specific skills (for example, operation of the equipment, and general IT and customer service). In contrast, training in French SMEs emphasized communication, teamwork and problem-solving. A third of all firms were found to train employees to perform roles other than their job-specific tasks, with a quarter identifying quality within their training activities.

Half of all firms deemed internal promotion to be important for retaining employee loyalty, and a quarter reported job security to also be an important aspect of their employee relations interests, with UK firms most likely to report equity in employees' terms and conditions.

Does a particular *system* of high performance exist in UK or French SMEs?

Is it possible to conclude that British firms adopt greater overall levels of HPWPs? Do these results suggest a preference by British firms for an integrated and strategic approach? In order to glean a more detailed picture, binary logistic regression was employed to illustrate the probability of firms utilizing various HPWPs as a function of being British or French. The result of this analysis proved very interesting.

Table 3 highlights how French firms were found to use a collective range of high-involvement work practices. Emphasis appeared to focus on taking a

strategic route to process improvement/innovation. French employers also concentrated on the involvement of employees through quality circles and teams. Indeed, downward communication methods, including the use of the management chain, were found to be negatively associated with the growth of French firms. Furthermore, French firms appeared to take a conscious approach towards the adoption of problem-solving skills, a practice found to be positively related to growth. In contrast, no variables were found to discriminate British SMEs within the high-involvement management practices.

Although British firms were found to be utilizing almost twice as many human resources practices, it is the complementary nature of such practices that adds greater depth to the analysis. Whereas British firms used a disparate set of human resource practices, French firms placed greater emphasis on quality-related skills, as well as the development of human resources policies and practices, which would appear to support their high-involvement approach. British firms did highlight the importance of quality within their business strategy, but they appeared less likely than French firms for this to result in the adoption of quality-related standards. In addition, while British firms recognize the importance of skill development within the business strategy, such development appears to be dominated by a statutory and task-focused approach, an approach proven to be negatively related to growth.

The findings within the reward and commitment HPWP component would appear to strengthen the aforementioned outcomes. French firms were more likely to place a greater collective importance on employee job satisfaction, pay and reward systems and internal promotion opportunities, with such practices reinforcing job security. British firms, in contrast, placed greater importance on the measurement of labour turnover and absenteeism. Individualization also seemed to be more important to British firms, with an emphasis on employee share options and profit-related pay.

A set of contextual variables also appeared to strengthen the French employers' integrative approach. French SMEs were more likely to possess a business strategy and record productivity. In contrast, the importance placed on skill development by British firms appears to relate to more job-specific or statutory related training (for example, in health and safety and equipment operation). Furthermore, the British workplace was characterized by downward forms of communication (for example, through managers) and long working hours.

Table 3 Results of detailed statistical analysis

Practice	UK firms		French firms	
	Significant variables	β / sig	Significant variables	β / sig
High involvement			Quality circles	12.416***
			Culture/change programmes	9.945***
			Sharing information (notice board)	9.091***
			Strategic process improvement	6.223**
			Communication skills	5.322*
			Problem-solving skills	3.997**
			Team briefings	2.769**
			Teamwork	2.207**
Human resources	Harmonized conditions	−11.696***	Strategic employment practices	19.383***
	Strategic skill development	−11.433***	Quality management system (ISO 9000)	5.452***
	Strategic quality improvement	−9.743***	Quality control skills	4.093**
	Staff induction	−9.223***		
	Staff appraisal	−8.744***		
	Formal recruitment and selection	−7.574***		
	Selection testing	−5.203		
	Equipment operation skills	−2.011**		
Reward and commitment	Employ share options	−12.054***	Staff job satisfaction	7.071***
	Labour turnover records	−8.211***	Internal promotion	5.583***
	Absenteeism records	−3.817***	Job security	3.103**
			Formal pay system	2.976***
			Performance-related pay	2.112*
Other	Reliability/time management training	−8.041***	Productivity records	3.667**
	Health and safety training	−6.577***	Export	3.398***
	Long working hours >35 hrs/wk	−6.571***	Business strategy	2.654*
	Customer service training	−3.865***		
	Communicate by e-mail	−3.264**		
	Skill development is important	−3.040***		
	Communicate through managers	−1.919*		

* Significant to 0.10, ** Significant to 0.05, *** Significant to 0.01.

▷
This research demonstrates a clear divergence in the nature and performance effects of HPWSs. Although British small firms were found to adopt a wider range of HPWPs, French firms were found to exhibit a higher degree of integration, portrayed through a collective range of practices that highlighted the apparent use of employee participation and commitment practices.

Source: Based on Gilman and Raby (2010)

Questions

1 Why are SMEs seen as the potential beneficiaries of a high-performance approach?
2 Having considered the above results, what are the key differences in approach taken by British and French firms to the adoption of human resources practices associated with a model of high performance?
3 How can the difference in approach taken by British and French SMEs be attributed to a firm's institutional setting?

References

Andrews, A. O. and Welbourne, T. M. (2000) The people/performance balance in IPO firms: the effect of the chief executive officer's financial orientation. *Entrepreneurship Theory and Practice*, 1: 93–100.

Andrick, J. (1998) Providing modern information services for small and medium sized enterprises. *World Patent Information*, 20(2): 107–10.

Angelis, J. and Thompson, M. (2007) Product and service complexity and high performance work practices in the aerospace industry. *Journal of Industrial Relations*, 49(5): 775–81.

Arthur Anderson and Binder Hamlyn (1996) *The 1996 Pulse Survey: Survival of the Fittest*. London: Arthur Anderson/Binder Hamlyn.

Ashton, D. and Sung, J. (2002) *Supporting Workplace Learning for High Performance Working*. Geneva: International Labour Organization.

Bacon, N. and Hoque, K. (2005) HRM in the SME sector: valuable employees and coercive networks. *International Journal of Human Resource Management*, 16(11): 1976–99.

Bacon, N., Ackers, P., Storey, J. and Coates, D. (1996) It's a small world: managing human resources in small business. *International Journal of Human Resource Management*, 7(1): 82–100.

Bamber, J., Lansbury, R. D. and Wailes, N. (2004). Introduction. In Bamber, G. J., Lansbury, R. D. and Wailes, N. (eds) *International and Comparative Employment Relations* (4th edn). Sage: London.

Barney, J. B. (1991) Firm resources and sustainable competitive advantage. *Journal of Management*, 17(1): 99–120.

Barrett, R. (1999) Industrial relations in SMEs: the case of the Australian information industry. *Employee Relations*, 21(3): 311–24.

Barrett, R. and Rainnie, A. (2002) What's so special about small firms? Developing an integrated approach to analysing small firm industrial relations. *Work Employment Society* 2002, 16(3) 415–31.

Bartram, T. (2005) Small firms, big ideas: the adoption of human resource management in Australian small firms. *Asia Pacific Journal of Human Resources*, 43(1): 137–54.

Beer, M., Spector, B., Lawrence, P., Mills, Q. and Walton, R. (1984) *Managing Human Assets*. New York: Free Press.

Birch, D. (1979) *The Job Generation Process*. Cambridge, MA: MIT Programme on Neighbourhood and Regional Change.

Blasi, J. R. and D. L. Kruse (2006) U.S. high-performance work practices at Century's End. *Industrial Relations*, 45(4): 547.

Bolton, J. E. (1971) *Report of the Commission of Inquiry on Small Firms*. Cmnd 4811. London: HMSO.

Bryson, A., Forth, J. and Kirby, S. (2005) High-involvement management practices, trade union representation and workplace performance in Britain. *Scottish Journal of Political Economy*; 52(3): 451–91.

Cardon, M. and Stevens, C. (2004) Managing human resources in small organizations: what do we know? *Human Resource Management Review*, 14: 295–323.

Caspersz, D. (2006) The 'talk versus the walk': high performance work systems, labour market flexibility and lessons from Asian workers. *Asia Pacific Business Review*, 12(2): 149–61.

Chandler, G. N., Keller, C. and Lyon, D. W. (2000) Unravelling the determinants and consequences of an innovation-supportive organizational culture. *Entrepreneurship, Theory and Practice*, 25(1): 59–76.

Chartered Institute for Personnel and Development (2009) *Annual Survey Report 2009: Recruitment, Retention and Turnover*. London: CIPD.

Chua, J. H., Chrisman, J. L. and Steier, L. P. (2003) Extending the theoretical horizons of family business research. *Entrepreneurship Theory and Practice*, 27(4): 331–8.

Davidsson, P., Lindmark, L. and Olofsson, C. (1998) The extent of overestimation of small firm job creation – an empirical examination of the regression bias. *Small Business Economics*, 11: 87–100.

Davidsson, P., Leona., A. & Naldi, L. (2005) *Research on Small Firm Growth: A Review*. Brisbane: Queensland University of Technology.

Davis, S. J., Haltiwange, J. and Schuh, S. (1996) Small business and job creation: dissecting the myth and reassessing the facts. *Small Business Economics*, 8: 297–315.

De Kok, J. and Uhlaner, L. M. (2001) Organisation context and human resource management in the small firm. *Small Business Economics*, 17(4): 273–88.

De Menezes, L. M. and Wood, S. (2006) The reality of flexible work systems in Britain. *International Journal of Human Resource Management*, 17(1): 106–38.

Denton, D. K. (2006) What's your big picture? *International Journal of Productivity and Performance Management*, 55(5): 423.

Department for Business Enterprise and Regulatory Reform (2008) *High Growth Firms in the UK: Lessons from an Analysis of Comparative UK Performance*. Economic Paper No. 3. London: BERR.

Dess, G. G. and Beard, D. W. (1984) Dimensions of organizational task environments. *Administrative Science Quarterly*, 29: 52–73.

Department for Business, Innovation and Skills (2010) Business Population Estimates for the UK and Regions 2010, Statistical release. Available from: http://stats.bis.gov.uk/ed/bpe/ [accessed 26 September 2011].

DiMaggio, P. and Powell, W. W. (1991) Introduction. In Powell, W. W. and DiMaggio, P. (eds) *The New Institutionalism in Organizational Analysis*. Chicago: University of Chicago Press, pp. 1–38.

Drummond, I. and Stone, I. (2007) Exploring the potential of high performance work systems in SMEs. *Employee Relations*, 29 (2): 192–207.

Eddleston, K. A., Kellermanns, F. W. and Sarathy, R. (2008) Resource configuration in family firms: linking resources, strategic planning and technological opportunities to performance. *Journal of Management Studies*, 45(1): 26–50.

Edwards, P. (2003) The employment relationship and the field of industrial relations. In Edwards, P. (ed.) *Industrial Relations*. Oxford: Blackwell, pp. 1–36.

Edwards, P. and Ram, M. (2006a) Surviving on the margins of the economy: working relationships in small low-wage firms. *Journal of Management Studies*, 43(4): 895–916.

Edwards, P. and Ram, M. (2006b) *Employment Relations in SMEs*. EIRO report TN0602101s. Dublin: European Industrial Relations Observatory.

European Commission (2005) The New SME Definition: User Guide and Model Declaration. Available from: http://ec.europa.eu/ [accessed 18 September 2011].

European Commission (2009) *European SMEs Under Pressure*. Annual report on EU small and medium-sized enterprises, EIM Business & Policy Research.

European Commission (2010) *Employment in Europe 2010*. Luxembourg: Publications Office of the European Union.

Forster, N. and Whipp, R. (1995) Future of European human resource management: a contingent approach. *European Management Journal*, 13(4): 434–42.

Gentle, C. and Contri, R. (2005) To spur growth, focus on process, not product. *American Banker*, 170(174): 12.

Gibb, A. and Davies, L. (1990) In pursuit of frameworks for the development of growth models of the small business. *International Small Business Journal*, 9(1): 15–31.

Gilman, M. W. and Raby S. O. (2011) *National Context as a Predictor of High Performance Work Systems in Small Firms: A British–French Comparative Analysis*. Working Paper Series No. 252. Canterbury, Kent: University of Kent Business School.

Gilman, M. and Edwards, P. (2008) Testing a framework of the organisation of small firms: fast growth, high-tech SMEs. *International Small Business Journal*, 26(5): 1–25.

Gilman, M., Edwards, P., Ram, M. and Arrowsmith, J. (2002) Pay determination in small firms in the UK. *Industrial Relations Journal*, 33(1): 52–67.

Golhar, D. Y. and Deshpande, S. P. (1997) HRM practices of large and small Canadian manufacturing firms. *Journal of Small Business Management*, 35(3): 23–34.

Goss, D. (1991a) *Small Business and Society*. London: Routledge.

Goss, D. (1991b) In search of small firm industrial relations. In Burrows. R. (ed.) *Deciphering the Enterprise Culture: Entrepreneurship, Petty Capitalism and the Restructuring of Britain*. London: Routledge, pp. 152–75.

Guest, D. E. (1997) Human resource management and performance: a review and research agenda. *International Journal of Human Resource Management*, 8(3): 263–76.

Harney, B. and Dundon, T. (2006) Capturing complexity: developing an integrated approach to analysing HRM in SMEs. *Human Resource Management Journal*, 16(1): 48–73.

Harney, B. and Dundon, T. (2007) An emergent theory of HRM: a theoretical and empirical exploration of determinants of HRM among Irish small to medium-sized enterprises (SMEs). *Advances in Industrial and Labor Relations*, 15: 109–59.

Harrison, B. (1996) The small firm myth. *California Management Review*, 36(3): 142–58.

Hendry, C. and Pettigrew, A. M. (1990) The practice of strategic human resource management. *Personnel Review*, 15(5): 3–8.

Hiltrop, J. (1996) The impact of human resource management on organisational performance: theory and research. *European Management Journal*, 14(6): 628–37.

Hornsby. J. S. and Kuratko. D. F. (1990) Human resource management in small business: critical issues for the

1990's. *Journal of Small Business Management*, 28(3): 9–18.

Ingham, G. F. (1970) *Size of Industrial Organisation and Worker Behaviour*. Cambridge: Cambridge University Press.

Jayoram, J., Droge, C. and Vickery, S. (1999) The impact of human resource management practices on manufacturing performance. *Journal of Operations Management*, 18: 1–20.

Jonash, R. S. (2005) Driving sustainable growth and innovation: pathways to high performance leadership. *Handbook of Business Strategy*, 6(1): 197–202.

Kaman, V., McCarthy, A. M., Gulbro, R. D. and Tucker, M. L. (2001) Bureaucratic and high commitment human resource practices in small service firms. *Human Resource Planning*, 24(1): 33–44.

Katz, J. A., Aldrich, H. E., Welbourne, T. M. and Williams, P. M. (2000) Guest editors' comments. Special issue in human resource management and the SME: Towards a new synthesis. *Entrepreneurship Theory and Practice*, 25(1): 7–10.

Kearns, G. and Lederer, A. (2003) A resource-based view of strategic IT alignment: how knowledge sharing creates competitive advantage. *Decision Sciences*, 34(1): 1–29.

Kerr, G., Way, S. and Thacker, J. (2007) Performance, HR practices and the HR manager in small entrepreneurial firms. *Journal of Small Business and Entrepreneurship*, 20(1): 55–68.

Kotey, B. and Sheridan, A. (2004) Changing HRM practices with firm growth. *Journal of Small Business and Enterprise Development*, 11(4): 474–89.

Lado, A. A., Boyd, N. G, Wright, P. and Kroll, M. (2006) Paradox and theorizing within the resource-based view. *Academy of Management Review*, 31(1): 115–31.

Lavie, D. (2006) The competitive advantage of interconnected firms: an extension of the resource-based view. *Academy of Management Review*, 31(3): 638–58.

Little, B. L. (1986) The performance of personnel duties in small Louisiana firms: a research note. *Journal of Small Business Management*, 24(4): 66–9.

MacMahon, J. (1996) Employee relations in small firms in Ireland: an exploratory study of small manufacturing firms. *Employee Relations*, 18(5): 66–80.

Marlow, S. (2006) Human resource management in smaller firms: a contradiction in terms? *Human Resource Management Review*, 16: 467–77.

Marlow, S. and Patton, D. (1993) Managing the employment relationship in the smaller firm: possibilities for human resource management. *International Small Business Journal*, 11(4): 57–64.

Marlow, S., Taylor, S. and Thompson, A. (2010) Informality and formality in medium-sized companies: contestation and synchronization. *British Journal of Management*, 21(4): 954–66.

Matlay, H. (1999) Employee relations in small firms. *Employee Relations*, 21: 285–96.

Mayson, S. and Barrett, R. (2006) The 'science' and 'practice' of HRM in small firms. *Human Resource Management Review*, 16: 447–55.

Miner, J. B. (1973) Personnel strategies in the small business organisation. *Journal of Small Business Management*, 11(3): 13–16.

Moule, C. (1998) The regulation of work in small firms. *Work, Employment and Society*, 12: 635–54.

Nguyen, T. and Bryant, S. (2004) A study of the formality of HRM practices in small and medium sized firms in Vietnam. *International Small Business Journal*, 22(6): 595–618.

Office for National Statistics (2009) *International Comparisons of Productivity: New Estimates for 2008*. Government Statistical Bulletin. Cardiff: ONS.

O'Gorman, C. (2001) The sustainability of growth in small- and medium-sized enterprises. *International Journal of Entrepreneurial Behaviour and Research*, 7(2): 60–75.

Osterman, P. (2006) The wage effects of high performance work organization in manufacturing. *Industrial and Labor Relations Review*, 59(2): 187.

Paauwe, J. (2004) *HRM and Performance: Achieving Long Term Viability*. Oxford: Oxford University Press.

Pearson, T. R., Stringer, D. Y., Mills L. H. and Summers, D. F. (2006) Micro vs small enterprises: a profile of human resource personnel, practices and support systems. *Journal of Management Research*, 6(2): 102–12.

Pfeffer, J. (1994) *Competitive Advantage Through People*. Boston: Harvard Business Press.

Porter, M. (1985) *Competitive Advantage: Creating and Sustaining Superior Competitive Performance*. London: Collier Macmillan.

Rainnie, A. (1989) *Industrial Relations in Small Firms: Small Isn't Beautiful*. Routledge: London.

Ram, M. (1994) *Managing to Survive*. Oxford: Blackwell.

Ram, M. (1999) Managing autonomy: employment relations in small professional service firms. *International Small Business Journal*, 17(2): 1–14.

Ram, M. and Edwards, P. (2003) Praising Caesar not burying him: what we know about employment relations in small firms. *Work, Employment and Society*, 17(4): 719–30.

Rubery, J. (1997) Wages and the labour market. *British Journal of Industrial Relations*, 35(3): 337–62.

Scase, R. (1995) Employment relations in small firms. In Edwards, P. (ed.) *Industrial Relations: Theory and Practice* (2nd edn). Oxford: Blackwell, pp. 470–88.

Scase, R. (2003) Employment relations in small firms. In Edwards, P. (ed.) *Industrial Relations: Theory and Practice*. Oxford: Blackwell, pp. 470–88.

Scase, R. and Goffee, R. (1987) *The Real World of the Small Business Owner* (2nd edn). London: Croom Helm.

Schmitt, J. and Lane, N. (2009) *An International Comparison of Small Business Employment*. London: Centre for Economic and Policy Research.

Schuster, F. (1986) *The Schuster Report*. New York: John Wiley & Sons.

Scott, M., Roberts, I., Holroyd, G. and Sawbridge, D. (1989) *Management and Industrial Relations in Small Firms*. Department of Employment Research Paper No. 70. London: HMSO.

Sels, L., De Winne, S., Maes, J., Delmotte, J., Faems, D. & Forrier, A. (2006) Unravelling the HRM-performance link: value-creating and cost-increasing effects of small business HRM. *Journal of Management Studies*, 43(2): 319–42.

Shih, H.-A., Chiang, Y.-H. and Hsu, C.-C. (2006) Can high performance work systems really lead to better performance? *International Journal of Manpower*, 27(8): 741–63.

Simpson, M., Tuck, N. and Bellamy, S. (2004) Small business success factors: the role of education and training. *Education and Training*, 46(8/9): 481–91.

Sirmon, D. G. and Hitt, M. A. (2003) Managing resources: Linking unique resources, management, and wealth creation in family firms. *Entrepreneurship Theory and Practice*, 27(3): 339–58.

Sisson, K. (1993) In search of HRM. *British Journal of Industrial Relations*, 31(2): 201–10.

Small Business Service (2004) Statistical Press Release, Department of Trade and Industry. Available from: http://www.dti.gov.uk [accessed 26 April 2005].

Smallbone, D., North, D. and Leigh, R. (1992) *Managing Change for Growth and Survival: A Study of Mature Manufacturing Firms in London During the 1980's*. Middlesex Polytechnic Planning Research Centre Working Paper No. 3. Hendon: Middlesex Polytechnic.

Smith, A. and Whitaker, J. (1998) Management development in SME's: what needs to be done? *Journal of Small Business Management and Enterprise Development*, 5(2): 176–85.

Stanworth, J. and Curran, J. (1981) Size of workplace and attitudes to industrial relations. *British Journal of Industrial Relations*, 19: 14–25.

Starbuck, W. H. (1976) Organizations and their environments. In Dunnette, M. D. (ed.) *Handbook of Industrial and Organizational Psychology*. Chicago: Rand McNally, pp. 1069–123.

Storey, D. J. (1994) *Understanding the Small Business Sector*. London: Routledge.

Sung, J. and Ashton, D. (2005) *Achieving Best Practice in your Business. High Performance Work Practices: Linking Strategy and Skills to Performance Outcomes*. London: Department of Trade and Industry/CIPD.

Tansky, J. W. and Heneman, R. (2004) Guest Editor's note. Introduction to the Special Issue on Human Resource Management in SMEs: a call for more research. *Human Resource Management*, 42: 299–302.

Thompson, M. (2002) *High Performance Work Organisation in UK Aerospace – the SBAC Human Capital Audit*. London: Society of British Aerospace Companies.

US Small Business Administration (2010) Table of Small Business Size Standards Matched to North American Industry Classification System Codes. Available from http://www.sba.gov/ [accessed 18 September 2011].

Van der Wiele, T. and Brown A. (1998) Venturing down the TQM path for SMEs. *International Small Business Journal*, 16(2): 50–68.

Wagar, T. (1998) Determinants of human resource management practices in small firms: some evidence from Atlantic Canada. *Journal of Small Business Management*, 36(2): 13–23.

Way, S. A. (2002) High performance work systems and intermediate indicators of firm performance within the U.S. small business sector. *Journal of Management*, 28: 765–85.

Way, S. A. and Thacker, J. W. (2004) Having a human resource manager in Canadian small business: what difference does it make? *Journal of Small Business and Entrepreneurship*, 17(4): 293–300.

Welsh, J. and White, J. (1981) A small business is not a little big business. *Harvard Business Review*, 59(4): 18–32.

Whittington, R. (1994) Sociological pluralism, institutions and managerial agency. In Hassard, J. and Parker, M. (eds) *Towards a New Theory of Organizations*. London: Routledge, pp. 53–74.

Wilkes, N. and Dale, B. (1998) Attitudes to self assessment and quality awards: a study in small and medium-sized companies. *Total Quality Management*, 9(8): 731–9.

Wilkinson, A. (1999) Employment relations in SMEs, *Employee Relations*, 21(3): 206–17.

Wilkinson, T. and Brouthers, L. E. (2006) Trade promotion and SME export performance. *International Business Review*, 15(3): 233.

Conclusion

Robin Kramar and Jawad Syed

Human resource management (HRM) is not what it used to be – the developments of the last two to three decades have changed the face and practice of business. These changes have confronted managers with many opportunities and challenges, and nowhere are these opportunities and challenges more pronounced than in the area of HRM.

The chapters in this book highlight eight recurring themes that have emerged in HRM. These themes define the domain of HRM and confront academics and practitioners with many theoretical and practical issues. The chapters clearly highlight that these themes and issues are not mutually exclusive but interact and overlap. Among the most powerful themes to emerge include:

- the powerful role of factors in the external, international environment on business, management and HRM;
- a need to consider HRM at a number of levels, particularly at the macro or national level, the meso or organizational level, and the micro or individual level;
- the continuing debate surrounding the convergence and divergence of HRM practices across the globe;
- the framework of strategic HRM (SHRM);
- the theoretical explanations of the links between organizational performance and HRM practice, as captured in the universalistic, configurational and contingency theories;
- the role of ethics in HRM;
- debates about measuring the effectiveness of HRM;
- the difficulties surrounding the implementation and consistency of human resources policies within organizations.

Although scholars differ in their views about the extent to which HRM should serve different stakeholders, there is consistent agreement that the interests of the owners of an organization are supported by HRM (Kramar et al., 2011). During the last 15 years, there have been developments, such as the policies of the World Trade Organization, which have championed business interests

(Bakan, 2004). In addition, the deregulation of many economies has encouraged an emphasis on financial returns to shareholders.

This view is most sharply brought out in the SHRM approach, which represents a distinctive approach to the management of people doing the work of an organization so that the organization achieves competitive advantage as well as financial and, possibly, other results in both the short term and the longer term (Kramar et al., 2011). However, the approaches to SHRM and the involvement of various stakeholders in the process of formulating and implementing HRM policy vary between organizations. Although there are converging forces of international legislation such as the International Labour Organization Conventions and Declarations that have specific implications for employment relations (Kellerson, 1998), the enactment of such laws, the roles of trade unions and governments and their agencies are not consistent across national contexts. For instance, in private sector companies in the USA, trade unions play a more limited role in HRM formulation than they do in private sector organizations in some Australian industries. Other contextual factors such as culture and values are equally relevant. For example, based on their comparative study of work-related attitudes and organizational change in post-socialist countries, Alas and Rees (2006) highlight that HRM practices are inextricably linked to conceptions surrounding culture and society, as well as to variables such as job satisfaction and organizational commitment.

In this book, Chapter 1 by Syed and Pg Omar provides very useful frameworks that identify aspects of what they term the 'macroenvironment'. This chapter argues that HRM strategies and practices need to be understood in the context of their legal and political, economical, sociocultural and technological environments. This theme is consistent with the institutional theory proposing that the institutional environment, consisting of regulative, normative and cultural-cognitive aspects and their activities, will influence the organizing principles and shape the behaviour of stakeholders in an economy and labour market (Di Maggio, 1988; Reay and Hinings, 2009). This does not, however, preclude complexity in the environment, which enables the coexistence of institutions with competing approaches; this complexity is reflected throughout many of the other chapters of the book.

An explicit acknowledgement of these macro-contexts provides insights into the convergence/divergence debate. Although globalization of business, culture, information transfer, technology and international standards has occurred and has contributed to some convergence of HRM, the chapters in this book demonstrate that the particular arrangements in national economies and societies are effective in maintaining divergent HRM policies in different countries. This is clearly brought out in the chapters on 'Performance Management' and 'Reward Management' (Chapters 9 and 10, respectively), which identify the influential role of cultural factors in the conduct and process of evaluating performance and designing rewards. These chapters also highlight the difficulties of conducting evaluations and designing reward strategies in an international context, particularly in multinational corporations.

A very strong theme running through the book is the importance of understanding HRM in terms of not only the macroenvironment, but also the meso-organizational and micro-individual levels. This approach enables us to consider the influence of collective factors operating within the organization, such as teams, people on different terms of engagement (for example, subcontractors) and employees, as well as individual differences and characteristics. By acknowledging the influence of these three levels, it is possible to explicitly think about the influence of non-rational responses and influences on the development and implementation of HRM policies and practices (Syed and Özbilgin, 2009). Such an approach enables explanations for the difficulties associated with implementing HRM policies, which are frequently based on assumptions about individuals being rational rather than complex social, emotional and political creatures. It enables a consideration of the rhetoric of HRM (Legge, 1995) and the reality of HRM. The chapter on training, development and learning (Chapter 11) implicitly acknowledges the influences of these three levels, while other chapters such as those on diversity (Chapter 4) and equal employment opportunity (EEO) and human resource planning (Chapter 6) explicitly use this framework.

The book clearly highlights the fact that management adopts varies approaches to HRM in different organizations, as well as for different employees in the same organization. Managers therefore make choices about HRM policies and practices. Two approaches that are often referred to either explicitly or implicitly are the 'hard' HRM and the 'soft' HRM approaches. Hard HRM focuses on the development of HRM strategies that further business strategy and consistently support its achievement. Soft HRM, however, focuses on using HRM to develop employee commitment, flexibility and highly competent staff. An acknowledgement of the various HRM approaches highlights how HRM policies and practices are not value-neutral; instead, they involve making choices about the development of policies that have different outcomes for the various stakeholders of an organization, and different ethical implications for these stakeholders and the broader society.

The chapter on ethics and HRM (Chapter 5) provides the basis for considering the ethical dimensions of all areas of HRM and reveals some of the assumptions embedded in HRM practices. It also emphasizes that ethical practice is broader than just applying to current employees and the current generation: it also involves taking future generations and world ecology into account. When this broad approach to HRM is adopted, it has implications for the nature of the metrics used to measure the effectiveness of HRM policies and practices (Syed and Kramar, 2009). Metrics will also vary according to the theoretical approaches that are used to explain the link between HRM and organizational performance. These metrics could include a range of mediating factors that, according to the theories, will influence business performance. The chapter 'A Critical Perspective on Strategic Human Resource Management' (Chapter 2) discusses the ambiguity surrounding performance metrics.

A number of the chapters, particularly 'A Critical Perspective on Strategic Human Resource Management', refer to three popular theoretical explanations known as the universalistic, the contingency and the configurational or resource-based views. These theories explain the link between HRM and organizational performance and focus on business outcomes as measures of organizational performance. These theoretical explanations are not, however, mutually exclusive. They also accord alignment with business strategy and other mediating factors different weights of influence. For example, according to the configurational view, HRM policies and practices are critically important for developing a unique culture that is unique and inimitable. Although culture is the mediating factor in this approach, behaviours required to achieve the strategy are frequently identified by writers on contingency as the mediating factor. The universalistic approach is somewhat diverse and incorporates writers on high-performance work systems, 'high-involvement management' and 'high-commitment management'. According to these writers, particular HRM practices such as sharing information, teamwork, involving employees in decision-making and selective hiring are able to develop employee motivation and commitment (Boxall and Purcell, 2008), and these will contribute to organizational outcomes.

These theories are based on assumptions about the economy, organizations and individuals that are similar to the assumptions informing the SHRM framework. All of these theories and the SHRM framework itself assume that people are value-creating assets, that they are rational and that they can be influenced by HRM policies and practices. In reality, however, people are often irrational, emotional, political and social individuals (Kramar, 1992). People also have qualities that are ignored by these explanations, such as passion, spirituality and creativity (Zappala, 2010). Similarly, these theories are framed within the context of a mechanical view of organizations, rather than a view that sees organizations as organic, non-linear, evolving and one form of a complex adaptive system. Finally, the explanations are framed within the context of a neo-liberal economy in which the interests of the owners of the business are accorded priority over those of other stakeholders.

Ideas about the nature of individuals and the implications for HRM developed during the 20th century, and these ideas are addressed in some of the chapters. Although the complex motivations and needs of individuals were identified through the work of Herzberg, Elton Mayo and Trist and Emery, these complexities are not explicitly addressed in the theoretical approaches that inform the theory and frameworks of HRM.

A major theme emerging from this book concerns the variety of stakeholders who have interests in HRM and its outcomes. For instance, stakeholders such as employees, the community and governments have a stake in the outcomes. The pluralist view confronts the unitarist view that informs most of the theoretical frameworks on HRM. This pluralist view highlights possibilities that different stakeholders could have different interests and/or different priorities. The chapters highlight that it is essential to adopt a pluralist view when considering HRM in a global environment. In particular, the chapters on 'Diversity Management' (Chapter 4), 'Work–Life Balance in the 21st Century' (Chapter 14), 'Human Resource Management and Ethics' (Chapter 5), 'Human Resource Management in Contemporary Transnational Companies' (Chapter 3) and 'Human Resource Management, Productivity and Employee Involvement' (Chapter 13) indicate that when HRM operates in an international labour market and a global business, it is essential to adopt a pluralist view.

The chapters in this book highlight a number of challenges and opportunities for scholars and practitioners of HRM. The development and growth of business, especially developments emerging from globalization and technological advances, suggest that the existing approaches to HRM require re-evaluation. In addition, ecological developments and the impact of business on the environment raise issues about appropriate measures of organizational performance and whether the focus and priority should remain on financial measures of success. It also raises debates about the time frames that should be used to assess organizational outcomes – should the focus be predominantly on short-term outcomes, or would it be more appropriate to consider outcomes in the longer term? These challenges have implications for both scholars and practitioners.

Similarly, the transformation of people management to SHRM and the development of universalistic, contingency and configurational theories have a limited capacity to explain the role of HRM in satisfying stakeholder requirements in the 21st century. These theories adopt a narrow view of the contribution of HRM to organizational outcomes and their impact on a range of stakeholders. This raises a need to reconsider the measures and metrics of not only organizational performance, but also the performance and effectiveness of HRM.

The opportunities raised for scholars and practitioners of HRM are numerous. The most compelling opportunities are the need to consider HRM at a number of levels simultaneously – national, organizational and individual – and to integrate these levels into a framework acknowledging the complexities of individuals, the diverse processes and cultures in organizations, and the varying institutional arrangements operating in different national contexts. The ability to do this will become even more important as business continues to internationalize and companies need to manage global workforces. This provides practitioners and scholars with the opportunity to integrate a wide range of knowledge available from disciplines as diverse as psychology, chaos theory, politics and economics.

The book also challenges the traditional terrains of international HRM (IHRM) and HRM. It highlights that the globalization of business has also globalized HRM. Although this book does not explicitly deal with the difference between IHRM and HRM, it does reveal the fact that global HRM is not synonymous with IHRM. This poses further exciting opportunities for HRM scholars to recast the scope of HRM and its many representations.

We anticipate that this book will provide insights into the framing and operation of HRM in a global environment. Although not all organizations have a global workforce, all organizations now operate in a global, international labour market. This raises the opportunity for HRM to be reconceptualized, and provides many wonderful opportunities for scholars and practitioners.

References

Alas, R. and Rees, C. (2006) Work-related attitudes, values and radical change in post-socialist contexts: a comparative study. *Journal of Business Ethics*, 68(2): 181–9.

Bakan, J. (2004) *The Corporation*. London: Constable.

Boxall, P. and Purcell, J. (2008) *Strategy and Human Resource Management*. Basingstoke: Palgrave Macmillan.

Di Maggio, P. J. (1988) Interest and agency in institutional theory. In Zucker, L. (ed.) *Institutional Patterns and Organizations: Culture and Environment*. Cambridge, MA: Ballinger, pp. 3–21.

Kellerson, H. (1998) The ILO declaration of 1998 on fundamental principles and rights: a challenge for the future. *International Labour Relations Review*, 137(2): 223–35.

Kramar, R. (1992) Strategic human resource management: are the promises fulfilled? *Asia Pacific Journal of Human Resources*, 30(1): 1–15.

Kramar, R., Bartram, T. and De Cieri, H. (2011) *Human Resource Management in Australia*. Sydney: McGraw-Hill.

Legge, K. (1995) *Human Resource Management: Rhetoric and Realities*. London: Macmillan Business.

Reay, T. and Hinings, C. R. (2009) Managing the rivalry of competing institutional logics. *Organizational Studies*, 30(6): 629–52.

Syed, J. and Kramar, R. (2009) Socially responsible diversity management. *Journal of Management and Organization*, 15(5): 639–51.

Syed, J. and Özbilgin, M. (2009) A relational framework for international transfer of diversity management practices. *International Journal of Human Resource Management*, 20(12): 2435–53.

Zappala, G. (2010) *Beyond Corporate Responsibility: The Spiritual 'Turn' and the Rise of Conscious Business*. CSI Background Paper No. 6. Sydney: Centre for Social Impact.

Index